OUTSIDER THEORY

OUTSIDER THEORY

INTELLECTUAL HISTORIES OF UNORTHODOX IDEAS

Jonathan P. Eburne

University of Minnesota Press
Minneapolis
London

The University of Minnesota Press gratefully acknowledges the generous assistance provided for the publication of this book from the College of Liberal Arts at Pennsylvania State University.

Portions of the Introduction and chapter 7 were previously published as "Sztuka outsiderska / teoria outsiderska," in *Kultura Współczesna* 3, no. 87 (2015): 84–96. Chapter 5 first appeared in *African American Review* 47, no. 1 (2014): 1–19; copyright 2014 The Johns Hopkins University Press and St. Louis University.

Published by the University of Minnesota Press
111 Third Avenue South, Suite 290
Minneapolis, MN 55401-2520
http://www.upress.umn.edu

Printed in the United States of America on acid-free paper

The University of Minnesota is an equal-opportunity educator and employer.

22 21 20 19 18   10 9 8 7 6 5 4 3 2 1

Library of Congress Cataloging-in-Publication Data
Names: Eburne, Jonathan P. (Jonathan Paul), author.
Title: Outsider theory : intellectual histories of questionable ideas / Jonathan P. Eburne.
Description: Minneapolis, MN : University of Minnesota Press, [2018] | Includes
    bibliographical references and index.
Identifiers: LCCN 2018008937 (print) | ISBN 978-1-5179-0554-5 (hc) |
    ISBN 978-1-5179-0555-2 (pb)
Subjects: LCSH: Facts. | Common fallacies. | Errors. | Philosophy, Modern—20th century. |
    Intellectual life—20th century. | Philosophy, Modern—21st century. | Intellectual
    life—21st century.
Classification: LCC B105.F3 E28 2018 (print) | DDC 001.9—dc23
LC record available at https://lccn.loc.gov/2018008937

We have reached a point where all destinations, all bright lights, arouse mistrust. The light at the end of the tunnel turns too quickly into the interrogator's spotlight.

—William Kentridge, *Six Drawing Lessons*

There are so many questions, and so much Dogmaturd to clear aside before anything makes sense, and we are on the point of destroying the Earth before we know anything at all. Perhaps a great virtue, curiosity can only be satisfied if the millennia of accumulated false data be turned upside down. Which means turning oneself inside out and to begin by despising no thing, ignoring no thing.

—Leonora Carrington, "The Cabbage Is a Rose"

Theory is absence, obscure and propitious.

—Édouard Glissant, *The Poetics of Relation*

CONTENTS

Acknowledgments   ix

Preface: Enemies of the Truth   xiii

Introduction   1

PART I. ALIEN GODS

1. The Alien Knowledge of Nag Hammadi   37

2. Gnostic Materialism   67

PART II. MYTHOMORPHOSES

3. So Dark, the Con of Man   113

4. The Chalice, the Blade, and the Bifurcation Point   159

PART III. SOVEREIGN INSTITUTIONS

5. Garveyism and Its Involutions   201

6. The Sade Industry   237

PART IV. PRODUCTS OF MIND

7. Cartographorrhea: On Psychotic Maps   269

8. Communities of Suspicion: Immanuel Velikovsky
   and the Laws of Science   305

Coda: Thought from Outer Space   345

Notes   365

Index   421

ACKNOWLEDGMENTS

THIS IS A LONG BOOK, and it took a long time to write. During the process, my thoughts often strayed from the common authorial apprehension about the odds of surviving the book's completion to a more daunting anxiety about the odds of there being a future at all. I am grateful for the scholars, artists, scientists, teachers, booksellers, and intellectual workers who persist in fighting not only for a political and ecological future on this planet but for an imaginative one as well.

To this end—and by way of a deep expression of gratitude—I take the liberty of citing something my colleague Robert Caserio wrote as we corresponded about our current scholarly preoccupations: *Outsider Theory,* he writes, "is not only about the romance and errantry of intellectual life, in which we are all quixotes; it is also about vulnerability and mortality as occasions of death as well as of birth. One can't tell, of course, if one's error will be mortal or natal." I wish to thank Robert for his tireless dedication to intellectual romance, as well as for his recognition of the necessary vulnerability of the work of scholarship—not only for the mortality that always haunts it, but also for the inevitability of entangling error with correctness.

In this regard, *Outsider Theory* has come to resemble its object of study in rather discomfiting ways. This book perpetually teeters on the verge of becoming an iteration of some of the more preposterous ideas it studies, an "interdisciplinary synthesis" as long on ambition and as short on credibility as some of its more overreaching subject matter. Its aims, however, are far more pedestrian. This book represents *not* an attempt to synthesize disparate intellectual fields but an exercise of indiscipline, however romantic in its errantry. It explores how certain fields of study—and how thought itself—can and have been deformed and reformed according to their encounters with ways of thinking and knowing alien to their own. Such "outsider" thinking both strains and exercises the social and epistemological mechanisms of what we consider to be expertise—and, in some cases, stretches its borders or even erodes them altogether.

As a consequence, this book represents a series of forays into fields of study that are not my own: theological heresies of late antiquity, archaeology, entrepreneurial business ventures, psychoanalysis and psychiatric medicine, astronomy, ancient history, the philosophy of science, and the sociology of knowledge. Yet it is an insistence of this book that such spheres of inquiry not be demarcated according to professionalism or prestige alone; my wanderings are, I hope, neither a colonial venture nor a perfunctory Grand Tour of the marvels and curiosities of knowledge. These are wanderings conducted very much on foot.

I offer thanks to the many friends, colleagues, and collaborators who have read or contributed in other ways to this project, whether as general readers and interlocutors, comrades-of-the-pen, and/or experts in their fields. I have turned to them less for shoring up the credibility of my wayward ventures—though I have been spared many a false trail on account of their generosity—than for their guidance and tolerance in reading, hearing about, and participating in the adventures chronicled herein. Thus, a warm, deep expression of cosmic gratitude to Martha Schoolman, Caitlin Wood, Jamie Taylor, Andrès Villalta, Janet Lyon, Michael Bérubé, Jamie Bérubé, Jeremy Braddock, Hoda El Shakry, Courtney Morris, Magalí Armillas-Tiseyra, Ebony Coletu, Ben Lee, Lisi Schoenbach, Kate Conley, Mary Ann Caws, Judith Roof, Susan Aberth, Gabriel Weisz, Catriona McAra, Effie Rentzou, Ben Schreier, Sarah Koenig, Susan Squier, Gowen Roper, Charles Tung, Gloria Fisk, Lisa Uddin, Debarati Sanyal, Gabriel Rockhill, Michael Gillespie, Marijeta Bozovic, Jean-Michel Rabaté, Patricia Gherovici, Amanda Williams, Nigel Roth, Patrick North, Beth Freeman, Mary Richardson-Graham, Patrick Richardson-Graham, Donald Becker, Aaron Jaffe, Helen O'Leary, Brent Green, Mary McClanahan, Charlotte Eubanks, Cynthia Young, Shuang Shen, Julia Kasdorf, Mark Morrisson, Aldon Nielsen, Kevin Bell, Nergis Ertürk, Jeffrey Nealon, Rich Doyle, Bruno Jean-François, Ellie Goodman, Abram Foley, Laura Anderson Barbata, Angela Naimou, Michael LeMahieu, Grant Farred, Matthew Hart, Sam Ladkin, Patricia Allmer, Toni Jensen, Dalia Judovitz, Nathan Grant, Aileen Keenan, Sarah Mesle, Sarah Blackwood, and Andrew Epstein, as well as my many other excellent friends and colleagues, both at Penn State and elsewhere—even beyond Pennsylvania.

For those who read portions of the book and offered careful thoughts, a special note of thanks: Michael Bérubé, Robert Caserio, Ebony Coletu, Michelle Commander, Patrick Durgin, Edgar Garcia, Michael Gordin,

Karen Jacobs, Phil Jenkins, James Kopf, Warren Liu, Shaoling Ma, Daniel Purdy, Gabriel Rockhill, Judith Roof, Edgar Schmitz, Susan Squier, and Jamie Taylor.

I also thank my colleagues in ASAP: The Association for the Study of the Arts of the Present, which offers a resounding creative stimulus and a model for intellectual camaraderie across the arts. I have had the pleasure of presenting portions of this project and receiving invaluable feedback from a number of colleagues and friends, including Pam Thurschwell, Sara Crangle, and the Centre for Modernist Studies at the University of Sussex; Marius Hentea, Sarah Posman, and the University of Ghent; Roger Rothman, John Westbrook, and the Bucknell University French and Art History departments; Jonathan Goldman and the New York Modernism research group; Andrea Goulet and the University of Pennsylvania Department of French and Francophone Studies; Diederik Oostdijk and the Vrije Universiteit Amsterdam Faculty of Language, Literature and Communication; Marcin Napiórkowski and the Polish Vernacular Culture research group at the University of Warsaw; John Wilkinson, Matt ffytche, and the members of the Outsider Writing consortium at the Neubauer Collegium for Culture and Society at the University of Chicago. I also thank Peter Potter for his early support of this project.

My experiments in inexpertise have been sanctioned—or at least sustained—by the great privilege I have of teaching in the Departments of Comparative Literature and English at Penn State and, more recently, in the Department of French and Francophone Studies. I thank Robert Edwards and Mark Morrisson for their support of my work, as well as Carey Eckhardt for her wisdom and mentorship. Thanks also to the Institute for the Arts and Humanities for supporting my research during a semester-long residential fellowship in 2012, and to the Penn State College of the Liberal Arts for allowing me to stretch a "teaching release" into a four-month residency abroad in 2014. I also wish to acknowledge the members of my graduate seminar, Oddity, Unreason, and Modernity, for their keen contributions to the study of alternative epistemologies, both then and now; as well as the brilliant current and former graduate and undergraduate students with whom I have had the pleasure of working closely.

I wish to thank Arnaud de Sède for offering me a copy of his father's memoir, as well as hosting me for lunch in the foothills of the Pyrenees in fall 2014. Thanks also to Irwin Chusid, Gail Lettick, and Rafael Sharon for permission to reprint archival materials, as well as the special collections and library staffs at the Bibliothèque Nationale de France, the University of Chicago, Princeton University, and Penn State. I thank Marcin Napiórkowski for his Polish translation of portions of the introduction and chapter 7 in *Kultura Współczesna*.

At the University of Minnesota Press, I thank Doug Armato for his interest in the project and his guidance through the publication process, and especially for his tolerance for long books—and willingness to read them with care and insight. Thanks also to Gabriel Levin for his intrepid stewardship of the manuscript, and to Rachel Moeller, John Donohue, and Emily Hamilton for their expertise in finalizing the book for publication. I am grateful, too, for the two readers who reviewed the manuscript, John Wilkinson and an anonymous second reader; my book has benefited immeasurably from their insights and suggestions for revision.

A fond shout-out to Amy Elias, with whom I have collaborated weekly for the past five years as founding coeditors of *ASAP/Journal:* here's to you, my comrade, friend, and partner in schemes. Thanks also to Margaret and Timothy Eburne, Samantha and Cal Morgan, Jordan Eburne and Gabriella Garcia-Eburne, and Maureen and Carl Blum, as well as the late Phoebe Eburne, for their love and support. Many of my surrogate family of core peeps have already been mentioned above, but here's to you again, dear ones. I would also like to thank my long-suffering domestic animals, who not only tolerated the many hours of distraction this book demanded in the making but also helped with some of the typing and occasionally volunteered to settle in and dwell on portions of the manuscript as well.

And finally, to Adelaide and Hester: I cannot imagine, in however visionary a fashion, a more fortunate way to spend time on this fractured earth than with two such luminous, magnificent people. This book is a testament to our shared adventure in life—and the rays of hope that animate it owes everything to your strength, brilliance, courage, and love.

PREFACE
Enemies of the Truth

A NUMBER OF YEARS AGO, as I was beginning to write this book, I came across a notice on Craigslist advertising used occult books for sale. The seller was offering hardcovers for a dollar apiece and paperbacks for a quarter. I contacted the seller and asked how much it would cost to purchase the collection outright. The response was an agreeable one: for fifty dollars, I could carry home the lot. Given the scarcity of bookstores in my region of the world, I considered this incentive enough to undertake the several hours' drive necessary for the pickup. A few days later I made the trip to retrieve what I presumed would be a box or two of used books. Who knows? I might find one or two treasures among them, I thought. What awaited me instead was a small library, a treasure in itself: the seller was unloading hundreds upon hundreds of titles, the bulk of his ailing mother's library. They filled the car: front seat, back seat, trunk.

I have since been slowly working my way through the pages of this acquired library of popular esoterica. It would be absurd to measure my lucky find against those far greater troves of hermetic wisdom uncovered in recent centuries, from posthumous caches of visionary writings to major archaeological discoveries such as the Dead Sea Scrolls and the Nag Hammadi Library (the latter of which forms the object of study in chapters 1 and 2). All the same, my little discovery was remarkable in its own right. For one, it comprised the sum of decades of accumulation, representing a set of reading habits that were not my own. As secondhand property, located digitally but acquired manually, the collection represents both a library of popular occult books and an archive of half a lifetime's reading.

I now keep the books in one large cabinet, with the paperbacks stacked double on every shelf. Studies of "psychic archaeology" and biblical history flank testimonials to lost worlds and paranormal activity, UFOs and crop circles, lycanthropes and life after death. The covers are often as understated as the titles are extravagant, as if assuaging readers as to the levelheadedness of their contents. The individual works are rarely playful or smug. Insisting on the profundity of their insights and furnishing elaborate proof of their assertions, they collectively form a genre of marginal nonfiction that obeys well-established codes and expectations. Each beckons toward a horizon of wonder, promising to flout scientific or historical dogma as necessary. To some readers, such works of popular superstition and pseudoscientific fancy dance at the borders of religion and myth, artfully embracing conjecture. To others, they are nonsense, preying on the credulity of their readers in their endless quest for "our planet's secret history."[1]

Are readers so gullible, though, as to believe everything they read in such texts, whether concerning the fate of Noah's ark or the alien geniuses who built the pyramids? Are we to read the claims and suppositions of such works as pure fantasy, or as something more heterogeneous: fabulation, sensationalism, or bullshit? As a subgenre of popular literature, such work might tug pleasantly at our imaginations. As texts whose claims jockey for the status of scientific or religious authority, however, they might give us greater pause. One might wonder how their former owner and original reader interpreted their claims—and whether they furnished tokens of belief or counterhistories of human knowledge. But what if they offered both at once? As with other literary subgenres, popular critics are often suspicious of the commercial appeal and ideological pull of parapsychology, mysticism, pseudoscience, occultism, and counterfactual history. "If the public wants to shell out cash for such flummery," wrote the popular mathematician and pseudoscience debunker Martin Gardner in 1952, "what difference does it make? The answer is that it is not at all amusing when people are misled by scientific claptrap. . . . It is hard to see how the effects can be anything but harmful."[2] Beyond the wasteful expenditure of mental energy that reading (and writing) them entails, popular occult and pseudoscience books dangerously muddy the waters of intellectual discernment. "The more the public is confused," Gardner warned, "the easier it falls prey to doctrines of pseudo-science which may at some future date receive the backing of politically powerful groups. . . . If the German people had been better trained to distinguish good from bad science, would they have swallowed so easily the insane racial theories of the Nazi anthropologists?"[3] Yet to the unnerving extent that the science upon which German eugenics and genocide were based was accepted and promoted by mainstream scientific institutions in their time, the question of how "intellectual discernment" might best be regulated raises questions

FIGURE 1. A secondhand library of popular esoterica. Collection of the author.

that far surpass the idiosyncratic reading habits and belief systems of the public. Instead these questions pertain to the ways in which the traditions and institutions of the so-called mainstream can be shaped and coopted. Nearly seven decades later, Gardner's skepticism finds regular refrains in the popular media and in academic scholarship alike: the public is perpetually seduced into entertaining deceptions—as well as racism and tyranny—on account of the titillating falsehoods of the internet, or of popular esoterica, the bibliographic shock troops of the culture industry in our "post-truth" age.[4] Perhaps our institutions are to blame? Such, at least, is the position that has gained increasing traction among antiscience, antiuniversity, and antijournalism politicians—a position that is alarming not only for its bald antiintellectualism but also for its equally bald solicitation of "politically powerful groups," from corporate lobbies to ultra-right-wing ideological factions.

With such denunciations in mind, *Outsider Theory* takes up a detailed investigation of the ways in which marginal or otherwise underground, hermetic, or far-fetched ideas circulate. It studies how, and according to what means, such theories gain acceptance or encounter rejection, as well as how they are revised and transformed over time. This book maintains that attention to the particulars of distribution and redistribution, and to the curiosities of readership and belief, is fundamental to any critical examination of so-called junk thought and its currency in modern intellectual history. A sustained reckoning with the circulation of outlandish ideas, as much as with the ideas themselves, is likewise fundamental to any attempt to uphold intellectual endeavors—whether artistic, scientific, or popular—against their institutional discreditation or ideological mobilization.

This is no minor undertaking, and the aim of *Outsider Theory* is to invite further inquiry rather than to exhaust (or to claim definitively to comprehend) this virtually limitless field of relations. In the chapters that follow I concentrate on the material and institutional forms through which heterodox thinking circulates: archives, libraries, periodicals, electronic databases, bibliophile societies, corporate entities, scientific communities, and the book market. Some of the more industrialized and institutionalized of these forms exert considerable interpretive and cultural power upon the way ideas form and travel, whether newspapers or college textbooks, policy think tanks or Facebook. Even so, such forms are never fully consistent with themselves, opening up interpretive gaps for invention, misinterpretation, or reappropriation. Other forms, by contrast, are significant for their capacity to persist in the face of implicit or explicit suppression. For instance, the theories and intellectual frameworks established through the traditional knowledges of indigenous peoples, or the intellectual labor of socially marginalized populations, is often discounted or trivialized as a rite of passage within mainstream institutions. As the environmental biologist Robin Wall Kimmerer has written, "Getting scientists to consider the validity of indigenous knowledge is like swimming upstream in cold, cold water."[5] Such acts of trivialization and suppression determine neither the veracity nor the content of the ideas they police, yet they go far to restrict their circulation to isolated or marginal spheres of influence. Even so, as the sociologist Patricia Hill Collins maintains, the intellectual resistance to such suppression can also dialectically foster "new angles of vision" and new specialized forms and communities of knowledge.[6] The rhetoric of this epistemological struggle has, however, also been rhetorically taken up by right-wing and white supremacist groups, whose own "marginalized" values and documents, they claim, deserve the same recognition that any other socially disenfranchised population might wish to claim. The circulation of ideas is ultimately a political struggle, and with real, mortal consequences. *Outsider Theory* is, above all, a book about the troubled waters of discernment—whether muddy, cold, or tempestuous, whether stagnant or acidic—in which contemporary intellectuals find ourselves immersed and from which we nevertheless continue to slake our thirst.

At the same time, it is important to note that attention to the particulars of circulation and consumption cannot fully exhaust the mystery of the books and other media that constitute outsider theory, much in the same way that obtaining a library through Craigslist does not begin to account for the task of reading its individual volumes. Such mysteries remain curiously powerful—dangerous, scandalous, deceptive, mind-expanding, visionary, reactionary—even as the allure of their truth effects and revelations can often fade into generic predictability. Likewise, the revelatory truth of an idea can demand a spiritual or epistemological upheaval regardless of whether such upheavals are heeded or betrayed, pursued or trivialized. *Outsider Theory* attends to the epistemological demands that even the most cynical or invidious works of conjectural nonsense levy upon our varied experiences as readers and thinkers, and which even the most authoritative or well-intentioned canons often neglect to take seriously. Such works confront us, most of all, with a demand to read, and to think, in more than one dimension, beyond the static contemplation of individual works or theories, and beyond the phenomenological self-improvement of our current methods.

Suspicions nonetheless abound. As the philosopher Harry Frankfurt reminds readers of his best-selling chapbook *On Bullshit,* the problem is not just that popular works of pseudoscience or archaeological fantasy might contain erroneous or falsified claims but that such claims tend to be spun out independently of any real concern with truth. It is one thing to enter seriously into the fray of truth and falsehood; it is another to wander through the no-man's-land of improper speculation. Frankfurt makes a number of strong assertions about this tendency: whereas errors and lies respond to facts by unintentionally or intentionally defying the authority of the truth, bullshit ignores these demands altogether. "By virtue of this," Frankfurt writes, "bullshit is a greater enemy of the truth than lies are."[7] Are popular books on UFOs and ancient mysteries analogously "enemies of the truth"? When a book such as Rupert Furneaux's 1977 *Ancient Mysteries* "captures the imagination and astonishes the mind," as the cover blurb from the *New York Times Book Review* tells its readers, does this capacity for apprehension amount to a literal act of ideological entrapment? To what extent, in other words, have "astonishment" and "capture" become synonyms? Furneaux's book hardly presents itself as an enemy of the truth. On the contrary, Furneaux is dedicated to exploding, rather than inflating, popular speculations about mythical history. *Ancient Mysteries* purports to demystify religiously themed fantasies as naturally occurring phenomena: it sets itself firmly *against* bullshit. Skeptical accounts of ancient mysteries appeal to the same audience as more seemingly far-fetched accounts, as Martin Gardner knew all too well; his own widely read *Fads and Fallacies in the Name of Science* (1957) remains in print as part of the Dover Books on the Occult series, part of the very genre he sought tirelessly to debunk. Doubt, or even a kind of critical paranoia—rather than credulity or belief—may well be the genre's fuel.

Doubt takes many forms, however. In France, for instance, contemporary esoterica has maintained a strong degree of intellectual prestige over the past century and a half; this owes largely to the field's "unification" as a refuge for a general, wide-ranging intelligence unmoored from professional scholarly or ideological fixations. Incorporating the work of established figures such as Raymond Abellio, René Alleau, and René Guénon, and not just of crackpots or popularizing hacks alone, the field bears continuities with the literary avant-garde as well as with philosophy and the history of science.[8] As we will see in chapters 3 and 4, this field of inquiry often positions itself paradigmatically at odds with more specialized institutions of knowledge, mobilizing doubt as an active epistemological force. In the United States and worldwide, the 1960s and 1970s saw a surge in popular forms of mysticism and the occult, itself largely a reprise of earlier occult revivals in the late nineteenth and early twentieth centuries. In a period of global political upheaval and insurgence, 1960s and 1970s movements in New Age spirituality, psychedelia, anticolonial and Black Arts collectivism, and countercultural epistemologies likewise mined the history of magic, witchcraft, hermeticism, Eastern mysticism, and ancient religions for alternative forms of knowledge and belief.[9] For some, such litanies might warrant little more than an eye roll of dismissal; the countercultural embrace of irrationality and mysticism has long since seen its day. For others, such reading lists might instead arouse a pang of nostalgia for the Aquarian days of yore, when students read Wilhelm Reich on the crowded lawns of "antiuniversities."[10] Today, pundits and critics often view such recuperations—as well as the motive forces of doubt and desire that fuel them—as symptoms of more sinister ideological functions. In an era of increasing political extremism worldwide, the skepticism at work in the circulation of occult and underground books harks back less to the rationalist doubt brandished by the likes of René Descartes, Frankfurt, and Gardner than to a far more corrosive form of suspicion: an empty nihilism that threatens the very foundations of rationalism itself. Questions about the deceptive allure of popular pseudoscience and mysticism fuel contemporary debates about the prevalence of "junk thought" in an increasingly "aliterate" United States.[11] For many journalists and commentators, a skepticism toward *real facts* and legitimate knowledge has become commonplace in the contemporary marketplace of bad ideas, both in its cheap paperback form and in its more insidious incarnations on Fox News and Breitbart, in politics, in the pulpit, and, for many, in academic mumbo jumbo. Skeptics are often skeptical of the other skeptics. In an age in which the general knowledge of history and geography has eroded nearly as apocalyptically as the education system itself, this genre testifies to an imaginative horizon no less fantastic, and no less mysterious to the supposed common reader, than the real contours of the living geopolitical word. Atlantis is no more unreal to many contemporary American readers than, say, the Canary Islands or Lichtenstein. Without a concrete frame of reference, everything looks like bullshit.

For this very reason, the massive production of books on occultism and paranormal activity holds something of a reliquary fascination. As *mere books*—given that books are so often considered to be things of the past—how dangerous could their allure possibly be? J. K. Rowling's Harry Potter series yielded no shortage of nervous fundamentalists in its heyday, to be sure. But the greatest marvel of the series' popularity may simply have been that it enticed children (and many adults) to read long books. Likewise, the ultimate acceptability of fantasy, pseudoscience, or other esoteric fancies seems to involve a kind of wager on behalf of the common reader, whereby the ideological idiosyncrasies of a work are measured against the genre's capacity to influence a reading public. According to what criteria should we deem the works of Sigmund Freud, or Martin Heidegger, or Ayn Rand, or the Marquis de Sade too dangerous to teach in schools? According to what criteria might Helena Blavatsky's theosophical writings, Ignatius Donnelly's *Atlantis,* Trofim Lysenko's antigenetic theories of heredity, L. Ron Hubbard's *Dianetics,* or Malachi Z. York's Nuwaubian movement warrant curricular attention?[12] I would propose that such questions—keeping in mind the ideological pitfalls flagged by Gardner—hinge far more readily on the education system itself, and the corporate technologies and "best practices" that sustain it, than on its reading material.[13] However intrepidly skeptics such as Gardner might strive to prune pseudoscience from science, rubbish from reason, they rarely manage to distinguish between the "fads and fallacies" they debunk and the industrialized cultural institutions that promulgate them. For Gardner, pseudoscience and phony religion are the products of crackpot demagogues whose work appeals to a public "hungry for sensational discoveries and quick panaceas."[14] The masses flock to bad ideas, it seems, of their own accord. Surely, though, the overwhelming plenitude of *unpopular* bad ideas—not to mention the overwhelming plenitude of unpopular *good* ideas, including books, magazines, sketches, letters, documents, lifeways, traditions, languages, and other cultural repositories that remain consigned to obscurity—already begins to controvert such a fearsome depiction of the credulous public. Such publics exist insofar as they are *made* rather than merely satiated. And however influential a best-selling work of popular nonsense might be, it is not the books themselves in isolation, nor the ideas within them alone, that forge the ideological susceptibility to which professional skeptics persistently appeal. As the historian Michael Gordin suggests, the "demarcation problem" of distinguishing science from pseudoscience, reason from unreason, is a political rather than purely conceptual struggle.[15] So too is the tendency to distinguish professional or legitimate forms of intellectual endeavor from locations and populations—people with disabilities, nonnative speakers, women of color, indigenous peoples, workers—who are not commonly perceived as intellectuals, as Patricia Hill Collins has argued.[16]

Curiously, in spite of its dangers, the capacity for slippage between occult thinking and the sphere of common knowledge policed by skeptics often elicits a begrudging respect. Even a stalwart pragmatist like Harry Frankfurt avers that bullshit bears a creative function, a kind of artistry beyond the mere technical proficiency demonized, for instance, by the historical opponents of alchemy and witchcraft. And yet this degraded mode of artful composition nonetheless occupies a different order of creativity from both analytical reason and, most important of all, truth. As Frankfurt writes, "the mode of creativity upon which [bullshit] relies is less analytical and less deliberative than that which is mobilized in lying. It is more expansive and independent, with more spacious opportunities for improvisation, color, and imaginative play. This is less a matter of craft than of art."[17] For Frankfurt, the danger of bullshit lies precisely in this art: it is neither sincerity nor credulity that defines its unfaithfulness to reason, but rather a "liberty" with the truth.

Frankfurt's account makes sense when this "liberty" bears worldly consequences beyond those we associate with art—such as when it begins to compete, say, for political or institutional authority. Dated, counterfactual, or ideologically suspicious works might be safely packed away in libraries along with the works of Paracelsus or the *Malleus Maleficarum*. But when they provide fodder for active beliefs and ideological positions, any such liberty with the truth becomes far more perilously charged with significance. What happens, though, under circumstances in which the truth is not self-evident, but unknowable or actively contested—or when it refers to an open-ended set of contingencies? The excesses of "improvisation, color, and imaginative play" to which Frankfurt alludes are often indistinguishable from their speculative deployment in the very name of rationalism and truth. We do not like to think of surgeons or heads of state as engaging in "imaginative play." Yet even under the best of circumstances their expertise often extends to the speculative, even improvisatory, deployment of their knowledge. Other methods and disciplines for distinguishing expertise—systematic training, methodology, rigor—each encounter their limits, after all, on the rocky shoals of whatever we mean by the notions of "experience" and "experiment," which accumulate according to other means.[18] What situated or embodied knowledges come into play, what intuitions and inventions become expedient, within the very deployment of expertise?[19] One might propose that it is ultimately an ethical question that underwrites any such authority, any such deployment of expertise, in the name of truth. But according to what forms of discernment does this "name," this set of intentions, become legible? Such questions haunt pragmatist philosophy and the sociology of knowledge—not to mention critical theory—well beyond the domain of occult books and "junk thought." But they leave an especially deep impression on both the public reception and the rhetoric of such books. As Arthur Koestler puts it in the opening pages of his "excursion into parapsychology" from 1972, *The Roots of Coincidence*, "Half of my friends accuse me of an excess of scientific pedantry; the other half of unscientific leanings toward preposterous subjects such as extra-sensory perception (ESP), which they include in the domain of the supernatural. However, it is comforting to know that the same accusations are leveled at an élite of scientists who make excellent company in the dock."[20] Unlike Frankfurt, Koestler does not presume "truth" as a manifest category for judgment; he instead outlines a more ambiguous investigation that faces up to its uncertainties. Koestler thus articulates here the ambiguities of speculative thinking that preoccupy many philosophers of science and writers of allegedly "preposterous subjects" alike. Yet he does so, no less characteristically, in terms that strikingly resemble the rhetorical devices of even the most outlandish works in the genre: *no matter how crazy my theories might seem*, the logic runs, *there are real scientists whose claims resemble my own*.

Such identifications characterize the "demarcation problem" of distinguishing pseudoscience or nonscience from legitimate scientific practice, as formalized by Karl Popper in the 1930s and advocated with renewed vigor by contemporary scientists bent on corroborating the authority, as well as the limits, of scientific expertise.[21] Yet such demarcations remain untidy and all the more difficult to discern within the sphere of reading and writing, and especially in the kinds of speculative thinking we find in metaphysics, philosophy, and the arts. We might propose, with Popper, that the distinction between science and nonscience, or between rationalism and bullshit, hinges on the pursuit of "falsifiable" experimentation: the point is less to measure good intentions, in other words, than to weed out empirically disprovable theories from the living body of theories that circulate actively. Or else we might recognize the difficulty—and even the arrogance—of formalizing the pursuit of truth in terms other than ethical ones. The alternative has been to take a longer view of the ways in which concepts like reason, truth, science, and knowledge have been both upheld and resisted. For centuries, scientists and philosophers have devoted serious attention to the epistemological status of "prescientific" theories and myths that inform scientific practice, even as they are dismissed for their factual or methodological shortcomings. In an era of "culture wars" and funding cuts for the arts and letters, by contrast, the humanities are only beginning to contend with their relationship to the margins of their practices. This book offers a step in this direction: it takes stock of the ways in which outmoded or otherwise outlandish ideas persist in shaping—as well as distorting—contemporary thought.

Who reads this stuff? The hundreds of books I purchased over the internet all belonged to a single reader, J.M., who signed her name in the inside front cover of each volume. Whereas I had acquired the books all at once, the collection itself had been carefully assembled over the course of several decades, from the mid-1960s through the late 1980s. The books are united by something more than a genre; they are also bound together by their common purchase and accumulation, bearing the signature of their common reader. The question of how such practices—buying, collecting, reading, signing one's name—impinge on the status of the books, and the outlandish claims they so often bear, presents its own set of methodological challenges. The history of J.M. as a reader (as well as my own reading history) is no less significant to the claims and theories her books advance than the technology of the book industry or public debates about truth and nonsense. Having discovered her signatures only belatedly, I had neglected to interrogate the seller more fully about his reasons for liquidating the collection. Had J.M. given up reading altogether, or had she simply downsized her collection?[22] What were her ideological predilections? How did she read? How did she vote?

A more public collection of literature, science, art, or ephemera might legibly disclose its principles of accumulation, at once exercising and revealing the aesthetic and ideological viewpoints that guided its formation. But one can only speculate about the kind of reading exercised on and through J.M.'s collection of popular esoterica. Unlike the "provisional institutions" of modern art and literature—or of scientific research—that establish authority according to principles of accumulation and discernment, the once private occult library of J.M. is the result of cultural practices that might seem limited, at least on first blush, to the intimacies of consumption.[23] This was not a collection housed in a public library, or in a church, literary salon, or art gallery. In their initial purchase and secondhand procurement alike, the accumulation of individual titles was bound up instead in the vicissitudes of taste, selection, and the marketplace of cheap popular books. Other than her signatures, the books bear few traces of the attentions bestowed upon them: they contain no marginalia, no underlined passages, no dog-eared pages, no wayward bookmarks. Unlike scrapbooks or diaries, the collection offers few macroscopic hints about the ways these books were read and digested beyond the shape of the collection itself. To generalize about its reader(s) on the basis of the titles would be to exercise a reductive typology no less conjectural than any of the hermetic mysteries "explained" by the books themselves. The reader cannot be deduced from the collection, whether freethinker or naive, reactionary or dupe. Yet it is in the name of such readers that scholars and pundits so often seek to legitimate or police the truth effects of esoterica and pseudoscience. In fact we tend to know far less about the way such books and ideas have been gathered, read, interpreted, and thought about than we do about their credibility or shock effects. How, and for whom, do collections of esoterica such as J.M.'s constitute bodies of knowledge?

Beyond such individual considerations, the collection bears other impressions; it offers, for instance, a portrait of the paperback publishing industry in its analogue prime, bolstered by ready distribution and the circulation of book reviews and cover blurbs. Throughout the 1970s and 1980s, it seems, virtually all these books on UFOs and life after death could lay claim to best seller status or rave reviews in prominent newspapers. Even a brief survey of the books' covers dramatizes how the industry changed over a period of several decades. Today the mass-market appeal of such books has dispersed rapidly in the age of internet sites such as Educating Humanity and The Conspiracy Zone,[24] which now contend with the print industry for both circulation and advertising space, if not for "truth." J.M.'s collection now comprises a set of paperback curiosities, notable less for their scarcity than for their evidentiary appeal to a marginalized culture of print.

My secondhand collection of popular occult books thus offers a counterpoint, I hope, to any discussion about the cultural status of such popular speculation and the pitfalls or pleasures of their truth claims. *Outsider Theory* is a book about the volatile status of such truths and falsehoods in modern intellectual history; it studies the marginalization and recycling of repositories of questionable knowledge. Rather than offering a compendium of epistemological curiosities—and there is no shortage of such compilations[25]—this book takes heed of the secondhand and often compromised forms in which readers encounter them.

INTRODUCTION

OUTSIDER THEORY is a book about outlandish ideas. It studies errant, unfashionable, or otherwise unreasonable thinking and its role in the intellectual life of the present. The term *outlandish* refers to a relational rather than an evaluative criterion: it designates an unfamiliar or alien contingency particular to what is known or normate. Rather than describing an isolated anomaly, it beckons toward a world of ideas whose status as truth or falsehood may be indeterminate or even suspect, but whose many forms nonetheless constitute the very horizon of the thinkable.

Outsider Theory attends to the complexity and dynamism of this ever-shifting horizon. I am interested in the extent to which speculative inquiry extends beyond the work of professional intellectuals (e.g., clinicians, scientists, philosophers, and critics) to include the work of nonprofessionals, whether amateurs, unfashionable observers, the clinically insane, or populations not commonly perceived as intellectuals. This book features the work of a variety of such figures, from self-taught philosophers to psychiatric patients and "outsider artists," from the Marquis de Sade to pseudoscientists. In doing so, however, my aim is neither to canonize so-called nonprofessionals nor to evaluate their worth, whether in affirming the relevance of their ideas or rejecting them as falsehoods. Whereas the term *outsider* often designates a social type or sociological category (as does *crank* in writings about pseudoscience),[1] *Outsider Theory* attends instead to the construction and reception of ideas rather than the social or cognitive faculties of their authors. *Outsider* does not refer here to a category of insanity or disability. In fact, I will argue that it does not refer to a category at all. Nor does it appeal to some critical or conceptual "beyond" as a vantage point from which thought arrives. This book instead studies the processes of interpretation, synthesis, and association through which idiosyncratic theories form—and by which they inform others. Some of these ideas circulate within contemporary popular culture; others are restricted to the archive or the asylum, or fall out of circulation entirely. Regardless of their origin or familiarity, such ideas have left their impression on twentieth-century thinking and continue to exercise a role in its continued evolution. This book looks beyond the arena of immediately recuperable knowledge to consider instead the complexity and dynamism of intellectual circulation. Far from demarcating a singular encounter with oddity or a susceptibility to ideological fads and fallacies, *Outsider Theory* traces the various and multiple currents of intellectual production, reception, and transformation that make up the oceanic expanse of modern intellectual history. It examines the relations among a wide array of thinkers and their evolving systems of thought—whether timely or untimely, fashionable or unfashionable.

OUTSIDER ART / OUTSIDER THEORY

Throughout the nineteenth and twentieth centuries, the many incarnations of mysticism, automatic writing, New Age holism, hermeticism, and pseudoscience have just as often been taken up as cast aside by other intellectuals. Offering concepts and traditions alternative to mainstream thinking, such bodies of knowledge have promised visionary flights, opened up underground currents of suppressed political intensity, beckoned to countercultural forms of intellectual exchange, and, on occasion, yielded nostalgic retroformulations justifying intolerance. Such deployments demonstrate the extent to which modern intellectuals have approached such "alternative" knowledges as something other than curiosities or aberrations of thought. Such heterogeneity reminds us not only that theory and intellectual creativity are "not the province of a select few but instead emanate from a range of people," as Patricia Hill Collins has written, but also that the range of forms through which such thinking inhabits the world is no less expansive.[2] Even the ravages of mental illness—paranoia, schizophrenia, bipolar disorder—have been recognized for their systematic functioning as much as they have been exploited for their romantic excesses. Writings and works of art collected from psychiatric patients have left an indelible impression on the history of art; but they have also contributed no less profoundly to the history of psychiatry, sociology, and philosophy, serving as models and forming genealogies as well as providing objects of clinical and critical study. The history of modern thought is incomplete without an account of the "discontinuous" and often pathologized systems of thought immanent in it. How, though, do contemporary intellectuals and cultural workers accommodate themselves to such systems? To what extent do these systems of thought fall outside the

definitions and traditions of rational thinking we might continue to maintain, or to what extent do they underwrite, haunt, or otherwise preoccupy
these very definitions and traditions?

Heterogeneous ways of thinking have long fueled new directions in
critical thinking and offered paradigms for frustrated or persecuted intellectuals. A key example for the present study is the French polymath Georges
Bataille, who in the early 1930s devised a form of cultural analysis he called
"heterology." Though Bataille has himself been subsequently canonized as a
major figure in French poststructuralist thought, his "science" of heterology
marshaled a discomfiting mixture of religion and politics, ethnography and
critical theory. It proposed to study unorthodox cultural phenomena normally
disavowed by classical theories of philosophy and political economy—such
as Sadean perversion, Nietzschean philosophy, popular front politics, and
sacrificial religions—and modeled its own methods of study upon the provocations such phenomena introduced. First adopted in an unpublished 1932
essay on the Marquis de Sade (who features in chapter 6 of this book), Bataille's "heterological theory of knowledge" resists the systematic incorporation of all data into a secure, homogeneous body of knowledge. It instead
participates in the disorderly production of waste, excretion, appropriation,
and discontinuity it proposed to study: for Bataille, theory and waste were
constitutive elements of other systems of knowledge that functioned normally
by casting them out.[3] The French artist and writer Jean Dubuffet picked up
on Bataille's ideas in developing his collection of *l'art brut* (literally, "raw" or
"crude" art)—what is known in English as *outsider art*—a general term for
the artistic production of self-taught, disabled, visionary, insane, or folk artists. Bataille's and Dubuffet's efforts to document the knowability of heterogeneous cultural material bore distinctly avant-garde credentials, particularly
to the extent that such material posed an implicit challenge to the closed
systems of the bourgeois art world at midcentury, as well as the human sciences more broadly.[4] The study and reclamation of heterodox knowledge is
often flush with revolutionary rhetoric as a result: oddity will set you free!
The foundation of outsider art as an aesthetic category coincided with its
formation as an object, as well as a means, of study. The history of such rec-
lamations is thus consistent with modern thinking about the complexity
and stochastic processes of intellectual history, insofar as ideas circulate in
ways other than according to a triumphalist narrative of forward technological progress.

Outsider Theory extends its purview from visual art to intellectual work
more broadly. Much as the notion of *l'art brut* acknowledges forms of artistic creativity once considered negligible or merely the source material for truly

great artists, this book seeks to enrich contemporary intellectual and critical inquiry by devoting serious attention to marginalized thought.[5] In the art world, the category of "outsider" is a tendentious one. Coined in the early 1970s by the art historian Roger Cardinal as a way to translate Jean Dubuffet's notion of *l'art brut,* the term *outsider* designated the kinds of artistic production typically excluded from the sanctioned realms of institutionalized high art, such as the work of self-trained and folk artists, cognitively or physically disabled artists, and the anonymous producers of "found" and ethnic art objects. The assimilation of such figures under a common category has come increasingly under fire in recent years, especially as outsider art has become a lucrative and critically appraised industry within the very art world against which it once positioned itself. The popularity of works by figures such as Henry Darger, Madge Gill, Martín Ramirez, Judith Scott, Bill Traylor, and Adolf Wölfli, among many others, has fueled the careers of numerous dealers, curators, and critics. Such successes have at times eclipsed the working conditions of the artists themselves, who often lived and died in obscurity, poverty, or institutional confinement. The criteria for assimilating the work of such disparate artists under a common rubric point largely to the tastes of collectors rather than to intrinsic properties of the works themselves. All the same, collecting art under the *outsider* rubric—or its alternative semantic rubrics, such as *self-taught, visionary,* or *intuitive art*—can also function as a curatorial recognition of cognitively disabled artists as intellectually and aesthetically gifted; for this reason it is impossible, as art critic Roxana Azimi reminds us, "to comprehend the full territory of outsider art," just as it is impossible fully to dismiss it as a heuristic for interrogating aesthetic criteria and the institutions, media, and concepts that shape and sustain them.[6]

The term *outsider* bears conceptual as well as sociological overtones. According to Cardinal, the term recalls the works of writers such as Albert Camus and Richard Wright, as well as existential philosophers such as Simone de Beauvoir, Martin Heidegger, and Jean-Paul Sartre, for whom the notion of alienation signified more than just a name for social deviants or the clinically insane *(aliénés).*[7] Cardinal's existentialist inflection differs markedly from the best-selling typologies of alienation published by Colin Wilson and Howard Becker in previous decades, whose titles it nonetheless recalls: in 1956, Wilson rose to celebrity on the countercultural claims of his book *The Outsider,* which ascribes brooding revelatory power to the sovereign outcast as a modern literary type. Becker's 1963 study of drug use in *Outsiders* is a landmark text in the sociology of deviance.[8] Rather than romanticizing the alien outsider as a rebellious or tragic exception to social norms, Cardinal's "outside" instead invokes alienation as an existential condition of our *Gewor-fenheit* (thrownness) into the world, whose ubiquity is at once disclosed and relativized by the marginalized figures it casts out.[9] Cardinal's genealogy thus shakes a critical fist at the institutional and ideological structures that perpetuate alienation insofar as they deemed marginal art, not to mention marginalized peoples, to be worthy of forgetting. This, too, was the polemical thrust of Dubuffet's notion of *l'art brut:* to challenge the cultural conditioning that sustains the tautology whereby forgotten or overlooked art is aesthetically inferior precisely because it is neglected. The term *outsider* is thus less a category or type than a provocation: it induces contemporary spectators to judge works individually rather than blindly heeding "the prevailing wind emitted by the Establishment, [whereby they] could consent to find objective beauty only in the place marked out by a superior order."[10] In the spirit of post-1960s revolt, the challenge of outsider art was to revolutionize the way people look at and think about art—rather than necessarily ascribing revolutionary force to the work of self-taught, visionary, anonymous, or intellectually disabled artists.

"An alternative art exists," writes Cardinal. "It need not be geographically remote, nor need it have a single location. It crops up in all the places where Art is considered to have no place."[11] In spite of the tendency for advocates of such alternative art forms to champion its "brutal purity," as Cardinal puts it—privileging its authenticity and newness—the notion that such alien forms *in fact exist already* is key to Cardinal's ecology of alternative art worlds. Their marginality and alienness can be plotted on a map whose centers and peripheries are no longer drawn from the imperial European model of "civilization" and its colonial margins but from the shifting ideological terrains of what we understand to be art. It thus occupies an altogether different sort of map, charted according to virtual rather than geographically or structurally fixed coordinates.

Cardinal's outsider refers, in other words, to an open set of practices, a field of dynamism and emergence that, for him, embodies the very truth of artistic creation. "If *art brut* is not a static place on a map, it can be a horizon," Cardinal tells us. "Its rare light beckons toward an impossible horizon where the most intensely human merges into the abhuman."[12] Were it to be measured according to geopolitical or institutional coordinates, such a statement might bristle with an all-too-familiar colonial fascination with alien forms—a primitivism of the mind. But the imperative of outsider art, as Cardinal describes it, is to alter our very conception of any such map. Outsider art does not refer to a set of artists whose aesthetic production occurs "outside culture," as Dubuffet understood the countercultural provocation of *art brut* to signify. Yet even for Dubuffet, "culture" referred to an "asphyxiating" ideological tendency rather than a localizable category, a set of inexorable yet unbearable laws within which the emergence of heterogeneous possibilities constituted a necessarily subversive act.[13] Cardinal's outside registers this process of emergence: even minor elisions of convention, regardless of their intention, enable the spontaneous production of new artistic energy. As a result, "alternative systems[s] of ideas and behavior" begin to emerge, in ways that are conducive to the satisfaction of individual psychic needs and yet also pull away from the normate, as Cardinal's "abhuman" indicates. Even to claim that such alternatives can be deduced from the history of conventions themselves, to cite the sociologist Pierre Bourdieu's more cynical view, is to suggest that such systemic alternatives nonetheless yield all kinds of invented solutions, theories, methods, and sources of inspiration.[14] The key is that the origin of such alternative logics is not the cognitive, sociological, or geographical alienation of the individual outsider artist but the functional discontinuities within convention itself, to which such logics call attention in turn. The very notion of an outside thus points to the functional creation of insides and outsides, a set of dynamic processes rather than a romanticizable category of abnormality or eccentricity that lies beyond the borders of normative convention.

Arriving in the heyday of postmodernism, Cardinal's recourse to outsides sought not only to redistribute the criteria of artistic value but, more significantly still, also to reengineer the very protocols of aesthetic experience. Cardinal's outside proposed what the philosopher Gilles Deleuze once referred to as a "pragmatics of the multiple," describing sets of variable combinations rather than a discernible position within or beyond existing fields of convention and expertise.[15] The result is a complexity theory of aesthetic and philosophical creation. In articulating his ideas about how such a cultural outside might function, Cardinal draws upon the work of the neo-Kantian German biologist Jakob von Uexküll, who furnishes him with a theory of contingent outsides drawn from the physiological study of living systems and organic feedback cycles. Published in 1920, Uexküll's *Theoretical Biology* introduced the notion of *Umwelt* (environment or lifeworld) as the immediate surroundings particular to an individual organism; it represents the specific milieu to which an organism responds, which is both constituted and represented according to the inner workings of the organism. Each living organism develops its own outside, in other words, in tandem with its own formation as an organism. Uexküll's *Theoretical Biology*, whose theories inform modern phenomenology and systems theory alike, enables Cardinal to "talk about a large number of independent artistic worlds that ought not to be envisaged as a forming a block, much less a school," but instead as comprising discrete, autonomous, and contingent realities.[16] Cardinal's differentiation of multiple, autonomous art worlds corresponds to Uexküll's project of describing the physiology of living organisms in terms of dynamic systems—that is, as the interdependent processes of apparatuses and functions, and of indicators and thresholds, rather than the work of discrete, static organs. The "worlds" to which Cardinal refers thus correspond to Uexküll's designation of *Umwelt,* providing Cardinal with a wholly different set of forms and causes for the characterization of outsider art.[17] Procedural rather than categorical, ecological rather than evaluative, Cardinal's translation of Dubuffet's *art brut* describes a set of entanglements that point to the complexity and interdependence of multiple art worlds rather than the discernment of individual works or discrete categories of social organization.

In *Outsider Theory,* I adopt this art historical provocation as a heuristic for the study of modern intellectual history. It is not enough to lament the fallen state of knowledge in a "post-truth" age. Rather, it is incumbent upon contemporary intellectuals and culture workers to expand rather than restrict our horizons of study in order to consider the dynamic and often convoluted ways in which conceptual schemes form, adapt, persist, and change in meaning. I challenge the presumption that only the best ideas deserve remembrance and that bad thinking should be immediately disavowed. I propose instead that modern intellectual life owes as much to outlandish or otherwise idiosyncratic thinking as it does to the dominant concepts and ideologies that populate the public sphere. Such entanglements also extend to one's own critical methodologies, which are often far too eager to slough off the fancies and aspirations of allegedly antiquated thought. It may be delusional to think that the earnest, oppositional strategies of even the recent past can be unproblematically imported into the present, but it is no less of a mistake to abandon them as categorically obsolete and thus insignificant. The tendency to accept or dismiss certain ideas—or, for that matter, to fetishize them as hermetic sources of wisdom while disavowing their currency as intellectual labor—is itself a site of ideological and political struggle. Some outsider theories stay outside more tenaciously than others, and this often owes as much to prevailing epistemologies that discount the work of certain populations, particularly women and people of color; it thus also depends on who or what determines the parameters of the normal and the marginal. The question, as Jeffrey Nealon puts it, thus becomes that of how thought systems and institutional and political forms are related and how they configure "a kind of odd, multiple totality."[18]

Such a proposition already bears its own intellectual genealogy. Beyond the innumerable occult revivalists and amateurs of esoterica from centuries past, the modern interest in outsider theory owes much to the pioneering work of the psychiatrist Hans Prinzhorn and the philosopher of science Gaston Bachelard. Prinzhorn's 1922 *Bildnerei der Geisteskranken* (Artistry of the mentally ill) sought to recognize and diagnose the creative output of psychiatric patients, whose drawings and paintings he collected and displayed as "artistry" or "image making" *(Bildnerei)*. Whereas Prinzhorn's work became a major sourcebook for avant-garde artists, his study was interested less in assessing the work of psychiatric patients as art *(Kunst)* than in recognizing it as part of the "odd, multiple totality" of *thought*. Bachelard, in turn, mobilized the study of alchemy, reverie, and other wayward practices in scientific history toward a reflexive epistemology that understood scientific progress as the product of ruptures within our self-assurance. The value of alchemy and dreams lay not in their claim to truth, in other words, but in their capacity to challenge the closed-minded certainty that stands in the way of truth, as one of the principle epistemological obstacles to new knowledge. Forming a kind of oppositional pair, Prinzhorn and Bachelard exemplify two complementary tendencies in modern epistemology: the former heeding, however incompletely, the insights and truth claims of intellectual work by marginalized subjects and populations, and the latter heeding the salutary *effects* of one's own (scientific) encounter with so-called epistemological obstacles or anomalies.[19]

Beyond Bachelard's instrumental recourse to epistemological oddity, other twentieth-century thinkers have sought to articulate the power, as well as the appeal, of the various mysticisms and eccentric belief systems that have taken hold of artists, writers, and politicians alike over the past several centuries. In her landmark 1980 book *Powers of Horror*, for instance, the French poststructuralist Julia Kristeva outlines an updated version of Bataille's heterology, undertaking a study of abject cultural material that yields a theory of psychic and social force rather than an epistemology. In her own dynamic of cultural outsides and forms of exteriority, Kristeva names abjection as "one of those violent, dark revolts of being, directed against a threat that seems to emanate from an exorbitant outside or inside, ejected beyond the scope of the possible, the tolerable, the thinkable."[20] The archaic resonances of such exorbitant emanations bear the force of the sacred and the profane, marking the fragile limits of the human individual and the social fabric alike. Building on anthropological studies of boundaries and taboos, Kristeva approaches the exclusion and reappropriation of heterogeneous cultural material in largely psychoanalytic and structural terms, measuring the power of transgressions against the implicit or explicit boundaries of the self, of propriety, of taboos. Kristeva's *Powers of Horror,* as both a study of ideologically suspect French writers such as Louis-Ferdinand Céline, participates in its own system insofar as it collapses the comfortable distance between their thinking and Kristeva's own. Writing over a decade later, the poet and philosopher Édouard Glissant outlines a complementary "poetics of relation" that posits *errance*—a thinking characterized by nomadic roaming, or "errantry"—as a heterological system of thought that likewise rejects the self-evident transparency of the world in favor of its opacities. In place of a "dark revolt of being," however, Glissant recasts the shock appeal of Kristeva's violent transgressions as a necessary and politically recuperative insistence on the limits of understanding. "One who is errant," he writes, "strives to know the totality of the world yet already knows he will never accomplish this—and knows that is precisely where the threatened beauty of the world resides."[21] Glissant outlines a poetic system of knowing that demands "the right to opacity" in the face of totalizing and appropriative forms of comprehension. The thinking of errantry instead "conceives of totality but willingly renounces any claims to sum it up or to possess it."[22] Such thinking exercises the right, in other words, to remain alien to the universalizing and all encompassing myth of clarity brandished by European and U.S. colonial worldviews: it describes a poetics, as well as a politics, of outlandishness.

My own work is methodologically invested in the intellectual demands of such "errant" participation. Rather than merely seeking better tools for describing—or dismissing—the power, creativity, or danger of outsider thinking, this book instead studies the asymmetrical circuits of creation, rejection, absorption, and transformation according to which modern theories circulate. The relationships between the ideas we take seriously and those we find on the rummage heap of intellectual history are complex and numerous, ranging from critical fascination to salvage and reconstruction.[23] By tracing such relationships, and by studying the way intellectuals reflect upon them, *Outsider Theory* aims to expand both the range and the archive of critical thinking in the humanities while prompting contemporary culture workers to rethink how we classify and respond to the philosophical, literary, and scientific currents that make up contemporary intellectual life. Our task should certainly be a little different from Dubuffet's or even Cardinal's; my aim is less to revolutionize aesthetic tastes—although I hope that this book might induce its readers to reflect anew on the "objective beauty" of conceptual prose—than to confront guiding assumptions about the contours of intellectual history. In an age of increasing political and economic pressure on the usefulness (as well as the profitability) of humanistic inquiry, it is time to reconsider the intrinsic value of demarcating proper from improper thinking and accommodating our methods to industrialized standards of intellectual "progress." It is time to reflect anew—to reflect again, and continually—on the currency of any claim to truth. This is not because all such claims have turned suspect, as if corroded by the acids of postmodernity, but because the stakes of their intelligibility are so high. So too is it time to persist in interrogating the "powers of the false," to cite Deleuze's Nietzschean formulation for the artistic and philosophical capacity to invent new concepts.[24] Such ideas are real—a part of our intellectual and political environment. They shape our lives, our intellectual and creative practices. Even if we wish to protect ourselves from the dangerous effects of "bad" ideas, it is all the more important to know where and how they function, how they impress themselves upon what we think and how we know. So too does the function of marginal thinking within twentieth-century intellectual history extend beyond its stylistic or methodological imitation by individual writers, artists, scientists, philosophers, or pundits. As Bataille's "science" of heterology seeks to demonstrate, marginal thinking discloses the entanglements and discrepancies within and among the disciplines of humanistic and scientific inquiry, as well as among their respective asymmetrical histories and repositories of partly or wholly discarded ideas.

Outsider Theory presents an open set of thinkers and works of creative speculation that correspond with such entanglements, demanding a renewed interrogation of our investment in the security and methodological self-evidence of modern intellectual history. Though some chapters of this study will treat relatively canonical figures, such as Marcus Garvey and the Marquis de Sade, their main purpose is to suggest that the corpus of "outsider theory" may be at once endless and, in many cases, anonymous. From the occult fascination with Gnosticism to the cartographic drawings of psychotic asylum patients, the case studies featured in this book make no claim to the encyclopedic or taxonomic; I nonetheless consider it imperative to devote sustained critical attention to specific figures and texts, lest our ideas about outsider thinking be reduced to a purely conceptual language, a set of ideas put forward by a critical lineage little different from any other intellectual history. Indeed, from Bachelard and Bataille through Maurice Blanchot, Gilles Deleuze, Michel Foucault, Édouard Glissant, Félix Guattari, Nathaniel Mackey, Fred Moten, Avital Ronell, Michel Serres, Isabelle Stengers, and others, readers have inherited from contemporary theory a set of concepts that consider the "outside" as a philosophical problem that beckons to discontinuities immanent within the world systems of language and thought, not to a metaphysical beyond: murmur and stammer; void and fold;

rupture and discontinuity; overcoding and nondiscourse. Such terms disclose contemporary theorists' recognition of the extent to which, even in spite of our efforts to the contrary, our thinking is subject to a retreat from instrumentality, a frustration of ready meaning, and even an errantry in its development as a truth procedure. Our thinking must instead accommodate itself to the vicissitudes of experience, its conditions of mediation and even erasure.

Yet such terms still refer to the concepts of so-called major thinkers in philosophy and art, rather than the ever-expanding ranks of discarded, unpopular signifiers that often characterize such noise, such stammering, such breaches within the fabric of communicative understanding. It is one thing to cite Michel Serres as an authority on communicative interference, or Gilles Deleuze on schizoanalysis. What does it mean, though, to direct our own critical attentions toward schizophrenic thinkers, or toward interrupted communication? Such asymmetrical entanglements may not necessarily yield the kind of return on our investments one might seek in tarrying dialectically with the negative elements of intellectual history; it might instead pull our own thinking out of orbit. Not all interruptions are salutary, moreover; far from it. It is thus especially crucial to examine such distortions and interferences in detail, on account of their capacity for alienation, their residuum of destruction, their pain. Alice Walker has written, for instance, about the "preposterous" deception of Joel Chandler Harris's fictional Uncle Remus, a racist invention whose name and figuration "placed an effective barrier" between Walker and the African American folktales Harris appropriated. This disruption represents an act of cultural theft whereby African American folklore has been "ridiculed and tampered with"—an oppressive instance of communicative interference that is especially pernicious because folklore is already "full of the possibilities of misinterpretation, full of subtleties and danger." In her drive to know and assimilate African American folklore and the writings of Black women, Walker seeks both to redress the interruptive silencing of such voices and to restore their capacity for discomfiture, their disruptiveness, their stammer and void. "We needn't pull away from [folklore] because of the pain," she stresses. The ideas that compose us—as individuals, as cultures—are not always "good," nor do they always require a proper name, but it is imperative for us to acknowledge them even at the risk of "learning too much about one's self."[25] Indeed, this is a risk we must increasingly confront as contemporary intellectuals, regardless of whether the ideas we study and fashion into theories are outlandish or not. Without a concrete frame of reference—or in an environment wherein all frames of reference have been liquidated—every theory risks sounding like a crackpot one.

In this light, the notion of "having a theory" takes on particular significance as an index of such asymmetrical entanglements. A theory, in its more scientific usage, refers to a rational explanatory framework that remains "speculative"—according to the Greek root of theory, *theoria* (θεωρία)—insofar as its assertions maintain a provisional openness in the face of empirical data. The consequences of a theory are not limited to what is already known, moreover: its explanatory framework also helps to predict and conceptualize that which is not yet known.[26] As a conceptual scheme, a theory designates a product of mind rather than a natural phenomenon—although, as numerous scientific thinkers remind us, our very observation of nature is conditioned by the products of mind one brings to bear upon it, from concepts to habits and technological forms. And in turn, "mind" is itself a product of the world, sustained by the bodies (whether human or composite, animate or computational), networks, and social forces that give them form. Thus, Newtonian gravity remains a theory insofar as it offers an explanation of why things tend to fall to the ground; though it names a measurable force, gravity denotes neither the fall itself nor an inherent property of celestial bodies. As we will see in chapter 8, the psychoanalytically trained popular science writer Immanuel Velikovsky attempted to "disprove" gravity, advancing instead his own hypothesis about planetary electromagnetism. Without the resources or the institutional credibility to test his hypothesis, however, Velikovsky was unable to substantiate anything resembling a "theory," whether according to the notions of falsifiability put forth by Karl Popper or in accordance with contemporary scientific paradigms. All the same, Velikovsky's broader body of work incorporates this antigravitational hypothesis within its grander explanatory framework about the behavior, as well as the age, of interplanetary events; Velikovsky, in this sense, *had* a theory, although it was far from a disembodied product of mind. Not only were its propositions worked out by means of the "paper tools" of psychoanalytic interpretations of biblical, historical, and scientific texts, but its polemical entanglements with contemporary scientific opinion also formed part of its methodology.[27] To "have a theory" may suggest a private intellectual idiosyncrasy, but to begin circulating it—or even to *work on* it (or to think it)—is to enter into the fray of discourse, a worldly system: an *Umwelt*.

In the arts and humanities, *theory* has taken on a different set of valences altogether, wherein the speculative component of an explanatory framework derives its claims to rationalism less from its relationship to empirical data than from its conceptual attunement with a discursive field of other speculative propositions. *Theory* has come to designate an autonomous field of abstract or otherwise speculative inquiry rather than a discrete explanatory framework. As the literary critic Jonathan Culler writes, "we use the term *theory* to designate discourses that come to exercise influence outside their apparent disciplinary realm because they offer new and persuasive characterizations of problems or phenomena of general interest."[28] Sounding very much like Cardinal or Dubuffet here, Culler describes theory itself in terms of its fundamental, if healthy, discontinuity with disciplinary norms. Rather than debate whether *theory* in this sense designates a heroic rupture with "the prevailing wind of the Establishment" or a rightly marginalized tangle of conjectures, I wish to point out instead how quickly the distinctions between scientific "theories" and humanistic "theory" collapse at the moment they fall under suspicion. Any theory can come to look like nonsense under the glare of total skepticism; the challenge is thus for us better to understand, as well as to exercise, the vicissitudes of intellectual circulation rather than striving to map out the firmest ground upon which to anchor our self-assurance. The cemetery of prescientific theories is replete not only with popular fads and fallacies, but also with the earnest thought systems of philosophers, artists, prophets, and nonprofessionals from across the political spectrum. To reject any such theory as categorically inadmissible to discourse would represent an impoverishment of that discourse, as well as an impoverishment of the notion of theory itself. The categorical rejection or dismissal of the intellectual labor of marginalized populations has long been a characteristic gesture of cultural imperialism; Collins notes, for instance, how African American women's experiences "as well as those of African descent transnationally have been routinely distorted within or excluded from what counts as knowledge."[29] With the long history of such distortions and exclusions in mind, this book focuses on breaks in the routine: the seemingly agentless or magical persistence, recursion, influence, or renewal of marginalized ideas themselves. Few ideas stay dead for very long—and many continue to stagger along as zombie concepts in spite of their death.[30] Consigned to the cemetery though they may be, such theories nonetheless continue to circulate among us, in countless forms.[31] *Outsider Theory* proposes to begin studying these forms and the means of their persistence, rather than simply cataloging the relative truth claims and outrages of each discarded theory.

For over two decades, scholars and journalists have proclaimed "the death of theory" as both an allegory and a symptom of a troubling set of historical conditions, from the spectacular rise of Fox News to the fiscal and ideological crises in the academic humanities, the decline of print and other analog media, and, most generally, the demise of liberalism and humanism in the contemporary world. Yet are current intellectual and political conditions so dire as to disrupt the very possibility for thought altogether? This book presupposes instead that the forms of intellectual inquiry one might designate as "theory" have tended always to face conditions of crisis and instability, subject to reciprocal questions of legitimacy and veracity. Rather than the occasion for the death (or bankruptcy) of speculative inquiry, such crises—from doubt and dwindling popularity to censorship and discreditation—are instead continuous with the processes of speculative thinking. The uneasy syntheses of unorthodox philosophy, psychoanalysis, and critical writing that make up humanistic theory derive historically as well as procedurally from conjecture and debate about the limits of epistemology, the boundaries between the humanistic and scientific disciplines, the contours of sanity and the neurotypical human subject, and the ethical stakes of intellectual discourse.

No less resonant for the study of *Outsider Theory* is the recognition that certain of the interactive fields and systems that constitute "theories" can themselves bear the capacity to think. Beyond the question of their credibility as explanatory and predicative frameworks, in other words, there lies an uncanny possibility that such frameworks themselves bear the capacity for analysis, for the generation of concepts. Though no longer an outlandish claim in itself, perhaps, the notion that theories can think nonetheless smacks of a certain degree of solipsism, if not of the academic imposture decried by the likes of Susan Jacoby: some theorists are so enchanted with their theories that they ascribe cognitive faculties to a set of conjectural abstractions! Such claims come as no surprise to readers of posthumanist philosophy and science studies; the kinds of feedback loops and self-regulating systems studied by systems theorists since Jakob von Uexküll and simulated by cyberneticists has certainly demonstrated the pragmatics of so-called artificial intelligence. Drawing from cybernetics in their 1991 inquiry *What Is Philosophy?*, Gilles Deleuze and Félix Guattari attribute the generation of concepts—the very work of philosophy—to an autopoietic function within the field of discourse. Thinking is a function, a set of processes rather than a faculty; a concept, in turn, is a self-referential and self-creating instance of this process: "it posits itself and its object at the same time as it is created."[32] Such notions of the capacity for systems and theories to think were likewise intimated by psychoanalysts earlier in the century. As Sigmund Freud famously remarked in his case study of the paranoiac German judge Daniel Paul Schreber, Schreber's delirious interpretations of his own nervous illness revealed "a striking similarity with our theory," as we will see in chapter 7.[33] This was a reversible likeness: describing how Schreber's paranoid interpretations simulated the theories used to diagnose it, Freud's own theory of paranoia emerges as a second-order simulation of that same illness. The risk, of course, is that in making such a claim, psychoanalysis exposed its own susceptibility to a kind of phenomenological infection. In claiming that viable theories could be produced by illness itself, Freud disclosed the extent to which madness was constitutive of his "science." Subsequent thinkers and practitioners have taken this literally. For the psychoanalyst Jacques Lacan, paranoia offered both an object of study and a form of delusional interpretation that could be appropriated and simulated as a clinical theory; this could be done, he claimed, because the illness already functioned as a theorizing apparatus in its own right. Such propositions suggest the extent to which classical psychoanalysis recognized the unconscious mechanisms of symptom formation and systematic interpretation alike. Yet this recognition also demands that we reflect anew on the shaky ground that such recognitions reveal to be the methodological bases of sciences such as psychoanalysis. Does this epistemological openness reveal the dynamism of psychoanalytic thinking, or disclose its fundamental poverty?

Outsider Theory charts the contours of this shaky ground by considering a range of twentieth-century thinkers, including philosophers, public intellectuals, critics, scientists, political figures, and writers. It does so with chapters on Gnostic libraries and ecofeminist world histories, on Marcus Garvey and the Marquis de Sade, and on maps drawn by psychiatric patients and theories about the extraterrestrial origins of knowledge. I examine the intersections between pseudoscience and philosophy, between bibliophilia and religion, and between conflicting ideas about the storage and retrieval of knowledge. Looking beyond Popper's "demarcation problem" of distinguishing legitimate scientific practice from pseudoscience, this book studies the constitutive role such demarcation crises play in the very foundation of theories and methods of humanistic thinking. The ambition of this project is not, therefore, to demand an uncritical embrace of all occulted knowledge, or to propose that the full force of past unreason should be brought to bear on the present. Rather, in order better to contemplate our own relationship to intellectual history at a moment when the future of many institutions of higher learning—from the printed book to the university itself—has come into question, I propose that the work of thought be measured in terms of its encounters with outsider theory.

PERMANENT MOBILIZATION

This is not a book about the culture wars, or the science wars, or the other lines of demarcation that carve up the contemporary cultural and intellectual landscape. Nonetheless, the high stakes of such divisions are impossible to ignore. This owes less to the weighty significance of truth and reason alone than to the determinative pressures such "wars" exert upon the environments in which we think, the fiscal and ideological resources they muster, and the kinds of damage they inflict. But what are the consequences of giving serious scholarly attention to—reading, or perhaps methodologically absorbing— potentially poisonous material, whether that of Hitler or Heidegger, heresy, or climate change denial? Certainly, the stakes of normalizing dangerous falsehoods are potentially catastrophic; yet the thresholds for defining what a dangerous falsehood looks like have become polarized, subject to an "epistemic asymmetry," as Barbara Herrnstein Smith has written. This asymmetry describes the reciprocal set of automatic conclusions according to which people believe that the things they believe to be true and sensible are, in fact, true and sensible, whereas those who contest this belief must be devils or fools—suffering, in other words, "from defects or deficiencies of character and/or intellect: ignorance, innate incapacity, delusion, poor training, captivity to false doctrine, and so on."[34] It is hardly my intention to entertain the legitimacy of ideologically pernicious material. On the contrary, this book argues for the urgency of studying how—the means through which—such legitimation occurs. Precisely because the stakes are so high, it would be remiss to ignore the demand of such patterns and systems of circulation, which tend to become obscured at the very moment scholars seek to erase problematic works from their memories and purge them from their grand narratives of intellectual progress. For this reason, *Outsider Theory* takes issue with the moralistic attacks on European philosophy and postmodern scholarly thinking by the likes of Susan Jacoby, Alan Sokal, and others.[35] Along with innumerable other hoax revealers and skeptical inquirers, such critics seek to chasten the outlandishness of much "fashionable" theoretical work in the humanities and sciences, upbraiding scholars, thinkers, and the public alike for their seduction by certain kinds of speculative thinking. This book seeks to open up new inroads for thinking across the idiosyncratic histories of the humanities and sciences. It pursues rather than polices the entanglements and demarcations between good and bad thinking, and between legitimate and illicit ideas.

Intellectual historians and philosophers of science have long been fascinated by the intersections of scientific knowledge and the occult, of enlightened reason and mysticism. From the vantage point of the contemporary age, for instance, early entanglements between alchemy and science legibly document the variety, if not the fecundity, of wayward turns along the path of intellectual history. Sir Isaac Newton was an alchemist; we can forgive the mathematician Pythagoras for his aversion to beans. The history of ideas is incomplete, as Ilya Prigogine and Isabelle Stengers contend, without the inclusion of failed, bad, outmoded, or unimportant ideas.[36] For unless contemporary thinkers recognize such efforts as part of our intellectual "heritage," we end up inventing arbitrary starting points for the systems of knowledge we claim to study and adapt as our own. Unless we take into consideration the evolution of any set of "starting points," that is, we render knowledge homogeneous and thus ultimately tautological. (As Smith puts it: we believe that the things we believe to be true are true because they are true.)

Neither intellectuals nor concepts are sui generis inventions—they do not simply emerge fully formed from either laboratory experience or from the crania of history's great geniuses. Such triumphalist myths of intellectual progress owe their sovereignty to the habit of relegating "local, discontinuous, disqualified, illegitimate knowledges" to the margins of intellectual history, as Michel Foucault argued. Rather than taking heed of the errors and idiosyncrasies of the great scientists, the alien excesses of their theories, and even the unfortunate beliefs to which they might have ascribed, traditional accounts of intellectual progress purge or relativize such heterogeneous material.[37] Like Foucault, Prigogine and Stengers seek not simply to resist such normalizing tendencies but to recast them altogether. In their 1979 collaboration *Order out of Chaos*, they propose an epistemology grounded in the notion that intellectual communities, like other complex systems, are turbulent, multifarious, and evolving rather than closed and isolated. Their approach to intellectual history is itself modeled on the complex thermodynamic systems they analyze in their research, which demonstrate chaotic and seemingly irrational processes at odds with the laws of classical physics. Prigogine and Stengers propose a nonlinear relationship between authorized theories and "discontinuous knowledges" in the name of a dynamic and evolutionary conception of scientific process. As they put it,

> The growth of science is quite different from the uniform unfolding of scientific disciplines, each in turn divided into an increasing number of watertight compartments. Quite the contrary, the convergence of different problems and points of view may break open the compartments and stir up scientific culture. These turning points have consequences that go beyond their scientific context and influence the intellectual scene as a whole. Inversely, global problems often have been sources of inspiration to science.[38]

Such dynamic and reversible approaches to intellectual history took on particular relevance during the 1960s and 1970s, resonating strongly with the antiestablishment politics of the civil rights and post-1968 era, as well as with continued scientific popularizations of quantum mechanics and dynamic systems theory. In place of a traditional "ascesis of reason" that conceived of science as a community of knowledge bound together by "freeing itself from outmoded forms of understanding nature," antifoundationalist sociologists of science—as well as philosophers and many scientists themselves—increasingly stressed the permeability of scientific "insides" and "outsides," whether defined in terms of paradigms, shared tacit assumptions, or specialist communities of knowledge.[39] Along with the work of French poststructuralist philosophers and process-oriented artists (including the outsider art collected and described by Cardinal and Dubuffet), Paul Feyerabend's landmark treatise *Against Method* (1975) galvanizes this fundamentally pluralistic and process-oriented approach to the sociology of knowledge. Rather than capitulating to the traditional assumption that scientific theories, observations, and argumentative principles are timeless, autonomous entities, Feyerabend argues that "science is a complex and heterogeneous *historical process* which contains vague and incoherent anticipations of future ideologies side by side with highly sophisticated theoretical systems and ancient and petrified forms of thought."[40] Feyerabend's argument is twofold: outlandish ideas are not only a fundamental part of the intellectual-historical landscape but are also constitutive of its development and transformation, a necessary part of its feedback loop.

To reorient intellectual history around the incorporation of discontinuous theories, notions, tendencies, beliefs, and other scraps of wayward knowledge is thus not only to propose a more realistic historiography of ideas but also to reassess our own intellectual investment in its ongoing evolution. In this light, science comes to delineate a *medium* rather than a discipline, a convergence of methods, materials, and problems rather than the professional ethos of closed or isolated communities of researchers. Such convergences are no less apposite to the arts and humanities, whose intellectual history is continually buffeted by aesthetic, conceptual, methodological, and institutional inventions and recursions alike, however prone to specialization the academy might be. Such a "complex medium containing surprising and unforeseen developments" demands complex procedures, Feyerabend argues, and it in turn "defies analysis on the basis of rules which have been set up in advance and without regard to the ever-changing conditions of history."[41] Far from outlining a program of pure chaos or a utopian condition of open-mindedness, Feyerabend's epistemology acknowledges the extent to which the very catholicity of scientific thinking can be determinative in itself: the contingency of this "complex medium" is a cause, rather than an effect, of new ideas and discoveries. Feyerabend thus challenges categorical notions about the kinds of ideas and concepts that are admissible or inadmissible to science.[42] Like Gaston Bachelard before him, Feyerabend proposed that epistemology was *part of* scientific practice rather than ancillary to it. One of the principal tasks of scientific practice was, as Bachelard wrote in the 1930s, to disabuse itself of its "epistemological obstacles," its tendency to naturalize inherited formal principles as laws, as methodological common sense. In an abstruse formulation that both names and pokes fun at this so-called sleep of reason, Bachelard cites "the abusive endosmosis of the assertoric within the apoditic," arguing instead that scientific culture must be placed "in a state of permanent mobilization, to replace closed and static knowledge with an open, dynamic understanding."[43] Science thrives, in other words, as an open system: as a medium for intellectual practices that exchange ideas, language, beliefs, and material forms with their surrounding cultural environment. This is not to recast science as a humanistic enterprise so much as to assert its common recourse to invention and contingency, reverie and surprise.

Though conceived as a corrective to the isolation and even secrecy of Cold War science, the antifoundationalist stance put forth by Feyerabend and others came under fire once again during the culture wars of the 1980s and 1990s, reaching a peak, we might say, with the Sokal hoax of 1996. Whereas many scientists had fought hard to popularize and democratize scientific thinking during the 1960s and 1970s—and continue to do so—the Sokal hoax was predicated on the opinion that this democratization had been hijacked for ideological purposes incommensurate with its own rational ends. Playing on the popularity of "science studies" among postmodernist thinkers in the humanities and social sciences, NYU physicist Alan Sokal submitted an essay to the humanities journal *Social Text* that sought to expose the egregious political demands that "postmodernists" in the humanities had levied upon the "open, dynamic understanding" of scientific progress. Sokal's essay, "Transgressing the Boundaries: Towards a Transformative Hermeneutics of Quantum Gravity," was an unsolicited submission to a special issue of the journal dedicated to the so-called science wars, a series of critical responses to the intensifying lines of political demarcation within recent debates about objectivity and reason, as epitomized by a 1994 volume on "the academic Left and its quarrels with science" titled *Higher Superstition*.[44] Sokal's essay, which he revealed to be a hoax upon its publication, exaggerated the epistemological anarchy of Feyerabend, Stengers, and others toward an appeal for a "liberatory science," putting forward a fatuous argument that quantum gravity was itself a linguistic and social construct. Sokal thus served up a version of "science" for which he considered the journal's editors to be desperate to the point of credulity: science was such an open system as to be infinitely permeable. As both an institution and a set of fungible theories it was so "discontinuous and non-linear" as to offer a model for leftist politics, receptive to all comers. It thus caricatures the avant-garde ambitions of any such claims to heterogeneity: postmodern openness and difference beckoned to a model of liberal inclusivity that could, in one fell swoop, also issue a slap to the face of establishment taste.

As the annals of academe have recorded it, the principal target of Sokal's mock-utopian hoax was not the political Left, but left-leaning, humanist cultural studies theorists who demonstrated their susceptibility to sloppy or fraudulent thought by accepting his "intellectual imposture" for publication.[45] Sokal's hoax thus doubly targeted postmodern humanities theorists, at once presuming their ignorance of *real* quantum physics and exploiting their desire for the scientific legitimation of epistemological relativism and uncertainty. Sokal misjudged the criteria for publication in humanities journals, however: an essay's acceptance, even by peer review—which was not the case in *Social Text*—does not automatically signify either an affirmation or a corroboration of its truth claims. The open-armed liberalism Sokal sought to expose as a methodological shortcoming may have pointed instead to a form of "tacit knowledge" within humanities publishing. More tellingly, Sokal's hoax also represented a broader about-face regarding the epistemology of "cognitive relativism" in the sciences.[46] For Sokal, as for other debunkers of intellectual imposture such as Paul Gross and Norman Levitt, antifoundationalism itself was a product of, rather than an epistemological reckoning with, a susceptibility to sloppy or fraudulent thought that threatened science—and reason—from the outside. Sokal and other like-minded scientists thus sought to purge "science" of epistemological self-reflection as if it were an alien intrusion. Writers who argued for the constitutive role of epistemology within scientific practice—such as Paul Feyerabend, Donna Haraway, Bruno Latour, Michel Serres, Barbara Herrnstein Smith, Isabelle Stengers, and others—could now implicitly be relegated to the very "cemetery of prescientific theories" they sought so vigorously to reconsider.

In many respects, precisely the reverse has happened. The result of the Sokal hoax and the science wars has been, we might say, an increasing relegation of science to the margins of public culture, whereby scientists must struggle to convince government officials about the viability of their theories of global climate change while occasionally receiving death threats for doing so.[47] Corporations and neoliberal politicians are all too happy to become relativist in the name of cost-saving measures and the privatization of public institutions. Though occasionally policed by rationalist skeptics such as Sokal, the contemporary marketplace of ideas has become regulated by forces other than truth, falsifiability, or even postmodernist unreason. In their place, one finds an embarrassment of sociopolitical effects such as funding cuts to universities, libraries, and arts organizations; the corporatization of the education system; and the consolidation of radical ideologies through government lobbies, all of which have increasingly transformed the "marketplace of ideas" into a closed shop. Rather than purging science of postmodernist self-reflection, Sokal's article marked a shift in political beliefs about the value and means of distributing knowledge, both in the United States and throughout the world. Rather than a rational distribution of expertise, we find instead a restricted field of discourse whereby data must now be argued about and rhetoricized as if it were purely speculative: *all* ideas—even those that concern the very survival of human civilization and the global biosphere—can be made to look like bullshit.

On the humanistic front, too, we might say that postmodern self-reflection has metastasized to the point of a near-tautological insistence. In an era marked by a revolutionary turn against the arts and letters as a public good, we witness the professional retrenchment of cultural workers within the illusory sanctity of artistic specializations and scholarly disciplines. Sokal's admonishment sought to shore up the boundaries of expert knowledge against the excesses and appropriations of "the postmodernists of the left, the fundamentalists of the right, [and] the muddle-headed of all political and apolitical stripes," he later explained.[48] It is a gesture that has subsequently been upheld both by and against political intervention into the institutions and methods of the arts and sciences alike, a kind of pact that renders administrative support contingent upon the proviso that the boundaries between disciplines remain self-evident, at once absolute and, paradoxically, transparent and accessible to all. Weird, rule-breaking, "interdisciplinary" collaboration is welcome as potential innovation so long as it can be sustained by "outside funding," whether grants or donor support—that is, monetized in advance. To conduct scholarship or intellectual creativity otherwise, presumably, is to participate in a crackpot industry.[49]

For all the efforts to dismiss the Sokal hoax as a mean-spirited but ultimately inconsequential attack against interloping humanist outsiders, it marked a powerful shift in the way professional scholars in the humanities and sciences demarcate the boundaries of their research. Whereas Feyerabend, Stengers, and others have sought, in the name of scientific "progress" and "realism," to open up scientific practice to the historical forms of knowledge heterogeneous with it, the Sokal affair instead reinforced the distinctions between "hard" scientific and "soft" humanistic worldviews, as well as between "insides" and "outsides" of discipline and academic rank. As Smith has written, the notion of "the two cultures" first articulated by C. P. Snow in 1959, however crude a caricature of the epistemological divide between humanists and scientists, has nonetheless become reified as an institutional ideology on many college campuses, not only ingrained in the thinking of students, faculty, and administrators but also reinforced by preemptive course requirements and vocational demands.[50] In the context of a broader erosion of state funding for the arts and humanities in the United States and Europe, and an intensified ideological divide between "rational" and fundamentalist or "alternative" worldviews, Sokal's hoax marks a historical return to Popper's demarcation problem—as well as to Mertonian social categories—on the broader scale of popular culture. That is, intellectuals are increasingly held accountable to the notion that "real" thought is categorically distinct from nonsense on account of its untestability as "practical" knowledge—the likelihood, that is, that it will fail to net a financial return on its investment.

Twenty years later, Sokal's prejudices seem downright providential, as even the most empirically grounded scientific theories find themselves increasingly subject to skepticism, no longer simply from postmodernists and ideologues but from policy makers and the voting public as well. While certainly egged on by corporate interests and the religious Right, such popular thinking harbors its own opinions about the veracity of Darwinism or global climate change. What better moment to insist anew on the fundamental *discipline* of the scientific worldview and to cast out *Nonsense on Stilts*, to quote the title of Massimo Pigliucci's book on the subject, in a campaign against the scourge of obscurantism and divisiveness?[51] In stark contrast to Feyerabend, Foucault, and Stengers, such entrenchment amounts to a loss of faith, so to speak, in the self-regulatory functioning of scientific systems of apprehension and experiment. Its boundaries compromised, the scientific worldview must now be shored up, defended, and even policed. What happens to scientific pluralism when even science finds itself subject to relativization from without? What happens, in other words, when "reality" describes a set of sociopolitical and economic conditions rather than a set of empirical data about the natural world? Laboratories, too, can be closed; government funding can be cut. And scientists, like humanists—as well as many generations of women, indigenous populations, and people of color—can be shouted down, trivialized, threatened (or incarcerated, exiled, deported, assassinated, murdered), or simply ignored.

The science wars of the 1990s drew new lines of demarcation between reason and unreason, between orthodox and unorthodox knowledge, that continue to shift and evolve today. As with any war, it becomes the task of future analysts to revisit the battlefields and determine anew the meanings and repercussions of events that have taken place. The humanities have yet to own up fully to their own cemetery of prescientific theories to the extent that the sciences have done so fervently over the past century. One of the risks of this underinterrogated epistemological formation is that the humanities themselves—art, literature, criticism, history, philosophy—come to populate that cemetery as the doddering extended family of the true sciences. It is certainly important, as Harry Frankfurt advises, to ponder humanistic knowledge in its break from myth—that is, in its relation to truth. Yet such a task also necessarily confronts us with the far greater question of how—in what way, and according to what processes, institutions, and other mediating forms—humanistic knowledge evolves over time. What, for instance, is the status of myth? As Walker reminds us, folklore traditions have long been "ridiculed and tampered with" to the point where their intrinsic "possibilities of misinterpretation," their subtleties and danger, pervert and alienate rather than constitute humanistic knowledge.[52] Myth, folklore, and vernacular and traditional knowledges are relegated to outsider status and distinguished categorically from "humanistic knowledge" only through an exercise of power. The task, however, is hardly to mine heterogeneous outliers for their intrinsic resistance to convention and authority. For as Bourdieu, Cardinal, and Walker each describe in their turn, such outlandish outsides emerge as involutions—stammers, recombinations, returns, interferences—within the very governing systems that exclude or pervert them. In tracing the circuits of discontinuous knowledges, we can more fully recognize how thought functions within the continuing evolution of the intellectual life of the present, in spite of—or more accurately by means of—the innumerable restrictions and excesses levied upon it.[53]

Beyond attending to the "lure of the arcane"—to cite the title of Theodore Ziolkowski's 2013 study of conspiracy fiction—*Outsider Theory* approaches the mediating forms and logical deformations of modern systems of thought in their encounters with ideas alien to them.[54] Such relations are necessarily unstable, and often reflect rhetorical, institutional, or political rather than logical lines of demarcation, since neither a system of thought nor an "alien" discourse denotes a static category. In spite of the all-too-familiar litany of Atlantean lost worlds, UFOs, New Age cults, kabbalistic calculations, hermetic formulations, conspiracy theories, Nazi science, and so on, that delineates recognizable genres of popular occultism, such material circulates throughout modern art, science, philosophy, literature, and political thought in multifarious ways. The profound heterogeneity of unorthodox thinking throughout the humanities and sciences thus directs our attention to variations immanent in the forms and media through which outlandish ideas come in and out of circulation. *Outsider Theory* studies the intricacies of this circulation: How, for instance, did the Marquis de Sade, the author of violently pornographic works of torture and sexual cruelty, become the darling of twentieth-century European philosophers? As I discuss in chapter 6, Sade's evolution as a modern philosopher owed much to the bibliophiles and syndicalist publishers who singled him out as a thinker of contemporary life rather than to the machinations of Sadean cruelty alone.

In addition to tracing such mechanisms of reception and recirculation, this book also asks us to reflect on our own individual encounters with the limits of our knowledge, the points at which expertise and self-assurance break down. Such moments of uncertainty bear, on the one hand, the potential for exploitation through fraudulence, con artistry, and bullshit—or for the further depreciation of already marginalized thinkers for their disability, madness, or minoritarian status. On the other hand, they also bear the potential for disclosing epistemological obstacles and uncertainties, to which Bachelard points as the constitutive event of the scientific mind, to be reconstituted anew at every turn. To think wildly—even badly—is to exercise a right to creativity that underwrites rational, independent thinking precisely because it poses a threat to its self-assurance.

Outsider Theory urges us to rethink simplistic demarcations according to which correctness or truth serves as a central axis against which all illegitimate truth claims become peripheral. Not all bad ideas are bad in the same way. This book thus takes up a number of the oft-maligned "higher superstitions" of twentieth-century thought as its objects of study rather than as points of contention. Paul Gross and Norman Levitt's "relativism of social constructions, the sophomoric skepticism of the postmodernists, the incipient Lysenkoism of the feminist critics, the millennialism of the radical environmentalists, the racial chauvinism of the Afrocentrics" stand, in this book, as pejorative terms whose arrogance and hostility nonetheless reveal much about the recourse to "alternative" logics characteristic of so much contemporary thought.[55] *Outsider Theory* revisits the antifoundationalist project of thinkers such as Bachelard, Feyerabend, Foucault, Stengers, and others in contemplating the unsettling contingency of our contemporary systems of thought and belief. In doing so, however, the book resists the temptation to erect such figures as a new philosophical canon, thereby tracing a linear, teleological narrative of intellectual progress and "great genius" of its own. Rather than continuing to demarcate acceptable and unacceptable intellectual categories, *Outsider Theory* examines the systems of relations between unreason and reason that unfold within and among the fields of art, literature, philosophy, science, and political theory.

Ranging from the psychoanalysis of the early 1930s to the religious history and feminist epistemology of recent decades, *Outsider Theory* testifies to the persistence of outlandish thinking while, at the same time, grappling with the methodological difficulties of studying it. It thus attends in particular to the means and systems through which thought circulates. Regardless of how outlandish certain theories might seem, they do not come from outer space. Even when they are attributed to an "alien God" (as in the case of the philosopher Hans Jonas, writing about the resurgence of Gnosticism after the rediscovery of key Gnostic texts in the Egyptian desert), or to interplanetary collision and extraterrestrial intelligence (as in the case of the popular science writer Immanuel Velikovsky and the jazz musician Sun Ra), such theories circulate according to intellectual and material circuits of transmission. Like "good" ideas, outlandish ideas also draw from all sorts of conceptual backgrounds and circulate through books, lectures, conversations, institutional affiliations, and computer networks, even though they may follow different paths.

THE MEDIUM OF HISTORY

Imagine a different kind of war altogether from the science wars. Consider instead an epic war of attrition that would determine whether occult knowledge belonged to the forces of progress and liberation or to the strongholds of conservatism and reactionary violence. Ishmael Reed's 1972 novel *Mumbo Jumbo* envisions precisely such a crusade. In Reed's brilliant allegory of the civil rights era, the Jazz Age in the United States becomes the immediate battlefield for an epic struggle to secure a hermetic power—holy grail, secret book, or spontaneous force that "jes grew"—whose origins date from antiquity. Set in a Prohibition-era New York scarred by segregation, lynching, and colonial expansion, this millennial crusade plays out intradiegetically as a racial struggle with mortal consequences. For Reed, the stakes of this war are not limited to the immediate conditions of racism and oppression alone, but extend to the long historical legacy of their perpetuation. That is, the struggle between reason and unreason—or more accurately, between liberatory unreason and a regressive bureaucratic rationalism—is nothing less than the epochal clash of universal histories: the white supremacist narratives of Western civilization such as those of Emile Gaborieau, G. W. F. Hegel, and Max Nordau, which contrast starkly with competing historiographies of ancient African Empires, as forwarded by Edgar Wylmot Blyden, Marcus Garvey, J. A. Rogers, Frank Snowden, and, more recently, Martin Bernal, as discussed in chapter 5. A number of such texts flesh out the bibliography of Reed's novel. Yet *Mumbo Jumbo* also ascribes living agency to such episte-mological warfare, its fictional characters fighting to "teach . . . the differ-ence between a healer, a holy man, and a duppy who returns from the grave and causes mischief."[56] In its zombie history of recursive, universalizing theories, *Mumbo Jumbo* seeks less to enforce the demarcation between good and bad theories than to dramatize the stakes of their intelligibility.

I invoke *Mumbo Jumbo* here to signal the political intensity, as well as the long transhistorical reach, of many of the "outlandish" theories I exam-ine in this book. More than a paean to the intrinsic freedom of the hetero-geneous and spontaneous, *Mumbo Jumbo* stages epistemological conflict as an epic political struggle. Occult or otherwise discontinuous knowledges are not intrinsically countercultural or politically reactionary in themselves; they belong neither to the Left nor to the Right. Nor, however, is the generation of conceptual outsides and short-circuits in truth production a neutral or nat-ural process in the ecology of knowledge. Rather, as Reed dramatizes, they have been mobilized to serve interests across the political spectrum: tales of Hitler's fascination with the occult populate the public sphere just as exten-sively as the New Age movement's reclamation of ancient religions for spiri-tual uplift.[57] *Mumbo Jumbo* gives names to these warring factions in framing their battle for occult knowledges—for unreason, for spirit, for the power of soul—as a transhistorical epic. The novel pits the Wallflower Order, a conspiratorial sect upholding the privilege and racial purity of Western civi-lization, against its ancient opponent, the adherents (or inductees) of "Jes Grew." Readers first encounter Jes Grew as the outbreak of a dance craze at the novel's opening, hitting the newswires like a sort of zombie plague; but as we learn from the novel's protagonist, Papa La Bas, Jes Grew describes the spontaneous eruption of a life energy that, "for some, [is] a disease, a plague, but in fact it is an anti-plague."[58] The "zombies" are not the dancers but the legions of ideological automata mustered by the Wallflower Order to suppress the dance; their lockstep accord with white supremacy is epito-mized by the Haitian zombie, the "duppy who returns from the grave and causes mischief," itself an allegorical figure for the literally dehumanizing effects of colonialism and slavery. Reed's novel thus recasts the history of U.S. racial persecution since the Middle Passage: instead of a violent history haunted by the "prescientific" myths and pseudoconcepts of racial superior-ity, we find an active millennial struggle for the occult sources of these myths. It is a struggle for life.

Outsider Theory begins, we might say, at a moment in intellectual his-tory at which the scope and scale of that very history had already emerged as an object of contention, as well as a methodological substrate, for twentieth-century thinkers. The sweeping transhistorical concepts and figures we find throughout these early chapters were already common to the universal histories of the nineteenth century. The poetic gathering of world-cultural and world-historical traditions forms likewise constitutes the very project of modern ethnographic folklore; the psychoanalytic archetypalism of Joseph Campbell, Robert Graves, and Carl Jung; and the synthesizing mysticisms of figures such as Helena Blavatsky, Aleister Crowley, George Gurdjieff, and Rudolf Steiner. Such synthetic projects were pursued and reshaped in turn by the methodological investments of the poets and artists of the European avant-garde. The "grand narratives" of the nineteenth- and twentieth-century epics are not in themselves the kind of outlandish ideas I study in this book. Rather, such narratives—with their requisite theories and formal structures of rising and falling empires, archetypes, lost civilizations, degeneration, Viconian cycles, romance plots, and so forth—instead constitute a medium for cultural and historical transmission in their own right. Such theories, forms, and concepts are themselves historical; they develop in time, and circulate according to a variety of mechanisms and ideological investments that could just as readily become pernicious as liberatory. This is Ishmael Reed's contention in *Mumbo Jumbo*, and it is one of the central contentions of *Outsider Theory* as well: such metahistorical models of recursion and return, rise and fall, are never ideologically neutral; nor are they ideologically stable. They are, on the contrary, the very battleground of truth.

Outsider Theory consists of four parts. Part I, "Alien Gods," contains two related chapters that discuss tendencies in twentieth-century thought that measure their conceptual or political exigency according to their understanding of Gnosticism, a proto-Christian body of heterogeneous texts and ideas asserting special knowledge—gnosis—of an utterly otherworldly, alien God superior to the Judeo-Christian Creator. Chapter 1, "The Alien Knowledge of Nag Hammadi," opens with a consideration of the epistemological impact of the Nag Hammadi discovery—the retrieval of a set of third- or fourth-century codices found in the Egyptian desert outside Nag Hammadi, near Luxor, in 1945. The discovery constituted a major intellectual event: it fundamentally transformed a centuries-long modern interest in Gnosticism. Before 1945, the Gnosticism known to modern poets and philosophers such as William Blake, Helena Blavatsky, Johann Wolfgang von Goethe, G. R. S. Mead, and others was an occult religion gleaned largely from the heresiological writings of early Christian Church Fathers. The Nag Hammadi discovery, however, brought to light an empirically verifiable set of Coptic codices, suddenly complementing a largely archival body of hermetic knowledge with an extant set of Gnostic books. In doing so the discovery provided both a resonant instance of and a set of writings about a body of knowledge that seemed to appear out of the blue, as if from an otherworldly source. Chapter 1 studies the resonance of such a "myth of discovery" within both the sphere of visionary reflection and in the history of religions as a scholarly discipline.

Chapter 2, "Gnostic Materialism," follows directly from the first chapter. It studies how modern intellectuals before and after the Nag Hammadi discovery understood Gnosticism, in both its heresiological and revised incarnations, as a model for a modern materialism. Considered alongside G. W. F. Hegel's *Phenomenology of Spirit* and Karl Marx's dialectical materialism, the ancient mysteries of Gnostic theology offered twentieth-century philosophers and scholars new ways to think of worldly matter itself as fundamentally alien, as in the case of work by Georges Bataille, Hans Jonas, Henri-Charles Puech, and Jean Wahl. For more recent scholars, it has also shifted the terms of countercultural movement as well, as in the case of Elaine Pagels's influential work in the 1970s, which brings Gnostic materialism into dialogue with the political theology of St. Paul, as another material witness to the power of the otherworldly. This chapter thus examines how outsider theory functions at the very heart, we might say, of European philosophical and religious thinking, rather than at its fringes; in the context of the thinkers surveyed in chapter 2, "Gnosticism" points to the unsettling disruptiveness of matter itself, whether encountered as material evidence or as a set of worldly contingencies.

Part II, "Mythomorphoses," extends the intersecting spiritual and material interests of Part I. Echoing Reed's epic transhistorical sweep, the section contains two chapters that examine the surprising shifts and returns of ancient "wisdom" considered to be metaphysical, visual, mythical, or purely fantastic. It features popular writings that found speculative claims on the basis of ancient secrets and revelations that are often no less speculative in their own right, from the mysteries of Gnosticism to the archaeological speculation of popular, scholarly, and fictional reconstructions of human prehistory. Part II begins with an investigation into the scholarly and parascholarly roots of Dan Brown's best-selling 2003 novel *The Da Vinci Code* and concludes with a study of the ecofeminist deployment of "goddess religion" as a form of social theory during the 1980s.

Chapter 3, "So Dark, the Con of Man," studies the more fanciful forms of historical mythmaking that emerged concomitantly with Gnostic materialism, and which drew from its revelatory discoveries about the curious fungibility of material evidence. Focusing on hoaxes and speculations about the last resting place of the Holy Grail, which gained worldwide popularity (or notoriety) with the publication of *The Da Vinci Code* in 2003, the chapter discusses the questions of fraudulence and hoax formation that arise in the (often profitable) industry of alternative historiography. Counterfactual and revisionist historiographies have long presented a lightning rod for debates about the politics and historical memory. Yet the majority of these debates hinge on the rhetoric of authenticity—even the outright claim to positivism—put forward by even the most outlandish of works that explore "history's mysteries." The chapter focuses instead on the deliberate historical mythmaking—and mythomorphic historiography—at work in such mysteries, with the aim of questioning whether the con artistry of alternative historiography explodes or sustains the genre. In particular, it treats the work of Gérard de Sède, the former surrealist parahistorian and student of Gaston Bachelard whose accounts of the Holy Grail, and the secret societies that preserved it for centuries, later formed the basis for the best-selling 1982 nonfiction work *Holy Blood, Holy Grail.* This latter text was famously co-opted, in turn, by the former art historian Dan Brown in *The Da Vinci Code.* In Brown's novel, the "con" of Sède's Grail legend stands as a revelatory, metaphysical challenge to Christian orthodoxy—rather than presenting, say, a political or ethical critique or a secular or religious set of alternatives. With such adaptations of Sède's work as its basis, chapter 3 considers how a con can be maintained as a spiritual, mystical, or even politically emancipatory enterprise.

Working in the same medium of universal historiography as the book's earlier chapters, chapter 4, "The Chalice, the Blade, and the Bifurcation Point," examines the ecofeminist counterhistoriographies of the 1980s and 1990s that likewise found their way into the archetypal symbolism of Brown's novel. With Riane Eisler's influential 1988 study *The Chalice and the Blade* as its central focus, the chapter studies the historical reception of ecofeminist world histories, from revisionist "herstories" about matriarchal goddess religions and social systems that predate patriarchy to alternative ways of knowing and inhabiting the world. Such ecofeminist theories have long been decried by the likes of Susan Jacoby (and many others) as a form of crackpot scholarship and counterfactual New Age fabulism, yet they are resurgent in contemporary discourses about global climate change and the ethics of sustainable life on earth.

In each of the book's first four chapters—as in subsequent sections of the book—we witness how occulted concepts and theories resurface to impress themselves on popular culture and scholarly method alike rather than resting quietly beneath the desert sands or in the cemetery of prescientific thinking. Herein lies the very logic of interrogating them: How do such returns come about, and what conceptual and political priorities are bound up in the myths, as well as the means, of rediscovery? The epic historical scale of the intellectual formations treated in each of the first four chapters is itself central to this resurgence, offering a metaphysical architecture for their own return to circulation. The monumental scale of a millennial return often belies, however, the often modest and even homespun tasks of disinterring, conserving, studying, translating, reinscribing, disarticulating, and reimagining even the most epic claims of so-called ancient wisdom.

Part III, "Sovereign Institutions," centers squarely on the social and institutional forms that mediate such struggles for meaning. It begins with an examination of the fraternal organizations and corporate institutions founded by Marcus Garvey in 1920s New York, and concludes with a chapter on the nonprofit bibliophile societies used to reintroduce the works of the Marquis de Sade as "philosophy" in 1920s France.

Chapter 5, "Garveyism and Its Involutions," studies the formal—rather than strictly political or ideological—significance of the life and thought of Marcus Garvey. Though heeding the ambivalent and often paradoxical reception of Garveyism by Black intellectuals and writers since the early 1920s, it focuses on Garveyism as a conjoined set of institutions and narratives. In one of his more generous assessments of Garvey's independently financed Black business enterprises and the short-lived but deeply influential "back to Africa" movement with which his name became synonymous, C. L. R. James writes that "when you bear in mind the slenderness of his resources, the vast material forces and the pervasive social conceptions which automatically sought to destroy him, [Garvey's] achievement remains one of the propagandistic miracles of this century."[59] The chapter studies how this so-called propagandistic miracle came about, through the leveraging of financial and political claims upon historical narratives that ran counter to white supremacist world history, and which had persisted in diasporic Black literature and thought since the Middle Passage. The phenomenon of Garveyism was neither based wholly on propaganda, nor was it an otherworldly miracle; it instead comprised a set of institutions that extended from the formation of the Universal Negro Improvement Association to the establishment of the "Black Star Line" of shipping and passenger freighters, as well as to aspirational claims to Black nationalism that led to Garvey's investigation by the U.S. government. Chapter 5 considers Garveyism as a system of thought that sought literally to capitalize on Black counternarratives and counterhistories in order to redress the deep historical crises of white supremacist violence, colonial exploitation, and the legacy of slavery throughout the African diaspora.

Chapter 6, "The Sade Industry," studies how one of the more inadmissible writers of eighteenth-century pornography became a leading philosopher of the twentieth century. During the 1920s the work of the Marquis de Sade was republished as a corpus of "philosophical novels," thus entering into the sphere of philosophical discussion. The centrality of Sade to modern European philosophy dates from this period, further intensifying in the years after the Second World War. The postwar period, indeed, witnessed the rise of what I call the Sade industry, the corporate body of French intellectuals—from Georges Bataille and Pierre Klossowski to Roland Barthes, Simone de Beauvoir, Maurice Blanchot, Gilles Deleuze, Michel Foucault, Luce Irigaray, Annie Le Brun, and Jean Paulhan—who looked to Sade as a radical theorist of intellectual agency. The chapter studies the "industrial" means through which such an occasion became possible, including bibliophile societies and the publishing organs of the intellectual Left. The rise of Sade as a philosopher mediates, in turn, a major shift in European thinking during this period, which was characterized by a growing rift between an intellectual style rooted firmly in Hegelian philosophy and, on the other hand, a nascent but no less resolute antidialecticism. Sade, while never the cause of such transformations, nonetheless provided the occasion for much of this work, thereby galvanizing his curiously central eccentricity to the sphere of European political thought.

Part IV, "Products of Mind," shifts from intellectual institutions to the strategies used to comprehend the experience of being institutionalized. Addressing the institutional forms of psychoanalysis, the two final chapters study the role of formal psychiatric institutions in the clinical study and clinical experience of psychotic mental patients, as well as the role of informal "schools" of post-Freudian psychoanalytic training and affiliation in the career of Immanuel Velikovsky.

Chapter 7, "Cartographorrhea: On Psychotic Maps," studies the maps drawn by paranoiac asylum patients. I consider how such maps—as well as the theories of paranoia developed by Gilles Deleuze, Sigmund Freud, Félix Guattari, and Jacques Lacan, among others—seek to understand the ravages of institutional power. Ultimately, my goal in the chapter is to address the work of psychosis as a clinical and epistemological apparatus. In other words, I focus on the critical function toward which psychosis has been directed by twentieth-century clinicians and theorists.

Chapter 8, "Communities of Suspicion: Immanuel Velikovsky and the Laws of Science," discusses the networks of association, both logical and social, that fuel the controversial historicoscientific theories of the psychoanalytically trained science writer Immanuel Velikovsky. With the publication of his best-selling *Worlds in Collision* in 1950, the Russian-born Velikovsky blazed a trail for religiously themed pseudoscientists who would later capitalize on the popularity of his work, such as Erich von Däniken and L. Ron Hubbard. Velikovsky's detractors, on the other hand, questioned both the factual basis and the speculative fancy of his claim that biblical texts offered an historical record of catastrophic interplanetary events. Viewed within the context of postwar reassessments of the politics of knowledge and the means of historical change, Velikovsky's relations with other scientists and historians present a fascinating set of debates about the nature of scientific truth and the role of institutions in shaping scientific knowledge. In particular, the backlash of the scientific community against Velikovsky's work, coupled with his own insistence on scientific positivism, had the effect of marshaling a broad group of supporters who praised his epoch-shifting genius and decried his character assassination at the hands of the "scientific mafia." The Velikovsky Affair and its aftermath subsequently became a countercultural model for critiquing scientific orthodoxy, and in later decades offered a case study in the political and institutional forces that regulate scientific knowledge. Chapter 7 examines the Velikovsky Affair as a major event in the redeployment of "Copernican" negativity in postwar thought, which yielded its own avant-garde groupings replete with magazines, manifestos, and the rhetoric of cataclysmic liberation.

The book concludes with a brief meditation on otherworldly sources of hermetic wisdom and the extraterrestrial battlefields of political epistemology. "Coda: Thought from Outer Space" extends the book's discussions of colliding planets and the Gnostic conception of an "alien god" to the more literal ideas about the cosmic and intergalactic origins of enlightenment that emerged in New Age discourses and Scientology, in the parapsychoanalytic theories of Carl Jung and Wilhelm Reich, and in the pseudoarchaeology of Erich von Däniken and others. In particular, it focuses on the jazz artist and Black Arts intellectual Sun Ra as an experimental thinker about the frontiers of human knowledge, a theorist of outsider theory. Sun Ra's literally outlandish self-presentation as an intergalactic traveler belies the notion that even the farthest reaches of the cosmos have long been colonized as white, whether in concept or in historical actuality. Looking beyond Sun Ra's reception as an Afro-futurist creator of wild sonic landscapes informed by Afrocentric history, the coda discusses Sun Ra's ideas about the sources and politics alike of experimental knowledge; in doing so, it situates his work within contemporary discourses about the cosmic and intergalactic origins of enlightenment. At stake in Sun Ra's work, I argue, is the notion that outer space offers less a refuge from worldly racism and exploitation on a human scale than a vast and inhuman universe of possibility whose openness to empirical encounter risks becoming foreclosed, restricted according to that same all-too-human scale.

Ideas—bad ones as well as good ones—are far from timeless entities. For this reason, *Outsider Theory* maintains that the epistemological debates and concerns of twenty, forty, or eighty years ago continue to pose pressing questions about the way we think and about the way ideas circulate, precisely on account of their ever-increasing historical remove. One of the standard defenses against accusations of intellectual sloppiness, mindlessness, ideological pollution, or the disciplinary erosion of value has been to insist that there are no intrinsic relations of cause and effect between intellectual systems: there are, in other words, no *inherent* similarities between pseudoscience, mysticism, liberatory counterdiscourse, and hateful ideologies. This is a safe and perfectly reasonable contention.[60] One of the contentions of this book, however, is that there *can be* and *have been* relationships between popular and unpopular ideas, and that these relations deserve to be studied in their particularity. Are all readers, writers, and thinkers equally susceptible to "the seduction of unreason," as Richard Wolin has claimed?[61] Certainly the value or distinctiveness of such theories and worldviews cannot be presumed as inherently stable or influence-free. It is imperative to study precisely where and how such heterogeneous knowledges become linked, thrown in or out of circulation, assimilated, conflated, or adopted. These are the vicissitudes of *Outsider Theory*.

PART I

ALIEN GODS

THE ALIEN KNOWLEDGE
OF NAG HAMMADI

Where the painter and poet are silent, the scholar must, from its fragments, reconstruct the vanished world and with his feebler means bring its form to life. He can do so better now than ever before, as the sands have begun to yield up some of the buried trust. This resuscitation is of more than antiquarian interest: with all its strangeness, its violence to reason, its immoderateness of judgment, that world of feeling, vision, and thought had its profundity, and without its voice, its insights, and even its errors, the evidence of humanity is incomplete.

—Hans Jonas, *The Gnostic Religion*

In the cosmic procession through every phase of consciousness there are new experiences to be gained, and more complex conditions to be met; more temptations to be overcome; more negations and illusions to be dispelled by Light and Truth.

—Frances Swiney, *The Esoteric Teaching of the Gnostics*

BEARING THE FULL METAPHYSICAL HEFT of Christian epiphany—the manifestation of divine essence in earthly form—the discovery of the so-called Gnostic Gospels has become known as one of the most significant archaeological finds of the twentieth century. It also constitutes a major event in modern intellectual history, as much for the saga of discovery as for the scriptural treasures it brought to light. In December 1945, two Egyptian peasants unearthed an ancient library: a cache of thirteen leather-bound codices, dating from late antiquity, buried in an earthenware jar at the base of a cliff in the desert outside the city of Nag Hammadi, near Luxor. Containing a set of Coptic religious tracts known mainly through the antiheresy writings of the early Christian Church Fathers, the Nag Hammadi Library appeared, in the words of one of its earliest scholarly witnesses, to be "the

FIGURE 2. The Gnostic Gospels: the Nag Hammadi codices. All the codices stacked together in the home of Maria Dattari, n.d. Photo by Jean Doresse. Institute for Antiquity and Christianity, School of Religion, Claremont Graduate University.

sacred library of an ancient sect, to all appearances complete. Pharaonic literature had never bequeathed to us a whole set of books so rich and homogeneous."[1] Like Tutankhamen's tomb in 1925 and the Dead Sea Scrolls in 1947, two other archaeological breakthroughs of the period, the library presented an exceptional, even miraculous, case of protracted conservation across more than sixteen centuries. The clay jar, and the desert sands of the talus in which it lay buried, had preserved a set of scriptural artifacts against the ravages of time—as well as against the repressions that had necessitated their burial in the first place. Offering a tantalizing glimpse into the thought and politics of a forgotten age, the discovery both documented and in many ways reversed the orthodox suppression of a radical set of teachings traditionally known as Gnosticism—a "mutant thought," in the words of one modern writer, that emerged in late antiquity "in the lands of apocalypse and revelation."[2]

Contributing to the singularity of the find was the fact that the Gnostic tracts bound together in the library had never been the explicit target for archaeological investigation. Unlike Howard Carter's success in Luxor, there had been no swashbuckling Egyptologist searching for the Gnostic Gospels. Their discovery was wholly accidental, and thus all the more spectacular. But the story does not end there: the fate of the Nag Hammadi Library beyond its initial moment of discovery was no less contingent on chance, fate, or wondrous occurrence. The library's entry into international scholarship was at once circuitous and, at times, precarious. Shortly after its discovery the bound codices were divided and sold; the retrieval and preservation of its scattered parts was, like the labors of Isis to reassemble the body of Osiris, a task of epic—if largely invisible—proportion. In turn, the slow process of its study and dissemination, as well as its broader repercussions in modern religion and thought, have been every bit as protracted as the discovery itself was sudden and epiphanic. It is for this very reason that the Nag Hammadi Library offers profound insights into the scholarly, bureaucratic, and conceptual means through which a secret trove of lost heretical wisdom could return to circulation in the modern world—even, it would seem, according to miraculous principles consistent with its own cosmic architecture.

Since at least the second century CE, Gnosticism had designated a body of knowledge that was doubly alien to orthodox thought: considered heretical by the early Christian Church Fathers and thus suppressed, it was also considered to postulate a transcendental spiritual hierarchy alien and superior to the "jealous" creator god of the Old Testament. The writings of the heresiologists of the early Christian church confirmed this fundamental dualism, as did a number of ancient texts rediscovered and compiled throughout the eighteenth and nineteenth centuries. In Gnosticism, that is, not only was worldly matter exceeded by a transubstantiate divinity, as in Judaism and orthodox Christianity, but this creator god or demiurge was also exceeded in turn by a higher god: an "alien god," as the philosopher Hans Jonas describes it, totally exterior to the Old Testament cosmology. The fallen condition of the material world was attributable to its botched creation by the biblical god and his host of lowly archons (ruling angels and demons). The *true* divinity, on the other hand, occupied a transmundane realm of pure spirit, or pneuma, and whose powers and emanations *(Aeons)* came together in their fullness *(pleroma)* as the sum total of divine illumination.[3] Across various schools and iterations, Gnostic teaching proffered salvation through esoteric knowledge of the divine pneuma: it was founded on a kind of knowledge, or gnosis, rather than on faith, sacrifice, or ritual. The Nag Hammadi discovery was noteworthy—and newsworthy—to the extent that it confronted this spiritual discourse with a substantive corpus of written evidence testifying to its worldly return. The empirical basis for our knowledge of Gnosticism thus appeared to shift categorically: after 1945 the existence of a secret, repressed tradition dedicated to the knowability of the divine essence was now itself knowable again in material form. The notion that Gnosticism now had its own library—its own set of Gospels bearing a claim to biblical legitimacy—at once complicated the religious history of late antiquity and disclosed, in turn, the persistence of esoteric thought within modern epistemology.

I begin *Outsider Theory* with the Gnostic discoveries at Nag Hammadi because, for one, such discoveries are often the principal intermediaries for the public encounter with new, unfamiliar, or otherwise alien knowledge. Beyond the scientific and archaeological finds that continue to make headlines on a regular basis today—and in spite of the innumerable acts of destruction and ignorance that often *fail* to gain public attention—the notion that scientific research could create a world-changing event is, as one can imagine, an alluring prospect. This is all the more alluring when the discovery promises to disclose a hidden trove of ancient wisdom. As the religious historian Philip Jenkins has argued, much of the appeal of such "myths of discovery" lies in the very fact of their hiddenness and retrieval, "with all the intrinsically dramatic implications of secrecy, persecution, escape, refuge, rescue, buried treasure, even burial and resurrection" this entails. In both scholarly and religious contexts, moreover, such concealment themes offer a useful way to justify "a revolutionary chance or revival, in which the purity of ancient religious truth is restored" or in which an epistemic shift can be marked with the decisiveness of a major event.[4] Certainly, most intellectual labor does not happen that way. On the contrary, it tends to proceed slowly, at times even tediously, exercising various degrees of discipline and invention along the way. And as we will see in this chapter, the Nag Hammadi discovery was no less subject to the vicissitudes of scientific and scholarly labor. Its story unfolds as a drama of scholarly (as well as theological) devotion, rather than magical accident alone. For this very reason the "myth" of discovery offers a profound insight into the means and consequences of intellectual labor, even at its most protracted and meticulous. Such discovery events are often necessary in turn for rendering public the significance, and even the worldly existence, of knowledge that might otherwise remain overlooked or undervalued.

Such discoveries find their complement, moreover, in some of the most paradigmatic stories about the posthumous fate of "discontinuous knowledges," whether ancient hermetic secrets, suppressed indigenous traditions, collections of outsider art, or neglected masterpieces. Such, for instance, is the story of Henry Darger, a hospital janitor who lived in the same small, junk-filled room on Chicago's North Side from 1931 until he was moved into a nursing home in 1972, the year before his death. A student helping to clean out the apartment, after having removed numerous piles of trash, found the fruits of a lifetime of creative labor: three massive, hand-bound albums—each roughly two feet high and twelve feet wide—containing Darger's images; fifteen bound volumes containing the narrative of Darger's epic *In the Realms of the Unreal*, over fifteen thousand typewritten pages; and trunks filled with his materials, tracings, clippings, and piles of photographs and magazines.[5] Now reconstructed at Intuit: The Center for Intuitive and Outsider Art in Chicago, Darger's room testifies to the decades of creative labor—devotional, relentless, inspired, obsessional—that subtend the belated discovery of their epic culmination. However effusively the magisterial creativity of his "inner visions" might be celebrated in the decades since his death (to cite the common rhetoric of outsider art exhibitions), the discovery myth of Darger's *In the Realms of the Unreal* disclose the worldly drama that undergirds the fantasies and spiritual visions of Darger's imagination. The sui generis epic is a testament not only to the "realms of the unreal," in other words, but also to the mundane practical details of Darger's working life as a janitor, devout Catholic, and furtive writer-artist. This includes the material practices of collecting, storing, tracing, copying, composing, and binding that made up his work. At the same time, the discovery story also sheds light on the economic, institutional, curatorial, scholarly, and aesthetic practices and decisions that spared Darger's work from the trash heap and brought it into public circulation.[6]

Such stories are far from unique—and they are not always happy ones. The work of the artist Sam Steinberg, for instance, who had been a street-corner fixture near Columbia University in New York from the 1930s until his death in 1982, was gathered for a posthumous exhibition at Columbia in 2015, but then accidentally thrown away by maintenance workers after the exhibition closed.[7] And just as the concepts, inner visions, and mystical realities of countless thinkers have been ignored, trivialized, expunged, or deliberately persecuted according to all-too-worldly means, so too does the very possibility of accounting for their truths likewise demand material interventions. Like Alice Walker's mission to find the unmarked grave of Zora Neale Hurston, who had died in poverty in 1960, the possibility of acknowledging even the most spirit-rending achievements often hinges on a set of unglamorous but indispensable material practices.[8] So too do epiphanies, for all their miraculous agency, presuppose a set of concrete operations, without which their spiritual ballast might otherwise go unheeded. In her collected early essays on women's knowledge, Walker cites a statement attributed to Jesus in the Gospel of Thomas (one of the most notable tractates in the Nag Hammadi Library) to mark the significance of such projects: "If you bring forth what is within you, what is within you will save you. If you do not bring forth what is within you, what is within you will destroy you."[9] The repercussions of such labor of "bringing forth" are no less material than their means: at stake for Walker is the radical transformation in value that extends from the recuperation of Black women thinkers to the spiritual and political urgency of their thought.

In this regard the Nag Hammadi discovery offers an especially note-worthy object of study because the rediscovered documents pertain to a cosmological drama of inner visions and otherworldly "outsides," of hidden truths and revelations, bound up in the material practices of knowledge collection, recollection, and salvage. Spiritual knowledge, I propose, is no less subtended by "specific practices through which the world is differentially articulated and accounted for" than any other kind of knowledge. The very drive to transcend the degradations of the mundane often beckon to alternative ways of knowing whose minutiae can warrant political struggle or even martyrdom.[10] In turn, the textual specificity of the Gnostic Gospels discloses the archival continuities between mystical or visionary experiences, the work of neglected writers and thinkers (especially women and writers of color), and so-called outsider art and writing: the documentary traces of such work consist of the innumerable texts, diaries, bound books, collages, letters, and other artifacts its authors produce, much of which ends up discarded or destroyed, or whose creators remain anonymous or otherwise overlooked.[11] The teachings of Gnosticism might seem to contradict such an emphasis on the mundane and material; gnosis generally refers to a specialized form of supramundane knowledge (as opposed to faith) through which divine truth can be experienced as a revelatory gift. "What you look forward to has already come," says Jesus in the Gospel of Thomas, "but you do not recognize it."[12] Gnosticism, it seems, professed a world-transforming recourse to transcendental, cosmic knowledge rather than to insights contingent upon worldly entanglements. For this reason the dramatic rediscovery of a suppressed Gnostic library *in the realms of the real* is all the more compelling, both because the "myth of discovery" seemed so strongly to resemble Gnostic epiphany and, more fundamentally still, because the minute particulars of textual preservation, translation, dissemination, and exegesis would come to take part in its ancient cosmic drama. Indeed, the very definition of Gnosticism as both a historical phenomenon and a theological system would change dramatically on account of such procedures.

The Nag Hammadi Library, like its discovery in Egypt in 1945, is a testament to profound devotion. Bearing concrete evidence about the body of early Christian theology that had come to be known as Gnosticism—named after the grounding notion of gnosis, or redeeming knowledge—the Nag Hammadi story was newsworthy for the possibility that it might yield new information about early Christianity, perhaps even about the life and teachings of a historical Jesus. Was Jesus married to Mary Magdalene? Did he have a twin brother?[13] But beyond sensational ideas about their historical or theological import, the discovery of the so-called Gnostic Gospels resonated throughout twentieth-century thought on account of their protracted rather than immediate effects on biblical scholarship, religious history, and philosophy. For all the insights the texts may offer about the nature of early Christianity, their significance has as much to do with the tangled set of material circumstances surrounding the discovery itself, as well as the ensuing conservation and translation of the Coptic texts. The discovery points, we might say, to the concrete, worldly status of Gnosticism's spiritual concerns as a heretical tradition. Gnosticism holds a singular place in the study of outsider theory, in turn, on account of the unusual circumstances that made the sudden, alien appearance of a cache of ancient books so noteworthy within modern thought. Commentators have long looked to Hans Jonas's characterization of the Gnostic "alien god" as a general figure for the transcendental nature of Gnostic cosmology, as well as Gnosticism's exteriority to Christian orthodoxy in turn, whether on account of its theological discontinuities, its alternative spiritual or political emphases, or its heresiological exclusion from the canon. My use of the term "alien" throughout this chapter retains these numerous registers of exteriority while noting that in Gnosticism such exteriors always tend to be figured as either manifest or readily attainable: what you look forward to has already come. This was especially the case in the wake of the Nag Hammadi discovery; the transcendental spiritual beyond to which Gnosticism had historically been understood to testify now opened up to the vicissitudes of textual preservation and scholarship, a set of concrete operations for recognizing what had "already come" in the form of earlier interest in this forgotten, heretical faith.

INDIRECT TESTIMONY

Modern scholars, amateurs, and occultists had long known Gnosticism to designate a heretical form of mysticism anathema to Christian orthodoxy. First studied systematically by religious historians in the nineteenth century, Gnosticism represented by turns a syncretic, "oriental" antecedent to Christian beliefs, and a "Hellenistic" distortion of Christian doctrine. Gnosticism, signifying at once the idea of gnosis and the practices dedicated to it (whether scriptural, textual, discursive, or institutional), had long been of interest within modernity as a particularly esoteric class of outsider theory. A parasite on the body of Christianity, according to the nineteenth-century historian Adolf von Harnack, Gnostic thought distinguished between the supreme god and the biblical creator, and hence between redemption and creation. The jealous god of Genesis created the world of matter, whereas the supreme god was absolute and fundamentally discontinuous with the material world, accessible only through spiritual knowledge.[14]

Yet the conditions of knowability for such accounts of the Gnostic cosmology were strikingly material in themselves. Separated by nearly two millennia, Gnosticism was accessible to modern investigators largely through its fragmentary preservation in the heresiological discourse of late antiquity. The antiheresy writings of the Christian Church Fathers in the second and third centuries CE record citations, names, and other information about Gnosticism as part of their rhetoric for eliminating its worldly existence. The traces are thus both partial and fragmentary, subject to the violent ideological and theological opposition of the heresiarchs. As Henri-Charles Puech puts it in his field-synthesizing 1934 essay on the "problem" of Gnosticism, "what we know about Gnosticism, on the whole, are the indirect testimonials, almost always polemical, that have transmitted it to us."[15] For Puech, one's knowledge of Gnosticism is subject to the vicissitudes of its documentary preservation: the Gnostic archive necessarily raised concerns about the status of its holdings and the administrative powers that sustain it. Gnostic ideas nonetheless managed periodically to elude their orthodox archons: indeed, other Gnostic and heterodox sects continued to appear over the centuries, some well into the middle ages; likewise, certain scriptural traditions persisted under the auspices of occultists, fueled by archaeological finds such as the Bruce Codex, purchased in Egypt in 1769 and acquired by the British Library in 1842 and, most notably, the Coptic *Pistis Sophia,* presented to the British Museum in 1785 and translated into German, French, and English around the turn of the twentieth century.[16]

"However superhuman the efforts of the early Christian fathers to obliterate the Secret Doctrine from the very memory of man," wrote Helena Blavatsky in 1888, "they all failed. Truth can never be killed."[17] Efforts to stifle such "secret doctrines" as heresies against the true church were, however, both numerous and exceedingly well documented. Unlike the scriptures they sought to suppress, works by second- and third-century CE theologians such as Clement of Alexandria, Irenaeus of Lyon, Origen, Plotinus, and Tertullian were actively preserved in apostolic libraries and reprinted by Renaissance philosophers as early as 1520, with Erasmus publishing Irenaeus's *Against Heresies* (ca. 180 CE) in 1526.[18] In the work of Irenaeus, such ironic means of conservation were the result of an effort "with brevity and clearness to set forth the opinions of those who are now promulgating heresy." In opposition to the esoterism and secrecy of gnosis, in other words, such "brevity and clearness" would subject all heresies to the rigors of ecclesiastical plain speech. As Irenaeus continues, "I shall also endeavor, according to my moderate ability, to furnish the means of overthrowing [such heretics], by showing how absurd and inconsistent with the truth are their statements. Not that I am practised either in composition or eloquence; but my feeling of affection prompts me to make known to thee and all thy companions those doctrines which have been kept in concealment until now, but which are at last, through the goodness of God, brought to light. 'For there is nothing hidden which shall not be revealed, nor secrets that shall not be made known.'"[19] Citing the (nonheretical) Gospel of Matthew, Irenaeus proceeds to document the cosmology of the Valentinian school of Gnosticism according to the logic that doing so will disclose "in their naked deformity" the errors and heresies concealed within the doctrine's outward "attractive dress" and clever imitation of Christian piety.

Rhetorically evacuating any claims to his intellectual or spiritual authority, Irenaeus's exposition sought to "furnish the means of showing their falsity" according to a faith in the heavenly power of revelation itself. Complicating his project were the very claims to superiority and revelation he considered heretical in the Gnostics: "These men falsify the oracles of God, and prove themselves evil interpreters of the good word of revelation. They also overthrow the faith of many, by drawing them away, under a pretense of [superior] knowledge, from Him who rounded and adorned the universe; as if, forsooth, they had something more excellent and sublime to reveal."[20] Irenaeus's method, at least rhetorically, was to present the Gnostic cosmology in all its concealed evils and contradictions, thus allowing them to disclose themselves. The result of such suspicious hermeneutics was an ironic form of heresiological conservation through which the very medium for denouncing Gnosticism served as a means for sustaining it as an occult religion for nearly two millennia.

What appeared suddenly in the desert in 1945—only to enter far more gradually into scholarly and popular inquiry—was a body of scripture that both substantiated and supplanted the heresiological accounts of so-called Gnosticism to which intellectuals, artists, mystics, religious historians, and occult enthusiasts had been turning since the Renaissance, bolstered by a small but significant corpus of Greek and Coptic papyri.[21] The defiant, transcendental truth celebrated by Blavatsky was no longer hidden in "subterranean stores" deep in the bowels of the earth.[22] Blavatsky and her fellow theosophist G. R. S. Mead had, among others, been instrumental in making texts such as the *Pistis Sophia* available to turn-of-the century occultists and freethinkers; after 1945 the Gnostic Gospels become subject to renewed scientific and philological inquiry, as well as public interest, on a far wider international scale. This did not mean that the Nag Hammadi discovery was unprecedented; earlier discoveries of papyri scrolls and codices from late antiquity had fueled the occult revival in Europe and the United States, much as they provided new evidence for historians of religion. Rather, it meant that the 1945 event, arriving in the era of modern archaeology and in the wake of the Holocaust and the hydrogen bomb, would mark a new, secularized era in biblical scholarship that would be galvanized two years later by the discovery of the Dead Sea Scrolls.

The revelatory scope of the Nag Hammadi discovery seemed nonetheless to rhyme with the doctrines it unearthed: the very sands of Egypt opened up to present us with the promise of new knowledge about an obliterated past. For this reason, the discovery has come to serve as an allegory for the fortunes of knowledge in the modern age, whereby the objects of study and the stories we tell about them are inextricably bound together. For some, the discovery testified to the insistence of theological "divine knowledge" as a concern for modern intellectual history: the return of thirteen buried codices marked the advent, we might say, of a postsecular age. For others, the discovery shook the very foundations of Judeo-Christian metaphysics, unsettling the patriarchal stranglehold on Christian orthodoxy. Critics of such revisionist positions noted, in turn, that the "heresy" of Gnosticism's appeal to transcendental knowledge was already the province of a long-standing idealist tradition in Western thought. Indeed, the German political philosopher Eric Voegelin decried Gnosticism for this very reason, deeming its appeal to superior celestial knowledge a delusional political mythology characteristic of modern political figures and movements, from G. W. F. Hegel and Karl Marx to psychoanalysis, fascism, and Stalinism. According to Voegelin, Gnosticism's transcendental claims amounted less to an act of faith than a will to power, whereby a mystical knowledge—gnosis—seeks to exert "dominion over Being." The result was not true knowledge, he claimed, but a "demonic mendacity."[23] In spite of the Nag Hammadi discovery, the Gnostic legacy still bore heresiological overtones; Gnosticism, for Voegelin as for the orthodox Christian theologians of late antiquity, was the first pseudoscience.

Most scholars have leveraged far more liberatory claims on Gnostic epiphany and on the "myth of discovery" itself. Most notably, the American religious historian Elaine Pagels famously celebrated the Nag Hammadi find as an evidentiary challenge to the authority of orthodox Christianity, as exercised throughout the centuries following the ecumenical councils at Nicaea. In place of an accepted tradition of ecclesiastical power, the Gnostic

Gospels revise the biblical canon and unsettle the institutions of Christian authority that labeled Gnostic texts as heresy in the first place. The Nag Hammadi Library thus discloses a more heterodox Christian past. Pagels, in other words, reverses the charge of Voegelin's critique: after Nag Hammadi, we recognize that it was the Nicene-era church and the ante-Nicene Church Fathers, rather than Gnosticism alone, that exercised a will to power under the aegis of its transcendental claims. No longer buried in the desert sands of history, the Gnostic Gospels exercised a critical function in the present, thus bearing worldly significance in addition to otherworldly knowledge.

The Nag Hammadi discovery demonstrated the extent to which gnosis, the "alien" knowledge of the divine essence, or pneuma, possesses both a history and—in the form of a real, verifiable set of leather-bound books—a material substrate. For all Gnosticism's ties to modern occult traditions and esoteric fantasies about the immediate, noumenal access to transcendent wisdom, the retrieval and study of the Nag Hammadi Library bears out the very "problem" of Gnosticism as a set of evidentiary and testimonial concerns. Even beyond the question of how—or whether—otherworldly essences could be revalued and comprehended in substantiate form, the Gnostic Gospels raised the question of whether material evidence could ever be fully self-evident. The very processes of gathering, conserving, documenting, and translating the pages of the Nag Hammadi Library demonstrate at once the resilience and the ontic particularity of even the most spectacular moments of revelatory experience. And the "myth of discovery" dramatized in turn the extent to which the Gnostic Gospels derived their revelatory significance from the confirmation and reconsideration of archival materials that were already known, however disparate or fragmentary this knowledge might have been: the "epiphany" was an assemblage or synthesis rather than a totally alien discovery. In short, the archival preservation of ancient Gnosticism may have divulged its meaning most dramatically at the moment when its heresiological archive suddenly gave way to a library; but the spiritual meaning of the Nag Hammadi Library continues to be bound up in the persistent demands of its status as physical, corruptible, and thus necessarily archival material. In its recovered Gospels, the historical status of Gnosticism as a spiritual discourse thus became inverted: for centuries an outsider theory demarcated in heresiological terms, its return to textual specificity in the decades after World War II confronted the metaphysical architecture of Gnosticism with the material labor and institutional conditions of its return to circulation. Like other forms of outsider theory, such epiphanies needed to be gathered up and, if necessary, reassembled shard by shard. Their capacity for wonder—or for any kind of visionary experience—depended on it.

FRAGMENTS OF A FAITH FORGOTTEN

Sometimes, it seems, knowledge comes to us from out of the blue. At once unexpected and curiously foreign, the suddenness of an epiphany bears the force of a historical event. For this to occur, however, such an advent would have to rely less on cognition than on the concrete, material conditions of knowledge itself. The paradox of epiphanic revelation has to do with substance rather than astonishment, after all: it accommodates the means through which transcendental knowledge suddenly manifests itself ex nihilo in concrete form. It cannot just be an idea; it must instead collapse the distance between otherworldy noumena and worldly phenomena. Such thinking is remarkably consistent with modern ideas about Gnosticism itself. As the German scholar Kurt Rudolph put it in 1977, "All Gnostic teachings are in some form a part of the redeeming knowledge which gathers together the object of knowledge (the divine nature), the means of knowledge (the redeeming gnosis) and the knower himself. The intellectual knowledge of the teaching which is offered as revealed wisdom has here a direct religious significance since it is at the same time understood as otherworldly and is the basis for the process of redemption."[24] Though scholars have increasingly come to contest the presumption that any such integrated body of "Gnostic teachings" might ever have existed as such in late antiquity, Rudolph's generalization articulates the conceptual stakes of the means through which the Gnostic Gospels came to be known in the mid-twentieth century. At once transcendent and immanent, gnosis raises knowledge to the status of a truth procedure, whereby the supramundane beyond introduces itself within the empirical as a radical suspension of mundane expectation. How could the discovery of the Nag Hammadi Library not be consistent with the theology of Gnosticism itself?

The retrieval of the Gnostic codices from the desert sands of Egypt has been mythologized, indeed, as an act of divine intervention in its own right—if not a deus ex machina, then at least a vox clamantis in deserto. The story of its discovery, dispersal, and reclamation remains no less striking seventy years later in spite of how canonical this story has become.[25] What is especially significant about this story, as I have begun to suggest, is the work it does to suture together concepts and processes, spiritual meanings and material practices, as mutually dependent components of the discovery. In December 1945, only months after the end of the Second World War, two Egyptian peasants digging for nitrate-rich soil in the talus of the Jabel al-Ṭārif cliffs outside the city of Nag Hammadi came across a sealed clay jar. Muhammed and Kalifah 'Ali of the al-Samman clan were treading care-

FIGURE 3. Site of the Nag Hammadi discovery under the Jabel al-Ṭārif cliffs, near Luxor; Jean Doresse with Egyptian dignitaries and crew at the foot of the cliffs, 1950–51. Photograph by Marianne Doresse. Institute for Antiquity and Christianity, School of Religion, Claremont Graduate University.

fully, the story goes, as they were then in the midst of a blood feud with a family from a rival village near the site where they were digging for fertilizer. 'Ali's father, a night watchman, had been murdered earlier that year after killing an intruder while he guarded farm machinery in the fields. Muhammed 'Ali later claimed to have avenged his father's death some time after the discovery of the earthenware jar.[26]

Though hesitating at first in case the jar might contain some supernatural element, such as a jinn or curse, Muhammed 'Ali soon smashed it open, deducing that something valuable might be hidden inside, such as gold. Immediately, 'Ali later recalled, the jar released a halo of golden particles that swirled into the sky and disappeared. The contents, according to James M. Robinson, the religious scholar who assiduously tracked 'Ali down for his story, were "neither jinns nor gold, but perhaps papyrus fragments!"[27] For Robinson, this was a sign portentous: what outwardly resembled a supernatural event materialized instead as a worldly drama of textual conservation.

What Muhammed 'Ali found, and subsequently tucked inside his clothes to carry home, was a trove of papyrus manuscripts, written in Coptic and bound in leather volumes. The bindings, and the manuscripts themselves—as well as the surviving lid from the shattered jar in which they were stored—date from the early fourth century CE; the Coptic texts are translations from earlier Greek documents that date from at least the second century CE, and possibly earlier. The number of codices found remained unclear for some time, and the library itself was subjected to all kinds of monstrous abuses. Robinson writes, for instance, that Muhammed 'Ali's mother incinerated an unspecified portion of the find: "Thinking the books were worthless, perhaps even a source of bad luck, the widow of 'Ali [*père*] had burned part of them in the oven (presumably Codex XII, of which only a few fragmentary leaves remain)."[28] Robinson later added that the cache was divided up between the 'Ali brothers and their friends, which meant splitting up some of the individual volumes.[29] As if succumbing to the orientalist allure of his tale, Robinson adds that "illiterate Muslim neighbors purchased the remainder [of the library] for next to nothing," and describes the ensuing pageant of profiteering gold merchants and "one-eyed outlaw[s]" who traded in on these spoils.[30] Whether narrated as adventure story or bibliographic catastrophe, the result was a dispersal of the codices on the Cairo antiques market. What began as a tale of epiphany soon found itself subject to the tortuous vulgarities of the marketplace. The fate of the books was anything but otherworldly.

Under such circumstances the work of scholars and conservators became especially urgent. And indeed, the story of the subsequent retrieval, conservation, and eventual publication of the Nag Hammadi codices is no less eventful then that of their initial discovery. The temporal framework of 'Ali's golden aureole of suspended papyrus fragments finds itself inverted, however, in the recovery portion of the tale: where there had once been a singular moment of revelation, there was now a prolonged drama of scholarly procedure.[31] The fate of gnosis lay in the circulation of its fragments throughout the politically charged sphere of international collectors, dealers, conservators, and scholars of the postwar decades. The micropolitics of this effort to recuperate, preserve, and publish the texts are literally constitutive of our contemporary knowledge of their content and significance. Far from a relativistic "social construction" of Gnostic cosmology, the minutiae of such social and institutional practices were the very sphere of operations in which the status of an outsider theory such as Gnosticism became available for renewed consideration.

For a while, moreover, the procedural drama was about as much as most scholars had to go on. As W. C. van Unnik wrote in his 1958 study of the *Newly Discovered Gnostic Writings*—a book composed and published while the Nag Hammadi Library remained all but unpublished and its contents largely unknown, as they would remain until the 1970s[32]—there was plenty going on behind the scenes:

> Anyone who, like the present writer, has had the privilege of seeing a little of what goes on behind the scenes, realizes that [the published reports of the discovery] do not tell the whole tale. Some future historian in this field of learning is almost certain to find in this story plenty of material for a fascinating book. For the way to deciphering these manuscripts and laying open what they contain has been a thorny path to tread: and when one day soon the texts come within our grasp, published and translated, one might do well to remember that the greater the difficulties encountered, the greater must be the credit for having unlocked their secrets. In particular, there have been a number of changes in the political field which have played some part in this business and prevented access to these treasures in a manner scarcely serviceable to the cause of scholarship.[33]

As van Unnik suggests, the difficulties encountered behind the scenes inaugurated a kind of archaeological mystery of a second order: the rigors of scholarly pursuit, even in the process of merely assembling the library, became a form of encryption whose "thorny path" surely offered an index of the marvelous secrets they contained.

A basic outline of the difficulties encountered on this thorny path might proceed as follows: near Nag Hammadi, a local schoolteacher came into possession of one of the codices and sold it to the Coptic Museum in Cairo in 1946, under threat of arrest for trafficking in ancient goods. The director of the Coptic Museum, Togo Mina, showed the codex to a former classmate, the French graduate student Jean Doresse, who was studying at the École pratique des hautes études under the influential religious historian Henri-Charles Puech (whose own work on Gnosticism features in chapter 2). Another codex was smuggled out of Egypt and circulated through the clandestine international antiquities market before being tracked down by the Dutch religious scholar Gilles Quispel and purchased by the Jung Institute in Zurich; it became known as the Jung Codex, after the psychoanalyst Carl Jung, who viewed Gnosticism's cosmic drama as a productive analogue to the human psyche. The remaining books were eventually purchased and gifted to the Egyptian government, but an extended period of political unrest—which came to a head with the Suez Crisis of 1956—restricted access to the collection throughout the 1950s. Under pressure from Quispel and Puech, UNESCO intervened during the early 1960s to advocate for compiling, conserving, and photographing all the contents; eventually, a multinational team of Canadian, Egyptian, French, German, and U.S. scholars contributed to the publication of a facsimile edition, the first volume of which appeared in 1972. An English translation, edited by Robinson, appeared in 1979. From reassembly to publication, the process lasted for more than three decades. What it yielded was the preservation and study of forty-six discrete works of ancient religious literature—out of fifty-two tractates in all, including several repetitions. Did these tractates, these Gnostic Gospels, change the shape of knowledge altogether? Were the "secrets" unlocked in their translation and dissemination worthy of the drama of their discovery?

Though the pace at which it unfolded was excruciating, and though its significance may have been overshadowed by the political events of the immediate aftermath of the war (as well as by other great discoveries in religious archaeology, such as the Dead Sea Scrolls), the Nag Hammadi event introduced a library, a physical collection of bound books, into a spiritual and scholarly discourse that had existed principally in archival form to that point. The Gnostic Gospels gave both tangible form and concrete textual support to a discourse on Gnosticism that had flourished throughout modernity—or at least since the early seventeenth century[34]—but which had been based largely on archival traces, the extant corpus of ancient texts that had been collected (and in some cases published in translation), as well as the citations and descriptions gleaned from the heresiological writings of the early Christian Church Fathers. The Nag Hammadi codices presented an altogether different kind of repository whose fragmentation, hermeneutic mysteries, and even political and ideological nuances were now a function of the material circumstances of the library itself.

The notion that the Nag Hammadi Library brought about a revolution in scriptural knowledge may be the most salient aspect of its myth of discovery. As Philip Jenkins and others—including the philosopher Hans Jonas—have maintained, most of the contents of the library were either known or guessed at well before its discovery; turn-of-the century scholars actually knew a great deal about Gnosticism.[35] This does not mean, however, that we should discount the significance or question the veracity of the discovery. Quite the inverse: the myth is significant on account of the way in which the administrative and scholarly labors of gathering and conservation came to materialize this earlier knowledge, in the form of a story about the sudden, epiphanic reemergence of ancient scriptures. Because of the way Gnosticism had been historically understood, the discovery story bears a strong resemblance to earlier occult or countercultural ideas about Gnosticism as a secret buried within the history of religions. At once sudden epiphany *and*

FIGURE 4. The back of the leather cover of Codex IX. Photograph by Jean Doresse at the home of Maria Dattari. Institute for Antiquity and Christianity, School of Religion, Claremont Graduate University.

passionate "thorny path," the discovery myth of the Gnostic Gospels both narrated and allegorized the second coming of a body of spiritual teachings whose ideas they also reflected. What is especially intriguing about this second coming is that it bore the heterodox—and heretical—force of an epistemological shift: not only an epiphany but also an upheaval in thought and belief.

Beyond the textual conditions of its survival as a heresy and its subsequent study by religious historians, Gnosticism had long been considered a kind of visionary archive in its own right—a repository for occult wisdom and countercultural self-identification that had attracted eighteenth- and nineteenth-century poets and freethinkers, from William Blake, Johann Wolfgang von Goethe, and Mary Wollstonecraft to Martin Buber, G. W. F. Hegel, and Thomas Mann. Before the Nag Hammadi discovery, Gnosticism's "fragments of a faith forgotten" designated a largely subterranean heritage, a heterodox assortment of ancient religious traditions that was discontinuous with, and thus cast out by, Christian orthodoxy. The standard perception of this heritage was famously described in the late nineteenth century by the German religious historian Adolf von Harnack as "the acute Hellenising of

Christianity," though by 1932 a German scholar such as Hans Lietzmann could consider Gnosticism instead as a "regression" toward the "oriental origins" of Christianity.[36] Bearing evident Neoplatonic tendencies in the dualistic form of its celestial architecture, and incorporating vernacular pagan practices, Gnosticism entailed a "secular" contamination of Christian dogma wherein "ideas and principles foreign to Christianity force their way into it, that is, are brought in under Christian rules."[37] Harnack's assessment, underwritten by the dissent of the Christian Church Fathers, has proven oddly resilient, as Eric Voegelin's suspicion attests. Much of Gnosticism's countercultural appeal can likewise be attributed to this dialectical entanglement with Christian dogma. The English writer and theosophist G. R. S. Mead, writing at the turn of the twentieth century—and thus still forty-five years before the Nag Hammadi find—merely inverted the chronology of Harnack's evolutionary description in his *Fragments of a Faith Forgotten* (1900), the follow-up to his translation of the *Pistis Sophia* in 1896. For Mead, Gnosticism constituted the raw, primitive heart of Christianity, anterior rather than external to Nicene orthodoxy. Still striving imperfectly toward unknown ideals, Gnosticism formed a powerful repository of both the Near Eastern beliefs and practices that predated Christianity and Christianity's own evolving spirit.

For Mead, Gnosticism thus offered a fitting counterpoint to the restlessness of the contemporary age, an archive of spiritual striving available to thinkers seeking theological forebears. In language that would be reflected in countless subsequent accounts of Gnosticism as an archetype for the modern mind, Mead noted that "it requires no great effort of the imagination for even the most superficial student of history to see a marked similarity between the general unrest and searching after a new ideal that marked the period of brilliant intellectual development which preceded the birth of Christianity, and the uncertainty and eager curiosity of the public mind in the closing years of the nineteenth century."[38] For Mead, in other words, Gnosticism was not simply a fragmentary mirror in which the modern spirit might recognize its own tortured reflection but the very wellspring of spiritual enlightenment, the occult repository of a "higher faculty which transcends the reason," to which any modern enlightenment strives to return.[39] "The soul of man," he explained, "returns again and again to learn the lessons of life in this great world-school. . . . It may well be even that many of the identical souls who were embodied in the early centuries of Christianity are continuing this experience among ourselves to-day. For why otherwise do the same ideas recur, why do the same problems arise, the same ways of looking at things?"[40] Upholding the mystical logic of an eternal return, Mead recasts the lineage of great gnostic thinkers—from Blake, Goethe, and Hegel to the theosophists and Rosicrucians of his direct acquaintance—as new vessels for the "primitive" originary spirit of Christian enlightenment, even the very souls of its earliest thinkers. The fragmentary remnants of Gnosticism's "faith forgotten" are both the historical traces and the living remnants of this original wellspring, a conduit to its spiritual resource. Gnosticism, though suppressed and buried, was for this very reason a repository for the raw spirit of Christianity, a hermetic archive of secret knowledge in its own right. It is instructive to consider the similar terms used by Jean Dubuffet to formulate the significance of *l'art brut* as the return to a "youthful" artistic fecundity discontinuous with the sterility of the contemporary world, with its "asphyxiating culture."[41]

Such esoteric impressions persisted well beyond the Nag Hammadi discovery, in ways that cast Gnosticism itself as the transcendent, redeeming knowledge it might otherwise attribute to divinity. In his 1960 preface to Mead's *Fragments,* for instance, the poet Kenneth Rexroth gently revises Mead's ideas about transhistorical persistence in light of the news—if not the precise contents—of the Nag Hammadi find. For Rexroth, the Gnostic tradition was the subterranean store for transhistorical wisdom, of which the earthen vessel served as the physical form. For Rexroth, as for other theosophically inclined modern poets, the beliefs and practices of the Gnostic schools of Basilides and Valentinius offered a secret repository of ancient wisdom that nonetheless responded to contemporary existential conditions of estrangement and suspicion. Concluding a survey of the syncretic admixture of pre-Christian elements brought together in Gnostic thought, Rexroth notes that "Gnosticism is the main funnel through which [pre-Christian] rites and doctrines reach modern times. The mystery deity of the Templars or the erotic revels of the witches or the ceremonies of the Masons or Rosicrucians, all are aspects of a special heterodoxy that began with Gnosticism. For better or worse, the Gnostics were the founders of what we call occultism."[42] Gnosticism, in other words, speaks less to a special knowledge of the divine essence (pneuma, or spirit) than to a "secret doctrine," as Blavatsky called it, a special relationship with the sublime expanse of ancient Near Eastern religious forms and practices. For Rexroth, as for other theosophists and mystics, it became a medium through which the elements of this secret doctrine could persist into the modern era, including "serpent worship, erotic mysticism and ritual, the mystic marriage, the slain redeemer god" and a "strong matriarchal or at least anti-patriarchal emphasis."[43] The archival persistence of such elements designates at once the province and the promise of occult movements, Rexroth suggests. Even Eric Voegelin, in his hostility toward such movements, nonetheless upheld this notion of transhistorical continuity.

For Mead and Rexroth alike, Gnosticism *was* an archive, a metaphysical trove that existed in the contemporary world according to the paradoxes of archival preservation: at once remembered and forgotten, fragmented and preserved intact. Indeed, their shifting designations for the transhistorical function of the Gnostic faith bear out the ambiguous etymology of the term *archive*. Divided between the Greek notion of *arkhé* (ἀρχή) (origin, or "first cause") and the Roman-Latin notion of *arca* (strongbox, coffin), the term's etymology corresponds to its central axiomatic question of whether an archive designates a set of material holdings (texts, documents, artifacts, images) or whether it offers a general heuristic for the processes of storage and retrieval, inscription and loss, for which archives are the locus. For scholars of religion such as Harnack and his nineteenth-century contemporaries, including Wilhelm Bousset and Eugène de Faye, the problem of Gnosticism was largely an evidentiary one. We know about a variety of Gnostic "schools" attributed to the ancient theologians Basilides, Marcion, Valentinus, and others from the accounts of the Christian Church Fathers, who cited them directly, often at length, even while targeting them for suppression. But we know far less about when or where such thinkers lived, or precisely what the texts reveal about their religious practices.

Such evidentiary questions owe much, as I have suggested, to the paradox of Gnosticism's preservation in the heresiological archive. Once again, the contemporary stakes of Gnostic truth emerge as a function of the material and institutional circumstances it might otherwise seem to transcend. In the case of theosophists such as Blavatsky, Mead, and, much later, Rexroth, any such "truth" refers to Gnosticism's capacity for transmitting knowledge transhistorically across the ages, as much as to the spiritual register of that knowledge itself. Such truths are anything but otherworldly. Even the British feminist and mystic Frances Swiney, whose 1909 study of *The Esoteric Teaching of the Gnostics* came illustrated with colorful drawings by "a woman under spirit control,"[44] considered the "pneumatic" essence of Gnostic revelation to be an evolutionary principle attuned to the truth of life. For Swiney, Gnosticism proscribed the *abandonment* of worldly "sense-experience" in favor of "the higher consciousness of things unseen." Even so, the resulting wisdom amounted to a "harmony with the Universal Consciousness, wherein the [human] unit is perfected."[45] This meant, for one, reversing the absurdity of patriarchal social and sexual relations in favor of the supremacy of the "divine feminine" within the Gnostic cosmology. More broadly, it also meant that "the natural law of our spiritual progress is our renunciation of and disentanglement from the lower sense life." This did not entail a denial of or disengagement from the world; rather, it meant "living *in* it, but not *of* it. The Soul makes the great and eternal choice."[46] Gnosticism thus served as an archive for human potential as an antipatriarchal evolutionary principle; like Mead, whose work she cites in her study, Swiney considered Gnosticism to be "imbued with the imperishable memories of the past" and thus bore the wisdom necessary for an "ascendant humanity." And though Gnosticism's feminist spirituality involved sloughing off the baser, material elements of earthly, bodily life, such a procedure nevertheless unfolded (albeit negatively) according to material processes of renunciation and purification. "The Soul," she writes, "is, as it were, suspended in space and time, in the midst of spiritual, intellectual, and material phenomena."[47]

For Mead, in turn, the evidentiary or material specificity of Gnosticism as a "funnel" or strongbox for the preservation of occult wisdom opened up continuities between the work of the critic and the work of the heretic. Both forms of labor, Mead suggests, draw their power from the rigors according to which archival preservation and philological and critical investigation alike take place. For Mead, as for Rexroth in turn, the power that both conserved Gnosticism and relegated it to an esoteric tradition emanated from Gnosticism itself. The heterodox, "primitive" body of knowledge exercises its own claims to authority; its millennial resilience draws from the restless intensity of a manifest spiritual force, a spiritual "first cause" that conserves its truth in subterranean defiance of the ages. So too does the work of the biblical critic. "Criticism," Mead writes in the introduction to *Fragments*,

> does not end with the investigation of the text; it proceeds to a higher branch and busies itself with research into the date and history of the sacred books, the analysis and comparison of their several contents, and their relations with other writings; in brief, it surveys the whole field of Biblical literature as to contents in all its parts. The results of this investigation are so stupendous, that we seem to enter a new religious land. But before we enter the sun-lit waters of the harbour of this new country, we must have battled through many storms which no bark of blind faith will ever survive; the only vessel that can live through them' is the ship of a rational faith.[48]

Like Swiney's appeal to an evolutionary life force, Mead's theosophically inflected insistence on the subterranean power of the archive as an autonomous transhistorical imperative derived its authority from the devotional—even disciplinary—rigor required of critical and spiritual faculties alike. As Mead puts it, understanding Gnosticism's "higher faculty which transcends the reason" requires a union between the scientist-scholar and the mystic. "The mystic will not submit himself to the discipline and training of science; the scholar refuses to attach any validity to the methods of the mystic. And yet without the union of the two the child of understanding cannot be born."[49]

Such notions of unification—which, for Mead, found their synthesis in theosophy—likewise animate the innumerable esoteric accounts of Gnostic wisdom that continue to appear in print today, most often bearing Jungian ideas about their psychic value as transhistorical archetypes for spiritual human truths. Given that Carl Jung, himself an amateur of Gnosticism (among his many other forays into comparative religion), was instrumental to the conservation of the Nag Hammadi codex that came to bear his name, the refashioning of Mead's archetypal wellspring into a Jungian archetype is hardly surprising. Theosophists and Jungians may cling, in other words, to the transcendentalism implicit in any such outsider theory, whether designating a causal force or a spiritual meaning that supersedes the immanent register of worldly phenomena and worldly discourses. Certainly the appeal of Gnosticism as an ancient alternative to the Western dichotomy of faith and reason derives largely from its recourse to gnosis as a radical awakening whose mystical comprehension surpasses belief and reason alike.[50] My aim is hardly to purge such visionary investments of their wonder, but instead to account for the material specificity with which Gnosticism functions as their archival form and medium, and thus as the aggregate set of practices and discourses through which its drama of knowability can be encountered anew.

VARIATION IS THE LAW

The discovery of the Nag Hammadi Library at once literalized and complicated this archival function. In the decades after 1945, the paradox of preservation and erasure came to characterize the physical condition of the codices themselves; it also emerged as a problem within the very notion of Gnosticism as a metaphysical system. The meticulous study of the Coptic script, bindings, cartonnage (the papyrus scraps used to stiffen the leather covers of the books), and other material components of the recovered codices has sought to establish with greater certainty the conditions under which the Coptic library was compiled and preserved in the first place. However otherworldly its cosmology might have been, the library itself was hidden with no small degree of practical attention to its immediate circumstances.

Under what pressures, and according to what imperatives, was the library sealed up inside a jar and buried beneath the walls of a desert cliff? Elaine Pagels, among others, surmises that fourth-century monks from the nearby Basilica of St. Pachomius, which now lies in ruins, hid the books to preserve them from burning. As heretical texts denounced by the Christian Church Fathers as early as the second century, the books were essentially contraband. Did this mean that the tractates, or at least their contents, had been in clandestine circulation up to that point? Or were the books instead brought together for the sake of preservation? Coptic scholar Marvin Meyer proposes, for instance, that Pachomian monks "brought the codices together at the time of their burial or before that, even a considerable time before that, out of several smaller collections. In this sense the Nag Hammadi library may be called the Nag Hammadi libraries."[51] The material evidence presented by the newly extant library thus opened up an array of historical questions about the conditions of archivization, to the point of questioning the functional totality of the library itself.[52] We can only speculate as to whether the Nag Hammadi Library was, in fact, an active library or a collection of disparate texts bound together under the pressure of censorship and persecution. Might the codices themselves have been a product of their very storage, compiled and hidden as a means for preserving them?

At the same time, the survival of the codices for more than a millennium and a half has enabled the theological particulars of Gnosticism to receive extensive philological and hermeneutic attention. A more concrete picture of Gnosticism has emerged as a result—even if this has led to a virtual disintegration of Gnosticism itself as a category for describing a single religious phenomenon or movement, as Puech anticipated in 1934.[53] For one, other Gnostic texts, such as those in the Berlin Codex (discovered in 1896 yet untranslated until after the Nag Hammadi discovery on account of accident, death, and war), have come increasingly to light.[54] Older sources for information about Gnosticism were likewise brought to bear on the field, such as the Latin Corpus Hermeticum, which had been considered a likely forgery of fifteenth-century Neoplatonists until corroborated by parallel texts in the Nag Hammadi Library.[55] A new scholarly industry was thus founded: the 1945 discovery led to a surge in scholarly activity and the formation of new institutions of knowledge. Beyond the intrigues of its collection and dissemination, the Nag Hammadi Library yielded innumerable international conferences and symposia, research institutes, and publications. The result, we might say, is the collective scholarly administration of Gnosticism as an exploded field of intellectual discourse rather than as a distinct movement within or prior to early Christianity, heretical or otherwise. As Puech anticipated in 1934, the "prejudicial question" arises as to whether "we might even ask ourselves if we have the right to approach Gnosis [*la Gnose*] as a whole, when 'variation' is the very law of Gnosticism?"[56] Once a portent, the very notion of Gnosticism seems increasingly to have dispersed and disseminated its meaning, a halo of golden particles.

For a while, the early categorical definition of the Gnostic heresy retained its shape. It did so, however, according to scholarly decree. In Messina, Sicily, in 1966, the International Congress on the Origins of Gnosticism formalized a working definition of Gnosticism that would stabilize the terms by which scholars and theologians would refer to their common object of study. Outwardly provisional, the definition demarcated a body of "alternative" Christian thought with certain "connected characteristics," even though such characteristics were connected only heuristically, as scholars conceded even before the Nag Hammadi find. The Messina definition nonetheless retained a definitive spiritual core, confirming

> the idea of the presence in man of a divine "spark" . . . which has proceeded from the divine world and has fallen into this world of destiny, birth and death and which must be reawakened through its own divine counterpart in order to be finally restored. This idea . . . is ontologically based on the conception of a downward development of the divine whose periphery (often called Sophia or Ennoia) has fatally fallen victim to a crisis and must—even if only directly—produce this world, in which it then cannot be disinterested, in that it must once again recover the divine "spark" (often designated as pneuma, "spirit").[57]

In the Messina definition we find less a confirmation of Gnosticism's status as an outsider theory, orphaned in time, than a contemporary theory of the "outside" as an animating otherworldly presence in humankind. Significantly, the Messina definition largely decoupled the cosmogony of Gnosticism from the historico-religious language characteristic of both Harnack's "acute Hellenising of Christianity" and Jung's and Mead's archetypal wellspring. Recast according to a field of contemporary discourse *about* a historical religion, the provisional definition forwarded at the 1966 conference constituted, we might say, a suspension of disbelief toward the ontology of Gnosticism as a historical phenomenon. It concentrated instead on the ontological claims made *within* Gnostic discourse. No longer a historical aberration within or prior to Christianity, Gnosticism instead formulated an "outside" by means of its own cosmological principles, which here take ontological (or at least definitional) priority.

The more or less parliamentary construction of the Messina definition likewise bears out this scholarly, discursive turn. Insofar as it appears to cast off the shroud of historicity in favor of more explicitly phenomenological terms, moreover, the Messina definition bears the strong historical impression of the star participant of the congress, the former Heideggerian protégé Hans Jonas. One of the twentieth century's preeminent philosophers of Gnosticism, Jonas's own first study of Gnosticism appeared the same year as Puech's, 1934. In his highly influential 1958 study *The Gnostic Religion* (which will be discussed further in chapter 2), Jonas offered a typology of gnosis as a "knowledge from without" that both derives from and opens up to a transmundane, pneumatic God as something profoundly alien to the world. In place of archives and traditions, we find instead the alien—albeit a *concept* of the alien drawn from the philosopher's earlier studies of the Gnostic religion. "The alien," as Jonas puts it, "is that which stems from elsewhere, does not belong here. To those who do belong here it is thus the strange, the unfamiliar and incomprehensible." In gnosis, he adds, "the transmundane penetrates the enclosure of the world and makes itself heard therein as a call. It is the one and identical call of the other-worldly."[58] Sometimes, Jonas tells us, knowledge comes to us from out of the blue, though any such "call of the other-worldly" rings no less strongly from the cloisters of philosophical discourse, as we will see in chapter 2.

The Nag Hammadi Library has been mythologized as the very materialization of this call. Thanks to the rediscovery of the lost codices, the traditional, occult interest in Gnosticism as a widespread historical aberration has given way to stories about an otherworldly singularity that entered the world as if from beyond. The Coptic library both arrested the proliferation of occult Gnosticisms extrapolated from archival sources and returned gnosis—knowledge itself—to active circulation, at least allegorically. As I have suggested, however, this mythology accounts for only part of the epiphanic appeal of the Nag Hammadi find. To the extent that Muhammed 'Ali's discovery of the codices was phenomenal, it yielded not, in fact, a single treasure but a fragile set of bound documents whose appearance in the world, and whose very availability as knowledge, were subject to an agonizing range of administrative, scholarly, and interpretive processes, from the exhaustive textual exegesis of fragmentary pages to the critical disarticulation of historical commonplaces about the very meaning of the term *Gnosticism*. Even the "phenomenological" definition from 1966 was itself based on intensive scrutiny and the painstaking process of studying and translating the texts. In light of the Nag Hammadi discovery, moreover, scholarly attention has unsurprisingly tended toward the particular and the multiple, yielding progressively finer distinctions and an intensified field of expertise. The knowability of so-called Gnosticism has been unsettled, suspended rather than fully granted, by the epiphany in the Egyptian desert. As the poet Nathaniel Mackey put it in a 2016 interview, "if you're in a bungled universe you have to figure that error and misconception permeate everything, even your knowing, even what you have to call a pretension to gnosis. I mean, why would your gnosis be exempt?"[59]

In place of an esoterically knowable Gnosticism conceived as a repository of ancient wisdom, that is, we now contemplate this very knowability by means of the worldly set of documents available for study, both ancient and contemporary. This availability has, moreover, become a virtual commonplace. Meticulously photographed and translated throughout the 1960s and 1970s, the Nag Hammadi Library is now available online as a free digital archive. Hosted by the Claremont Colleges Library, the Nag Hammadi Archive conserves the documentary traces of the discovery as well as the texts themselves; the site features photographs of the conservation process and the discovery site, and includes the individual pages of the Coptic tracts. The online Gnosis Archive publishes parallel translations of the individual tractates, along with the heresiological context.[60] In print and in digital form, lines from the scriptures can be retranslated and subjected to intensive philological scrutiny, as well as reinterpreted in light of the ever-expanding library of new scholarly and popular studies. The scholarly field, too, continues to grow, with both new archaeological discoveries and the crossover appeal of numerous scholarly works animating the ongoing popularity of Gnostic thinking. Yet even as the textual basis and scholarly study of so-called Gnosticism has become increasingly ready at hand, the questions about what we know on account of such texts have only continued to multiply. Do the texts point to a discrete set or sets of Christian doctrine, or are they simply a subset of the syncretic dualisms that proliferated throughout the ancient Middle East? Does anything resembling "Gnosticism" even exist as a viable category for assimilating such belief systems? Of what, in other words, are the texts representative? Was the Nag Hammadi Library a working library that sustained a group of practitioners, or already a clandestine archive of "heretical" thought? Under what conditions, and according to what pressures, were the codices buried? The availability of the Nag Hammadi Library has intensified rather than exhausted the epistemological demands Gnosticism poses as a historical, theological, philosophical, and textual discourse.

Whether epiphanic library or suspensive archive, the two paradigmatic stories of Gnosticism's contemporaneity that emerge in light of the Nag Ham-

FIGURE 5. The Nag Hammadi Archive homepage, Claremont Colleges Digital Library.

FIGURE 6. Codex II, opened at pages 50–51, the conclusion and subscript title of the Gospel of Thomas. The hand is that of Marianne Doresse. Photograph by Jean Doresse in the home of Maria Dattari. Institute for Antiquity and Christianity, School of Religion, Claremont Graduate University.

madi Library each cast the retrieval of Coptic books from the Egyptian desert as a profound and historically resonant allegory for the fortunes of knowledge in the modern age. Yet they also serve as illustrative *instances* of the profound entanglements between and among transcendental concepts and mundane working practices, the insuperability of spirit and matter within even the most esoteric field of knowledge. The discovery of the Gnostic Gospels confronted ancient heresy with its uncanny textual complement, and the reassembled fragments of the texts exploded the scholarly field in turn. At stake in these encounters was the relationship—or, more accurately, the identity—of immaterial, "alien" knowledge with the material specificity of its worldly adventures. This, we might say, is a governing concern not only of Gnosticism as it was historically understood but also of its contemporary relevance and circulation as a popular, scientific, and theological field of study. Whether this "alien knowledge" bears strictly religious or more methodologically oriented overtones—whether it refers to the redeeming knowledge of God or the inherent strangeness and implicit unknowability of historical origins and causes—the question of how it becomes manifest, and under what conditions it does so, underwrites the myths and allegories of Nag Hammadi that I have discussed in this chapter.

Reciprocally, the material form and medium for this manifestation (whether book, scriptural text, logos, or scholarly network), is no less central to the provocations it introduces within the sphere of knowledge. Gnosis is literally unthinkable without such supports. As we will see in chapter 2, questions about the status of concrete worldly materiality—the "fallen" state of matter—determine many of the conceptual stakes, as well as historical and political ambitions, of the twentieth-century attention to Gnostic texts and ideas. For modern European and American thinkers—from Georges Bataille, Hans Jonas, Henri-Charles Puech, and Jean Wahl in the 1930s to Elaine Pagels and James Robinson in the late 1970s and beyond—the study of Gnosticism has offered a means for contemplating how knowledge comes into the world as the phenomenal advent of a fundamentally discontinuous, alien "outside." Far from rehearsing the implicit dualism of the spiritual and the mundane implied by such terms, these thinkers are concerned with the deferrals and short circuits to which the Nag Hammadi codices were likewise subject. The conditions according to which knowledge circulates form a constitutive part of that very knowledge, no less bound up in its ontology than any otherworldly metaphysical "content." Even in allegorical form, the function of the library, the archive, and the material text remains active throughout the Gnostic drama, informing—imposing or impressing itself upon—the very being of what is known and knowable. For twentieth-century thinkers such as those discussed in chapter 2, matter (the mundane, the physical, the tangibly material) is bound up with even the most alien, extracognitive, and transcendent movement of knowledge. Rather than merely the form that bears its otherworldly truth, the material constitutes its inalienable substrate, its medium, bearing the attendant hypomnesic conditions of storage and retrieval, commodification and preservation, fragility and intelligibility. As we will see in the ensuing chapter, the consequences of this recourse to Gnosticism are ethical and political as well as methodological.

In spite of its continued appeal for mystics and occultists—and perhaps even spurred by it—the "alien knowledge" at question in Gnosticism fuels a provocative discourse on the immanence or transcendence of knowability throughout twentieth-century intellectual history. As a paradigmatic instance of how outsider theory circulates throughout contemporary thought and culture, Gnosticism is far from simply a curiosity of popular religion, in spite of its numerous reprisals in works of Jungian archetypes and pseudoreligious epiphany, from *Raiders of the Lost Ark* and *The Da Vinci Code* to Immanuel Velikovsky's biblical theories of interplanetary collision, which form the basis of chapter 8.[61] Rather, in framing the coming into knowledge as a world-rupturing event, the study of Gnosticism demands critical self-reflection about one's expectations about the origins and pathways of knowledge, whether secular or religious, ideological or mystical. The "divine spark" of an outsider theory owes no small degree of its transhistorical resilience and heretical force—its "strangeness, its violence to reason, its immoderateness of judgment"[62]—to the work of heresiarchs and prophets as well the work of librarians, philologists, translators, and scholars.

GNOSTIC MATERIALISM

Found a family, build a state,
The pledged event is still the same:
Matter in the end will never abate
His ancient brutal claim.

—Herman Melville, "Fragments of a Lost
Gnostic Poem of the Twelfth Century"

WRITTEN MORE THAN A HALF CENTURY BEFORE the Nag Hammadi discovery in 1945, Herman Melville's "Fragments of a Lost Gnostic Poem of the Twelfth Century" evinces the suppression of the Gnostic heresy by the early Christian Church Fathers. Whereas Gnostic writings might be said to maintain that worldly creation was exceeded by a superior, transmundane realm of pure pneuma, or spirit, Melville's lines testify to the ineluctable finality, the "ancient brutal claim," of worldly matter. The message is a dour one: this fictitious "fragment of a lost Gnostic poem" testifies to the victory of the fallen world in whose name Gnosticism was suppressed.[1]

Melville's deposition applies just as strongly to the heresiologists, however, as to the Gnostics: the "pledged event is still the same." Like a *vanitas* painting, the poem dwells on the fleeting nature of all things, whether worldly or abstract, cultural or spiritual. Its attribution to a twelfth-century document suggests, however, the possibility that even a humble textual fragment could partake in that same ancient, brutal claim. Indeed, by naming a twelfth-century (rather than second- or third-century) Gnostic fragment, Melville's poem echoes the occult tradition according to which Gnosticism's "secret doctrine" managed to survive throughout the centuries, in spite of relentless efforts to suppress it.[2] The persistence of such fragile cultures of idealism and heterodoxy may be recognizable only in their extinction; yet even in extinction, matter prevails. The poem asserts the resilience of the material trace itself, the very fragment whose testimony survives in tragic defiance of the orthodoxy that suppressed its assertions. Gnosticism may have died, along with its aspirations and worldly trappings, but so too have its detractors. We are left with the obstinate material remnants of its pneumatic cosmology. As we saw in chapter 1, Gnostic writings testify, however paradoxically, to both the endurance and the metaphysical heft of such materials. Rendered brutal and ancient in Melville's "Fragments," matter, by this dialectical logic, comes to exercise something of a cosmic, even otherworldly, capacity for persistence.

For Melville, as for a large number of modern thinkers, the esoteric appeal of Gnosticism owes much to this paradox of destruction and survival. In witnessing the worldly traces of an obliterated faith, we encounter the alien singularity of matter itself, less the "call from without" of a superior god than the resounding shock of the ancient. Thinking historically about Gnosticism confronts the spiritual and political architecture of human invention with its pitiless inhuman substrate: the material frames that undergird and mediate it. Even before the Nag Hammadi discovery, in other words, the study of ancient Gnosticism furnished twentieth-century thinking with a signal example of the way knowledge is entangled with the obstreperous "claim" of matter, a very old materialism bound up with the fragility of human aspirations and the limits of worldly invention.

"The whole world is a tomb," as Hans Jonas put it, "to the soul or spirit, that alien injection in what is otherwise unrelated to life. There, one might be tempted to say, the matter rests to this day, with the difference that the tomb has meanwhile become empty."[3] Gnosis may aspire to the spiritual and otherworldly, but the sphere of its preparation remains insistently terrestrial. Herein lay its fascination for ancient and modern thinkers alike, as a model for sloughing off such terrestrial intermediaries. As Frances Swiney put it in 1909, "The Gnostics taught the true meaning of the 'Going Forth out of Egypt,' the eternal cosmic process of the soul's progression from the material to the spiritual."[4] And a fascination it has continued to be, to the extent that Gnostic dualism plays a major role in the development, and ultimately the transformation, of European philosophy between and after the two world wars. In both its heresiological and scholarly forms, Gnosticism's dialectic of pneumatic spiritual essence and brute materiality animates the development of modern materialism as a philosophical as well as political imperative. A resistant kernel of mysticism at work in the field of continental philosophy, Gnosticism's history as a scandal or heresy within Christian orthodoxy likewise offered an *evidentiary* model for an epistemology of scandals and resistant kernels. This "Gnostic materialism" proposed, in short, that the spiritual aspirations of Western humanism—whether the "soul's

progression" or the political emancipation of human subjects—was a function of the disruptive, unremitting claim of matter upon orthodox systems of
abstract thought. Even though Gnostic teachings may have sought to transcend the physical, the role of Gnosticism itself served as a perpetual witness
to such material demands.

Indeed, one of the more counterintuitive modern theories about Gnosticism was the notion that it offered a theory of materialism in its own right.
Whereas eighteenth- and nineteenth-century idealist philosophers appealed
to ancient religions as vehicles for visionary experience, a number of key
twentieth-century thinkers approached the study of Gnosticism as an exercise in materialist thinking. Approachable only through fragments and traces,
the task of gathering up evidence about the ancient religion was no small
undertaking, a "coming to know" whose relation to the material documents
at hand was anything but immediate.

Nor was it always easy to tell these traditions apart. For some thinkers,
such as the German political philosopher Eric Voegelin, modern Gnosticism
brandished decidedly idealist credentials, naming an elitist belief in the
power of special knowledge to comprehend and change the world. For other
modern thinkers, by contrast, Gnosticism's tenuous historical survival was
evidence of a restless dialectic of spirit and matter from which no "superior"
knowledge could ever fully extract itself. In proposing the phenomenal
advent of a discontinuous, alien "outside" within the spiritual architecture
of early Christianity, Gnostic dualism exceeded the spiritual architecture of
biblical cosmology. For the modern thinkers I examine in this chapter, such
an "outside" did not so much augur the availability of superior knowledge
as demand a way of thinking that was itself subject to the "ancient, brutal
claim" of matter. In place of conviction, we find instead a truth procedure
grounded in the evidentiary overturning of existential or spiritual guarantees,[5] an "impossible horizon where the most intensely human merges into
the abhuman."[6]

Melville allegorizes this mediating entanglement in the form of a
twelfth-century document that survived its own obliteration. His poem draws
its pathos from our capacity as readers to recognize how the Gnostic fragment both exercises and bears the evidentiary trace of the ancient, brutal
claim of its material. The poem goes so far as to personify matter as the
pronominal "he" that stands in the place of divinity: where one might look
for God, one finds matter instead. And yet the tragic force of our recognition is not itself a property of this matter; rather, it is a function of its
unabated "claim"—an insistence that refers less to mortality or divine
power than to vanity, naming a fundamental discontinuity with human

conceits and expectations. Matter, in this sense, is doubly alien; itself onto-logically agnostic, it interrupts rather than guarantees our knowledge and survival alike, thereby creating the medium of our fallen existence.[7] Yet it is also alien to itself: its "claim" does not bear the power to sustain our faith, but only to impose its own force of negation—yielding, at best, only the possibility of a compromised, dialectical relation with knowledge.

Even before the administrative and philological concerns of its textual reception after the Nag Hammadi discovery of 1945, the modern intellec-tual discourse on Gnosticism dwelled on the evidentiary problems it pre-sented. German idealist philosophy had long been associated with the Gnostic tradition, with the dialectical philosophies of Jakob Boehme and G. W. F. Hegel recognized for their spiritual inheritance from its transcen-dental cosmology. Approaching Hegel through the lens of Marxism and phenomenology in turn, a range of twentieth-century thinkers inverted this association, pursuing the study of Gnosticism for its worldly, counterortho-dox political and textual specificity rather than for its spiritual associations. As the trace form of an obliterated heresy, Gnosticism's surviving material ar-tifacts testified to a historical way of thinking at odds with the celestial architecture and ecclesiastical politics of nascent Christianity. Recasting nineteenth-century notions of the Gnostic religion as a foreign or vestigial element in Christianity, a number of influential modern thinkers considered the Gnostic heresy as a resistant kernel *within* the development of Christian theology, an "outsider" formation immanent to its historical development. What remained alien in Gnosticism was the extent to which it resisted, even negated, the spiritual hierarchy of Christian orthodoxy. The novel insight was the proposition that such negation drew its heretical power from the "ancient brutal claim" of matter rather than from the numinous authority of a higher god, or a cosmological appeal to unmediated wisdom.

As we will see in this chapter, modern thinkers from the polymath critic Georges Bataille to the philosophers Hans Jonas and Jean Wahl, and from the French religious scholar Henri-Charles Puech to the contempo-rary U.S. scholars Elaine Pagels and James Robinson, thus approached Gnos-ticism as something far more than a general influence within the history of dialectical thought. Rather, Gnosticism demanded attention for its insistent particularity on account of its discontinuous place in the material world. Modern materialist thought, as it developed in France through the recon-sideration of Hegelian phenomenology, and in Germany in confrontation with the work of Martin Heidegger, was profoundly informed by Gnosticism. What might seem to have been a purely antiquarian interest for certain modern thinkers was in fact an animating concern in continental philoso-

phy of the twentieth century on account of its paradoxically material entanglement with the problem of knowability. For as we saw in chapter 1,
even in the century before the Nag Hammadi discovery the term *Gnosticism*
referred not to a discrete religious movement or doctrine but to a complicated set of historical traces that testified variously to the problems of
spiritual and worldly knowledge. As a methodological rather than purely
theological concern, it became significant to modern thinkers on account of
its discontinuity with idealist philosophies and histories of knowledge, demanding instead an evidentiary turn toward the concrete.

In early writings by Georges Bataille, the claim of matter finds its complement in the notion of a "base materialism," a philosophical and political
espousal of phenomena "external and foreign to ideal human aspirations," as
Bataille put it.[8] Gnosticism features as a historical example in Bataille's
writing in the late 1920s and early 1930s, pointing to a methodological imperative consistent with the work of other twentieth-century thinkers who
likewise found Gnosticism appealing for its discontinuities with conventional systems of philosophical idealism. Gnosticism and base materialism
each named potent and potentially revolutionary challenges to such "ideal
human aspirations" because their insistence on matter implicated thought to
the point of abolishing the spiritual comforts of critical distance or abstraction. As Bataille noted, this negation of philosophical idealism necessarily
took place on the terrain of method or even, most broadly, among the complementary sets of entanglements that comprise the act of knowing itself.
Gnostic materialism thus staged a confrontation within the very sphere of
knowability, in which matter and spirit encounter one another.

Further confrontations emerged in 1934, when Hans Jonas and Henri-
Charles Puech each published important studies of Gnostic religion. In
spite of their methodological differences, both studies are resolutely up-to-
date with contemporary developments in continental philosophy, and they
both articulate the hefty theological concerns animating that philosophy in
turn. For these and other modern European thinkers, Gnostic dualism could
be said to incorporate the classical opposition between two conceptions of
knowing: the idealist premise that perception is grounded in human cognition, and the materialist premise that the physical world exercises its determinative forces upon our perception. The history of so-called Western
philosophy in the twentieth century is, in many ways, the history of such
incorporations, with movements such as phenomenology and pragmatism
interrogating the mutual entanglement of consciousness, concepts, and the
empirical world. Likewise, in physics the study of atomic theory, Einsteinian
relativity, and quantum mechanics plumbed the procedural inextricability of

matter and observation, if not matter and spirit. To what extent was human thought a product of the very world it studied—and to what extent, conversely, was the "world" we observed a product of mind? European and American thinkers from William James and Edmund Husserl to Alfred North Whitehead and Martin Heidegger increasingly resisted the "bifurcation of nature into two systems of reality," as Whitehead put it.[9] In the writings of the so-called Gnostics, we find claims about the reciprocal movement between these two premises: the pneumatic spiritual intensity of gnosis makes itself known on account of a mutual participation by both the thinking subject *and* the material world—even if such participation amounted to defiance and strife. Each way of knowing—the idealist and the materialist—mediates the other in the name of a higher truth procedure that superseded the all-knowing subjectivity of both the biblical god and Hegel's panlogistic spirit (*Geist*).

Lest we fall into abstract generalization ourselves, it is worth citing an instance of this reciprocal mediation in Gnostic thinking. Thus, for instance, one of the texts collected in Codex II of the Nag Hammadi Library, The Gospel of Thomas, attributes to Jesus the following aphorism:

> Come to know what is in front of you, and that which is hidden
> from you will become clear to you.
> For there is nothing hidden that will not become manifest.[10]

As we saw in chapter 1, Irenaeus of Lyon cites the orthodox version of this statement from the book of Matthew in denouncing the Gnostics: "for there is nothing hidden which shall not be revealed, nor secret that shall not be made known" (Matt. 10:26). The version of this statement in the Gospel of Thomas renders such revelations hortatory: procedural rather than passive, the call of the unknown can be heeded by coming to know concrete things—that is, "what is in front of you."[11] This process is not necessarily a straightforward one, however, as the double negative of the final assurance suggests: ᴍ̄·ⲗⲁⲁⲩ ⲅⲁⲣ ⲉϥ·ϩⲏ̄ⲡ ⲉϥ·ⲛⲁ·ⲟⲩⲱⲛϩ ⲉⲃⲟⲗ ⲁⲛ—literally, "nothing being hidden will appear forth not," according to Michael Grondin's interlinear translation.[12] Rather than designating an immediate reckoning with that which is present-at-hand, the Gospel of Thomas instead professes to a dialectical movement whose logic of negation suspends the hidden within the manifest, and the manifest within the negative. "Coming to know" is a restless and perhaps even infinite process, not a given.

This chapter dwells on the twin priorities of this aphorism—that is, of "coming to know what is in front of you" and of "becoming manifest." As I have begun to suggest, these conjoined processes inform the governing methodological and political concerns of the philosophers and scholars who studied them under the aegis of Gnosticism.[13] The modern approach to the study of the ancient religion, which began in the mid-nineteenth century but reached its speculative peak in the early 1930s, was concomitant with the rise of both pragmatist philosophy (particularly the Jamesian variety) and phenomenology, movements that each framed the process of "coming to know" as a central problematic. In the decades before the Nag Hammadi discovery, philosophers and other intellectuals sought to understand the dynamic logical and historical processes through which concrete phenomena became knowable to consciousness, and by which products of mind circulated in the world. This was as much a question of method as it was, for some, of spiritual revelation and political awakening.

For modern intellectuals interested in the problem of Gnosticism, the rise of phenomenology and pragmatism in philosophy at once resembled and conditioned the study of a religious movement whose evidentiary basis was as fragmentary as its beliefs were speculative. The study of Gnosticism thus demanded a careful attention to the contingency of any set of premises about its meaning, or about the significance of studying it. Reciprocally, the study of Gnosticism contributed to modern European philosophy in its move away from positivism, the naive empiricism of turn-of-the-century neo-Kantian and neo-Thomist thinking that presumed the self-evidence of data. Stefanos Geroulanos has described this movement as an "antifoundational realism" that reached its peak in the 1930s. In terms that resonate with the work of scientific thinkers such as Paul Feyerabend (see the present volume's Introduction), Geroulanos defines this tendency as "a kind of philosophical 'realism' that denies man any kind of transcendental separation *from* the reality he finds himself in, attributes to him a contribution to this reality, and forces him to accept his powerlessness to radical change—or escape from—it."[14] Human knowledge was imbricated in the fallen world of creation, in spite of the transcendental outside it was capable of imagining. The tragic existential condition of being suggested by such a cosmology would feature heavily in Hans Jonas's writings on Gnosticism, which bore the strong impression of Heidegger's existential philosophy. For others, however, the movement of an "unhappy consciousness" familiar to readers of Hegel would give way to a more redemptive and even politically charged methodological investment. In either case, Gnosticism dramatized the fundamental recognition that any philosophical idealism was necessarily subject to concrete evidence and worldly material circumstances. The result was an "empiricist mysticism," as the philosopher Jean Wahl put it.[15] It was the task of philosophy to heed the call of the outside—but such an outside referred neither to a metaphysical beyond nor to the conceptual privilege of an elite critical perspective; rather, the outside arrived as the claim of worldly matter exercised *in the name of* transcendental religion.

In this chapter, I study the critical forms of this empiricist mysticism in modern materialist thinking, examining how twentieth-century thinkers confronted Gnosticism's transcendental spiritual horizon as a function of the dialectical entanglements of matter and spirit, materialism and idealism, heresy and orthodoxy. In this context the alien in Gnosticism referred less to an otherworldly god or spirit, I maintain, than to the untimeliness and phenomenological interruptiveness of the empirical: the ancient, brutal claim of matter itself. For these thinkers, the relations between and among such "alien" forms bore the living demands of concrete thought, applicable not only to the history of religions but also to the exigencies of life in the modern political world.

The discussion that follows consists of three sections, tracing an evolving history of the entanglements between Gnosticism and "concrete" neo-Hegelian philosophy from the early 1930s through the late 1970s. As we will see, the modern intellectual reception of and approach to ancient Gnosticism takes a variety of forms. Yet what renders it significant to the study of outsider theory is the degree to which the worldly and the material begin to take on something of an otherworldly significance in exercising its ancient brutal claim upon and within abstract philosophical speculation. The three sections of this chapter thus each register the systematic deformations induced by the advent of Gnosticism within modern Anglo-European thinking.

The first section focuses on Georges Bataille's account of Gnosticism in a brief but conceptually significant essay he published in 1929 in *Documents,* the experimental journal he edited. Bataille understood Gnosticism as a religious and intellectual movement dedicated to debasing the spiritual architecture of orthodox Christianity; such an understanding was fundamental, in turn, to his ideas about modern materialism. His essay "Le Bas matérialisme et la gnose" (Base materialism and Gnosticism) engaged in dialogue with the work of the philosopher Jean Wahl and his influential colleagues at the École pratique des hautes études in Paris who would later found the journal *Recherches philosophiques;* this group included the religious scholar Puech, who contributed two essays of his own to Bataille's journal. Bataille's essay contributed in turn to a broader revision of Hegelian philosophy in interwar French thought in its epistemological as well as political turn "toward the concrete," to quote the title of Wahl's 1932 study of the philosophers William James, Gabriel Marcel, and Alfred North Whitehead.[16] For Bataille,

Gnosticism travestied the Christian spiritual hierarchy, pitting god against god in a manner parallel to the rupture in contemporary philosophy as it broke with the panlogism and idealism attributed to Hegel by his earlier admirers. In doing so, Gnosticism also disclosed concrete, "base" material phenomena whose resistance to knowability would reenact this travesty time and again, with dogged persistence.

The second part of the chapter shifts from Bataille's methodological investment in material documents and artifacts to the concrete existential and ethical considerations that animate the work of the German philosopher Hans Jonas. For Jonas, a former student and protégé of Martin Heidegger, Gnosticism addressed the fundamental existential alienation of our being-in-the-world, both allegorizing and literalizing the violence of historical reality. Though deeply informed by Heideggerian philosophy, Jonas's work on Gnosticism offers an explicit rejoinder to the fatal passivity of Heidegger's Nazism. And whereas Jonas's system shares the "antifoundationalist realism" of Bataille, Puech, and Wahl, it nevertheless recasts the dialectical cosmology of the Gnostic "alien God" as a realist ethical demand. Rather than a travesty, in other words, Jonas presents the phenomenological resistance to thought as the very medium for intelligibility. The historical conditions that threaten our existence—and our concepts—are nonetheless the medium through which we can begin to comprehend that existence. Jonas's work thus also conceptualizes the extent to which living historical, political, and ecological realities generate new modalities of accident and exception—new "outsides." To "heed the call" of the beyond is not a mystical or transcendental fantasy, but a recognition of the demands imposed upon our judgment by living systems whose dynamism is fundamentally discontinuous with the abstract or purely formal laws through which we might otherwise presume to know the world.

The final section of this chapter extends its focus to the methodological and ethical priorities of scholars writing after—as well as about—the Nag Hammadi discovery itself. In the 1970s and after, the American scholars Elaine Pagels and James Robinson stressed the political value of Gnosticism as an evidentiary rejoinder to long-standing orthodox Christian (and scholarly) beliefs about religious history. Demonstrating both the methodological persistence and the ethical and political intensity of a "Gnostic materialism," Pagels and Robinson each pursue the study and dissemination of the Nag Hammadi Library as a "new" set of Gospels that indicated how ancient religious evidence could complement contemporary liberationist thinking. Their approaches to the study of Gnostic religious documents are informed by contemporary feminism and counterculture leftism; yet more profoundly still, Pagels's work recapitulates the antifoundationalist realism of the earlier thinkers studied in this chapter in a revised historical understanding of early Christianity as an open, contested discourse. Gnosticism in this light demands a suspension of universalizing assumptions in favor of the ancient, brutal claim of material evidence. Such a shift exemplifies, in turn, the extent to which outsider theory comes to denote dynamic sets of local entanglements with concepts rather than a general category of sovereign or alienated reason.

BATAILLE'S COINS

Well before the Nag Hammadi discovery focused renewed attention on the relationship between material evidence and theological speculation, Georges Bataille's ideas about a new kind of materialism—a form of Marxist inquiry fully divorced from its idealist, Hegelian roots—invoked Gnosticism as both a precursor and a model. A later touchstone for French intellectuals of the 1960s and 1970s, Bataille's materialism was, at its origin, idiosyncratic and self-consciously unorthodox. Working at the scholarly margins of the French avant-garde, Bataille developed his ideas in the pages of his short-lived but epoch-marking journal *Documents,* which brought together ethnography and politics, art and the study of religion. His writing and editorial work upholds the capacity for documentary evidence to resist rather than corroborate our concepts and hypotheses. For Bataille, material facts constitute a form of alien knowledge whose dialectical resistance to conceptualization constituted a generative, if volatile, movement of thought.

In Bataille's thinking, Gnosticism refers above all to an ancient source for such material evidence, whose worldly leavings consisted of coins, textual fragments, heresiological tirades, and an inherited body of legends. His approach thus resembles Melville's in many respects: for Bataille, Gnosticism designates at once a fragmentary set of archaeological and heresiological findings, and a cosmology preoccupied with the otherworldly strangeness and power of the mundane. For all its attention to the transcendental nature of divinity, Gnosticism was a vernacular religion that extended to numerous mystery cults throughout the Near East. Drawing heavily on scholarly historiographies of the religions of late antiquity, Bataille's ideas about Gnosticism reflect, on the one hand, the coin and intaglio "gem" collections of early modern European antiquarians, who used the term *Gnostic* to describe the various mystery traditions of late antiquity. On the other hand, they also reflect the work of later European scholars to supplement the heresiological record by studying its archaeological traces: such physical

FIGURE 7. Bataille's coins. On the left, "God with human legs, serpent's body, and rooster's head. Gnostic intaglio"; on the right, "Headless god crowned with two animal heads; Gnostic intaglio." Cabinet de médailles, Bibliothèque nationale de France. This image originally published in *Documents* 2, no. 1 (1930).

evidence substantiates Gnosticism's continuity with Near Eastern mystery cults and other occult traditions rather than designating merely a confusion of categories.[17] Bataille seeks to literalize this heterodox fascination as both a methodological insistence in his own work and as the historical truth of Gnostic cosmology: physical evidence of the material culture of the Gnostics is, he asserts, evidence of a culture of materialism. The crude forms available to Bataille through the archaeological and numismatic record disclose a Gnosticism notable, that is, for its fixation on the mundane, the bestial, and the fallen condition of the terrestrial world—a kind of negative theology. Bataille's approach thus deploys material evidence in a twofold manner: it testifies to a powerful Gnostic investment in the mundane fundamentally at odds with the iconography of Hellenism and orthodox Christianity alike and, in doing so, overturns the "idealist" tradition of considering Gnosticism as a transcendentalist religion.

As we will see, Bataille's project resonated strongly with the other major contemporary studies of Gnosticism with which it came in contact—particularly with the work of Puech and his colleagues in *Recherches philosophiques,* a journal of science and philosophy founded in 1932, as well as on the French intellectual Left more generally.[18] Puech, a founding editor of *Recherches philosophiques*, would go on to become one of the leading French scholars of Gnosticism until well into the 1970s, and a major figure in the initial interpretation of the Nag Hammadi codices. Though articulated from the experimental edges of the avant-garde, Bataille's ideas about the disruptive "claim" of matter took part in a broader discourse on materialism during this period, particularly as it developed through the philosophical reconsideration of Hegelian dialectics as a philosophy of the concrete.

Anticipating his own movement toward the concrete, Bataille began his career as an archivist. As a student of medieval manuscripts at the École des chartes, he completed a thesis in 1922 on a manuscript version of the thirteenth-century verse epic *L'Ordre de Chevalerie* (The chivalric order) before taking a position at the Cabinet de médailles (Coins and Medals Department) of the Bibliothèque nationale.[19] Though the thesis has been lost, a brief summary appeared in the annual bulletin of theses submitted to the école for its "diplôme d'archiviste paléographe," a professional degree for an archivist (and thus a civil servant) specializing in paleography, the study of ancient handwriting. A brief glimpse of Bataille's later intellectual positioning appears even in the summary of this thesis: he describes the thirteenth-century poem as bearing "no literary value, no originality, and no interest other than as an old and curious document on chivalric ideas and their rites of accolade [*adoubement*]."[20] The notion that a cultural artifact could be more significant as a document—that is, as ethnographic evidence and a record of ideas—than as a discrete work of artistic, literary, or even monetary value soon became Bataille's signature analytical insight.[21]

Even before founding the journal *Documents* in 1929, thereby launching his long, if circuitous, career as an avant-garde critic and theorist, Bataille exercised this analytical position in a series of essays and reviews published in *Aréthuse*, an art and archaeology journal coedited by Bataille's colleagues at the Cabinet de médailles, Jean Babelon and Pierre d'Espezal, who would each collaborate with Bataille on *Documents* as well. Bataille's insights about Gnosticism would extend directly from this work, as would his forays into modern materialism as a kind of negative economy or even, as Bruce Holsinger has described it, as a negative theology.[22]

Though largely dismissed by his biographers, Bataille's early numismatic writing codified his language for assessing the kinds of impressions stamped and engraved on coins and medallions.[23] Coins were, for Bataille, literally a medium for bearing historical impressions. The historical value of such objects had less to do with their artistic or monetary value—they were, after all, no longer in circulation—than with the indications they bore of impersonal social and conceptual functions. Numismatics was the study of historical currency. Methodologically, this signified a shift from the traditional contemplation of idealized forms and representations of historical periods toward a "concrete" assessment of how ancient coins constituted historical evidence in the first place. As he writes in a 1927 review of Jean Babelon's book *La Médaille et les medailleurs* (Medals and medalists), for instance, the portraits of sovereigns on coins attended to political rather than physical likenesses. This was true even during periods of great representational art. Numismatic portraiture lacks "the taste for individual expression," as Babelon puts it; "the king's effigy is but an immobile image." What is portrayed is the king's power, rather than his personhood, "a simple expression of the majesty and will of the power of the king."[24] The "interest" held by coins and medals was thus evidentiary rather than aesthetic or pecuniary, Bataille concludes, reprising his earlier assessment of the *L'Ordre de Chevalerie*. Anticipating the more explicitly political thrust of his future writing, moreover, he begins to suggest the consequences of such numismatic portraiture considered as an archive of power. Political power was, for Bataille, predicated on a restricted system of exchange and exploitation with real historical, material, and metaphysical limits; power, no less than aesthetic or pecuniary value, could fall out of circulation. However stridently a numismatic portrait might point to the force and majesty of a historical epoch or sovereign, the status of the coin itself levies a tax upon the historical power it depicts in effigy: once it falls out of currency, it becomes subject to the numismatic system of representation that preserves it in bas-relief. Such representations may lack "interest," but they nonetheless both record and ultimately suspend the smooth functioning of their claim to power.

Bataille's numismatic concerns extend into the vast archival range of *Documents*. The journal's inaugural issue, for instance, features an essay on Gallic coins, "Le Cheval académique" (literally, "The academic horse"), in which he discusses the coins' resistance to conventional Roman stylization. Modeled on Greek coins, the "crude" iconography of Gallic coins of the fifth through first centuries BCE offers an archive of the anticolonial imagination, their crudity more a travesty of imperial power than a reflection of Gallic backwardness. Bataille notes that "the absurdities of barbaric peoples [i.e., the Gauls] stand in contradiction with scientific arrogance; their nightmares are at odds with geometric drawing; their monstrous horses conceived in Gaul are at odds with the academically styled horse."[25] This contradiction, however stark, is generative on account of its extremity, whereby the foreignness of such "nightmares" bears both epistemological and affective repercussions. "It has to do, in fact, with everything that had necessarily paralyzed the idealist conceptions of the Greeks: aggressive ugliness, raptures linked to horror or the sight of blood, immoderate screaming—that is, whatever is without sense or utility, introduces neither hope nor stability, confers no authority."[26] The traces of this ancient civilization bear evidence of its inadmissibility within classical empire. Such traces thus document the political intensity of Gallic resistance, sketching out a broader set of figural tendencies foreign to and discontinuous with the "academic" regime of classical representation. Such litanies of excessive affect ("without sense or utility . . . neither hope nor stability") are characteristic of Bataille's early writings; his essays on coins at once rehearse his nascent ideas about base materialism as a repudiation of classical ideals, and thus also anticipate his later notion of "heterology" as the methodology proper to the study of its effects.

It is through coins, too, that Bataille approaches Gnosticism. In his 1930 essay "Le bas matérialisme et la gnose" (Base materialism and Gnosticism), published in the eighth issue of *Documents,* he attributes the sovereign power he describes in his review of Babelon's book to the crude, insurrectional force of "primitive" forms (as opposed to the "majesty and will" of orthodox or ideal forms of authority). For Bataille, the stone amulets "on which [the Gnostics] engraved the figures of a provocative and especially indecent pantheon" testified to the currency of such a force in Gnostic material culture as it was understood by continental scholars.[27] In a manner that would bear significantly on the French reception of Gnosticism, as well as the predilections of French leftist philosophy, Bataille inverts the conventional understanding of the Gnostic celestial hierarchy, with its transcendent deity remaining alien and superior to the mundane universe of the demiurge—the jealous creator god of the Old Testament—and the demonic archons who oversee it. Bataille proposes instead that Gnosticism was fixated on the iconography and power of the material universe, however robustly it may have aspired to otherworldly transcendence. This insight draws principally from numismatic evidence: the carved gemstones and amulets that illustrate his essay are decorated with serpents, donkey-headed figures, and acephalous gods who would populate Bataille's own critical imaginary in turn. The iconographic imperative in such Gnostic coins resides in their depiction of the archons, the creators of all things mundane and sensory. It is to the "despotic and bestial obsession with outlawed and evil forces" that the Gnostics devoted their most scrupulous attention; this is the power to which their work testifies most centrally.[28] In Bataille's account, Gnosticism becomes a religious movement devoted—obsessively, if negatively—to the disruptive materiality of this emphatically mundane power.

FIGURE 8. The archons: duck headed gods. Cabinet de médailles, Bibliothèque Nationale de France. This image originally published in *Documents* 2, no. 1 (1930).

Far from a betrayal or disavowal of its theological value as a religion, this "obsession with outlawed and evil forces" constituted Gnosticism's very strength as an epistemological and political movement. As a faith that never served as a state religion or calcified into an orthodoxy, Gnosticism was insistently heterodox, functioning according to the unruly and even violent entanglements of mundane forces and systems of power. At once heterogeneous in its syncretic origins and heretical in regard to its reception by the church, its perverse fixation on the fallen world of the archons levies the transcendental power of the supreme being upon the "base material" that might otherwise seem anathema to it. Matter, not God, is alien—whether coin, fragment, document, beast, or body part. In place of Melville's melancholic reflection we find defiance: what Bataille finds in Gnosticism is not a system of divine transcendence but a negation of orthodox "idealisms."

In his approach to Gnosticism as a heterodoxy, Bataille nevertheless rejects the traditional world-historical understanding of Gnosticism as "a strongly Hellenized intellectual form of primitive Christianity too popular and indifferent to metaphysical development," as he puts it, paraphrasing Adolf von Harnack's classic formation. By focusing on the iconography of fourth- and fifth-century Gnostic coins, Bataille instead levies their

"provocative and especially indecent Pantheon" against the limits of Hellenism and Christianity alike. The figural images represented on the stones, as
well as the myths they portray, certainly corroborate "the bad opinion of the
heresiologists," but they also establish a far older origin for Gnosticism—in
Zoroastrianism, for instance, rather than in Christianity or Hellenistic Neoplatonism. Bataille also rejects other, largely Protestant efforts to recuperate
the "principle protagonists of Gnosticism—Basilides, Valentinus, Bardesanes,
Marcion"—as "great religious humanists."[29] Noting that the writings of the
Gnostic theologians were "systematically destroyed by the orthodox Christians," he turns his attention to the impersonal manufacture of coins. In place
of humanist authors, we find instead the authorless "impurity" of its figural
engravings.

The syncretic "crudity" of the coins extends to Bataille's version of
Gnostic cosmology as well. Inverting the hierarchical system of the cosmos
presumed by earlier scholars of religion, he outlines the basic dualism of the
Gnostic creed as a dialectical rather than a transcendental distinction between the fallen world and the otherworldly realm of the pneumatic supreme god. Not only does the mundane world serve as the paradoxical
medium for any possibility of pneumatic transcendence—as we saw in
chapter 1—but it also does so, according to Bataille, in scandalous fashion,
in defiance of the spiritual authority of the transmundane. In opposition, that
is, to the "profoundly monistic Hellenistic spirit, whose dominant tendency
saw matter and evil as degradations of superior principles," the Gnostics saw
matter as "an active principle having its own autonomous existence" ruled
over by a special tier of monstrous archons, the degraded pantheon of cosmic
authority. Bataille singles out the "troubled concession to evil" and "monstrous taste for obscene and lawless archontes" as dialectical characteristics of
Gnosticism, in spite of the presumption that "good and perfection" may well
have constituted the "supreme object" of their spiritual activity.[30] Where
Melville saw an enduring reminder of our fallen state, Bataille finds a principle of epistemological insubordination: for Bataille, that is, Gnosticism
demonstrates matter's resistance to any celestial architecture that might assimilate its spiritual and causal authority. It thus demonstrates, by extension,
the resistance of empirical phenomena to abstract logical systems more
broadly. Concrete phenomena suspend and interrupt thought rather than
merely illustrating its abstract pursuit of truth.

Why study Gnosticism? As a model for a new kind of dialectical thinking, Bataille's idiosyncratic approach to the ancient religion draws from the
"unambiguous interest" it shares with other mystical philosophies.[31] This
might suggest an explicit fascination with the occult, or with the perverse

"mysticism of sin" bound up in the history of fetishizing heresy.[32] Consistent with his numismatic and paleographic work, however, this interest is a resolutely professional one, "analogous in practice to that of an uninfatuated psychiatrist toward his patients," as he puts it.[33] Though certainly aware of the perverse allure of "monstrous tastes" and "the troubled concession to evil," Bataille's approach to such outsider theories is a clinical or at least disinterested one, grounded in a careful attention to methodology. His attraction to Gnosticism has very much to do with religious knowledge, but not his own belief; his interest is instead epistemological, a study of the inner workings of Gnosticism that is simultaneously a reflection on the contemporary stakes and methods of knowledge production.

As I have suggested, Bataille's interest in Gnosticism emerged in tandem with the work of other contemporary French philosophers. Most notably, his contemporary Jean Wahl sought to recast Hegel's dialectic as a more "concrete" form of realist philosophy by approaching him through the lens of American and British pragmatism and process philosophy (William James, Alfred North Whitehead) as well as through the work of Martin Heidegger and Gabriel Marcel. For Wahl, as for Bataille, the dialectical resistance of empirical phenomena to conceptualization constituted an important movement of thought. Earlier French philosophers had evaluated Hegel on account of his idealism, a philosophical system that subsumed the violent tribulations of historical change within the panlogism of a transcendental consciousness, or *Geist* (spirit). By contrast, Wahl radically recast Hegel's system to privilege the dynamism and incompleteness of dialectical movement rather than the abstract totality of spirit. This meant that dialectical negation operated as something other than a logical formula or a world-historical pattern; rather, it described the dynamic functioning of consciousness in its relationship to the world. Wahl thus sought to open up Hegel's dialectic to a broader phenomenological encounter with "realism," as the necessary resistance of phenomena to thought. This project extended, moreover, to the other philosophers, religious historians, and philosophers of science affiliated with the journal *Recherches philosophiques,* to which Bataille and Wahl each contributed, along with other notable phenomenologists such as Gaston Bachelard, Henry Corbin, Alexandre Kojève, and Alexandre Koyré.

Consistent with the work of Wahl's influential 1929 study *Le Malheur de la conscience dans la philosophie de Hegel* (The unhappy consciousness in Hegel's philosophy), Bataille—as well as other vanguard thinkers of the period, such as the surrealists—understood the work of consciousness as intrinsically restless, incomplete, and self-contradicting.[34] For some, this restlessness is productive: both poetic creation and historical change are dynamic processes that come about through negation. The unfolding of the human world over time, like the unfolding of human thought, takes place according to a process through which closed, knowable entities (such as an object, the self, or a nation) become divided and begin to oppose themselves, negating their former, limited totality. In traditional Hegelian dialectics, this divided, antithetical condition could be surmounted in turn by various forms of *Aufhebung*, or synthesis, a provisional "negation of the negation" that yielded a new arrangement in turn. For Bataille, however, any such recuperation already heralded a return of the idealism against which his work set its sights. In tandem with the surrealists (with whom he nonetheless engaged in a series of disagreements over this very subject), he maintained that the appeal of dialectical negation consisted in its restlessness rather than its resolution. Art and revolution were not the utopian fruit of dialectical synthesis, but the concrete forms of persistent negation, at once the result and the medium for a necessary "crise de conscience" (crisis in understanding), as the surrealist writer André Breton put it.[35] Likewise, Bataille's engagement with Hegelian thought was itself dialectical, rejecting Hegel's own systematics in favor of a movement "toward the concrete," as Wahl would later phrase it.

Bataille's approach to such a "crisis in understanding" extends, I maintain, from his work in numismatics and, in particular, from his interest in the iconography of Gnostic coins. Like Bachelard, Corbin, Koyré, Puech, Wahl, and other philosophers associated with *Recherches philosophiques,* Bataille's movement "toward the concrete" involves a dialectical encounter with systems of belief—Gnosticism, Jewish mysticism, Islam, early Christianity—that would likewise overturn totalizing abstractions with material artifacts, logical contradictions, and historical data. Far from a return to nineteenth-century positivism, this "mystical empiricism" is charged with the metaphysical intensity of its theological medium; it nonetheless occupies a concrete historical scale on account of its existential and methodological relation to worldly matters. For Bataille, such matters are as much a political as an epistemological concern. His own movement toward the concrete is shot through with revolutionary political exigency: viewing ancient coins as a material archive for power, he considers the overturning of that power as an immanent empirical demand thrust upon the very project of studying it. "It is difficult today," he writes, "to remain indifferent even to partly falsified solutions brought, at the beginning of the Christian era, to problems that do not appear noticeably different from our own (which are those of a society whose original principles have become, in a very precise form, the *dead letter* of a society that must put itself in question and overturn itself in order to rediscover motives of force and violent agitation)."[36] The resistance of empirical phenomena to conceptualization bears an emphatically political charge; the "dead letter" refers to orthodoxies of both thought and ideology that warrant upheaval.

Forming a kernel of resistance to Christian orthodoxy, Gnosticism interrupted the smooth functioning of Christianity's ideal form, the totalizing abstraction of its "original principles." Gnosticism thus not only resembled modern dialectical materialism—such as Bataille sought to define it, as both a theory of historical change and as a rejection of idealist philosophical abstractions about the causes of historical change—but also exercised its own rejection of systematic abstraction. It was on account of this rejection that Gnosticism, like materialism, created a method, a way of knowing.

The donkey-headed and acephalic archons carved on Gnostic gemstone coins demonstrate this fixation on the power of the negative—the "base" and "ignoble" forces of the mundane, which were incommensurate with the idealist principles of classical orthodoxy and Hegelian spirit alike. It is ultimately on this "fixation" that Bataille concentrates. "Thus it appears," he writes,

> that Gnosticism, in its psychological process, is not so different from present-day materialism, I mean a materialism not implying an ontology, not implying that matter is the thing-in-itself. For it is a question above all of not submitting oneself, and with oneself one's reason, to whatever is more elevated, to whatever can give a borrowed authority to the being that I am, and to the reason that arms this being. This being and this reason can in fact only submit to what is lower, to what can never serve in any case to ape a given authority.[37]

In place of an ontology of "matter"—or, conversely, a humanist metaphysical architecture for redemptive "elevated" knowledge—Bataille proposes a phenomenology of insubordination. What he refers to as "base matter" evacuates the function of transcendence in Gnostic idealism, thereby suspending even its own cosmic architecture. "Base matter," he writes, "is external and foreign to ideal human aspirations, and it refuses to allow itself to be reduced to the great ontological machines resulting from these aspirations."[38] Denoting matter's stubborn resistance to conceptualization—rather than matter in itself—this alien quotient produces epistemological effects through its very exteriority to humanistic reason. For Bataille, modern materialism heeds the "ancient brutal claim" of matter that presents it as alien and inassimilable to idealizing systems of thought. The result is a discomfiting and heterogeneous freedom that extends from the persistent overthrow of any such system. Materialism, for Bataille and his philosophical contemporaries, is an outsider theory.

Bataille's ideas about Gnosticism likewise developed in concert with those of Henri-Charles Puech, Wahl's colleague at the École pratique des hautes études and, later, in *Recherches philosophiques*. Bataille's essay "Le Bas matérialisme et la gnose" draws directly from the work of Puech, who contributed two essays of his own to subsequent issues of *Documents*; Bataille—as the journal's editor—had access to Puech's texts in advance of their publication and alludes to them directly in his essay. A historian of religion and founding editor of *Recherches philosophiques*, Puech devoted his career to the study of heresies and religious syncretisms within early Christianity, particularly Gnosticism and Manicheanism. Puech's scholarship proposed that Gnosticism was knowable through its concrete expressions rather than as a generalized concept (in contrast to nineteenth-century scholars such as Harnack, who approached it as a "tendency," or to Christian orthodoxy itself, which posited it as a heresy). Consistent with his own interest in "realist" philosophy, Puech's scholarship likewise took aim at the specious authority of metaphysical abstraction.

Of Puech's two essays for *Documents*, only the later contribution deals explicitly with Gnosticism. The work that resonates most strongly with Bataille's abhuman materialism, however, is the earlier essay, which addresses an altogether different topic that nonetheless articulates the core existential drama he attributed to Gnosticism. The political charge of Puech's approach to the religions of late antiquity emerges with striking clarity in his 1930 meditation on the imaginary prisons of the eighteenth-century Italian artist Giovanni Battista Piranesi. It is here, I propose, that Puech equates the "prison" of classical order and philosophical idealism (as targeted by Bataille) with the fallen worldly dominion of the archons in Gnostic cosmology. According to Puech, the traditional Gnostic antipathy toward the mundane takes on architectural form in Piranesi's nightmarish assemblages of staircases, arches, crosses, and giant wheels. The recognizably Greco-Roman form of these assemblages casts the ideal order of neoclassicism as an architecture of oppressive imperial power, giving way to "a perfectly inhuman vision of things." As Puech writes, in Piranesi's prison etchings "Man is definitively overwhelmed by what he has created and which, bit by bit, annihilate him utterly."[39] Like Bataille, Puech ascribes the inhuman degradation of the fallen world to the "metaphysical scaffolding" of classical order, the dead letter of a society that has not yet "overturned itself."

These terms return in Puech's Gnosticism essay for *Documents*, to which Bataille likewise alludes in "Le bas matérialisme et la gnose."[40] Reciprocally, Bataille invokes Puech's notion of metaphysical scaffolding as a general term for the idealist abstractions he seeks to slough off. Dismissing

FIGURE 9. Giovanni Battista Piranesi, *Le Carceri d'Invenzione*, plate V, 1761. Public domain.

the cosmological trappings of early Christianity, Bataille writes that the "abstract God (or simply the idea), and abstract matter" represent only "the chief guard and the prison walls. The variants of this metaphysical scaffolding are of no more interest than the different styles of architecture."[41] Bataille, for his part, seeks to suspend the imaginative dominion of this imperialistic scaffolding in favor of the "Gnostic" intensity of base materialism. Puech, on the other hand, sees the dehumanizing effects of this metaphysical scaffolding as the source of a profound existential crisis. "Man traces out a thin line between God and the machine," he writes, "and attains a perpetually threatened equilibrium only rarely, by chance."[42] Throughout his long career as a scholar of Gnosticism, this existential crisis would become the foundational problematic he identified within the Gnostic faith, throughout all its forms and incarnations. For Puech, even more so than for Bataille, Gnosticism opened up questions and exigencies that exceeded their historical delimitation as a problem within Christian doctrine or their comparative place in the history of religions. Gnosticism was, in short, a reflection on worldly problems. As he writes in the synopsis of his five-year course cycle on the "phenomenology of gnosis" at the Collège de France in the early 1950s, his work looks beyond the transcendentalism of the Gnostic celestial architecture. Instead, he writes, "our inquiry concerns, in the end, a more ample and general object: the 'world,' the *kosmos,* such as gnostics perceived and assessed it." This world was a fallen one, Puech concludes, a bungled creation whose "hideousness, mediocrity, and nothingness" the Gnostics decried, and to whose chaos they refused to submit.[43]

Like Bataille's materialism, Puech's approach to the study of Gnosticism drew from and in many ways synthesized both phenomenology and pragmatism. On the one hand, Puech's work approached its object of study by way of a reflexive discourse on method rather than through timelines and taxonomies; on the other hand, it also considered the practical difference that such thinking could make in our own lives. In the 1934 essay "Où en est le problème du Gnosticisme?" (The problem of Gnosticism today), Puech lays out his approach to the study of the ancient religion. Though the issue was complicated by a relative paucity of evidence and a surfeit of "Gnostic" schools such as the Marcionites, the Valentinians, and so forth, Puech advocates approaching "the problem of Gnosticism" schematically as a movement in and about thought rather than merely tracing its origins or speculating as to whether it constituted an adaptation or perversion of Christianity.[44] "As opposed to the comparatist position," he later explains, "it is on account of the whole [of Gnosticism] and its internal organization that the parts can be analyzed, comprehended, and organized dialectically. We can thereby

discern its essential themes (whether constant or general, calculated or implicit), from which, above all, we can derive the mutual implications of these
themes, as well as their relation to the phenomenon as a whole."[45] Gnosticism
thus doubly challenged our abstractions and commonplaces, both in presenting an evidentiary problem for study and in creating the spiritual response
to a concrete set of worldly problems in late antiquity whose "essential
themes" emerged dialectically from its fragments.

Puech reiterates this claim in a late, synoptic preface to his collected
essays. "Gnosis [La Gnose]," he writes in 1978, "does not exist in itself, independently of its expressions, apart from 'Gnosticisms' and Gnostics. It
would likewise be pointless to reduce it to an abstract concept, to an utterly
ideal notion, thereby giving it a definition that would be too oversimplified,
too general, not to be insignificant."[46] Gnosticism names a field of inquiry
that beckons reflexively to the concrete ways in which religious teachings,
spiritual needs, and scholarly categories exist in the world. Insofar as it
designates an organic and multifarious set of "myths, doctrines, speculations, and practices," Gnosticism has to be measured in terms of its concrete
forms and immanent concerns. For Puech, in other words, Gnosticism's
constitutive intellectual and spiritual processes draw their metaphysical
charge from the worldly conditions (material, political, psychic) they might
otherwise appear to supersede. As he explains, "The sequence of reflections
and deductions that comprise [the Gnostic process]—which arise in response to a series of successive illuminations that lead to an ever-deepening
revelation—remains . . . managed and oriented at every moment by practical and concrete sentiments and emotional exigencies."[47] By the end of his
career, the concreteness of a Gnostic "materialism" has come principally to
refer to psychic and existential phenomena: the concrete sentiments and emotional exigencies of living in a fallen world, whose metaphysical scaffolding
is no less a kind of prison.

For Bataille, the singularity of the Gnostic spiritual "process" had to
do with the discontinuous effects its dualism produced within totalizing systems of knowledge. For Puech, the major impact of Gnosticism upon modernity lay in the methodological repercussions of its response to existential
crisis. This position not only reflects the broader neo-Hegelian turn to antifoundationalist realism in French philosophy but, I propose, was also constitutive of it. The mystical and evidentiary detour of Gnosticism is an
example of a "concrete" investigation within philosophy that indicates
the conceptual stakes of any such detour insofar as the obstacles to "ideal"
comprehension become the very medium for voicing existential problems.
Though this turn "toward the concrete" is most often attributed to a

decidedly philosophical lineage (from Søren Kierkegaard to Alfred North Whitehead and Martin Heidegger), an outsider theory such as Gnosticism constituted a significant obstacle in its own right. It was, moreover, an obstacle that offered its own theory of knowledge. At issue in the study of Gnosticism for Bataille and Puech, in other words, was ultimately the question of its participation in the abhuman turn in modern philosophy—no longer as a system of faith, but as the trace form of a theoretical system or systems that bore methodological consequences of its own. In this light, Gnosticism's fragmentary leavings formed a procedural as well as archival basis for a new philosophy that recast materialism as a dynamic theory of life.

THE CALL FROM WITHOUT

Bataille, Puech, and the *Recherches philosophiques* group helped change the face of European philosophy, leveraging Gnostic materialism against the panlogism of Hegelian idealism. With the work of the German philosopher Hans Jonas, Gnosticism entered the New Age. Published in English in 1958, Jonas's *The Gnostic Religion* was an enormously influential study of the Gnostic "message of the Alien God" that proved at once to serve the interests of scholarship, philosophy, and the growing counterculture. Above all, Jonas's ideas about Gnosticism sought to reclaim some of the transcendental possibility—if not the transcendentalist logic—that the French intellectuals of the 1930s largely abandoned. For Jonas, Gnosticism was remarkable for upholding its faith in the midst of a fallen world, to the point that the worldly historical forces that always threatened to destroy it became the very medium for its claim to knowability, to gnosis.

Jonas himself was already known for his philosophical approach to Gnosticism well before the English publication of *The Gnostic Religion*. In a survey of the contemporary field in 1955, Puech named Jonas as one of the major figures in the phenomenological turn he identified within the field of religious history; Jonas had been writing on the topic since the early 1930s, with his first book, *Gnosis und spätantiker Geist* (Gnosticism and the spirit of antiquity), appearing in 1934. Like Puech himself, Jonas sought to move beyond the world-historical speculation characteristic of turn-of-the-century German scholarship, and to assess instead what Gnosticism was in itself, "in its totality." The goal of this shift was to attend to the inner workings of Gnosticism as a unified religious and philosophical system rather than relativizing it within the history of Christianity or Near Eastern religions—or, as Karen King reminds us, of seeing it as merely a conglomeration of disparate elements.[48] The result of such an approach was a definition of Gnosticism as "a style of life, a concrete, existential comportment," as Puech explained. Gnosticism was a mechanism for asking basic questions about the nature of worldly existence. The trinity of "worldly" questions Puech derived as a result—"'Where did I come from? Where am I? Where am I going?,' that is, '*What* was I? *What* am I? *What* will I be?'"[49]—become the interrogative basis for disclosing a more authentic state of subjective being. By the early 1950s Puech's "worldly" phenomenological questions had thus picked up on postwar French philosophical language in formalizing the medium of consciousness through which the Gnostic phenomenon could be encountered. Its turn toward the concrete defined in existentialist rather than strictly evidentiary or materialist terms, Puech's phenomenology sounded less like Bataille here than Jean-Paul Sartre. The work of Hans Jonas, on the other hand, bore a different set of intellectual coordinates; rooted in existential philosophy from the very beginning, Jonas's work sounded more like Martin Heidegger.

Like his French peers, Jonas approached Gnosticism as a historical form of outsider theory grounded in and responsive to the vicissitudes of the material world. What attracted Jonas to Gnosticism was likewise its existential bearing; rather than representing a religion of the soul (psyche) governed by moral and spiritual laws, Gnosticism asserted an "authentic freedom of the self" founded on the "spirit" (pneuma), defined as "the indefinable spiritual core of existence, the foreign spark."[50] Like Bataille, Jonas asserted that this "foreign spark" constituted a negation of the intelligible world: this negative transcendence, he wrote, "is not the essence of that world, but its negation or cancellation. The gnostic God as distinct from the demiurge is the totally different, the other, the unknown. In him the absolute beyond beckons."[51] On account of this fundamental negation, Gnosticism amounted to a negative theology. Jonas would thus integrate the language of pneuma into his existential philosophy as the very obstacle to totalizing conception that spurred a turn "toward the concrete": pneuma was itself a negation of intelligibility. Unlike Bataille, Jonas did not identify this obstacle as "material," though it exercised the same abhuman call or claim that defined Bataille's materialism and was no less evidentiary or experiential in the jarring disruptiveness of its effects.

Jonas, a student of Heidegger and one of "Heidegger's Jewish followers," began working on Gnosticism for his doctoral dissertation at the University of Marburg in the 1920s.[52] He published the first volume of the resulting book in 1934, having emigrated to London the previous year after the Nazis seized power; he later moved to Palestine and finally to Canada and the United States. The second volume of his study did not appear until

1954. In both volumes of *Gnosis und spätantiker Geist*, as well as in his later *The Gnostic Religion*, Jonas famously articulates in Heideggerian terms the "worldly" imperative described by Puech. In this sense Jonas's work on Gnosticism can be said to shift from phenomenology to ontology: he is concerned less with the "internal structure" of Gnosticism, that is, than with its "contents"[53]—namely, the disclosure of an inexorable cosmic injustice as the very condition of worldly existence. In *The Gnostic Religion* he describes the "constantly recurring expression [in Gnostic literature] for the ensouling of man by his unauthorized creator" as an ontologically prior condition of *Geworfenheit* (thrownness). The term, developed in the courses Heidegger taught on the phenomenology of religion in the early 1920s, which Jonas attended, derives from Heidegger's *Being and Time* (1927); it describes the "facticity of life," as Heidegger put it, the condition of "being thrown" *(geworfen)* into the world, indicating the fundamental alienation of being. For the Gnostics, Jonas argues, it likewise designates the jarring violence of worldly existence, as "an attribute qualifying the given existential situation" of estrangement and cosmic separation from the supramundane realm of true divinity.[54]

What distinguishes Jonas's work on Gnosticism, however, is the extent to which this "jarring violence" constituted a concrete historical reality. Unlike Heidegger, Jonas takes such violence literally; it refers to the political conditions that were ontologically prior as well as historically anterior to Gnostic cosmology and that likewise characterized its modern reception. "Gnostic myth," he writes, "is precisely concerned with translating the brute facticity experienced in the Gnostic vision of existence . . . into terms of an explanatory scheme which derives the given state from its origins and at the same time holds out the promise of overcoming it."[55] The fallen state of the historical world designates the conditions through and against which Gnostic eschatology initiates a separation. Jonas thus embraces the very "metaphysical scaffolding" of Gnostic transcendentalism that Bataille and Puech reject—but he does so for reasons similar to theirs. Gnosticism's alien cosmology offered Bataille and Puech a dialectical model for matter's evidentiary resistance to conceptualization; for Jonas, Gnosticism's capacity for resistant conceptualization lends its negative theology a liberatory force. Less revolutionary than eschatological, the rigor of Gnostic thinking makes itself receptive to the advent of exceptions within the existential conditions of our fallen world: a call from without.

The notion of a "call" bears distinctly Heideggerian credentials, and Heidegger's language likewise suffuses Jonas's other cardinal formulations about Gnostic spirituality, as we will see. In particular, the notion of the Gnostic message as a "call from without" bears an especially charged resonance.

This call designates the means through which the alien god of Gnosticism, whose absolute transcendence is both the cause and aspiration of gnosis, makes its appearance in the world. Signaling Jonas's intellectual debt to his philosophical mentor, this notion of the call would also become the foremost means through which Jonas would articulate his subsequent break with him after the debacle of Heidegger's pro-Nazi rector's speech in 1933. For Jonas, the alien call from without accommodates at once the cosmogony and the soteriology of Gnostic belief—naming, that is, the transcendent origin and eschatological point of salvation for revelatory experience. Jonas describes something wholly other than a metaphysical abstraction: Gnosticism is instead a living procedure of transcendence made possible by the speculative, ruptural call of the alien within the material world.

This latter, aspirational emphasis would be of great significance to Jonas's thinking. "It is this 'beyond,'" he writes, "which really qualifies the new conception of the physical universe and of man's position within it. Without it, we should have nothing but a hopeless worldly pessimism. . . . The total Gnostic view is neither pessimistic nor optimistic, but eschatological: if the world is bad, there is the goodness of the outer-worldly God; if the world is a prison, there is an alternative to it; if man is a prisoner of the world, there is a salvation from it and a power that saves."[56] Explaining the notion that such a salvation involves "a process of gathering in, of re-collection of what has been so dispersed," Jonas likens the eschatological process of gnosis, of heeding the call from without, to the "gathering" function Heidegger attributes to logos—that is, to language as well as thinking.[57] Yet whereas for Heidegger this gathering refers to a basic ontological procedure—the paradoxical calling into nearness and remoteness of that which logos names—it is for Jonas an eschatological gesture. To illustrate this point, Jonas cites a fragment of the Gnostic Gospel of Eve preserved by Epiphanius: "He who attains to this gnosis and gathers himself from the cosmos . . . is no longer detained here but rises above the Archons."[58] Rather than simply disclosing the basic condition of being, in other words, Gnostic gathering proposes a line of flight: less a command to be obeyed than an inducement toward a new form of being. For Jonas, Gnostic "knowledge" (gnosis) evokes, but ultimately supplants, the function of logos in Heidegger's philosophy. And in doing so it outlines a Gnostic materialism oddly consistent with that of Bataille and Puech insofar as it looks to the imbrication of matter and meaning as the living, dynamic medium for an emancipatory truth procedure.

Far from simply translating Gnosticism into Heideggerian terms, Jonas's approach to it is constitutive of his own philosophical career, which, like the ancient religion he studied, unfolded through and against the brute

facticity of historical violence. Such violence would condition Jonas's intellectual career in ways that left a profound impression on his philosophical
work. His turn "toward the concrete" bears the force, that is, of a specifically twentieth-century *Geworfenheit,* registering the geopolitical realities of
Nazism and the Holocaust, as well as the Cold War and the ecological ravages of late capitalism. Jonas was not a scholar of religion, as a number of his
critics were prone to pointing out.[59] Instead, Gnosticism offered at once an
incitement and an apparatus for his evolution as a philosopher: what began
in the 1930s as the study of a religious articulation of existential conditions
became the point of departure for Jonas's development of an ethics of responsibility in the years after the Second World War.

Interrupted by the war, Jonas's study of Gnosticism offered an interruptive, resistant philosophical kernel of its own. More than an analogue for
the restlessness and struggle faced by contemporary intellectuals, Gnosticism became the very medium for this struggle. Most of all, Gnosticism
offered a means for thinking through—as well as against—Heideggerian
philosophy, much as it offered Bataille and the *Recherches philosophiques* group
a means for rethinking the Hegelian system. With Heidegger's "call of conscience" *(Gewissensruf)* increasingly in mind after the betrayal of Heidegger's
brief but indelible Nazi affiliation, Jonas sought his own version of the call
from without that would inaugurate a countermundane orientation of its own.
Jonas would famously reject both Heidegger and Heideggerian philosophy
for its nihilistic passivity toward the "call" of being. As he wrote in 1964, for
Heidegger, "Hitler was also a call. *Such calls are drowned in the voice of being
to which one cannot say No.*"[60] Jonas's own project sought, we might say, to
separate the despotic "voice of being" of the worldly demiurge—the jealous
creator god that Heidegger increasingly came to resemble in Jonas's Gnostic
imaginary—from the true "call from without" of the utterly alien. This latter call would, in Jonas's later work, increasingly derive from the insistent and
irremediable demand of organic life itself: no longer the ultimately humanist ontological discourse of "being," but the inhuman causal and regulatory
functions of living systems, whose effects were perceivable but whose organic
existence, whose reality, superseded anthropocentric conceptions of life. The
alien god of Gnosticism would come to stand in for this more explicitly
worldly dynamic of immanence and transcendence.

Jonas's work on Gnosticism unfolded over a period of more than four
decades; while certainly marked by the Nag Hammadi discovery, these years
were far more profoundly interrupted and altered by the rise of Nazism, the
Holocaust, and the foundation of Israel. The call of "life itself" announced
itself foremost as an immanent historical emergency. A secular Jew from an

assimilated bourgeois family, Jonas became a Zionist in the early 1920s and immigrated to Palestine in 1935, joining a vibrant group of intellectuals that included the mathematician Hans Lewy, the Marxist historian George Lichtheim, the Egyptologist Hans-Jakob Polotsky, and the religious scholar Gershom Scholem. His philosophical career encountered a significant hiatus during the war, however, when Jonas, having written a famous appeal for Jewish men to volunteer for the war effort, served in the British Army's First Palestine Anti-Aircraft Battery, later serving in the Jewish Brigade Group through the end of the war. His work on Gnosticism was marked by a corresponding historical interruption, as illustrated by the twenty-year gap between the first and second volumes of *Gnosis und spätantiker Geist.*

In his memoirs, Jonas offers a striking reflection on this publication gap, which narrates an accident of historical preservation reminiscent of archaeological accidents like the Nag Hammadi discovery. The first volume of *Gnosis und spätantiker Geist* was published in Göttingen in 1934 by the Vandenhoeck und Ruprecht publishing house, after Jonas had already left Germany for Palestine. Before departing, he arranged to send the second volume from Jerusalem, in regular installments. Part of the volume had already been typeset while Jonas was en route; but after Kristallnacht he broke off contact with the firm and sent no further texts. The war took place; the Holocaust; the eradication of lives, books, and histories. Returning to Germany as a soldier in the conquering army in 1945, Jonas visited the publisher seven years after his last contact. To what fate had his books—the stock of volume 1 and the typeset portions of volume 2—succumbed? The event is memorable enough to warrant citing Jonas's memoirs at length:

> "Herr Ruprecht, I've traveled a great distance to meet you at last. My name is Hans Jonas." The effect was dramatic. "You're Hans Jonas? We've been waiting for years to see you!" What he told me next is one of the chapters of my life that deserves to be recorded for posterity. "Yes," he said, "your *Gnosticism* is one of our most important books. It wasn't until the war began that we thought it would be prudent to withdraw it from circulation"—he mentioned a year, 1940 or so—"and store the remaining inventory in a secure location." So the books had been moved to caves in the mountains somewhere. "How about the sections of volume two?" I asked. "Also in safe storage."[61]

Rather than putting their remaining stock of Jonas's Gnosticism book at risk of Nazi book burning, Vandenhoek und Ruprecht hid their stock, thereby replicating almost uncannily the gesture of certain Pachomean monks in the early fourth century, who buried a cache of endangered books in a clay jar in the Egyptian desert. Though Jonas admits that the firm had not "been complete heroes either," making concessions to the Nazi-favored "literature of the day," he praises their lack of compromise toward his own book: "They said, 'We didn't want to expose the book to danger. And we wanted to keep the book on our list. We didn't believe the Hitler period would last.' Their editorial meetings took place during the war, after all, when it was becoming clear that the Thousand-Year Reich wouldn't last for a thousand years."[62] Jonas's silence, and the underground storage of his books, opened up a hiatus recognizable only once it outlasted the truncated historical span of the Third Reich. By the time Jonas had retrieved his books and had completed the second volume of *Gnosis und spätantiker Geist*, the Nag Hammadi discovery had become known to the world. The Coptic texts would, however, play a relatively minor role in Jonas's work because, he claimed, they did not really offer much in the way of new information.[63] As his memoirs suggest, such instances of archival storage and retrieval could occur as the fulfillment of a kind of historical principle rather than as isolated events.

Indeed, his later work on the Gnostic religion, particularly his English-language book by that title, attempted to conceptualize the repercussions of such historical phenomena. Amid the violence and atrocity of the fallen world, the survival of religions in the very face of their obliteration was nonetheless an empirically verifiable form of historical accident. Yet for Jonas, it was less survival alone that interested him than the uncanny phenomenal gap it opened up within that fallen world, an exception to its worldly, archontic laws. In other words, the ancient, brutal claim according to which Reichs and religions would always fall—yet according to which their traces and artifacts might also persist—was the very principle of such historical accident and exception. What distinguished Jonas's philosophy was his insistence on the imperative to respond with judgment and care, rather than with acquiescence, to such gaps. Accident was not the same thing as fate.

This methodological imperative amounted above all to reconciling Jonas's early Heideggerianism with the all-too-evident demands of historical emergency. This reconciliation takes two primary forms, each seeking to replace, rather than simply reject, the "cruel and bitter disappointment" of Heideggerian philosophy in its susceptibility to fascism.[64] First, Jonas particularizes the historical development of Gnosticism itself as a syncretic, heterogeneous religious tendency, thus incorporating the comparative "history of religions" approach within his own methodology. He does this, I maintain, in order to render concrete the worldly terms of Heideggerian existentialism. More than just an system of individual belief, Gnosticism as a movement was subject to the historical conditions of its own genetic structure, its own

Geworfenheit. Jonas draws on a concept from mineralogy to explain his ideas about this historical development: Gnostic beliefs are an amalgamation of syncretic elements that filled the structural void left behind by the decay of other, earlier beliefs. This concept—pseudomorphosis—helps to explain how Gnosticism occupies the place of Near Eastern syncretisms without necessarily extending from them, resembling these historical precursors in form while being different from them in origin and substance.

Jonas's second means for reconciling his prewar and postwar work is more explicitly political in tenor. In its recourse to Gnosticism as a "primary source" for philosophical reflection, Jonas's unfolding work seeks to address the Gnostics' eschatological resistance to the archon-governed world into which it had been thrown. His career as a philosopher of gnosis constitutes, as I have suggested, a phase in his broader project to develop an ethics of responsibility, a project that was both interrupted and radically transformed by Nazism. Gnosticism comes to serve as the medium for Jonas's movement toward an ethical "philosophy of life," a means for both gathering and keeping at a distance the basic priorities of Heideggerian existentialism—another instance of pseudomorphosis through which Jonas's thinking could resemble Heidegger's in form but differ from it in origin and substance.

Rather than either heeding or exorcising the Heideggerian logos, Jonas doubly relativized his mentor after his spectacular failure in the face of national socialism. Whereas in his early career Jonas approached Gnosticism in Heideggerian terms, in the decades after the war Gnosticism instead came to supplant Heideggerian philosophy in his thinking, occupying its place as if through pseudomorphosis. Jonas's mineralogical metaphor for historical replacement finds its complement, moreover, within Gnostic cosmology, whereby Heidegger becomes the philosophical demiurge: a jealous creator god bound up in the violently corrupted worldly empire of the fascist archons. What replaces Heidegger in these schematics is not, of course, Jonas himself—narcissism was hardly the point of such maneuvers—but an encounter with an altogether alien system that demanded ethical judgment rather than blind obedience. Gnostic religion was superior to Heideggerian philosophy because it was, in short, more attuned to the real, wrenching exigencies of world history.

Heidegger's downfall lay in his presumption of passivity in heeding the call from without as if it were the authentic voice of existence itself. "As to Heidegger's *being,*" Jonas writes in a sensational 1964 speech to Christian theologians, "it is an occurrence of unveiling, a fate-laden happening upon thought: so was the Führer and the call of German destiny under him: an unveiling of something indeed, a call of being all right, fate-laden in every sense."[65] In place of the uncritical submission to the alien call of being, Jonas highlights the work of mediation that any such unveiling necessarily entails—a mediation that conditions our acceptance of its revelation. Even fate "work[s] out its own destiny, using human minds as its organ." Likewise Christian salvation, which purports to abandon such worldly fates, nonetheless requires the crucifixion. Jonas's point—consistent with the Gnostic materialism of his French peers—is to account for the extent to which even the most alien and otherworldly elements of belief are mediated through earthly forms, whether mind or body; whether concept, language, or material trace. Gnosticism's call from without was an interruption of worldly thought and worldly judgment, not a demand to abandon it altogether. It was the task of philosophy to take heed of the interruption as a renewed call to ethical judgment.

Such an approach meant recognizing, in turn, an analogously mediating function in the Heideggerian "call," an ethical demand that Heideggerian philosophy dismissed. The "cruel and bitter disappointment" of Heidegger's own decision-making in the face of Nazism signified the need for "a norm by which to decide how to answer such calls." Yet for Heidegger, there was no norm other than "depth, resolution, and the sheer force of being that issues the call." Far from a return to orthodoxy or philosophical idealism, Jonas argues that such "norms" are a function of the *deregulatory* function of language and the likewise *extraregulatory* function of complexity in living systems, whether the circulation of concepts or the ecological limits of sustainability: the language of the call, logos, is provisional and not be heeded with deaf ears. The role of norms and judgment was to recognize this provisional language *as such*, as a myth rather than the true unmediated voice of God or of being. Only in this way could the call from without open up to a truth procedure. Jonas borrows here from the language of Gnosticism: to the believer, he continues, "ever suspicious of this world, depth may mean the abyss, and force, the prince of this world. As if the devil were not part of the voice of being!"[66] One must not mistake archons for alien gods or the true voice of being. Faith, even more than reason, is a necessarily suspicious enterprise.

In *The Gnostic Religion*, Jonas likens Gnosticism to a form of moral skepticism insofar as moral laws—Mosaic codes, human opinions—were themselves part of the fallen, biblical world it rejected. The radical transcendence of Gnostic dualism constituted a purgation of the worldly, subjective, and humanist means through which the knowability of the beyond expressed itself and the provisional language to which it was conceptually restricted. The voice of this beyond, Jonas reminds his theological audience, "comes not out of being but breaks into the kingdom of being from without."[67] It is imperative, therefore, not to become *enchanted* with God, or the call, as if these could be immanent in knowledge or being in a way that rendered them fully present to consciousness; this would reduce God or pneuma to a mere concept again. Rather, the task is to recognize the world of appearances as such. This might suggest a shift toward Richard Wolin's anti-Heideggerian claims about the "seduction of unreason"—or even toward Voegelin's critique of Gnostic "immanentism"—but Jonas's position is far from any such abandonment. He advocates not clarity, but opacity; not the demarcation of reason from unreason, but a recognition of the dynamism and responsibility alike of anything resembling philosophy or even faith.

This is ultimately what separates Jonas from an anti-Heideggerian political philosopher such as Voegelin, who decried the "Gnostic" tendency in modern political thought on account of its fantasy of unmediated access to truth. For Jonas, such fantasies are indeed a dangerous illusion, but they represent a contemporary ideological problem, not a historical attribute of the Gnostic religion. In "Heidegger and Theology," Jonas challenges theologians to interrogate their own fatalism toward contemporary philosophy and take stock of the conceptual language they borrow. As the example of Heidegger all too painfully reveals, theologians cannot simply "wait for the consensus of philosophers, nor even necessarily trust its authority," but need instead to rely on their own judgment for appraising *which* philosophy is adequate to its task.[68] A "call" is not a command; historical exceptions do not amount to fatalism. Not only is philosophical language subject to the historicity of the material world, but its concepts are thereby necessarily destabilized and mediated through the mundane.

In place of the hubris of presuming that philosophy (or theology) can bear the essential voice of being, Jonas advocates the provisional acceptance of philosophical and theological concepts alike as *myths* through which the call from without can be approached as "in a glass darkly."[69] As he explains, "to keep the manifest opaqueness of myth transparent for the ineffable is in a way easier than to keep the seeming transparency of the concept transparent for that, to which it is in fact as opaque as any language must be."[70] Concepts, Jonas reminds us, are far from transparent. The historical contingencies that disrupt, sway, and threaten to destroy their worldly circulation comprise at the same time the medium of their knowability. Such archontic conditions thus become the means for their own suspension, in bearing out the simultaneously regulatory and deregulatory function through which the call from without becomes conceivable.

Jonas's Gnostic conception of radical exteriority—the call from without—posits that any such "outside" is indeed alien to the material and existential conditions of its intelligibility. This outside is not a *product* or function of existing conditions and processes of knowing, in other words, but the organic and inorganic sum of existence itself, a lifeworld whose "call"—or whose ancient, brutal claim—was the phenomenal indication of the very limits of such conditions. Though he hardly shied away from metaphysics, Jonas would increasingly come to illustrate this point in ecological terms: the full complexity of a living system such as the planetary biosphere dwarfs and exceeds the concepts used to describe how, in turn, it dwarfs and exceeds anthropocentric understanding, whether its notions of higher logic, divine order, Gaia, or world system. Such concepts mediate the alien imperative that surpass and elude them, the inorganic force of death, the "divine spark" of life itself. This, for Jonas, is the ultimate "outside" whose call the Gnostics sought to heed.

THE PNEUMA OF HISTORY

Jonas's efforts to recognize the instability of philosophical concepts find their complement in the political imperatives of Gnostic scholarship in the late 1970s. Yet whereas Jonas attributed eschatological force to the otherworldly bearing of the Gnostic religion, he largely downplayed the Nag Hammadi discovery. For the scholars most instrumental in translating and disseminating the Gnostic Gospels, however, the magnitude and scope of the discovery bore liberatory significance on account of the "good news" it introduced within the Christian canon. As the material trace of a hitherto unknown set of practitioners—or at least conservators—of Gnostic belief, the Nag Hammadi codices destabilized many of the concepts and categories according to which religious historians understood the theological politics of late antiquity, as we saw in chapter 1. With the Coptic library as its textual basis (considered alongside other extant sources such as the Berlin Codex[71]), the field definitively shifted its focus from the "oriental" syncretism characteristic of nineteenth-century religious histories—and still prominent in the work of Bataille, Jonas, and Puech—to the birth pains of early Christianity. The Nag Hammadi Library constituted testimonial evidence to the practice of nonconformist or heterodox movements within early Christianity, as opposed to the heresiological recording of its treachery. Scholars had long approached Gnosticism according to its suppression; the Gnostic Gospels offered resurgent evidence of its positive worldly circulation in late antiquity.

In this context, the Nag Hammadi Library testified to the historical reality of a Christian counterculture. It indicated, that is, the positive existence of living, alternative cultures of Christian knowledge and practice, rather than merely an aberrant or "alien" intrusion from other Middle Eastern religions. For James Robinson and Elaine Pagels, two of the most influential U.S. scholars of early Christianity who were both instrumental in publishing and popularizing the texts, the Nag Hammadi Library helped to recast ante-Nicene Christianity as heterogeneous and experimental in itself. The idea that Christian sectarianism and radical reform movements were in fact intrinsic to historical Christianity rather than later offshoots was in the early 1970s a concept largely alien to the American public, and it granted no small evangelical charge to the findings of textual scholars. The various schools of Gnostic theology (such as the followers of the early Christian thinkers Marcion and Valentinus) constituted a set of "alternative" communities that functioned independently of ecclesiastical authority, although they would eventually be shunned, persecuted, and ultimately suppressed under the evolving orthodoxy of the Church Fathers. Robinson and Pagels thus patently resisted Voegelin's tendency to view Gnosticism in Heideggerian terms as an elitism fundamental to the belief systems of totalitarian politics. Though still informed by Jonas's and Puech's existentialist approaches, Robinson and Pagels shifted the terms of their respective views of Gnostic soteriology to reflect the political demands of civil rights–era collectivism and feminism. The study of Gnosticism thus adopted new terms for upholding the redemptive possibilities of alien knowledge; by the 1970s, as we will see, Gnostic materialism had evolved into a politics of reading.

With gospels—"good news"—that could now be disseminated in material form, Gnosticism became an extant theology of liberation rather than the anguished record of alienation and resistance. The first English translation of the Coptic library bears out this political argument in its editorial framework. As if calculating the New Age predilections of his readership, Robinson claims that the writings propose a radical form of communal pacifism: not only had the Gnostics been purged from Church history, but their own theology also advocated "dropping out." Reminding readers that early Christianity was itself a radical movement, Robinson describes the Gnostics as a radical subset of that movement who adhered to "an ideal order that completely transcends life as we know it, and a life-style radically other than common practice." The priorities they maintained sound remarkably familiar: for Robinson, the Gnostics were a lot like hippies. He continues,

> This life-style involved giving up all the goods that people usually
> desire and longing for an ultimate liberation. It is not an aggressive
> revolution that is intended, but rather a withdrawal from involvement
> in the contamination that destroys clarity of vision. As such, the focus
> of this library has much in common with primitive Christianity, with

eastern religions, and with holy men [*sic*] of all times, as well as with
the more secular equivalents of today, such as the counterculture
movements coming from the 1960s. Disinterest in the goods of a
consumer society, withdrawal into communes of the like-minded
away from the bustle and clutter of big-city distraction, noninvolvement in the compromises of the political process, sharing an
in-group's knowledge both of the disaster-course of the culture and of
an ideal, radical alterative not commonly known—all this in modern
garb is the real challenge rooted in such materials as the Nag Hammadi library.[72]

Reflecting the popular ideology of the counterculture and, as we will see,
his own endeavors in the scholarly field, Robinson's introductory prose
depicts the Gnostics as precursors to the contemporary politics of liberation.
In doing so he explicitly dissolves the materialist emphasis at work in the
writings of Bataille and Puech in favor of a defiant idealism that nonetheless
translates into a concrete practice of life. He instead recasts the language of
archetypes and esoteric transhistoricism favored by Carl Jung, G. R. S. Mead,
and other mystics (see chapter 1) to describe a Gnostic political intentionality. Whereas Robinson no longer attributes historical causality merely to the
"equivalency" between ancient and modern countercultures, his ideas about
the exigency of the Nag Hammadi Library nonetheless draw heavily on the
New Age currency of such mystical interpretations, with one exception: for
Robinson, the "alien" visionary idealism is no longer to be transmitted hermetically through secrecy and indoctrination, whether in occult or scholarly
circles, but rendered common and available to all. He argues vehemently, if
tacitly, against Voegelin's charge of elitism. Framing the Gnostic "elite" as a
community of withdrawal rather than direct spiritual or cognitive access—his
own version of Jonas's negative theology—Robinson maintains that the
means for such withdrawal could and should be held in common. It is a matter, first of all, of reading the material texts themselves—which means having the means to get one's hands on the books in the first place.

The idealist communitarianism Robinson attributes to Gnostic writings
is both reflected in and underwritten by his own role in bringing the Nag
Hammadi texts into the public sphere. The Nag Hammadi discovery offered
a millennial opportunity for the Gnostic Gospels to transcend their historical relegation to esoterica, elitism, and hearsay provided that the texts could
be made available to common readers. Yet in the 1950s, he explains, a new
set of worldly concerns arose to restrict access to the Gnostic Gospels. Puech,
for one, had enshrined himself as a gatekeeper to the Jung Codex, restrict-

ing scholarly access even to his own student, Jean Doresse, as well as to his colleague Gilles Quispel, who had retrieved the codex from the antiquities market in the first place. Only when Puech was denied access to the codices in turn, this time by the Coptic Museum in Cairo, did he seek the aid of UNESCO to exert international pressure on the Egyptian government toward publishing a facsimile edition.[73] This process was protracted and fraught, as we saw in chapter 1. As Robinson has explained on numerous occasions, the codices (and especially Codex I, the Jung Codex), remained subject to a governmental and scholarly monopoly throughout he 1950s and 1960s; Robinson's calling, we might say, was to break the monopoly and make the texts universally available in an affordable translated edition.

On behalf of the greater good, Robinson took it upon himself to compile various sets of photographs, negatives, and transcriptions of the Jung Codex, which had deteriorated significantly during its years on the black market. Robinson then circulated these documents privately among a broad, international group of "cooperating scholars," along with transcriptions and images of the other Nag Hammadi documents. The result was an underground means of circulating the texts, which soon yielded an inexpensive translation overseen and edited by Robinson. "Thus," he writes, "the monopoly of the Jung Codex was broken two years before the *editio princeps* was completed."[74] Through his agency the texts' circulation became consistent with their inherent political message; withdrawn from the degraded "political processes" of scholarly monopoly and international intrigue, their entry into the public sphere enabled collective access to Gnosticism's counterculture of withdrawal and noninvolvement. Robinson's collectivism was nonetheless fueled by individual agency, an apostolic calling through which the "radical trend of release from . . . dominion" required a worldly intermediary.

Though hardly without personal reward, Robinson's apostolic contribution to the countercultural framework for the Nag Hammadi Library's popular reception also virtually inaugurated the scholarly institution of Gnosticism studies in North America.[75] His monopoly-busting collectivism impressed itself on the reception of the codices with particular profundity, moreover, because it took place after the fact: like St. Paul, we might say, Robinson was neither an eyewitness to nor a participant in the original "miracle" of the Nag Hammadi find. It was instead to the strength of his conviction in the event, and his dedication to spreading the "good news" of the resurrected texts, that the scholarly industry owes much of its foundational strength. With the initiation of research institutions such as the Institute for Antiquity and Christianity at Claremont Graduate University, others, too, could participate in studying the body of the resurrected codices without having to travel to Cairo, or having been present at the scene of the original Nag Hammadi find. The Claremont Colleges Digital Library now offers open online access to its entire Nag Hammadi Archive, providing public access to digital images of each page of the thirteen codices as well as a trove of historical photographs documenting the discovery site and ensuing research. Consistent with Robinson's Pauline imperatives for liberatory access, the Nag Hammadi Library is now available virtually as an open-access digital resource. Though hardly unmediated, it is readily available to anyone with an internet connection and a command of written English or Coptic.

In her own field-building work on Gnosticism, Elaine Pagels literalizes the Pauline overtones of Robinson's project of making the Nag Hammadi texts accessible to a popular audience. In *The Gnostic Paul* (1975), and in her best-selling *The Gnostic Gospels* (1979), Pagels addresses the countercultural and liberationist valences of Gnostic "heresy" in explicitly Pauline terms. Whereas Robinson might be said to invoke the epiphanic Paul as a figure for countercultural dissemination of the contemporary English translations—the ersatz Saul struck blind on the road to Damascus—Pagels considers the apostolic tradition of Pauline exegesis, interpreting the way in which the Gnostics read St. Paul's writing. At the vanguard of the post-1960s movement in religious history, Pagels's reintegration of the Gnostic Gospels within the Christian apostolic canon means interpreting the documents comparatively, in relation to other (often canonical) Biblical texts that circulated in late antiquity. This means viewing the various schools and sects known to the heresiologists as Gnosticism as active participants in the politics of reading in early Christianity, a political hermeneutics vested with the profound theological stakes of knowing, witnessing, and interpreting—that is, of spiritual access and spiritual authority—upon which organized Christianity was founded. The result of this research was an epistemological and theological upheaval that brought renewed attention to the political struggle for Christian orthodoxy in late antiquity—as well as in the present.

Pagels's *The Gnostic Gospels,* first published as a series of essays in the *New Yorker* in 1974 and later decreed by the Modern Library as one of the one hundred best nonfiction titles of the century,[76] is not only a key text in the active revision of the history of Christianity but also a key text in the history of contemporary feminism. Its aim is to open up a fuller picture of early Christianity, albeit less by bearing witness to the "real" Jesus than by chronicling the formation of the church, whose historical remove from the historical Jesus becomes starkly apparent. Pagels depicts early Christianity as a struggle for knowledge and power in the face of Roman persecution and the church's own administrative imperatives. Orthodox Christianity did not spring fully armed from the temple of Christ, but developed historically as an outsider religion in its own right, subject to the same ancient, brutal claim as any Gnostic heresy. In *The Gnostic Gospels*, Pagels reminds us of the very real threat of persecution and martyrdom faced by early Christians: "the orthodox who expressed the greatest concern to refute 'heretical' gnostic views of Christ's passion were, without exception, persons who knew from firsthand experience the dangers to which Christians were exposed—and who insisted on the necessity of accepting martyrdom."[77] Pagels's work thus offers a revisionist history of early Christianity writ large, recasting Gnosticism from an alien tradition anterior or exterior to Christianity to an expurgated tradition within it, an "accursed share," as Bataille might say, testifying to its former heterogeneity. Ecclesiastical authority is a worldly phenomenon, in other words, the product of political machination rather than direct spiritual access—a notion that has been profoundly influential to subsequent critics and historians of early Christianity. Pagels's aim is less simply to undermine ecclesiastical authority than to confront its living institutions with their own suppressed history: namely, the plurality and social inclusiveness the church purged in order to institutionalize its claim to universalism.

The repression of this history of dissensus becomes especially resonant in taking heed of the figuration of women in the Gnostic Gospels. In texts such as the Gospel of Thomas, for instance, one finds a testimony to Jesus's preference for Mary Magdalene as an apostle in spite of Peter's attempts to dismiss her. Such a position explicitly contradicts the canonical Gospels, where Mary Magdalene is reduced, at best, to an elusively described penitent (and, in many popular traditions, a prostitute or fallen woman). The Nag Hammadi Library also contains numerous depictions of a divine mother, as does the *Pistis Sophia*, which was influential to an earlier generation of feminist thinkers (see chapter 1). While Pagels admits that the texts are diverse and that there is no singular Gnostic way of depicting such a divine mother, she sketches out a number of basic characterizations—as one-half of an original divine couple in the Valentinian school; as the primal intelligence *(epinoia)* that complements the originary mind *(nous)* of the universe; as the Holy Spirit; and as wisdom *(Sophia)* in the first universal creator.[78] Such figurations run counter to the patriarchal cosmos of orthodox Christianity, wherein women are either relegated to saintly (but eminently earthbound) virgin mothers or, in the case of Mary Magdalene, rendered as fallen women.[79] For Pagels, this evidence does not so much contest or subvert the Christian canon as form part of its greater totality. She notes that "one might expect that these texts [in the Nag Hammadi Library] would show the influence of archaic pagan traditions of the mother goddess," alluding to the syncretism championed by Bataille and Puech (as well as by poets such as Kenneth Rexroth), among others. "But for the most part, this language is specifically Christian, unmistakably related to a Jewish heritage. Yet instead of describing a monistic and masculine God, many of these texts speak of God as a dyad who embraces both masculine and feminine elements."[80] Here, in other words, the dualism attributed by earlier scholars to Gnosticism's rejection of the Judeo-Christian cosmos becomes a positive attribute of its function within Christian theology: God embraces both masculine and feminine elements, just as Christianity harbored plural elements during the tempestuous period of its formation.

Pagels is careful to avoid idealizing the Gnostic "good news" as an instrumentally retrievable model of pluralistic democracy or an ethical belief system, however. In *The Gnostic Gospels* she depicts the political context of anti-Christian persecution within which heresiological discourse emerged: universalism, rather than Gnostic separatism or even elitism, become the strategy for shoring up the worldly continuity of the Christian faith. "Desiring to open that church to everyone, [the orthodox leaders] welcomed members from every social class, every racial or cultural origin, whether educated or illiterate—everyone, that is, who would submit to their system of organization."[81] Such universalism was a historical and political strategy rather than a theological or philosophical given. Pagels thus portrays early Christian debates about the "true" church and the nature of gnosis, enlightenment, and pneumatic interpretation as a ruptural event of its own, levying new claims upon church history as the basis for historical truth. Pagels breaks, that is, with the axiomatic principle of ecclesiastical necessity that continued to govern the history of early Christianity, inaugurating a new universal instead: Christianity is, and was, a political theology.

Dating from the very foundation of the apostolic church in the first and second centuries (rather than Nicene orthodoxy), this political theology draws heavily on the Pauline system of interpretation. The Gnostic reception of Pauline writings becomes Pagels's evidentiary means for approaching the liberatory possibilities of Gnosticism as a political and social formation. The results are arresting: rather than considering Paul to be the enemy and persecutor of the Gnostics, as the Synoptic Gospels (i.e., the New Testament) had come to portray him, Gnostics of the Valentinian school considered Paul to be a Gnostic himself. As Pagels argues, Valentinian Gnostics claimed that in his epistles Paul spoke to two audiences. The first group only read the scriptures literally, *psychically,* whereas the Gnostics learned to read scripture symbolically—that is, *pneumatically.* "Only this pneumatic reading yields 'the truth' instead of its more outward 'image,'" Pagels explains.[82] Couched squarely in the idealist terms of Neoplatonist dualism, such a distinction approaches Pauline claims about the superiority of pneumatic knowledge and faith as a hermeneutic principle: Paul's foundational claim that the old notion of salvation according to the law was superseded by spiritual redemption through grace becomes, in Gnosticism, a hierarchy of interpretation as well. The claim in Paul's letter to the Galatians that "there is neither Jew nor Greek, there is neither bond nor free, there is neither male nor female; for ye are all one in Jesus Christ" (Gal. 3:28) both names a new hierarchy (between Jews/Greeks and Christians) and becomes legible in terms of it, according to the interpretative hierarchy between the Gnostic elect (the pneumatics) and the literalist remainder (the psychics). As a result, Pagels explains, the outward terms *Jew* and *Greek* are not to be taken literally but allegorically, on a pneumatic level: Paul's discussion of Jews and Greeks refers to different groups of Christians. The worldly knowledge of mundane things is the province of "psychic" knowledge (i.e., of Jews and Greeks); the pneumatics, on the other hand, reflect Paul's own privileging of a higher spiritual access. The claim of gnosis could thus be attributed to St. Paul himself: knowing the resurrection in spirit (pneuma) is superior to having merely witnessed it in the flesh (psyche).

As fascinating as Pagels's map of Gnostic dualism may be, what is perhaps most significant about her work is that it bases its claims about such transcendental "spiritual access," as well as the pneumatic reading of Paul himself, on textual evidence. The Gnostics' spiritual one-upmanship—which dramatically alters our understanding of early Christianity—rests not on a "spiritual" or transcendental one-upmanship on the order of method; it instead requires acknowledging the full implications of the Nag Hammadi discovery: namely, reading it in the context of the apostolic tradition. The "outsider" status of the Gnostic Gospels is a historical product that belies their historical immanence within the contested field of political theology in late antiquity.

When we compare the heresiological accounts of Gnosticism with the "newly available evidence" of Nag Hammadi and the Berlin Codex, as Pagels proposes in her 1975 study, what we find are two antithetical traditions of Pauline exegesis that began in the late first century CE and extended through the second century: "Each claims to be authentic, Christian, Pauline: but one reads Paul antignostically, the other gnostically."[83] The result is a radically expanded archive of Christianity itself. Gnosticism—Pagels concentrates on the Valentinian and Naassene schools most centrally—constituted an autonomous, if diverse, set of Christians who, like the "pneumatic" Paul whose writings they looked to for textual support, believed in their own spiritual version of Christianity. "Gnostic Christians," Pagels explains, "assert that what distinguishes the false from the true church is not its relationship to the clergy, but the level of understanding of its members, and the quality of their relationship to one another."[84] Rather than viewing Gnosticism as a belated perversion of, atavistic root for, or heretical "protest movement" within early Christianity, in other words, Pagels depicts it as an alternative set of beliefs within the evolving theological imagination of early Christianity, in the years before it became fully systematized. We see this this most dramatically in the paradox of Pauline exegesis: Paul's greeting to the Corinthians, for instance, "discloses to the Valentinian initiate how he discriminates between the psychic and pneumatic aspects of himself, his audience, and his message. As in his greeting to the Romans, he acknowledges first himself in psychic terms, as one 'called,' and secondly designates himself as a pneumatic apostle 'through the will of God.'"[85] As if allegorizing the post-Heideggerian shift in both Jonas's work and in the field at large, the Gnostic Paul shifts from the psychic heeding of a call to the pneumatic invocation of grace. This hermeneutic distinction, which derives from heresiological evidence and the Nag Hammadi material alike, had the effect of particularizing the dualism of Valentinian Gnostic discourse as a textual practice, the material evidence of its spiritual insistence.

The consequence of Pagels's insistence upon a scriptural tradition of Gnostic exegesis is twofold. First, it relativizes the heresiological depictions of Gnostic belief by foregrounding polemical opposition and multiplicity rather than relying on the citational absorption of one (lost) tradition by another. The interpretive struggle over the meaning of Pauline texts demonstrates that Gnosticism—at least in its Valentinian and Naassene forms—drew as heavily on Pauline texts as did any other movement in early Christianity. Its "heresies" were not the consequence of syncretic or "oriental" mysteries but the result of divergent interpretations. Gnosticism bore textual and hermeneutic priorities of its own, which demonstrate the political and theological intensities of early Christian hermeneutics. In place of an alien, heretical cult obsessed with unmediated thought, we find instead an alienated Christianity, no longer a testimonial lineage extending from the crucifixion but an embattled field of experimental theology whose otherworldly theories struggled for spiritual authority in the historical world of late antiquity.

Second, whereas Pauline testimony may have provided the spiritual authority that grounded the Christian church, Pagels demonstrates that the precise nature of Paul's spiritual authority was hardly a given. Traditionally,

Paul's theology of grace over law explains how the church could come to be centered in Rome rather than Jerusalem. The justification for the church's temporal and geographical remove from the scene of Christ's death and resurrection was modeled, in other words, after Paul's own belated, even alien, experience of epiphany. But how did this happen? The nature of "spiritual authority," and of the pneumatic as opposed to the physical or psychic basis for this authority, was subject to exegetical divergence and administrative debate that bore deep political repercussions.

Christianity—and not Gnosticism alone—emerged as a political theology by means of such divergences and debates, whose passions ranged from textual hermeneutics to violent martyrdom. The liberationist charge of Pagels's work thus has less to do with refashioning early Christianity as a liberal enclave for women and freethinkers, or as an archive of occult traditions, than with confronting Christian orthodoxy with the evidentiary testimony of its own heterodox formation. Pagels certainly depicts a far more inclusive Christianity than most contemporary orthodoxies continue to maintain; she reminds us, for instance, that the ethnic and racial constitution of the early Christians—as of the Roman Empire in general—was profoundly diverse. More substantively, however, what Pagels underscores as the revelatory thrust of her research is the extent to which this "diversity" was in fact maintained through the political purgation of Gnostic elitism by the early Church Fathers. Early Christianity suspended its theological heterogeneity in favor of cosmopolitan universalism, privileging the worldly diversity of an empire over the theological diversity of competing interpretations. On the methodological front, Pagels's work suspends any such universalizing function in turn by confronting Christianity with its own textual archive, a reclaimed history. However otherworldly its interpretive systems may have sought to be, the deformations Gnosticism introduced within the history of Western religion—and the history of thought more broadly—are as concrete, material, and historical as they are theological. Whereas for Bataille, Jonas, Puech, and even Robinson, Gnostic spiritual dualism offered both a model and a reflection of contemporary intellectual and political demands, for Pagels it offers an empirical instrument: Gnostic idealism forms the evidentiary basis for the reintegration of its outsider, alien status within Christian church doctrine, with the effect of disintegrating the universalizing spiritual authority of the orthodox church. Early Christianity itself becomes heterogeneous, discontinuous, and even profoundly syncretic—on account not simply of its adaptation and absorption of older, indigenous religions but also of its own sectarian inconsistency. In turn, Pagels's study of the Gnostic Gospels offers a model for rethinking the politics of canon formation more broadly, whether the so-called Great Men heralded as the pillars of Western civilization or the literary classics taught in schools.

Such entanglements with Gnosticism offer a microcosm of twentieth-century intellectual history in Europe and North America, whose contours and dialectics I have begun to trace in this chapter. The significance of Gnosticism in modern thought owes less to its contentious place in the imperial history and quasi-hegemonic status of Christianity in the Western world—though this does at least partly motivate the political charge of studying a "heresy" such as Gnosticism—than with the discursive and spiritual paradoxes that rendered it heretical in the first place: the problem of knowability; the tragedy of alienation; the disruptive, brute facticity of the material world, and the speculative formulation that the truth of this world exceeded human comprehension, even our concepts of the divine. The magical, mystical, heretical, or otherwise heterogeneous kinds of thinking associated with faith and unreason both permeate and motivate the scholarly and philosophical concepts developed to approach it. This "susceptibility" to Gnostic thinking within the very heart of European philosophy and American religious history is thus anything but a sovereign claim to direct, immediate apprehension of the truth. Rather, the thinkers discussed here recognize the negative movement of any such dialectic of apprehension: far from direct and immediate, it struggles actively toward the truth through its tortured, contested relations to material things and worldly concepts. Knowable by means of what it rejects, such a truth procedure is subject to the ancient, brutal claim of its own Gospels.

PART II

MYTHOMORPHOSES

SO DARK, THE CON OF MAN

Mystical explanations are considered deep. The truth is that they are not even superficial.

—Friedrich Nietzsche, *The Gay Science*

FOR A TWENTY-FIRST-CENTURY COMPLEMENT to the passions of Gnostic materialism, we need look no further than *The Da Vinci Code*. The sudden discovery of a trove of textual evidence—which may or may not pose a threat to the grand spiritual designs founded upon its suppression—is the basic premise of Dan Brown's best-selling 2003 novel. Indeed, the secret revelations at work in the novel draw directly on the scholarly and political repercussions of the Nag Hammadi discovery: Christianity has a checkered past, insofar as the Gnostic Gospels disclose the heterogeneity of belief at the heart of the church's struggle for spiritual and worldly authority. Still arguing about the true knowledge of God for centuries after the death of Jesus, the Church Fathers weighed in on the proper boundaries and interpretive forms of its scripture. The biblical canon was ultimately a political judgment that granted sacred authority only to certain accounts of the life and death of Jesus.

Scholars of Gnosticism present such claims as the interpretive result of textual exegesis and scholarly research. Brown's novel, on the other hand, presents them as actively guarded secrets at the heart of a millennial conspiracy. The dark secrets of early Christianity are buried not in the desert sands, in other words, but in the codes and crypts in which even contemporary "church fathers" continue actively to traffic. Such secrets can be discerned only by an elect few, yet Brown's novel lets us in on them. Through the novel's adventure plot we witness the Gnostic drama of discovery, translation, and interpretation as an unfolding series of illuminations rather than the slow yield of scholarly deliberation. For Brown, the disclosure of such knowledge is a populist project by default, readily available to a general reading audience. Moreover, *The Da Vinci Code* raises the exhilaration of its revelations to the status of an organizing principle, setting forth a cryptographic worldview whereby the everyday world is saturated with hidden secrets. Watch for the italics: "As someone who had spent his life explaining the hidden interconnectivity of disparate emblems and ideologies, Langdon viewed the world as a web of profoundly intertwined histories and events. *The connections may be invisible,* he often preached to his symbology class at Harvard, *but they are always there,* buried just beneath the surface."[1] Disclosing a landscape shot through with reliquary evidence of the ancients, such a worldview is more than merely cryptographic or conspiratorial; its web of lightly concealed secrets instead testifies to the presence of the sacred within the profane.

Robert Langdon, the tweedy protagonist of Brown's novel, is a professor in the so-called religious symbology department at Harvard University, a testament to his expertise in the fields of religious history and, more pertinently still, the interpretation of symbols. In *The Da Vinci Code,* Langdon becomes entangled in an adventure plot that begins as a murder mystery, continues as a treasure hunt and conspiracy thriller, and culminates as a work of alternative historiography that both proves and supplements his scholarly expertise. The novel concludes, that is, with the discovery of the true nature of the Holy Grail, having illuminated, along the way, a centuries-long network of conspiracies and counterconspiracies always machinating to protect or destroy it. As it turns out, the Holy Grail or San Graal is not a holy cup of wine or blood but a human "vessel" for bearing the holy bloodline: *sang réel,* the living embodiment of a direct bloodline to Christ.[2] The revelation encapsulates several centuries of conjecture about Christian apocrypha—as well as the more recent disclosure of the Nag Hammadi texts—that speculate about the life of Jesus and the status of Mary Magdalene as a "favored" apostle. The historical Jesus was, in short, married to Mary Magdalene and had a family whose descendants live among us today. The historical mission of the church is therefore less to phase out heresies than to police this ancient secret, whose truth poses a threat to its sacred authority. In *The Da Vinci Code* this revelation takes the condensed form of a pun, albeit a pun with mortal consequences: the San Graal is really *sang réel,* real blood, a holy family lineage descending from Jesus and Mary Magdalene to the present day.

As our apparatus for facing up to such revelations, Langdon's credentials as a professional academic are rehearsed periodically throughout the novel. Langdon is no mere adventurer; though we quickly learn of his physical resemblance to Harrison Ford—evincing the actor's roles in such swashbuckling fantasies of biblical-archaeological discovery as *Raiders of the Lost Ark* (1982)—he is less Indiana Jones the tomb raider than Indiana Jones the dishy, if distracted, Marshall College professor. His scholarly expertise thus anchors the novel's claims to credibility: the church may sway unsteadily on its foundations, but the intellectual credentials of our protagonist are immaculate. In spite of the apparent outlandishness of some of his historical claims, in other words, we are assuaged as to the rigor of his research methods. We witness such assurances in a conversation between Langdon and his editor on the subject of a forthcoming book:

> "This manuscript claims *what?*" his editor had choked, setting down his wineglass and staring across his half-eaten power lunch. "You can't be serious."
>
> "Serious enough to have spent a year researching it."[3]

Ever willing to throw himself headlong into his scholarship—a whole year!—Robert Langdon is dedicated to investigating the "web of profoundly intertwined histories and events" that form the basis of his research into the *longue durée* of religious symbols, whose original meanings have become occluded: male and female symbols from pagan goddess cults, for instance, such as the pentagram, the chalice, and the blade. Like his nonfictional counterparts in the study of religious symbols, such as Mircea Eliade, Elaine Pagels, Gershom Scholem, Jean Seznec, Edgar Wind, Frances Yates, and Ioan Culianu—the last of whom was assassinated by Romanian spies in the bathroom stall of the University of Chicago divinity school[4]—Langdon studies the survival of pagan myths within the iconography of Western art as well as the broader survival of sacred traditions within post-Renaissance culture.[5] Langdon's character holds legitimate scholarly bona fides in spite of his fictional departmental affiliation; this premise is central to the novel's cryptographic imagination. (As we will see in chapter 4 of the present volume, by contrast, many of the real-life feminist scholars and intellectuals who studied such goddess religions struggled for legitimacy, regardless of their university affiliation or authoritative status in the field.) Yet as his tendency to "preach" to his symbology classes attests, Langdon is not only a scholar but also something of a mystic. For all his expertise in the history of religious symbols, his career is dedicated to their "symbological" power to make up the very logos through which "profoundly intertwined histories and events" become knowable. In this respect, Professor Langdon professes to be a phenomenologist of the sacred as described by the philosopher Paul Ricoeur, whereby the "revealing power of symbols" addresses itself to him as a participant in and nonneutral subject of the revelatory truths they bear.[6]

Espousing a Gnostic materialism of its own, Langdon's worldview extends to the fictional universe of the novel, wherein—as it turns out—the histories and events it narrates *are* in fact intertwined.[7]

Such connections extend, moreover, to the novel's own network of relations with other sensational histories of Christian heresy and popular occultism. *The Da Vinci Code* erects its fable of evidence and discovery on a well-trodden intertextual substrate. This is not to insinuate that the novel is plagiarized, though this was the contention of a quickly dismissed lawsuit filed in 2006. Rather, it is to propose that in its literary recourse to the history of religiously themed millennial secrets and mysteries, Brown's novel joins the ranks of other late modern fictions of occult synthesis, from grail quests and lost crusades to the paranoid trappings of Umberto Eco's 1988 novel *Foucault's Pendulum*. As in such other stories, the cryptographic worldview espoused by the *Da Vinci Code*'s fictional characters serves as a vehicle for the novel's research, the deep esoteric and often pseudoscientific archive of its own construction. The result is a metafiction of bibliographic proportions, with the claims to truth and revelation professed within appealing as much to an esoteric textual inheritance as to a holy bloodline. This chapter explores the textual genealogy from which Brown derives the encrypted secrets of *The Da Vinci Code*.

I refer to Langdon as a mystic on account of his scholarly access to and "sacred" participation in this genealogy. However far-fetched his claims may seem, his notions about the interconnectedness of all things—of symbols and histories, beliefs and real events—are borne out in the novel's fictional universe. Langdon is not only serious; he is also right. Even so, we nonetheless face something of a lag or gap between his professional theories and the cryptographic revelations that unfold throughout the novel. Langdon professes—and perhaps believes—that the world is a "web of profoundly intertwined histories and events," yet the conspiracies and persecutions outlined in his symbolic universe remain at a historical remove from the professor's experience until the events of the novel plunge him directly into their midst. By decoding the secrets thrust upon him throughout the novel, Langdon's interpretive prowess as a religious symbologist is doubly exercised and doubly rewarded: not only do the novel's revelations confirm Langdon's theory, but they also embroil him in the continuity to which his theory professes. The codes and ciphers he unlocks in the novel amount to a mystical experience insofar as they provide Langdon, and the novel's readers, access to the world of profundity and interconnectedness that the quotidian struggle of political and textual transparency might otherwise render inaccessible.

Like *The Da Vinci Code* itself, Langdon's mysticism is worth taking seriously insofar as it constitutes the novel's historical and epistemological
project. Indeed, the novel *has* a project, one that has received a great deal of
attention for both its mythohistorical excesses and its own extensive literary
genealogy—that is, for the fact that its truth claims are at once entirely *made
up* yet also profoundly, marvelously unoriginal, appropriated more or less
wholesale from other sources. This unoriginality is hardly unique to Dan
Brown's novel, since so many books about mysticism and the occult are themselves compendia. As Mircea Eliade writes in a late essay reflecting on the
"explosion" of occult interest in the 1970s, "even when these ideas are naïvely or even ludicrously expressed, there is always the tacit conviction that
a way out of the chaos and meaninglessness of modern life exists and that
this way out implies an *initiation* into, and consequently the revelation of, old
and venerable secrets."[8] For Eliade, the medium is *not* the message; he instead chalks up popular interest in occultism to a fantasy of initiation, a kind
of direct spiritual access into ancient secrets. *The Da Vinci Code* offers an
alternative fantasy of *scholarly* access to those secrets.

For all its generic resemblance to other narratives of quest and conspiracy (and there is no shortage of such narratives), Brown's novel emerges
most strikingly as an allegory of scholarship. This allegory, as we will see in
this chapter, plays out on two fronts: the first, and more commonly discussed,
is the novel's dialectic of interpretation, according to which Langdon's wild interpretations of religious symbology become virtually transparent to readers
of the novel. Scholarship, removed from academia's ivory tower and proffered
to the common reader, provides universal access to the occult secrets of antiquity and conspiracy. Second, this dialectic of interpretation extends to the
novel's own recourse to source material, through which it comes also to allegorize the contemporary history of university scholarship in the humanities.

The novel's research, like its portrayal of Langdon's thought processes,
leapfrogs the irritating complexities of plodding scholarly procedure. My task
in what follows is to return some of this plodding to our understanding of
the novel. For I would hazard that at least part of the book's appeal lies in the
mystical interplay of faith and suspicion it induces, rather than in a fantasy
of religious access alone. This dialectic of doubt and longing is continuous
with the epistemological drama of outsider theory. The novel's fictions of direct interpretive access are founded, I maintain, on the very difficulties it
purports to spirit away, insofar as *The Da Vinci Code* incorporates the claims
and methods of an extensive genealogy of popular mythohistorical writing. In doing so, it also literalizes the implicit stakes of both mystical and
scholarly interpretation in the perils of its adventure plot: Is the pursuit of

esoteric secrets a path to enlightenment and liberation, or a site of regressive ideological intensification?

The novel bears a direct bloodline to its historical antecedents. *The Da Vinci Code* gleans much of its mystical historiography from an earlier best seller, *Holy Blood, Holy Grail,* which likewise traces the interconnectedness of histories and symbols. Though Brown makes no secret of it in his novel, this lineage became especially well known after a 2006 plagiarism lawsuit filed against Brown by two of the earlier book's three coauthors. *Holy Blood, Holy Grail* began as a series of BBC documentaries penned by the screenwriter Henry Lincoln in the early 1970s, and was published in book form in 1982 with the aid of Michael Baigent and Richard Leigh. The names of the two latter coauthors are condensed in Brown's novel to form the name of Leigh Teabing (an anagram for Baigent), the renowned British historian who turns out also to be the diabolical Teacher, a covert Vatican operative who seeks to destroy the secret society sworn to protect the *sang réel.* It was, interestingly enough, Leigh and Baigent who filed the plagiarism lawsuit against Brown, which they lost more or less summarily.[9]

It would be tempting to elaborate more fully on the reasons why the lawsuit failed, as well as why Baigent and Leigh filed it in the first place. For our purposes here, suffice to say that Baigent and Leigh lost their plagiarism suit because *Holy Blood, Holy Grail* itself draws heavily from other primary sources in turn. In addition to their general continuity with occult histories and archaeologies of the British Isles, the documentary and book owe their existence to an earlier body of texts, a series of books published by the Trotskyite journalist and wartime surrealist Gérard de Sède beginning in the early 1960s. Of particular relevance is Sède's 1967 book, *L'Or de Rennes* (The gold of Rennes, later republished as *Le Trésor Maudit* [The accursed treasure]), which levies a far different set of ideological priorities upon the speculative historiography and interpretive play in which it indulges, as we will see in what follows. Itself a best seller in France, Sède's book investigates a set of local legends and rumors that had been circulating around a village rectory in the southwest of France, in the picturesque but otherwise forgettable hilltop village of Rennes-le-Château. Sède's books draw in turn upon a vast tradition of mythohistorical fact and folklore that extended from the study of ley lines and sacred geometry to grail romances and the history of medieval "Gnostic revivals" such as the Albigensians and Cathars of the Languedoc region in France.

The Da Vinci Code has spawned—or at least reawakened—an entire industry of "code"-obsessed documentaries and books exploring the religious secrets and conspiratorial groups alluded to in the novel.[10] Yet as this industry likewise recognizes, Brown's novel is already a work of synthesis, if not of explicit pastiche. However vexed its legal entanglements may appear, *The Da Vinci Code* all but advertises its recourse to such sources. The novel's relationship to its lightly occulted source material is telling in itself, for it reveals continuities that belie the fictional normalization of outsider thinking. As a second-order fiction of historiographic mythmaking—or of what Gérard de Sède referred to in his own work as the deployment of "mythomorphic facts"[11]—Brown's 2003 novel popularizes the very hermeneutics of such mythmaking. *The Da Vinci Code* takes up the modes of interpretation proper to the counterfactual histories, grail myths, goddess cults, Gnostic Gospels, secret societies, conspiracies, and historical falsifications that continue to fuel the books and films that follow in its wake.[12] Torn between deep suspicion and poetic longing, the code-deciphering work undertaken by the (fictional) Professor Langdon and his (likewise fictional) cryptographic partner Sophie Neveu both trusts and mistrusts the capacity for texts, symbols, and "facts" to bear hidden meanings. Yet their interpretive labors are themselves undergirded by the history of interpretation itself, which haunts the novel's actions no less strongly than the history of the Christian church. In its efforts to popularize the discursive undercurrents of its interpretive system, *The Da Vinci Code* opens up to the broader archive of its own research, revealing a volatile set of ideological tendencies and unresolved political demands about the possibilities and limits of inventive interpretation. The significance of this archive lies, I propose, in the extent to which it outlines a theory of knowledge inseparable from belief and suspicion: a speculative system of ideas whose function in the name of truth has less to do with the status of its "facts"—which often idiosyncratic or erroneous, borrowed or even invented—than with the nature and means of one's participation in their web of "connections" and symbols.

LONGING AND SUSPICION

As a religious symbologist, Langdon's version of contemporary scholarship presumes giant leaps across the chasms of time, historical memory, material evidence, and factuality. The nature of these gaps has much to do with contemporary ideas about interpretation and the nature of university scholarship in the humanities. For the narrative drama of Langdon's discoveries hinges on the accessibility and the authority of his interpretive methods—and thus the meaning and legitimacy of his claims to knowledge—rather than on ancient bloodlines and conspiracies alone. Langdon's—or rather, Brown's—approach to spanning these gaps is, as I have suggested, a mystical one, by which I mean that he seeks to transcend the phenomenal alienation from meaning such gaps necessarily indicate.

The religious historian Gershom Scholem defines mysticism in precisely these terms in his 1941 classic of dialectical religious historiography, *Major Trends in Jewish Mysticism*. For Scholem, mysticism refers to a phase in the historical development of a religion characterized by the attempt to surmount an alienated condition of religious experience in which people no longer feel connected to God. It thus describes something far more historically specific than a pseudobelief or a set of occult practices. The phenomenon called mysticism "is connected with, and inseparable from" the conditions of its historical emergence, Scholem maintains.[13] Whereas the first stage of religious consciousness, the "mythical epoch," represents the world as "being full of gods whom one encounters at every step," the subsequent period represents the "break-through of religion," which Scholem describes literally as a radical negation of this mythical unity. "Religion's supreme function," he writes, "is to destroy the dream-harmony of man, universe, and God," inaugurating an absolute abyss between a transcendent deity and a finite man.[14] Mysticism, by contrast, "strives to piece together the fragments broken by the religious cataclysm," but on a new plane: it does not "deny or overlook the abyss," but instead "proceeds to a quest for the secret that will close it in, the hidden path that will span it." Neither a redemptive nor a strictly reactionary tendency, mysticism "coincides with what may be called the romantic period of religion," a dialectical phase characterized by a poetic longing that becomes, in turn, the foundation of its hermeneutics.[15] Even as Robert Langdon's poetic longing traverses the episodic codes and conflicts of his novelistic quest, the poetic longing of *The Da Vinci Code* extends to the body of speculative historiography from which it draws, as well as to scholarly debates about the limits of interpretation that reached their peak in the late 1980s. As we will see below, Brown's own mysticism hearkens not only to the possibility of direct contact with, or at least a bloodline to, the Christian god, but also to the possibilities of interpretation that might otherwise be crushed underfoot in the plodding, workaday world of American academia. In this sense Brown's novel offers a "Gnostic" approach to scholarly hermeneutics that is remarkable for its textual and historical specificity; rather than a fantasy of unmediated access or initiation, one finds instead a fiction that "strives to piece together the fragments" of meaning that had, in university scholarship as in conventional religion, become broken and hollow.

The novel's breathless quest for and discovery of an ancient secret yields a rather literal identification with Scholem's account of religion's "romantic" phase. In the novel's conclusion, Langdon and his companion, the police cryptographer Neveu, indeed find the Holy Grail: the literal, millennial lost treasure for which they have been searching, pursued at every step by Opus Dei, a sect of ultra-orthodox defenders of "the Way" in search of their own mystical return to Inquisition-era Catholic militancy. The novel's "secret" revelation discloses two transhistorical continuities. The first is the notion that religious symbols—the field of Langdon's scholarly expertise—refer to real, historical conflicts and pressures, a premise long maintained by religious historians of the nineteenth and twentieth centuries. That is, like folktales, nursery rhymes, and other forms of vernacular expression, religious symbols—pentagrams, chalices, grails, and saint's days—are the residual forms of ancient, indigenous cultural and religious systems that have since been appropriated by Christianity. By this logic, the Holy Grail of medieval romance refers not only to the Christian iconography with which it was associated—or, say, the vessel Jesus used at the Last Supper or which Joseph of Arimathea used to collect a blood offering from the crucified Christ—but also to more ancient formal representations of the "eternal feminine," by which Brown designates matriarchal agrarian folk rituals of hearth and home rather than, say, Johann Wolfgang von Goethe's patriarchal myth.[16]

The second continuity is the notion that such symbols and traditions retain their political charge in the present. Thus the grail, by this second logic, is not in fact an object but a genealogy. For Brown, that is, the San Graal consists in the clandestine perpetuation of a holy bloodline, the *sang réel* that traces an unbroken dynasty from the historical Jesus through the present day, preserved in face of persecutions and across a vast historical tableau of Merovingian kings and Templar Knights. In addition to preserving the trace forms of pagan fertility religions, in other words, the grail also bears evidentiary testimony to the historical status of Jesus in ways that contradict Christian orthodoxy.[17] It also bears an extensive fictional and political genealogy, from Reformation-era secret societies to the genres of historical romance and conspiracy fiction. As such, the *sang réel* poses a fundamental threat to the institutional forms of Christianity, whose militant wings have, Langdon tells us, always sought to destroy the link and obliterate its traces. This is an idea that owes much to the counterhegemonic language of Pagels's *The Gnostic Gospels*, which, as we saw in chapter 2, depicts the variety of ante-Nicene Christianities as a counterculture to later Christian orthodoxy. Yet in Brown's novel this counterculture has retained an active corps of covert agents, as well as a militant counterinsurgency, whose underground persistence over the millennia rears its head in the novel's early pages. The holy bloodline has been protected by a secret society that underlies virtually all other Western occult groups, a metaconspiracy known as the Priory of Sion, which, in the novel's epigraph, Brown declares to be a factual organization, its veracity corroborated by "parchments known as *Les Dossiers Secrets*" discovered in 1975 in the Bibliothèque nationale de France. (Perhaps it is needless to say here that these "secret dossiers" were discovered in 1975 because they were also *deposited* in 1975, as part of an elaborate hoax carried out by a man named Pierre Plantard, who had produced maps and other occult calculations for Gérard de Sède in the 1960s.[18]) This double revelation yields a third in turn, true to the mystical synthesis Scholem describes: toward the novel's conclusion, we find out that Sophie Neveu is herself the living heir to this secret bloodline. Across the abyss of millennia, and against the persecutions of religious orthodoxy, gods and women encounter each other at every step, and have been doing so, literally, all along. *The connections may be invisible,* Langdon preaches, *but they are always there, just beneath the surface.*

As Brown's Clive Cussleresque spin on the grail legend—and indeed, in his acknowledgments Brown thanks Cussler, the author of counterfactual adventure thrillers such as *Raise the Titanic!*—*The Da Vinci Code* develops its adventure-thriller plot as a vehicle for reverse-engineering a kind of historiographic sublime. The text acknowledges the phenomenal "abyss" of millennial Christian history and conspiracy, rattling the chains of ancientness while simultaneously assuaging us that such mysteries lie within a reader's grasp. The result, as Jean-Michel Rabaté has argued, is a travesty of Freudian "wild interpretation" whereby the mysterious aura of antiquity gives way to the nearness at hand, or the sleight of hand, of the "forceful deciphering of traces, more often than not imaginary traces." As Rabaté puts it, "the hidden truth about the foundation of Christianity turns into a series of coded rituals, Fibonacci numbers in scrambled order, society's puzzles ripped from a specific culture and turned into trivialized pursuits that can be leisurely cracked one after another."[19] Whereas the historiographic sublime might threaten to take possession of one's senses, to sweep readers up into its utter discontinuity with contemporary understanding, the "forceful deciphering of traces" instead indulges a fantasy of ready access. In this light, what I have been referring to as the novel's mysticism resonates strongly with the analogous Christian neofundamentalisms that have sprung up throughout the contemporary United States and elsewhere, whether in Catholic, Mormon, New Age, or Protestant incarnations. In spite of its ostensible attack on religious orthodoxy as a murderous régime, *The Da Vinci Code* galvanizes postsecular Christianity through its staged encounter with a scandalously anthropomorphic Jesus and the deep evidentiary archive of a millennial bloodline, however counterfactual or simply wro ng this evidence may be.

What is most outlandish about *The Da Vinci Code*, however—and what continues to make it an object of interest and scorn alike—is the meta-fictional apparatus by which the novel indulges this longing. As Rabaté puts it, describing the novel's "hermeneutics of suspicion gone wild," the book's gamelike assortment of codes and puzzles purports to offer us a ready-made, fantastical access to the deepest "secrets" of religious longing. As employed by Paul Ricoeur, the notion of a hermeneutics of suspicion describes the "ascetic" project of approaching the interpretation of symbolic language as a process of unmasking or demystification, as exemplified in the work of Sigmund Freud, Karl Marx, and Friedrich Nietzsche.[20] Such a project presumes to decipher the expressions of an ever-untrustworthy world of opaque, equivocal, and duplicitous symbols that are, at the same time, our only means for expressing and understanding the world. Significantly, however, Ricoeur stresses that in modern thought—as well, ultimately, as in Freudian psychoanalysis—the hermeneutics of suspicion does not function alone, but in dialectical conflict with a mythopoeic insistence that "tries to grasp, in the symbols of faith, a possible call or kerygma."[21] Ricoeur describes this latter insistence as a hermeneutics of the sacred, a "propaedeutic to the revelation of meaning" that demands a phenomenological investment of faith as the precondition for any such revelation or call. The "wildness" Rabaté attributes to *The Da Vinci Code* thus describes the hasty resolution of this dialectic, stripped of the messy conflicts and resistances of the entanglements between the process of unmasking ("suspicion") and the heeding of a call ("sacred"). It is the "wildness" Freud attributes to "wild analysis," a rush to interpretive conclusions without the proper working through and without regard for necessary patient–analyst relations of resistance and transference. "If we succeed in all these trials and ordeals," Rabaté asks, "can we prove that we, too, are made of a divine mettle? After all, who hasn't dreamed of descending directly from Jesus?"[22] (I, for one, have not.) Rabaté's key insight is a valuable one here: In the name of a subversion of Nicene Christian orthodoxy, one instead finds a mystical confirmation of a concrete relationship to the divine for which, ironically, the machinations of conspiracy and orthodoxy become a medium.

Such fantasies of unmediated interpretive access also reflect the novel's position toward the work of scholarship in the arts and humanities. The dialectical mysticism of Brown's novel extends, as Rabaté suggests, to its hermeneutics, which unfold throughout the interpretive gymnastics of our intrepid religious symbologist and his cryptographic companion. On the terrain of interpretation, too, *The Da Vinci Code* exercises a poetic longing no less exacerbated by historical belatedness. Yet here the orthodoxy whose heavy tread has scarred the Edenic landscape of religious symbology is less that of the Christian Church Fathers, I propose, than of the modern university: that is, the bureaucratization and professionalization of academia that has taken place since the Second World War, and—in the United States—increasingly in the wake of the culture wars of the early 1990s, the Gulf Wars, the state of domestic politics after 9/11, and the withdrawal of university and educational funding. Let us not forget that Robert Langdon is a professor at Harvard. As a drama of evidence and interpretation—however wild, counterfactual, or twice told—Brown's 2003 novel manifests nostalgia for an academically centered hermeneutics that could at once wield unimpeachable scholarly authority and bear wide-ranging, even earthshaking, cultural significance. Writing about the ambitions of Freudian psychoanalysis, Ricoeur notes that "by interpreting culture [psychoanalysis] modifies it: by giving it an instrument of reflection it stamps it with a lasting mark."[23] It is curious to consider how, in the post-9/11, postrecession intellectual milieu, such claims on behalf of real-life university professors—a professional livelihood not only short on departments of religious symbology but on tenure-track jobs—might seem either quaintly misinformed or downright hostile to the real conditions of scholarly research, higher education, and peer-reviewed historiography. The "wildness" to which Rabaté alludes in referring to the "hermeneutics of suspicion gone wild" in *The Da Vinci Code* thus has less to do with the outlandishness of the novel's claims or the trivialization of historical puzzles than with its wild longing for a bygone era of scholarly practice that presupposed a textual world pregnant with significance. It was a bygone era in which scholarship *mattered*, and in which professors could travel the world precociously thanks to their expertise and flexible teaching schedules.

Remember when one of the most exigent questions that literary critics faced was whether or not interpretation had become too free? Neither do I, but the question went something like this: Had the rise of deconstruction and "French theory" ushered in a new era of overinterpretation, an eschatological lapse into relativism and nonsense? Brown's novel is as invested in this less-than-ancient war between pragmatists and deconstructionists, the incipient culture wars of 1980s American academia, as it is in the heresies and conspiracies of early church history. Its well-masticated system of codes and cyphers conjures up the excesses of "overinterpretation" and "communicative action" alike—scholarly imperatives that may since have been eclipsed by more contemporary expressions of scholarly urgency but whose partisans and counteragents, Brown suggests, nonetheless continue to machinate in secret just beneath the surface. As an invented scholarly practice of its own, Langdon's religious symbology both registers and spans the abyss of twenty-first-century scholarly orthodoxy, wherein, needless to say, it sometimes takes even longer than a whole year to research a book—or, for that matter, to find a tenure-track academic position in the humanities. In doing so it offers a romantic synthesis of the debate between interpretation and overinterpretation characteristic of the scholarly culture wars, as Umberto Eco named it, to which it harkens as a scene of mythic unification.[24] *The Da Vinci Code* thus positions itself alongside other recent returns to such questions of hermeneutics in the work of Rita Felski, Bruno Latour, Eve Kosofsky Sedgwick, and other proponents of "surface," "distance," "reparative," or other alternative, adjectival forms of reading that seek, as Felski puts it, new methods of scholarship motivated "by a desire to articulate a positive vision for humanistic thought in the face of growing skepticism about its value."[25] Such scholars seek not a mystical synthesis, of course, but a viable—realistic, meaningful, ethical, "valuable"—vehicle for spanning the abyss of contemporary scholarly alienation and the contemporary politics of knowledge in the ongoing culture wars in and beyond the academy. However "wild" its own interpretations might be, Brown's novel offers an important counterpoint to such realist efforts insofar as it acknowledges (for better or worse) the extent to which this abyss is not a new one, even if the conditions of crisis, alienation, and even violence have only continued to intensify.

Langdon's and Neveu's narrative immersion in the world of secrets and cyphers begs a question posed by Umberto Eco: was history—or a book, or a text—an *opera aperta,* an open work to be shaped actively by its interpreters? Or did it require specific criteria for validating its meaning, lest readers lapse into wild "unlimited semiosis" unbound by historical context, material evidence, and ethical imperatives?[26] Eco, the author of his own work of counterfactual historical mythmaking and conspiratorial adventure in *Foucault's Pendulum* (1988), elaborated on this question in a well-known series of lectures at Cambridge University in 1990. In response to the critical divide between poststructural "openness" and pragmatist "limits"—or, for that matter, between "deep" or symptomatic reading and surface reading, to cite a more recent set of terms—the semiotician-novelist proposed to take a long view of the problem, reaching back into the vast library of ancient and medieval texts to which *The Da Vinci Code* likewise seeks to anchor its fictions of interpretation.

For Eco, the question of overinterpretation names a transhistorical concern within Western reason itself, an ancient rather than contemporary problematic. He describes something akin to Brown's and Langdon's mysticism in a historical survey of hermetic interpretation from Koranic and kabbalistic exegesis through counter-Enlightenment esotericism. In such modes of interpretation, he writes, "Every object, be it earthly or heavenly, hides a secret. Every time a secret has been discovered, it will refer to another secret in a progressive movement toward a final secret. Nevertheless, there can be no final secret. The ultimate secret of hermetic initiation is that everything is secret. Hence the hermetic secret must be an empty one, because anyone who pretends to reveal any sort of secret is not himself initiated and has stopped at a superficial level of the knowledge of cosmic mystery."[27] For Eco, hermetic semiosis is a hermeneutics of suspicion gone awry, perpetuating an inconclusive game of hide-and-seek under the guise of truth seeking. In place of true suspicion—or true conviction—we find instead a confidence trick. This condition might be said to describe Brown's fictional universe, though *The Da Vinci Code* offers a fictional solution to the ultimate emptiness of the hermetic secret: we, the readers, are the initiated, and our suspicions will be rewarded, since at the novel's conclusion the truth of the *sang réel* stands right before us in the character of Sophie Neveu.

Like Eric Voegelin before him, Eco is suspicious of the elitism that hermetic semiosis presumes, which he likewise attributes to Gnosticism and its long inheritance in poetry and philosophy. Exercising what he calls the "syndrome of the secret," the hermetic and Gnostic heritage cultivates a will to power rather than, say, outlining a path to enlightenment or a "positive vision" for thought: "If the initiated is someone who understands the cosmic secret, then degenerations of the Hermetic model have led to the conviction that power consists in making others believe that one has a political secret."[28] This, by implication, is the same problem faced by the "hermeneutics of suspicion" as described by Ricoeur, an interpretive attitude whereby, Eco claims, language is "unable to grasp a unique and preexisting meaning" and leads instead to an "open-ended universe where the interpreter can discover infinite interconnections."[29] Suspicion, for Eco, is always "wild." This is not necessarily a pathological condition in itself—as it can be salutary when wielded by detectives and scientists in the process of sorting through evidence, for instance; but it requires an economy of judgment rather than some kind of obsessional method. Interpretation requires a set of critical judgments to keep it in check; this judgment is, however, anything but a matter of iconoclasm, or taste versus distaste. Rather, it is a historical and epistemic construct. Eco invokes the *history* of Gnosticism and other ancient hermetic movements as the discourse that functions as such a limit in his own thinking, outlining an esoteric genealogy that subtends and delimits his position in the contemporary debate about interpretation in which he has participated. Interpretation is historically continuous and relational, he argues, rather than unique or absolute. For this very reason it is always mediated, subject to the historical and evidentiary demands of semiosis itself, the particularity of meaning-making. Open interpretation, as a hermeneutics of suspicion that plumbs deep meanings between the coded surfaces of texts and images and deconstructed commonplace assumptions, is necessarily constrained by the material, historical, and epistemic specificity of the works they interpret, as well as their relations to other works, concepts, and histories. To do otherwise would be to fall prey to a dangerous delusion.[30] Only fiction can invent in virtually limitless ways, though fiction does not always remain fictional for very long: "narrative imagination," Eco writes parenthetically, almost as a joke, "has no limits."[31] Like Brown, Eco's approach to the debate between interpretive openness and pragmatism, between revelation and procedure, between depth and surface, is to have both—albeit in dialectical tension rather than mystical synthesis.

For Brown, the animate crux of academic hermeneutics is likewise both ancient and contemporary; the meaning of worldly things is neither given nor open-ended, but tangled, slippery, and pregnant with meaning. We can nonetheless be assured of the reality of such meanings; the connections may be invisible, but they are all around us. The work of scholarly research may be streamlined to the point of near revelatory immediacy, but the secret is far from hollow. For Eco, however, the solution to the crisis in interpretation cannot be quite so easily manufactured: the answer is not mystical access or revelation but hard work—a working-through, in Freudian language, without which analysis becomes "wild." Transhistorical wonder and the interconnectedness of all things are still very much conceivable, but in the realm of scholarly pursuits such effects are anything but immediate. Research and learnedness are the result of accumulated labor rather than Gnostic revelation. Hermetic semiosis could, however, be *studied* as a historical phenomenon with concrete textual and ideological forms, but this is not the same thing as becoming an initiate into its dangerous shell game. And yet, Eco reminds us, such games could nonetheless be synthesized in fiction. Thanks to the power of fiction, that is, pure invention can produce reality, at least in textual form. As he demonstrates in *Foucault's Pendulum*, the networks of association about which his characters fantasize can, in a novel, come true, yielding a point of totalizing comprehension but also of imminent peril. Eco's point is that invention is not the same thing as interpretation; invention is a form of fiction making, an artful con rather than a truth procedure. Interpretation, on the other hand, is inventive only to the extent that its creative freedoms are attuned to the forms within and upon which it exercises its faculties. Eco's response to debates about interpretation and overinterpretation was thus not, in the end, to demarcate the hermeneutics of suspicion from its pragmatic constraints but to propose a dynamic entanglement between them, linking depth with surface, openness with historical specificity. The mystical synthesis of hermetic semiosis, by contrast, was either a political deception or, at best, a fiction in its own right.

In an interview for the *Paris Review,* Eco proposes, to this end, that Dan Brown is himself Eco's own invention. In response to the suggestion that *The Da Vinci Code* "seems like a bizarre little offshoot of *Foucault's Pendulum*," Eco replies,

> The author, Dan Brown, is a character from *Foucault's Pendulum*!
> I invented him. He shares my characters' fascinations—the world
> conspiracy of Rosicrucians, Masons, and Jesuits. The role of the
> Knights Templar. The hermetic secret. The principle that everything
> is connected. I suspect that Dan Brown might not even exist.[32]

This statement has less to do with an authorial claim of priority over Dan Brown's writings than with rehearsing Eco's ideas about hermetic semiosis and the limits of hermeneutic suspicion. Eco disparages Brown by suggesting that he has fallen prey to his own semiotic invention, like the character Belbo in *Foucault's Pendulum,* who suddenly comes to realize that his invented metaconspiracy theory had stumbled dangerously into the proximity of truth. Eco's novel functions as a kind of moral fable for his own hermeneutics; it demonstrates, not without humor or wonder, the consequences of believing in the possibility of one's own access to the interconnectedness of all things.[33] The result is a nightmarish entanglement in an act of political will that, for the novel's characters, bears mortal consequences. Hermetic semiosis was, in other words, a con—and as Eco dramatized in *Foucault's Pendulum,* it is a con we tend to play on ourselves. The scholarly apparatus in *The Da Vinci Code* is precisely such a con, to the extent that Brown insists that he did not make it up himself: as a prefatory note to the novel states, "All descriptions of artwork, architecture, documents, and secret rituals in this novel are accurate."[34] Far from heeding Eco's injunctions, Brown's novel enlists the possibilities of genre fiction to will itself into a suspension of disbelief. The serial epiphanies of Robert Langdon and Sophie Neveu (who just happens to be the direct descendant of Christ) furnish readers with a mystical synthesis of accessible secrets, infinite suspicion, and living proof all at once. Such a synthesis may be the fruit of Dan Brown's narrative imagination, but it also serves as the device for stitching together the "descriptions of artwork, architecture, documents, and secret rituals" that have become the author's trademark. It is for this reason that Eco, albeit with his tongue in his cheek, finds it impossible to believe that Dan Brown is anything other than one such character himself; his gambit is to suspend the author within one of the fictions to which Langdon and Neveu always seem to possess the key.

Eco's remark about Brown also provides an example of the Italian author's strategy for extending, rather than demarcating, fictional invention from the interpretive limits he otherwise advocates. For Eco, the recourse to a fictional premise ("Dan Brown is a character in my book") discloses the experimental rather than purely restrictive nature of such limits: rather than dismissing the "lure of the arcane" and the enticements of outsider thinking, Eco insists on the ethical imperative of laboring through their interpretive complexities and attending to their textual and historical specificity. The narrative imagination may have no limits, but a real, published work of fiction inevitably becomes subject to its own semiotic claims, a participant in numerous sets of interpretive relations. This dialogic and dialectical participation makes all the difference; to proceed otherwise is to succumb to a narcissistic fantasy of access whose consequences could be very real, in misrecognizing as "revelation" what is actually, for Eco as for Voegelin, a will to power. The "hermeneutics of suspicion" could, in theory, come to resemble hermetic semiosis—with each secret leading to the next in an ever-widening chain of credulity. It was thus important to remain suspicious of one's own suspicion.

In some ways Eco was right to be suspicious of Langdon's hermeneutics. Early in *The Da Vinci Code*, we are faced with a crime scene in the Louvre that Langdon and Neveu are forced to interpret under the suspicious eyes of the police. This involves deciphering a number of inscriptions and anagrams left by the dying victim, the famous curator Jacques Saunière, Sophie Neveu's estranged grandfather. We read, along with our protagonists, the cryptic lines inscribed by the dying man on the gallery walls: "O, Draconian devil! Oh, lame saint!" which turn out to be "a perfect anagram of 'Leonardo da Vinci! The Mona Lisa!'"[35] Saunière evidently had the tenacity and foresight to add exclamation points to his cryptogram as he died, perhaps in deference to the bathos of "encrypting" the English title for an Italian painting housed in a French museum. The trail of premortem ciphers continues until our protagonists discover a final message scrawled (in a special black-light pen, only visible under an ultraviolet light) across the plexiglass panel covering the face of the Mona Lisa. The hidden message reads, "So dark the con of man." The phrase becomes the basis for a double interpretation; the first is Langdon's "wild," research-driven overinterpretation, which links the "con" to the hegemonic warfare of Christian Church Fathers against competing sects, naming its simultaneous obliteration and appropriation of pagan goddess cults. Christianity has erected man—the figure of Jesus, as the filial representation of a patriarchal god—in place of the female divinities whose iconography it absorbed. In addition, the message also "proves" the curator's involvement in a centuries-old secret society called the Priory of Sion, which had allegedly been operating since 1188:

> "The Priory," Langdon whispered. "This proves your grandfather was a member!"
>
> Sophie looked at him in confusion. "You *understand* this?"
>
> "It's flawless," Langdon said, nodding as his thoughts churned. "It's a proclamation of one of the Priory's most fundamental philosophies."
>
> Sophie looked baffled in the glow of the message scrawled across the *Mona Lisa*'s face.
>
> SO DARK THE CON OF MAN
>
> "Sophie," Langdon said, "the Priory's tradition of perpetuating goddess worship is based on a belief that powerful men in the early Christian church 'conned' the world by propagating lies that devalued the female and tipped the scale in favor of the masculine."
>
> Sophie remained silent, staring at the words.
>
> "The Priory believes that Constantine and his male successors successfully converted the world from matriarchal paganism to patriarchal Christianity by waging a campaign of propaganda that demonized the sacred feminine, obliterating the goddess from modern religion forever."[36]

Putting aside the historical inaccuracies of Langdon's breathless interpretation—not to mention Neveu's silence and apparent befuddlement in the face of his account of obliterated femininity—his reading is soon followed by a second, far simpler, account of why the dying Saunière would have written such a phrase. Even as Langdon's mind "was still grappling with the bold clarity of Saunière's outward message" (and Langdon dwells on this: "So dark the con of man, he thought. So dark indeed"), Neveu's subsequent interpretation reveals the phrase to be another simple anagram. It points to Leonardo da Vinci's nearby painting, *Virgin of the Rocks* (or *Madonna of the Rocks)*, where the dying curator has cleverly stashed a key. The "code" is not, in fact, an elaborate historical commentary on ideological and epistemic struggle but a message in the form of an anagram that yields a pragmatic result: a set of letters that manage, in spite of a minor digression, to arrive successfully at their destination. Saunière had raised his granddaughter to crack codes—and to do so in English rather than her native French. And here, in the dark recesses of the Louvre at night, he has communicated with her across the abyss of death.

FIGURE 10. Leonardo da Vinci, *Vergine delle Rocce (Virgin of the Rocks)*, 1483–86. Musée du Louvre, Paris. Public domain.

Yet as it turns out, Langdon's "wild" interpretation does not stray that far from the mark, either. For the key they find hidden behind *Madonna of the Rocks* sets their quest in motion, a quest which, in the end, both "proves" and redresses the historical impact of the church's "con of man": that is, their quest reveals the underground persistence of a secret bloodline that extends from Jesus's marriage to Mary Magdalene, whose reputation was sullied by church propaganda. Even Saunière's choice of painting, *Madonna of the Rocks,* confirms this narrative validation of Langdon's reading: while reflecting that "Sophie's quick thinking had been impressive" in recognizing a second anagram at the crime scene, Langdon notes that "*Madonna of the Rocks* was yet another fitting link in the evening's chain of interconnected symbolism. Saunière, it seemed, at every turn, was reinforcing his fondness for the dark and mischievous side of Leonardo da Vinci."[37] The painting is replete with "explosive and disturbing details" that forward a scandalously counterorthodox set of figurations, including a baby Jesus who appears to submit to the authority of John the Baptist, and a Mary who seems to be conspiring with the angels to eliminate the competition. Langdon subsequently indulges in a few more paragraphs about the particularities of the Louvre's version of the painting, which represents merely one such investigation into the deep mysteries of Leonardo's multifarious hidden symbolism.[38]

The con of Brown's novel is also the source of its ingenuity. Its efforts to ground the factuality of its wild interpretations in concrete narrative acts of concealment and discovery all but advertise the extratextual sources of any such authority. Neither the Da Vinci code, the Fibonacci sequence, nor the anagrams are pure inventions; the novel is, like Eco's *Foucault's Pendulum,* a pastiche. Even so, Langdon's interpretations (which he attributes to the murdered Saunière) are sustained by their narrative ties to the conspiratorial plotline, which both confirms their claim to plausibility and gives their speculative historiography a revelatory, hermetic allure. We do not have to go outside the text to find context for such interpretations: the explanations are all furnished for us, between Langdon's expertise and the confirmation of the novel's own revelations. We even have the novel's paratextual claims to guide us, safe in the assurance that "All descriptions of artwork, architecture, documents, and secret rituals in this novel are accurate."[39] This has not stopped thousands—even millions—of readers from seeking other interpretive keys to such descriptions, to the point of buying, reading, and writing innumerable compendia, exposés, and studies about the novel's claims to historical accuracy. The present chapter is itself one such supplement.

In many ways, however, the novel already incorporates its own outside, as I have suggested. *The Da Vinci Code* is already a kind of library or compilation in its own right, of which *Holy Blood, Holy Grail* and Sède's writings about the French southwest represent but a fraction of the holdings. In spite of the volumes of responses, guides, and rebuttals that have appeared in the years since its publication, Brown's novel already functions as a second-order interpretation and synthesis of the sources from which it gleans. Brown's work is, in a sense, reminiscent of Eco's here, except that *The Da Vinci Code* seeks to transcend the generic separation Eco establishes between the contextualizing labor of erudition and the fantasy of total knowledge: whereas such fantasies may be possible in the "narrative imagination," for Eco they become pernicious in real life, amounting to a "syndrome" that can never be anything other than a fascinating but potentially fatal con. For Brown, on the other hand, the labor of erudition is itself a kind of grail quest in its own right, wherein scholarship and hermetic semiosis come together in the machinations of the art-historical novel. Scholarship is no less perilous than the unbounded initiatory pursuits of starry-eyed occultists, and no less bound up in the quest for cosmic mysteries. This, I maintain, is the animating fantasy of *The Da Vinci Code*.

MYTHOMORPHIC FACTS

By suspending what Umberto Eco calls its "hermetic semiosis" within the free indirect discourse and pandering dialogue of Brown's thriller plot, *The Da Vinci Code* domesticates what might otherwise lapse into interpretive delirium. In place of a paranoid or purely inventive recourse to the historical sublime of mystical revelation, the novel embeds such revelations within a narrative framework and set of "trivial pursuits" that are both procedural and unremarkable in themselves. "So dark the con of man" is an anagram. Of course, this strategy of confirming Langdon's wild interpretation as both "hidden" and as a safely delivered secret message is something of a con in its own right. As numerous critics and debunkers have noted, the validation of Langdon's conspiratorial counterhistory—which occurs both intradiegetically and extradiegetically in citing the facticity of the Priory of Sion in the novel's epigraph—may be the novel's supreme fiction.

This "con," however, is by no means unique to Brown's novel. As I mentioned earlier, the *Dossiers Secrets* testifying to the existence of the Priory of Sion, which were "discovered" in 1975 at the Bibliothèque nationale, are themselves part of a hoax. These *Dossiers Secrets* are a series of forgeries and elaborately contrived genealogical fictions engineered by two Frenchmen: Pierre Plantard, a hermetic royalist and militant Pétainist during the war, and Philippe de Cherisey, an actor and journalist who wrote playfully experimental texts in the spirit of Alfred Jarry's 'pataphysics. This hoax unfolded over the course of several years, and in spite of Cherisey's acknowledgment of the forgeries, continues to attract believers and conspiracy theorists to this day. A large part of this belief owes its perpetuation to Plantard, who—far more dogged and conspiratorial in his hoax making than Cherisey—continued to uphold the veracity of his counterfeit through the end of his life.[40] In spite of its ring of familiarity, the Priory of Sion is modeled less on the notorious, anti-Semitic *Protocols of the Elders of Zion*—itself a forged document published in Russia in 1903—than on the hermetic societies formed throughout the nineteenth and early twentieth centuries, such as the Rosicrucians and theosophical groups such as the Hermetic Order of the Golden Dawn. Indeed, much like the Rosicrucian movement, whose self-invention in the early seventeenth century formed the kernel for later occult revivals, the history of the Priory of Sion has been made up in installments and thus bears its own tangled history of invention and appropriation.[41]

As the unsuccessful plagiarism charge against *The Da Vinci Code* suggests, Dan Brown's novel was hardly the first text to spin out an elaborate counterhistory based on the secret dossiers. In 1982, *Holy Blood, Holy Grail* uses Plantard's "evidence" of the priory to introduce the notion of a secret, sacred bloodline that dates back not only to the Crusades but also to Jesus and Mary Magdalene as the true meaning of the Holy Grail. The pun on San Graal is, in fact, theirs.[42] Without necessarily testifying to the veracity of the *Dossiers Secrets*, the text leaves it ambiguous as to whether Baigent, Leigh, and Lincoln were in on the con or duped by it. *Holy Blood, Holy Grail* nonetheless speculates about such millennial conspiracies, framing its own capacity for historiographical conjecture against scholarly orthodoxy and the rules and structures of contemporary academia. In many ways, *Holy Blood, Holy Grail* takes advantage of the early 1980s discourse on the "relativism" of historical experience and empirical facts, claiming that novelists are more capable of understanding historical truth than scholars.

Responding to critics of their methods and conclusions in the preface to the paperback edition of the book, the authors write,

> By established academic research standards our methods had been highly unorthodox, irregular, and heretical. We had not observed certain enshrined protocols of scholarship, certain dogmatically cautious approaches to material, and had thereby (in their opinion) betrayed ourselves as amateurs who did not warrant serious consideration and who had, moreover, committed the transgression of trespassing on the sovereign domain of experts.[43]

Noting that the strongest supporters of their work had been (male) novelists and "American feminists, who were quick to discern the implications of what we had said," the authors explain that "unlike the professional historian, the novelist is accustomed to an approach such as ours. He is accustomed to synthesizing diverse material, to making connections more elusive than those explicitly preserved in documents. He recognizes that truth may not be confined only to recorded facts but often lies in more intangible domains—in cultural achievements, in myths, legends, and traditions; in the psychic life of both individuals and entire peoples."[44] Robert Langdon, on the other hand, manages to reconcile such unorthodox investigations with the "established standards" Baigent, Leigh, and Lincoln propose to flout. As both a fictional construct and a university scholar, Langdon is at once an interloper *and* a professional.

The hermeneutics of *Holy Blood, Holy Grail* are no less founded on what the authors call "the need for synthesis," a mystical project of its own. In opposition to the "ever-increasing specialization" of modern scholarship which, "as the modern university attests, implies and entails the segregation of knowledge into distinct 'disciplines,'" Baigent, Leigh, and Lincoln embrace the speculation intrinsic to "an interloping approach," which they define as "a mobile and flexible approach that permits one to move freely between disparate disciplines, across space and time." "Finally," they conclude, "it is not sufficient to confine oneself exclusively to facts."[45] In this regard *Holy Blood, Holy Grail* falls squarely in line with other contemporary works of fantastic archaeology, a genre that included works such as Erich von Däniken's *Chariots of the Gods?* (1968) and, in England, John Michell's *The View over Atlantis* (1969), which likewise sought to "move freely" between (and beyond) disciplines. *The Da Vinci Code* is animated in turn by Baigent, Leigh, and Lincoln's suspicions toward academia, ultimately recuperating its authority by fictional means. American academia—and the orthodoxies of interpretation—had already changed dramatically in the two decades between the books, with the "mobile and flexible approach" favored by the authors of *Holy Blood, Holy Grail* resembling, in hindsight, the rhetoric of poststructuralist epistemes and discontinuities. By 2003, such poststructuralist interlopers were old hat, already fully assimilated within the scholarly establishment, albeit under the tenuous mantle of "theory" rather than, say, revelatory historical fact. Baigent, Leigh, and Lincoln, writing before 1982, attribute the power of relativism instead to novelists and "certain American feminists."

Like the nineteenth-century French historian Jules Michelet, the authors of *Holy Blood, Holy Grail* appeal to fabular historiography as an "eternal Poesy" of greater standing than the plodding academic recourse to positive facts and dates.[46] Yet whereas Michelet, writing in 1862, would frame this "eternal Poesy" as the irrepressible spirit of folk wisdom, the authors of *Holy Blood, Holy Grail* attribute it to the truth effects of their own inventiveness. In place of the persistence of suppressed folk culture, we find if not an outright con, then at least a free rein with the inventive capacity of historical longing. Likewise, whereas poststructuralist and antifoundationalist thinkers may have interrogated the formation and status of "facts," the authors of *Holy Blood, Holy Grail* are eager to make them disappear altogether, noting that "facts, in short, are like pebbles dropped into the pool of history. They disappear quickly, often without a trace. But they generate ripples."[47]

In spite of its revelatory claims, therefore, *Holy Blood, Holy Grail* ultimately exercises neither a hermeneutics of suspicion nor even a capitulation to Eco's hermetic semiosis. In place of a "tearing off of masks" or an esoteric initiation, one finds instead a dissemination of surface effects, a romantic proposition for readers to suspend their disbelief. What stimulated the creation of *Holy Blood, Holy Grail*—and *The Da Vinci Code*, in turn—was ultimately not academic scholarship at all but a chance encounter with another popular work of conjecture: Gérard de Sède's *L'Or de Rennes (Le Trésor Maudit)*, later published in English as *The Accursed Treasure*. Sède's book, published in 1967, first lays out the story of a country priest's sudden and mysterious access to wealth as he transformed a Visigoth-era rectory in the hilltop village of Rennes-le-Château in southwestern France into a sumptuous set of houses, chapels, libraries, and gardens. As Sède describes it, the village's rectory, once a near ruin, became the object of local lore around the turn of the twentieth century when a its rector, Bérenger Saunière (the namesake of Dan Brown's murdered museum curator) began refurbishing the church. Though of decidedly modest means, Saunière spared no expense in restoring the church and creating a virtual pleasure palace in its surrounding gardens. Where did the money come from? Sède's proposition was that Saunière had unearthed a treasure of far greater value than monetary worth: he had discovered a secret that, in the history-laden hills of southwestern France, bore epic proportions, with its origins dating from the Albigensian Crusades, the Knights Templar, or even the Temple of Solomon itself. The authors of *Holy Blood, Holy Grail* were impressed with Sède's tale of Rennes-le-Château on account of its inventive historiography. In exploring the mysterious sources of Saunière's wealth, the book unfurls a trail of encrypted messages and historical coincidences that draw speculative energy from regional lore as much as from documentary "facts." Sède's work nonetheless obeys a different set of interpretive principles than the syntheses Baigent, Leigh, and Lincoln—as

FIGURE 11. Tour Magdala, Rennes-le-Château. Photograph by the author.

well as Brown—would ultimately pursue, a politics of interpretation that bore left-wing populist rather than academic (or antiacademic) suspicions. Even so, its contribution to the holy bloodline myth discloses how suspicion and speculation could be deployed not only in a variety of combinations but also according to a variety of ideological effects. Much like scholarly and fictional accounts of the historical Jesus and the formation of the early Christian church, there are also left-wing and right-wing tendencies in religious symbology, each of which figures prominently in popular culture.[48]

Henry Lincoln, who did not participate in the *Da Vinci Code* lawsuit, fully acknowledges his debt to Sède, and has since published a translation of *L'Or de Rennes,* upon which his original BBC documentary was based.[49] As Lincoln writes in his postscript to a recent French reprint of Sède's book, "How many people have admitted that a single book has changed their life? In my case, this expression is an understatement. When I bought a bundle of secondhand paperbacks from a bookseller at the Vendôme in 1969, I never imagined that one of these books would lead me to my life's work."[50] As Lincoln likewise writes in the introduction to *Holy Blood, Holy Grail,* the "primal scene" of his own investigation was not an archaeological discovery but a hermeneutic investment in Sède's historiographic mythmaking. As he wrote in 1982,

> In 1969, en route for a summer holiday in the Cévennes, I made the casual purchase of a paperback. *Le Trésor Maudit* by Gérard de Sède was a mystery story—a lightweight, entertaining blend of historical fact, genuine mystery, and conjecture. It might have remained consigned to the postholiday oblivion of all such reading had I not stumbled across a curious and glaring omission in its pages.[51]

Lincoln is drawn to a set of "secret messages" to which Sède alludes but does not reproduce as evidence in the book—which, it turns out, are the secret dossiers fabricated by Plantard and said to have been later deposited in the Bibliothèque nationale in 1975. For Lincoln and his coauthors, the fact of the counterfeit was hardly a deterrent to their investigation, which amounted to an appreciation of and participation in Sède's (and Plantard's) aesthetic system of "historical fact, genuine mystery, and conjecture." Even as Baigent, Leigh, and Lincoln's research for *Holy Blood, Holy Grail* unfolded, new "priory" documents continued to appear, highlighting the contemporaneity of their pursuit. Such new documents, some of which appeared in print, "only compounded the mystification." As they concluded, "someone was obviously producing this material."[52] Baigent, Leigh, and Lincoln were willing to overlook the counterfactual or counterfeit nature of the documents in order to participate in the labyrinthine historical construction to which they beckoned.

Sède's *L'Or de Rennes* approaches such fiction making as a work of art in its own right, to the extent that it is an art that belongs to local or marginalized populations rather than to a privileged elite. Sède develops this premise along two distinct axes. First, such an art of fabrication describes Bérenger Saunière's own acts of reconstruction and even forgery as the set of procedures Sède pursues in tracing the mystery of the village rector's sudden wealth. We find, in other words, a treasure hunt narrative whose evidentiary trail follows and reconstructs Saunière's *own* treasure hunt, a logic Brown would later fold into his story of Robert Langdon and Sophie Neveu. Second, and more broadly, the book traces Sède's ideas about "mythomorphic facts," his term for the historical value of rumor and local legend, which became "facts" through their social currency and resilience within popular imagination. *L'Or de Rennes* outlines a historiography of sensation that draws, as we will see below, on Sède's background as a surrealist poet and resistance fighter during World War II, as well as on his investment in the cultural particularity of the French southwest, the Languedoc region known for its long affective tradition of legend making and resistance to clerical orthodoxy. Sède's account of the Rennes-le-Château rectory proceeds according to this double insistence. Long a subject of modern popular lore in the region, Saunière's precipitous rise from virtually penniless village rector to sovereign overseer of a massive construction project unfolds according to a series of hermeneutic intrigues. The story proceeds from odd, cryptic architectural flourishes and mysterious documents to the secret contours of the surrounding landscape, whereby the very terrain of the Languedoc region becomes invested with the intricacy and mystery of Sède's historical conjectures. In turn, the hermeneutic tradition he explores ultimately bears less on revealing a set of hermetic secrets than on perpetuating the historical practice of mythomorphic interpretation proper to Saunière and the Languedoc region more broadly.

The story of Bérenger Saunière and the possibility of a secret buried treasure was first popularized in the early 1950s, when the rectory's owner, Noël Corbu, having converted the property into a hotel after the war, began publicizing the mysteries and treasures of the isolated rural church as a way to drum up business. It was Sède, however, who transformed a series of local legends about an essentially material treasure—the "gold" of Rennes le-Château necessary to renovate the church—into a primarily epistemological trove of cryptographic and historiographic intrigue. Though he stops short of making the genealogical claims about a Magdalenian bloodline on which *Holy Blood, Holy Grail* and *The Da Vinci Code* capitalize so resolutely, Sède's *L'Or de Rennes* opens a very wide door for speculation. As Sède notes, over a period of twenty years Saunière spent the "vertiginous sum of 659,413 francs—or, that is, 23,079,455 francs in today's [1980s] currency."[53] Where did this sudden wealth come from? Saunière was rumored to have unearthed an ancient parchment while restoring the interior of the church; the nature of the parchment is unknown, though Sède retraces the pastor's journey to Paris, where he brought the document for expert consultation and consorted with a group of wealthy amateurs with ties to Rosicrucianism.[54] The money seems to have rolled in subsequently. What did the parchment say?

In tracing the origins of Saunière's finances, Sède's work lays out a marvelous assemblage of textual and figural allegories, puns, rebuses, numerological determinations, and geographical allusions inaugurated by the priest in his restoration of the village rectory in Rennes-le-Château. Saunière seems also to have rearranged some graves in the parish cemetery, according to Sède, curiously erasing the inscriptions on two nineteenth-century tombstones. What secrets was he hiding by erasing the tombstone inscriptions? Had he discovered treasure hidden in the walls or the crypt of the Visigoth-era

FIGURE 12. Noël Corbu's advertisement for Rennes-le-Château, in the form of a newspaper article in *La Dépêche du Midi*, January 12, 1956.

church? In tracing the story of Saunière's renovation project, Sède describes the lavish, even garish, details of the restored church, dense with hermetic symbolism. For Sède, a cryptic language emerges from studying the renovations, an elaborate series of coded images and icons that lay out an elaborate coded language of rebuses, allegorical figurations, plays on words, pseudo-etymologies, and deliberate error.[55]

In transforming his poor village rectory into an elaborate forest of symbols, Saunière's renovations testify to his access to a hidden source of great wealth, to which their elaborate symbolism points in turn. In Sède's account, Saunière emerges as a "da Vincian" figure in both Brown's and Freud's senses of the term, at once sneaking disguised symbols into his paintings and, possibly, hiding something of great historical value within them as well. The trail of icons and images left behind by Saunière—supplemented, of course, by the forged documents of the *Dossiers Secrets*—become legible for Sède by means of their topographical and historical legendary correspondences with the physical landscape around the village of Rennes-le-Château as geographical sites for further interpretation. In a manner rendered in narrative form by Dan Brown, Sède constructs an interpretive treasure hunt whose effect, we might say, is to charge the entirety of French history with an almost paranoiac intensification of significance. It is challenging at times to determine where Saunière's cryptographic imagination ends and where Sède's begins; how much of Sède's account is interpretation and how much is invention, or conjecture, or con?

Certainly, like the history-mysteries that followed in its wake—not to mention the countless other works of fiction and reportage that continue to appear today—Sède's extrapolation of the Saunière mystery into a centuries-old secret history of the Occitan region draws much of its appeal from the generic trappings of conspiracy fiction, what Theodore Ziolkowski calls the "lure of the arcane" at work in the genre from antiquity to postmodernism.[56] Yet as Henry Lincoln himself maintains, there is something especially alluring about the premises and methods of Sède's book that distinguishes it from the genre of conspiracy fiction and history-mystery as a whole; Sède's writings bear, that is, their own intrinsic project, an interpretive system of code making and breaking that draws heavily upon popular, regional folklore traditions. In contrast to the excesses of hermetic semiosis criticized by Eco, Sède's writing aims at once to explicate and participate in the poetic forms of Occitan folklore and living history. His goal is to multiply rather than unmask the meanings and correspondences hidden just below the surface. Baigent, Leigh, and Lincoln likewise invoke the poetic to justify their liberal approach to facts, as a license to speculate; Sède's ideas about poetry, by contrast, may be no less liberal toward facts, yet they bear a more specific ideological charge as well. Informed by his ties to the surrealist and Trotsky-ite movements, Sède's approach to poetry and hermeneutics identifies the semiotic machinations of linguistic excess, interpretive delirium, and ideo-logical defamiliarization as both significant ideologically and consistent culturally with the counterhegemonic popular forms and traditions of the region. Set in the land of the Cathars and troubadours, Sède's work offers a reflexive popular historiography that playfully reminds its readers that the French southwest has long been a site of religious tolerance and antiauthori-tarian dissent. In spite of the direct line of heavy borrowing that extends from Sède to Lincoln to Brown, their investments in imagining a cryptic universe thus reveal markedly different sets of intellectual and political priorities—or at least different environments within which their hermeneutics function ideologically.

For Sède, the appeal of such popular myths, lore, and wordplay had less to do with scholarly debates about interpretation, as it did for Brown and Eco, than with the significance—even the political exigency—of the "treasure" such interpretative investments exercised in their deployment. In this con-text, Sède's writings are illuminating not only because they constitute the aggregate source material for these better-known books but also because they suggest how open the ideological stakes of such historical mythmaking can be. In contrast to the ultimate suspicion *toward* scholarly overinterpretation at work in Brown's populist fantasy of miraculous hermeneutics—whereby all codes become legible under the expert tutelage of the Harvard expert, rather than remaining either hermetically sealed or open for continued "wild" interpretation—Sède's work bears a far more explicit mode of left-wing populism. For Sède, the fantastic proliferation of crypts and encryp-tions in Rennes-le-Château has less to do with a mythical access to legibil-ity than with local, vernacular practices of hermeneutic play that comprise and extend the suppressed history of a political and religious counterculture in the Languedoc region.

Sède's occult history of the region unfolds against a landscape already charged with historical significance. Even before the mysterious village rector enters the scene, we find ourselves spirited away into a region "wild and fur-rowed, which nature and History have long persisted in tormenting."[57] In the early pages of *L'Or de Rennes*, Sède describes a rock formation known popularly as "la Main du Diable" (the Devil's Hand), writing, "In this area the Devil has greatly enriched the toponymy: over here is his Breast [*Sein*]; over there, his Armchair [*Fauteuil*]. And toward the South, toward Serbaïrou, we can feast our eyes upon a raised stone in the form of a gaming die, geometrically perfect. This is a phantasmagorical landscape, in which we are hard pressed to distinguish the art of early humans from the inventiveness of nature, a landscape that soon sets our minds careening down the slopes of an imaginary archaeology."[58] Bérenger Saunière's discovery can lead to a profound historical mystery because the landscape in which he resides is already scarred by history, overwritten by lore, and brimming with hidden ancient treasures. These treasures, Sède contends, are historical rather than monetary: the scarring *is* the treasure; the investiture of the landscape with folklore, imagination, and historical memory is not only the code but also the treasure to which the code leads. Without completely letting his readers off the hook in the quest for some ulterior revelation, Sède makes this point consistently throughout his other regional historiographies: the "hollow secret" Eco attributes to hermetic insiderism is a vernacular historical trace rather than an esoteric lure.

In the book that immediately precedes the story of Bérenger Saunière, entitled *Le Sang des Cathares* (The blood of the Cathars) and published in 1966, Sède offers a broader survey of regional lore and history about similarly ancient, hidden treasures. Addressing the admixture of fact and myth in the living history of the Languedoc region, he describes, as above, the legacy of its haunted past. The countryside around the medieval cities of Carcassonne and Toulouse has seen, over the millennia, a long sequence of suppressed civilizations—Cathars, Templars, troubadours, and Visigoths—whose long and tragic history of religious syncretism remains a living cultural memory. The "treasure" left behind by the Templars, or by the kingdoms of Occitan, thus refers to the paradoxically common and clandestine traces of its legacy as much as to any material hoard of artifacts: the living memory of its resistance, available in songs, popular legends, *langue d'Oc* turns of phrase, and a legacy of hermetic language consistent with its medieval worldview. The titular Cathar treasure thus designates both an evidentiary trove and a semiotic legacy, the testimonial traces of an archaic past that persist, Sède maintains, in the present. Referring to the treasure of Montségur, the Cathar fortress destroyed in 1244 by papist forces in the final year of the Albigensian Crusade, Sède writes,

> The treasure of Montségur is nowhere and everywhere. It is a treasure of faith, of culture, of military feats and sacrifices in service of a people's freedom, its vision of the future of humanity. In other ages, and beneath other skies, this treasure has belonged to Joan of Arc, the German Anabaptists, the Hussites of Bohemia, the Cévenol Hugenots, and the soldiers who fought at Valmy, Verdun, Guadalajara, and Stalingrad. Man's only treasure is mankind itself, and it is inexhaustible.[59]

Sède's treasure belongs to the people, the common folk whose histories are so often absorbed or erased altogether by the grand narratives of kings and nobles. Like the holy, suppressed "eternal feminine" to which Langdon repeatedly alludes in *The Da Vinci Code,* Sède's treasure is ultimately a repository of embodied historical memory—a myth, perhaps, but a myth that exercises a significant semiotic and ideological function even in guarding its secrets.

This vernacular treasure is preserved, in turn, by means of a set of regional idioms and modes of signification. "In the labyrinth of Occitan mythology," Sède writes early in *Le Sang des Cathares,* "language is thus Ariadne's thread. The etymologies of our ancestors were often fanciful; but we have pulled this thread a great deal. We have given them the right of way; this is because such fantasies are hardly gratuitous for the deciphering of legends, any less than those in dreams are for a psychoanalyst. In both cases a play on words is often the link between the scattered elements of an absurd totality whose hidden meaning it reveals. In both cases, double meanings, the approximation of images, the figuration of ideas by objects or people, obeys but one sole logic: that of the pun or rebus."[60] By the middle of his investigation of Saunière in *L'Or de Rennes,* this historical language of puns and double entendres becomes instrumentalized as the very trail of codes and cyphers Sède attributes to the village rector. Mobilized as a discrete medium of expression, it approximates the Freudian language of dreams: legends and dreams alike appeal to the same processes of distortion and concealment, he writes, listing "rebuses, the pays on words, pseudo-etymologies, telling errors of detail, figurations of abstract notions by people or through invention, etc.," as the medium for this game of hide-and-seek. Analyzing legends is likewise a process of discerning historical dates or "episodes" that have been unconsciously repressed. For Sède, "the fantastic always conveys, in cryptic form, traditions that return to positive data, albeit in a mediated form."[61] Even singular Christian treasures such as the Holy Grail, whose objective form remains uncertain—a philosopher's stone or cup—become legible through this method, and thus become continuous with their expressive medium: the grail is likewise "invisible to anyone unfit to approach it, but it miraculously restores whoever knows how to crack its secret and thereby become part of the lineage of the 'Kings of the Grail.'"[62] Sède's hermeneutics fully collapse the distinction between "open" interpretation and hermetic elitism delimited by Eco: the knowledge of "how to crack its secret" was a privilege not of expertise or power but of shared vernacular wisdom—a counterhegemonic "hermeneutics of suspicion" that for Sède was participatory, ritualistic, and even sacred. Analogous, but hardly limited, to the work of psychoanalysis, this language of symbols and ciphers was inseparable from its physical and cultural environment. This was not because of some cryptofascist bond with "the soil" (although similar logics can and have been used in the service of genocidal nativism and xenophobia) but because the dynamic networks of association between a language and its living (social, natural, institutional) environment are precisely what distinguish a participatory hermeneutics from a mere story. Like psychoanalysis, in which the clinical relationship forms a key component in the interpretative process, it is a practice that functions through the demands and resistances, the process of working through, of its vernacular deployments.

The village rector Bérenger Saunière figures as an agent within this signifying chain, a spinner of Ariadne's thread. The recourse to labyrinthine fantasy as a bearer of historical knowledge was, for him, a conscious rather than an accidental or unconscious cultural practice. This is not a contradiction for Sède. The seemingly anonymous capacity for vernacular wisdom to retain as well as disfigure historical knowledge may resemble the workings of the Freudian unconscious, but this does not mean that individual subjects were necessarily unaware of their contribution to its forms and portent. If Saunière discovered and hid historical secrets within the rectory at Rennes-le-Château, erasing monuments and decorating the church with a baroque confusion of symbols, he did so in the manner of the troubadours, who composed in the very idiom Sède ascribes to the hermeticism of legend in the Occitan. In their language of inventive misdirection, that is, troubadour poets could express ideas that might otherwise have been scandalous or heretical, yet which inventive auditors could participate in as fully as the troubadours themselves. Sède describes the fundamental ambiguity toward language (as well as love) through which "the troubadour is always loyal and deceptive at once: untrustworthy toward this husband who remains attached to bodily needs, and loyal to the lady, she with whom he can be freed from such needs through the mutual enthusiasm for chastity."[63] Linguistically as well as sexually, a little cheating is tolerable, even commendable, when it heeds the double language of love and legend alike. Such hermeneutics amount to an open secret or even, in Eco's terms, an open work whose encryption enabled the transmission and exercise of desire and knowledge rather than its censorship or restriction to an elite. Thus, Sède notes that "not only are legends often based on historical facts whose traces they help us recover, but we also know, through Marx and Freud, that the products of the human imagination, even the most fantastic ones, draw their forms and images from the history of societies and individuals. In the face of these imaginary creations, the work of the historian should be parallel to that of the psychoanalyst."[64]

This parallel means two things for Sède. First, cons, hoaxes, and forgeries such as Pierre Plantard's Priory of Sion documents—or even Bérenger Saunière's own possible traffic in documents—were *part of* the historical chain of hermetic signification. (One of Sède's principal suspicions was that Saunière began trafficking in forged documents among the Rosicrucians, having disclosed his discoveries at the rectory to an influential group of occult enthusiasts in Paris.) Like Plantard, Saunière may have been a con artist, in other words, but even so, the con was also a form of devotion—just as the motives for cheating were often, in the case of troubadour songs, as faithful a record of historical wishes and ideas as any factual evidence. By demanding that the historian become more of a psychoanalyst in turn, Sède proposes less a position of expertise for "unlocking" such codes than a set of modern parameters for participating in this transhistorical exchange.

Second, Sède's work levies this same demand upon his own readers. This means, by implication, that his narrative historiography is as prone to the con as any other potentially duplicitous document. As his "Avertissement" (which means both "preface" and "warning") to *L'Or de Rennes* reads, "there exists a resemblance between the facts recounted in this book and an imaginary construction, but this is the result of pure chance. This is not the least bit strange, because the resemblance is striking."[65] What regulates or even motivates the deliberate liberty with historical facts in such works? Viewed alongside one another, the most outlandish propositions of Sède's books seem to have less to do with Christian legacies than with the kinds of interpretation in which they invite readers to participate: a hermeneutics of suspicion that has not so much gone wild as to have become a poetic extension of vernacular history. Play and insincerity are as integral to historical interpretation as they are to poetic invention. There may be a con, in other words, but we are all invited to be in on it. The limits of such open interpretation—which is to say, its conditions of possibility—have less to do with credulity than with the parameters of the cultural tradition of which it is an expression and into which it is also an invitation: it may presume an initiated elect, but it performs this initiation itself.

Sède's work is a forest of symbols in its own right: even a "primary source" of parahistoriography such as *L'Or de Rennes* is already a synthesis, an amalgamation of legend, fact, and poetic invention. According to this same logic, the "cons" of Plantard's *Dossiers Secrets* likewise became part of Sède's archive; in a later revision of his work on Rennes-le-Château published in 1988, the con becomes part of the transhistorical treasure itself. The secret knowledge of the Visigoth church was, in this late account, not that it housed Merovingean gold, or the Holy Grail, but a traffic in forged documents. It remains unclear as to whether Saunière really did discover something, thereafter embedding crypts and symbols in his restoration of the church, or whether he raised money through forgery and the traffic in sermons, either dabbling in or cynically appealing to the popularity of occult knowledge and France's mystical past. For Sède, the difference is virtually negligible; regardless of their veracity, Saunière's activities become part of the living archive of the French southwest.[66]

What might look like an "imaginary construction" could thus also become a fact for precisely this reason. The doubleness or reversibility of Sède's preface/warning to *L'Or de Rennes* thus placed the responsibility of participatory understanding on the reader—rather than on a truth-telling author or a Harvard-affiliated prosopopoeia. None of these figures stands outside history, able to judge its truth claims and facts from a transcendental position. This is a dangerous game, of course, for this very reason; it suggests the volatile status of "facts" in our so-called postfact age. But in the case of mythomorphic facts, as well as local and indigenous knowledges and vernacular theories of all kinds, the status of such "facts" is always volatile: immanently politicizable, subject not only to the ideological leanings of the polis but also to the sovereign biopolitical systems that shape (or eradicate) these leanings. Yet rather than presuming regional lore to be politically suspect, as even Bruno Latour does in criticizing the cultural exhaustion of "suspicion" as a viable critical mode, Sède's work rehearses both the semiotic richness and ideological specificity of vernacular knowledge in the Occitan.[67] In place of Robert Langdon's mystical scholarly authority, Sède discloses his readers' imbrication in the labyrinth of historical signs and traces that likewise rehearses an ideological history of the French southwest. This participatory, entangled mode of historiography offers a hermeneutics of suspicion distinct from Brown's or Eco's notions of interpretation for the very reason that it renders historical mythmaking and even falsification as a mode of communicability, even solidarity. The medium, in other words, is the secret, but it is an open secret.

TREASURES IN OUR MIDST

At the opposite pole of the political spectrum from the royalist Pierre Plantard, whom he nonetheless consulted as an expert in hermeticism, Gérard de Sède was a lifelong Trotskyite and militant anti-Stalinist who had been active in the underground French Resistance during World War II. His historiographic insistences—including his fascination for clandestine speech and the double language of the troubadours—bear the impression of his broader political and poetic career as well as his regional interests. Born in 1921, Sède's schooling at the Sorbonne was interrupted by the war, and he spent the Vichy years working for the clandestine Trotskyite Parti ouvrier internationaliste (POI), as well as for the semiclandestine wartime surrealist group, La Main à plume, which published books of underground poetry while conducting resistance activities of its own. Whereas Sède's work for the POI was more ostensibly militant—he was imprisoned by the Germans for smuggling false papers—La Main à plume was hardly less so. The group's name alludes to this: drawn from a line in Arthur Rimbaud's *Un Saison en enfer* (A season in hell), the Main à plume name both evinced the contemporary wartime "season in hell" and cited the poem's claim that "La main à plume vaut la main à charrue" (The hand that holds the pen is as good as the hand that holds the plow). Poetry, in other words, was a form of labor—and of political labor in particular. Of the roughly twenty-five young poets and artists affiliated with the group, Sède counted seven who lost their lives on account of their resistance activities.[68] As Sède writes of the group in his unpublished memoir,

> The track record of La Main à plume was more than honorable. Not only did this group take up the torch of surrealist revolt in a period when Stupidity and Atrocity coupled in obscene fashion, but they paid a heavy toll for it as well. Jean-Claude Diamant-Berger was killed in uniform in Normandy; Hans Schoenhoff and Edith Hirschowa died after being deported; Robert Rius, Marco Menegoz, and Juan Simnpoli were shot by the Nazis in Arbonne, and Jean-Pierre Mulotte, who was only 17, was gunned down in central Paris after executing an SS officer on the Austerlitz bridge.[69]

Though he would only turn to writing popular books of "mythomorphic" regional historiography later in life, the political charge of Sède's underground activity as a militant poet and resistance member during the war remained a persistent spur throughout his career. After the war, Sède worked on a doctoral dissertation in philosophy at the Sorbonne before turning fully to journalism, though his political militancy did not wane. Working for the Parti socialiste unitaire (in its early, postwar incarnation) and writing for the anti-Stalinist Marxist journal *Revue internationale*, Sède traveled extensively in Yugoslavia after Josip Tito's break with Joseph Stalin. On returning to France, he briefly tried his hand at farming, while remaining active in leftist political circles. The political intensity of his wartime surrealism and extraliterary activism persisted in the fabular methodology of his more popular work, I maintain, particularly in articulating a populist revolutionary imagination that broke from the ideological strictures of Stalinist social realism. This is not to suggest that his popular books of the 1960s were wholly unmanipulative or indelibly marked as socialist. Nor is it to suggest that Sède, by then a freelance writer, was wholly unmotivated by material gain. Rather, my point is instead to consider Sède's historiography of "mythomorphic facts" as a project that bore ideological significance other than the largely epistemological concerns of 1980s scholarship as embodied by Robert Langdon, with its culture war–era concerns for demonstrable truth and overinterpretation. As a freelance writer, Sède was not concerned with any such crisis in the humanities. His interpretive project, like its Occitan setting, reflects a historical and political investment in clandestine speech and vernacular expression that was hermeneutically consistent with his pan-leftist politics of global liberation. *The connections may be invisible,* in other words, *but they are always there,* buried just beneath the surface.

The Main à plume group, which published surrealist poetry anonymously and conducted semiclandestine operations in Nazi-occupied Paris from 1941 through 1944, lived a furtive existence, using "whatever feeble means that remained at their disposal," historian of surrealism Gérard Durozoi has written. "They carried out their duplicitous acts daily, as much in order to live as to publish; they were led to taking very real risks in printing and distributing texts that were so many signals of exigency and ardent resistance against all possible forms of spiritual enslavement."[70] As the anarchist poet and future detective novelist Léo Malet wrote to his Main à plume comrade Noël Arnaud in 1943, "There is never a shortage of schmucks [*cons*] and dipshits [*emmerdeurs*] in the occupied zone"; it was important instead "to affirm our intransigence and right against all those dogs with writing-desks, whether they be democratic or authoritarian."[71] In this context, the Main à plume group turned to surrealist poetry as a mode of resistance against Vichy-era ideological warfare, but it was a surrealism itself rendered "methodical, ideologically intransigent, active, scientific," as Boris Rybak put it in his 1943 "Introduction to Scientific Surrealism."[72] Championing the "redistribution of poetic values," the group sought to invest the contemporary phenomenal world with something other than a "mummifying" reflection of its oppressive ideological and geopolitical realities. It did so by creating concrete instances of irrational possibility, discontinuity, and play within "the immanent nature of objects and the phenomena to which they give rise."[73]

For Sède, surrealism offers a "general crisis in the notion of the object" that challenged the self-evidence of objective reality: material objects, as he puts it, are really products. Such a fungible notion of reality means that it could be replaced with a new set of poetic products, a "*concrete* that bears the exigency of materialist dialectics such as contemporary physics had mobi-lized."[74] Fusing the hermeneutics of suspicion with experimental poetry, Sède asserts the political significance of making things up.

In the 1943 essay "Theoretical Objectivity and Lyric Objectivity," writ-ten during his involvement in the surrealist resistance movement, Sède in-vokes the notion of "poetic knowledge" as a collective scientific practice that replaces "art" with "myth." Drawing from the past twenty years of the sur-realist movement's interest in "contemporary collective myth," he develops the notion of what he calls lyric objectivity: a knowing lyricism significant for its capacity to disrupt the "determinism of thought."[75] Rather than sim-ply creating individual works of art, in other words, Sède advocates a poetic practice through which the "reflexive consciousness" by which we encounter art objects becomes the medium for experiment and transformation. These are ideas he subsequently developed further in a dissertation on Jean-Jacques Rousseau and sociological method he began writing at the Sorbonne after the war, under Gaston Bachelard, before turning to a career in journalism.

At stake in this project of historiographic mythmaking was less the mystical longing for a lost condition of hermeneutic unification than a strik-ing convergence of "facts" and "imaginary constructions" rooted in wartime surrealism's poetic recourse to myth. What this project demanded, accord-ing to Sède and his comrades in the Main à plume group, was a "redistribu-tion of poetic values" that subjected the ever-expanding archive of the known and knowable to the upheavals of poetic thought. The distinction of such "lyric objectivity" from the kinds of hermetic semiosis described by Eco was an explicit one—as, I maintain, were Sède's later compilations of "mytho-morphic facts." Whereas hermetic or mystical revelation is marked by fa-cility, as Eco claims, Sède's own project bears a dialectical provocation that exacerbates rather than satisfies poetic longing. "All occult doctrines," Sède writes in his book *Les Templiers sont parmi nous* (The Templars are among us), "aim to present their births as the fruit of a tradition as old as the world itself and to lay claim to divine initiations."[76] Sède's project proposes instead to recognize both the vernacular history and the contemporary exigency of such doctrines. The point, in other words, is not so much to "relativize" his-torical facts as to redeploy them as a medium for imaginative provocation, both in dislodging ideological commonplaces and in promoting reflexive, as well as collective, thought.

Sède's political priorities in the years between his Main à plume ac-tivities and his turn to mythomorphic history were consistently Trotskyite; his ideas about mythmaking and politics likewise continued to develop along anti-Stalinist lines, as articulated in a 1946 essay for the Trotskyite magazine *Jeune Révolution* entitled "Marxist Philosophy and Stalinist Philosophy," which directly extends his surrealist ideas of lyric objectivity into the sphere of postwar leftist politics.[77] In the essay, which he retyped in its entirety for inclusion in his memoirs, Sède seeks to disentangle a living Marxist theory from its fatal abstraction in the semiotics of contemporary Stalinism. In the latter, he argues, dialectical materialism had come to stand for a brute form of pragmatism that "authorized avant-garde proletarian militants to deny a priori the dialectically neutral character of political deviations and treasons," and thus to consider all political deviations or disagreements as counterrevolutionary activities worthy of eradication.[78] Sède instead champions such deviations and even "treasons" as necessary functions of history and, in turn, of theories and accounts of the way history unfolds.

Anticipating the role of regional myths and legends in his account of Bérenger Saunière, Sède argues that Marxist historical thought needed to accommodate the distortions, double entendres, and interpretive delirium that comprised the dialectical movement of history. Stalinist communism suffered, by contrast, from a limited conception of what Marx meant by "history," privileging an almost mystical self-evidence rather than a truly dialectical struggle for meaning. Marx may have written that "the only reconciliation of nature and man is history, the transformation of history into humanity; the only truth that unites materialism and idealism is this active [*réalisé*] humanism, which is communism."[79] But the all-too-common tendency (on the Right and Left alike) was to think of history as purely metaphysical rather than as the volatile fusion of materialism and idealism, the concrete and the metaphysical. To think this way was to reduce the historical project of communism from a transformative set of confrontations to an abstract horizon of futurity that rendered it indistinguishable from bourgeois philosophy. Under such conditions, Sède notes, idealism and materialism once more become mutually exclusive positions, yielding a bifurcated communist orthodoxy whose metaphysics amounted to a utopian, purely formal abstraction of Marxism and yet whose operatives, by contrast, shot dissenters and invaded countries according to a utilitarian, "realist" orthodoxy. The result was, of course, Stalinism.

Seeking to break with Stalinism's "capitulation" to such a split between historical idealism and practical realism,[80] Sède concludes that a new Marxist philosophy is necessary to overcome this murderous dualism. He urges new modes of speculative thought that could accommodate the dialecticism of historical knowledge within their very logic or could even do away with formal logical systems altogether. He thus advocates the serious Marxist investigation of contemporary philosophical currents such as existentialism and phenomenology—movements labeled as "bourgeois" by the party—as new terrains for leftist thought. "For if speculative form is the limit of all realism," he writes, "realism is a limit surpassed today by speculation. Since Heisenberg and Broglie, since Husserl, Bachelard and Sartre, the class character of bourgeois philosophy no longer resides in its ontological dilemma [regarding the opposition between idealism and materialism]. The concept of substance has run dry. Today, the advanced bourgeois dialectics have far surpassed old-fashioned realism. It is a matter precisely of showing what might be 'progressive' in them, while also determining their full significance." In the nineteenth century, Marx had literalized Hegel's idealist speculation, recasting Hegelian panlogism as proletarian struggle; but in the twentieth century, Sède proposes, the philosophical move "toward the concrete" had in fact superseded the limits of this literalization (see chapter 2). Instead of the literal, Sède offers the conjectural: the necessarily reflexive and often duplicitous work of speculation that recasts Marx's "reconciliation of nature and man" as living thought.[81]

Existentialism and phenomenology were necessary for communists because they posited being and thinking as mutually unsettling and mutually constitutive processes of dialectical struggle. Sède's notion of "speculation" introduces ideological struggle within the very heart of ideology itself, as the very enigma of Marxist theory. This extension of lyric objectivity into the sphere of leftist thought colored Sède's long career as a journalist and freelance writer, which brought him to sites of continuous ideological ferment around the world, from Hungary in the 1950s to Czechoslovakia in the 1960s and Nicaragua in the 1980s. Most pertinently for my discussion here, it likewise formed the methodological core of Sède's fabular books of popular historiography which—however invisibly to their popular audience—remained consistent with their imperative toward speculative provocation and lyric objectivity.

Sède became quite famous for the popular works of imaginative historiography he began writing in the early 1960s. In his late memoir, he dismisses the overall significance of this work, claiming that he "churned out some twaddle, of which I was not especially proud, on account of their strong contribution to the subculture." He professes to the "sad courage" of foolishly signing his own name to such works, if only in "refusing to hide the poor conditions of a hack writer in 1960s France behind a pseudonym."[82] Books such as *L'Or de Rennes* did not brandish the Trotskyite credentials of his journalism or wartime poetry, particularly from the militant perspective of his late unpublished memoirs. All the same, the books reveal a methodological consistency with his speculative Marxism, in however clandestine a fashion. In their approach to the idea of "history" as dynamic and experiential, Sède's regional tales of crypts and treasures incorporate the dialectic of speculation and historical action, text and living memory, as well as the material traces of suppressed resistance. Unlike Dan Brown's novel, Sède's elaboration of the "resemblance" between facts and imaginary constructions is fueled not by mysticism but by a dialectic of aura and trace, of archaic mysteries and present-at-hand semiotic evidence. His "twaddle" remains open to all kinds of interpretations—even to the point of mystification or appropriation to other ideological ends. In his popular writing Sède is hardly casting about for a party line or an instrumental form of ideology critique, as his self-disparagement suggests. Yet his work nonetheless plays out its interpretive treasure hunts in the name of ideological provocation—if not the wondrous revelatory participation of a sacred hermeneutics, then at least a vernacular participation in a common forest of symbols. In a manner consistent with his ideas about history in 1946, he recasts the contemporary Occitan landscape as a living historical text whose interpretation, even overinterpretation, remains open. This, again, is the treasure we find at Rennes-le-Château and in the secret history of the French countryside: lyric objectivity, a treasure that is nowhere and everywhere at once.

The first of these books, published in 1962, is *Les Templiers sont parmi nous,* an investigation into the popular regional legends and even eyewitness claims that there was a secret Templar enclave hidden deep beneath a local castle in the village of Gisors, north of Paris. The book is dedicated "to the marvelous" [*à la merveille*], testifying not only to its surrealist inheritance but also to its own lyric objectivity. It is here that Pierre Plantard first appears in print as an expert "hermeticist" cited by Sède, who invokes the existence of something called the Priory of Sion in a self-consciously esoteric afterword to the book. In 1966, Sède shifted his sights to the French southwest in publishing *Le Sang des Cathares,* which expands upon the ideas about hidden buried treasure begun in the Templars book. Sède's subsequent book, published in 1967, was *L'Or de Rennes;* this, of course, is the immediate source for *Holy Blood, Holy Grail,* and thus of *The Da Vinci Code* in turn.

For Sède, the monuments, images, and documents of local history (from the medieval period to the present) become a medium for speculative experimentation. The title of Sède's unpublished memoir, "La Chimère expérimentale" (The chimera of experiment), is instructive here: though it dismisses his popular mythohistoriography as hack work, the memoir casts Sède himself as a kind of speculative construct, however "teratological" or subject to deformation.[83] History, for Sède, is likewise teratological: composite and dynamic, it comprises far more than facts alone. But so too does the conceptual framework of historiography. Sède's ideas about lyric objectivity extent to the politically charged practice of historiographic mythmaking, which has less to do, in this case, with the practice of constructing ideologically reactionary "alternative histories" than with surrealist poetics of ideological rupture. His recourse to history as an artistic medium—whether for fabulation, game, or outright con—bears a self-conscious methodological imperative that proposes neither to insult our intelligence nor to pass off revisionist history as truth but instead to provoke, through the very marvels of its interpretive curiosities, a kind of poetic self-consciousness about our own concepts of history and our ideological attachments. One finds gestures toward this imperative in the tourist Paris of *The Da Vinci Code*, which presents an almost pedagogical exposition of such histories.

Far from seeking to deploy semiotic and historical constraints on "open" interpretation, as Umberto Eco does—and far from spiriting them away, as Dan Brown does—Sède's work offers a rationale for their speculative and experimental synthesis in chimerical form. What is strained, what is put to the test, is first and foremost our credulity—that is, our susceptibility, but also our resistance, to being conned. This is hardly a new idea, but it is an idea worth revisiting. One might invoke the roughly contemporaneous work of the psychoanalyst Jacques Lacan in pointing out, with regard to the hidden messages in Edgar Allan Poe's "The Purloined Letter," that it is the nonduped who err, that we are at our most credulous when we think ourselves free from the con, as if standing on the solid bedrock of authority or facts. Sède invokes Poe's "Purloined Letter" in *L'Or de Rennes* in proposing that the language of Saunière's code remains hidden to tourists because, like the words written across the face of a map, they are too visible to be seen.[84] For Sède, Saunière's code was instead an *invitation au voyage*, a gesture of initiation into the depths of historical meaning that was inscribed upon the very surface of things, in plain view. In the words of Sède's wartime colleague Christian Dotrement, "Thought is born in the mouth. And on paper. In words."[85] For Sède—and even for Dan Brown—thinking begins in the con. This is not because hoaxes—or fabrications, or myths—represent either a legitimate claim to belief or a clever form of subversion, but because this realm of suspicion and overinterpretation becomes the very terrain of speculation within which, as Sède argued in 1946, historical alternatives could remain open, in spite of everything.

SUB ROSA

Gérard de Sède was never considered to be an outsider artist, even though his writing is often relegated to the fringe of pseudohistorical mythmaking that his work helped popularize in France and throughout the English-speaking world. Like Umberto Eco, Sède was as much a theorist of such historiographies as a practitioner and popularizer, and in no less resolute a fashion than the famous semiotician. Sède, Eco, Brown, and even Lincoln each recognize "mythomorphic facts" (and, we might say, factomorphic myths) to be a terrain of ideological struggle animating the literary subgenre of grail fiction and conspiratorial investigation to which they contribute. And they each approach this terrain more or less from the political Left, albeit with variable degrees of intensity. Their theories nonetheless diverge, in spite of the seemingly direct bloodline of literary inheritance that connects them. For in spite of their convergent interests in Templars and buried treasures, Mary Magdalene and the Holy Grail, their claims about interpretation and access to special heterodox forms of knowledge bear very different methodological and procedural insistences. What distinguishes them in particular is their relationship to a hermeneutics of suspicion, the insistence that appearances belie hidden underlying meanings. Do counterfactual history mysteries challenge the certainty of orthodox histories and their so-called facts, or do they simply con readers into a fantasy of ready access to powerful secrets?

In his own study of the appeal of conspiracy, secret societies, and mystery fiction, Theodore Ziolkowski proposes that the "lure of the arcane" may be a basic human need. Tracing a genealogy of conspiracy fictions from Euripides and the Rosicrucians to Ishmael Reed and Dan Brown, Ziolkowski argues that such fictions, like secret societies themselves, "share as their attraction the promise to make sense of a world grown incomprehensibly chaotic and to provide a meaningful structure linking past and present."[86] Such attractions do not presuppose that readers give credence to the mysteries or conspiracies, or that the political intentions are either right-wing or left-wing. But Ziolkowski can make this claim largely by dismissing popular fiction such as *The Da Vinci Code* for its "easy access to material that might otherwise require extensive historical sociological, political, or psychological knowledge and research."[87] His basic premise is that mystery fiction is popular because it duplicates in narrative form the "lure" of the secret society itself; it gives "easy" access to this human need, only without the "real" labor. Ziolkowski thus stresses the distinction between a mere fantasy of access and proper scholarly diligence, a distinction which, like other forms of demarcation, threatens to become a lure of its own. For Eco, the stakes of this distinction are political as well as epistemological, whereby the "easy access" Ziolkowski dismisses is characterized not by a lack of work but by a will to power. Such a will is no less present in the investment in scholarly legitimacy one finds in the contemporary academy, as an elitism based on scholarly prestige rather than on scholarly labor. In her recent study on *The Limits of Critique*—an echo of Eco's *The Limits of Interpretation,* a book published a quarter century earlier—Rita Felski makes this claim on behalf of the ends to which literary-critical recourse to the hermeneutics of suspicion has been levied, even in the very name of subversive or liberatory interpretation. "Suspicion" has come to serve as an easy way out, or an easy way in, whereas questions about the historical circulation of texts, readers, ideas, authors, and other "actants" can recall us to the fuller richness of interpretive labor.[88] It is on account of this distinction, I maintain, that Robert Langdon's "mystical" form of scholarship seeks to bridge the divide between too easy an interpretive access and too daunting, or too remote, a model of scholarly expertise. Sède, on the other hand, is less concerned with access than with readerly participation in the production and transmission of historical countermemory: a will to power on behalf of the common, the vernacular, and even the proletariat. Like Eco's ideas about the open work, the scholarly labor cited by Ziolkowski thus becomes continuous with mythohistorical fantasy, the very labyrinth into which we are all invited.

Yet however universal Ziolkowski might claim the lure of the arcane to be, we have seen how particular the deployments of any such lure can become, as well as what political dangers and possibilities it can take on even in the name of interpretive openness. Such is the contention of the radical feminist scholar Mary Daly, whose writings Langdon paraphrases (in however patronizing a fashion) as he glosses the religious symbology of Leonardo da Vinci's *Madonna of the Rocks* for Sophie Neveu. Even the claim to openness and participation is a lure, a con, whose alleged universalism perpetuates and naturalizes the distinctive will to power of patriarchy itself. According to Daly, "patriarchy preserves its deception through myth." Daly is citing Simone de Beauvoir's *The Second Sex* here, but rather than disparaging (or unmasking) myths for the ideologically pernicious ends they have been made to serve, Daly argues that these very myths have themselves been stolen and perverted from women as a very part of this deception. The symbolic forms and icons that make up myths about the "eternal feminine" or the sacred status of maternity have been appropriated from the matrilineal and matriarchal societies whose very existence such myths serve to disavow. So dark, indeed, the con of man. Daly's recourse to a hermeneutics of suspicion is to unveil *further*, as well as to recapture, the very means of deception. As we will see in chapter 4, moreover, such deceptions also form an analytical medium in turn. Because they are stolen, myths "are something like distorting lenses through which we *can* see into the Background," she writes. "But it is necessary to break their codes in order to use them as viewers; that is, we must see their lie in order to see their truth. We can correctly perceive patriarchal myths as reversals and as pale derivatives of more ancient, more translucent myth from gynocentric civilization."[89] Such code breaking amounts to a "metaethics" (a concept Daly developed over the course of her career, which began, like Robert Langdon's, with something resembling religious symbology) that demands more than mere interpretation. Rather, such codes and myths needed to be broken, dismantled, and radically reimagined.

For a number of feminist thinkers, the truth claims of historical myth lay less in their facticity than in their ethical deployment or redeployment in the name of historical justice and even the very fate of the earth. Certainly, as Sède maintains, myths maintain the capacity to bear out certain "mythomorphic" facts; but since such facts are themselves derived from myths, their truth value is subject to interrogation and reinvention. This double process of code breaking and recoding (or overcoding) entails what might thus be called a project of metainterpretation: we must see their lie in order to see their truth. Rather than engaging in debates over "open" interpretation and overinterpretation, veracity and implausibility, Daly contends that the work of interpretation must be altogether reconsidered: it is not simply a matter of deciphering codes or participating in their semiotic labyrinths but of breaking the codes and reweaving the labyrinths, dismembering the logic of deception and concealment through which they function and rectifying their theft. "Failing that," Daly writes, citing Monique Wittig, "invent."[90]

THE CHALICE, THE BLADE, AND THE BIFURCATION POINT

When it comes to silencing women, Western culture has had thousands of
years of practice.

—Mary Beard, *Women & Power*

CITED BY DAN BROWN in his acknowledgments to *The Da Vinci Code*,
Riane Eisler's *The Chalice and the Blade* was itself something of a runaway
best seller when it appeared in 1987, selling 181,000 copies in paper and
24,800 in cloth over a five-year period.[1] The book, which presents itself as a
study of human cultural evolution, offers an alternative to the social order of
the contemporary world, the global sphere of late capitalism marked by ecological unsustainability and relations of domination and exploitation. This
social order, Eisler argues, constitutes an evolutionary wrong turn, of
which late capitalism represents a fatal extension. It is a wrong turn that
has yielded not only capitalism but also feudalism, fascism, imperialism,
and, most broadly, patriarchy (or androcracy, as Eisler renames it, in order
to denaturalize "emotion-laden and conflicting images of tyrannical fathers and wise old men" that do not "even accurately describe our present
system").[2] Such political formations are all manifestations of an underlying
structure of social competition and domination we have come to naturalize
as "human" rather than historical. Western history has, in short, cultivated
a necropolitics, a global cult of death that is rapidly accelerating toward its
apocalyptic conclusion. Where did we go wrong? What hope remains for
our survival?

Threatened by encroaching ecological and nuclear disaster, the survival
of the human race depends on a bold shift away from such relations of domination. Human survival instead demands an alternative model of human

interaction, Eisler tells us, based on cooperation, heterarchy, and harmonious relations with the natural world. This model of social organization is neither utopian nor new, she insists. It is, in fact, very old. It derives from the vestiges of Neolithic social forms that date to prehistoric agrarian cultures, civilizations that worshipped mother goddesses of birth and fecundity and celebrated partnership rather than hierarchy and competition. Eisler refers to such social forms by means of their common iconography, the chalice or grail, a form that symbolizes the hearth, the earthenware vessel, the womb of life. Available only in trace form as the glimmer of a repressed prehistorical inheritance, the chalice preceded the "blade" of the warlike dominator societies with which we have become all too familiar. Thus the "ancient chalice or grail" symbolizes "societies that worshiped the life-generating and nurturing powers of the universe," she writes, whereas the "lethal power of the blade" symbolizes "the power to take rather than give life that is the ultimate power to establish and enforce domination."[3]

Tellingly, the titular artifacts of Eisler's study are misrepresented somewhat by Robert Langdon, Brown's protagonist in *The Da Vinci Code,* in his hermeneutic recourse to their explanatory value as symbols spanning the ages of human civilization. As we saw in chapter 3, Langdon deploys "the chalice" and "the blade" as archetypal forms within his theory of religious symbology: for him, the chalice (or grail) symbolizes the "eternal feminine," the pre-Christian heritage of ancient fertility cults and matriarchal forms of social organization. The blade, on the other hand, symbolizes masculinity, as well as its political enshrinement in the form of "phallic" patriarchal authority. As in Eisler's book, the symbolic value of the terms corresponds roughly to pictorial abstractions of male and female genitalia. But in Brown's novel, this schematic amounts to something of a holy battle between the sexes rather than an alternative model for human survival. Certainly, Langdon's deployment of such archetypal symbols correlates with Eisler's theories about the vestigial power of repressed historical material. "*The connections may be invisible,* [Langdon] often preached to his symbology class at Harvard, *but they are always there,* buried just beneath the surface."[4] Yet unlike the sacred geometry of Landon's fictional universe, Eisler's work asserts the ethical and political possibilities of an alternative social form in the present, a political eschatology rather than a fiction of millennial inheritance. The stakes of this distinction have everything to do with the prospect of outsider theory, on account of the appeal—but also the volatility—of deploying powerful ideological symbols as a medium for visionary synthesis.

Even as Langdon and Sophie Neveu encounter the (fictionally deployed) evidence for the living historicity of chalices and blades, their own partnership never quite lives up to Eisler's model of partnership societies and horizontal power structures. Their code-breaking partnership remains painfully asymmetrical, with Neveu ever playing the Watson to Langdon's Holmes.[5] Langdon does virtually all the explaining, after all, in spite of Neveu's lifelong training as a cryptographer. Even though *The Da Vinci Code* recasts the titular "chalice and the blade" of Eisler's study as a resurgent feminist and egalitarian secret at the origin of Christianity, its contemporary protagonists act as though such oppositional terms for gender difference were somehow determinative of their access to knowledge. Men are from Mars; women are from Venus.

Eisler's 1987 study, by contrast, explicitly mobilizes such appeals to deep history toward the exigencies of the contemporary political world. In place of Langdon's "preaching" about the hidden connections between symbols, that is, Eisler's recourse to ancient symbols aims to recalibrate human social behavior altogether. Invoking the salutary return of a repressed ethos of collaboration and connectivity, *The Chalice and the Blade* responds holistically to the apocalyptic ecological and geopolitical conditions of the contemporary world. In doing so, it takes up the premise of a body of spiritually and archaeologically oriented feminist writing from the 1970s and 1980s in positing the "goddess hypothesis"—namely, the notion that Neolithic cultures throughout Europe and the northern Mediterranean worshipped a mother goddess rather than the patriarchal sun gods of later antiquity (whether Islamic, Judeo-Christian, or pagan). There is, in other words, a prehistorical alternative to the destructive social relations we take for granted; it has simply been forgotten. "Gradually," Eisler explains, "a new picture of the origins and development of both civilization and religion is emerging," thanks to recent developments and discoveries in archaeology.[6] Such studies, pioneered by feminist archaeologists such as Marija Gimbutas, establish the Neolithic agrarian economy as the basis for the development of civilization. "And almost universally, those places where the first great breakthroughs in material and social technology were first made had one feature in common: the worship of the Goddess."[7]

Eisler thus distinguishes her work from the primarily sexual and bodily overtones to which Langdon ascribes her basic terms. The opposite of patriarchy or androcracy is not matriarchy, for instance, but a society of partnership she names as "gylany," describing a nonhierarchical model of social organization by fusing the Greek roots *gyn* (woman) and *andro* (man).[8] Eisler borrows from earlier archetypal theories in establishing the conceptual architecture of her 1987 study, as well as from feminist theology and, in particular, the nonlinear systems thinking or "chaos theory" of influential science writers such as Gregory Bateson, Fritjof Capra, Stephen Jay Gould, Ilya Prigogine, and Isabelle Stengers. In this regard the terms *chalice* and *blade* explicitly refer to social systems rather than the iconography of wombs and phalluses, a heuristic that enables a holistic, macrohistorical survey of the "totality" of human history. As Eisler argues early in the book, "underlying the great surface diversity of human culture are two basic models of society";[9] such basic models are neither essentially female nor essentially male, but organizational.

The Chalice and the Blade examines the evolutionary shifts throughout human history between these two models of social organization. Eisler's recourse to archetypal sexual forms is thus largely rhetorical in the sense that her theory proposes to unite rather than police the separation between men and women, the "two halves of humanity." In spite of the heteronormative binary that undergirds any such conception of "halves"—Eisler's models have little to say about same-sex relations, intersex or transitional bodies, or nonnormative genders, for instance—her model of partnership or "gylany" seeks to de-hierarchize, if not fully to eradicate, sex and gender difference as criteria for social organization. "Partnership" and "dominator" signify in turn the basic forms of two opposing sets of social orders, patterns, and "systems of configurations." Such systems, she writes, "organize the relations between the two halves of humanity [i.e., women and men] for the *totality* of a social system" according to fundamentally opposed sets of social values and technologies.[10] Like the New Age physicist Fritjof Capra, on whose work Eisler reflects, the chalice and the blade both represent paradigms of cultural value and behavior; Eisler's chalice corresponds to the holistic worldview of complementarity and nonlinear relation attributed to systems thinking, ecology, evolutionary biology, and the new physics. Capra draws on the I Ching, the ninth-century BCE Chinese "book of changes," as his model for this "new" paradigm, which combines yin and yang, the interlocking cosmic forces of masculine and feminine, rationalism and intuition, in dynamic mutual participation. The outmoded paradigm, by contrast, is represented by the rigid, mechanistic worldviews of patriarchy, as well as Newtonian physics and Cartesian philosophy; though already in decline, this system of thought continues to force its ideas on phenomena to which its methods are increasingly insufficient, yielding, as Capra puts it, "narrow perceptions of reality which are inadequate for dealing with the major problems of our time."[11]

Like Capra, Eisler not only champions the social values of the new paradigm—which she models on the chalice rather than the I Ching—but also deploys them methodologically. Her holistic "systems analysis" of human cultural change thus aspires to a radical expansion of the scale of modern historiography, which has so often been restricted to a historical record populated and recorded by men. Eisler's study instead comprehends both pre-history and women. The binary opposition between chalice and blade plays out as a transhistorical epic of methods and paradigms that asserts its feminist politics on the order of metahistorical forms and structures rather than individual bodies and selves. Championing the rights less of silenced women than of a silenced goddess culture, Eisler argues that we humans currently find ourselves in the midst of a "dominator" society whose innumerable wars, genocides, and hierarchies have scarred the earth to the point of impending nuclear and ecological disaster. "The time of the lone wolf, Capitalism, for instance, is indeed over," writes Alice Walker in a similar vein. "It cannot possibly sustain itself without gobbling up the whole."[12] This system of social configurations has remained in place for over five millennia, to the point where we have come to regard it as natural and inevitable. Yet as Eisler and Walker each insist, dominator society does not represent a victory for humankind, nor do its relations of power constitute an evolutionary advance over prehistoric partnership societies. Quite the reverse: the blade is killing us. "Be they religious or secular, modern or ancient, Eastern or Western," Eisler writes, "the basic commonality of totalitarian leaders and would-be leaders is their faith in the power of the lethal Blade as the instrument of our deliverance. A dominator future is therefore, sooner or later, almost certainly a future of global nuclear war—and the end of all of humanity's problems and aspirations."[13] Eisler's book proposes the study and promotion of an alternative set of social networks that, she claims, preceded our dominator society; in contrast to this partnership model, contemporary social relations represent a fatal and even accidental wrong turn.

The Chalice and the Blade marks something of a watershed moment in American public intellectualism, as well as a signal shift in feminist thinking of the 1980s. Whereas it retains the familiar gender binaries of early second-wave feminism, its transhistorical archetypalism was in many ways out of step with the increasingly microhistorical or poststructuralist theoretical focus of much feminist scholarship in the Anglo-American academy during the era of the culture wars. The book's epoch-spanning archetypalism seems more in line with New Age metaphysics than with leftist historiography or scholarly archaeology, in both its expanded historical frame of reference and its abstraction of "patriarchy" to an archetypal structure of power.[14] In doing so, Eisler's book signals a general turn away from the individual human subject as the site of political debate, and instead toward the networks of social and ecological relations that are organized according to such transhistorical structures of power. As I have already begun to suggest,

Eisler was certainly not alone in making this shift. Her book draws from numerous works of spiritually and archaeologically informed feminist cultural studies from the 1970s and 1980s, including writings by Paula Gunn Allen, Carol Christ, Mary Daly, Marija Gimbutas, Starhawk, Merlin Stone, Alice Walker, and others. Eisler's work is notable, too, for its recourse to systems theory in situating the goddess hypothesis in the context of dynamic political and ecological systems. Her work spans this implicit but wholly artificial divide, even as its reception marked a growing separation between "serious" historical and political thought and New Age pseudohistory.

In the context of outsider theory, *The Chalice and the Blade* is significant for the visionary, eschatological urgency of its rehabilitation of holistic thinking on a geopolitical scale. Such a project self-consciously confronts the field of social theory with methods heterogeneous to its culture war–era prerogatives, a discontinuity that becomes especially clear in its critical reception. The book's idiosyncrasy derives largely, I propose, from its explicit appeal to a popular audience in reconciling systems theory with feminist archaeology. Unlike other popularizations of the goddess hypothesis, such as Clarissa Estes's *Women Who Run with the Wolves* (1992), Monica Sjöö and Barbara Mor's *The Great Cosmic Mother: Rediscovering the Religion of the Earth* (1987), or Merlin Stone's *When God Was a Woman* (1978), Eisler's study elides the generic classifications that might render it immediately legible as, say, a work of folklore, religion, memoir, mysticism, self-help, or Jungian metapsychology. Its generic classification is as open as its project to address the "totality" of human history is holistic. The book is thus notable for the intensity and scope of its ambition and reception alike, offering a critical insight into the methodological lines of demarcation drawn by scholars and critics in the late 1980s and early 1990s, even as it sought definitively to blur them.

Though praised effusively by some critics, *The Chalice and the Blade* was lambasted by others, who belittled or dismissed it altogether as a work of New Age pseudoscience or pseudoarchaeology, an ersatz political theory based on misrepresented archaeological evidence and loose appeals to technofuturists such as Fritjof Capra, Hazel Henderson, and Alvin Toffler. This chapter studies the fate, as well as the genealogy, of Eisler's efforts to construct an inclusive vision of human evolution in the face of global catastrophe. Her book grounds its appeal for an alternative future in speculative theories about the survival of repressed archaeological and cultural knowledge; for this reason alone the book garnered criticism, as we will see in what follows. Yet *The Chalice and the Blade* is also a synthesis of other such theories, from living systems theory and feminist spiritualism to the study of countercultural phenomena and the history of myth, including archaeological fantasies and conjectures about the location of the lost city of Atlantis. Unlike Brown's *The Da Vinci Code*, however, Eisler's project seeks not to reward or induce wild interpretation but instead to allegorize the return to circulation of disavowed political possibilities: if not the "return of the Goddess," then at least a revived partnership model of social organization.[15]

Eisler is not herself an archaeologist, after all, but a synthesizer and cultural theorist. In addition to bringing together goddess discourse with chaos theory and systems theory, her work also delves into the longer history of archaeological and mythical speculation about ancient matriarchal and goddess religions, which began in the nineteenth century with works such as Johann Jakob Bachofen's *Das Mutterrecht* (1861; published in English as *Mother Right*), Jules Michelet's *La Sorcière* (1861; published in Engish as *Satanism and Witchcraft*), and Jane Ellen Harrison's *Prolegomena on the Study of Greek Religion* (1903). In spite of Eisler's tendency to invoke such work as the factual basis of her theory, any such archaeological evidence is necessarily speculative, as Eisler herself admits. The claim to speculative archaeology ultimately forms a methodological rather than evidentiary spur for her project insofar as feminist archaeology already sought to overhaul a scientific field that tended not only to be predominantly male in its personnel and predilections but also fundamentally conjectural, even fabular, in its methods. What *The Chalice and the Blade* draws from such works is a model of conjecture, even a metaphysics, derived from their proto-Freudian notions of an archaeological unconscious. The human past has, in short, been repressed, and the traumatic causes of this repression continue to haunt our present. Itself "haunted" by nineteenth-century archaeology, *The Chalice and the Blade* is ultimately a theory of such haunting. Its aim, in other words, is to open the field of social thought to its own repressed antecedents and possibilities—thereby offering, in turn, a vehicle for synthesizing the systems thinking and chaos theories of the natural sciences within social thought. As Eisler and David Loye wrote in a 1987 article, such "intervening requirements" of a new social science were necessary for establishing "a bridge from natural science to social action."[16]

Eisler's work thus differs in this key regard from the writings of a physicist such as Capra, whose own systems theory was sure to keep one foot firmly planted in the rationalist yang of physics research; in spite of his forays into mysticism and interdisciplinary synthesis, Capra never failed to assert his scientific bona fides. Eisler, while drawing on Capra's writing, instead posits an empirical field whose very claim to legitimacy is a function of the competing paradigms she uses it to measure. Even the more dubious presumptions of Eisler's theory are grounded in a broader system of methodological inferences and adaptations that constitutes her chaos theory of cultural transformation. Through Eisler's recourse to such methods we can witness, in turn, the cultural transformations that take place within the figural ecology of contemporary intellectual history, as much as within the geopolitical world to which *The Chalice and the Blade* appeals.

In the polarizing discursive climate of the United States during the era of Presidents Ronald Reagan and George H. W. Bush, such speculations took on a heightened political significance as the factuality of scholarly history—as well as the nature or even existence of anything resembling "human evolution"—became flashpoints in public and scholarly debates. *The Chalice and the Blade* was published in the midst of the culture wars of the late 1980s (the same "prehistory" toward which Dan Brown's novel directs much of its epistemological nostalgia, as we saw in chapter 3). Criticism of Eisler and other feminist and ecofeminist texts zeroed in on their capriciousness toward facts and data; broader attacks on the duplicity of feminist spirituality arrived from virtually all points on the political spectrum in a period of increasing pressure on the instrumentality and self-evidence of scholarly truth claims. From "intelligent design" to Afrocentric history, the 1980s and 1990s were awash with public and scholarly attacks on alternative historiography. On the left and the right alike, critics took aim at the latent ideological consequences of nonsensical, counterfactual claims or of totalizing theories that offered easy promises for future gain.[17] The methodological basis and textual inheritance of such counterhistories often seemed to take priority in determining the ideological stakes, as well as the popularity, of such attacks—even if the ideological lines of demarcation were fully drawn in advance. Did such histories draw from the Bible or from Charles Darwin, from G. W. F. Hegel or from Carl Jung, from Mao Zedong or from the I Ching, from Michel Foucault or from Marcus Garvey? Were its principal intellectual coordinates men (as in the previous sentence) or women? And were those women and men principally white? Such questions certainly fell upon Eisler's study and other works of holistic and spiritual feminism, though this suspicion was based less on the excesses of their methodological influences than on a broader tendency to point out their factual shortcomings.

Despite its popularity in the public sphere, Eisler's study—and the broader surge in "goddess" religion and feminist spirituality in which it took part—has since fallen into relative obscurity as a late flowering of New Age thinking—as well as, perhaps, a victim of the culture wars. *The Chalice and the Blade* has largely been marginalized as a kind of outsider theory in the most dismissive of senses, disparaged as an outmoded or alien idiosyncrasy within feminist theory and sociopolitical analysis alike. Regardless of whether one considers such work to be legitimate or misguided, however, its methods are decidedly out of step with both positivist and dialectical, neo-Marxian historiography. *The Chalice and the Blade* proposes an interference within the discursive commonplaces of contemporary historiography and social theory; however pressing its apocalypticism may be—or may remain today, thirty years after its publication—the book emphatically foregrounds its untimeliness in stressing both its "inherited" speculations about prehistoric goddess cultures and its recourse to a sweeping, macrohistorical analysis of social systems over the entirety of human history.

Such untimeliness is constitutive, moreover, of the very field of inquiry it might otherwise seem to compromise: Eisler's work was out of step with contemporary archaeological methods on account of the *urgency* of being out of step. Rather than seeking to "trouble" political and ideological formations in a manner consistent with the emergent left wing of academic cultural theory (particularly in the work of Judith Butler and Slavoj Žižek), or with the dogged right-wing culture warriors of the late 1980s, Eisler's "cultural transformation theory" was troublesome, even alien, with regard to contemporary epistemological formations. The alleged methodological sloppiness of goddess theory, along with its speculative recourse to historical and archaeological evidence, is less its failing than its guiding insight and even, perhaps, its fundamental ambition. Rather than seeking refuge in New Age utopianism and claims to self-improvement, Eisler's study and others like it locate the search for alternatives to the political and ecological disasters of the modern world in the pressing need for new—or very old—systems of knowledge, ethics, and belief that run counter to the contemporary epistemic regime. As a number of recent scholars have begun to suggest, moreover, Eisler's recourse to systems thinking and attention to ecological and social relations on a global scale can be seen as prescient and worthy of serious reconsideration in an era of impending ecological disaster, as Eisler herself anticipated in 1987.[18] *The Chalice and the Blade* has proven easy to dismiss, but as Eisler reminds us, our imperatives for doing so might lay at the very heart of all our woe.

SPECULATIVE ARCHAEOLOGY

"At the very dawn of religion," writes the art historian Merlin Stone in 1978, "God was a woman. Do you remember?"[19] Before there was a god, there was a goddess: the deity of hearth and home, birth and life, which preceded the warlike Olympians and jealous creator gods of antiquity. How else to account for the figurines that regularly turn up at Neolithic excavation sites throughout the world, from the Venus of Willendorf (discovered in Austria in 1908) to the Orkney Venus (discovered in Scotland in 2003)? The notion that a prehistoric mother goddess–worshiping society existed before the onset of patriarchy (or "dominator" society) is a hypothesis necessarily based on an incomplete or even nonexistent historical record. The ancient and the contemporary thus converge as mutual restrictions on the knowability of prehistory. Do you remember?

The evidentiary challenge faced by proponents of the goddess hypothesis is thus twofold. As Eisler puts it early in *The Chalice and the Blade*, "Prehistory is like a giant jigsaw puzzle with more than half its pieces destroyed or lost. It is impossible to reconstruct completely." The reason for this is not only the relative scarcity of evidence but also the ideological vantage point from which scholars attempting any such reconstruction approach the problem. "The greatest obstacle to the accurate reconstruction of prehistory is not that we are lacking so many pieces; it is that the prevailing paradigm makes it so hard to accurately interpret the pieces we have and to project the real pattern into which they fit."[20] The problem of prehistory is both a hermeneutic one and, by extension, an ideological one: the "prevailing paradigm"—according to which Neolithic prehistory precedes "history" as its unknown or unknowable past—necessarily forms the negative condition of any attempt at interpretation. For Eisler, this "prevailing paradigm" is the contemporary incarnation of the blade itself, an ideology of domination that conditions what we do and do not learn about the history of human civilization, and which establishes the methods and priorities through which we determine the admissible content of the archaeological record. The process of reclamation thus entails a double methodological challenge, whereby one must not only determine the evidentiary "puzzle pieces" but also interrogate the contemporary paradigms that mediate how we assimilate evidence into the "jigsaw puzzle" framework. History, by this logic, comes to reckon with its own fundamental incompleteness. No longer the sovereign record of human civilization, it becomes the medium according to which we measure basic conceptions of what is known and unknown, knowable and unknowable, about the past. And it thus is subject, in turn, to seismic shifts as well as striking counterfactual reversals.

Eisler's comparison of prehistory to a jigsaw puzzle itself has a history. Adapted from a remark by Arthur Basham in his 1954 study *The Wonder That Was India*, the statement has become a historiographical commonplace, a rhetorical device for acknowledging the epistemological challenges presented by the gaps in the ancient historical record. Not only is a comprehensive understanding of the past impossible, but in attempting to reconstruct it we also necessarily resort to speculation; Basham refers to this as "controlled imagination."[21] Such a reckoning mitigates the direct appeal to poetic truth of folktales, fables, and myths characteristic of certain nineteenth-century historiographies; a jigsaw puzzle bears a more determined framework of gaps and cuts, after all, than an inherited set of local legends. The jigsaw puzzle becomes all the more difficult to reconstruct, however, when chronicling the history of women, as the classical scholar Sarah Pomeroy noted in a land-mark 1975 study: "In ancient history there are few certainties. We are trying to assemble a puzzle with many pieces missing. In a period when the history of men is obscure, it naturally follows that the documentation for women's lives is even more fragmented."[22] Under the patriarchal conditions of the clas-sical age, there were simply fewer records kept of the lives of women than of the lives of men; this scarcity has been compounded over time, in turn, by the relative lack of study dedicated to redressing it. Women's history thus looks all the more speculative, all the more subject to the uncertainties of the archaeological jigsaw puzzle.

Pomeroy's solution to this fragmentary condition is, notably, to intro-duce a methodological shift that involves recognizing and even naturalizing the inevitable disagreements that arise when scholars reconstruct the history of women in antiquity on the basis of limited documentation. Instead of pre-suming that the conclusions derived from fragmentary information should be either categorically accepted or categorically rejected, she acknowledges the "various interpretations of scholars" and seeks to "indicate reasons for the divergence in opinion."[23] Given that the very existence of mother goddesses in prehistory has been contested by scholars, Pomeroy seeks neither to prove that such religions existed nor to assert that a matriarchal or egalitarian "chal-ice" society existed prior to classical patriarchy. She instead assesses the ideological stakes of prevailing and emerging paradigms for interpretation. The mother goddess theory offers, for instance, a convenient explanation for a number of evidentiary questions—such as why there are so many more extant Neolithic female figurines than male figurines. It also offers an at-tractive and emotionally resonant theory of female dominance, a counter-hegemonic model of political possibility. For Pomeroy, such speculation necessarily has its limits. To use goddess theory as a way to draw specific conclusions about the social structure of Neolithic societies—particularly regarding the high status of human females during this period—would, she writes, be "foolhardy."[24] Archaeological speculation about women in antiq-uity (or prehistory) may be inevitable, but it should be deployed judiciously.

The study of women in archaic societies is no less pressing a concern for archaeology, Pomeroy maintains. In spite of her assertions about the limits of reconstructing the "jigsaw puzzle" of prehistory, Pomeroy's aim is hardly to disqualify the project or, for that matter, to admit defeat. On the contrary: as a major feminist contribution to the human sciences, her work takes issue with prevailing paradigms of contemporary historiography that might dismiss or exclude such hypotheses about women from their thinking. By maintaining the existence of a puzzle to be solved, however incompletely, Pomeroy stresses the importance of studying the imperfect traces of ancient women's lives and, perhaps even more significantly, also relativizes any contemporary paradigm that would categorically ignore or dismiss such evidence. "It is as foolish to postulate masculine dominance in prehistory," she writes, "as to postulate female dominance."[25] The unknowability of female prehistory should never preclude its study, however inconclusive, or emotionally charged, or politically resonant such studies might be. And whereas the scarcity of definitive evidence renders the archaeologist's project oddly consistent with poststructuralist "archaeologies of knowledge" that dwell on discursive formations and institutional structures of knowledge, Pomeroy stresses the importance of pursuing the search for positive evidence by and about women. As the archaeologist Margaret Ehrenberg put it fourteen years later in 1989, "The degree of social and political power held by women in prehistoric societies is a subject to which little attention has as yet been paid by archaeologists, although archaeological evidence may be able to provide indications of wealth and status, and hence of the degree of social stratification within a society. The origin of social hierarchies is a key topic within current archaeology, and, together with analysis of the position of women within the system, it also plays a major part in feminist theories."[26] For Ehrenberg and Pomeroy alike, the study of women in archaic societies—not to mention the participation of women researchers in the fields of archaeology and cultural anthropology—is a fundamental intellectual and scholarly priority.

For such archaeologists, the exigency for studying Neolithic and preclassical women thus hinges on the active "discursive formations" and institutional conditions of the scholarly field rather than on the evidentiary results of their investigations alone. The study of women in prehistoric cultures is important regardless of whether or not matriarchy (or "partnership" societies) preceded patriarchy. The point is not to supplant the unknowability of ancient history or prehistory with plausible fantasies, but to confront the conditions of knowability and unknowability in pursuing the investigation. Eisler inverts this proposition, we might say: in *The Chalice and the Blade*, she grounds the evidentiary credibility of the goddess hypothesis on the political credibility—and methodological subtlety—of feminist archaeology. What is a "key topic" in Ehrenberg's and Pomeroy's estimation of the field becomes a virtual premise in Eisler's work, a jigsaw puzzle picturing the origin of social hierarchies that appears far more complete.

However quick she might be to formalize such degrees of social stratification in her "chalice" and "blade" heuristics, Eisler is anything but foolhardy in her presumptions about the jigsaw puzzle of prehistory. Taking up Pomeroy's methodological justification for investigating the roles of women in prehistoric cultural systems, Eisler's project is to leverage its heuristic "reality" toward a paradigm shift in contemporary thinking about cultural transformation. The chalice is a blind spot in the archaeological and historical record, a symptom of its capacity for disavowal. Her inversion of Ehrenberg's and Pomeroy's judiciousness is thus proleptic: rather than framing the study of ancient or prehistoric women as a "topic" important to both archaeologists and feminists, Eisler posits the reconstructed prehistory as the very object cause for their research. The violent eclipse of matriarchal societies by dominator societies at the dawn of human history is the origin of the "current paradigm" against which feminist science must struggle. In making this claim, Eisler thereby challenges the self-evidence of the "prevailing paradigm" by introducing another   partnership, chalice, synthesis, living system—as both evidence and method at once. Like other systems theorists, Eisler proposes that the models and methods one uses to describe reality *and that reality itself* are simultaneously in flux because they are complementary phenomena, each leaving its impression upon the other. Such a model for cultural transformation strays radically from the causal principles of social change presumed by most contemporary scholars and pundits. In place of rising and falling empires, revolutions, market competition, and other such conflicts and upheavals, Eisler instead posits the far more sweeping temporal scale of human cultural evolution over five millennia. She does so less as a rhetorical sleight of hand for disparaging academia or duping readers, I maintain, than as a methodological provocation. Eisler seeks to introduce a principle of error within both history and historiography alike. Not only does she depict the "error" of patriarchy as an evolutionary false step, but in doing so she also illustrates the broader, stochastic processes of cultural transformation to which, we will see, she refers throughout her study as the very principle for false steps and restitutions alike. What may save us is, in other words, a kind of error as well.

Eisler's recourse to prehistory as the model for a possible future is significant for its very discontinuity with contemporary historiography. In this regard, Eisler's paradigm shift is far more outlandish than even her critics might admit. In *The Chalice and the Blade* she confronts her readers with an alternate reality wherein both historical judgment and the errancies of cultural transformation start to look very different from what they have come to expect. "Like travelers through a time warp," she writes, "we have, through archaeological discoveries, journeyed into a different reality. On the other side we found not the brutal stereotypes of an eternally depraved 'human nature' but amazing vistas of possibilities for a better life. We saw how in the early days of civilization our cultural evolution was truncated and then completely turned around. We saw how when our social and technological evolution resumed it was in a different direction. But we also saw how the old roots of civilization were never eradicated."[27] Eisler's "different reality" refers at once to the "vistas of possibilities" to which it opened up and to the means by which one can witness them in old roots. Her time warp amounts to a methodological gesture whose relationship to goddess archaeology and other feminist alternative historiographies has less to do with the status of its truth claims than with the alien gesture itself. As in *The Da Vinci Code*, moreover, this alien gesture is founded on the disclosure of a repressed archaeological past; its "different reality" is the result of an uncanny return rather than a purely invented or otherworldly form.

Such ideas about long-repressed historical memories are not unfamiliar in themselves; the task of remembering when God was a woman has a history of its own. Indeed, one of the key reference points in Eisler's prehistoric futurism is Johann Jakob Bachofen's 1861 study of archaic matriarchies, a work that lays out the basic methodological terrain for a speculative historiography based on fragments and myths. Like Sigmund Freud, whose psychoanalytic methods he anticipates, Bachofen proposes nothing less than a Copernican shift in our approach to historical knowledge. Rather than deducing from the known, or inducing from discrete, verifiable facts, we must instead proceed from the unknown. "An unknown world opens before our eyes," writes the Swiss antiquarian and philologist in the introduction to his volume *Mother Right*, "and the more we learn of it, the stranger it seems." In venturing forth into the "virgin territory" of preclassical ancient times, Bachofen alerts his readers to a matriarchal world alien to the imperial nation-states "we commonly associate with the glory of the ancient world." The matriarchal organization of such cultures "seems strange in the light not only of modern but also of classical ideas. And the more primitive way of life to which it pertains, from which it arose, and through which alone it can be explained, seems very strange beside the Hellenic."[28] Drawing from Hesiod and Herodotus, Bachofen locates matriarchy as a phase in cultural development—albeit a "primitive" one—that preceded patriarchy and began to decline only with the "victorious" development of patriarchy as a cultural system. Unlike the "eternal feminine" [*Ewig-Weibliche*] of Johann Wolfgang von Goethe's *Faust, Part II* (1832), which locates motherhood as a transhistorical principle akin to the Gnostic *Sophia*, Bachofen's *Mother Right* outlines a social system, at once a "paradigm" and a system of governance.

The idea of motherhood, Bachofen explains, "produces a universal fraternity among all men, which dies with the development of paternity." It possesses, therefore, a discrete set of sociopolitical and metaphysical characteristics. As the more primordial form of human social organization, the matrilineal family is material rather than spiritual in character: "Obedient in all things to the laws of physical existence, [such cultures] fasten their eyes upon the earth, setting the chthonian powers over the power of uranian light. . . . In a wholly material sense they devote themselves to the embellishment of material existence, to the . . . practical virtues."[29] Sounding a bit like a nondialectical Georges Bataille, Bachofen links matriarchy with the pre-Olympian gods of the earth and the underworld; yet even in metaphysical form it is a belief system connected to the elements of "material existence," which he naturalizes as an essential characteristic of femininity. In addition to concentrating on agriculture and the erection of walls, such matrifocal cultures were dedicated in particular to the generative powers of the womb: "Every woman's womb," he writes, is "the mortal image of the earth mother Demeter, [and] will give brothers and sisters until the day when the development of the paternal system dissolves the undifferentiated unity of the mass and introduces a principle of articulation."[30] For all its universalizing claims about the inherent connections between wombs and walls, mothers and material existence, Bachofen's theory insists on the strangeness of such "mortal images." The advance from primitive matriarchy to patriarchy is inevitable—Bachofen, unlike Eisler, is hardly proposing a *return* to undifferentiated unity—but it is also tragic, a loss of primordial innocence. In portraying the essential fragility of this primordial stage in human cultural development, soon to be extinguished under the heavy tread of patriarchy, Bachofen's own interests have less to do with feminism than with the possibilities of historical knowledge.

Like Bachofen's French contemporary Jules Michelet, whose fabular historiography of witchcraft, *La Sorcière,* likewise furnished feminist thinkers with a narrative (however imperfect) of repression and uncanny return, Bachofen championed myth as a form of historical evidence. What might appear to be pseudohistory or imaginative fancy was, for such historians, a legitimate medium for the evidentiary retrieval of repressed, vestigial cultural memory, as well as a "living expression" of that repression. Anticipating Eisler's discussions about "prevailing paradigms," Bachofen justifies the use of myth as a viable medium for historical knowledge because it bears the impression of the mythmakers who disguised and modified it according to their own cultural values. Myth is a record not only of the repressed past but also of the repression itself. Beginning with Herodotus's account of matrilineal inheritance of the Lycian people, he advocates the "mythical tradition" as an "authentic, independent record of the primordial age" that proves that "mother right prevailed in Lycia" as well as in the archaic phase of culture more generally. The basis of this authenticity was, ironically, patriarchy rather than matriarchy: the story of Laodamia's hereditary priority over her brothers in the succession of Lycian kings can serve proleptically as evidence for the authenticity of myth, Bachofen argues, because the preferential treatment of a daughter was unimaginable—and thus impossible to fabricate—within Hellenic thought in the age of Herodotus. As he writes, anticipating the later recourse to puzzles as a metaphor for Neolithic archaeology,

> The older system represented an utter puzzle to the patriarchal mind, which consequently could not have conceived any part of it. Hellenic thought could not possibly have fabricated Laodamia's priority, for it is in diametric opposition to such a conception. The same is true of the innumerable vestiges of matriarchal form woven into the prehistory of all ancient peoples—not excluding Athens and Rome, two most resolute advocates of paternity. The thinking and literature of any period unconsciously follows the laws of its life form. So great is the power of such laws that the natural tendency is always to set the new imprint on the divergent features of former times.[31]

In his proto-Freudian delineation of an archaeological unconscious, Bachofen justifies the recourse to mythic evidence through the very outlandishness of the traces of prior cultures that appear vestigially within it. Myths are reliable insofar as they are alien; their value lies in their incommensurability with the "laws" of the age that records them as myth. This suggests in turn that such myths also offer a living expression of the transformations imposed by later ideas. He notes, "Since the changes [to a myth] usually result from the unconscious action of the new ideas, and only in exceptional cases from conscious hostility to the old, the legend becomes in its transformation a living expression of the stages of a people's development, and for a skillful observer, a faithful reflection of all the periods in the life of that people."[32] Such ideas were taken up by some of the most influential popularizers of myth—and matriarchal goddesses—in the nineteenth and twentieth centuries, such as Joseph Campbell, James George Frazer, Joselyn Gage, Robert Graves,

E. O. James, and Erich Neumann, not to mention Friedrich Engels, Sigmund Freud, and Carl Jung, who likewise considered ancient myths to represent the rituals of earlier civilizations in disguised, vestigial form.

Though hardly a Freudian thinker, Eisler nonetheless upholds the basic Freudian consequences of Bachofen's premise—namely, that the uncanny strangeness of "mother right" is itself a product of historical repression, exercised so thoroughly as to defamiliarize women and "practical virtues" even in our current ideological proclivities. More dramatically, the repressed knowledge is never fully eradicated, but leaves an indelible impression on the very mechanism that erases it. This knowledge thus has the tendency to return in disguised or accidental forms, as Eisler demonstrates in a survey of "gylanic" irruptions or accidents throughout the ages, from the practice of witchcraft to the Nag Hammadi discovery. Even the neologism "gylanic" bears its own uncanny or at least unfamiliar impression of the partnership society it names. The conditions cited by Bachofen as alien and unfamiliar become for Eisler, more than a century later, a perfectly natural conclusion: Eisler's "time warp" disorients us in our contemporary coordinates in order to recognize anew the buried "old roots" of archaic civilizations that occasionally flare up, as if at random, throughout recorded history. For Eisler, Bachofen's uncanny archaeology anticipates a redemptive return of the repressed, a return that registers not only in evidentiary form but also in apocalyptic portent. Eisler cites the discovery of the Gnostic Gospels at Nag Hammadi as a key example of such a return: the buried codices testify to the systematic repression of partnership-oriented Gnostic material by the orthodox dominator society that labeled Gnosticism a heresy—a systematic repression later overturned by a random, chance occurrence. Such uncanny returns—and for Eisler the instances were numerous—testify to the immanence, as well as the exigency, of a paradigm shift.

Riane Eisler's alien archaeology thus pursues a far more literal set of conclusions than Bachofen's *Mother Right* and its twentieth-century analogues. Beyond the procedural challenges of reconstructing the jigsaw puzzle of prehistory, the ballast of knowledge at stake in this recovery project confronts us symptomatically, from all angles, with the psychopathology of everyday life in the contemporary world. Because we are not accustomed to looking at history in terms of partnership and dominator models, their profound effects remain difficult to see. We must instead turn to myth, Eisler argues, as a corroborating source for the change in our cultural evolution that took place roughly five thousand years ago. This source is not new, she reminds us: "In fact, it is something we already know, something long implanted within our minds: the storehouse of the sacred, secular, and scientific mythology of Western civilization, which can only now be seen to reveal the reality of an earlier and better past."[33] This is how something so alien can seem so completely natural and familiar. Do you remember?

For Eisler, the jigsaw puzzle of prehistory constitutes an archive of social forms, a kind of Gnostic Gospel of its own that testifies to alternative political and spiritual realities that have been largely, albeit incompletely, obliterated. Myth thus becomes a medium for both historical knowledge and active ideological conflict. Unlike some spiritually oriented feminists, who sought a "return of the goddess" by means of largely metaphysical or metaphorical quests, Eisler's "cultural transformation theory" recognizes this project as an explicitly ideological one. It bears, that is, on prevailing paradigms of critical judgment and political belief, as contemporary iterations of the organizational forms designated by "chalice" and "blade." Such paradigms are themselves a product of the cataclysmic change Eisler describes, whose effects they serve to naturalize as scientific givens, and whose causes and alternatives they repress and trivialize as pseudoarchaeology or utopian feminist mumbo jumbo. For Eisler, the return of the repressed thus demands active intervention, a manipulation of unconscious processes on account of the sheer scale of their operation. As she writes near the conclusion of *The Chalice and the Blade*,

> Often unconsciously, the process of unraveling and reweaving the
> fabric of our mythical tapestry into more gylanic patterns—in which
> "masculine" virtues such as "the conquest of nature" are no longer
> idealized—is in fact already well under way. What is still lacking is
> the "critical mass" of new images and myths that is required for this
> actualization by a sufficient number of people.[34]

Shifting her metaphorical language from jigsaw puzzles to textile manufactory, Eisler rewrites the fragmentation and loss of prehistorical knowledge as an immediate political task rather than a historiological problem. The value of myth lies not only in its capacity to remember but also in its active capacity to forget. The "return" of the chalice or the goddess amounts to an unraveling of the "tapestry" of dominant ideological forms, which can then be rewoven anew. The project begins, moreover, on the terrain of method, the ideological basis of the very way we think. Eisler draws here from ideas about the recourse to myth as textile work developed throughout the 1970s by a number of feminist thinkers, particularly by the feminist theologian Mary Daly. "Absorbed in Spinning," Daly writes in 1978, "in the ludic celebration which is both work and play, Spinsters span the dichotomies of false consciousness and break its mindbinding combinations."[35]

Eisler's metaphorical language likewise adopts the terminology of so-called women's work, itself a challenge to the tendency to trivialize domestic labor and feminism alike as care work rather than "serious" political thought. *The Chalice and the Blade* rejects this very hierarchy as an effect of the dominator ideology. The sphere of domestic and sexual relations is bound to the sphere of social and political relations by means of the organizational paradigms that form the titular opposition of Eisler's study. One of the book's principal aims is thus to disarticulate the prevailing paradigm that enforces and naturalizes this division of political and domestic labor, a tendency to which many of even the most revolutionary modern political movements have succumbed. "During the nineteenth and into the twentieth century," she writes, naming Leon Trotsky's late observation about the failure of communism to question patriarchy, "other modern humanist ideologies—abolitionism, pacifism, anarchism, anticolonialism, environmentalism—also emerged. But like the proverbial blind man describing the elephant, they each described different manifestations of the androcratic monster as the totality of the problem. At the same time, they failed to address the fact that at its heart lies a male-dominator, female-dominated model of the human species."[36] Eisler's rejoinder to such blindness is to discuss cultural transformation and weaving in the same breath. But there's more to it than mere rhetoric: her project demands reweaving as well as unraveling, after all, suggesting the extent to which her recourse to weaving and spinning begins to both perform and conceptualize the ideological work proposed in the book.

The complementary tasks of disarticulation and rearticulation—that is, the processes of "unraveling" contemporary ideological forms, denaturalizing and delegitimating their hegemonic function, and of "reweaving" their strands to inaugurate a new "critical mass" of ethical and sustainable ideologies—is in fact consistent with the social theory of leftist thinkers such as Ernesto Laclau and Chantal Mouffe, who in *Hegemony and Socialist Strategy* (1983) take issue with the agonism of the political Left, whose revolutionary disarticulation of dominant ideological formations often fails to accommodate their own ready tendency to rearticulate themselves as "prevailing paradigms" in turn.[37] We see here, too, the appeal of Bachofen's proto-Freudian mythic prehistory: the alien encounter with a "different reality" opens up the possibility, as well as the urgency, of disarticulating and rethinking the orthodoxies of contemporary political beliefs and theories. At the same time, the repressed familiarity of the chalice remains a methodological insistence, at once a storehouse of archaic social forms and an imperative for rearticulation. This latter insistence would ultimately prove to be the most contentious aspect of Eisler's book, which was criticized as much for the ersatz politics of its utopian-apocalyptic approach to cultural transformation, as for the conjectural nature of its evidence. Eisler's claims, to some, were neither original nor revolutionary—which, I propose, was precisely the point. Much as her metaphors of unraveling and reweaving seek to synthesize feminist and leftist discourse, her cultural transformation theory fuses speculative archaeology with ecological systems thinking in a manner that troubled critical and political ideas about historical cause and effect throughout the decades of the culture wars.

Eisler's chaos theory of cultural transformation posits, as we have seen, that the shift from partnership to dominator societies was an evolutionary wrong turn that nonetheless offers a model for its restitution. The prehistoric disaster of the blade thus directly prefigures our own, to the extent that Eisler describes the ravages of Bronze Age invaders in the present tense. "As prehistoric excavations evidence," she writes, "the archaeological landscape of Old Europe is transformed. Not only do we find increasing signs of physical destruction and cultural regression in the wake of each wave of invasions; the direction of cultural history is also profoundly altered."[38] The destruction of millennial traditions brought about by a shift from partnership to dominator models of social organization was, Eisler argues, "a punctuated equilibrium," an aberration—triggered by events that were relatively sudden and, at the time, unpredictable.[39] Eisler draws from numerous systems thinkers to characterize cultural transformation as a dynamic and interrelated set of self-organizing processes that, as Capra summarizes, exhibit most of the phenomena characteristic of organic life, including the complementary processes, on the one hand, of "self-renewal, healing, homeostasis, and adaptation" and, on the other hand, of "self-transformation and self-transcendence."[40] The shift from chalice to blade was the cataclysmic result of the latter process of self-transcendence. "Systems transformations arrive at critical 'bifurcation points,'" Eisler writes, citing the thermodynamics-based work of Ilya Prigogine and Isabelle Stengers, "when 'the system can 'choose' between or among more than one possible future.'"[41]

The unsettling of "gylanic" equilibrium or near equilibrium by "peripheral isolates" such as the Bronze Age invaders could occur, Eisler writes, because the interventions took place at precisely such a bifurcation point.[42] Contemporary human civilization has now reached another such bifurcation point: "Human evolution is now at a crossroads. Stripped to its essentials, the central human task is how to organize society to promote the survival of our species and the development of our unique potentials."[43] *The Chalice and the Blade* colors this task with the poignancy of lost Neolithic societies, but it also directs contemporary efforts according to the model of systemic transformation it proposes. While invoking chance and complexity as historical motive forces, Eisler nonetheless sides with technofuturist thinkers in claiming that the consolidation of major changes in human systems comes down to a matter of choice, albeit a "choice" exercised by collective systems rather than by individual human actors. Eisler believes, in other words, that we can avert destruction—if we heed the claims of archaeological speculation and accumulate the peripheral isolates of partnership as the seeds of a new hegemony.

POSTMODERN FARCE

As a work of "cultural transformation theory" seeking to demonstrate and redress how human society made a wrong turn in shifting from a (prehistoric) partnership model to a (historical) dominator model, Riane Eisler's *The Chalice and the Blade* was hailed by the archaeologist Ashley Montagu as "the most important book since Darwin's *Origin of Species*," an encomium cited on the book's front cover. For in opposition to Darwin's evolutionary model of natural selection—and especially its dominator-like bowdlerization as "the survival of the fittest"—Eisler's book targets the ecological and political unsustainability of competition and domination, offering its feminist countermodel of ecological partnership as the last, best hope for human survival on the planet. As a work of historical and archaeological proposition, by contrast, the book received no shortage of criticism, some of it as exaggerated in hostility as Montagu's statement was in praise. In her review for the *New York Times Book Review*, for instance, the neoconservative historian Elizabeth Fox-Genovese accuses Eisler of a "dubious reading of history and a perhaps more dubious reading of human nature." The book "chronicles the sweep of human history in the manner of a morality play," Fox-Genovese explains, to the extent that "inconvenient details do not figure prominently in her account." Passing lightly over changing social and economic systems, Eisler "does not seem to notice that, whether we find it unpalatable or not, violent conflict has historically been midwife to some of the greatest leaps toward freedom from oppression." Ultimately comparing the book (unfavorably) to the utopian speculations of science fiction, Fox-Genovese dismisses *The Chalice and the Blade* as both politically quietist and historically inaccurate. In her recourse to "Manichean" terms, Eisler is a bad dialectician: her efforts to forge a totalizing system are fundamentally at odds with the implicit Hegelianism behind Fox-Genovese's claim that true historical change is unimaginable without violence, "whether we find it unpalatable or not."[44]

Many of the sharpest dismissals of *The Chalice and the Blade* came from historians and feminist writers who confronted its reliance on questionable archaeological evidence and its recourse to largely outdated works of historical scholarship. But as Fox-Genovese suggests, implicit within such criticism lies a broader rejection of Eisler's holistic—rather than positivist, dialectical, or pragmatist—mode of macrohistorical speculation. By relegating "dominator" societies to a historical form rather than to a historical process, as in Hegelian and Marxist philosophies of history, Eisler opens historical change to the forces of chance, error, and contingency that enabled dominator societies to establish their foothold in the first place. Her model for salutary cultural transformation is no less random: is it possible to save the world merely by saying so? Rather than presuming that history progresses through opposition and conflict—the very notion of "progress" indicating that chance could never fully account for true historical change—Eisler's book merely seeks to distinguish "human evolution" from history. It thereby offers few concrete propositions for instrumentalizing transformation, instead appealing to the accumulation of "peripheral isolates" as the virtually accidental motor for social change, a concept drawn from Niles Eldredge and Stephen Jay Gould's 1972 study of "punctuated equilibria" in evolutionary biology.[45] Progress, by this logic, has less to do with political agency than with mere appeal to a higher phase of human development, which Eisler posits as a return to the developmental path we left behind in abandoning the partnership society of the chalice. For its critics, *The Chalice and the Blade* thus amounted to a theory purged of any recognizable recourse to practice beyond the metaphorics of spinning, weaving, and jigsaw puzzles.

As the basis for this theory, Eisler's understanding of prehistory was perhaps the greatest source of consternation for opponents of her work. One of her more strident critics is the religious scholar Cynthia Eller, herself the author of an earlier study of the feminist spirituality movement entitled *Living in the Lap of the Goddess* (1993). In *The Myth of Matriarchal Prehistory* (2000), Eller launches a sustained attack on the "goddess myth" of which Eisler's book remains a landmark popular exemplar, taking on such works for their blindness in "the face of evidence that challenges its veracity," a reliance on myth, and even the pseudoscience that postures as documented fact; this, as a result, "leaves feminists open to charges of vacuousness and irrelevance that we can not afford to court."[46] For Eller, the ideas embedded in the myth of matriarchal prehistory are, moreover, "neither original nor revolutionary" insofar as they draw on works by Bachofen, James, and other earlier studies that proposed a matriarchal prehistory under the premise that ancient patriarchy constituted an evolutionary *advance* over primitive mother cults. Thus, the inherited terms of "the myth of matriarchal prehistory" have not only been used to serve patriarchal interests, but the gendered stereotypes on which they rest also "persistently work to flatten out differences among women; to exaggerate differences between women and men; and to hand women an identity that is symbolic, timeless, and archetypal, instead of giving them the freedom to craft identities that suit their individual temperaments, skills, preferences, and moral and political commitments."[47] Books such as *The Chalice and the Blade* are thus wrong twice over: both factually erroneous and ideologically suspect.

As a historical premise the appeal to goddess worship is, for Eller, likewise hopelessly backward, and not simply on account of the claim that it antedates patriarchy. In spite of the feminist notion that matrifocal or "gylanic" Neolithic societies featured "elder women or heads of clans [who] administered the production and distribution of the fruits of the earth, which were seen as belonging to all members of the group,"[48] Eller argues that such depictions enforce gender binaries that yoke women to their traditional, essentializing identification with the hearth, the family, and the soil. Works such as *The Chalice and the Blade* may "grope around for alternative terms (never very successfully) [and] hedge themselves about with disclaimers," but they ultimately "wade right back into the morass of gender stereotypes they profess some interest in escaping."[49] Here, as in Fox-Genovese's criticism, we likewise find a broader methodological rejection of Eisler's claims beyond the charge of counterfactual historiography alone. In Eller's case, the problem lies in the extent to which Eisler's feminist "alternative" amounts to an accidental *inheritance* of ideological domination through the adoption of an essentially patriarchal, as well as paternalistic and patronizing, "myth of matriarchal prehistory."

Eller's complaint that *The Chalice and the Blade* and other forms of goddess feminism uphold "traditional, essentializing identification[s]" instead of giving women "the freedom to craft identities that suit their individual temperaments" ventriloquizes a common neoliberal critique of organized social movements more broadly, which "rob" individuals of their freedom in the name of a more formalized horizon of social change.[50] Eller's anxiety over an "embarrassing" susceptibility to wish fulfillment and a coercive faith in dodgy evidence also resembles other culture war–era concerns.

The most dismissive critiques of Eisler's book, as well as of the spiritual feminisms, gaia hypotheses, and systems theories from which it drew, ultimately came from the scholarly Left. For Marxist critics, the problem with a book like *The Chalice and the Blade* was less its shaky evidence (often generalized as a failing of the goddess movement during the culture wars), or even its archetypalism, than its occultation of socioeconomic cause and effect. Eisler's leftist critics viewed her mythohistorical cultural transformation theory as an ideological stand-in for the real work of socioeconomic transformation. Whereas archaeologists and historians had a problem with credibility, for many other feminists the problem lay in the conclusions to which such work leapt, an essentialism that likewise eliminated "intervening arguments" about the complexities of gender and social formations. This is a position taken up by critics of the goddess hypothesis more broadly. In her 1987 book *Is the Future Female?*, for instance, the Australian socialist Lynn Segal notes her disturbance at the "apocalyptic feminism" that emerged as "the public face of feminism in the eighties," which "portrays a Manichean struggle between female virtue and male vice, with ensuing catastrophe and doom unless 'female' morality and values prevail."[51] The problem, for Segal, as for many others, is that "the evidence that both 'masculinity' and 'femininity' are socially constructed and variably expressed across class, ethnic, regional and national groupings, drops out of such feminist thinking."[52] Such Manichean dualism was not only reductive in its understanding of gender, but its reductivism also cartooned the complexity of real social forces.

In *Matriarchs, Goddesses, and Images of God* (1989), the Austrian Marxist theologian Suzanne Heine makes a similar critique of goddess spirituality. Rather than making comparisons with a better past in order to "prove" inequality, the point should be to find concrete strategies for changing the world. "The decisive factor, Heine writes, "is what women want and what they are prepared to do in order to accept a position of strength and equality." Noting how Bachofen's work has been adopted on the far left (such as by Friedrich Engels, who discusses *Mother Right* in *The Origin of the Family, Private Property, and the State*) and the far right (as in the Third Reich's myth of motherhood), Heine argues that "it is no loss to the cause of women to bid farewell to the retrospective utopia of a matriarchal primal period."[53] The notion of matriarchy is a shortcut in thought that envisions social change on the basis of inherited models rather than a critical engagement with sociopolitical reality.

Viewed within the context of the culture wars, the question of whether *The Chalice and the Blade* and other works of spiritual feminism were allegories or fantasies of cultural transformation was indeed a pressing one. The methodological invention—or inheritance—of speculative archaeology posed a fundamental problem, at once potentially "embarrassing" to the truth claims of feminism and, more substantively, ideologically coercive in its recourse to cultural transformation through attractive propositions alone, fantasies of belief. It is instructive to consider Eisler's work in light of the contemporary shift in feminist theory away from spirituality and identity politics during this period, which gave way instead to more systematic discursive analyses characterized by Judith Butler's *Gender Trouble*, published in 1989, and Donna Haraway's *Simians, Cyborgs, and Women*, published in 1990. In this context, the "archaeology of knowledge" referred more to the work of Michel Foucault and Sandra Harding than to Johann Jakob Bachofen or Marija Gimbutas—that is, to a "practice of objectivity that privileges contestation, deconstruction, passionate construction, webbed connections, and hope for transformation of systems of knowledge and ways of seeing," as Haraway put it, rather than to the revelation of evidentiary treasures buried beneath the sands of time.[54] Eisler's "cultural transformation" approach to social systems (and the status of goddess myths more generally) suddenly looked all the more alien in its retrospeculation about prehistoric models of social organization, as opposed to the performative sphere of contemporary discourse on which Butler set her sights.

In this light, the problem with *The Chalice and the Blade* was thus that its recourse to speculative archaeology undermined both its truth claims *and* its ideas about political and ideological consequence. For the Marxist-Lacanian philosopher Slavoj Žižek, on the other hand, it was ultimately the redemptive promise of propositions such as Eisler's that rendered such thinking problematic. Žižek extends the Marxist critique of the pragmatic failings of "spiritual" feminism to the New Age and "deep ecology" movements in general. Such movements lack, he argues, "a concrete social analysis of the economical, political, and ideological roots of ecological problems" in facing up to the apocalyptic scenarios that animate such work. "It is not enough," he contends, "to demand an ecological reorganization of capitalism, but neither will a return to pre-modern organic society and its holistic wisdom work. What is needed first of all is a fresh look at the uniqueness of our situation."[55] Žižek is not referring directly to Eisler here, and it is telling that her work no longer comes under direct attack in such a way; yet his disagreement with technofuturists, deep ecologists, and New Age thinkers such as Capra is nonetheless a categorical one. Žižek does not take issue with the notion that human society has reached a fatal crossroads. A hard look at the concrete political situation of the contemporary biosphere certainly corroborates Eisler's apocalypticism: the "blade" of dominator society is indeed killing us. But to advocate a return to a prior historical moment or an alternative paradigm of organic self-transcendence is, for Žižek, an ideological fantasy that disavows both the causality and the facticity of this condition.

Far from exaggerating the ecological threat, for instance, Žižek claims that even ecocritics underestimate its cataclysmic proportions. He writes that "the recent uncertainties about global warming signal not that things are not too serious, but that they are *even more* chaotic than we thought, and that natural and social factors are inextricably linked."[56] The decisions we face today, as in 1987, cannot simply presume the reversibility of history or its paradigms (as in replacing "blade" with "chalice"), nor can it presume that we can simply accommodate ourselves to or even fully understand the global order of being. According to Žižek, we must instead presume the apocalyptic conditions of ecological and political disaster as a starting point for the difficult decisions that face us now, which have to do with the radical redefinition of sovereignty and the development of new forms of global cooperation necessary for making political and economic decisions in a world defined by shortage, crisis, and remobilization. Whereas Eisler proposes that human choice bears the capacity to catalyze and reinforce cultural "bifurcation points" that might save us from the blade, Žižek maintains that the problem is not an ideological but a tactical one. His answer for this condition reverts to communism, a logical extreme that certain "New Age spiritualist" ideas of nonhierarchical organization approximate but do not fully deliver. Žižek thus offers his own ironic twist on the kinds of historical return and revision he criticizes: a "return" to communism emerges as the only concrete possibility in an apocalyptic present within which any moderate or otherwise "realistic" political solution is impossible. Eisler's chalice of partnership society is insufficient, in other words, because it is not outlandish enough. Its loose resemblance to communism as a sustained political apparatus invokes nonhierarchical social organization and an ethics of cooperation while retaining an ideological form (utopia) that shortcuts the difficult—perhaps impossible—political mechanisms and discomfiting political choices necessary to face up to the chaotic ecological and historical unknowns we face in the "end times" in which we live.

Whether or not it takes into consideration the full scope of anthropocentric and ecological complexity in its theory of cultural transformation, *The Chalice and the Blade* has few qualms about grounding its historical speculations on unknowns. Eisler's epistemology confronts the problem of cultural transformation by becoming more, rather than less, outlandish in its claims. Consistent with its general methodological reflections on the "jigsaw puzzle" of prehistory, the book articulates its ideas about historical change in the same language of archaeological speculation upon which it founds its historical claims about the nature of cultural predictability. That is, the disastrous advent of our dominator society is, in Eisler's study, at once the result of unpredictable permutations of macrohistorical causality and, at the same time, something we already know. Her speculations about the evolutionary perversion of cultural domination—and her assertions about our recourse to cultural transformation in turn—look to discrete moments of historical uncertainty that are themselves resoundingly familiar. Eisler's case studies and "bifurcation points" are drawn from an existing inventory of mythohistorical phenomena whose status as evidence is, at first blush, severely compromised by their familiarity as historical "mysteries" rife with pseudoarchaeological fantasy and mystical explanation. But such "known unknowns," as Žižek puts it (citing President George W. Bush's defense secretary, Donald Rumsfeld, with deliberate irony),[57] establish a familiar relationship with the unknowable or indeterminate whereby the mystery of historical cause and effect is artificially delimited. How outlandish, how truly conjectural, are the implicit pictorial borders of Eisler's jigsaw puzzle?

Communism—even Stalinism—may be Žižek's wild, "unrealistic" response to contemporary apocalypse, but Eisler preemptively offers us an even more outlandish atavism in its place: rather than looking to the Soviet Union, we should think of ancient Crete. Her first case study in *The Chalice and the Blade* is the "archaeological bombshell" of Minoan civilization on the island of Crete, a peripheral isolate of its own that represented a vestigial form of prehistoric partnership society that lasted well into the Bronze Age. According to Eisler, Cretan civilization was a goddess-worshiping society that made "slow and steady technological progress" for over two thousand years "in pottery making, weaving, metallurgy, engraving, architecture, and other crafts, as well as increasing trade and the gradual evolution of the lively and joyful artistic style so characteristic of Crete."[58] This "bombshell" dates to archaeological discoveries that began in the 1860s and reached their speculative peak in the modernist reconstructions of the Minoan palace of Knossos by Sir Arthur Evans in the early twentieth century. Anything but sudden, this discovery was deeply, fundamentally, overlaid with the mythological investments that fuel Eisler's study, at once a model for theorists of ancient matriarchy and an archaeological site framed and reconstructed according to such theories.[59] For Eisler, in turn, the "bombshell" of Crete dramatizes both the apocalyptic and eschatological registers of her study, a model of destruction and reweaving alike.

Minoan civilization lasted "well into the Bronze Age," Eisler notes, "a time when in the rest of the then civilized world the Goddess was steadily being displaced by warlike male gods."[60] Again naturalizing rather than substantiating her theory of cultural transformation, Minoan Crete stands as a Bronze Age vestige of partnership society. Relatively isolated from the mainland, Crete was an outlier, a "peripheral isolate" whose poignancy and significance had to do not only with its architectural and iconographic testimony to the last surviving goddess-worshiping partnership society but also with its eventual destruction. "The violent end of Crete is particularly haunting—and instructive," Eisler writes. "Because it was an island to the South of the European mainland, Crete was walled off for a time from the warlike hordes by the mothering sea. But at least here too the end came, and the last civilization based on a partnership rather than a dominator model of social organization fell."[61] Narrated as tragedy, the fall of Crete unfolds as the Achaean takeover of Minoan rule, which may have involved some adoption of the "more civilized Minoan ways," but which ultimately cemented "a social and ideological organization oriented more toward death than life." This conquest was compounded, moreover, by geological disaster, "a series of earthquakes and tidal waves that so weakened Minoan civilization [that] it could no longer resist the barbarians pressing down from the North."[62] Invoking chance and conquest alike, the fall of Crete "instructively" beckons to the ecological and geopolitical spheres of uncertainty within which we currently find ourselves "in our time of growing systems disequilibrium."[63]

In her scholarly history of the modern fascination with Crete, Cathy Gere refers to such reinventions of Minoan civilization as a "postmodern farce."[64] The myth of a matriarchal society in Crete was, she argues, a quintessentially modernist invention, the work of the British archaeologist Arthur Evans, who was himself a proponent of Bachofen's—as well as Friedrich Nietzsche's—myth-saturated theories about the classical and preclassical world. According to Gere, Crete was less a late outlier of prehistoric matriarchy than the mother of all subsequent historical fantasies. Cold War reinventions of Evans's modern reconstruction "assumed many guises," she writes, "from the spiritually nostalgic to the militantly political." Her litany of scorn is worth repeating here, insofar as it offers a virtual cross-section of the "alternative" histories that would become flashpoints of culture war scholarly debate:

> In the 1950s ancient Crete was reinvented as a beatnik Eden of
> creative spontaneity and existential joy. At the end of the next decade,
> these neo-Dionysian Minoans were reborn as the exemplary peaceniks
> of the ancient world, before emerging from their hippie haven to star
> in an outrageous feminist fable about the matriarchal beginnings of
> culture. As the cold war arms race escalated, this feminist Eden was
> retooled for the nuclear age, reenacted by lesbian antinuclear activists
> as an embattled refuge of Amazonian eco-warriors. At the same time
> the Afrocentric interpretation of matriarchal, peaceful Minoan Crete
> was revived to stir up unending controversy in the grove of academe.[65]

What Gere lampoons as farce, however, Eisler adopts as symptom: that is, as a set of overdetermined "falsehoods" and fantasies bristling with political and imaginative intensity. Beyond a mere liberty with archaeological facts and dates, Eisler's account of Crete steps deliberately onto shaky archaeological ground on account of the ideological intensity of such investments. Eisler's "known unknowns" recuperate such mysteries as evidence of both repression and an emergent paradigm shift, even in the "grove" of academia, for the very reason that their dismissal as pseudohistorical fantasy renders them consistent with the theory of causality she proposes in *The Chalice and the Blade*.[66] The point is not that readers should succumb to an "outrageous feminist fable," but that enumerating such fables testifies to the persistence of "ways of perceiving, ordering, and valuing reality" alternative to the mastery of nature and the conquest of space by "rational man."[67] There are scientific, as well as ideological and spiritual, alternatives to the rationalist Enlightenment worldview that seeks to cure the human mind of its "old irrationalities, all the old errors and maladies of humanity." What becomes evident, Eisler maintains, is that "the great transformation of Western society that begin with the eighteenth-century Enlightenment did not fail but is merely incomplete," demanding—for the sake of human survival—taking such "irrational" alternatives seriously.[68]

Eisler's social theory hinges on the familiarity and even the folkloric extravagance of such claims as an index of her chaos theory of cultural transformation. From New Age commonplaces to tragic indexes of our evolutionary wrong turn, the goddess cultures and Minoan civilizations of *The Chalice and the Blade* are both "known unknowns" and, as Eisler claims, "unknown knowns": that is, they are indexes of a knowledge that is not (consciously) known, archaeologically preserved but not historically acknowledged. Such mythohistorical "farce" thus contributes to Eisler's Bachofean investment in an archaeological unconscious. Here, though, they have to do not only with repressed data but also with the nonconscious, dynamic historical and ideological processes of repression and return themselves, in a way that is no longer truly archaeological at all but synthesizing, a systems theory of social organization. Through her entanglements with "prevailing paradigms" and propadeutically discredited evidence, Eisler presents her ideas about ideological transformation as both an allegory and an instance of world-historical catastrophe and methodological surprise.

One of the big surprises of the book is its account of the lost city of Atlantis, the mother of all archaeological fantasies. The "archaeological bombshell" of Minoan Crete bears an aftershock: Eisler's claim that Crete was Atlantis, that other legendary ancient civilization cataclysmically engulfed by the sea, according to Plato's account of it in the *Timaeus*. As if soliciting Fox-Genovese's charge that *The Chalice and the Blade* is a work of science fiction, Eisler's peripheral isolate of Bronze Age "gylanic" civilization reaches a kind of mythic apotheosis in her proposal that "the story of Atlantis is actually the garbled folk memory . . . of the Minoan civilization of Crete."[69] Her claims are hardly a pure invention, however; in a manner consistent with the overall logic of the book, her claims are drawn from other scholars and sources, whether skeptical or sincere. In proposing that the fall of Minoan civilization also resonates in and as the mythohistorical legend of Atlantis, Eisler both redoubles the poignancy of her archaeological bombshell and compounds the fabular construction of her theory. Far from limiting herself to "postmodern farce," she invokes the very centerpiece of pseudoarchaeology.

In short, Eisler follows the postwar classicist J. V. Luce in positing that the myth of Atlantis bears a striking resemblance to the Minoan empire, which flourished during the sixteenth century BCE and was rocked by cataclysmic volcanic eruptions around 1450 BCE. This move, which features in Luce's 1969 study *The Ends of Atlantis,* seeks to skirt the pseudoarchaeological consequences of its literal reading of Plato's Atlantis story popularized by Ignatius Donnelly in his 1882 best seller *Atlantis: The Antediluvian World* and its innumerable and ideologically heterodox successors. Luce does so by proposing that the Atlantean myths themselves can be "stretched" to line up with historical data rather than making outrageous demands on scant physical evidence. But he nonetheless maintains that "some dim far-off historical reality lay behind" folk belief and historical myth.[70] Even "stretching" Platonic myth in this fashion suggests a literalist approach to the story of Atlantis that reads Plato's account as a historiography rather than, say, a political allegory, as the philosopher Pierre Vidal-Naquet has argued.[71] By invoking Luce's theory that Minoan civilization lay at the basis of the Atlantis story, Eisler's work falls into a long line of archaeological speculation and fabulation that fuses the occult sciences with geographical specificity in order to uphold the possibility of alternative civilizations and histories. For this reason there has been "no staunching the flow of 'realistic' interpretations [of Atlantis]," laments Vidal-Naquet, himself more interested in the way the Atlantis story offers a genealogy of political myth, a history of speculative thought that dates from antiquity. Why insist on citing Atlantis as a peripheral isolate? As the prolific pseudoscience skeptic (and popularizer) L. Sprague de Camp wrote in 1954,

> Several sources supply the Atlantis theme with its singular vitality.
> The search for lost continents enables the bumptious amateur in the

sciences to play at being a historian, an archaeologist, or a paleogeog-
rapher. The borderland between the known and the unknown is the
most fascinating field of human knowledge to study, and statements
about times and places for which no real history exists are hard to
disprove. Atlantis provides mystery and romance for those who don't
find ordinary history exciting enough, and can be readily turned to
account to point a moral lesson—in fact, any of many different and
contradictory moral lessons.

But most of all it strikes a responsive chord by its sense of the
melancholy loss of a beautiful thing, a happy perfection once possessed by mankind. Thus it appeals to that hope that most of us carry
around in our unconscious, a hope so often raised as often disappointed, for assurance that somewhere, some time, there can exist
a land of peace and plenty, of beauty and justice, where we, poor
creatures that we are, could be happy. In this sense Atlantis—whether
we call it Panchaia, the Kingdom of God, Oceana, the Classless
Society, or Utopia—will always be with us.[72]

Linking Atlantis to communism by way of a transhistorical longing for utopian societies, Sprague de Camp upheld the poetic longing (and epistemological fascination) at work in such myths while trivializing their pursuit as
historical or scientific realities as the terrain for "bumptious amateurs." Eisler's
Chalice and the Blade not only fell prey to such dismissive criticism for its approach to historiography; it also invoked them as part of its methodological
synthesis.

Eisler's recourse to the literalism of Luce's Atlantis theory lies, I propose, at the heart of her own political myth, the causal crux of her holistic
allegory of chalices and blades. Her reasons for delving into such fantastic
archaeology are twofold: first of all, it furnishes the story of a vestigial chalice
society in Minoan Crete with an equally idiosyncratic conclusion, a series of
political and environmental disasters that erased it not only from existence
but also from historical memory. The very contentiousness of the myth shows,
in turn, how potent the forces of historical erasure and repression remain,
animating scorn and scholarly (as well as crackpot) persistence alike. This
counterfactual insistence thus constitutes Eisler's provocation: like Bachofen's
account of prehistoric matriarchy, Luce's proposition that the Platonic story
about the destruction of Atlantis had a real, geographical basis dramatizes
the epistemological tension between myth and fact, knowledge and belief.
"We have," Eisler reminds us, "journeyed into a different reality." The very
contentiousness of the claim demonstrates how subject to historical erasure

and repression that reality has become. The "postmodern farce" of Eisler's Cretan-Atlantean excursus neither ignores nor invents facts. It instead accumulates and synthesizes speculative, eccentric, or otherwise counterintuitive historical examples in order to interrogate the ideological structures that reinforce our credulity or incredulity toward them.

This very synthesis both substantiates and exercises Eisler's ideas about historical causality in turn. The sheer persistence of the Atlantis myth throughout the Enlightenment and into the twentieth century—and the fascination it continues to hold for archaeologists, popularizing hacks, and occult enthusiasts alike—already testifies to its capacity to resist or supersede dominant evidentiary paradigms, or at least to hold them in abeyance. The "responsive chord" struck by myths such as that of Atlantis is an index of a shift in worldview, the "turning point" that Eisler, like Capra, stresses as both necessary and underway, however subject to serendipity it might appear. Returning to Prigogine's and Stengers's "bifurcation points" late in the book, Eisler extends their thermodynamic systems theory to the study of social systems, wherein chance events at certain moments can determine whether a temporary equilibrium of a complex system is disrupted or shifts gradually. The destruction of Atlantis allegorizes one such cataclysmic eruption of a radically chaotic peripheral isolate. But so, too, Eisler maintains, can more gradual or subtle transformations emerge, whereby minor fluctuations and new, spontaneous modes of functioning can accumulate and become amplified to the point where they produce a new bifurcation point, yielding radical changes from ostensibly modest causes. This becomes Eisler's explanation for the historical persistence of "gylanic" outliers throughout the millennia, as well as the basis for her counterhegemonic theory of cultural transformation and human survival. "Like a plant that refuses to be killed no matter how often it is crushed or cut back," she writes, "gylany has again and again sought to reestablish its place in the sun."[73] Eisler's recourse to outlandish archaeological speculation is thus allegorical rather than historical, a millennial narrative of the persistence of and perpetual need for a partnership society, in the face of its innumerable persecutions. This is less a Freudian "return of the repressed," therefore, than the evolutionary thrust of a living system, the autopoietic substrate of ideology that functions as a kind of life drive.

SPINNING

What use is a political allegory? What are the stakes of spinning out a new—or rather, a very old—tapestry of social myths? The irony of Žižek's dismissal of New Age spiritualism is the extent to which its critique of ideological complicity strongly resembles the radical feminist work that was itself incorporated into—and often dismissed as—New Age thinking. Beyond its rhetorical appeal to a new historical epoch, the term *New Age* holds little empirical value in itself, designating the loose synthesis of "Eastern" philosophy and religion, occult history, and parapsychology that gained new countercultural currency in the 1960s and 1970s. The looseness of this category already demonstrates how the occultation of cause and effect of which Žižek accuses New Age thinking exercises itself in the categorical slippages at work in the very term itself.

For Eisler, however, it is on account of this very slippage that New Age thinking heralds the kind of social transformation her work seeks to substantiate. Such "alternative" thinking is significant, in other words, for aspiring methodologically to the kinds of counterintuitive and even counterfactual syntheses she posits as the key to human survival on the planet. Capra's fusion of yin and yang is based on the premise that contemporary advances in quantum physics, thermodynamics, and biology resemble the more "intuitive" insights of indigenous thought, "feminine" values, and humanistic philosophy. Eisler inverts the implicit hierarchy even in Capra's approach. Her cultural transformation theory posits goddess religion as the methodological kernel from which her own "contemporary advances" extend rather than as the spiritual complement to the world of leading scientists. The complex terrain of belief, myth, archaeological speculation, ideology, worldview, and paradigms is as central to systems thinking as the subatomic, chemical, and molecular worlds of the other sciences. She thus approaches New Age thinking with a pseudosuspicion that carefully rehabilitates it as a methodological "bombshell," however tarnished and defused by scholarly dismissal. "A great deal is being written about a New Age," she writes, "a major and unprecedented cultural transformation. . . . But in practical terms, what does this mean? A transformation from what to what? . . . Most importantly, what changes in social structure would make such a transformation possible?"[74] For Eisler, the New Age designates the ideological and cultural terrain she synthesizes in *The Chalice and the Blade*. It both names the technofuturist horizon toward which her study gathers its forces and assembles an array of heterodox and technofuturist thinkers (from Gimbutas and Stone to Capra, Stengers, and Toffler, among many others) in accordance with the partnership model she advocates.

Orchestrating their diverse intentions, Eisler overwrites such thinkers as organic participants in the allegorical theory of partnership to which she gives voice in *The Chalice and the Blade*. Thus, whereas Žižek travesties New

Age thinking for its wish fulfillment and nebulous ideas about political causality, Eisler offers a corrective to such accidental forms of complicity by exercising her own mode of co-optation upon this thinking itself, forging a counterhegemonic formation across the broad field of spiritual feminism, deep ecology, technofuturism, New Age religion and ideology, archetypalism, and archaeological speculation. *The Chalice and the Blade* thus fashions its own synthetic form of outsider theory, a methodological assemblage exercised in the name of partnership within the very discourse of social thought. Method, more than "fact" or even allegory, becomes the evidentiary basis for her claims to the possibility of cultural transformation.

Eisler's methods are predicated, moreover, on a defense of such trivialized ways of thinking insofar as trivialization is an ideological weapon. Accused of factlessness and hyperbole by her detractors, Eisler notes how such accusations are themselves an iteration of the "dominator" ideology, a screen for the facts of patriarchal oppression that we too often universalize or naturalize in the name of scholarly and scientific credibility. As Mary Daly writes in *Beyond God the Father* (1973), "there are many devices available both to women and to men for refusing to see the problem of sexual caste," including the very "spiritualization" of "concrete oppressive facts" to which Žižek alludes.[75] However spiritually inclined or holistic they may be, feminist ideological critiques of the 1970s and 1980s were already exercising the Žižekian insistence that "ideology" was not a false consciousness but a set of unconscious identifications that structure our sense of reality, and which exercise themselves in the "innocent" references to clarity and utility.

What Daly, Eisler, and others identify as the perverse core of this patriarchal ideology is the de facto dismissal of women's thought altogether, the premise that feminism abandons method in favor of intuition and belief (and can, perhaps, be rehabilitated paternalistically as one of the softer, "yin" forms of intuitive knowledge). In this light, the mythohistorical fantasies of Eisler and other spiritual feminists might seem precisely to uphold the sublime kernel of misogyny in advocating for a happy utopia of women. Indeed, Cynthia Eller describes her rage and suspicion at how "matriarchal myth" leaves "feminists open to charges of vacuousness and irrelevance that we can not afford to court."[76] As Eisler notes, however, the use of ridicule and trivialization has long served as a means for maintaining male control over women. This device operates as much within the historical record as upon archaeologists and theorists who seek to contradict the self-evidence of patriarchy as a biological and historical given.

Eisler is not trying to fool anyone, or to cash in on the popular allure of ancient mysteries; nor is she so naive as to misrecognize conjecture for empirical fact. Her synthesis of archaeological speculation and sociopolitical theory seeks not to domesticate an invented set of counterhegemonic feminist "beliefs" but instead to assemble a corpus of hypotheticals that extend to the very methodologies we use to assemble our understanding of historical and contemporary reality. The significance of such methods has less to do, as Žižek has often noted, with one's faith in the truth claims they yield than in the ideological functions they exercise, whether one believes in them or not. We do not, in other words, need to believe in an ideological construct in order for it to work. Reciprocally, in refusing to be taken in by an ideological construct, by refusing to be duped by it, we can come to obey it most recklessly. Eller's volte-face from goddess proponent to debunker exemplifies such a scenario: "If a lot of snickering was all that prehistoric matriarchies could get me, who needed them?"[77] Eisler's study ultimately proposes that we interrogate our suspicions toward the *disjecta membra* of intellectual history, to question our inherited certainties about the (im)possibility of partnership and the self-evidence of the dominator model. Eller, by contrast, sees a trap—not an interrogation, but a flight of fantasy that invites ridicule and therefore corroborates the convictions of patriarchy.

Eller's inclinations toward a less ridiculous feminism have, ironically, made her a champion of trivialization. Her book-length refutation of "the myth of matriarchal prehistory" discusses an incident in a college class in which a professor raised the "Minoan hypothesis" Eisler invokes in *The Chalice and the Blade*, only to have the students react with laughter and disbelief. Eller recalls that she was "annoyed with the professor for bringing it up and then letting it degenerate from archaeological observation to cheap joke." Eller went on to write a dissertation on this very topic, yet she paradoxically deploys the anecdote two decades later as a gesture of dismissal in its own right, noting "the evangelical tone of the converted" in the speech and writing of the women she studied, for whom the theory of prehistoric matriarchy "underwrote their politics, their ritual, their theology (or understanding of the goddess), and, indeed, their entire worldview."[78] Eller admirably takes issue not with the truth claims of the "myth" but with its ideological effects, a "deeper discontent" for which her "irritation with the historical claims" served as a vehicle. As we have seen, her criticism is that the theory of sex and gender embedded in this myth "is neither original nor revolutionary," since it springs from the work of nonfeminist writers such as Bachofen and confirms gendered stereotypes about the symbolic, timeless, and archetypal qualities of women.[79] Heine writes similarly in 1989 that such modes of feminism represent a "second-hand avant-garde" that no longer cause much of a stir. "Is this progress?" she asks, then answers, flatly, "No. What may mean liberation for the feminist insider is mocked by outsiders or is welcomed in paternal, patronizing ways as a way in which women who are discriminated against by 'fate' can cleanse their souls: 'that's all right, if it helps them.'"[80] Such accounts warn of the dangers of unoriginality and ridicule, urging readers to avoid the ideological trap such outsider thinking represents. "The enemies of feminism," Eller writes, "have long posed issues of patriarchy and sexism in pseudoscientific and historical terms. It is not in feminist interests to join them at this game."[81] Certainly, her critique does not mean that she has implicitly joined the chorus of derisive laughter in the college classroom, but it does offer a telling illustration of the ideological elasticity at work in counterhegemonic discourses.

Mary Daly's radically playful—or playfully radical—approach to this ideological conundrum is to err methodically, explicitly, and in militant fashion. Her work fixes on the sublime object of the patriarchal ideology itself, which, as Daly puts it, functions in the service of a "methodolatry," a "false god" that "prevents us from raising questions never asked before and from being illumined by ideas that do not fit into pre-established boxes and forms."[82] The god Method is, moreover, "a subordinate deity, serving Higher Powers," which Daly names as "the social and cultural institutions whose survival depends upon the classification of disruptive and disturbing information as nondata."[83] Isolating the methodical dismissal and trivialization of women's thought as the perverse core of the "dominator society" itself, Daly proposes "methodicide," a "high treason" against the prevailing paradigms of patriarchal thought that she describes as "an effort to begin asking non-questions and to start discovering, reporting, and analyzing nondata."[84] For Daly, this involves nothing less than "an ontological, spiritual revolution, pointing beyond the idolatries of sexist society and sparking creative action in and toward transcendence. The becoming of women implies universal human becoming. It has everything to do with the search for ultimate meaning and reality, which some would call God."[85] Daly's "methodicide" thus amounts to a kind of Gnostic replacement of the "subordinate deity" of Method in favor of this ultimate meaning, a task she figures, incidentally, through the Minoan axe: a double-headed blade (as opposed to Eisler's chalice) called the Labrys, a pun on the female "sex which is not one."[86]

During the 1980s and 1990s, such positions toward reason and belief became increasingly unpopular, not only among proponents of patriarchal cultural literacy but also among many feminist scholars and activists. As we will see further in chapter 8, such methodological challenges—and the trivialization and critique they both garnered and resisted—confront the problem of demarcating reason from faith, and science from pseudoscience, characteristic of the "pseudoscience wars" of post–World War II intellectual culture in the United States.[87] Indeed, Eisler's speculations about goddess cultures and "gylanic" forms of social organization mark a far broader crisis of epistemology during the culture wars. The very language of intellectual controversy suggests how readily feminist speculation could be relegated to the same dustbin of historical bad ideas into which creationism, intelligent design, climate change denial, or other pseudoscientific theories are repeatedly cast. In a 1990 *New York Times* article, for instance—printed, with no small degree of historical irony, beneath a story about the so-called Star Wars missile defense system—a group of experts discuss the "controversy" surrounding the goddess archaeology of Marija Gimbutas, a major source for Eisler's claims. Indeed, one such expert notes Gimbutas's influence in the no less "controversial" *Chalice and the Blade.* In narrating the controversy, we find a striking instance of the paternalistic derision anticipated by Eller and Heine; as one anthropologist notes, "most of us tend to say, oh my God, here goes Marija again," describing how the feminist archaeologist leaps "to conclusions without any intervening argument."[88] Analogously, Cathy Gere later notes how Gimbutas "has compensated for her loss of academic credibility with a profitable spot on the lecture circuit and a shadowy second career as a high priestess of the goddess movement."[89]

Lurking beneath such critiques, however, is a stronger and perhaps more anxious position toward "methodicide"—that is, the possibility that such problems of credibility and conclusion had less to do with a lapse in aptitude or judgment (in the *New York Times* article on Gimbutas, the same colleague remarks that her peers consider her "immensely knowledgeable but not very good at critical analysis") than with the stakes and boundaries of the "ontological and spiritual revolution" of which Daly writes. Lynn Segal, for one, is openly contemptuous of the idealism she sees in such claims to "revolution." For Daly, she writes, "reality is reduced to language. . . . I would love to take pleasure in this familiar nineteenth-century pagan romanticism, with all its rites this time reserved for women. I would love to chuckle along with my friends, both women and men, at Daly's so 'absolutely Anti-androcrat, A-mazingly Anti-male' fiery poetics. . . . But there is a snag. Mary Daly's writing is also A-mazingly anti-woman, as well as anti-political." Such romanticized Gnostic pronouncements are not only "constructed from within the discourse of [the very] deceptions" they claim to revolutionize, but they also describe only the salvation of "the chosen few."[90] Segal takes issue, in other words, with a "methodicide" that targets epistemology in totalizing strokes rather than targeting specific institutions and frameworks of meaning and making finer distinctions between the agents and forms of oppression.

As Heine puts it all the more definitively, such "methodicide" in fact amounts to a blindness to method. "Method," she writes, "is not self-sacrifice to the God science but literally the way of distinguishing the actual from the conceivable, the empirical from the conceptual, and at the same recognizing how they are related to one another. What feminists claim to be feminine science is a false kind of thinking which takes short cuts. . . . However, one can make a virtue of feminine illogicality by declaring logic itself to be a vice and disqualifying all those who concern themselves with it, both men and women."[91] It is less a shortcut that theorists such as Daly and Eisler seek, however, than a short circuit: a unilateral suspension of the "law" of method that sustains the ideological effects of patriarchy or androcracy. The point of this suspension is not to celebrate the provisional, heuristic "castration" (as Daly puts it) of method as a victory in itself, but to pursue the redirections of conceptual and speculative energy it permits. The short circuit of methodicide opens up to new syntheses and discloses disavowals or otherwise impossible practices and possibilities. As the poet and critic Audre Lorde puts it in her 1979 "Open Letter to Mary Daly," itself a critique of Daly's work for its limited recourse to Black women's writing, "When I speak of knowledge, as you know, I am speaking of that dark and true depth which understanding serves, waits upon, and makes accessible through language to ourselves and others. It is this depth within each of us that nurtures vision."[92] The "dark and true depth" to which Lorde refers as knowledge is as much the effect as the mystical object cause of such methodical short circuits: the spiritual reservoir, rather than the evidentiary basis, for a potential shift in prevailing paradigms.

My aim here is not simply to defend the work of Daly, Eisler, and others against its contemporary detractors, however, but to recognize such controversy as part of the very medium from which Daly and Eisler derive their theories of cultural transformation. As sprawling, epic syntheses of historiography, archaeology, philology, ecology, systems theory, pseudoscience, and myth, their work situates itself squarely within and against the prevailing paradigms that regulate the truth claims and admissible conclusions of such fields. It also suspends as well as fuels the continuities and discontinuities within the paradigms that prevail in its wake. Unlike Daly, however, Eisler does not present *The Chalice and the Blade* as a work of radicalism or militancy, which would champion individual or collective agency even in revolutionizing language. It is instead a decidedly rehabilitative work that seeks to gather and popularize such "methodicide" in the name of new possibilities for social thought. For this reason, *The Chalice and the Blade* offers an instructive case study for outsider theory on account of the extent to which such increasingly unfashionable ideas animate the methodological imperative of the book: our conscious hostility to outdated, conjectural, or otherwise "embarrassing" ideas may be no less dangerous than the risks of believing them.

In the decades since *The Chalice and the Blade* appeared, ecofeminist scholars and activists have continued to wrestle with the power of such work—in both its epistemological and even spiritual registers—for precisely this reason. Like Eisler, they seek to move beyond the "false opposition of politics and spirituality" and to recognize even the metaphorical language of methodicide and cultural transformation as resonant provocations. As Frances Devlin-Glass and Lyn McCredden note in 2001, for instance, even metaphors "are never 'mere' language but are sources of both creativity and suspicion."[93] Writing similarly in 2000, Stacy Alaimo warns "against the hasty dismissal" of spiritually and ecologically oriented feminism, arguing that "the ease with which many ecofeminist texts are labeled essentialist betrays a narrow rigidity on the part of the predominant feminist positions." Rather than dismissing such feminisms, "it would be more productive to bring its perspective to bear on the continuing debates about strategic essentialism, performative identities, postmodern feminism, and difference" that have persisted in its wake.[94] Adopting the systems thinking to which Eisler alludes in *The Chalice and the Blade,* materialist as well as "cultural" ecofeminists have increasingly come to view the methodological debate within the field among and between scholars, activists, and theorists as a constitutive problem to be confronted "with scholarly rigor and in the light of historical and archaeological findings" rather than being content with "nostalgic and romantic recuperations of a past golden era or a present that has somehow evaded the problems of late capitalism (as does some New Age 'scholarship')."[95]

The political scientist Irene Diamond looks, for instance, to grassroots activism (as well as to Foucauldian theory) to argue that the Western discourse of instrumental rationality, which forms the ideological basis of capitalist technological advancement and political agency alike, has in fact impeded feminist discourse. Inverting Segal's critique of Daly's apoliticism, Diamond proposes that a restrictive sense of what counts as "real" politics has created ideological rifts as well as blindnesses to alternative capacities for transformation and agency. If we look to already existing grassroots political movements, we can witness the extent to which feminist appeals to nature and goddesses—in all their visionary, utopian, and mythical components—manifest their ethical priority. Rather than dismissing such appeals as fantasies or ideologically complicit reductions of "real" political cause and effect, Diamond, among others, questions the instrumental limits of conventional political theories in favor of "webs of connection and social justice" that incorporate human and nonhuman forms of social and ecological production. Diamond's contention is that the Western discourse of reproduction and sexuality, focused so centrally on instrumentalist ideas about regulation and control, has made it difficult for many women in the West to see why the ecological activity of women must be considered integral to the feminist project.[96] Instrumental reason can be blinding.

Method, in this context, is neither a "self-sacrifice to the God science" nor a cartoonish rejection of all logical parameters, but instead the open and often contentious system of practices, theories, and forms of expertise whose necessary diversity accommodates itself to the diversity that sustains life. Such a proposition may be no less outlandish than Eisler's recourse to the legend of Atlantis. As Mary Mellor put it in 1997, "a book on ecofeminism(s), feminism(s), and ecologism(s) must necessarily be a tangle of ideas, and interweaving of many threads that will sometimes gather into untidy knots or trail out in numerous loose ends."[97] Such work may err, even outlandishly, but in its ethical and ideological commitment such a tendency to err is not only human but also inhuman, attentive to the systemic demands of a set of global conditions that are organic as well as social, ecological as well as political, spiritual as well as historical. Such errancy animates Eisler's holistic project in *The Chalice and the Blade,* which assembles a chaos theory of human cultural evolution in order to introduce the possibility of gathering new "peripheral isolates" toward a change in the catastrophe-bound direction of human civilization. "For at stake at this second evolutionary crossroads," Eisler writes, "when we possess the technologies of total destruction once attributed only to God, may be nothing less than the survival of our species." Such stakes are, for Eisler, worth the price of trivialization.

PART III

SOVEREIGN INSTITUTIONS

GARVEYISM AND ITS
INVOLUTIONS

Speculative thought is presence rather than argument, a presence whose efficacy is to infect every justificatory argument with the adventurous questions of what is demanded by the position whose legitimacy it expresses, of what it recruits to endure or propagate, and of the way it is liable to be affected by the encounter with another position.

—Isabelle Stengers, *Thinking with Whitehead*

THE ARCHAEOLOGICAL SPECULATION that forms the basis of Riane Eisler's cultural transformation theory found critics who associated this type of feminism with other revisionist histories, from Nazi myth to Afrocentrism. If social theory relied on myth rather than fact, then what was there to distinguish such theories from pure ideological posturing? Without an evidentiary means for demarcating pseudohistory and pseudoarchaeology from their more respectable scholarly cousins, what truths could we possible learn about our past, or about the historical forces that shape our future? The result, presumably, would be an open field of unregulated ideological contestation—a concern that fueled some of the more hard-fought scholarly debates of this period. During the final decades of the twentieth century, the topography of the American professoriate become one such field, a terrain "cratered by a series of epistemological canyons," as Jacques Berlinerblau put it in 1999, describing the scarred academic landscape of the culture wars.[1] Not only have those scars yet to heal, but the scale of epistemological warfare has only increased in recent decades, exceeding the confines of academia to reveal a far vaster and more entrenched siege upon institutions of knowledge and cultural transmission. The repercussions of this protracted cultural warfare are global and apocalyptic, as Eisler anticipated.

One of the key skirmishes of the culture war era in the United States centered on the publication of Martin Bernal's three-volume *Black Athena*, the first volume of which appeared in 1987, the same year as Eisler's *The Chalice and the Blade*. A study of "the Afroasiatic roots of classical civilization,"[2] Bernal's work is likewise an interdisciplinary synthesis that draws upon over two centuries of African American, African, and diasporic scholarship and speculation alike in arguing that ancient Greece had been colonized by Egyptian and Phoenician cultures rather than by Indo-Europeans. The alleged whiteness and Europeanness of ancient Greece was, in other words, a European invention. Bernal's amalgamation of philological, archaeological, and historical precedent gave contemporary scholarly immediacy—and, given that the author was white, counteridentitarian voice—to theories about suppressed North African and Levantine influences on Western civilization that had circulated for nearly two centuries as a veritable counterculture of modernity.[3] The book met with significant backlash on behalf of the sanctity of Western (that is, white) canons and traditions. Alongside her critiques of Riane Eisler and Marija Gimbutas, for instance, historian of science Cathy Gere takes aim at Bernal's study for misrepresenting the history of Minoan civilization in order to support its ideological project. "Coinciding with the development of the pacifist-feminist Minoan utopia," she writes, "was one of the most infamous interventions in the politics of ancient Crete"—namely, *Black Athena*, a study that urged the "overthrow" of a culturally imperialist, Aryan model of history that denied the extension of Greek civilization from its African and Near Eastern roots.[4] Gere singles out Bernal's "revival of the Afrocentric view of Greek origins first promulgated by George Wells Parker" as the epitome of "postmodern farce," whose utopian proceedings were founded on the chimerical reconstructions of Sir Arthur Evans and other nineteenth- and twentieth-century "prophets of modernism."[5]

Yet whereas the "postmodern farce" of ecofeminism tended largely to encounter dismissal and trivialization, Bernal's *Black Athena* became a hotbed for debate insofar as it represented—for many white scholars, as for conservative pundits and critics—not only a learned but dilettantish work of historical revisionism but also an outright attack on the foundations of Western civilization.[6] For Gere, as for other culture warriors like the classical scholar Mary Lefkowitz, right-wing pundit Dinesh D'Souza, and others, Bernal's work gave apparent credibility to the outlandish counterfactual histories of Afrocentric thinkers such as Cheikh Anta Diop, Frank Snowden, and Ivan Van Sertima, as well as earlier figures such as George Wells Parker, J. A. Rogers, and, most controversially of all, Marcus Garvey (1887–1940), the founder of the Universal Negro Improvement Association, whose own synthesis of earlier theories about the African origins of Western civilization had fueled his commercial and political speculations during the 1920s. What made Bernal's theory "infamous" for critics was its scholarly credentials—Bernal was a professor of government and Near Eastern studies at Cornell University—as well as its popularity among general readers, not only in the United States but in Egypt, Europe, and throughout the African diaspora.[7] As Gere puts it, whereas a thinker such as Diop "was pretty much kept away from the elite centers of Anglo-American academia," Bernal's "massively learned version of the African Minoans exploded right in the face of the Ivy League, bringing Afrocentric scholarship to the attention of a much wider public."[8]

Whereas Gere depicts Bernal as a consummate insider, Lefkowitz considers him an ideological interloper. Lefkowitz, a classical scholar who dedicated two books to attacking Bernal's premises, notes that the popularity of *Black Athena* owes largely to "the appeal of iconoclasm in an age where everything traditional has been questioned and found wanting"; she herself sides with the defenders of canons and traditions of (white) Western civilization against the excesses of contemporary humanities disciplines, in which "much that is written by Europeans, and especially European males, is regarded with suspicion."[9] She notes that Bernal's "speculations about Egypt and Greece convey a determination at once poetic and assertive," but takes pains to depict Bernal—in spite of his Ivy League credentials—as an "armchair archaeologist" who was anything but an expert in the preclassical periods about which his theories speculated.[10] Such depictions already suggest the extent to which "controversy" over *Black Athena* had as much to do with scholarly conventions, practices, institutions, and infrastructures as with the ideological portent of its contentions: the two were, it seems, inseparable.

At the heart of these debates stands, for complicated reasons, the historical figure of Marcus Garvey, the Jamaican-born race leader who mobilized ideas about a repressed historical legacy of great African civilization toward a corporate and media empire in the early 1920s. Anticipating Bernal's multidisciplinary synthesis by nearly seven decades, Garvey's writings and speeches—along with his commercial and organizational ventures—formed the polemical seed for both later Afrocentric history and Pan-African nationalism alike. The association of *Black Athena* with Garveyism was itself a polemical device, however, often used to depict such "Afrocentric" thought as "a historically monolithic intellectual device" and to subject its intellectual premises to a priori skepticism, as Maghan Keita has argued.[11] "When Marcus Garvey first spoke about the Greeks' stealing from the Africans," Lefkowitz writes, "he was not creating a new historiography, he was creating a new mythology. The reasons are not far to seek. For black Americans (many of whom now prefer to be known as African Americans), the African origins of ancient Greek civilization promise a myth of self-identification and self-ennoblement, the kind of 'noble lie' that Socrates suggests is needed for the utopian state he describes in Plato's *Republic*. . . . But hope is not enough of a reason for illusion."[12] The specter of Garveyism recurs throughout Lefkowitz's crusade against the "desire to rewrite history in support of new political and social claims" that characterized both *Black Athena* and the "resurgent nationalism and ethnic self-assertion" of the 1990s; indeed, one of Lefkowitz's major public opponents was the Garvey scholar (and her Wellesley College colleague) Tony Martin, who clashed with her in a series of inflammatory books and libel cases during this period.[13] Afrocentrism, for Lefkowitz and other Cold Warriors (as for white supremacists as well), was a myth. As Keita notes, such a positioning not only disparages "the merits of Afrocentrism as a body of legitimate academic arguments" by discounting them as myth but also "casts a blind eye on the general utility of 'myth' itself. This means that serious considerations of myth in the construction of 'useable pasts' are slighted; and, most specifically, that its formidable power in the construction of a world and intellectual discourses that have subordinated or excluded peoples of colour, women, the poor, the gendered different, and so on in the pursuit of myths of modernity and the histories that might undergird them is, for the most part, ignored."[14]

This chapter studies the institutional forms of Garveyism as both the bearers of such myths and, more significantly, as the medium for their synthesis as an operational theory of Black sovereignty. Garveyism, which the historian Adam Ewing views "not as an ideology but as a method of organic mass politics,"[15] is central to the study of outsider theory on account of such institutional forms, which both capitalize on the plasticity of historical narratives and demonstrate the capacity for institutions to think. Beyond Garvey's individual legacy as a historical persona, this chapter studies the conceptual labor incorporated under his name.

The repercussions of Lefkowitz's paternalistic brand of racism, and the reception of Bernal's *Black Athena* more broadly, have been exhaustively discussed over the past two decades; this chapter is not about the contemporary stakes of Afrocentrism. It instead addresses the thinking that animates and haunts it, the work of Marcus Garvey as the founder of institutions such as the Universal Negro Improvement Association (UNIA), the *Negro World* newspaper, and the Black Star Line (BSL). Founded in Jamaica in 1914, the UNIA was a fraternal organization that served as the umbrella structure for a movement "to establish a universal confraternity among the race."[16] Re-launched in New York in 1917, the UNIA quickly began accumulating subsidiary institutions that both generated capital and expanded the public reach of the association, from the *Negro World* newspaper in 1918 to the purchase and operation of Liberty Halls, the establishment of the Negro Factories Corporation, and the launching of the Black Star Line in 1919. The organization's most visible and ambitious undertaking, the BSL was a group of steamships launched as a shipping and passenger fleet designed to connect the port cities of the African diaspora, and which promoted Black repatriation to the African continent. Though associated primarily with Black emigration movements that had begun in the nineteenth century, Garvey's organization program was embedded in a theory of history and, as I will discuss in this chapter, a practice of historical and commercial speculation. Garvey did not, however, create either a new historiography or a new set of myths out of whole cloth. Instead, much like Bernal, he synthesized existing research and speculation about the imminent resurgence of an ancient African promise, mobilizing such eschatological narratives toward his project of "universal negro improvement."[17] The result was a mass movement notable for its effectiveness and global scale in an era of violent racist oppression in the United States and the colonial world.[18]

Seeking his own "bifurcation point" in the millennial evolution of world civilizations, Garvey staked his political and commercial claims on grand narratives of historical repression and return that likewise fueled the political mythmaking of numerous other social movements in the decades before and after the First World War. Garvey's emergence and reception as a world-historical figure was bound up in the unfolding of these narratives, but so too were the commercial and paragovernmental organizations that formed the medium for his thinking. Far from purely abstract inventions, such mythohistorical patterns of rise and fall, resurrection and awakening responded to pressing contemporary exigencies: the distinctly nonprogressive tendencies of the so-called Progressive Era of 1920s America; the carving up of Africa by the white League of Nations after the First World War; the campaigns for home rule in Egypt, India, and Ireland; the Zionist movement in Palestine; and the writings and speeches of other contemporary Black nationalist thinkers. Garvey's indictment (1922), conviction (1923), and subsequent imprisonment on the trumped-up charge of mail fraud (from 1925 until his deportation in 1927) were based on the highly speculative means through which the UNIA raised money for the BSL. But they were also largely a function of a federal Bureau of Investigation eager for an opportunity to prosecute or otherwise undermine Black leaders. As early as 1919, J. Edgar Hoover, head of the bureau's General Intelligence Division, had singled out Garvey as an "undesirable alien" who could not yet be deported because he had "not as yet violated any federal law."[19] Emerging in a political environment of subterfuge and resurgent white supremacist violence, and amid accusations and counteraccusations of fraud and conspiracy, paranoia, messianism, mythohistorical mumbo jumbo, and even fascism, Garvey's institutions drew upon and were subject to historical narratives that have played out in his reception ever since.

Indeed, like the organizations he founded, Garvey's reputation is bound up with a similar set of mythohistorical structures and narratives according to which critics and admirers alike have formulated his legacy. Whether they embrace or decry his ideological and political priorities, judgments of Garvey's historical significance are sustained, I propose, by the very narratives of prophecy, belatedness, and return according to which the phenomenon of Garveyism played out historically. This is the case whether one embraces Garvey as a heroic visionary or persecuted witness to the rise of Black nationalism (as Kwame Nkrumah and subsequent nationalists have done);[20] or whether one decries his spectacular politics of racial empire as paranoid or fascist (as Paul Gilroy and C. L. R. James have insisted, citing Garvey's own claim to have anticipated Benito Mussolini).[21] It is likewise the case whether one dwells on the ambiguities of Garvey's place in history or strikes him from the historical record altogether.[22] In each case the assessment of Garvey's consequence—as an ideologue or demagogue; as a figure in world history, politics, or intellectual history—is both sustained and structured by the metahistorical narratives through which we measure such consequences: rise and fall; tragedy, farce, *Bildung*, or epic; persecution and messianic return; or psychoanalytically inflected patterns of repression, outburst, and recovery. It is for this reason that Garvey's thinking—more so than his individual motives or accusations about his alleged "madness"[23]—functioned so powerfully as an outsider formation in modern intellectual and cultural history, as both a synthesis and an instrumentalization of "universal" historical forms.

I refer to this recourse to historical forms as one of the "involutions" of Garveyism as a cultural phenomenon, invoking a sociological term for nonrevolutionary, nonevolutionary change described by Clifford Geertz as "the overdriving of an established form in such a way that it becomes rigid through an overelaboration of detail."[24] For Geertz, *involution* describes a set of colonial relations whereby the demands of colonial trade and the demands of subsistence economy are superimposed, yielding an intensification of labor and productive technology without a corresponding shift in power relations. For Geertz, such an intensification leads to a reification of existing economic relations, resulting in a "shared poverty."[25] Such a stalemate certainly describes the consequence of depicting Garvey as "controversial" insofar as such contestation obscures the enormous range—as well as the lingering forms and effects—of Garvey's influence throughout the United States and the African diaspora alike, as Mary G. Rolinson argues in her study of grassroots UNIA organizing in the rural U.S. South. Even groups that sought actively to obscure and invalidate Garvey's leadership, such as the National Association for the Advancement of Colored People (NAACP), nonetheless adopted some of his principles.[26]

More concretely, the notion of involution describes the historical conditions of white supremacy Garvey sought to redress in his organizational work, whereby people of African descent had "no possible way of extricating [themselves] from [their] environments."[27] Yet so too, I propose, was Garvey's system for redressing these conditions profoundly involutionary in turn, in a more politically expedient sense of an investment in the intricacies of such environments. In the context of Garveyism's massive sphere of operations in the 1920s, that is, the "overdriving of an established form" refers to the institutional means through which his speculative theories of Black sovereignty functioned historically and financially. From the UNIA to the BSL, Garvey's commercial enterprises and paragovernmental institutions operated within the same "established forms" of capitalism and universal history according to which the prospects of people of African descent had, since the Middle Passage, been violently foreclosed. Garvey did not look for radical possibilities outside capitalism or beyond the frontiers of history as the basis for "improvement," but within their very folds. Leveraging the historical grand narratives of Western civilization toward the construction of a massive global infrastructure, Garveyism staked a claim to Black sovereignty on an intensification of existing metahistorical patterns of rise and fall, redemption and return, that had hitherto naturalized European colonialism and white supremacy. For Garvey, involution was the very engine of speculation, which made itself known through the presence of institutions rather than through argumentation or hortatory rhetoric alone. For this reason the intensities of Garveyism continue to resonate throughout contemporary theories of race, Pan-African leadership, and the history of diasporic thinking in ways that testify to the persistence of outsider theory within the conceptual entanglements of twentieth- and twenty-first-century intellectual history.

Such metahistorical narratives lie at the heart of Garvey's own thinking, a corporate body of work that extends from his speeches and writings to the administration of institutions he founded in Jamaica and the United States. His speculations also incorporate, react to, and resonate among the work of other thinkers with whom he collaborated and fought, as well as the discourses on race and power with which he came into contact. Within the historical environment of the 1920s, Garveyism comprised its own singularizing corollary, an involution that could at once appeal to the innermost hearts of many and appear alien and threatening to others. However strongly Garvey may continue to resonate as a historical figure, the metahistorical figurations of his writings, speeches, and administrative enterprises are no less provocative. His body of work operated according to a narrative logic through which historical justice and geopolitical sovereignty alike hinged on the narrative economies of speculation and return. This chapter approaches Garvey as a *theorist*, a term I want to take very literally as one engaged in the work of speculation—by which I mean the work of theory, exercised in terms of finance, Black history, and collective organization.

UNIVERSAL SPECULATION

Early in his 1972 novel *Mumbo Jumbo*, Ishmael Reed characterizes Marcus Garvey's singular place in Black history with a characteristically multifarious line. Following a passage that outlines the lynchings and racial injustices of the early 1920s, Reed writes, "Until Marcus Garvey came along to rescue the American Negro he was basking in his lethargy like a crocodile sleeping in the sun."[28] As is the case with the majority of Reed's historical coordinates in *Mumbo Jumbo*, this syntactically ambiguous line can be read in a variety of ways, registering at once the ambivalences of Garvey's career and the counterhegemonic project of his flagship organization, the Universal Negro Improvement Association.

Read satirically, Reed's allusion invokes the earliest criticisms of the UNIA, which from its origin garnered hostile responses in Jamaica and the United States for the hortatory rhetoric of lethargy, degradation, and eventual awakening through which Garvey promulgated its message of "improvement."[29] Reed's *Mumbo Jumbo* registers such criticism in attributing the line about lethargy to a "Guianese art critic," Hank Rollings, a colonial subject who has chosen to assimilate European values and is thus suspicious of, albeit also fascinated by, any such claims to racial self-awakening. Reed's art critic thus amplifies the ambivalences of Garvey's earliest critics, who struggled to distinguish the ambitions of Garvey's organizations from the excesses of his rhetoric. Characteristic of such rhetoric is his assertion in an early pamphlet from 1914, *The Destiny of the Negro*, that "you have consistently been unfair to yourselves, because you hate and despise yourselves."[30] Such prejudice toward one's own race, Garvey insisted, must be abandoned in order to "claim the appreciation and honest comradeship of the more advanced races who are to-day ignoring us because we are so lethargic and serfish."[31] The irony of Garvey's rhetoric lay in its own tendency toward racial self-accusation, a fact rarely lost on his critics; this tendency became only more adamant in subsequent writings, such as when Garvey declared ten years later that "there is no doubt that the Negro is his own greatest enemy."[32] This latter assertion, written from Atlanta Federal Penitentiary after Garvey was indicted for mail fraud, was exacerbated by the sustained governmental opposition his organization had encountered by the early 1920s; it reflects at once the implosion of his immediate commercial ventures and, in particular, his tendency to impugn his former colleagues and associates in defense of his own personal integrity.

Even at its most paranoiac and defensive, however, such accusatory rhetoric characterized one of the principal strategies of Garvey's "universal improvement" project. Black people were responsible for their own history, Garvey claimed, a task that meant awakening from the "lethargy" of subjugation whereby, he wrote in 1919, the condition of the "Negro Universal" had, in a span of five years, gone from "sleeping on his bale of cotton in the South of America . . . seeing no possible way of extricating himself from the environments" to rising as the "new man" in order "to rule and to teach man how to live."[33] Yet this call for responsibility was itself already a double-edged proposition insofar as it sought agonistically to uphold its commitment to self-determination in a period of acute persecution in the postwar United States during which Black self-determination faced murderous opposition.[34] Unlike many of his contemporaries, Garvey did not formulate Black historical self-determination as a revolutionary or even strictly political movement. The UNIA project to foster "appreciation and honest comradeship" among the races proceeded neither from militant struggle nor from liberal arbitration, but from a speculative investment in a historical position of Black sovereignty that would be measurable in terms of its equivalence with other "advanced races." Reed's one-line assessment of Garvey's "improvement" project stresses the ambiguities of his campaign to reject victimhood as a legitimate historical or political position, even at the expense of reifying white supremacy and exploiting the very people whose exploitation he rejected.

Reed's allusion to Marcus Garvey through Hank Rollings is thus anything but dismissive. The very conflation of grammatical subjects in the Guianese art critic's line about sleeping crocodiles gestures toward the powerful and immanent awakening to which Garvey's work attended: an awakening measured "universally," as Garvey would put it—that is, according to a grand historical narrative of reciprocity and recompense drawn from the universal histories of writers such as G. W. F. Hegel, Max Nordau, Oswald Spengler, and Lothrop Stoddard, as well as from biblical hermeneutics[35]—rather than through individual or collective activism. The immediate context for Reed's invocation of Garvey is a commentary on the historical moment of persecution during which Garvey's UNIA movement first rose to prominence in the United States, a moment characterized by a violent reversal of Black fortunes in the aftermath of the Great War. Reed notes that

> 61 lynchings occurred in 1920 alone. In 1921, 62, some of the victims, soldiers returning from the Great War who after fighting and winning significant victories—just as they had fought in the Revolutionary and Civil wars and the wars against the Indians—thought that America would repay them for the generosity of putting their lives on the line, for aiding and salvaging their hides from the Kaiser who had been tagged "enemy" this time. Instead, a Protestant country ignorant even of Western mysteries executes soldiers after a manner of punishments dealt to witches in the "Middle Ages." Europe and the Catholic Church were horrified but not surprised at this "tough guy" across the waters whose horrendous murders in Salem led Europe to reform its "witch laws."[36]

Reed's allusion to Garvey proceeds from this tragic balance sheet of unreconciled historical accounting. The historical and contextual frames for invoking Garvey thus stipulates that he is by no means the target of suspicion here. What comes under fire instead is the irrational surge in "medieval" forms of murder in the interwar United States, as well as the governing historical logic according to which the memory of centuries of persecution became indistinguishable from "lethargy"—that is, subject to *lethe*, memory loss, oblivion. Like Reed's own epic counterhistory of race relations in *Mumbo Jumbo*, Garvey sought to inaugurate a new system of historical relation that sloughed off the lethargy of canonical Western historiography— the historical erasure carried out by a "dominator society," as Riane Eisler might put it.[37] Reed's novelistic version of the 1920s envisions a similar refashioning of historical logic: it offers, as Reed puts it, a "gros-ben-age" of the times, a pun on the Haitian *gros bon ange* of vodun metaphysics that already marks its etymological distinction from the Germanic *Zeitgeist*. Reed and Garvey each invoke the metaphysics of historiography, the very "spirit" of the times, as a mechanism for awakening their audiences from its obliviating effects.[38]

Garvey's 1922 Easter Sermon in Harlem invoked precisely this sense of lethargy as an ideological construct, the amnesic "sleep of the past" that constituted an erasure of persecution and potential greatness alike. Heeding the liturgical context of his Easter address, Garvey advocated a "resurrection" from this historical loss of consciousness, thus suggesting that his charges of lethargy had less to do with assigning responsibility for the immanent realities of racial persecution than of proselytizing a narrative of Black sovereignty that would balance the accounts on the scale of universal history.[39] He thus spoke of the "great need for a resurrection—a resurrection from the lethargy of the past—the sleep of the past—from that feeling that made us accept the idea and opinion that God intended that we should occupy an inferior place in the world." Reed's own ironic historiography expands similarly on this assessment of lethargy as a force of historical repression, depicting the bankruptcy of a culture that had eradicated the very possibility of historical reciprocity or "repayment" on the order described in *Mumbo Jumbo*. Just as it was "ignorant even of Western mysteries," the postwar U.S. nation-state could guarantee no return on the social, legal, moral, human, and financial capital expended by African Americans. In this context, Garvey emerges as a figure and symptom of this failed reciprocity, one who both advocated against it and voiced its terms. In approaching him as a theorist of Black sovereignty, therefore, what is called for is less a judgment of his successes or failings as a leader than a rethinking of the historical terms he brought into play, the metahistorical structures upon which such expectations of reciprocity depended, whether provisionally upheld or flagrantly ignored in periodic outbursts of "medieval" violence.

Garvey, whose litany of executive titles grew to include the president general of the Universal Negro Improvement Association and the provisional president of Africa, certainly cut a spectacular historical figure. His surfeit of sartorial, rhetorical, and institutional signifiers attests to his leveraging of cultural capital as the basis for his efforts to secure credit in return for credibility.[40] As scholars have noted, Garvey's self-fashioning was, by design, metonymic of the UNIA project as a whole, which was to establish what Garvey later referred to as a "grand racial hierarchy" that would simultaneously unite and levy distinction upon the Black race beyond "clime, border, or nation." The notion of a grand racial hierarchy was an administrative rather than evaluative category, referring to the sovereignty of the Black race rather than to a set of categorical distinctions akin to W. E. B. Du Bois's "Talented Tenth." It thus proposed that sovereignty was a corporate project to be carried out by the organization of Black people worldwide rather than by an elite class of intellectuals alone. By "inspir[ing] a literature and promulgat[ing] a doctrine of our own without any apologies to the powers that be," Garvey argued, people of African descent could forget the history of forgetting in which they had been inscribed and instead reclaim their place among the great civilizations of world history.[41] In forwarding such claims, Garvey's project fused the Tuskegee Institute's vocational notions of uplift rooted in economic pragmatism with a Pan-African attention to world-historical clashes for sovereignty in the era of the Great War and the League of Nations. Garvey's program of "universal negro improvement" proposed to do so without sacrificing either the economic or the "universal" exigencies upon which its claims to sovereignty were grounded. In other words, Garveyism both proposed and institutionalized a large-scale program for racial self-fashioning that could bear immediate material and social results.

The Garveyite project drew its authority, as I have suggested, from the narratives and metahistorical structures through which this self-fashioning played out on the scale of universal history, which framed political struggle in terms of the rise and fall of great civilizations. This meant not only the retrieval of a suppressed Black historiography but also the heeding of its narrative terms—that is, the impending resurgence of a once great Pan-African civilization. "When we come to consider the history of man," Garvey wrote in 1922, "was not the Negro a power? Was he not great once? Yes, honest students of history can recall the day when Egypt, Ethiopia and Timbuctoo towered in their civilizations, towered above Europe, towered above Asia."[42] Garvey's system proposed the reintroduction of this racial inheritance understood in terms not only of greatness, or technological and intellectual authority, but also wealth—an inheritance he solicited *in the present* through the promissory note of universal history. This recursive logic of return presents another involution (rather than revolution) characteristic of Garveyism, here describing the proleptic historical return that underwrote its financial and organizational possibility. Even as Garvey may have wagered heavily on the credibility of his spectacular self-presentations, his thinking and organizational work was founded on the credit of speculative historiography.

The theories and institutions for which Garvey became known were not in themselves unique to him—Garvey did not invent the concepts or organizational forms he developed through the UNIA. I stress the unoriginality of Garvey's thought because its core insight, its visionary involution, pertains to its function as an assemblage of institutions and other thinkers. His theories are, in other words, corporate, assimilating the work of the writers and thinkers he brought into the UNIA and the *Negro World* newspaper he founded: Dusé Mohamed Ali, John E. Bruce, Wilfred Domingo, William Ferris, Amy Jacques Garvey, Hubert Harrison, and J. A. Rogers, along with earlier figures.[43] As his detractors noted in particular—and with no small degree of contempt—Garvey's particular talent lay in making ideas about racial self-fashioning and world-historical sovereignty seem possible—that is, in bringing them to life, however fleetingly, in all their spectacular appeal. E. Franklin Frazier's oft-repeated 1926 assessment that Garvey "has the distinction of initiating the first real mass movement among American Negroes" was intended as an admonishment: Garvey's appeal to the uneducated masses derived from the rhetorical charm of his appeal to a "lost paradise" whose time "is always almost at hand."[44] Because he lacked formal education Garvey was, according to Frazer, one of "those so-called cranks who refuse to deal realistically with life," an opinion that was repeated during the culture wars of the 1980s and 1990s.[45] Yet even as such portrayals of Garvey's troublesome success as a "mass leader" impugn the questionable ideological calculations at its base, they also articulate in their very disbelief the unique speculative conditions of Garvey's thought as it played out institutionally.

Garvey's innovation as a thinker and organizer had very much to do with the broader project of bringing together conflicting and often mutually exclusive administrative and ideological priorities. As Du Bois put it in 1922, in one of a long series of critiques of Garvey's "black demagoguery," Garvey's singularity lay in this very synthesis. Referring to the Black Star Line of steamships launched by the UNIA in 1919, whose advertising and accounting practices would soon fall under government scrutiny, Du Bois wrote that "autonomous African Negro States have been forecast by scores of Negro leaders and writers. But a definite plan to unite Negrodom by a line of steamships was a brilliant suggestion and Garvey's only original contribution to the race problem."[46] I wish to take Du Bois's assessment literally here, exploring what even he considered to be the originality of Garvey's work. Beyond his personal talent or propensity toward spectacular promises, his work offers a narrative theory of Black power that both accounted for and sought to manage its own historical and material contingencies. Insofar as it outlines a theory of sovereignty, that is, Garvey's thinking is notable for its systematic—albeit composite and unfolding—approach to combining two oppositional forms of speculation. On the one hand, it envisioned a world-historical structure of racial resurgence that situated historical change according to an epic timeline; on the other hand, it instituted a form of financial speculation—in selling shares in the Black Star Line—that sought to raise enough capital to bring about this epic change in the immediate present. Garveyism inaugurated what we might refer to in Deleuzian terms as a desiring machine of social and libidinal investment that literalized historical desire—promise, power, awakening—as a financial promise.

"YOUR DAY IS COMING"

Whatever ideological and rhetorical warfare may have come to divide them, Garvey's UNIA shared with Du Bois and the NAACP a common interest in redressing the European and American redistribution of Germany's African colonies at the 1919 Paris Peace Conference.[47] In addition to creating the League of Nations and ratifying the Treaty of Versailles, the conference dealt a blow to home rule and anticolonial movements throughout the continent, awarding German overseas possessions to the other major colonial powers—Belgium, France, and Great Britain—a decision made without the participation of those colonial possessions (on account of their status as colonial possessions, which meant that they had no legitimate indigenous governmental status). The Garveyite slogan "Africa for the Africans," while designating by the early 1920s a project of Black recolonization, began as an assertion of home rule and, more broadly, as a shared sense of outrage at the fact that the nascent League of Nations neither represented nor addressed the political interests of "the darker races."

But the resemblance between Garveyism and Du Bois's nascent Pan-Africanism largely ends there. As we will see, the methodological apparatus through which Garvey's UNIA confronted the politics of race both abroad and on the home front contrasted starkly with that of the NAACP and *The Crisis,* the magazine Du Bois edited in its name. Du Bois famously traveled to Paris as a special envoy to the Paris Peace Conference, organizing the Pan-African Congress, which sought to represent the interests of colonial subjects to the League of Nations; the Pan-African delegates went so far as to draft a code of law "for the international protection of the natives of Africa," though it went largely unheeded at the conference.[48] Impatient with Du Bois's diplomatic mode of advocacy, Garvey would express increasing hostility toward Du Bois's claim to racial leadership throughout the 1920s, contesting not only the concepts but also the financial and administrative practices of the NAACP. He levied Du Bois's institutional reliance upon liberal white patrons—as well as Du Bois's wartime call to "forget our special grievances" in favor of the war effort—toward galvanizing the UNIA's notions of racial purity in opposition to the NAACP's program of racial integration. Such charges were fueled, in turn, by Du Bois's own public critiques of the UNIA and the BSL. Yet the principal difference between Garvey's early Pan-Africanism and Du Bois's position at the Paris Peace Conference was, I maintain, as much a methodological as an ideological one, based on the material form as much as the evidentiary content of their programs for redressing white supremacy and enabling "racial uplift."

The particularity of Garvey's institutional and corporate recourse to me-tahistorical narratives and patterns comes into relief against the social-scientific presentation of data in *The Crisis*.[49] With a striking consistency, the Du Bois–helmed magazine represented cartographically the geographical distribution of global and domestic events, as in its documentation of Afri-ca's colonial distribution, the national origins of the delegates in attendance at the Pan-African Congress in 1919, the locations of NAACP franchises throughout the United States in 1922, and the incidents of lynching throughout the country from 1889 through 1921. In a manner that reflects Du Bois's sociological training, the editorial apparatus of *The Crisis* docu-mented world history and murder alike through statistics and maps. Gar-vey's speeches and editorials were, by contrast, quintessentially narrative and epic in scale, grounded in versions of world history consistent with the works of G. W. F. Hegel, Oswald Spengler, and Lothrop Stoddard, as well as the revisionist Black historiographers Edward Wilmot Blyden, Hubert Harrison, and George Wells Parker. Du Bois himself had published a work of Black historical reclamation in 1915; his study *The Negro* sought to re-dress the curious effect of "modern prejudice that most of this splendid his-tory of civilization and uplift is unknown to-day, and men confidently assert that Negroes have no history."[50] Yet he also sought to dislodge the study of "the darker part of the human family" from the claims to scientific catego-rization of nineteenth-century ethnography, stressing that "race is a dynamic and not a static conception."[51] Unlike the universal histories of Hegel, Speng-ler, and Stoddard, Du Bois organized his deep historiography of *The Negro* according to the geography of Africa and the diaspora rather than heeding the inherited categories of race or merely tracing the fate of racialized world empires.

Garvey's histories, on the other hand, were governed by the waxing and waning of greatness and power. In place of sociological data, we find the "gros-ben-age" of universal history—that is, Garvey's historical schemes resembled in methodology the Hegelian–Spenglerian world histories in maintaining the premise that the dominance of the European empires was currently in decline. Yet rather than a cause for panic—or for increased militancy against the "rising tide of color," as Stoddard notoriously put it[52]—Garvey's historical patterns were emphatically promissory, even in the financial sense. In contrast to Du Bois's epistemic reclamation of Negro history, Garvey charted a narrative return to sovereignty in the era of Spen-gler's *The Decline of the West* (1922) and the political "awakening" of Africa.

The sweeping historicism Garvey adopted was voiced in countless speeches and tracts but formalized most succinctly in his 1925 editorial

Africa and the World Democracy

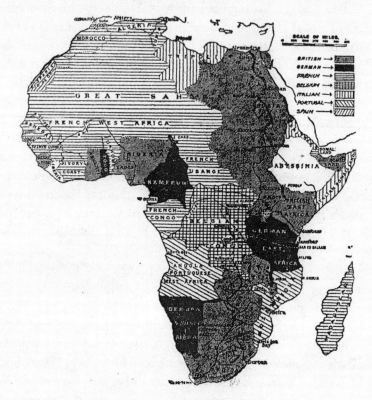

HOW AFRICA WAS DIVIDED UP AMONG THE NATIONS
OF EUROPE BEFORE THE WAR

Country	Area Sq. Miles	Populat'n	Country	Area Sq. Miles	Populat'n
British Empire	3,700,000	52,325,000	Belgium (Belgian Congo)	909,000	15,000,000
France	4,641,000	29,577,000	Spain	88,000	660,000
Germany	931,000	13,420,000	INDEPENDENT STATES		
Portugal	749,000	8,244,000	Abyssinia	432,000	8,000,000
Italy	593,000	1,579,000	Liberia	40,000	1,800,000

175

FIGURE 13. Africa's colonial distribution, as published in *The Crisis* 17 (February 1919): 175.

110 DELEGATES TO THE PAN-AFRICAN CONGRESS BY COUNTRIES

 卐 卐　　　卐 卐 卐　　　　卐 卐

United States of America

R. P. Sims, Bluefield, W. Va.,
  West Virginia Teachers' Association.
H. A. Hunt, Fort Valley, Ga.,
  Ga. Ass'n Advancement Negro Education.
G. R. Hutto, Bainbridge, Ga.,
  Knights of Pythias.
Mrs. A. E. Hutto.
P. F. Haynes, St. Joseph, Mo.,
  Odd Fellows.
Dr. Henry R. Butler, Atlanta, Ga.,
  Ancient Free Masons.
H. R. Butler, Jr., Atlanta, Ga.,
Mrs. Viola Hart Felton, Americus, Ga.,
  Eastern Star.
Lydia G. Brown, Washington, D. C.,
  Dunbar High School.
Florence Kelley, New York City,
  N. A. A. C. P.
Rev. W. H. Jernagin, Washington, D. C.
  National Race Congress of America.
Jessie Fauset, New York City,
  Delta Sigma Theta Sorority.
William S. Nelson, New York City,
  Omega Psi Phi Fraternity.
Dr. A. Wilberforce Williams, Chicago, Ill.,
  Chicago Defender Pub. Co.
Bishop C. H. Phillips, Nashville, Tenn.,
  C. M. E. Church.
Bishop John Hurst, Baltimore, Md.,
  A. M. E. Church.
Mrs. John Hurst.
Dr. R. T. Brown, Birmingham, Ala.,
  C. M. E. Church.
Dr. C. H. Phillips, Jr., St. Louis, Mo.,
  Missouri Negro Republican League Club.
Mrs. C. H. Phillips, Jr.
Mrs. H. R. Butler, Atlanta, Ga.,
  Colored Parent-Teachers' Association.
Miss Lavinia Black, New York City.
Mr. and Mrs. Arthur Spingarn,
  N. A. A. C. P.
C. H. Tobias, New York City,
  International Committee, Y. M. C. A.

Bishop Cary and Mrs. Cary, Chicago, Ill.,
  A. M. E. Church.
Mrs. French, St. Louis, Mo.
R. R. Wright, Jr., Philadelphia, Pa.,
  A. M. E. Church.
Capt. and Mrs. N. B. Marshall,
Walter F. White, New York City,
  N. A. A. C. P.
Dr. W. E. B. DuBois, New York City,
  N. A. A. C. P.

England

Dr. John Alcindor and wife
Alice Werner
George Lattimore
Ruth Fisher
Dr. F. Hoggan
Robert Broadhurst
Mrs. Fisher Unwin
J. R. Archer, ex-Mayor of Battersea
Roland Hayes
Rev. Mr. A. M. Chirgwin
Rev. Mr. Frank Lenwood

France

Deputy Barthélémy
Félicien Challaye
Mrs. Ida Gibbs Hunt
Sénateur Aubert
Dr. George Jackson
Rayford Logan
Mme. L. Chapoteau
Mrs. Charles Young

Belgium

Paul Otlet
General Gillain
Jean Baugniet
Sénateur La Fontaine

Belgian Congo

Paul Panda
Members of Union Congolaise (18)
Madame Soroléa

Sierra Leone

Mr. Sutton
Dr. Ojo Olaribigbe
Rev. Mr. E. G. Granville

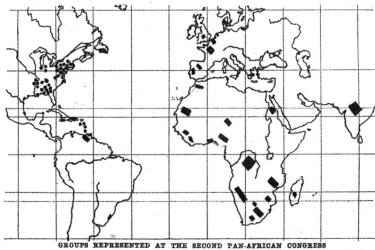

GROUPS REPRESENTED AT THE SECOND PAN-AFRICAN CONGRESS

68

FIGURE 14. National origins of the delegates in attendance at the Pan-African Congress in 1919, as published in *The Crisis* 23 (December 1921): 68.

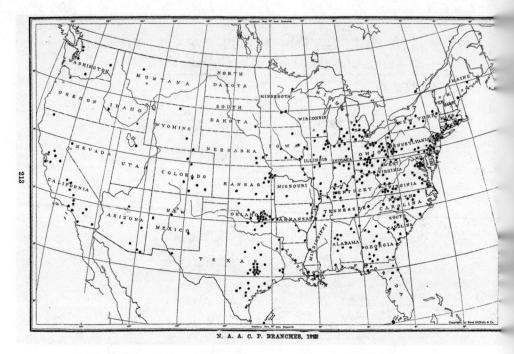

N. A. A. C. P. BRANCHES, 1922

FIGURE 15. NAACP locations throughout the United States in 1922, as published in *The Crisis* 23 (March 1922): 213.

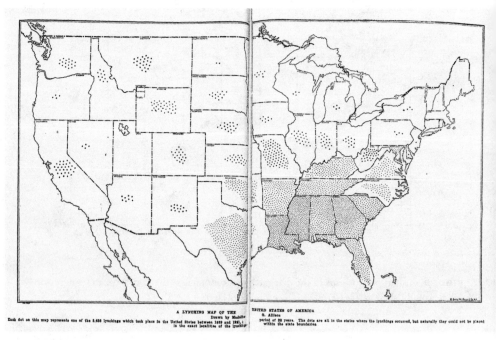

A LYNCHING MAP OF THE UNITED STATES OF AMERICA
Drawn by Madeline G. Allison
Each dot on this map represents one of the 3,436 lynchings which took place in the United States between 1889 and 1921, a period of 32 years. The dots are all in the states where the lynchings occurred, but naturally they could not be placed in the exact localities of the lynchings within the state boundaries.

FIGURE 16. Incidents of lynchings throughout the United States, 1889–1921, as published in *The Crisis* 23 (February 1922): 168.

"African Fundamentalism," a virtual manifesto of midcareer Garveyism written from Atlanta Federal Penitentiary. Here, as in other such writings, Garvey sought to relativize the current subaltern state of diasporic nations and subjects by advancing a long view of the ages of empire, a now familiar Afrocentric grand narrative that celebrated Africa as the ancient cradle of civilization rather than as a continent devoid of any history other than colonial exploitation. As Garvey wrote in one of the editorial's more measured statements,

> The world today is indebted to us for the benefits of civilization. They stole our arts and sciences from Africa. Then why should we be ashamed of ourselves? Their MODERN IMPROVEMENTS are but DUPLICATES of a grander civilization that we reflected thousands of years ago, without the advantage of what is buried and still hidden, to be resurrected and reintroduced by the intelligence of our generation and our prosperity.[53]

Garvey's ideas about the priority of Africa not only supplanted Greco-Roman antiquity as the origin for the "benefits of civilization" but also challenged the inheritance itself: rather than a direct bloodline from Athens to the splendors of contemporary democracy, we find a legacy of theft and imperfect duplication. Garvey's language thus anticipated the notions of unremunerated debt, pillage, and failed reciprocity to which Reed alluded in *Mumbo Jumbo* far more than it beckoned to the "noble lie" of self-ennoblement targeted by Lefkowitz.

As I have suggested, Garvey's appeals to the historical—if not ontological—priority of African civilization represent a synthesis of nearly two centuries of Black diasporic thought. In addition to their continuities with the work of his early contemporaries in Jamaica,[54] they reflect Garvey's early encounters in England with a number of African intellectuals who, in the years before the First World War, were already in the process of working out a distinctly historical (rather than political or moral) logic for home rule in India and Africa. These intellectuals included, most notably, Dusé Mohamed Ali, the editor of the *African Times and Orient Review* and author of *In the Land of the Pharaohs* (1911), a history of contemporary Egypt that made a strident case for home rule, and J. E. Casley Hayford, author of *Ethiopia Unbound* (1911).[55] Such intellectuals sought to promote racial "advancement" through both a discursive unification (in the form of a newspaper) and a world-historical narrative of the rising and falling of great civilizations, according to which African and "oriental" civilizations had once been powerful empires and would rise again once more. A call for contributions printed in the inaugural issue of the *African Times and Orient Review* in 1912 announces, for instance, that "your day is coming. Your place in the sun has been and will come again. As darkness overtook you for a space, it must also overtake Europe. The future of Africa, the future of India, will not be decided in the chanceries of Europe, but upon the hills of India and the plans of Africa."[56]

Garvey's own published essay in a 1913 issue of the *African Times and Orient Review* adopts this prophetic language explicitly: "As one who knows the people well," Garvey writes, "I make no apology for prophesying that there will soon be a turning point in the history of the West Indies; and that the people who inhabit that portion of the Western Hemisphere will be the instruments of uniting a scattered race who, before the close of many centuries, will found an Empire on which the sun shall shine as ceaselessly as it shines on the Empire of the North to-day."[57] In the editorial "African Fundamentalism," written twelve years later, this narrative has been fully formalized as the retrieval of a forgotten cultural treasure to be resurrected from historical oblivion *(lethe)* and reintroduced into contemporary Black life by the "intelligence of our generation and our prosperity." Yet by 1925 Garvey had fundamentally altered both the implicit contestation of his earlier model and its uncertain temporal conditions. Gone, for instance, is the allusion in the 1913 essay to a diasporic empire emerging "before the close of many centuries"; the time for resurrection was instead at hand. In the years of Garvey's most active organizational work, the abstract, teleological "some day," the suspended temporality of an eventual return to the sun, increasingly became a kind of historical guarantee that formed the basis for his pragmatic operations, the very means for the historical shift he envisioned. In place of an abstract horizon of eschatological fulfillment, Garvey furnished an instrumental logic for precipitating that fulfillment "by the intelligence of our generation and our prosperity." At stake, in other words, was not merely a nostalgic (or tragic) appeal to ancient history or a dialectical struggle between colonizer and colonized, but an alternative structure of historical change, one whose political prophesies were self-fulfilling in both world-historical and financial terms.

Garvey's "improvement" industries operated within a narrative framework that actualized the abstract horizon of prosperity as the work of corporate institutions such as the UNIA. Not only did such institutions provide him with the rhetorical platform for speaking on behalf of "400,000,000 Negroes" worldwide, but they also became the instrumental medium for the intelligence and prosperity they promoted.[58] This claim to sovereignty was structured, in turn, as a political and moral choice between two forms of repetition: the first, *return*, signified the resurgence of Black historical prominence; the second, by contrast, comprised the mimetic duplication of African civilization by European Empires—that is, theft, fraud, and persecution on a world-historical scale. By advocating return as a rejoinder to such fraudulent repetition, Garvey upheld the claim that African sovereignty came both historically and ontologically prior to Western empire. This priority then formed the standard against which the currency of Garvey's speculations could be substantiated through the financial return accumulated by UNIA corporations. His claim to Pan-African resurgence literally banked on a mode of world-historical and financial return whose tautological structure distinguished it from imitation, nostalgia, or other forms of fraudulent repetition, an insistence later rendered ironic by his prosecution for mail fraud for misrepresenting the ships in the BSL fleet and overestimating the future value of stock shares. Garvey's vision of a Black empire to come thus proposed a supersession not only of empires but also of metahistorical forms, replacing repetition (or, for that matter, dialectical struggle) with return; this epistemic shift owes as much to the tautological insistence of its own formal logic as to the more muscular interventions of revolution or warfare that commonly figure as the instruments of political transformation.

Garvey's claim that the resurgence of Pan-African sovereignty constituted a historical return rather than a mimetic duplication of other empires enabled him to gesture toward other nationalisms and independence movements without acceding to their ethical or political priority. Garvey could borrow freely from contemporary discourses of sovereign power, in other words, precisely because his world-historical narrative demanded the incorporation of such discourses as a form of reciprocity or compensation rather than as a gesture of imitation (as reflected in naming the Black Star Line after the Cunard White Star Line, with all its colonialist overtones). This logic applied as strongly to his appropriation of African American and anticolonial thought as to his oppositional aspirations in the face of white imperialism. In this respect Garvey's thinking about the exigency of an "African awakening" draws both from the diasporic intellectuals of the *African Times and Orient Review,* as well as from the work of Hubert Harrison, the socialist and former Industrial Workers of the World activist instrumental in introducing Garvey to Harlem audiences in 1916, and who became one of the editors of Garvey's *Negro World* newspaper. Indeed, Harrison would later claim, not without acrimony, that "Garvey appropriated every feature that was worthwhile in his movement" from Harrison's own earlier organization, the Liberty League, as well as from its flagship newspaper, *The Voice.*[59] Such recriminations notwithstanding, Harrison's work was instrumental in shifting the terms of "racial awakening" from a teleological horizon of expectation to the field of immediate economic and social relations upon which Garvey's ideas of contestation and reciprocity would play out.

In his articles for *The Voice* and *Negro World* alike, Harrison outlined a resurgent Black nationalism that could both redress the global imbalance of power and combat lynching and injustice on the U.S. home front. His ideas about an instrumental form of nationalism were modeled on the global logic of home rule advocated by anticolonial activists in Africa, India, and Ireland. As Harrison wrote in 1917, in language that answered to Garvey's earliest rhetoric of racial self-critique, "the new Negro race in America will not achieve political self-respect until it is in a position to organize itself as a politically independent party and follow the example of the Irish Home Rulers."[60] Political independence demanded independent politics, in other words; as Harrison explained in a 1923 article, "The original program of the Universal Negro Improvement Association was a good one, and it is still good. That program was based on the belief that Negroes should finance the foundations of their future and not go begging to the white race for help, leadership or a program."[61] Though it settled on finance as the basis for political self-organization, such an understanding of independence necessarily prioritized race because race formed the universal exception to other forms of political solidarity. "Every movement for the extension of democracy has been broken down as soon as it reached the color line," Harrison wrote. "Political democracy declared that 'all men are created equal' [but it] meant only all white men."[62] For Harrison, a "race first" practice of independent political organization coincided with the possibility of taking democracy at its word—that is, as a real system for distributing political power rather than a form of idealism alone. Substituting race consciousness for the class consciousness of his Marxist peers, Harrison cited the recent world war as an event that disclosed the categorical separation between democratic idealism and the real struggle for political sovereignty it overshadowed. The inevitable result was a violent confrontation between democratic principles and their exceptions, exposing the limitations of a merely rhetorical appeal to equality and human rights. As Harrison noted,

> The great World War, by virtue of its great advertising campaign for democracy and the promises which were held out to all subject peoples, fertilized the Race Consciousness of the Negro people into the stage of conflict with the dominant white idea of the color line. They took democracy at its face value—which is—equality. So did the Hindus, Egyptians, and West Indians. This is what the hypocritical advertisers of democracy had not bargained for.[63]

As the results of the 1919 Paris Peace Conference demonstrated, the First World War owed no small part of its violence to the role of African and overseas colonies in the struggle for imperial expansion. Its world-historical pressures also demonstrated that the "fratricidal strife" among colonial superpowers was consuming the very resources—ships, guns, men, and money—upon which their claims to sovereignty, "superiority," and civilization were founded.[64] The West faced its own decline and, correspondingly, its colonial subjects could no longer "be eternally coerced into accepting the sovereignty of the white race."[65] Harrison presented this condition as a prophetic choice: if the white race accepted this redistribution of power, then it would live in peace with it. But "if it insists that freedom, democracy, and equality are to exist only for white men," then bloodshed will inevitably follow."[66]

Remarkably, Harrison's terms self-consciously beckoned to Lothrop Stoddard's alarmist work of racist historiography, *The Rising Tide of Color against White Supremacy* (1920), which Harrison both reviewed in print and incorporated into his essay compilation that same year. In a profound gesture of *détournement*, Harrison levied Stoddard's anxiety about the "colored" threat to white supremacy as an ironic confirmation of his own argument about the "social theory of white domination" that undergirded the struggles for African territory so instrumental to the war and its aftermath.[67] Like Stoddard, Harrison claimed that the so-called Great War had more to do with racial domination than with the political ideals it advertised, such as the defense of democracy.[68] "Mr. Stoddard holds that his race is doomed," Harrison wrote, adding that "the present reviewer stakes his money on 'the doom.'"[69] Historical narratives, he suggested, bore real corporeal and material effects.

In its incrimination of European superpowers for the epistemological and material forms through which it carried out imperial domination in the name of democracy and civilization, Harrison's counterhistoriography might be said to anticipate not only Garvey but other anticolonial critics of Western humanism such as Aimé Césaire.[70] Harrison at his most rhapsodic asserts that "the white race has lied and strutted its way to greatness and prominence over the corpses of other peoples. It has capitalized, Christianized, and made respectable, 'scientific,' and 'natural,' the fact of its dominion. It has read back into history the race relations of today, striving to make the point that previous to its advent on the stage of human history, there was no civilization or culture worthy of its name."[71] Harrison's notion of race consciousness takes stock not only of the contemporary fact of white domination, but also of the historical narratives that sustain it ideologically. In doing so, it beckons to a form of reciprocity for, rather than an imitation or appropriation of, the corpus of white supremacist historiography, of which Stoddard's *Rising Tide of Color* represented the anxious culmination.

Harrison's counterhistory of Black resurgence does not so much strive to "naturalize" or "make respectable" the ennobling reality of African civilization as instead to crystallize the struggle for political and material power that operates under the aegis of such narratives. Like Reed's body count in *Mumbo Jumbo*, Harrison confronts the "advertisement" for democracy with the balance sheet of its unpaid mortal debts. As he writes in his continued discussion of the consequences of World War I, "The American Negroes, like the other darker peoples, are presenting their cheques and trying to cash in, and delays in the process, however unavoidable to the paying tellers, are bound to beget a plentiful lack of belief in either their intention or their ability to pay. Hence the run on Democracy's bank—'the Negro unrest' of the newspaper paragraphers."[72] Democracy may have been the ideal under which colonial power was redistributed among the European nations, but in furnishing a concept of equality and reciprocity, it also enabled the "cashing in" on the political and material currency it stood for. "The king-word of modern nations," Harrison writes, "is POWER," which he, like Garvey, understood in both historiographical and material terms—that is, both in terms of the "metaphysical" claim to "better manners, more religion or a higher culture" and "on the frankly materialistic ground that it has the guns, soldiers, the money, and resources" necessary to sustain its power.[73] Whether or not the formal powers of democracy can survive the run on its bank is another story: can whiteness tolerate a redistribution of racial sovereignty? For Harrison, the essential point is to take democracy at its word (to heed, that is, the "king-word" of power) and to seize a rightful share of power according to an ethical standard of reciprocity.

Harrison's notion that African Americans are "trying to cash in" on the politicoeconomic and epistemic "advertisement" for democratic reciprocity forms the basis, moreover, for his logic of ethical self-defense against the immanent crisis of lynching in the United States. In similarly grim actuarial terms, Harrison writes, "Suppose [the common Black man in Tennessee] lets it be known that for the life of every Negro soldier or civilian, two 'crackers' will die? Suppose he lets them know that it will be as costly to kill Negroes as it would be to kill real people?"[74] In its measurement of costs and balanced accounts, Harrison's notion of Black racial awakening thus constituted far more than an appeal to financial earning power alone. Black sovereignty was instead founded on the corporeal security of its "metaphysical" ideals: that is, power derived its currency from the bodily, material, juridical, and ethical resources—including the recourse to violence—it always held in reserve.

Harrison's economic metaphorics thus acknowledge that even "cash" constituted a form of credit, signifying an immanent potentiality whose future was assured by trust in a material reserve. One of the major peculiarities of Garveyism, on the other hand, was that it sought to render the "frankly materialistic ground" of which Harrison spoke all the more concretely, and thus was all the more bankable as the very *realization* of power rather than as its standard or its field of contestation. Indeed, when he incorporated the Black Star Line in 1919, Garvey literalized Harrison's economic terms: the system of reciprocity and bankable resources Harrison described became, for Garvey, an actual commercial enterprise, which stood as the principal attempt by the UNIA to actualize the logic of historical reciprocity that Harrison and other Black nationalist intellectuals advocated. Garvey's enterprise sought, in other words, at once to make possible and to render present the forms of historical return upon which Harrison and his peers speculated.

"THE ACME OF AMERICAN NEGRO ENTERPRISE"

The notion of undertaking—rather than merely advocating—commercial speculation as a means for underwriting this speculative historical program remains Garvey's most significant and characteristic intervention, as Du Bois reminds us.[75] The foundation of the Black Star Line, a steamship corporation that would carry freight and passengers throughout the major ports of the African diaspora, aimed to satisfy the twin imperatives of Garvey's theory of racial sovereignty. At once a Black-owned and -operated commercial enterprise financed through stocks and, like the *Negro World* newspaper, a means for bringing the Black populations of the Atlantic world into contact, the BSL presented a living example of Garvey's world-historical program. As Michelle Stephens has written, "imagining ships as the vehicles to facilitate circumatlantic performance and circumcaribbean movement, Marcus Garvey literally attempted to place ownership of the means of production in the hands of working Black populations," a project that acknowledged the historical overtones of a long legacy of Black transatlantic travel, including earlier pilgrimages and African repatriation movements that had sought to assert agency over the horrific legacy of the Middle Passage.[76] As with his recourse to narratives of world-historical return, Garvey's program in founding the Black Star Line was notable for its unprecedented scope—as well as, I maintain, for its theoretical function as the administrative basis for rendering *present* the horizon of futurity implicit in the historiography of Black resurgence. To this end, what made the BSL project especially brilliant—and what was most problematic about it—was the plan to finance the company through the selling of public shares. For all its emphatic presentism, the BSL was still funded through speculative means.

Shortly after its incorporation in July 1918, the UNIA was paired with a secondary organization, the African Communities League (ACL), a stock corporation legally incorporated later that same month; the purpose of the ACL was to raise capital through the sale of stock for an open-ended set of business ventures, from the management of grocery stores, restaurants, laundries, and real estate to the manufacturing of tin, clothing, and appliances, as well as the publication of newspapers, books, and music.[77] Yet it was in June 1919 that the UNIA launched its most characteristic—and most embattled—enterprise, the Black Star Line, which would be funded through the sale of one hundred thousand shares priced at five dollars each. Arriving at the moment when "the Huns have signed [the Treaty of Versailles]," as Garvey declared in a *Negro World* editorial the day after its incorporation, the capital campaign for the BSL offered a means for taking advantage of the "stepping stone to fuller independence for Negroes in the future" represented by the German defeat. Yet from the start, Garvey came under fire—both legally and editorially—for the timing and rhetoric through which he advertised BSL stock. The New York *World* and district attorney alike admonished Garvey for selling BSL stock before the company had been legally incorporated. For its part, the U.S. Post Office cited Garvey's published claim that the five-dollar stocks "may be worth one hundred dollars six-months from now" as reason to doubt his credibility. Having settled these claims—that is, after suing the *World* for libel and finalizing the company's legal documents—Garvey's publicity campaign to raise capital for the BSL exploded, shifting from a rhetoric of futurity to an adamant claim to historical imminence.[78]

In its effort to mobilize finance capital toward world-historical gain, Garvey's program of financial speculation was continuous, yet again, with the earlier economic strategies of Dusé Mohamed Ali and other intellectuals affiliated with the *African Times and Orient Review,* who endorsed the formation of Black-owned shipping and export ventures that could disrupt white European monopolies on the African continent.[79] Indeed, the *African Times and Orient Review* included numerous advertisements for such commercial enterprises, confirming Ali's socialist contention that financial interest, more than ideology or racial "superiority" alone, constituted the motive force of political struggle. "Conquest," Ali wrote in 1911, "is no longer the battle-cry of monarchs. Modern warfare is conducted in the interest of trade and dividends."[80] Launched in the wake of the Armistice, the Black

Star Line aimed to continue the massive dissolution of European empires that the war had begun in preparedness, Garvey noted, "for the next war, twenty, thirty or forty years hence."[81] By October 1919 Garvey's language had become all the more firm in advocating the instrumentality of the BSL toward the fulfillment of his narrative of historical resurgence, asserting that "we want the Black Star Line so as to launch out to the Negro peoples of the world, and today the richest people of the world are the Negro people of Africa. Their minerals, their diamonds, their gold and their silver and their iron have built up the great English, French, German and Belgian Empires. Men, how long are we going to allow those parasites to suck the blood out of our children? How long? I answer for those who are active members of the Universal Negro Improvement Association and African Communities League, 'Not one day longer.'"[82] An advertisement for the BSL put it even more succinctly: "Negroes Awake! The hour has come to save your Race from the burning stake."

Garvey was, again, not alone in making such claims. Nor was the mechanism of issuing stocks and bonds to raise funds for Black-owned businesses and nonprofit organizations unique to Garveyism.[83] Beginning in 1913, for instance, the Oklahoma-born Chief Sam began selling stock in the Akim Trading Company to finance passage to the Gold Coast aboard the SS *Liberia,* pioneering the "back to Africa" movement for which Garvey would become the more visible figurehead.[84] Even the leftist *Messenger,* whose editors would become some of Garvey's most adamant critics, themselves launched a funding drive in 1919 by urging supporters to take out "a Messenger humanity bond" that would also be "an anti-lynching bond, an anti-discrimination bond, an anti-peonage bond, an anti-Jim Crow bond, a bond-of-brotherhood bond, the only real bond worth while, [and] a race liberty bond."[85] Such organizations were generally careful, though, to distinguish their financial accounting from their historical accounting—that is, they submitted their social and political goals to a different measure of return from their pragmatic operations. Buying a "Messenger humanity bond" was not the same as buying a Liberty Bond from the U.S. government: the point was solely to support the publishing organization and its antilynching campaign rather than seeking an eventual financial yield, even if, as Ian Baucom has noted, that yield existed along an imaginary timeline.[86] Yet in issuing stock the Black Star Line sought to raise money for the express purpose of generating *profit* for its shareholders. For to do so, to establish the BSL as a functioning corporate enterprise measurable in terms of financial gain and working ships, would signify that the hour of historical return had come. Thus the BSL found itself doubly mortgaged: it was not only funded

FIGURE 17. Advertisement in the *African Times and Orient Review* 1, no. 3 (September 1912): 1.

through advance promises on its own future profitability but it also marketed, proselytized, this return as the very present of an otherwise speculative historical timeline.

Because available credit was scarce, at best, for a Black-owned business, the stocks sold by the UNIA were meant to serve as venture capital for the Black Star Line. Yet since the BSL operated at a staggering loss (as Du Bois

FIGURE 18. Advertisement for the Black Star Line, 1919.

carefully demonstrated in the pages of *The Crisis*), this venture capital in fact constituted the operating budget for a de facto nonprofit organization.[87] Not only did Garvey use share revenues to pay off other UNIA and ACL debts, but the ships themselves proved notoriously unseaworthy, and their operation was thus subject to steep repair costs, as well as to numerous incidents of profiteering and subterfuge.[88] Thus the Black Star Line generated stock in order to extend its own life, in a way that had the ironic effect of requiring the deferral of any measurement of its (unprofitable) returns in favor of keeping open the possibility of a miraculous reversal of its misfortunes somewhere down the line. The line was thus forced to operate according to the very suspended temporality that Garvey sought to revise, in both guaranteeing the actuality of a future present and rendering it near at hand. The profitability of the BSL, against which Garvey had levied the credibility of a historical return, a "time in the sun," was now relegated to an eventual horizon of profit sometime in the future. As the historian Judith Stein puts it, "Garvey's politics were hostage to the economic trouble of the BSL. The more difficult it was to operate a profitable business, the more frantically he turned to the political arena to gain capital and explain the line's problems."[89] The result was an involution in the more regressive sense of the term, as defined by Clifford Geertz: an intensification without the capacity for radical change. Like Charles Ponzi, to whom other writers compared Garvey both favorably (as in the case of John E. Bruce) and scornfully (as in the case of George Schuyler), Garvey set in motion a speculative operation that functioned along a hypothetical timeline of perpetual prospect, a present characterized by infinite progress but also by perpetually deferred completion.[90] Any attempt to bring it to a measurable conclusion would bring the whole system into collapse. And collapse it did, in spectacular fashion. Yet whereas Ponzi's pyramid schemes were designed to exploit—leaving its lowest-ranking investors holding the bag—the Black Star Line was short-circuited by specific historical circumstances; its collapse was a function, for one, of political resistance and subterfuge in the United States and West Africa alike, as well as of the sheer enormity of the undertaking.[91]

Garvey's Black Star Line venture could not sustain itself in real time. It is worth noting, however, that in Garvey's case, "real time" was itself predicated on the virtual impossibility of acquiring credit, the perpetual possibility of racist violence, and the political intensities of the postwar period in general. In an era, as Ishmael Reed suggests, not only of *restricted* access to political, social, and financial capital but of utter bankruptcy and unreciprocated historical capital, it seems problematic to naturalize the "real time" according to which Garvey's speculations collapsed. For even as Garvey—a talented publisher, editor, writer, and orator but hardly an expert in maritime commerce—proved incapable of managing the BSL successfully, the company's failure, like its ambition, was overdetermined from the start.

As Garvey would insist in his own defense, the BSL was plagued at once by internal sabotage, embezzlement, and profiteering, as well as persistent Bureau of Investigation surveillance and tampering. Theodore Kornweibel concludes his account of the BSL collapse, as well as Garvey's trial and imprisonment for mail fraud, by stressing the significant impact of federal investigation and infiltration upon the UNIA, as upon other radical Black movements of the years after World War I. "It might be argued," he writes, "that Garvey's guilt makes immaterial the long crusade of the Bureau of Investigation and other federal agencies to block his magnetic impact on the black masses. But such a conclusion ignores the repressive weight of federal activity during the Red Scare."[92] My aim here is not to rehearse the well-documented events surrounding the implosion of the BSL and Garvey's subsequent legal circumstances. Rather, I wish to note the extent to which the temporality of his double speculation—staking historical resurgence upon the selling of stock—was itself conditional, subject to both administrative and ideological demands. For indeed, the instrumental role of the Black Star Line in Garvey's universalist project for restoring Black sovereignty was speculative rather than ideal—a wager, we might say, but never simply an abstract notion. This was precisely the point: Garvey was not interested in merely *promising* racial sovereignty, but in yielding it historically and materially. His program rested on the very recognition that the financial and administrative speculation at the heart of the BSL's fortunes was contingent upon legal, actuarial, financial, and organizational exigencies. Such a recognition testifies not only to the ambition of the BSL but also to its operative short-circuit and suspended temporality. The Black Star Line was, in spite of itself, a promissory venture.

CONCLUSION: THE PROVISIONAL PRESENT

Garvey's career did not end with the Black Star Line, nor with his imprisonment for mail fraud and subsequent deportation. He would launch another shipping line in 1924, the Black Cross Navigation and Trading Company, though it, too, would prove short-lived. More significantly, the period leading up to the collapse of the BSL saw a discernible shift in Garvey's tactics, which would find their full expression during and after his prison sentence. In addition to an increasing emphasis on African repatriation, his speeches and writings during this time were spiked with accusations of duplicity and betrayal directed toward other Black leaders, as well as members of his own organization—the ironic hypostasis, we might say, of his characteristic hortatory rhetoric. Garvey's allies and critics alike reacted strongly to his tendency to blame his legal persecution on Black "enemies of the race" such as Du Bois rather than pointing fingers at the federal government for its longstanding surveillance program. At the same time, his work was punctuated by a dramatic, even shocking, series of diplomatic gestures toward white bodies of power, including the U.S. government and the Ku Klux Klan.[93] A dramatic shift in tactics, indeed—but one that constituted a reentrenchment rather than an abandonment of his speculative project. For as Garvey would proclaim at the 1922 UNIA convention, and reiterate in the two volumes of his *Philosophy and Opinions* published by Amy Jacques Garvey in 1923 and 1925, the mission of the UNIA would henceforth be directed toward a different kind of corporate enterprise, investing in statehood rather than finance capital. As Michelle Stephens has noted, Garvey's project with the Black Star Line had already offered, in spite of its struggles and eventual collapse, a "spectacular traveling portrayal of the race's right to statehood."[94] During the early 1920s Garvey turned progressively toward statehood itself—no longer as merely a right, but as a sovereign claim—as the executive apparatus for administering the temporal and material conditions of his historical narrative of African resurgence.

Though they had evolved simultaneously with his rise to prominence in Harlem, Garvey's ideas about statehood increasingly formed the administrative horizon of the UNIA. The projects of African repatriation and Liberian economic development, which had taken seed during the BSL campaign, now became formalized as part of the UNIA's core mission.[95] For Garvey, however, statehood designated not only a nationalist claim to the African continent as the seat of a new Black empire but also a general concept of the nation-state as an apparatus of sovereign power. States, rather than corporations, became the means for "cashing in" on the unpaid debts of geopolitical reciprocity, a currency measurable in terms of power itself. Thus Garvey's ideas about the historical and political comportment of a state apparatus likewise became formalized as a set of authoritative principles or, as his critics claimed, authoritarian demands. "Underpinning Garvey's predilection toward nationhood," writes Tony Martin in his 1976 study *Race First*, "were his own speculations on political theory."[96]

As Garvey wrote in the first pages of his 1923 *Philosophy and Opinions*, in language recalling the militancy of the now estranged Hubert Harrison, "the political readjustment of the world means that those who are not sufficiently able, not sufficiently prepared, will be at the mercy of the organized classes

for another one or two hundred years.—The only protection against INJUS-
TICE in man is POWER—Physical, financial and scientific."[97] Linking these
two notions of sovereignty within the concept of statehood, Garvey continues: "NATIONHOOD is the only means by which modern civilization can protect itself."[98] This "protection" occupied two temporal registers. On the one
hand, it continued the Garveyite project of securing the world-historical
fortune of the race, in defending its nearness at hand against an impossible
attenuation (that is, for "another one or two hundred years"). On the other
hand, unmoored from the precarious finances of capitalist adventure, it also
proposed an institutional future for this new balance of power, keeping in
place the restored authority of the race in face of whatever opposition might
come along to threaten it.[99]

The notion of statehood to which Garvey entrusted the protection of
the black race was, however, all the more speculative than even the Black
Star Line. For not only did a Pan-African state not yet exist, but the very
concept of an independent Africa that would underwrite the sovereignty of
the Black diaspora also constituted a far more ideologically encumbered—not
to mention logistically tricky—project than the launching of a fleet of ships.
As Robert Bagnall notes in his 1923 essay "The Madness of Marcus Garvey," "So Garvey sees himself president of the Republic of Africa, sees his
government established. Year before last, at his convention, he promised that
ninety days afterwards, he would have embassies at the court of St. James,
in Paris, Petrograd, Rome, etc. He has no conception of the gulf of difficulty between a plan and its fulfillment."[100] Unsurprisingly, as a consequence
of Garvey's tactical and conceptual shift, the post-BSL era witnessed an adjustment of Garvey's temporality for Black resurgence. As Garvey wrote in
1923, in prophetic and thus no longer presentist terms, "No one knows when
the hour of Africa's redemption cometh. It is in the wind. It is coming. One
day, like a storm, it will be here. When that day comes all Africa will stand
together."[101]

The reason for this shift, I maintain, is that the sovereignty Garvey now
proposed was necessarily provisional, even virtual: Garvey's redoubled focus
on Black nationalism meant that the formation of a Pan-African Black state
became less the figurative historical telos of UNIA activity than its operative means. Statehood, rather than a corporate enterprise, constituted the apparatus for rendering present the prospective future of Black resurgence. Yet
the existence of an African state was itself speculative, with Garvey elected
by the UNIA membership as the provisional president of Africa in August
1920, much to the ridicule of his detractors. Garvey was hardly unaware of
the "gulf of difficulty between a plan and its fulfillment." His declaration of

provisional statehood was designed precisely as a means for spanning this gulf: what this meant was that his subsequent activities—from UNIA meetings themselves to the project of African repatriation and colonization, and even to Garvey's decision to represent himself in court—themselves constituted a means for exercising the sovereign power of a Pan-African state in advance of its actual legal or political formation. By 1922 Garvey's shift from finance capital to virtual statehood had been confirmed by the legal dissolution of the BSL; in exercising the executive functions of this provisional state, Garvey's acquiescence to diplomatic relations with other state formations represented a categorical separation from the politics of activism and advocacy exercised by his contemporaries, resembling instead the "paranoid" politics of suspicion and protogovernmental excess decried by his critics.

Much of Garvey's UNIA infrastructure remained intact throughout the 1920s and after, though it unsurprisingly lost some of its intensity after his deportation in 1927. Yet many of the structures and networks of Garvey's organizations persisted throughout the Global South in altered form, whether in collective local and diasporic political movements, grassroots organizational networks, or Black-owned bookstores and business networks, as scholars have increasingly noted.[102] Rather than acceding to the various narratives according to which scholars and political thinkers have sought to balance their accounts of Garvey's historicity—by dubbing him a fascist, a "mass leader," or a visionary—it is the institutional presence of Garvey's speculations that stand as a significant body of twentieth-century thought. This is not to uphold (or reject) the full repertoire of Garveyism's ideological consequences, but instead to consider the extent to which the originality of this thinking emerged on the very terrain of "consequences," of consequentiality. Not only did Garvey desire to be a person of consequence in his own right—as his ever-increasing proliferation of diplomatic titles never fails to suggest—but his efforts to engineer consequence according to a radical, procedural foreshortening of universal history also testify to the resonance of his work as a major theorist of sovereignty. Even the excesses and shortcomings of UNIA ventures demonstrate the adventurous nature of the speculative thinking they embodied—as well as the economic, political, and personal risk they entailed. In turn, I propose, they also illuminate the necessarily speculative basis of any theory of historical or political change, precisely in their concentration on finance capital and the formation of a state apparatus. We would be wrong, however, to assign these procedural questions to a dismissive account of near success or deferred influence—or to judgments of madness, fascism, or demagoguery. For it is precisely in confronting such judgments and narratives on the terrain of working institutions and networks that Garvey's thought performs its most significant function. His systems reveal the involutions at work in the very claim to sovereignty, as well as in the work of speculation itself—any act, we might say, of theory, in keeping in play at once its internal resistance to narrative fulfillment and its persistent demand for consequence. Garveyism thus remains significant less for the question of whether it was right than for the question of how its material and institutional forms testify to the uncomfortable demands of any thinking about power.

Beyond its function as a talking point in culture war–era debates about the excesses of Afrocentric history, Garvey's thought is striking for its focus on instrumentalizing contemporary struggles to redress the historical imbalance of power between Western imperial superpowers and "the darker races" taxed by centuries of colonialism, slavery, and ideological justification. No less striking is the involuted, counterdialectical tautology according to which Garvey leveraged his "instrumental" corporate ventures, whereby an awakened Africa comprised both the (political) effect and the (narrative) cause for raising financial capital. Mary Lefkowitz's remark that the legacy of democracy—and all it stands for—is so compelling as to render it perfectly comprehensible that "other" (that is, non-Greek, non-Western) cultures or races might wish to claim it here takes on a significance beyond the patronizing Eurocentrism with which she employs it. Garveyism reveals the extent to which "democratic" institutions of social and governmental administration served as the means through which such ideals become institutionalized as historical legacies, birthrights, or promises in the first place. The seat of the debate was not "respectable" historiography, in other words, but the very technologies for "laying claim" that, in the aftermath of the First World War, decisively favored the Western superpowers whose balance of power was nonetheless in the process of redistribution.

What Lefkowitz and other culture warriors overlooked was that Garvey had already seized hold of such democratic institutions in the very process of using public fund-raising and public speeches to raise capital. As Harrison had explained, in seeking reciprocity after World War I, Black people were already taking democracy at its word—that is, exercising it as a claim to power. As a result, this revealed all the more starkly the exceptionalism used to uphold democratic and other allegedly Western principles only in certain cases. Incorporating the work of Harrison, Dusé Mohamed Ali, Chief Sam, and other Black nationalist thinkers, Garveyism proleptically reveals the later culture wars to be no less persistently a struggle to maintain such exceptionalism rather than a neutral set of scholarly controversies about the nature of truth claims or the Western intellectual canon. This was a world-historical contestation in which epistemology—including notions of evidence, myth, and the causal forms and structures of historical change—was but one of the technologies of struggle, one of the means of laying claim to and maintaining real political power. Garvey's concentration on other material technologies—including finance capital, nonprofit and corporate institutions, public media, and provisional statehood—aimed toward a redistribution of power predicated, as we have seen, on world-historical narratives of reciprocity and return rather than on myths, assurances, or pseudoarchaeological platitudes alone. Garvey thus inverts Lefkowitz's ideas about the Afrocentric "claims" to an illustrious ancient past, recasting it from a potential spoil of victory—the holy grail of a cultural crusade Lefkowitz impugns and which Ishmael Reed dramatizes in the epic pastiche of *Mumbo Jumbo*—to a narrative form whose implementation was concomitant with its deployment toward geopolitical and economic power. In this respect, Garveyism may remain speculative, even paranoid—as well as ideologically fraught—but it is nonetheless illuminating for its recognition that the plasticity or "relativism" of the historiographical terms so contested during the culture wars represented a concrete, constitutive investment rather than an irresponsibility with evidence. History was fungible because it had to be made.

THE SADE INDUSTRY

The critics who make neither a blackguard nor an idol of Sade, but rather a man, a writer, can be counted on the fingers of one hand. Thanks to them, Sade has returned once again to the earth, among us. But where might we properly situate him? What about him merits our interest?

—Simone de Beauvoir, *Must We Burn Sade?*

AS IF ANTICIPATING THE CULTURE WARS of the 1980s and 1990s more than forty years in advance, Theodor Adorno and Max Horkheimer diagnosed the "lapse into mythology" of Enlightenment reason in their 1947 *Dialectic of Enlightenment.* Writing in the shadow of the Holocaust as refugees from Nazi Germany, Adorno and Horkheimer offered their now-famous dialectical twist on the fate of Enlightenment principles such as reason, universal rights, and democracy. Their claim was that the causes for the Enlightenment's lapse into mythology—a regression that likewise formed the bone of contention for so many canon-preserving pundits and critics of the 1990s—were immanent rather than foreign to it. That is, the causes lay not so much "in the nationalist, pagan, or other modern mythologies concocted specifically to cause such a relapse" as instead in a reaction formation within the very heart of Enlightenment thought, a "fear of the truth which petrifies enlightenment itself."[1] It was this petrification, rather than a liberty with facts or scientific evidence, that stunted the Enlightenment's movements and brought about its regressive condition. The problem, in short, was the mechanized certainty with which Enlightenment principles came to be brandished, a reification that crystallized concepts into murderous dogmas.

Rather than singling out pseudoscience and mythohistorical revisionism as the acid lies corroding the foundations of democracy, the refugees of the Frankfurt school impugned "the concept of clarity in language and thought" characteristic of Enlightenment rationalism itself insofar as it rendered taboo "any thought which sets out negatively from the facts and from the prevailing modes of thought as obscure, convoluted, and preferably foreign."[2] In what sounded like a defense of outsider theory, Adorno and Horkheimer posited that the very cultural forms and institutions that sought aggressively to uphold Enlightenment principles against their perversion could themselves become the very perversions they feared. The false clarity of such entrenchments became "another name for myth," holding the mind captive "in an ever deeper blindness." Such a condition was a cultural product, Adorno and Horkheimer insisted, rather than a purely logical consequence. The "sanction by ideas and norms" that reified Enlightenment principles as commodities was trafficked by "the culture industry," the authors' term for the manufacture of self-evidence that yielded a "withering of imagination and spontaneity in the consumer."[3] Such principles became objects for consumption rather than stimuli for thought, through the "hypostatization of the rigidity and exclusivity which concepts have necessarily taken on whenever language has consolidated the community of the rulers for the enforcement of demands."[4] The resulting cultural apparatus does our judging for us. Even our perception that Enlightenment principles reflect our autonomous judgments has itself been shaped by those principles, well before our perceptions took place.[5] Enlightenment ceases when thinking gives way to regulation.

In the face of such a hypostasis, Adorno and Horkheimer championed the critical prowess of negation and disclosure, the dialectical movement that "teaches us how to read from its features the admission of falseness which cancels power and hands it over to truth."[6] The task of this rigorous critical practice was to disrupt the reification of Enlightenment concepts at the hands of the culture industry, and to open such concepts instead to the restless demands of a truth procedure that was opaque and harrowing.

On account of his capacity to "teach us to read," one of the heroes of *Dialectic of Enlightenment* is, perversely, the Marquis de Sade (1740–1814), the late eighteenth-century French writer whose pornographic fantasies of sexual cruelty and remorseless violence might otherwise seem to cast him as the very obverse of Enlightenment reason, its abject antithesis. Sade becomes a hero in Adorno and Horkheimer's book on account of his dialectical relation to Enlightenment rationality: on the one hand, Sade's work proceeds from the very "petrified" condition into which Enlightenment thought had lapsed, wherein the clarity of its formal logic has already turned against itself as a system of terror. Sade's most "scandalous" novels, *Justine* and *Juliette,* systematically invert the hierarchy of Christian moral virtues; they replace sacrament with sacrilege, piety with violation, innocence with crime. This inversion is reflected, too, in the fates of their titular heroines: Justine becomes a martyr to so-called virtues, whereas her sister Juliette inhabits this systematic inversion logically and scientifically, wielding "the instrument of rational thought with consummate skill."[7] She thrives in crime. In tracing the divergent fates of Justine and Juliette, Sade's fictions articulate the perversions of Enlightenment reason, the cultural procedures according to which it "turns against itself."[8] Like Friedrich Nietzsche nearly a century later, Sade realized that once reason had been formalized, a condition that was itself "the intellectual expression of mechanized production," pieties such as pity and compassion became vices according to the "law" of reason. They were, in other words, "left behind as a kind of sensuous awareness of the identity of general and particular, as naturalized mediation."[9] Torture and crime were the logical extension of this intellectual expression of mechanized production whereby "the means is fetishized: it absorbs pleasure" in the name of domination as an end in itself.[10] Fascism took this formalization to its "absurd conclusion" in "elevating the cult of strength to a world-historical doctrine."[11]

Sade does not himself drive the idea of enlightenment to this point. Rather, his work "lays bare the mythological nature of the principles on which civilization was based" after the formalization of reason and the demise of religion. Thus, on the other hand, Sade's writing represents rather than indulges the "story of thought as an investment of power," opening up a critical distance from the Enlightenment's ideology of clarity and self-reproducing rationalism. In "taking fright at the image in its own mirror," as Adorno and Horkheimer put it, Sade's fiction pitilessly expresses the "shocking truth of the identity of power and reason in Enlightenment ideology and opens thought to the possibilities of viewing what lies beyond it."[12]

In *Dialectic of Enlightenment*, Sade emerges as an almost autopoietic figure of negation within Enlightenment thinking. Contemporary with the French Revolution and the Terror, his writing voiced rather than resisting or disrupting the indissoluble alliance of reason and atrocity from which it seemed to emerge. Unlike Marcus Garvey (see chapter 5), Sade did not propose a further "involution" within the dialectic of enlightenment, nor did he seek to redress the horrors reflected therein. For Adorno and Horkheimer his work is a mirror, not a means. His libertines are perverts who uphold the laws of perversion with Enlightenment clarity. Sade's profane status, his exteriority as a critical figure, is likewise the result of taking Enlightenment "at its word," of pursuing the implications of reason resolutely and proclaiming them from the rooftops. For this very reason, Sade (like Nietzsche) is still vilified by many progressive thinkers, an outsider in the eyes of those who continue to uphold the myth of Enlightenment clarity and self-evidence even in the midst of contemporary atrocities carried out in its name.

Is it possible to read Sade's "truth" without the dialectical framework in which Adorno and Horkheimer situate his work? Is it only the recourse to prefabricated ideological positions that distinguishes readers who vilify Sade from the critics and philosophers who do not? This chapter proposes, on the contrary, that Sade is a figure through which such thinkers have developed and articulated their positions. In twentieth-century France, for instance, Sade became a major philosopher on account of his contemporaneity: he was "our neighbor," as the novelist and critic Pierre Klossowski put it, rather than a historical figure or, a case study of sexual deviance, or a bibliographic curiosity. Sade has come to occupy an oddly central place in modern European thought, leading the critic Éric Marty to dedicate a book-length meditation on why the twentieth century took Sade seriously.[13] Today Sade stands not only as a major philosopher but also as a household name. Once relegated to the Enfer, the bibliographic crypt for obscene works in the Bibliothèque nationale de France, Sade's work is now celebrated by the library as a centerpiece of its holdings.[14] In 2014 the surrealist philosopher-critic Annie Le Brun curated a major exhibition at the Musée d'Orsay in Paris that situated Sade in a history of visual culture from the Revolution to the 1950s. Entitled *Sade: Attacking the Sun,* it presented the crowds of tourists who throng the popular museum of nineteenth-century painting with a history of art organized according the priorities and principles of Sade's writing.[15]

This chapter addresses the means through which a writer once labeled as monstrous and obscene came to occupy such a position in modern European thought and culture. Sade offers a case study for the critical and institutional forms through which even the most rebarbative and frightening cultural products have entered into and functioned within the canon of "serious" thought, independently of popular taste and its oft-reviled susceptibility to bad ideas, the seduction of unreason. "Outsider theory" describes such oblique processes of reception rather than naming the self-evident unreason or reason of the ideas themselves.

The difficulty of approaching the work of Sade derives nearly as much from the imposing list of twentieth-century writers and thinkers who have confronted his work as from the violent, pornographic excesses of the writing itself. From poets Guillaume Apollinaire and Algernon Charles Swinburne to Georges Bataille and the surrealists; from Adorno and Horkheimer to Roland Barthes, Maurice Blanchot, Judith Butler, Angela Carter, Simone de Beauvoir, Guy Debord, Michel Foucault, Pierre Klossowski, Julia Kristeva, Jacques Lacan, Annie Le Brun, Yukio Mishima, Philippe Sollers, and many others, the litany of philosophers and critics who appeal to the rigors of Sadean thought is staggering. It discloses the extent to which he figures as a provocation immanent to European thought rather than an aberration or curiosity. The onus of entangling with Sade's other readers displaces no small proportion of the work's perversity from the text to the virtual library that surrounds it. As the French editor-critic Jean Paulhan put it in 1945, "for one hundred and fifty years it has been the custom to frequent Sade through the intermediary of other authors."[16] To take stock of this custom is to acknowledge an anxiety of influence—but what kind of influence?

Like a number of his postwar contemporaries, Paulhan was concerned by the fact that Sade's earlier readers could only approach his work through allusion or clinical diagnosis, whereby his name designated a psychosexual abnormality, a medicolegal category for the pathological "association of active cruelty and violence with lust."[17] Until quite recently the texts by Sade himself were largely unavailable, the majority consigned to the Enfer section of the Bibliothèque nationale or lost entirely. Paulhan's terms nevertheless resound ever more acutely today, even in the wake of the massive republication efforts that have since returned Sade's work to wide-scale circulation. For the availability of Sade's work in the years since the Second World War is complemented by a corresponding spike in Sade-related criticism and philosophy, which has yielded a veritable Sade industry in western Europe. For this very reason, the anxiety of influence remains acute. This is less because one cannot read Sade in private than because, as Adorno and Horkheimer suggest, the very availability of Sade's work for private consumption is itself a product of the Sade industry.

To read Sade is to enter into a relation of complicity, Pierre Klossowski suggested in 1947. But complicity with what? When we read a novel such as *Juliette* absentmindedly, we "let ourselves be taken in by a rather vulgar piece of literature," Maurice Blanchot noted in 1948, subject to the shock effects of its obscenity.[18] But to do otherwise—to recognize the broader patterns and systems that operate through Sade's work—renders us complicit instead with Sade's intermediaries, the host of philosopher-critics who propose the noncomplicity of Sadean discourse. Either way, we fall under the influence. This paradox is oddly consistent with the "law" of perversion described and upheld by Sade's characters: the formal absolute that prevails over any individual experience of judgment or erotic pleasure, itself the very profanation of Enlightenment principles. To what extent, in other words, is any experience of reading Sade—or not reading Sade—determined in advance of our perfection by this constellation of other readers, whose virtual imprint on any such approach constitutes, in turn, a Sadean effect par excellence? Paulhan diagnoses this perversion of judgment in taking stock of the intermediaries who haunt our reading. The shadowy corpus of intellectuals who materialize at the scene of any such encounter with Sade's writing presents a virtual cross-section of twentieth-century European critical thought. Paulhan notes the extent to which contemporary thought drew its very raison d'être from Sade. Far from finding this situation troublesome, he praises it, writing that the field of modern literature, or at least "in that area where it seems to us most alive—most aggressive, in any case—is . . . dominated, determined by Sade as eighteenth-century tragedy was by Racine."[19] Sade is as present at the scene of modern European intellectual life as his critics are present at the scene of reading.

This chapter seeks less to expunge this anxiety of influence than to chart its shift from the Enfer—wherein Sade's works formed part of a collection of obscene works to be cataloged but never circulated—to the sphere of modern philosophical and critical exchange. How, in other words, did Sade become an occasion for so many modern thinkers to reflect on the questions of legitimacy, complicity, ethics, and the agency of intellectual practice that emerge through their engagements with the revolutionary-era writer? This is not simply a matter of determining what made twentieth-century thinkers "take Sade seriously," as Marty asks; rather, it is a matter of interrogating the nature of such seriousness, as a reflection on the concepts and intermediaries through which they entangled with his work. The discourse on Sade in France mediates the shifts and crises in European thinking before and after the Second World War. Whereas Adorno and Horkheimer situate him as the by-product of the dialectic of enlightenment, an eighteenth-century figure whose work discloses its "fear of the truth," for Blanchot and others Sade becomes a conceptual persona that mediates the critical entanglements with the work of philosophy itself, the very concept of reason. Consistent with the "Gnostic materialism" discussed in chapter 2, Sade's emergence in twentieth-century French thought both illuminates and enables the general movement from an intellectual style rooted firmly in dialecticism to a nascent but no less resolute antidialecticism. The postwar focus on Sade's work marks a major epistemic shift in French thinking, for which Sade himself came to stand as an intermediary.

Sade marks a fundamental break or shift in continental philosophy characterized by Jean-Michael Rabaté as the "ethical leap out of metaphysics" undertaken by postwar intellectuals in the decades after World War II.[20] This "leap" stands in opposition to the explicitly metaphysical imperatives we saw in previous chapters, yet even so, the extent to which figures such as Gérard de Sède (chapter 3), Riane Eisler (chapter 4), and Marcus Garvey (chapter 5) approach metaphysical patterns and promises as plastic forms to be manipulated already suggests the extent to which metahistorical and epistemic concepts such as dialecticism had already "become absolute," reified as a formal abstractions. While never presumed to be the cause of such transformations, Sade nonetheless provided the occasion for much of this work, a prosopopoeia whose contemporaneity with the French Revolution and the Terror rendered his work capable of voicing the exigencies of his modern readers.

The Sade industry of the postwar era thus refers to the corporate body of French intellectuals who looked to Sade as a repository for radical ideas about the methods and ethics of intellectual transformation. The industry designates a set of critical and editorial practices that regulates the ways in which readers approach Sade and, in turn, constitutes Sadean discourse as a generative site of intellectual labor, of "taking Sade seriously," as Marty puts it. Sade thus stands not only as a case study for midcentury phenomenology—suggesting the extent to which Sade is a product of Sadean criticism—but also as a figure for the broader question of mediation itself. The history of Sade's reception is thus bound up with the history of European thinking about the possibilities of intellectual agency as well as the role of institutions in gathering and distributing the forces of historical change.

It is tempting, of course, to naturalize Sade's twentieth-century reception as an inevitable historical convergence insofar as he offered stricken postwar intellectuals an Enlightenment-era precursor in contemplating absolute atrocity.[21] Who better than Sade to voice the corrupt excesses of Enlightenment reason, carried out to their murderous extremes? Who better than Sade to diagnose—or perhaps, for some, to exercise—the toxic fantasy life of male power, of androcracy? Yet such notions are complicated by the extent to which Sade's singularity as a precursor was itself largely a historical product, the accumulated result of critical reflections that began far earlier than the 1940s or even the rise of fascism. Circulated in clandestine editions throughout the nineteenth century, his works were singled out as evidence of the author's sexual and mental abnormality. This largely "scientific" interest became to change, however, with Guillaume Apollinaire's attention to Sade in the early decades of the twentieth century, which emerged through the poet's collaborative project (with the writers Louis Perceau and Pascal Pia) of cataloging the contents of the Enfer. Sade's reception as a philosopher of the unthinkable was, moreover, already flourishing in France during the interwar period, when his writings began to reappear in print, supplemented with a strong editorial apparatus and archival attention to its author's biographical details. Most notably, Sade's *Dialogue entre un prêtre et un moribond* (Dialogue between a priest and a dying man), written in 1782; his *Historiettes, Contes et*

Fabliaux (Tales and sketches), written in 1787–88; and his *120 Journées de Sodom* (120 days of Sodom), written in 1785 and first published in an early transcription in 1904, all appeared in print between 1926 and 1935, under the auspices of a nonprofit society founded in order to return Sade's works to circulation. The Société du roman philosophique (Society for the philosophical novel) was founded by the left-wing bibliophile and editor Maurice Heine, a trained medic who dedicated the last two decades of his life to researching the life of Donatien Alphonse François de Sade and publishing critical editions of his work.[22] Heine died in 1940 before completing a biography of Sade; this task was left to his friend and protégé, the surrealist poet Gilbert Lély, whose massive biography *La Vie du Marquis de Sade*, dedicated to Heine, was first published in 1952, becoming a central reference point for French discussions about the revolutionary-era author during the postwar period.

The "return to Sade" proposed by Beauvoir, Blanchot, Paulhan, and others after World War II thus refers as much to a reprise of this earlier interwar activity as to an attempt to strip away the layers of historical intervention to locate the authentic figure of Sade.[23] Without proposing yet another such return, I seek here to understand the means through which Sade came to occupy such a singular position in twentieth-century thought. Such a task concerns the formation of Sade as a conceptual persona, a figure who comes to stand in for the concepts and discourses that converge around his name. Through the Sade industry the "historical, empirical, individual, anecdotal" Sade gives way to a "concept of what he represents," as Marty puts it. As a result, "the Sadean text becomes an operational mechanism for disclosing a well-established and formalized discursive approach [*dispositif*] that lies above and beyond the particularities of Sade's works."[24] My contention is that Sade emerges as such a mechanism on account of the ways in which his postwar reception itself became a site for reflection upon the capacity for a conceptual persona to mediate the field of philosophy. Sade became, in other words, the mirror in which contemporary thinkers could take fright; he thus came to stand for the repercussions of such a reflection, and thus on the agency or means through which an epistemic shift could take place (such as the Enlightenment's "turn against itself," as Adorno and Horkheimer describe it). Sade's function in the pantheon of twentieth-century European philosophers hinges, therefore, on his status as an outsider, though in Sade's case, this "outside" had less to do with foreignness, historical remove, or even obscenity than with an effect: the negation of critical distance and the comforts of assurance such distance presumes. This outsider status describes the aggregate capacity for mediation his work acquires, and according to which readers could exercise, as well as experience, the shock of Sadean perversion, atrocity, libertinism, and revolutionary criminality as a demand for—rather than a privileged recourse to—critical reflection.

THE MEDIATE AND THE IMMEDIATE

Adorno and Horkheimer present Sade as a kind of litmus test for distinguishing those who still adhered to the myth of Enlightenment from those who had wised up to its perversions. As Marty notes, the experience of the Second World War at once invited and yet ultimately negated the associations one might be tempted to make between Sade's authoritarian criminals and sexual torturers and the atrocities of Nazism. The extermination camps and systematic genocide had less to do with obscene literature or its libertines, after all, than with the murderous function of state power. Certainly Sade's work had something to say about the abusive excesses of such power, but one of the more discomfiting effects of reading Sade was its tendency to implicate readers in the work's own disciplinary formulations. From what vantage point was it safe to read? The French critic Maurice Blanchot opens his book *Lautréamont and Sade* (1949) with a meditation on the tenacity with which writing about Sade tended toward critical self-reflection rather than textual scrutiny, as if actually *reading* Sade's texts might immediately presuppose one's complicity in a set of propositions about the collapse between reason and atrocity. For this reason, Blanchot suggests, critics tended to attribute their desire for critical distance to the workings of Sade's own system, as a function of its levelheaded, systematic cruelty. But Blanchot also proposes that any such striving for critical distance exercises a determining influence on the way we understand the workings of this system.[25]

Sade, in this sense, became a major twentieth-century author on account of his unreadability. Blanchot addresses, for instance, the paradox of claiming that a book such as *La Nouvelle Justine* (1792) was the most scandalous ever written. The very statement garners attention for the book in proposing it to be singular, peerless in scandal: "We have, therefore, in some way, within our grasp, and in the very relative world of literature, a veritable absolute."[26] This "absolute" authorizes readers to persist in holding the book at arm's length rather than interrogate the nature or degree of its scandalousness. For this very reason the truth of Sade's writing has to do less with the extent to which his writing takes Enlightenment reason "at its word" than with the extent to which it establishes a proleptic relationship to one's own judgments, and one's own critical positions, insofar as those judgments and positions reveal themselves as already framed and constituted in our approach to his writing. Sade becomes Sade, in this sense, through the mediating role of literary experience, which Blanchot understands as "the capacity to negate and change," a capacity he ascribed to revolution earlier in his career.[27] Yet such an experience is tacitly shaped and sustained in turn by the role of critics such as himself, a second-order mediation that is both insignificant and determinative in framing such (non)encounters with the work of Sade as a "veritable absolute."

In attending to the way critics write about Sade's work, Blanchot proposes, we become aware of the paradoxical modesty and resonance of critical discourse more broadly. "Criticism is nothing," he writes, "but this nothingness is precisely that in which the literary work, silent and invisible, allows itself to be what it is. . . . Critical discourse is this space of resonance within which the unspoken, indefinite reality of the work is momentarily transformed and circumscribed into words."[28] By means of such mediation Sade's work itself comes to serve this function in turn, thereby becoming the "space of resonance" of Enlightenment reason—or its fearful "truth," the moving target it can never fully pin down. For Blanchot the question of a Sadean reason—that is, the possibility of Sadean thought, but also of a Sadean raison d'être—hinges on the transformations and mediations by means of which Sade has come to serve as a mediating figure in his own right, a veritable absolute in modern intellectual history.

The critic thus serves as both a witness to and, more consequently, an intermediary for Sade's currency in contemporary culture. Though modestly bound to a secondary, ancillary relationship to the work, the critic is no less responsible for its currency, its *actualité*. Sade, in turn, becomes a kind of prosopopoeia, a figure who stands in for the conceptual work of this contemporary self-reflection. Blanchot's depiction of the critic describes, too, the Sadean phenomenon in modern French thought; it also gestures, as we will see in what follows, to the critical and editorial apparatuses through which Sade came to occupy this position, illuminating the ostensibly modest labors of Maurice Heine and the Société du roman philosophique.

The question of mediation outlined by Blanchot is, by extension, a question of intellectual agency. Borrowing Martin Heidegger's image of a snowflake falling on a bell, Blanchot describes the agency of the critic in terms of the resonance made possible by a fleeting and virtually insubstantial element.[29] As Blanchot puts it, "Herein lies, if you will, the ultimate consequence (and a singular manifestation) of this movement of self-effacement which is one of the indications of criticism's presence: through its disappearance before the literary world, criticism recovers itself again in the world as one of its essential moments." Within this movement of disappearance and recovery "we locate a process that our era has seen develop in various ways. Criticism is no longer an external judgment placing the literary work in a position of value and bestowing its opinion, after the fact, on this value. It has come to be inseparable from the internal working of the text, belonging to the moment when it becomes what it is."[30] In a way that anticipates Sade's historical recovery by modern European thinkers, Blanchot's essay on the purpose of criticism reflects on the nature of mediation itself, understanding its claim to agency in methodological rather than purely instrumental terms. The radicalism of Sade's thinking lay in its hypostasis and formalization of the metaphysical support upon which the notion of intellectual agency typically relies. Instead of voicing the truth of enlightenment, Sade instead comes to reflect the truth of critical reason in the very course of its operation.

Blanchot's account of Sade as both mediator and mediated resonates, in turn, with the terms used by other critics and philosophers to untangle the formal structure of his works, with their institutions and schools of crime and libertinage. Here, too, "Sade" comes to signify a set of principles rather than the author's own capacity for thought: his works, in other words, suggest a principle for holding worldly phenomena—as well as the text—"at arm's length." Unlike the intellectual envisioned by Émile Zola as a figure whose authority derived from her position outside the fray of historical events, the Sadean libertine heeds desires and demands that are at once more egoistic and more formal than any such positioning. As Simone de Beauvoir put it in 1952, Sade was a man "who dared systematically to assume particularity, separation, and egoism."[31] The key here is the emphasis on systems, rather than on an individual author's special access to critical insight: Sade, like the libertines in his writing, becomes a "daring" conceptual persona but no longer a sovereign subject.

Other postwar French thinkers concur with such a decentering of the subject in favor of the systems they conceptualize in Sade's name.[32] In Sade's logic, the libertine's desire becomes a formal absolute replacing or even travestying moral and governmental laws, to the extent that this desire is no longer simply a form of individual egoism but, as Jacques Lacan explains in his essay "Kant with Sade," an impersonal formal principle. The libertine's egoistic desire is so absolute as no longer to belong to the libertine; it is instead an absolute law, subjective yet universal. Immanuel Kant refers to this as a categorical imperative; Lacan refers to it as the desire of the Other, the demand of a social rather than metaphysical system of codes, orders, and institutions.[33] In such conceptions the Sadean libertine is no less morally accountable for her acts. But to the extent that these acts are themselves the expression of a formal absolute that transcends the individual subject, the libertine—like

Sade himself—becomes at once a figure and medium for the causality of such formal absolutes. Much as Blanchot attributed Adorno and Horkheimer's dialectic of enlightenment to a critical relationship with Sade, other post-war thinkers attributed this critical relationship to the laws of Sadean perversion.

In his 1966 essay on Sade and Leopold von Sacher-Masoch, for instance, Gilles Deleuze further formalizes the Sadean system as a network of interfaces that exercises "reason" through impersonal rather than individual faculties. *Sadism* becomes the name for an institutional set of demands and functions that administer the formal laws described by Blanchot and Lacan, and which the Société du roman philosophique likewise prefigured as a social apparatus for restoring Sade's works to print. Revising the vernacular coupling of sadism and masochism (as in "S&M"), Deleuze distinguishes Sacher-Masoch's system of "coldness" from Sade's system of "cruelty" rather than necessarily dislodging Sacher-Masoch and Sade from their "scandalous" associations with sexual perversion. Deleuze's account goes something like this: Whereas masochism and sadism might presuppose two reversible iterations domination and submission, Sade's and Sacher-Masoch's libertines in fact operate according to two very different sets of relationships between master and victim. The sadist, he writes, is in need of institutions, whereas the masochist is in need of contractual relations. Sacher-Masoch and Sade each inaugurate systems of combinations that "make up a whole hierarchy of forms at which the individual may become fixated or to which he may regress."[34] For Deleuze, sadism and masochism are significant because they outline relations of power distinct from the Hegelian master–slave dialectic, wherein victimizer and victim are mutually bound up in their antagonism. Sacher-Masoch's perversions operate through contractual rather than dialectical struggle: the perverse charge of masochism derives from the presumption that both torturer and victim are "in on it." Sade's relations of perversion, on the other hand, explicitly suspend any such reciprocity. The subjects of Sadean perversion are instead mutually coerced and mutually implicated by institutions that structure their relations of domination and cruelty—such as the "society of friends of crime" in *Juliette* or the "school of libertinism" at the Château de Silling in *120 Journées de Sodom*. Such institutions differ essentially, Deleuze claims, "from both law and contract" as a formal rather than strictly material or moral system.[35]

Rather than putting institutions "at the service of their abnormality," Sade's libertines are subject to their laws of operation. Such institutions, that is, "determine a long-term status of affairs which is both involuntary and inalienable." What makes them significant is their artificiality, their distinction from any moral, natural, or dialectical law. As Deleuze explains, they establish a power or authority that takes effect against other structures or regimes, such as the allegedly "natural" Oedipal family, the "singularly unanalytical conception of the mother as representative of nature and the father as sole principle and representation of culture and law."[36] Through his analysis of such formalized relations of power in Sade's writing, Deleuze articulates his own philosophy of causality in turn, the basic movements of which resemble Sade's: Deleuze's "radical empiricism" describes sets of material phenomena whose principles of cause and effect proceed, like Sade's, according to an abstract law or concept of their functioning rather than according to linear or dialectical narratives of progression through conflict. Deleuze outlines, in other words, a hierarchical system whereby a higher principle emerges as a second-order accounting for the differences and repetitions that recur within the empirical. Sade's institutions serve as a figure for this kind of second-order philosophy of power, insofar as the institution supplants other laws and explanations. As a result, Sade—no less than Sacher-Masoch—becomes a pivotal conceptual persona in Deleuze's own thought, precisely insofar as he facilitates the abandonment of Hegelian dialectics.

Deleuze's radical empiricism itself has an empirical basis. His approach to Sade's textual institutions is at once informed by Klossowski's ideas about Sadean secret societies and anticipated by Heine's endeavor to collectivize critical attention to Sade through the formation of the Société du roman philosophique. In turn, the institutional form of Sade's reception produces "Sade" as the neighbor and contemporary of modern European thinkers. A critical institution in his own right, Sade, like the Sade industry, becomes a philosophical medium for supplanting existing laws or paradigms of thought, whether Enlightenment universalism or Hegelian dialecticism.

The notion that Sade might be thought of as the marker of a major epistemic shift in intellectual history is presented most explicitly by Michel Foucault in *The Order of Things*, his 1966 study of such shifts, only here the shift marked by Sade takes place during Sade's own lifetime, rather than during the 1940s, 1950s, or 1960s. As a contemporary of the French Revolution and thinker of the Terror, Foucault names Sade—and not, say, G. W. F. Hegel or Immanuel Kant—as the figure who marks the end of classical thought and the rise of a modern episteme through which "the enormous thrust of a freedom, a desire, or a will" would be "posited as the metaphysical converse of consciousness."[37] Whereas Hegel, Sade's contemporary, sought an idealist philosophy that would reconcile consciousness and freedom in the movements of the dialectic, Sade's modernity lies in his travesty of such a panlogical system. In *The Order of Things* Foucault cites Sade's body of work as writing that stages the "obscure and repeated violence of desire battering at the limits of representation." Sade's work at once epitomizes the sovereignty and autonomy of classical representation, and yet subjects this autonomy to an external and absolute law of desire. Through Sade, Foucault explains, the whole classical system of order "that makes it possible to know things by means of the system of their identities" closes in on itself.[38]

As I have already begun to suggest, a similar epistemic transformation occurs in postwar European philosophy through which the modern episteme Foucault describes as emerging through Sade also closes in on itself through Sade. Sade's emergence coincides, we might say, with a becoming-absolute of dialectical thinking, in which the Hegelian system of progression through negation no longer bears any pretense of naturalism or self-evidence but has instead reached its hypostasis as a purely formal principle of metaphysical contestation and even terror, as Adorno and Horkheimer suggest. Sade becomes the philosopher of this formal absolute, precisely on account of his work's capacity for terror. As Blanchot puts it in a later essay, "we come away from reading Sade less troubled in our sensibilities than belied in our manner of thinking."[39] Sade, for Blanchot, is a revolutionary thinker for this reason. This is not to say that he caused or even contributed to the French Revolution, even though he lived through it. Rather, as Blanchot claims, the mad excess of Sade's writing—which raises negation to an absolute truth—articulates the Revolution's "reason" in explicitly post-Hegelian terms. Sade's writings express, in other words, a truth played out in revolutionary experience: that insurrectional negation was not simply something that happened *in* thought, in the form of a concept, but was also something that happened *to* thought, as well as to morals, laws, and beliefs. For Blanchot, Sade is the figure in whose writing the dialectic becomes knowable in its absolute form as terror (rather than revolution), as a paradoxical hypostasis of freedom and exigency. Sade was so radical a dialectician, in other words, as to no longer be a dialectician—a formulation that largely inverts Adorno and Horkheimer's claim that he negated Enlightenment principles to the point of upholding their truth.

Through Sade's writing, the truth of revolution makes itself knowable. Blanchot puts it this way: "With Sade—and in a very high form of paradoxical truth—we have the first example (but is there a second?) of the way in which writing, the freedom to write, can coincide with the movement of true freedom, when the latter enters into crisis and gives rise to a vacancy in history."[40] This freedom, which is also terror, is not something Sade produces or even knows. Rather, he is the form of its mediation, not through his capacity for dialectical critique, as Adorno and Horkheimer suggest, but through its institutional form as a space of resonance. His writing coincides with this terror, and, in doing so, demarcates a point at which history is so fully mediated by reason—conceived as an utterly transcendent, infinite negation—that it paradoxically gives rise to the possibility of a suspension of history, a "flashing event" that is the time of revolution. Sade thus becomes, for Blanchot, the first post-Hegelian insofar as his work makes it possible to recognize that the infinite horizon to which the dialectic leads is no longer the "end of history" but a "vacancy in history," the opening up of a historical rupture in which, as Blanchot writes, being is nothing other than the movement of the infinite.

We are a long way here, of course, from Sade the pornographer, the Sade of the *Philosophy of the Boudoir* and *The Crimes of Love:* that is, the Sade of sadism. The transformation of the figure whose name came to stand for a personality disorder and a form of sexual cruelty into a figure whose name stood for the demands and ambitions of contemporary philosophy was an exercise of the very capacity for transformation he embodied.[41] Yet this transformation did not take place overnight, as if through some kind of cataclysm or revolutionary event. Rather, the postwar Sade industry that institutionalized the study of Sade according to the transformations and repercussions thinkers articulated in his name was the cultural product, in turn, of earlier industry. The very figure to which French philosophers responded was made possible by a transformation in the reception of Sade that began in the decades before the Second World War, the product not only of intellectual institutions but also of specific forms of intellectual and bibliographic labor. Once a figure relegated to medical treatises and the Enfer, the Sade of the twentieth century owes no small part of his canonicity among left-leaning philosophers to the project of publishing and researching his life and work that sought explicitly, if "modestly," to situate Sade among contemporary movements in continental philosophy, political and literary theory, and social thought. To the extent that Sade haunts the twentieth century as the mediating figure he becomes in the work of Beauvoir, Blanchot, Deleuze, and others, this presence owes much in turn to the mediating role of his own reception. The postdialectical turn to which Sade gives occasion was, however, rooted in the work of concepts, mediated not only by his writings but also by the *discourse* on Sade that precipitated his availability as a conceptual persona. The ethical "leap out of metaphysics" that institutionalized Sade as an outsider theorist was made possible in no small part by the industry of his editor, Maurice Heine.

FROM THE ENFER TO THE
SOCIETY OF FRIENDS

It was through Heine's editorial and publication practices that Sade's writing began to exert its pressure on the history of French thinking as the iteration of its own exteriority, its own leap out of metaphysics. Sade's modern reception stems from two principle mechanisms. The first has to do with Sade's largely archival persistence after his death in 1814; as numerous scholars have discussed, during the nineteenth century and into the early twentieth, the name Sade designated a perversion rather than the author of literary or even pornographic works. Sade became a figure of medicolegal attention, whereas the works themselves were relegated principally to private libraries and repositories of obscene works such as the Enfer. The second mechanism emerges discontinuously from the first. In the 1920s and 1930s, the artists and writers of the surrealist movement (André Breton, Luis Buñuel, Man Ray, and others) began to take Sade seriously as a political thinker and theorist of sexuality in a manner that would likewise be taken up, though with oppositional flair, by Bataille, Beauvoir, Klossowski, Paulhan, and others. The fruit of a revisionist history no less than of a history of revision, Sade's reputation among the interwar avant-garde owed much to the *actualité* of Sade, the contemporaneity made possible by the study and circulation of his works.

In his preface to the 1930 publication of Sade's *Infortunes de la vertu*—an early version of the more famous novel *Juliette* that had remained unpublished since Sade wrote it in 1787—Maurice Heine writes that "Sade is not only one of the least read of the writers we talk about most, but he also remains one of the least understood of the writers we've read in their entirety, since we have access to barely a quarter of what that extraordinary man wrote."[42] The transformation in the reception of the Marquis de Sade in France between the world wars was made possible largely through Heine's efforts to recover those remaining three quarters of the Sadean archive—a project undertaken, as we will see, as a continuation of Guillaume Apollinaire's earlier bibliographic and editorial attention to Sade in the years before World War I. Heine's archival, editorial, and critical work of the 1920s and 1930s brought Sade into circulation as a revolutionary thinker and an early theorist of sexuality, altering both the availability and epistemological consequence of his works. In dialogue with the surrealists as well as with Bataille and Paulhan, Heine's mediating role in Sade's reception not only arbitrated divergent avant-garde movements but also constituted the material labor that made possible the "historical fact" of Sade the philosopher.

Heine, who was trained in medicine and became one the founders of the French Communist Party in 1920, was responsible for returning Sade's unpublished manuscripts—many of which were owned by private collectors—into circulation, forming the Société du roman philosophique in order to do so. The Société was a nonprofit publishing collective modeled on other bibliophile societies popular in France from the 1890s through the interwar years, including the Société des médecins bibliophiles, of which Heine was a founding member, and Les muses françaises, Heine's own editorial imprint, through which he published his own early poetry during the First World War.[43] As its name suggests, the Société du roman philosophique presented to its circle of readers a Sade framed not as a figure of pornographic excess, nor as the Sade of sadism, but instead as the writer of philosophical novels. The Société took its name from the title of Sade's autobiographical novel *Aline et Valcour, ou, le roman philosophique* (Aline and Valcour, or, the philosophical novel, 1795). But the name was nonetheless an ironic one, invoking a common eighteenth-century tendency to ascribe pornographic as well as anticlerical and antimonarchic writings to the category of "philosophical books" in order to avoid censorship.[44] Heine's Société du roman philosophique takes this category seriously, however, naming not only the slippage between pornography and political or atheist diatribes characteristic of many eighteenth-century texts but also the practice of philosophy itself as a discourse that, like perversion, was mediated through its institutional forms.

This project began in 1923 with the formation of the Société, the statues for which outlined the association's "principal object," which was to "create a link between researchers and bibliophiles interested in the historical character of Donatien-Alphonse-François de Sade" and to prepare critical editions of his published and unpublished works.[45] The first publication of the Society was *Dialogue entre un prêtre et un moribond* in 1926, an early work, edited by Heine, that showed Sade to be more concerned with exploring the contours of atheism than with managing the extremities of sexual depravity. Heine also brought out a collection of Sade's short writings, *Historiettes, Contes et Fabliaux,* in 1926; an early incarnation of *Juliette* entitled *Les Infortunes de la vertu* (The misfortunes of virtue) in 1930; and, perhaps most influentially, a corrected version of *120 Journées de Sodom,* whose three volumes appeared between 1931 and 1935. Heine also published other manuscripts and letters in literary periodicals, including *Le Surréalisme au Service de la Révolution,* where he wrote a regular column on "L'actualité de Sade" (The currency of Sade); the surrealist-affiliated journal *Minotaure;* and the medical journals *Hippolyte* and *Progès médical.* This massive republication project continued after Heine's death with the publication of Sade's complete works by

Jean-Jacques Pauvert, beginning in 1947; this project led to a highly publicized obscenity trial in 1956, in which Pauvert was ultimately acquitted.[46] Heine's own collected writings on Sade preceded the full Pauvert edition of Sade's complete works by several years, appearing posthumously in 1950, edited and prefaced by Gilbert Lély, who published his own major biography of Sade in 1952.

Thanks to Heine's editorial work, the notion of Sade as either a perverted author of obscure works or a solitary genius fell subject to the imperatives of a new readership. Sade's texts no longer designated objects consigned to an archive or set of bibliographic curiosities, but became instead a site of conceptual labor, as well as the repository of its effects. Though Pauvert's editions of the 1940s and 1950s are rightly credited with providing public access—and countercultural flair—to Sade's writings in France, Heine's Société du roman philosophique is notable for presenting it as an object of collective study.

Whatever ulterior motives might have fueled Heine's lifelong dedication to Sade,[47] Heine's work extends from two collectivizing imperatives, grounded, respectively, in bibliographic and political friendships and commitments. Heine was a professional bibliophile who designed books throughout the early 1920s and whose extensive research on Sade was supported by his work for the art dealer Ambroise Vollard from the late 1920s until Vollard's sudden death in 1939—an event that left Heine jobless and, it seems, destitute.[48] Heine notably shared the bibliophilia of Guillaume Apollinaire, whom he admired and befriended early in his career, along with Apollinaire's friends Louis Perceau and Pascal Pia. The latter three writers had compiled and published a "descriptive, critical, and comprehensive icono-bio-bibliography" of the Enfer in 1913.[49] As Heine wrote in the preface to *Historiettes, contes et fabliaux* in 1926, his decision to republish Sade began with a conversation with Apollinaire lamenting the fact that of the eighteenth-century author's large corpus of work, only the eleven stories of the *Crimes de l'amour* remained in print (along with a twelfth story republished by Anatole France). In response, Heine wrote, "we resolved, oblivious to [Apollinaire's] premature death, to combine our efforts to research and publish the *disjecta membra* of Sade: a task interrupted by that disaster, but which has been taken up and pursued anew with the aid of the Society for the Philosophical Novel, founded specially for the study of the man and his work."[50] Apollinaire had already taken steps in this direction. In addition to the experimental poetry for which Apollinaire was famous—and whose Sadean overtones can be seen in a work such as *Les Onze mille verges* (The eleven thousand rods, 1907)—the Enfer catalog he published with Perceau and Pia offered an exhaustive descriptive bibliography of the Bibliothèque nationale's holdings in obscene literature, which yielded "many curious works full of interest for philosophers, historians, and persons of letters."[51] Their attention was directed primarily toward aesthetic and epistemological concerns, as much as to the titillating or scandalous content of the works themselves. Some of the writers represented in the Enfer, such as the "licentious satirists of the sixteenth and seventeenth centuries," were important poets whose exclusion from literary history represented a fathomless void in French literature.[52] Apollinaire, along with Perceau, had begun to fill that void, republishing a number of such works in collaboration with the poet Fernand Fleuret under the Bibliothèque des Curieux imprint. Its works heavily annotated and featuring a detailed bibliographical apparatus, the Bibliothèque des Curieux published writings such as the *Mémoires de l'Abbé de Choisy, habillé en femme* (The transvestite memoirs of the Abbé of Choisy) and *Les Procès du Sodomie* (Sodomy trials) in 1920. Though scholarly in their editorial framework, such projects nonetheless retained a tongue-in-cheek and semipornographic approach to their material. Choisy's *Mémoires* were edited, for instance, under the pseudonym of le Chevalier de Percefleur; the name fuses the surnames of its editors, Perceau and Fleuret, to form the pseudo-aristocratic "pierce flower," a crude allusion to the sexual conquest of virginity attributed to the patronymic Chevalier. Apollinaire himself edited a number of volumes under his own name for the Bibliothèque des Curieux, including *La Rome des Borgia* (The Rome of the Borgias), *Le Canapé couleur de feu* (The flame-colored sofa), *L'Oeuvre badine de l'abbé de Grécourt* (The playful works of the Abbé of Grécourt), and two volumes of *L'Oeuvre du Marquis de Sade*, published in 1909 and 1912. He also published his own pastiches of eighteenth-century erotic poems under a variety of pseudonyms, in addition to two erotic novels. Taking their cue from eighteenth-century book circulation, Apollinaire and his friends mobilized their editorial apparatus toward the erotic or pornographic charge of the books they prepared for "the curious."

Heine's pursuit of the project he first envisioned with Apollinaire continued the bibliographic attentions of this earlier society of friends; the critical attention to Sade was the resounding phenomenon of an editorial project that bore no small resemblance to Blanchot's image of a snowflake. As we will see, however, Heine exercised a far different set of intellectual and political priorities in doing so. Both in the editorial work of framing Sade as a philosopher rather than a pornographer and in the publishing venture invented for that purpose, Heine assembled a self-sustaining institutional collectivity rather than purveying a collection of rarities for "the curious." His republication of Sade's works was made possible through the nonprofit institution he founded for this purpose. One of several such organizations Heine proposed, the Société du roman philsophique was explicit in its organizational structures and principles, formalizing its legal status as a nonprofit organization for processing funds. The published statutes of the Société, printed on fine paper in pamphlet form, declared in legal language that "there is hereby formed between the two hundred persons to have accepted the present statutes, a scholarly and literary association which takes the name *Société du roman philosophique*." The document continued, describing the express mission of the association:

> As its primary objective, this Society aims to create a link between researchers and bibliophiles interested in the historical character of Donatien-Alphonse-François DE SADE (1740–1814).
>
> To this end, it proposes
>
> 1° To collect in critical and strictly private editions the works of this writer that remain in manuscript form or which have become rare;
> 2° To enable the publication of unpublished works of scholarly erudition about these texts, which would be agreed upon according to articles 12, 13, and 14 below;
> 3° To publish, as often as possible, a periodical bulletin keeping the literate and learned public informed about its work.
>
> The Society may, in addition, and as an exception, take an interest in the contemporary social milieu of D.A.F. de Sade and all the works similar to his or which may be judged useful to the principle aims of the association.[53]

Significantly, the French Association Law of July 1, 1901, according to which the statutes were formulated, was part of an administrative separation of church and state under the Third Republic, enabling nonprofit organizations to exist as legal entities independently of any religious affiliation. Such a separation already favored the work of a writer who professed atheism as a viable and organized philosophical system, as Heine noted in his preface to the *Dialogue between a Priest and a Dying Man*.

Later commentaries on Sade's work were certainly attentive to the administrative forms of Sade's own system of perversion. In his influential 1947 study *Sade, My Neighbor*, for instance, Pierre Klossowski likens the workings of Sade's language to the "code of perversion" exercised by his characters.

Sade's work operates, that is, according to the relations of complicity Klossowski likens to a secret society, whereby the membership is bound together according to a set of formal activities rather than through persuasion. Unlike Heine's society for publishing Sade's work, however, Klossowski depicts the administrative means of the Sadean secret society as in more clandestine terms, as a counternormative gesture whereby "the discourse of the pervert" emerges as a simulacrum or rite that the members of the secret society "do not explain to one another otherwise than by the inexistence of the absolute guarantee of norms, an inexistence they commemorate as an event that one can represent only by this gesture."[54] Heine's Société du roman philosophique was private—in the sense that it was noncommercial—but it was far from secret. Beyond the requirements of French nonprofit law, its priorities had more to do with circulation than with ritual or initiation. The texts published by the Société were soon republished by larger publishing houses for a broader reading public. The mission of the Société was fueled, in turn, by Heine's broader interest in collective organization, which sought to consolidate the administrative power and productive expertise of skilled workers. Rather than a secret society, a school of libertinage, or a "society for the friends of crime," the Société du roman philosophique functioned as a syndicate, a self-organizing institution whose function was that of the *syndikos*, the advocate or caretaker of an issue who acts on behalf of justice *(diké)*.

Heine himself was a committed syndicalist. Trained in medicine and stationed in Algeria during the early years of the First World War, he returned to Paris as a journalist before joining the Socialist Party. In the period leading up to the foundation of the Société du roman philosophique in 1923, he was active in the formation of the French Communist Party, particularly in an extreme-left faction of that was eventually purged from the party on account of its resistance to centralization. After the "schism of Tours" in 1920 (at which the French Communist Party formally broke off from the Socialist Party), Heine's party activism concentrated on organizational rather than ideological or theoretical prerogatives. In particular, he was involved in proposing and defending the "twenty-one conditions" of the local Féderation de la Seine, which recommended an executive federation of internal party governance for the nascent Communist Party. The syndicalizing proposal was modeled on the Bolshevik organization of rural soviets that granted authority to the masses rather than to a central bureaucratic power. The "twenty-one conditions" thus resisted the centralization and bureaucratization that ended up taking precedence throughout the Communist International in the name of a "united front."[55] Heine was instrumental in drafting the structure as well as the actual resolutions themselves; the propositions were ultimately rejected by the party, which considered his federalist position to be hostile to Moscow and part of a heterogeneous faction.[56]

My claim is less that these efforts somehow influenced Heine's later publication societies than that they disclose the ideological consistency running throughout Heine's recourse to syndicalism and collective organization. The Société du roman philosophique was a pragmatic federation consistent with Heine's earlier career in leftist politics insofar as it collectivized both the administration of and the access to the writings of Sade rather than centralizing it as the work of individual expertise. This was not, again, a secret society—nor, however, did it amount to the populist recourse to a commercial public. It was instead an elect society of skilled laborers (analogous to a trade union) assembled for the sake of consolidating and developing their access to specialized knowledge. This, incidentally, is how Heine describes Sade's own philosophical project in his introduction to *120 Journées de Sodom*, writing that "this immediate disciple of the Encyclopedists takes up . . . the full domain of the intelligence and addresses himself not of course to the public but to elites prepared by their culture to receive the absolute expression of thought."[57] Privileging Sade's address to readers rather than the figural laws or institutions of his libertines, Heine recasts Sade as an *instituteur,* an Enlightenment pedagogue. His notion of an "elite" demarcates an intellectual rather than a professional or class-bound hierarchy, an institutional structure for enabling access to specialized knowledge rather than limiting it to discrete professional conditions. Heine makes such a claim, I propose, in order to disaggregate Sade from the medicolegal context to which he had traditionally been consigned, whereby the only authorized readers of his work were psychiatrists and alienists. Heine's "elite" here stands in contrast, therefore, to the work of Richard von Krafft-Ebing, which, as Heine writes, citing the Austrian psychiatrist's translator, was so objectively medical as to discount "any incursion into the domain of pure philosophical speculation."[58] Heine's elite thus proposed to democratize rather than restrict access to Sade's work, formalizing its intended audience as an intellectual syndicate "prepared by their culture to receive the absolute expression of thought."

This same passage can also be read, mind you, as a precursor to Klossowski's depiction of Sadean perversion in terms of the quasireligious protocols of a secret society—or, for that matter, to Eric Voegelin's depiction of Gnosticism as an analogously elitist fantasy within modern political thought (see chapters 1 and 2). Heine's insistence lay, however, on the importance of research and the circulation of unpublished documents that distinguished a philosophical Sade from a subject of purely medical interest or a "perverse mythomaniac," as was characteristic in the nineteenth-century reception of

Sade. In a 1932 essay for the journal *Progrès medical*, for instance, Heine praised a 1930 doctoral thesis for distinguishing Sade from such obsolete designations, noting that an increasing number of researchers had begun to approach "a subject that had hitherto been considered unapproachable." Heine noted that the Société du roman philosophique was founded for this very purpose, and offered a brief bibliographic survey of recent publications. What he referred to as "the movement of interest in the power of Sade" as a philosopher, rather than as a case study of sexual psychopathology, demanded the circulation of research and expertise that the Société made possible.[59] "There are grounds for believing that Sade, having disturbed an entire century incapable of reading him, will be more and more read," Heine wrote in the 1930 preface to *Les Infortunes de la vertu*, a belief that "mitigates our disturbances with the following pages."[60] The aim of an erudite association was to supplant one set of disturbances with another.

Heine's syndicalist approach to institutionalizing critical and editorial attention to Sade's writing extended to the working conditions of editors, translators, critics, and other stewards of the book trade, on whose behalf he proposed another learned society, l'Association des écrivains bibliographes, traducteurs et commentateurs (The Association of bibliographic writers, translators, and commentators), in 1927. Here the aim was a more explicitly financial rather than archival form of advocacy. Describing the project in a letter to Louis Perceau that year, he wrote about the financial plight of bibliographers and the preparers of old books: "In order to defend ourselves we must group ourselves together. Does not the moment for constituting a professional Association for French "Editors" [in English] strike you as having arrived?"[61] Perceau, in his enthusiastic reply, agreed that the financial considerations of commercial publishing made it necessary to advocate for the "erudition rights" [*droits d'érudition*] that would make it beneficial to both publishers and the interests of editors and translators to produce carefully revised and annotated works.[62] He also proposed that Heine expand his purview from bibliographers to translators and "commentators." Two days after Perceau's letter, Heine had already drafted the statutes of l'Association des écrivains bibliographes, traducteurs et commentateurs, a society that would be open to "any French person of either sex, at least twenty-one years of age, who has published at least two works of either bibliography or translation, commented upon or annotated by him/her." The purpose of the association was to "unite, in a sentiment of solidarity, [such specialized writers] for the study and defense of their professional interests, economic as well as moral, outside of any political or religious matters."[63] The syndicalization of critical and bibliographic labor was itself part of a broader movement to recognize the significance of book manufacturing as a unionizable trade in the 1920s and 1930s.[64] Bibliophilia had itself shifted from a largely private practice of collection and ownership to a sphere of specialized labor and expertise. Heine's later bibliographic association seems never to have been formally launched; even so, he pursued other such projects. In addition to proposing to relaunch his earlier small press, Les Muses Françaises, as a bookstore in 1928, Heine also became a member of the Association syndicale de la critique littéraire, one of a number of related syndicates for authors and intellectual workers in interwar Paris who, unlike more prominent writers, critics, and artists of the period, had little professional means for subsistence.[65] The difficulty of making a living played no small a part in Heine's organizational efforts; his position with Ambroise Vollard began soon after.

As a nonprofit organization subject to the same legal status and statutory administrative form as other such organizations, the Société du roman philosophique was likewise collectivist in its aims; yet the object of its advocacy was less the welfare of intellectual workers than the writings of the Marquis de Sade. Heine was hardly mindless of the more sensational and troubling components of Sade and his work: Sade the pornographer, Sade the pervert, Sade the sexual deviant. Whereas his work with the Société du roman philosophique sought to extract Sade from his insalubrious place in literary and psychosexual history, Heine's broader critical project sought to analyze systematically, if not to rehabilitate, the genres of obscene writing and sexual perversion with which Sade was so intimately associated. Such "excitations" contributed to Sade's encyclopedic approach to human knowledge, a function of his philosophical project rather than the symptom of its monstrous excesses. Heine develops this position in his critical work on the *roman noir*, or Gothic novel, more broadly, a genre to which he assimilated much of the obscene writing Apollinaire and his friends had collected. In doing so, he thus aggregated it to Gothic terror rather than the eroticism and scandal to which the Bibliothèque des Curieux had catered. In a 1934 essay Heine decried the "spiritual tendencies" of postrevolutionary readers "infatuated" with such work. As if anticipating Adorno and Horkheimer's *Dialectic of Enlightenment,* he proposed that the popularity of Gothic romance suggested that the "convulsive changes of political regime had left no apparent influence" on popular tastes. "Let it suffice here," he added, "to denounce this black cloak of indifference that shrouds acts, works, and souls."[66] Taste was not a measure of the truth. Heine's response to such indifference was to inaugurate an encounter with the truth, a possibility the books themselves held in reserve but which popular indifference repressed. His later essays championed the "scandalousness" such writing retained, in spite of its potential appeal to popular taste, on account of what he referred to as its objectivity, its capacity to articulate the truth of such convulsive changes. In a similar vein, he wrote systematic essays on Sade's contemporary Rétif de la Bretonne, author of *Le Pornographe* (1769), *Le Paysan perverti* (The perverted peasant, 1775), and *L'Anti-Justine* (1793), a polemical response to *Justine*. Arguing that Rétif's "erotomania" was fundamental to his objectivity, Heine wrote in a 1934 article for the medical journal *Hippocrate*, "To write outside the excitation of the senses and the mind would be inconceivable to him."[67] Sade was no different: his philosophy extended from and incorporated perversion into the philosophical apparatus of his work as a constitutive element of its very approach to truth, which Natania Meeker has characterized as Sade's "epicurean materialism."[68]

In addition to recasting perversion as objectivity, Heine sought reciprocally to disclose the passions, if not the perversions, of the scientists who approached Sade as a case study of sexual deviance. He thus extended this imbrication of objectivity and excitation to the very field of medicolegal diagnosis that sought to pathologize it. Along with his meticulous research on Sade's life and criminal record, which brought him to numerous police archives and repositories of public records throughout the country, in 1936 Heine published the critical anthology *Receuil de confessions et observations psycho-sexuelles* (Psychosexual confessions and observations), which surveyed the categories of sexual deviance put forth by sexologists such as Havelock Ellis, Richard von Krafft-Ebing, and others. The anthology relativized the place of Sade within sexological discourse that, among its other taxonomic functions, classified homosexuality and exhibitionism as deviances continuous with narcissism, bestiality, and necrophilia. Heine's focus in presenting this continuum was to highlight the role of case studies and "confessions" in the very creation of such repressive classifications. As a result, the medical study of psychosexual abnormalities approached "the elements of curiosity, interest, and passion" we find in novels. "There is nothing unexpected in this," Heine assured his readers, "since doctors and novelists necessarily study the same psychological reality, albeit to different ends."[69] Heine's point was less to decry the biases and prurient interests of sexologists than suggest that such interests were in fact part of "direct observation." Excitation was fundamental, in other words, to any capacity for heeding the "intrinsic nobility of facts" through which "certain texts escape pure technicality in order to join and touch human sensibility."[70] For Heine, objective truth lay not in the sphere of critical distance or critical disinterestedness, but on an "excitation of the senses and mind." To the extent that such excitation could exceed the immediate egoism of an individual subject, it could offer its own kind of law or principle that resembled the Kantian categorical imperative, as Lacan suggested. For Heine it did so through the entanglements—one might even say the complicity—of subjective desires and sensations, both pleasurable and unpleasurable, with any such law. By this logic, Sade was not only a philosopher but also a sexologist; Heine noted that in *120 Journées de Sodom* we recognize the very first *psychopathia sexualis*.[71]

In his published essays and lectures, as well as the prefaces to Sade's texts, Heine advocated in similar terms for Sade's contemporaneity as a thinker of the twentieth century. This *actualité*, which became recognizable in the full complement of Sade's published and unpublished writings, stemmed from his paradoxically invested mode of social and psychosexual observation, which Heine referred to as "surromantic." In contrast to the confessional writings of such figures as Giacomo Casanova, Jean-Jacques Rousseau, and even Rétif de la Bretonne, Sade's "objective method" ushered in "the birth of documentary observation, as it would be taken up by the naturalist school with greater rigor but also greater dryness—and with such reluctance!"[72] Heine made this claim in the final section of his introduction to *Les Infortunes de la vertu* in 1930, entitled "Sade, Auteur Vivant" (Sade, a living author)—a title that proposed the extent to which Sade's work owed its contemporary relevance to its "naturalist" observation of its living environment, the intellectual and political circumstances of revolutionary France. Sade's objectivity extended from the documentation of sexual perversion to the violent forces of historical and epistemic transformation at work in the Revolution he witnessed. Sade neither caused nor chronicled the Revolution, and yet, as Adorno and Horkheimer would likewise suggest, his writing nonetheless articulated the otherwise inadmissible laws exercised through it. To the Revolution Sade thus brought "a philosophy, that which all societies had denied, combatted, reprimanded, but which circumstances permitted him to proclaim upon the social ruins: the sovereign, individual, and unformulatable law of instinct."[73] Sade's philosophy, whose iteration was a function of "circumstance," provided the circumstances in turn for the iterability of otherwise unformulatable laws—namely, the law of absolute egoism that accepted no social contract but only provisioned a "social compromise able at any moment to be renounced or renewed."[74] For Heine, Sade's testimonial to fundamental laws of political behavior lay at the heart of his own institutional endeavors to syndicalize—rather than contractualize—modern critical practices.

As we have seen, the variations on this notion of a Sadean "law" forwarded by postwar intellectuals reveals the persistence of Sade—his *actualité*—as a figure whose writings were notable for their ability to demarcate such laws. Sade, whose writing was coincident with but not immanent in the French Revolution, is an intellectual without agency in any explicit sense, as he likewise remains in Adorno and Horkheimer's *Dialectic of Enlightenment*. Yet as the figure around whom classical thought closed in on itself in favor of "the enormous trust of freedom, or desire, or a will," as Michel Foucault put it, we see how Sade comes to occupy a privileged position in twentieth-century thought on account of this very "excitation of the senses and mind," a formalization of its laws and desires. As a conceptual persona, Sade functions as an institution in his own right: the administrative totality of his "objective" documentary relations to a historical environment that comprised not only the Revolution but also the contemporary order of things.

In recognizing the extent to which the conceptual persona of the Marquis de Sade was mediated by the intellectual labor of Maurice Heine, we witness how the very notion of a conceptual persona hinges on Sade—that is, the aggregate labor of the Sade industry, from nineteenth-century sexologists to twentieth-century philosophers. As Gilles Deleuze and Félix Guattari have written, conceptual personae refer to mediating figures in philosophy, the "intercessors" who are not the biographical people but the figures who serve as the intermediaries through which philosophy "produc[es] movement by thinking it."[75] Such mediating figures emerge within the field of historical and discursive immanence that constitutes the environment for their enunciations.

Sade comes to serve as the very model for such conceptual personae. As the figure whose immanence in European philosophical discourse mediates its "leap out of metaphysics," Sade's work occasions new postwar thinking about negative dialectics (Adorno and Horkheimer), epistemic shifts (Foucault), formal absolutes (Blanchot and Lacan), intersubjective ethics (Beauvoir), and nonsubjective institutions and systems of thought (Deleuze, Guattari, and Klossowski). Blanchot notes that "we come away from Sade less troubled in our sensibilities than belief in our own manner of thinking. It is not that we are convinced; rather, we are offered as it were to a manner of understanding that escapes us and nonetheless draw us on. And thus despite ourselves and despite our desire for a simple logic, we again take up our own reading, carried along by a movement there is no stopping."[76] The "we" here can extend to the very field of critical thinking in twentieth-century Europe, in a manner that bears out the question Heine posed in the title of a 1932 lecture: "Will Sade, persecuted in the eighteenth century, ignored in the nineteenth, dominate the twentieth century?"[77] The answer suggests that mediation, rather than domination, would characterize this legacy.

In Sade's postwar reception, as Éric Marty puts it, "the Sadean text becomes an operator that discloses a discursive apparatus fully established and formalized well beyond the particularity of Sade's oeuvre."[78] Marty rightly notes the extent to which Sade maintained his exteriority to the midcentury philosophical discourse for whose "leap out of metaphysics" he nonetheless served as an intermediary: beyond a certain point, Marty proposes, it was no longer necessary to read his work. According to Heine, however, the inauguration of Sade as a conceptual persona was made possible by the very "historical, empirical, individual, anecdotal" Sade it might otherwise seem to supplant, a function of Sade's objectivity as a philosophical novelist. Heine did not live to see the explosion of interest in Sade's work that took place after the war; yet the Sade industry nonetheless bears the distinctive impression of his institutional labor in returning Sade's work to circulation as philosophy—and as historical, empirical, individual, anecdotal—rather than as pornography or as deviant works for the curious.

To reflect on the methodological significance of studying a mediating figure like Heine is a far cry, of course, from ushering in the heroic return of the Zolaesque intellectual. My aim here has been instead to complicate the genealogy of philosophers and theorists who, since the days of Maurice Blanchot, Simone de Beauvoir, Jean-Paul Sartre, and company have rightly been suspicious of the notion that intellectuals derive their authority from some sort of special metaphysical access. It is thus important to demonstrate the extent to which "Sade," the historical construct, does not end up reproducing this fantasy of metaphysical access by emerging out of history as a transcendent marker of epistemic shifts, however accidentally. The cultural production of Sade the philosopher is no accident. Nor, however, is it especially original or heroic in itself. As Heine insists in his introduction to *120 Journées de Sodom,* his own role was minor: "my very modest role is thus to prevent, if possible, the present age from subscribing to the iniquitous conclusions of a past accustomed to putting the mind on trial, out of surprise and misinformation."[79] Heine's efforts to syndicalize this role as an institutional one at once grounds this modesty in a set of social practices and extends the field of Sade's resonance to the intellectual responsibilities of the contemporary age. I thus propose that the discourse on mediation to which Sade contributes might be reconciled with the study of institutions and texts to which Heine's work directs our attention, as well as to the theoretical and political conditions of their circulation.

The emergence of the Sade industry demonstrates the machinations of outsider theory as a set of conceptual processes and relations characterized by the restless movement of thought Blanchot attributes to the very encounter with Sadean reason, "capable of an energetic becoming and . . . itself always in the process of becoming, being essentially movement."[80] This means two things. First, it suggests that the project of reclamation in which Heine participated be framed within the epistemic shifts to which the resulting Sade industry contributed, however modest in its editorial and critical forms Heine's role might have been. Second, it suggests that we look to the specificity of Sade's use by postwar thinkers, as well as to his construction as a figure of interwar and postwar intellectual life, as a way to think about the immanent practices of intellectual history as constitutive: they open up less to immediate political or even epistemological effects than to the intermediary concepts and personae that render such effects thinkable. For even as the philosophical discourse around Sade appears to displace the agency of the intellectual from a privileged—or perverted—agent to little more than an index of historical becoming, the syndicalist production of Sade by Heine and the Sade industry suggests that the work of such mediation remains grounded in the practices of textual circulation and critical discourse. There is agency here—a limited agency, to be sure, perhaps no more dramatic than a falling snowflake landing on the rim of a bell. But its significance lies in the capacity for such immanent technologies to yield a conceptual persona such as Sade in the name of philosophy—of truth—rather than crime, sadism, madness, and perversion. Sometimes, it seems, the bell does ring.

PART IV

PRODUCTS
OF MIND

CARTOGRAPHORRHEA

On Psychotic Maps

It is the use of paranoid modes of expression by more or less normal people that makes the phenomenon significant.
—Richard Hofstadter, "The Paranoid Style in American Politics"

Why . . . stigmatize in advance, as null and void, what issues from a subject who is presumed to be in the order of the meaningless, but whose testimony is more unusual or, even, entirely original? However disturbed his relations with the external world may be, perhaps his testimony still remains valuable.
—Jacques Lacan, *The Seminar of Jacques Lacan, Book III*

THE MARQUIS DE SADE became a conceptual persona of the twentieth century to the extent that his thought was salvaged from psychopathology, just as his writings were rescued from the Enfer of the Bibliothèque nationale de France. Not every author of obscene works or otherwise heterogeneous logical systems has been so fortunate, however, as to inherit a posthumous critical industry dedicated to the circulation and advocacy of her work. Far more common is a fate characterized by perpetual obscurity or, perhaps, by the lingering epistemological half-life of an occult or countercultural following. As we have already seen throughout this book, however, even the graveyard of human thought is a vast and heterogeneous landscape that opens up to a small variety of possible afterlives. In this regard, I have sought consistently in *Outsider Theory* to repudiate the supposition that there might be an easy line of demarcation between the living and the dead, or the normal and the pathological, in the history of ideas.

Such divisions crop up all the more starkly, however, in the treatment of thinkers diagnosed with mental illness or cognitive disability. The "alien landscapes" of thought systems discontinuous with our own—but who are "we"?—suddenly appear perilous and intractable when the sanity of their authors comes into question.[1] The writings of the insane have been readily admired for their beauty and prescience, but such judgments tend also to presume the social marginalization of their authors, if not their de jure disqualification from the work of reason.[2] Sade becomes a philosopher, after all, to the extent that we cease speculating about his madness and read (or do not read) his texts. The study of mental illness and disability interrupts, however, the automatic demarcation of "normal" from "pathological" conditions in citing not only the social construction of the evaluative terms themselves but also the heterogeneous array of individual conditions they name. No condition is strictly "normal" or "abnormal" in isolation, but instead represents thresholds and commonplaces within complex systems of cognitive, social, and discursive, interactions.[3] "There is no fact which is normal or pathological in itself," wrote the French philosopher and historian of science Georges Canguilhem in 1966. "An anomaly or mutation is not in itself pathological. These two express other possible norms of life. . . . The pathological is not the absence of a biological norm: it is another norm but one which is, comparatively speaking, pushed aside by life."[4] By this logic, the psychiatric designation of madness—cognitive dysfunction, personality disorder—or other cognitive disabilities describes a similar "pushing aside" mediated by social existence and clinical judgment alike. It is not an absolute condition, any more than it represents an abandonment of the faculties for thought. On the contrary, madness instead discloses the extent to which such faculties—reason, judgment, moral compass—can be measured according to thresholds and equilibria rather than full possession.

In this context, the history of paranoia as a psychiatric category offers a telling case study of the entanglements between normal and pathological thought. Such entanglements characterize both the psychic condition it names and the fields of psychoanalysis, social theory, and literary criticism that have studied paranoia and deployed it conceptually. Like other psychotic conditions, paranoia bears a remarkable capacity for producing intricate interpretive systems and theories of its own; the term itself designates, after all, a condition known for its nearness to (*para-* meaning "beside") or approximation of reason. This capacity has been widely recognized in turn and even emulated by the professional psychiatrists, philosophers, and social thinkers who have studied it over the past century and a half. Paranoia, I propose, reproduces the continuities between normal and abnormal cognition on the order of the theories developed in tandem with its clinical identification and treatment. For this reason the history of thinking about paranoia—as well as the history of paranoiac thinking—illuminates the dynamism I attribute to outsider theory, the open system of relations between normal and pathological ideas, between acceptable and inadmissible concepts.

Paranoia, in this sense, is theory's shadow. One seems inevitably to pursue the other: wherever speculative thinking rears its head, questions about its folly or delirium are rarely far behind. In political thought, as in psychoanalysis, the world is rife with persecutions, powerful influences visible only to the tortured souls chosen as their witnesses. Reciprocally, every sweeping historical claim, every conspiracy theory, gravitates toward the limits of reason; and yet even as the products of an unhealthy mind, such fabular constructions nonetheless often circle dangerously, seductively, close to the truth. Is this not how Hollywood films imagine the classic paranoiac, spinning a baroque tapestry of psychotic interpretation from the filaments of worldly events? The speculative faculty might likewise be said to manufacture its own evidence, madly scouring the empirical world for facts to suit its own imaginative ends. Theory, like paranoia, is "mad" to the extent that it recasts the world in its own delirious image—pushed aside, we might say, by life.

Such a diagnosis is hardly inconsistent with work of speculative inquiry itself. For many thinkers, after all, truth lies somewhere other than within the world of observable facts that has, since at least the Enlightenment, exercised a normative function on the known and knowable. As Eve Kosofsky Sedgwick argues in a well-known essay, the centrality of this kind of suspicion to contemporary critical practices has involved "a concomitant privileging of the concept of paranoia" to the extent that "paranoia has by now candidly become less a diagnosis than a prescription."[5] The practical insuperability of theory from its shadow lies at the very core of methodological self-interrogation, not to mention the critical project of articulating underlying structures or patterns that elude empirical observation. This is especially the case for thinkers whose work directly confronts the systematic functioning of psychotic illness itself. Indeed, one of the problems implicit in the widespread circulation of paranoia as an instrumental concept—a concept easily as commonplace in political discourse and literary criticism as it is in the history of psychoanalysis, as Sedgwick suggests—is that it is hard to distinguish the diagnosis from the disease. As Sigmund Freud famously remarked in his 1911 case study of Daniel Paul Schreber's *Memoirs of My Nervous Illness,* the psychotic's "delirious" interpretations of his own nervous illness reveal "a striking similarity with our theory."[6] This similarity had to do with the fact that both Freud and Schreber faced similar evidentiary challenges in conceptualizing and diagnosing psychic rather than behavioral or material phenomena; their accounts necessarily derive from speculative evidence.[7]

The German psychiatrist Hans Prinzhorn, whose 1922 study *The Artistry of the Mentally Ill* galvanized a professional interest in what would later be known as outsider art, makes a similar claim to Freud's. "Phenomenologically," he writes, "we cannot distinguish the reasoning of a mathematician, operating in a fourth dimension on the basis of completely abstract but logically correct assumptions, from that of a schizophrenic who posits an electric power station in whose current he swims as the cause of certain physical sensations. The former is not more correct, more real, or more valid than the latter. . . . The difference appears only in the role which the different hypotheses play in the life of the person who posits them."[8] The hypothetical, relational basis of such thought rendered it virtually impossible to disprove: the theory was pliable enough that all kinds of phenomena could be explained by it. As Karl Popper would later argue, this meant that psychoanalysis itself was, if not a form of madness, then at least a pseudoscience. Freud himself asked a different question, attending to the experimental question Prinzhorn raises: To what extent, Freud wondered, do psychotics speak the truth?

Paranoiac discourse bears a remarkable capacity for manufacturing truth effects. And by *paranoiac discourse* I mean both the corpus of clinical and theoretical writing about paranoia and the body of writings, drawings, diagrams, objects, scribbles, and maps produced by psychotic patients themselves. In his case study of Dr. Schreber, Freud describes the "ingenious delusional structure" developed by the patient, whom he encountered in textual rather than clinical form; his study is based on Schreber's published memoirs rather than on personal contact or direct observation. Freud is not the sole medical authority to comment on this structure. As the examining physician Dr. Weber writes in the book's preface, in spite of showing no outward "signs of confusion or physical inhibition," nor any impairment of the intelligence, the patient is "full of ideas of pathological origin, which have formed themselves into a complete system; they are now more or less fixed, and seem to be inaccessible to correction by means of any objective valuation of the actual external facts."[9] In Schreber's case, this "complete system" involved a delirium of persecution in which the patient's nervous system found itself under attack—by his physician, the "soul-murdering" Dr. Fleischig, as well as by God himself in the form of divine rays that conveyed instructions and produced miracles in him. The result was an elaborate interpretive cosmology that, for Freud, represents Schreber's attempt to reconcile his internal and external worlds. "The paranoiac," Freud writes, "perceives the external world and takes into account any alterations that may happen within it; and the effect it makes upon him stimulates him to invent explanatory theories."[10] The delusion function "is in reality an attempt at recovery," Freud continues, "a process of reconstruction."[11] In this sense the symptoms of the illness represent the patient's own form of autoanalysis, a psychoanalytic theory concomitant with the illness itself. More than a manufactory for truth effects, paranoia emerges as a means for grasping at the very truth itself, the psychological as well as social and relational reality of the patient's suffering. It thus functions as a kind of thinking rather than a purely inventive delusion. Freud concludes in turn that psychiatrists "should take a lesson from the patient," struck as he was by the unconscious and conscious processes that yielded such interpretations in the name of curing an illness they in fact composed. Psychoanalysis, in this sense, resembles paranoia to no small degree.

Indeed, as Freud demonstrates, psychoanalytic theories of paranoia are often reflexive in their awareness that they bear the methodological stamp of the delusional systems they study. Insofar as paranoiac thinking tends to posit an extrahuman source or cause for its cognitive effects—whether in conspiracies, networks of antagonists, or mystical God rays—the work of psychoanalytic theory likewise demands confronting the extent to which thought takes place beyond the thinking subject, the "I" of the cogito presumed throughout the history of Western humanism. In this sense paranoiac thought could be said to occur beyond (or "beside," *para-*) the mind, not as an aberration but as a fundamental displacement of its cognitive functions. For Jacques Lacan, who wrote his graduate thesis on paranoia and returned to the topic throughout his career, paranoia presented an important object of study precisely for this reason. Not only did paranoiac thinking attribute its truth to external causes, but its system of delusional interpretation was also reproducible elsewhere because the illness already manifested itself as a kind of theory in its own right.

Lacan's contribution to psychoanalytic discourse owes much to this phenomenologically resonant insight. As we will see in this chapter, Lacan developed his theories of subject formation on the basis of the extrahuman and systematizing functions of paranoid psychosis. The question was less simply that of whether psychotics spoke the truth than of how psychosis disclosed the production of truth to be radically nonhuman. What thinks? From where does the truth speak? For Lacan, the task of psychoanalysis was to suspend in turn any presumptions about its own normative, scientific entitlement to the faculty of thinking and to heed, through the lesson of psychosis, the "speech" of truth.

This chapter studies the work of psychosis as a clinical and epistemological apparatus. It focuses, in other words, on the critical but also proprioceptive function toward which twentieth-century clinicians and theorists such as Freud, Lacan, and others directed psychotic illness. Rather than rehearsing the symptomology of the illness, I examine the graphic production of paranoiac patients and analysts alike in order to interrogate the claim that such work "knows" more than the human subjects who produce it. This is as true of Freud's writings as of the writings and drawings of psychotic patients.

In turning to the drawings of psychotic patients, I seek to redress lingering critical apprehension about the pathology (or hypernormalization) of paranoia theory—and perhaps of "theory" more broadly—by pointing out ways of dislodging psychotic thinking from the patient–analyst binary that still haunts it. Psychotic drawings certainly testify to the subjective ravages of the illness—that is, its dominion over the imaginary, the terrain of the individual ego—as well as to the institutional conditions of treatment and incarceration such drawings often depict. Yet as signifying systems in their own right, they also bear their own interpretive possibilities as diagrams of the symbolic order, the nonhuman discourse of the Other. These drawings thus illustrate, in turn, dramatic shifts in the way analysts and philosophers conceptualize the production of thought—including their own—according to systems, relational structures, and abstract mechanisms.

THE DISCOURSE OF THE OTHER

Lacan began making claims about the autotheorizing function of paranoia as early as 1932, when he defended his doctoral dissertation "De la psychose paranoïaque dans ses rapports avec la personnalité" (On paranoid psychosis in its relations with the personality). He returned to the topic in his 1955–56 seminar on psychoses, shifting his attention from the singularity of paranoia to the broader spectrum of psychoses that included "paraphrenia," "dementia praecox," and the more contemporary designation of schizophrenia. For Lacan, the psychoses offered a fundamental case study for the extrahuman production of thought because, he explains, in psychotic delusions we find "a truth that isn't hidden, as it is in the neuroses, but made well and truly explicit and virtually theorized."[12] The question of what remained "virtual" in paranoia's theorization of certain kinds of truth would remain the determinant in distinguishing its clinical form from other modes of speculative inquiry, including the work of psychoanalysis itself.

Lacan was adamant, however, in his refusal to oppose psychotic "illness" to functional "sanity." Quite the reverse; in his essay "The Mirror Stage as Formative of the *I* Function" and in other major texts from the late 1940s he describes even "normal" human subjectivity as an imaginary construction whose formation within a "social dialectic" structures it as fundamentally paranoiac.[13] Paranoia refers less here to a type of mental illness than to a coherent delusional system, a dynamic structure within which a subject experiences a social construction—which Lacan refers to as the (primordial) desire of the Other—as her own identificatory desire. What Lacan calls "paranoiac knowledge" corresponds, in other words, "to certain critical moments that punctuate the history of man's mental genesis, each representing a stage of objectifying identification."[14] A subject's own knowledge of herself as a subject, according to the schema of imaginary relations he sketches out in his essay on the mirror stage, is itself paranoiac in structure: what we think of and recognize as our own consciousness is the result of a delusional reconstruction of a complex and fragmented set of social determinants. In this case, what renders such knowledge "virtually theorized," as Lacan puts it, rather than fully and autonomously conceptualized, is that it functions unconsciously. Its speculations are not deducible from rational, conscious imagination or choice; rather, as in Freud's diagnosis, this knowledge unconsciously reflects, identifies, and gives imaginary form to the vicissitudes of the subject's psychic and social environment. We can think about the world without knowing that we are thinking.

In his seminars on Freudian technique in the early 1950s, and especially in his 1955–56 seminar on the psychoses, Lacan further develops his ideas about the phenomenon of unconscious knowledge and unconscious thought by exploring cybernetic "thinking machines" whereby the faculty of thought becomes "embedded in an apparatus." Such protocomputers frame the basic operations of thought as the regulatory distribution of messages and relations, the function of a mechanical or even mathematical apparatus that inscribes sequences of signs within a feedback loop that registers and adapts to changes in the resulting system. He models psychotic delusion functions as similarly self-regulating systems.[15] As he demonstrates most famously in his seminar on Edgar Allan Poe's short story "The Purloined Letter," the purely mathematical repetition of "evens and odds" characteristic of games of chance and the binary logic of information systems yield sets of combinations whose laws of sequential possibility and impossibility are both self-organizing and self-regulating.[16] The point was less to stake a claim to the "artificial intelligence" of the computer age than to employ its terms to approximate the abstract, and fundamentally inhuman, functioning of the unconscious. The unconscious thus no longer refers to a cognitive faculty, but to a set of formal or mathematical possibilities, abstract machines whose functioning Lacan compares to digital code and the relational production of signifiers in structuralist linguistics: the "discourse of the Other," he called it. "Relations between human beings are really established before one gets to the domain of consciousness," Lacan explained in a May 1955 seminar lecture, summing up his characterization of unconscious desire as a kind of cybernetic operation that achieves a "primitive structuration of the human world" in advance of conscious understanding.[17] Indeed, Lacan's work on the unconscious production of thought is consistent as much with contemporary anthropology as with cybernetics insofar as structural anthropology attended to the laws and systems of culture that preceded individual human experience and made it possible in turn, a "primitive structure" that was irreducible to conscious determination.[18] "The discovery of the unconscious," Lacan explains, "such as it appears at the moment of its historical emergence, with its own dimension, is that the full significance of meaning far surpasses the signs manipulated by the individual. Man is always cultivating a great many more signs than he thinks."[19] Lacan thus opens up "thinking" to its broader social environment, the "cultivation" from which it emerges. He thereby dramatizes the extent to which such cultivation aggregates thinking to a set of operations that are alien to consciousness rather than the province of a sovereign act of cognition. Like psychoanalysis and "normal" subjectivity alike, the psychotic imaginary constitutes a second-order production of this cybernetic unconscious.

In his yearlong series of lectures on the Schreber case, which he refers to as Freud's Rosetta Stone, Lacan argues that the truth made explicit in and by psychotic delusion was the revelation that such thinking machines operated within so-called normal subjective experience and even determined its primordial conditions. The truth of psychosis, which Lacan also sees as the truth of psychoanalysis itself, is its ability to disclose "the effect of discourse within the subject."[20] Psychosis bears witness to the "discursive" forces of linguistic and cybernetic authority that structure existence prior to the development of subjectivity. The nature of this witnessing lay at the heart of Lacanian psychoanalysis to the extent that it acknowledges the necessary insuperability of observing and experiencing this extrahuman discourse as an alien phenomenon within the imaginary. This acknowledgment likewise undergirds and reflects Lacan's methodological investment in phenomenology insofar as the object and method of study are, in effect, mutually determinative. But for psychotics it means something more. Psychosis is unique, Lacan argues, in the degree to which it both records and suspends the effects of this unconscious: in psychosis, "the unconscious is present but not functioning."[21] Psychosis bears witness to the unconscious at work, but its means for doing so are unsuccessful and thus radically, painfully unsatisfying.

More martyrdom than insight, psychotic delusion witnesses the discourse of the Other as an experience of unfreedom and suffering. This is because the psychotic encounters this discourse on the terrain of the imaginary—according to subjective impressions and ideas—rather than through the production of symptoms, or, for that matter, through a symbolic approximation through mathematical or linguistic signifiers. The psychotic instead experiences the abstract machines of unconscious discourse as a disruption within the world of meaning and representation, which demands that the subject make sense of it. The psychotic's delirium thereby becomes an imaginary solution to this disruption, at once desperate and enslaving, to which the subject clings with the full force of identificatory attachment. As Lacan puts it, "the psychotic, in the sense in which he is a first approximation an open witness, seems arrested, immobilized, in a position that leaves him incapable of authentically restoring the sense of what he witnesses and sharing in the discourse of others."[22] However poignant, the humanistic drama of psychosis still constitutes a second-order mode of thinking: the delusional struggle to make sense of a fragmented world comprises at once a testimony to and an arrested function of the extrahuman mode of thinking Lacan privileges as the discourse of the Other.

Through paranoia, and through the psychoses more broadly, Lacan sought not only to revise psychoanalytic ideas about where thought comes from but also to transform the clinical and scientific practice—as well as theory—of psychoanalysis itself. Rather than seeking to eliminate it as a pathological condition, Lacan's renewed focus on the psychoses during the mid-1950s thus bore a critical imperative as well as a clinical function. As he argued throughout this period, the psychoanalytic profession had increasingly confined its clinical practices to the field of imaginary relations—that is, to the personal and subjective. Lacan's notable "return to Freud" sought to dislodge psychoanalysis from its humanistic focus on the health and strength of the ego, and instead to attend to the field of symbolic relations, the systems of nonhuman relations that structure human subject formation; this is the set of relations both disclosed by psychosis and foreclosed within its delusional system.[23] The point was to remove humanism from the picture—dislodging both the tendency for ego psychology to fixate upon healthy subjects, and the egoistic tendency for analysts to privilege their own authority as scientists—in order to invoke a truth that speaks through subject's entanglements with the extrahuman discourse of the Other, the truth of unconscious thought. Lacan's teaching urged analysts to think less like doctors or patients and more like psychosis itself.

Such a project meant recognizing the extent to which psychosis enabled the truth of unconscious thinking to "speak" itself. What forms of mediation, though, did such speaking require? Was there a special way of listening to what paranoiacs have to say? If the autotheorizing function was, as Lacan suggested, virtual, then the means through which it could become actual, material, textual took on renewed priority. As we see in the case of Schreber's memoir, paranoiacs produced texts, documents, writings, drawings, diagrams, and even machines that already mediate the "virtual theory" of their illness.

My aim here is to take seriously the claim that such virtual theories resemble psychoanalysis in offering complementary attempts to formalize extracognitive systems of functions and dysfunctions. Reciprocally, such a resemblance illuminates the extent to which psychoanalysis bears its own capacity for autotheorizing reflections on and alterations to its methods. In this sense, the proximity of psychoanalytic and psychotic theories renders psychoanalysis less reductive (as in the diagnosis that paranoia is "caused" by repressed homosexuality) and more receptive to truths that might lay beyond its immediate grasp. My focus in this discussion will be the schematic drawings, maps, and diagrams of paranoiac patients themselves, as a genre of visual theory from which Lacan, and later writers such as Gilles Deleuze and Félix Guattari, drew much of their insight about the social, political, and psychic functioning of paranoiac thought, as well as their own means for representing it figurally. The result is a theoretical and scientific practice modeled on the very operations of psychosis. Studying Lacan's graphemes and Deleuze and Guattari's diagrams of paranoia and schizophrenia alongside the drawings of clinical patients, we witness further methodological continuities—not only between paranoia and theory but also between Deleuze and Guattari's antipsychiatric philosophy and Lacan's "return to Freud." Though often considered as oppositional tendencies in twentieth-century thought, both projects approach the psychoses as epistemologically resonant processes rather than as fixed pathological states. These processes, moreover, are generative: they yield systems, maps, drawings, and texts that testify to a thinking that occurs beyond the individual subject and also theorize how it works. Paranoia is theory's shadow to the extent that both testify to the power of complex systems of relations, codes, and signifiers that exceed—but also form, tax, and buffet—the human mind.

CARTOGRAPHIC MACHINES

One of the earliest clinical cases of paranoia, which rarely figures in psychoanalytic discussions of the illness, is that of James Tilly Matthews, whose persecution fantasies involved the machinations of what he called an "air loom." Matthews was institutionalized in London's Bethlem Royal Hospital (Bedlam) in 1797 for his accusations that he, along with numerous members of Parliament—particularly the home secretary, Lord Liverpool—were being influenced toward treasonous acts of espionage with postrevolutionary France. The source of this influence, he later claimed, was the air loom, a pneumatic machine that emitted mind-controlling and "event-working" rays and also exacted torturous bodily punishments on its victims. The air loom was operated by a gang of seven villains whose roles and powers are outlined in the diagrams Matthews drew. Engravings based on these drawings—the first a figural depiction of the machine as a three-dimensional object, the second a schematic floor plan—were published in John Haslam's culpatory 1810 study *Illustrations of Madness.* The book was published by Haslam, Bethlem's apothecary, as proof (hence "illustration") of Matthews's incurable insanity, and as a rebuttal to repeated efforts by Matthews's family to sue for his release from the asylum. Herein lies one of the categorical distinctions between the case of Matthews and that of Senatspräsident Daniel Paul Schreber a century later, whose own theories about God rays strongly resemble the persecutory forces of the air loom: we do not have a memoir for Matthews, as we do in Schreber's *Memoirs of My Nervous Illness,* but instead a secondhand and overwhelmingly hostile account published by a representative of the medical-legal profession. Yet whereas Haslam's book proffered a testimonial against Matthews's liberty, its illustrations instead testify, on their own behalf, to the drama of Matthews's delusional system through the medium of their reproduction as engravings.

The diagram of the air loom schematizes many of the commonplaces of what we now think of as "political" paranoia, giving figural form to a conspiratorial agency guiding international relations beyond, or beneath, the allegedly reasonable politics of parliamentary debate. Haslam's book documents the architectonics of Matthews's delusional machine—its bodily and psychic effects and the gang who operates it. At the close of his account of the air loom, Haslam concludes that the very existence of the apparatus as a delusional construct provides an irrefutable illustration of the patient's dangerous insanity:

> Although the fable may be amusing, the moral is pernicious. The
> system of assailment and working events deprives man of that volition
> which constitutes him a being responsible for his actions, and persons
> not so responsible, in the humble opinion of the writer ought not to
> be at large.[24]

However "fabulous," Matthews's air loom becomes the clinically verifiable embodiment of his alienated condition, thereby sustaining Haslam's project

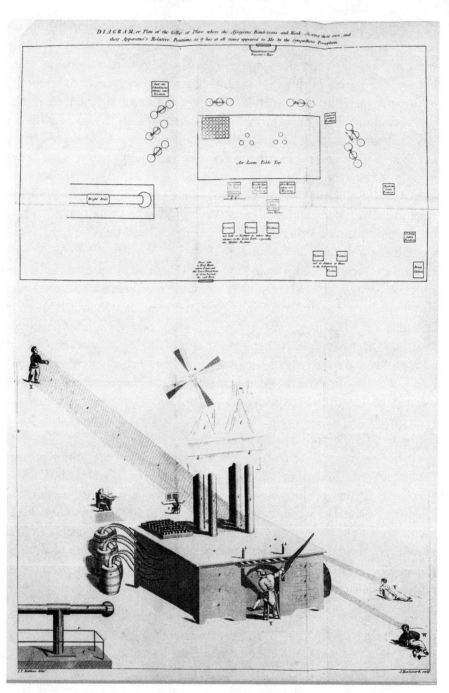

FIGURE 19. James Tilly Matthews's air loom: *DIAGRAM, or Plan of the Cellar or Place where the Assassins Rendezvous and Work. Shewing their own, and their Apparatus's Relative Positions, as it has at all times appeared to Me by the Sympathetic Perception.* Illustration for John Haslam's *Illustrations of Madness*, 1810. Wellcome Library, London (CC-BY 4.0).

to keep Matthews incarcerated. Matthews's delusional machinations remain confined within a diagnosis of criminality that documents their threat to public safety. Haslam's conclusions register a threat to subjectivity as well: presuming responsibility and reason to be inherent properties of the human individual, he considers the air loom drawings as documentary proof that Matthews's delusional system had already usurped his individual volition and responsibility; the air loom functioned, in other words, as the very apparatus for depriving Matthews of his sanity. The "illustrative" value of the drawings thus overshadows their status as images produced in and by the imaginary hyperproduction of psychotic delusion.

Viewed according to an order of representation beyond Haslam's normative judgment, however, the same images disclose an additional set of relations: Do they not testify, for one, to the very forms of authority levied upon them by Haslam in recasting them as "illustrations of madness"? For as Roy Porter notes in his introduction to a 1988 reprint edition of *Illustrations of Madness*, the air loom functions not just as a delusional machine but as an affective map of Matthews's immediate conditions. "It would be an exquisite irony," Porter writes, "if Matthews has cast the staff of Bethlem, including Haslam himself, as the *dramatis personae* in his fantasy world of persecutions."[25] The air loom gang, in other words, could conceivably designate the asylum workers; and the air loom itself, in addition to its function as an influencing machine for international politics, might also allegorize the event-working operations of Bethlem Royal Hospital. The air loom documents not only Matthews's experience of "madness"—a loss of psychic and bodily control, a subjection to harsh institutional conditions—but also his experience of power, an experience that includes his rhetorical as well as clinical encounter with Haslam's scientific authority. Even in their alienated form as reproduced engravings, Matthews's air loom drawings map institutional and ideological relations as well as affective or imaginary ones.

In this respect, Matthews's drawings—and, to a certain degree, their reproductions—might be said to resemble the "sociograms" developed by the anti-Freudian psychologist Jacob Moreno in the early 1930s. These schematic drawings graphed social relations in ways that allowed analysts to "grasp the myriad networks of human relation and at the same time view any part of portion of the whole which we may desire to relate or distinguish."[26] The sociogram's vectors of intersubjective relation offer a visual language for formalizing a set of complex data without straying into pure abstraction: human subjects are still recognizably the principle ordering unit of classification. Insofar as Matthews's air loom diagrams similarly allegorize relations of affective power—whether parliamentary or institutional—Porter's hypothesis is

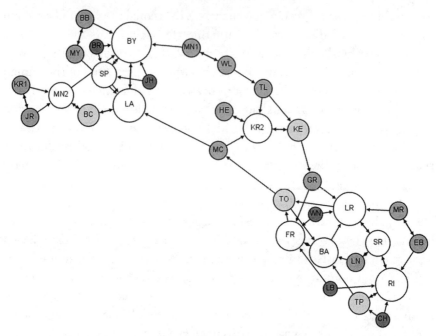

FIGURE 20. Jacob Moreno's sociogram (seventh-grade social relations), by Martin Grandjean. Wikimedia Commons, https://commons.wikimedia.org/wiki/File:Moreno _Sociogram_7th_Grade.png.

that the air loom presents a schematic map of the intersubjective relations of its dramatis personae, laid according to a spatial logic and figured as a machine.

At once a schematic diagram of invisible forces and an affective map of the Bethlem asylum, Matthews's delusional machine seems to borrow its technological apparatus from the popular imagery through which, as Mike Jay has put it, the brain "provides a ready explanation from the materials it has to hand. For some, the form is God and cosmic conflict, for others, it is technology—not real technology, but often a canny reading of where technology seems, or perhaps wishes, to be heading."[27] To the extent that pneumatics, mesmerism, and vacuum tubes compose the imaginative form of Matthews's machine, the air loom's cartographic function is no less "technological" as an apparatus for grasping networks of institutional relations. The Viennese psychiatrist Victor Tausk makes this case in his 1919 essay "The Influencing Machine," arguing that the machinelike constructions of psychiatric patients carry out a particular set of functions that perform real, if virtual, work. They work to produce concrete effects within the psychotic subject, at once provoking thoughts as a "suggestion-apparatus" and stimulating somatic responses. Yet making this claim, Tausk also distinguishes the mystical influencing machines he tied to schizophrenia from the ideas of persecution he considered specific to paranoia, thereby limiting the technological function of the machines to an "internal" subject-oriented system of representation.[28] For Tausk, the graphic production of such machines—consisting, he writes, of "boxes, cranks, levers, wheels, buttons, wires, batteries and the like"—represents persecution not from without but from within, originating "from the sensations of change accompanied by a sense of estrangement."[29] The machines, Tausk concludes, are ultimately a symbolic projection of the patient's own genitalia, represented in disguised form, and their functioning exercises fantasies of both masturbation and escape. Even so, Tausk notes how such machines function symbolically, as Lacan might put it; they do not simply depict imaginary constructions but work to formalize relations of desire and power that structure individual experience.

As a paradigmatic example of one such influencing machine, Jakob Mohr's drawing "Proofs" (c. 1910), part of the Prinzhorn Collection of asylum art, brings to mind the event-working rays of Matthews's air loom, as well as the more oft-studied God rays described in Daniel Paul Schreber's memoirs. Their system of representation is hardly limited, of course, to the internal (or even genital) object causes of their illness. Regardless of whether or not one accepts the genital symbolism of Tausk's theory, we can still view the machine images as mechanisms for formalizing the conditions and means of psychotic estrangement. As I have suggested, the graphic representation of such rays, and the bodily tortures they entail, allegorizes at once the delusional logic and the real institutional conditions of the illness. In doing so it resituates the causal insistence of their influences in a system both beyond and prior to the "interior" causality of the individual subject. The machine images map out, in turn, the relations of institutional and imaginary power through which their delusional apparatuses co-opt the more abstract authority of the Other—the symbolic order—over the subject. When considered as maps, in other words, the cartographic allegories of power such drawings provide become the very medium through which the discourse of the Other speaks its truth. Psychotic maps are not only testimonials to institutional and psychic suffering; they are also diagrams of the symbolic order, depicted in the refracted effects of its "influence."

For Lacan, the influencing machines at stake in psychosis were not only the air looms and God rays of the delusional subject but also the abstract machines of signification and system formation that make up the discourse of the Other. "It's not a question," he explains, "of the subject's relation to a link signified within existing signifying structures, but of his encounter under

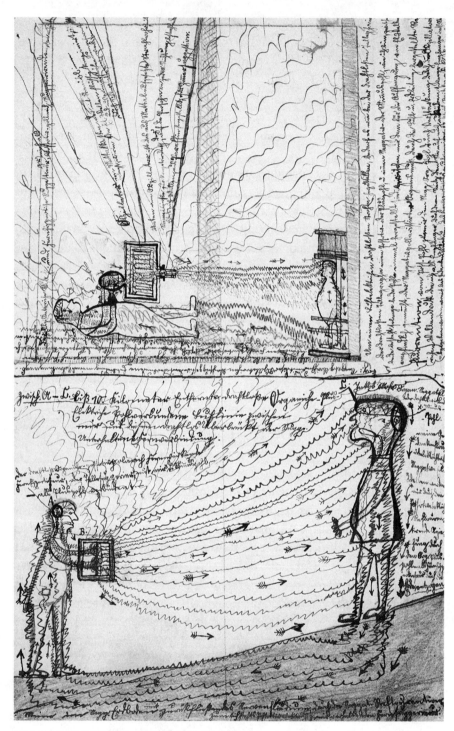

FIGURE 21. Jakob Mohr, *Beweiße* (Proofs). Inventory no. 627/1 (created around 1910), Prinzhorn Collection, University Hospital Heidelberg.

elective conditions with the signifier as such, which marks the onset of psychosis."[30] Lacan adopts, in other words, the formal rather than explanatory value of Tausk's notion of influencing machines. The "technological" or godlike apparatus of such delusional constructions registers the relations of power and influence as the medium within and upon which the nonhuman discourse of the Other exercises its effects. Psychosis describes a condition in which a subject no longer speaks out through the machines of unconscious thought formation "with all his being"—as in the case of neurotic symptoms—but in which such machines speak out through the imaginary relations of the subject. As Lacan explains, in the phenomenology of psychosis "everything from beginning to end stems from a particular relationship between the subject and this language that has suddenly been thrust into the foreground, that speaks all by itself, out loud, in its noise and furor, as well as in its neutrality. . . . If the neurotic inhabits language, the psychotic is inhabited, possessed, by language."[31] What this suggests, with regard to an apparatus such as Matthews's air loom, is that we consider it less a figural representation of the conspiratorial agency behind political, institutional, or psychotic influence than a second-order production of the order of discourse for which such "agency" or power is already an imaginary rendering.

Psychosis, Lacan argues, implies a persecution by discourse—an "oscillation in which a discourse that the subject experiences as foreign and as revealing a presence to him itself asks the questions and itself gives the answers."[32] To what extent, in turn, might we consider the air loom—in both its visual and speculative incarnations—as a second-order conduit for the "language" of governmentality, which plays the role of interrogator Lacan describes? We might consider Matthews's psychosis "political" insofar as the air loom formalizes the abstraction-prone problems of social ordering and hierarchical structure for which institutions such as parliaments and asylums serve as mediating institutions. The discourse that "speaks" its truth by means of Matthews's air loom might therefore be, in Lacan's terms, the same order of discourse that bears regulatory force upon the so-called normal subject, here extrapolated and collectivized under the aegis of the Hobbesian nation-state.

Lacan's own schematic diagram of the "dialectic of intersubjectivity," which schematizes this effect, figures heavily in his early seminars "from the theory of transference to the structure of paranoia."[33] This diagram offers a graphic depiction of the psychotic phenomenon whereby the Other's discourse speaks through the subject's delusion; in doing so, its own schematic form obeys the formal logic of drawings such as Matthews's and Mohr's. Lacan's schema represents visually, in other words, the structural logic through

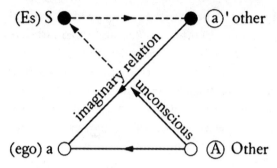

FIGURE 22. Jacques Lacan's "dialectic of intersubjectivity," from the seminar on Edgar Allan Poe's "The Purloined Letter," April 26, 1955.

which the Other (A, for *Autre*) exercises its effects upon a subject (S) through the imaginary relations that constitute its medium of "influence" (represented in Lacan's schema as the diagonal line (ego) a ← ⓐ' other). This influence includes both the construction of subjectivity in the first place and the constitutive illusion, as Lacan puts it, that the subject has found the symbolic order of the Other in her own consciousness. Topological rather than topographical, Lacan's schema is itself a machine for witnessing and conceptualizing the means through which the discourse of the Other speaks through the subject; yet it does so with an insistence that imaginary relations constitute the medium rather than the cause or source for these effects. What speaks—what "thinks"—is this discourse, whose abstract machines constitute what it is we imagine to be the unconscious. This is the truth to which psychoanalysis appeals in turn, a truth exterior to consciousness—an inhuman "outside"—that nonetheless forms its very condition of possibility.

DELUSIONAL THINKING

"The more one studies the history of the notion of paranoia," Lacan writes, "the more significant it seems and the more one appreciates the lesson that can be drawn from the progress, or lack of progress—whichever you like—that characterizes the psychiatric movement."[34] As Lacan's remark suggests, the consequences of the historical proximity between analysis and delusional "unreason" have been twofold. First, they give rise to the periodic assumption that "theory" is itself by nature hallucinatory—that is, the notion that the kind of analysis constituted by and through a clinical relationship to paranoia is pathological and abnormal, a symptom of what it studies.[35] In this view, theory and psychosis alike yield little more than an elaborate form of babbling aphasia wherein, as Lacan writes, the subject "employs enormous, extraordinarily articulate bla-bla-bla, but . . . can never get to the heart of what he has to communicate."[36] Second, the alternative view, which derives from the same uncomfortable proximity, holds that analytical reason distinguishes itself from psychosis only through the imposition of institutional authority—that is, the categorical distinction between sanity (the faculty for coherent thought, whether exercised in "theory" or clinical judgment and treatment) and madness is a product of epistemological and social forms of distinction, a territorialization of the analyst-theorist within a position of normative institutional empowerment, and the patient within the alienated realm of madness. The doctor or professor can theorize because she speaks as a knowing subject vested with the authority of an institution; the madman speaks from a position bound up within the constraints of the asylum, the therapeutic relationship, the haze of psychotropic medication, or simply the diagnosis. The same goes for the normalization of paranoia as a critical mode in humanistic scholarship, insofar as professional critics wield it as a "strong theory," as Sedgwick puts it, that reproduces its "powerfully ranging and reductive force" throughout the academy, at the expense of "weak theories" of local, diffuse, and otherwise queer phenomena it marginalizes and overshadows.[37] These twin sets of conclusions, drawn from the intimacy between delusion and analysis, recur frequently throughout contemporary intellectual discourse and reproduce their effects within the fields of politics and culture, often in the name of either an antitheoretical or an antipsychiatric humanism. According to this logic, critical theorists either think too much like mad people or brandish their faculties of thought only at the expense of others.

None of this, mind you, is especially new; the notion that the delusional structure of psychosis and the analytical form of speculative inquiry might be mutually subject to interpretive delirium and self-aggrandizing claims to authority has long been a cause for humanistic vigilance. What is peculiar about the discourse of psychotic thinking is that this disquietude arises from within an array of seemingly incommensurate ideological positions, even beyond the reactionary tendency to discredit speculative inquiry altogether for its rhetorical or epistemological excesses. Few things evince as much suspicion as the intricacies of psychoanalytical jargon. A version of this disquietude might even be said to characterize certain features of psychosis itself, characterizing a sense of certainty or urgency incommensurate with the delusional subject's sense of the real. At the same time, a similar crisis of demarcation has also troubled psychiatrists and psychoanalysts, for whom clinical treatment risks devolving into a struggle for power through transference and countertransference, the tangle of affective relations between analyst and patient. It is easy, after all, to demonize Haslam for his insistence on keeping Matthews under lock and key, and for leveraging his case study of Matthews's mental illness as evidence. For Lacan, however, this struggle reveals the basic truth of Freudian psychoanalysis: far from seeking to extract scientific truth from its messy entanglements with the intersubjective relations between patients and analysts, such entanglements are constitutive of the science itself. Transference, in its spoken and affective exchanges, constitutes the very medium through which the science of psychoanalysis emerged in the first place. Not only are analysts never fully neutral or objective observers of "madness," but their science is itself a product of this nonneutrality, the basic set of clinical conditions from which Freud and others developed their theories. As Lacan puts it, the objectivity of psychoanalysis is "strictly tied to the analytic situation," constituting "the science of the mirages that arise within this field."[38] Lacan's "return to Freud" proposed at once to refocus attention upon the primacy of language and aggression in Freud's work and demanded that analysts recognize their dependence on this discourse and thus abolish the "narcissistic mirage" of their scientific authority.[39] Much like the objectivity Maurice Heine attributed to Sade (see chapter 6), the truth of psychoanalysis lay in its capacity to register—to bear witness to—relations beyond the individual subject, but which nonetheless employ subjective impressions and relations as their medium. The point was hardly to ignore the suffering of psychiatric patients, but instead to challenge the self-assurance of the clinical mind as the normative guarantor of scientific authority.

This critique of scientific authority also galvanized the more activist political program of the antipsychiatric movement of the 1960s, whose proponents included Deleuze and Guattari and the admirers of so-called outsider art. For such figures—who wished to acknowledge the creative, even revolutionary, intellectual production of the clinically insane—it was the rationalizing and power-imposing institutions of diagnosis, treatment, and analysis that determined the extent to which psychosis represented a form of madness to be pathologized and incarcerated. The terms *paranoia* and *schizophrenia* came instead to describe mechanisms at work in the field of social, institutional, and economic relations whose limitation to the unhealthy mind, and to the discourse of psychiatry, was itself pathological. For such thinkers, the discourse of paranoia thus opened up to the contested terrain of social control and biopolitical forms of discipline, as much as to the formal machines of the Lacanian Other. Psychotic theories and theories of psychosis were profoundly political in their dialectical relations of form and content, message and medium.

The popular recourse to paranoia as a political metaphor is no less contentious. Indeed, the metaphorical uses of paranoia to describe conspiracy theories and other interpretive schemes for diagnosing—or perpetuating—systems of persecution and influence likewise bear an anxiety about demarcating normal from pathological forms of what might be called psychotic thinking. This latter concern has come into focus as an especially vivid motif in the U.S. politics and culture of the Cold War era. As Richard Hofstadter writes in his 1963 essay "The Paranoid Style in American Politics," the qualities of "heated exaggeration, suspiciousness, and conspiratorial fantasy" that he describes as paranoid are dangerous because they are the symptoms of a perverted historical judgment and a pathological understanding of political processes. Hofstadter writes, "The paranoid tendency is aroused by a confrontation of opposed interests which are (or are felt to be) totally irreconcilable, and thus by nature not susceptible to the normal political processes of bargain and compromise."[40] He levies this charge specifically against the American right wing of the McCarthy era, but the seriousness of his accusation is compounded by the structural similarities he cites between the Cold War United States and other paranoid regimes throughout history, from early American anti-Catholicism to the more recent totalitarian regimes of German fascism and Stalinist communism. For Hofstadter, as for Haslam a century and a half earlier, such political regimes share not only the conspiracy theory-driven symptomology of "paranoia" but, more dangerously, also the same fundamental alienation from the so-called normal political processes of bargain and compromise he attributes to democratic liberalism. By this logic, any movement whose political aims and means are either unrealizable by or unimaginable within the "normal" mechanisms of power become pathological.[41] Hofstadter's insistence on liberal normality belies a worldview overrun with dangerous regimes, an interpretive delirium of its own that begs the question of whether Hofstadter's own essay might be considered fundamentally paranoid according to the logic it sets forth.

But are all such "paranoid" tendencies alike? Must a critical theory of paranoia function only in the name of demarcating the pathological from the normal, "real" persecution from the false sense of persecution imagined by desperate political regimes eager for preemptive retaliation? Even if, as Emily Apter has written, political paranoia theory is "very much a symptom of what it critiques," the tendency for paranoiac modes of thinking toward "blotting out any sense of the possibility of alternate ways of understanding *or* things to understand" identified by Sedgwick refers to a critical paradigm rather than a clinical attribute.[42] This does not automatically discredit its function as a means for inaugurating both a mode of thinking and a scientific practice.[43] To argue for the epistemological value of paranoiac discourse is thus to consider it as something other than a disease of power, as Elias Canetti once put it, or as a medium of political or cultural struggle, as Sedgwick puts it. It is instead a theory of power's functioning—albeit a theory irrevocably bound up in this power, as the medium through which it thinks. What Lacan referred to as Freud's "Copernican Revolution" demanded that we dramatically rearticulate how, and from what register, such "power" exerted its effects. The nature of this "revolution" involved shifting from the project of revealing hidden underlying causes of observable phenomena—the suspicious hermeneutics so often characterized as paranoid—toward a science capable of recognizing structures and relations whose real existence could be measured only obliquely (that is, symbolically, in Lacan's terms). The psychoanalytic "revolution" resembled the psychoses insofar as its own obliquities gave conceptual form to the psychic and social forces to which analysts and patients were mutually subject.

Paranoia thus represents a totalizing clinical paradigm or "strong theory" only in the restricted sense that its efforts to map out the abstract laws and relational effects Lacan named as the symbolic, however erroneous such maps may be, nevertheless testifies to the real effects of such laws and effects. Scholars have long noted the ideologically resonant imprint of a "social dialectic" on the process of subject formation, in keeping with Lacan's early arguments about the paranoid structure of ego formation.[44] By this logic, human subjectivity emerges from its rocky cradle already buffeted by the vicissitudes of power and desire. By the mid-1950s, however, Lacan's focus on paranoia and persecution had shifted in attention from ego formation to the cybernetic laws and structures that come to light by means of it. The psychoses thus became a platform for examining how delusion gave living, tortured expression to formations that operate in the symbolic, within the discourse of the Other. It would be a mistake, in other words, to conflate the abstract machines through which structural laws and patterns emerge with political systems alone. The "thinking" of psychotic delusion is not limited merely to resembling or reproducing the effects of political conspiracies and global regimes of power or, for that matter, repressed sexuality. Rather, in its articulation through action, as a "discourse of error," it testifies to an expanded field of symbolic relations that both introduced and demanded a new set of methods to study their effects. In its tortured production of symptoms and interpretive schemes, psychotic discourse can "bear witness to the truth against the apparent facts themselves."[45] Truth itself speaks, by this logic, from the place where it suffers.

Lacan's 1955–56 seminar on the psychoses discusses how such abstract machines engineer the force of law upon the delusional subject. He describes how the formal insistence of even a random or automated repetition (based on the "insistence of the signifying chain") results in cybernetic laws of probability and logical necessity, an idea he introduced in his seminars on Freudian technique in 1954. Yet through the workings of the symbolic, such "laws" become mythologized, even personified, in figurations such as the Oedipal triangle, the classically Freudian structure of unconscious (male) desire. As Roy Porter notes of Matthews's air loom, unconscious thought gives imaginary form—complete with moving parts and figures of persecution and sexual desire—to abstract systems of relation that "speak" their truth through this medium. By this logic, political regimes and conspiracies are likewise part of this imaginary form, another such medium through which the "truth" of psychosis speaks.

As we will see, Lacan's recourse to the stock discourse of the Freudian imaginary nonetheless elicited critique from thinkers such as Deleuze and Guattari, who refused his acceptance of the Oedipal triangle as a set of "primordial signifiers" and considered it a delusional formation of psychoanalysis itself. As the very title of their book *Anti-Oedipus* announces, Deleuze and Guattari sought with polemical intensity to dismantle the mythologically laden terms used by Freud, Lacan, and other psychoanalysts to demarcate the machinations of the symbolic order. Even in doing so, however, their work extends Lacan's attention to the power and influence of systematic, extrahuman production of thought to which psychosis testifies. Their work elaborates an alternative vocabulary of social-libidinal economics, mechanomorphic functions, and "regimes of madness" replete with diagrams analogous to the conceptual visualizations Lacan uses in his work. For Deleuze and Guattari, however, such functions and regimes denote social and libidinal forces with real, material effects, rather than abstract machines of signs and codes. And the diagrams they offer as illustrations of such forces are modeled, in turn, on the graphic production of mental patients and outsider artists. Whereas Lacan's schematic renderings of the "dialectic of desire" generalize psychotic structures as fundamental to "normal" subjectivity, Deleuze and Guattari insert the political and institutional valences of paranoia within their abstractions. Lacan's diagrams are maps of abstract relations; Deleuze and Guattari's diagrams are, I propose, maps of power. Their conceptual visualizations attend to the function of psychotic thinking in its relation to the very real psychic and institutional conditions of power and influence to which it responds. My point here is not to claim that Lacan's or Deleuze and Guattari's schematic diagrams literally imitate patient drawings—although this is entirely feasible. Rather, it is to propose that the phenomenological proximity of theory with paranoia extends to the graphic production of both analysts and patients in the degree to which their figural logic contends with the persecuting force of the symbolic in pictorial form.

DIAGRAMS OF POWER

From what place does the truth speak? The institutional distinction between imaginary and symbolic relations Lacan draws in his schemas and graphs becomes discernible in the asylum maps drawn by psychiatric patients. Numerous such images in the Prinzhorn Collection of the art of the insane, for instance, similarly diagnose the accumulations of influence, discipline, law, and even tyranny to which psychotic patients are subject and to which, in the maps, they subject what they draw. Like Matthews's air loom, their figuration of the symbolic erupts as distortions within the figural logic of the imaginary, and encounter with the "signifier as such" that leaves its impression on the figural language of the drawings.

Franz Josef Kleber's rendering of the grounds of the Regensburg Institution, created over the course of seventeen years between 1880 and 1896, creates the illusion of an aerial map, but from the perspective of an emphatically grounded subject. The map, one of several by Kleber in the holdings of the Prinzhorn Collection, is exquisitely paradoxical: areal in scope yet painstakingly drawn from the ground up, the plan reflects the near symmetry of rural institutional architecture.[46] Yet it suspends this symmetry as well; whereas the four framing outbuildings at the corners of the image all resolve to a centralized and even quasi-panoptic vantage point, the walls of individual buildings within the grounds delineate exploded forms, perspectivally flattened in a way that renders facing sides and roofs contiguous on the same plane. As a drama of cartography, Kleber's map of the institution might be seen as an effort to gain a totalizing perspective of the Regensburg asylum in its entirety, as well as, perhaps, an image of the totalizing enclosure of the institution itself. The distortion and fragmentation of perspectives serves quite tragically as an allegory for the artist's chronically limited vantage points. In its aggregate form, the drawing offers less an overarching image of the asylum—an aerial view—than an agglomeration of innumerable measurements taken from within the grounds. The mapmaking subject is not, however, "trapped" at the image's center, as its near symmetry might suggest—such centralization would dramatize not only the subject's incarceration but also, dialectically, his totalizing mastery. Rather, the implicit subject is nomadic, wandering from courtyard to courtyard, looking up at the buildings from each side.

What is perhaps most impressive about Kleber's asylum map is the extent to which its logic radiates outward from its central focus. Regardless of where the perspectival flattening of buildings and forms locates its viewing subject, the map obeys an overarching spatial logic, reminiscent of gnomic

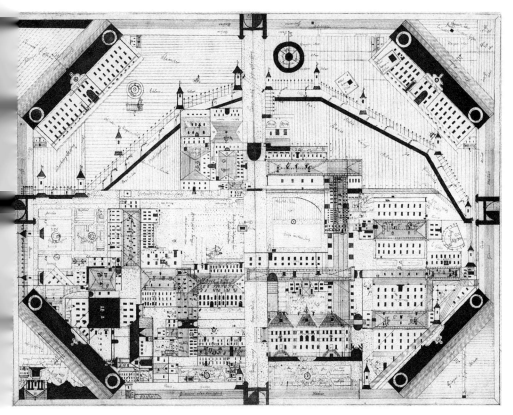

FIGURE 23. Franz Josef Kleber, untitled drawing (Lageplan der Anstalt Regensburg, Karthause Prüll). Inventory no. 4506 (created between 1880 and 1896), Prinzhorn Collection, University Hospital Heidelberg.

projection, wherein the geographical coordinates extend geometrically from a central focus like the measures on a sundial. Kleber's map thus registers a system of discursive production that organizes both the drawing and, in turn, the Regensburg Institution itself. It no longer does this through figural renderings of its spatial relations alone, but according to a distortional "law" of cartographic perspective. The map recasts the asylum as an influencing machine, no longer simply of its own medical-legal authority but of the impersonal laws and systems of order the map seeks endlessly to calculate: planes, surfaces, angles. By means of cartographic distortions, the carceral system finds its laws explicit and virtually theorized.

A second drawing from the Prinzhorn Collection further develops the calculative function of the psychotic map, extrapolating the radial logic of gnomonic perspective featured in Kleber's drawing to include the passage of time and the diurnal movement of celestial objects. Johann Knopf's untitled drawing of what looks to be a freestanding country cottage or chalet displays a similar perspectival flattening, depicting the front and sides of the building on the same surface plane, as if features of an elaborate facade. The image is likewise subject to radial distortion: the trees and gardens to either side of the cottage are laid out along a single axis, enforcing a parallelism between the two halves of the image. Otherwise the drawing appears more illustrative than cartographic, insofar as the facade of the house privileges the fanciful embellishments of its timber-frame design; the spherical motif of the roof is reiterated in the garden shapes and celestial bodies surrounding the house.

It is in the intersection of the garden spaces and the celestial bodies that the image discloses its function as something more than an architectural rendering. The sun, moon, sundial, and fanciful stars and birds depict—and possibly enforce—a cosmological system whose affect appears cheerful given the broad smiles the sun and moon each bear. Other drawings by Knopf recast these motifs in a far more anxious light, suggesting that their systematic or near systematic position in the chalet drawing has more to do with their configuration than their jovial affect. Indeed, Knopf's other drawings connect the iconography of the smiling orbs to an autobiographical narrative of persecution and murder reminiscent of paranoiac delusions—for example, his "Petition No. 2345 the mysterious affairs of the murderous attacks," an image that features a configuration of birds in flight consistent with the cottage drawing and numerous others, documents a bureaucratic search for "signs of the Mysterious Murderous Attacks."[47] Other drawings feature the grinning celestial orbs as the heads of totemic figures who either

FIGURE 24. Johann Knopf, untitled drawing. Inventory no. 1490, Prinzhorn Collection, University Hospital Heidelberg.

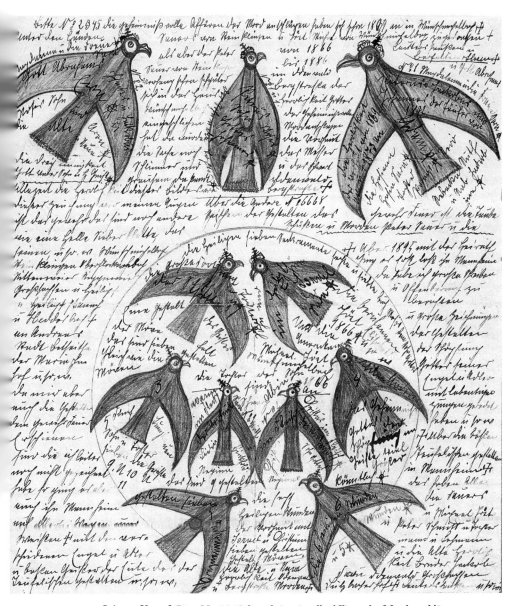

FIGURE 25. Johann Knopf, *Bitte No. 2345 die geheimnisvolle Affären der Mordanschlägen* (Petition No. 2345 the mysterious affairs of the murderous attacks), Inventory no. 1494/4, recto, Prinzhorn Collection, University Hospital Heidelberg.

brandish weapons or imply sacrifice, such as the drawing entitled "The Lamb of God."

The house, with its elements organized in a picturesque whole, thus might be seen as an unnerving cosmological chart of numerous persecutions, depicting less their violence alone than their relational totality. The

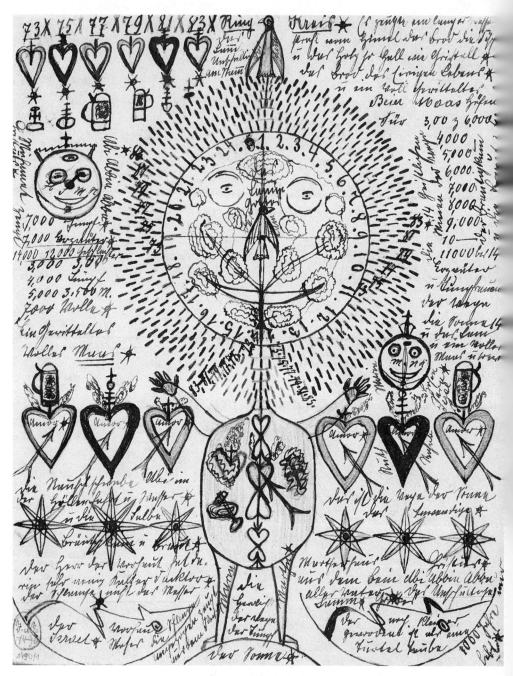

FIGURE 26. Johann Knopf, *Lamm Gottes* (The lamb of God). Inventory no. 1490/1, recto, Prinzhorn Collection, University Hospital Heidelberg.

drawing's radial order and cosmological projections disclose the instrumental quality of the map as a kind of calculating device, at once microcosm, orrery, and balance sheet. As the second-order machinations of a delusional system, its calculations would thus be consistent with the abstract, schematic function of the map as evidence of the intrusive presence of some other, alien system—some other discourse—whose questions and commands it strives to resolve in imaginary form.

In an essay on the art of the insane, Hal Foster emphasizes the tragic quality of such drawings, the tortured nature of their witnessing and theorizing. In a manner reminiscent of Tausk or even Freud, Foster argues that these maps neither implicate nor resist the machinations of power, law, or discourse to which they testify, but instead try "to *find* such law again . . . , at the very least to recompose its empty form, its absence." For to their horror, Foster continues, "this is what these artists often seem to see—not a symbolic order that is *too* stable . . . but rather a symbolic order that is *not* stable at all, that is in crisis or corruption."[48] Psychotic maps such as Kleber's are, for Foster, projections of a fantasy of restoration. They may say something about the general condition of modernity during the time of their composition, perhaps, but the knowledge they disclose is largely that of the artist's own suffering. And to the extent that these images have since found their way into the avant-garde imagination and clinical and scholarly study alike, institutionalized psychotic artists find themselves exploited all over again, this time as underacknowledged producers of aesthetic and critical objects.

Foster's principle intention in making such claims about the instability of the symbolic order is to problematize the tendency for avant-garde artists to fetishize outsider artists as countercultural heroes "in revolt against artistic conventions and symbolic order." And in this sense I concur with the assessment that such drawings not be co-opted as a medium for aesthetic or ideological struggle—as Sedgwick likewise contends regarding paranoiac discourse as a whole—but recognized as a medium of cognitive and emotional struggle. For Lacan, such efforts at synthesis and restoration describe the very "discourse of error" by which psychosis "bears witness" to the truth: what is in crisis is not the symbolic order—the abstract laws and structures of intersubjective relations—but the patient's tortured experience of this order. In the regimented maps of Kleber, Knopf, and others, the abstract machines or laws that the drawings at once testify to and reconstruct, piece together and obey, are ruthlessly self-regulating. In their cartographic function the images figure the Other's discourse as a territorializing concatenation of various systems of power, particularly in the extent to which the severity of abstract or metaphysical laws—voices from God, cosmic order—seem to line up with the figural regime of real clinical and institutional power. The maps, as maps, proffer what Lacan once referred to as an "immediate noumenal apprehension of oneself and the world,"[49] staging this apprehension as a condensation of powerful influencing machines—institutional, political, psychic, psychiatric—within a single morphological system. Yet insofar as such maps also function schematically as influencing machines in their own right, their symbolic testimony to the abstract machines of the Other can be considered differently: as gnomonic projections, we might say, of how the discourse of the Other "thinks" through the material and imaginary relations of its subjects. In this respect, psychotic maps do not so much represent this discourse as become apprehended by it, seized and held by it in its functioning.

LINES OF FLIGHT

Psychotic maps, a genre I take to include both the influencing machines of Matthews and Mohr and the asylum drawings of Kleber and Knopf, are conducive to thinking insofar as their cartographic systems function according to the laws of the symbolic order rather than the cognitive demands of the individual subject. This thinking is already twofold: it not only formalizes the medium through which the symbolic exercises itself upon the delusional subject (via institutions, persecutory figures, rays, and the entire lexicon of charged signifiers) but also testifies to the abstract machines that constitute the order of discourse that speaks its truth through this same medium, as Lacan maintained. It is to the political and epistemological exigency of this order of discourse, and to the thinking proper to it, that Deleuze and Guattari dedicate their collective project in *Anti-Oedipus,* a work that seeks radically to rethink the Lacanian "discourse of the Other" according to revisionist ideas about psychotic production. Unlike Lacan, Deleuze and Guattari formalize the abstract machines of the symbolic order as engines of production rather than mathematical contrivances, as virtual machines of social and libidinal investment—desiring machines—for which schizophrenia offers the fullest expression. "Schizophrenia," they write, "is the universe of productive and reproductive desiring-machines, universal primary production as 'the essential reality of man and nature.'"[50] Abandoning Lacan's painstaking phenomenology, Deleuze and Guattari seek to disclose the ontological priority of such virtual machines *as* machines, which they achieve by adopting the systematicity of psychosis as their privileged form of testimony.[51] The result is "schizoanalysis," Deleuze and Guattari's term for an analysis named and modeled after schizophrenia—a thought that extends rather than "cures" its function. Schizoanalysis is thus a critique of the psychoanalytic contract that transforms a patient's lived experience into fantasy,[52] and which, in proscribing Oedipal relations, substitutes "a classical theater" for "the unconscious as a factory."[53] Yet it does so by maintaining, even hypostatizing, the psychoanalytic insight that its theories both resembled and owed their existence to psychotic production.

Whereas Oedipus becomes the name for the normalizing prescriptions of psychoanalysis, paranoia becomes in turn the psychotic "regime" that reflects the imperialism of both Oedipal law and clinical power alike. And whereas Lacan progressively folds paranoia into the general category of the psychoses, Deleuze and Guattari enforce a categorical separation between paranoia and schizophrenia as systems that bear their own distinct laws about the distribution and figuration of power, both abstract and material. This very separation becomes part of the figural logic of their own conceptual diagrams, to the point of allegorizing their divorce from psychoanalysis. In *Anti-Oedipus* Deleuze and Guattari distinguish schizophrenia from paranoia as a mode of social libidinal investment that produces breakdowns, ruptures, and discontinuity through its very functioning; they describe paranoia, by contrast, as reactionary, despotic, and even fascistic. Paranoia, they claim, "enslaves" psychic and social mechanisms "to the gregarious aggregates that they constitute on a large scale under a given form of power or selective sovereignty."[54] Through this configuration of schizophrenia and paranoia as "two regimes of madness," Deleuze and Guattari revise the psychoanalytic model of the unconscious as a realm of psychic functions structured according to the family (Sigmund Freud), to object relations (Juliet Mitchell) or to discourse and signification (Jacques Lacan). They instead view schizophrenia and paranoia as twin yet oppositional configurations of psychosocial mechanisms. Casting off paranoia and its graphic productions as a regime of totalization constituted by and perhaps constitutive of political fascism and psychoanalytic method alike, they put forth schizophrenia as the natural state of desiring machines in their full, profligate excess. No longer bound up in the asylums and clinical relations that speak their own "truth" through the tortures of mental illness, Deleuze and Guattari's schizophrenia exercises the wild, nomadic machinations of unconscious thought.

In their own schematic diagrams of social libidinal investment, Deleuze and Guattari figure paranoia's despotic function as a trajectory that mirrors but diverges from the trajectory of schizophrenia. In the first figure, the central axis serves as a pivot along which paranoia's "molar," large-scale organization of aggregates, and schizophrenia's "molecular" fixation on submicroscopic detail, become distinct from each other. Paranoia and schizophrenia thus emerge as oppositional orders of configuration to which desiring machines resolve in their aggregate multiplicity; the former systematizes, whereas the latter deterritorializes and flies into bits. A second diagram further spatializes paranoia's relationship to schizoid deterritorialization. Along a trajectory of nomadic, nonorganic psychosocial functions, these functions can be reinvested, reterritorialized by a number of processes, of which paranoia is only one of several. On the order of representation, Deleuze and Guattari's mappings of such lines of flight disclose their polemical insistence upon paranoia as the "despotic" and "molar" system against which their holistic embrace of schizophrenic multiplicity defines itself.

Paranoia is thus no less central to Deleuze and Guattari's thinking as it is to Lacan's earliest work on the psychotic structure of subjectivity. Even as a structure of despotism, and even as an allegorical figure for the excesses of institutional psychiatry and psychoanalysis, paranoia gains dialectical utility as a mechanism of formalization. No longer comprising a totalizing

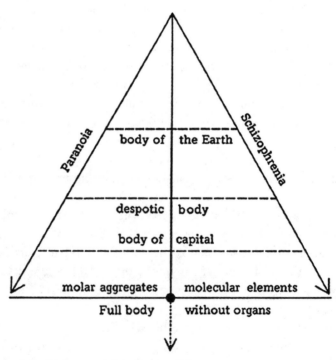

FIGURE 27. Gilles Deleuze and Félix Guattari, "Paranoia and Schizophrenia, The Two Poles of Libidinal Investment," from *Anti-Oedipus* (1972).

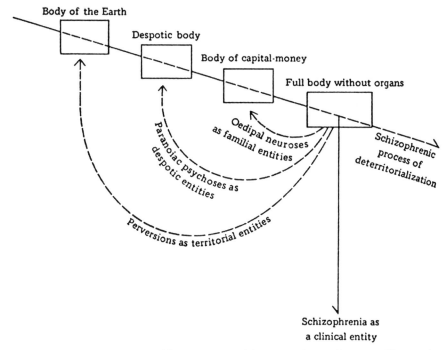

FIGURE 28. Gilles Deleuze and Félix Guattari, "The Schizophrenic Process as Universal Clinical Index," from *Anti-Oedipus* (1972).

system, it instead performs a partial function within their own broader epistemic and institutional economy.

The forms of mapmaking and graphic explanation paranoia often yields are likewise instrumental in *Anti-Oedipus* insofar as they provide theories of the imaginary and symbolic workings of power. In doing so they offer graphic depictions of the social and libidinal forces and investments that make possible the work of liberation Deleuze and Guattari undertake in the name of schizophrenia. In spite of the categorical distinction they draw between the two poles of psychosis, their own recourse to abstract modes of graphic production indicate how closely their antipsychiatric critique of paranoia resonates with earlier studies of the illness in the early 1930s, which appropriated paranoia as a tool for cultural and political critique.[55] At the same time, Deleuze and Guattari's recourse to delusional thinking becomes instrumental for epistemological purposes, both testifying to and also exercising the systems and graphemes of social libidinal production that form their biomechanical counterpoint to Lacan's abstract machines—a cybernetic attention Deleuze and Guattari explore, both individually and in collaboration, throughout their careers. Psychotic discourse functions as a thinking machine within philosophy itself; it does so not by replicating itself—a normalizing tendency Sedgwick rightly rejects—but by designating systems that operate beyond its reach.

As the precipitate of the psychotic mechanism Deleuze and Guattari call "fascizing" and "despotic," moreover, psychotic maps are no longer necessarily determined by, or legible in terms of, the psychotic apparatuses that produce them. The maps are still "theories" of the workings of both concentrations of power and abstract machines alike. But in their material form as graphic and textual products, they are hardly coterminous with the psychotic function itself. The map, in this sense, is not the territory. As Deleuze and Guattari later suggest in *A Thousand Plateaus,* such images already function according to the deterritorializing possibilities they attribute to maps—as opposed to considering them simply as the cartographic extensions of a sovereign power describing the contours of its domain. "The map," they explain, "does not reproduce an unconscious closed in upon itself; it constructs the unconscious. It fosters connections between fields. . . . The map is open and connectable in all of its dimensions; it is detachable, reversible, susceptible to constant modification." As a machine in its own right, the map "has to do with performance," and thus "has multiple entryways" and can be abstracted from its material substrate.[56] As map, as drawing, as material precipitate, psychotic "theory" is thus in turn both subject to and productive of its deployment within an intersubjective realm, within which it can be read or misread, appropriated or archived, obeyed or retheorized.

Deleuze and Guattari thus articulate with ontological intensity what Lacan refuses to state definitively: that the "unconscious" functions autopoietically as a set of infinitely interlocking machines of desiring production for which the human subject is only a "mere residuum" produced alongside other desiring machines, as one set of configurations among many.[57] Desiring machines are real. Virtual rather than metaphorical, they exist as a function immanent to the material world in all its dimensions, from the biomechanical to the geopolitical. The inhuman *ça* of the unconscious, the thing-that-thinks, "is at work everywhere, functioning smoothly at times, at other times in fits and starts," Deleuze and Guattari claim in the opening lines of *Anti-Oedipus.*[58] Their project seeks to play out the numerous pragmatic repercussions of such a radical empiricism, as Deleuze later called it, in philosophy and psychiatry as in political thinking, looking beyond the interactions of aggression and solidarity among human subjects toward the multifarious assemblages of desiring machines.

Lacan's own critical project accords no such liberatory potential to the cybernetic unconscious, which retains its etymological ties to governance in indicating an order—no less virtual or "abstract" than Deleuze and Guattari's machinelike unconscious—of rules, laws, and insistences whose effects are necessarily regulatory. Lacan instead gave increasing precedence to an analogous criticism of the "contract of psychoanalysis" itself, dedicating his own line of flight—his own speculative, but also political and ethical, project—to the institutional and epistemological framework that *Anti-Oedipus* names in its polemic against "oedipal" psychoanalysis. For Lacan, in other words, the methodological and "theoretical" consequences of his recourse to psychotic discourse was less to remake psychoanalysis in the image of schizophrenia (or in the image of a rhizomatic proliferation of abstract machines) than to confront the institution of psychoanalysis with its phenomenological stakes in the discourse of the Other. In a manner that heeds the double function of psychotic maps themselves, Lacan increasingly sought to reform the very practice of psychoanalysis according to the fundamental antihumanism of his cybernetic unconscious. Lacan recognized the extent to which the psychoanalytic "contract" constituted the very institutional, scientific, and clinical apparatus through which the symbolic might come to speak its truth. The institutional and imaginary relations of power constitutive of the psychoanalytic profession—which Lacan attributed to the centrality of transference in Freud's technique—occluded and paradoxically formed the medium for the discourse of the Other.

Lacan's teaching thus became the site of intensified activity—not to mention controversy—during the latter years of his career, as he sought to dislodge the institutional authority of the practicing analyst in favor of a disciplined withdrawal of her interference from the scene at which *ça* speaks its truth. As he explained in a 1967 lecture to the Faculty of Medicine in Strasbourg, "what we should be helping [analysts] to find, [is] namely the right situation of asceticism or what I would call 'destitution': that is the situation of the analyst to the extent that he is a man like any other, and one who must know that he is neither knowledge nor consciousness, but is dependent upon the desire of the Other, just as he is on the speech of the Other."[59] For Lacan, the "line of flight" consistent with the thought production of psychosis was not to commit oneself to the liberatory functioning of desiring machines but instead to enforce a kind of discipline. Yet it is discipline that serves the discourse of the Other rather than clinical expertise: "the discipline that is incumbent upon [the analyst] is therefore the opposite of the discipline incumbent upon a scientific authority"—that is, "the authority of he who knows and touches, who operates and cures through the presence of his authority alone."[60] The analyst must instead "know how to eliminate himself" from the clinical dialogue, "as something that falls out of it, and falls out of it forever."[61] It is only by knowing how to disappear from the scene of thinking—to become little more than a shadow—that an analyst could become an apparatus for the truth that speaks itself. The future of psychoanalysis depended on its capacity to remain an outsider theory, a science of immanence and multiplicity rather than the practiced deployment of clinical authority.

COMMUNITIES OF SUSPICION

Immanuel Velikovsky and the Laws of Science

Compared with [the] facts, theories and standards [of the time], the [Copernican] idea of the motion of the earth was as absurd as were Velikovsky's ideas when compared with the facts, theories and standards of the fifties. A modern scientist really has no choice in this matter. He cannot cling to his own very strict standards and at the same time praise Galileo for defending Copernicus. . . . The Galileans were content with far-reaching, unsupported and partially refuted theories. I do not criticize them for that; on the contrary, I favour Niels Bohr's "this is not crazy enough." I merely want to reveal the contradiction in the actions of those who praise Galileo and condemn the Church, but become as strict as the Church was at Galileo's time when turning to the work of their contemporaries.

—Paul Feyerabend, *Against Method*

AS WE SAW IN CHAPTER 7, Jacques Lacan approached Sigmund Freud's work as "a revolution of Copernican proportions," owing to the discovery that "the veritable center of human beings is no longer at the place ascribed to it by an entire humanist tradition."[1] The Copernican proportions Lacan describes were first outlined by Freud himself, in likening psychoanalysis to the "two major blows" to which "the naïve self-love of men has had to submit . . . at the hands of science."[2] The first of such major blows, Freud explained in 1917, was the Copernican moment itself at which humanity "learnt that our earth was not the centre of the universe but only a tiny fragment of a cosmic system of scarcely imaginable vastness." The second outrage was the evolutionary moment at which "biological research destroyed man's supposedly privileged place in creation and proved his descent from the animal kingdom and his ineradicable animal nature." As the "third and most wounding blow" to "human megalomania" in turn, psychoanalytic research followed Copernicus and Charles Darwin in seeking "to prove to the ego that it is not even master in its own house, but must content itself with scanty information of what is going on unconsciously in its mind."[3] By this logic, the scientific revolution amounted to an eviction notice—or, depending on one's metaphorical sensibilities, a domestic uprising.

Lacan, writing nearly forty years after Freud's pronouncement, called attention to the specificity of this gesture, inviting us to take its investment in "scanty information" [*kärgliche Nachrichten*] literally. The human subject was a "pseudo-totality" that no longer laid claim to the sovereignty of thought. Freud's writings, in their recourse to rebuses, puns, slippages, plays on words, and textual forms, instead testified to the capacity for the structural laws of language to speak in our place, in and as "us." Lacan called this the "discourse of the Other." Rather than depicting human thought as an inner act of cognition that draws masterfully upon the social field of language, Freud engineered a vertiginous reversal: the "I" of human thought turned out to be an instrumental function in its own right, a prosopopoeia for the broader system of language from which, and by means of which, the thinking subject takes shape as an imaginary totality. This was something more than a revocation of an illusory humanistic privilege. Rather, Freud's derivation of a science based on rebuses, jokes, and dream interpretation was Copernican in scope for its methodological revolution as well: it shifted the study of human cognition from a science that levied metaphysical presumptions on observable data—as had been the case in nineteenth-century psychiatry, with its ideas about the hereditary or somatic origins of psychic symptoms—to a science of "higher truths" that measured phenomena inaccessible to immediate observation and which could only be discerned elliptically, by detours or even by error, as Lacan explains.[4]

Intriguingly, this was not the "revolution" upheld by Freud's supporters and epigones, Lacan argued, who instead enshrined Freud as the figurehead for ego psychology to the point of exhausting the contemporary relevance of psychoanalysis by the 1950s.[5] What Lacan referred to as his "return to Freud" aimed to restore the founder of psychoanalysis to his proper place: rather than enshrining him, that is, it fulfilled Freud's Copernican ambitions by shifting attention away from his biographical singularity and toward his writing, and thus toward the "discourse of the Other" to which it beckoned. To take Freud at his word was to confront the idea that the center of the universe, the locus of truth, lay elsewhere than under one's hat.

All the same, Freud's Copernican claims have been roundly criticized for their egoism and ambition. Not only do they elevate psychoanalysis to the stature of a third great modern epistemological revolution, but they also enshrine Freud himself—rather than the field of psychiatric research—as the conceptual persona of this revolution.[6] More damningly, perhaps, the psychoanalytic reliance on "scanty information" has proven especially hard to digest. Karl Popper famously developed his ideas about demarcating science from pseudoscience by working through his skepticism toward Freud's "revolutionary theory" (as well as the theories of Alfred Adler and Karl Marx), which bothered Popper for their resemblance to myth rather than science. Exiled from the house of mastery, we relied far too heavily on the veriest scraps of news. What Lacan singled out as the fundamental truth of psychoanalysis was, for Popper, a misleading "explanatory power." There was no shortage of worldly phenomena that could be illuminated by its interpretive schemes; virtually any conjecture could be supported by citing repression or distortion. But this hardly meant that the theories were true, or that they held up to scientific scrutiny. Popper instead became suspicious of the presumption that "the world was full of *verifications* of the theory. Whatever happened already confirmed it."[7] In the eyes of its initiates the theory always fit: there was no human behavior that could not be interpreted in terms of the theory, which meant that the theory could not be tested—that is, subjected to the possibility of its falsification. Though perhaps no longer master of its own house, psychoanalytic thinking instead took up residence wherever it pleased; like Wallace Stevens's Tennessee jar, it took dominion everywhere.

According to Popper, the clinical observations of psychoanalysis were buttressed, moreover, by the evolving field of psychoanalysis, which institutionalized its explanatory power. Psychoanalytic observations were "interpretations in the light of theories; and for this reason they are apt to seem to support those theories in the light of which they were interpreted."[8] Psychoanalytic theory was tautological in its recourse to proof; this made psychoanalysis a pseudoscience, rather than a revolutionary breakthrough, in Popper's eyes. To levy clinical and institutional authority upon such a tautology would thus be even more irresponsible. The point of targeting psychoanalysis in this way was less to brand Freud as a crackpot, however, than to challenge his Copernican inheritance: the theories of Copernicus could be proven or disproven. Freud's could not.

At stake in such demarcations was not only the fundamental veracity of any scientific claim but also the processes and criteria for judgment it entailed. Yet the challenge of a Copernican claim, by contrast, was explicitly to overthrow such criteria. As Paul Feyerabend noted in 1975, "the situation becomes even more complex when we consider that the Copernicans changed not only views, but also standards for the judging of views."[9] What Paul Ricoeur referred to as the "hermeneutics of suspicion" described precisely such an overhaul; the term levied positive philosophical associations on the very thinkers Popper rejected. Ricoeur's "suspicion" described, in other words, the systems of interpretation developed by modern thinkers such as Sigmund Freud, Karl Marx, and especially Friedrich Nietzsche, who claimed that consciousness could not be trusted, and thus all expressions of truth required interpretation in order to purge "the illusions and lies of consciousness."[10] The result was a rejection of traditional empiricism that overturned the self-evidence of observable data in favor of a "symbolic" access to truth.

The project, in short, was ultimately to distinguish the real from the apparent according to "scanty information" that nonetheless disclosed the duplicity of appearances and opened up instead, as Freud put it, to a world system of a magnitude hardly conceivable. But this meant accommodating science to new ideas about testimony, as Avital Ronell has noted—that is, subjecting our illusions, as well as our conjectures, to endless repudiation and "repeated hypothetical positing."[11] And perhaps more dauntingly, it also meant according oneself to the fugitivity of truth. The Copernican claim levied on science—and the pursuit of truth more broadly—may have entailed a humiliating overthrow of conventional humanistic methods and worldviews. But in doing so it also demanded a humbling interrogation of where, and according to what means, truth might rear its head, even in the form of an "unfounded, opaque, and incoherent doctrine."[12]

The scandal of Freudian "pseudoscience" raises further questions about the very means of scientific upheaval—of how, for instance, it might be possible for a single person to "develop such extraordinary effectiveness," as Freud once put it. How much can one person do to incite such transformations? Or to what extent is such agency ever fully one's own, rather than collective or even impersonal, a function of the discourse of the Other?[13] The possibility of a Copernican revolution might be said to displace the means by which any such revolution could come to pass, given that Copernicus's own Copernican revolution was hardly the work of one person. Indeed, as Thomas Kuhn wrote in 1957, "Only the battle that established the concept of the planetary earth as a premise of Western thought can adequately represent the full meaning of the Copernican revolution to the modern mind."[14] The significance of Copernicus's *De Revolutionibus Orbitum Caelestrium* (On the revolutions of heavenly spheres, 1593) lay "less in what it says itself," Kuhn noted, "than in what it caused others to say." The book gave rise to "a revolution that it scarcely enunciated," a sentiment that laid the basis for Kuhn's own paradigm-shifting study of scientific revolutions.[15] To the extent that such questions articulate governing concerns proper to the experimental sciences, as well as to the history of thought more broadly, they present an inquiry about causation and agency that is every bit as procedural, historical, and even administrative as it is charged with radical ambition.

What does it take to revolutionize the way we think, interpret, and inhabit the world? The history of such procedures has, since Kuhn's work in particular, come to the forefront of debates about the problem of distinguishing science from pseudoscience, in pointing to the constitutive role of institutions, standards, and paradigms, as well as controversies and influences, in determining how and for how long a scientific utterance is acceptable or unacceptable as truth. For all the political and intellectual exigency we ascribe to experimental scientific and cultural production, sociologists of science have directed attention to the rather humble procedures and everyday activities of knowledge production and reception alike. "The course of science is mediated by its sources of external support, by institutional self-reinforcement, and by language," asserts Evelyn Fox Keller.[16] However radical or revolutionary their intentions might be, it is important to attend to their "molecular" as well as their "molar" practices. Such a shift demands that we look beyond the retrospective tendency to reify either the instrumentality or the intentionality of intellectual discovery—that is, the question of whether it worked, and of whether its intentions were good or evil—and instead to consider the battles, networks of association, institutional repercussions, and political pressures that make up any such practice of "revolution." Yet it also introduces the possibility of considering ambition, discovery, and creative thinking in similar terms, as equally bound up in the minutiae of producing, circulating, and reacting to new ideas.[17] Just as it would be preposterous to claim that all experiments proceed solely on the basis of trial and error, it would be equally preposterous to claim that one might simply decide to revolutionize things in general, as if the very stakes and consequences of a revolutionary empirical breakthrough or paradigm shift could be fully formalized or pursued in the abstract.

In this chapter, I examine a set of works and texts that nonetheless seems to be doing precisely this. For the controversial Russian-born polymath Immanuel Velikovsky (1895–1979), who first rose to public notoriety in the United States in 1950 with his best-selling book *Worlds in Collision,* the very scale of an epistemic shift could be so massive as to become cosmic, universal—that is, to transcend the grounded metaphorics and metaphysics of surges, shifts, ruptures, and other seismic cataclysms and instead take on interplanetary and transhistorical dimensions. Velikovsky's ambitions were, like Freud's, decidedly Copernican in scope, in the sense of demanding a radically counterintuitive and decentered understanding of the universe. The very titles of his first books remind us of this "major blow" to the geocentric universe so central to humankind's self-love: after *Worlds in Collision*, Velikovsky published *Ages in Chaos* in 1952, followed by *Earth in Upheaval* in 1955. As in the case of Copernicus's *De Revolutionibus*, Velikovsky's titles allegorize their epistemological upheaval by means of the interplanetary and metahistorical cataclysms to which they refer literally. Although, as we will see, Velikovsky clung fiercely to evidentiary particulars in proposing his theories of interplanetary collision and catastrophe, his work played out no less cataclysmically as a drama within the history of science. In the months leading up to the publication of *Worlds in Collision* in 1950, a number of leading scientists, spurred by sensationalized excerpts in the popular press, began to pen angry letters questioning why a reputable science publisher like Macmillan would stoop to printing a work of such obvious nonsense.[18] One of the more influential early opponents of Velikovsky's work was the Harvard University astronomer Harlow Shapley, who remained out of the public fray; all the same, the word on the street came to be that *Worlds in Collision* was a threat to Macmillan's reputation as a publisher and thus to future textbook commissions. Macmillan broke its contract, and Velikovsky's book appeared instead with Doubleday. The story of Velikovsky's ambitions is, for better or worse, bound up among his entanglements with the "scientific community." Velikovsky, no less than Freud, became a key figure in the demarcation of scientific "insides" and "outsides" in Cold War–era thought, through which scientists and sociologists theorized the complex sets of social relations that regulated scientific knowledge and established "a largely institutionalized reciprocity of trust among scholars and scientists," as Robert Merton wrote in 1971.[19]

In a late, unpublished memoir penned in the 1970s, the octogenarian Velikovsky reminisced about his decades-long confrontation with hostile astronomers, physicists, geologists, historians, archaeologists, and other academics about the truth claims of his catastrophism; he did so in terms whose classical and biblical overtones belied their apparent modesty: "I was fortunate enough," he reflected, "to kindle a light in the days preceding the beginning of a great revolution in science and the humanities. This candlelight has caused conflagration, but history will not accuse me of arson."[20] Presenting himself at once as an originary, light-bearing creator and as an interloping Titan, Velikovsky's claim to "conflagration" would, he insisted, not only be vindicated against the accusations of fraudulence and de facto rejection to which it had been subject for over a quarter century, but would also be recognized as having sparked the great revolution itself.

What was the nature of this "Copernican revolution"? With the publication of *Worlds in Collision* in 1950, Velikovsky blazed a trail for religiously themed pseudoscientists who would capitalize on the popularity of his work, such as L. Ron Hubbard and Erich von Däniken. Indeed, Hubbard's rapidly penned *Dianetics* appeared the same year as *Worlds in Collision*, six months after Velikovsky's fiery ideas first appeared in advance digest form in popular magazines such as *Harper's*, *Collier's*, and *Reader's Digest*. More dramatically, Velikovsky's work also incited the rage of prominent scientists, who attacked both the factual basis and the speculative fancy of his work even in advance of the book's publication. The efforts of a number of leading scientists to suppress *Worlds in Collision* bolstered, in turn, Velikovsky's rhetorical position as a persecuted heretic whose work flouted the repressive orthodoxy of contemporary scientific practice. Velikovsky's conflagration thus beckoned not only to Copernicus but also to Galileo and Giordano Bruno, martyrs to the cause of scientific revolution—a comparison to which Velikovsky's supporters and critics mutually resorted with no small degree of consistency over the course of three decades. His work thus also fueled what the historian Michael Gordin has called the "pseudoscience wars" of the Cold War United States, which wrestled with the problems of demarcation and epistemological revolution to which scientists and historians of science devoted increasing attention. In his 2012 book *The Pseudoscience Wars*, Gordin documents the hostile reception of Velikovsky's work and its polarizing effects on the popularization of science in the 1950s, 1960s, and 1970s, in a period when public access to institutions of higher learning was an increasing political demand.

Velikovsky was not a laboratory scientist; his experiments were speculative and hermeneutical rather than empirical. Yet it is precisely for this reason that the "substance" or medium of his propositions became especially significant to the history and sociology of science, as well as to the history of thought more broadly. That is, insofar as the "revolutionary" project of *Worlds in Collision* constituted at once the premise and the foregone conclusion of Velikovsky's work, its procedures extended from the enormous body of evidence it gathered from widely divergent scholarly disciplines to include the institutions and publications through which Velikovsky addressed his critics and supporters. This vast synthesis sustained, in turn, the very promise of Velikovsky's project, which studied and incorporated into its methods even the hostile reactions of the "scientific establishment." Science, we might say, was Velikovsky's medium; his project aimed less to find acceptance within the scientific establishment than to overthrow its basic assumptions. The project was thus an epistemologically revolutionary and even messianic one, in its dedication to a kind of truth procedure rooted, as we will see, in a scientific project derived from the work of Sigmund Freud.[21] But so, too, was the so-called Velikovsky Affair a medium for the developing discourse on scientific revolutions that consolidated the sociological study of science as an emerging field. Such collisions coincided with and substantiated a major shift in the history of science, wherein the discipline understood itself as a field of contestation and self-regulation rather than a heroic line of succession. Animating the pseudoscience wars, in other words, was the question of scientific revolution more broadly—that is, the question of how, and by what means, our understanding of knowledge could fundamentally shift in ways that changed the way science understood itself as a set of practices and institutions. Could scientific revolution ever be the work of an "outsider," an outlier within the established institutional and disciplinary norms of scientific practice? According to what lines of demarcation could such an event even be drawn? In the decades animated by the Velikovsky Affair, the very question of what constituted the borders and limits of scientific practice fell under serious consideration among historians and sociologists of science, as much as in the public and the counterculture.

THE CONFLAGRATION OF THE WORLD

Velikovsky's basic claim was literally outlandish: when examined alongside other works of ancient world mythology, the Old Testament record of violent events during the Mosaic era—the parting of the Red Sea (Exod. 14), the plagues of Egypt (Exod. 7–11), the "day the sun stood still" (Josh. 10)—was a fragmentary record of catastrophic interplanetary events.[22] The miracles of the Bible, ancient epic, and global myth commemorated real occurrences. Yet rather than testifying to the workings of some divine power, they instead bore witness to the intervention of real heavenly bodies whose cataclysmic effects, as traumatic to human memory as to the world itself, were later revised and misremembered as divine forces. The Bible was a historical record, albeit an amnesic one; Velikovsky's psychohistorical project lay in articulating the astronomical causes to which the biblical record and its disfiguration attested. Herein lay a strong Freudian impression: although Velikovsky's work was often misrecognized (even in prepublication) as a form of creationism or biblical fundamentalism, this was far from the case. Even the "literal" sense of the Old Testament lay in its value as testimony, as Gordin notes;[23] for Velikovsky this amounted to a form of witnessing that was subject to the unconscious processes of condensation and displacement, in its traumatized and fragmentary relation to historical disaster. Our historical memory of ancient planetary cataclysms was reduced to scanty information on account of the sheer magnitude of the trauma.

In short, Velikovsky claimed that two major catastrophes punctuated ancient human history: the first took place around 1500 BCE, during the Mosaic era, the second during the eighth century BCE, during the Homeric era and the days of Isaiah. Their causes, as he reconstructs through painstaking textual and astronomical exegesis, were, in the first case, the near collision of a comet with the earth, a comet whose massive electromagnetic discharge pulled the earth off its axis, reversing its orbit and shifting its poles, before raining debris from its body and tail. The comet would, moreover, find its own orbit and stabilize into the young planet Venus, having sprung fully armed from her parent planet Jupiter. (The "birth" of Venus, Velikovsky mentions in passing, was mythologized as the origin of the Goddess Athena, who sprung fully armed from her father's thigh—a characteristic displacement.) The second cataclysm was caused by the earth's near collision with the planet Mars. The first event wrought devastation throughout the world, a global cataclysm memorialized in the book of Exodus as the devastation of the Egyptian Middle Kingdom, an event that miraculously spared the fleeing Israelites and whose series of miracles seemed to confirm their station as the chosen people. The second event produced the fiery prophesies of the biblical prophets Hosea, Isaiah, Joel, and Micah. Velikovsky was loath to reduce his reconstructions to such unvarnished propositions, for reasons that may seem perfectly self-evident. For in their baldest form, such hypotheses resemble the conjectures of earlier cosmic fabulists such as Ignatius Donnelly, whose 1883 book *Ragnarok: The Age of Fire and Gravel* makes similar claims about the ravages of a comet strike on human civilization twelve thousand years ago.[24] Velikovsky's writing bristles with scholarly references and evidentiary documentation; the penumbra of facticity is a fundamental part of his work. His supporters noted his "strong distaste for summaries and popularizations" based on the "many erroneous criticisms" such reductions yielded.[25] Velikovsky asserted that his theories be judged on the terrain of science rather than, say, according to belief, fantasy, or fiction. This insistence was itself a major factor in his early reception, in the publication of what looked to be the science-fictional claims of a psychoanalyst as assertively scientific claims. For whereas we can easily accept the volatility of the solar system as a hypothetical condition, relegated to the deep time of the geological past, it strains both credibility and, in many cases, facticity to propose that it can be measured in historical time.

Velikovsky's contention, however, was that the cosmic volatility associated with the Big Bang persisted into the Holocene era, measurable no longer simply in geological time but in human history as well. Our ignorance of these "wars in the celestial sphere that took place in historical time" was attributable to their violence and devastation, a product of the amnesic effects of traumatic historical erasure.[26] Here the psychoanalytic understanding of repressed childhood trauma became literalized as a global catastrophe of apocalyptic proportions. "One of the most terrifying events in the past of mankind," Velikovsky writes, "was the conflagration of the world, accompanied by awful apparitions in the sky, quaking of the earth, vomiting of lava by thousands of volcanoes, melting of the ground, boiling of the sea, submersion of continents, a primeval chaos bombarded by flying hot stones, the roaring of the cleft earth, and the loud hissing of tornadoes of cinders."[27] The worst of such conflagrations, Velikovsky tells us, took place in the days of the Hebrew Exodus, for which the Torah offers a kind of shattered testimony. In the wake of this ancient holocaust the survivors "did not cease to learn and repeat the traditions, but they lost sight of the fearful reality of what they learned."[28] Religion and myth were the trace forms of an ersatz historical record, which later came to be understood as mere allegory or metaphor—or as testimony to divine interpretations. Velikovsky's psychoanalytically charged task was to reestablish the historicity of such stories, as the disfigured evidence of a repressed psychic—and for Velikovsky, physical and cultural—truth. He notes, for instance, that "the great discharges of interplanetary force are commemorated in the traditions, legends, and mythology of all the peoples of the world. The God—Zeus of the Greeks, Odin of the Icelanders, Ukko of the Finns, Perun of the Russian pagans, Wotan (Woden) of the Germans, Mazda of the Persians, Marduk of the Babylonians, Shiva of the Hindus—is pictured with lightning in his hand and described as the God who threw his thunderbolt at the world overwhelmed with water and fire."[29] With a certain amount of philological juggling, other ancient world religions could likewise be called upon to produce their testimony.

These claims were sensationalized in the popular press in early 1950, with excerpts and précis of *Worlds in Collision* appearing in *Harper's, Collier's,* and *Reader's Digest,* a publicity strategy by Macmillan that played no small role in the immediate scientific backlash against Velikovsky's claims. The *Collier's* articles were framed by illustrations by the well-known commercial artist Birney Lettick, whose epic depictions of biblical holocaust were matched, that same year, by a set of images depicting a nuclear holocaust on American shores. Lettick's illustrations played on the epic but still human scale of Velikovsky's "wars in the celestial sphere." Like the *Collier's* adaptations of *Worlds in Collision* (entitled "The Heavens Burst" and "World on Fire"), the images dramatize Velikovsky's literalization of the Old Testament based on his theory "that the miracles chronicled in the Bible actually happened," as the editorial put it.[30] In its first installment, the *Collier's* adaptation featured a short text, "The Greatness of the Bible," by the pastor Norman Vincent Peale, that courted the fundamentalist appeal of a scientist's attention to biblical truth—even if, as Peale noted, "it must be borne in mind that the Bible is essentially a volume of supreme spiritual law, and its truth does not depend upon any 'wonder' happening."[31] Lettick's illustrations, by contrast, implicitly challenge the status of "miracles" altogether. The events may have marked the Israelites as a chosen people, but they also brought about a virtual genocide for the Assyrians and Egyptians that Lettick depicted. We witness the holocaust, not the miracle. But as the Protestant minister Peale shrewdly noted in his brief statement, even the sensationalized literalism of Velikovsky's biblical treatment replaced God with comets and interplanetary near collision as the source of these "miracles."

FIGURE 29. Birney Lettick, illustration for "World on Fire," *Collier's*, February 25, 1950. Reprinted with permission.

FIGURE 30. Birney Lettick, illustration for "The Heavens Burst," *Collier's*, March 25, 1950. Reprinted with permission.

What remains most striking about this shift in biblical causality is its inverted claim about the transcendent source of ancient events. In reengineering theomachy as interplanetary near collision, Velikovsky's hermeneutic approach to ancient religions yields a spectacular negation of theological tradition and common sense alike, whose radical displacement of divine authority aspired to the Copernican. Our presumptions about a stable solar system are sustained, that is, by humanist myths and religions, if no longer by Ptolemy; such myths extended to the scientific view of the cosmos as fundamentally stable during the (relatively brief) period of human history. Velikovsky's contentions demanded not only that we view science as a form of such humanistic mythmaking but also that we overturn it in favor of a cosmology whose own claim to truth is levied on the history of scientific proposition, and thus on an experimentalist attunement to the insufficiency of human knowledge. Velikovsky opens *Worlds in Collision* with a screed against the presumptuousness of an anthropocentric cosmos:

> In an immense universe a little globe revolves around a star; it is the
> third in the row—Mercury, Venus, Earth—of the planetary family. It
> is of a solid core covered over most of its surface with liquid, and it

has a gaseous envelope. Living creatures fill the liquid; other living creatures fly in the gas; and still others creep and walk upon the ground on the bottom of the gaseous ocean. Man, a being of erect stature, thinks himself the prince of creation. He felt this way long before he, by his own efforts, came to know how to fly on wings of metal around the globe. . . . He knows the laws governing the living cell with its chromosomes, and the laws governing the macrocosm of the sun, moon, planets, and stars. He assumes that gravitation keeps the planetary system together, man and beast on their planet, the sea within its borders. For millions and millions of years, he maintains, the planets have rolled along on the same paths, and their moons around them, and man in these eons has arisen from a one-cell infusorium all the long way up the ladder to his status of Homo sapiens. Is man's knowledge now nearly complete?[32]

As his defamiliarized, mythologically laden snapshot of the contemporary world implies, "man's knowledge" is not only incomplete but also astronomically insufficient. No less than religious tradition, modern science was delusional in its presumption of a mastery of inhuman "laws" alien to itself. As the Velikovsky supporter Ralph Juergens puts it,

> In short, Velikovsky's research among the ancient records of man—records ranging from unequivocal statements in written documents, through remembrances expressed in myth and legend, to mute archaeological evidence in the form of obsolete calendars and sundials—and his examination of geological and paleontological reports from all parts of the globe led him to conclude that modern man's snug little world, set in a framework of celestial harmony and imperceptible evolution, is but an illusion.[33]

Velikovsky's propositions about interplanetary near collision were fueled by doubt and suspicion, rather than by delusion or faith.

Velikovsky's work exercised, we might say, a hermeneutics of suspicion so fundamentally suspicious as to divest scientific and humanistic reason of its authority. Yet he did so firmly within the sphere of "scientific" practice, carefully marshaling evidence, sources, and an almost paranoiac attention to scholarly minutiae; we see an early instance of such a practice in his 1945 study, "Cosmos without Gravitation," which seeks to discredit the theory of gravity. As he writes, "The fundamental theory of this paper of mine is: there is no such phenomenon as gravitation. There is no primary motion implanted in planets or satellites. Attraction, repulsion and circumduction govern their movements."[34] To say that this is experimental thought without actual experiments would simply accede to its ridiculousness or perniciousness.[35] Rather than either mocking or defending Velikovsky, it is worth considering how closely the shift from "primary motion" to "attraction, repulsion and circumduction" he proposes describes Velikovsky's thinking in general, a "circumduction" that rests on the fields of relations between evidentiary statements and established concepts as the basis for its conclusions, rather than on discrete and irreproachable facts. Velikovsky's "interdisciplinary synthesis" of world myth, archaeology, astronomy, and biblical hermeneutics derived its truth effects, as well as its hotly contested claim to truth, from its correlational logic—that is, the system of correspondences it spun out between and among the forms of evidence it gathered together. Unlike empirical data, Velikovsky's evidentiary material was necessarily distorted or incomplete, he argued, either because it had been largely altered or forgotten through secondary revision or, as in the case of astronomical data, it was not yet measurable and could only be predicted. If the evidence did not seem immediately to fit, it was because the evidence was wrong; this meant adjusting or "correcting" the dates for certain historical events in antiquity whose deviation from the system demonstrated the extent to which the historical record had symptomatically distorted them. *Worlds in Collision*, like his subsequent work, was thus a science of exceptions, its claims resting on the total system of idiosyncrasies and correspondences he constructed. Velikovsky's aim was to elaborate a new interdisciplinary synthesis that accommodated itself to this total system.

More remarkably still, the Copernican shift from singularities to relations has also come to describe the field of scientific inquiry itself in its relation to Velikovsky. The uncanny correlations and cataclysms he claimed on behalf of the empirical world, in other words, became that of scientific reason itself. What Gordin has called the "pseudoscience wars" of Velikovsky's quarter century of reception, the "attraction, repulsion, and circumduction" of his critics and supporters, took place during a period of rapidly growing sociological study of scientific communities and the nature of scientific revolution. Velikovsky's work was "revolutionary," I propose, less for its astronomical claims about biblical catastrophe than for its historical coincidence with the sociology of science as a developing scholarly field itself attuned to revolutionary shifts in knowledge. The explicit appeal to scientific truth in Velikovsky's work—albeit a truth fundamentally at odds with established claims, and which many practicing scientists found maddening—was an increasingly significant object of attention for sociologists of science who studied where scientific ideas came from and how accepted knowledge could

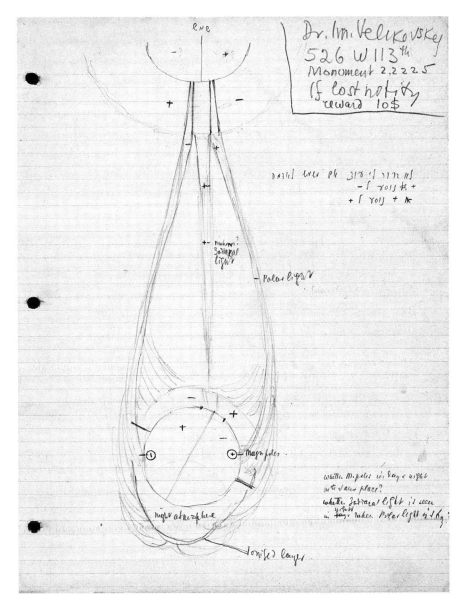

FIGURE 31. Immanuel Velikovsky, sketch for gravitation experiment, n.d. Immanuel Velikovsky Papers, box 1, item 1, Manuscripts Division, Department of Rare Books and Special Collections, Princeton University Library.

be altered and transformed by new ideas. Though branded as an outsider to proper scientific conduct, Velikovsky's psychoanalytically inflected attention to the distortions and errors of historical consciousness sketched out a conceptual history that no longer heeded the presumption that science was "master in its own house."

At stake in the sociology of science was a similarly Copernican structural imperative: to question the means through which scientific knowledge was tested, verified or disproven, as well as transmitted or rejected outright. The center of thought was not in the place ascribed to it. In place of the lone genius or the notion of science as an ideal, disembodied totality, the sociological study of science that emerged in tandem with Velikovsky's polarizing intellectual reception—and which was both informed by and reflected in it—attended to institutions and communities of knowledge that mediated insides and outsides, tacitly determining which theories were worthy of testing, or even worthy of consideration as theories. As Robert Merton put it in 1945, the "Copernican Revolution" in this area of inquiry

> consisted in the hypothesis that not only error or illusion or unauthenticated belief but also the discovery of truth was socially (historically) conditioned. . . . The sociology of knowledge came into being with the signal hypothesis that even truths were to be held socially accountable, were to be related to the historical society in which they emerged.[36]

Such a shift involved a certain humiliation—as Freud put it, an "outrage to man's self-love." The question of whether this humiliation concerned the ethos of scientific conduct, or whether it pointed simply to the Icarian flight of Velikovsky's ambition, would fuel the pseudoscience wars in the decades following the publication of *Worlds in Collision*.

Influential astronomers and physicists may have considered Velikovsky a crackpot, but this did not mean that his work was methodless. On the contrary, his conceptual trajectory played out according to distinct methodological imperatives, though they were the imperatives of a different science: they derived not from astrophysics but from applied psychoanalysis. The Velikovsky Affair thus also opened up continuing debates about the communities of knowledge that constituted science as a "self-correcting" system, as well as the means according to what criteria it measured and communicated the plausibility, and the truth, of its theories. By this logic, the conceptual history of science could—and did—measure its own experimental demands against the yardstick of Velikovsky's reception.

THE VELIKOVSKY INDUSTRY

Viewed within the context of postwar reassessments of the politics of knowledge and the means of historical change, Velikovsky's hostile reception from scientists and historians—and his ensuing rebuttals and counter-claims—present a fascinating set of debates about the nature of scientific truth and the role of institutions in shaping scientific knowledge. The fierce backlash of the scientific community against Velikovsky's work, coupled with his own insistence on piling up scientific and historical evidence, had the effect of marshaling a broad group of supporters who praised his epoch-shifting genius and decried his character assassination at the hands of the "scientific mafia."[37] For in addition to igniting the passions of scientists and critics, Velikovsky's "conflagration" was both sustained by and helped fuel the American counterculture; by the 1960s, and throughout the 1970s, his works became required reading for freethinking college students, campus radicals, and experimental "free universities," spawning study groups and a fleet of Velikovsky-themed scholarly journals, as Gordin has described.[38] It also inspired work by the minimalist composer Philip Glass, whose 1983 opera *Akhnaten* was based in part on Velikovsky's 1960 book *Oedipus and Akhnaton,* as well as work by the "avant-garage" rock band Pere Ubu, who titled their 1991 album *Worlds in Collision.* The Velikovsky Affair and its lengthy aftermath became a countercultural model for critiquing scientific orthodoxy, and, in later decades, it has offered a case study in the political and institutional forces that regulate scientific knowledge, as Gordin's work attests. Velikovsky thus became a figure for "experimenting" with science itself as a professional field of procedures and beliefs. It is thus as an avant-garde formation that we might approach Velikovsky's "catastrophic" work within the field of scientific discourse rather than as an alien collision. That is, the Velikovsky Affair was a major event in the redeployment of critical negativity in postwar American thought, which yielded its own avant-garde groupings—replete with journals, manifestos, and study groups—as well as a rhetoric of cataclysmic displacement to which Velikovsky and his supporters referred as a liberatory catastrophism.

I will not rehearse here the full details of the Velikovsky Affair, which began with the epistolary efforts by leading astrophysicist Harlow Shapley to pressure Macmillan into suppressing *Worlds in Collision.* The basic story of the affair has been told on numerous occasions, and its disclosure forms part of the very scientific controversy itself. The basic details were first elaborated in a 1963 essay by Ralph Juergens, entitled "Minds in Chaos," which appeared in a special issue of the journal *American Behavioral Scientist* dedicated to Velikovsky's case and brought a veritable Velikovsky industry in its wake.[39] In short, Velikovsky and his defenders claimed that scientists had attacked him without, in some cases, even reading the book; by misquoting it and then ridiculing what they had misquoted; and by taking his evidentiary claims out of context. This was less an issue of demarcation, they argued, than of dogmatism. Depicting the "scientific establishment" as fundamentally at odds with its own principles, the Velikovskians sought to establish not only that Velikovsky and his work had been unfairly slandered by many leading scientists—an egregious instance of cronyism and "abominable behavior"—but also that their "scientific" refutations were in fact unscientific, the result of bias and flawed judgment rather than careful testing and debate. The Velikovskians relentlessly took scientific discourse to task, as well as the "bureaucratic" forms and media of that discourse, in exhaustively documenting "the scholars, the learned societies, the professional journals which violated, in some cases quite outrageously, the canons of proper scholarly procedure in evaluating Velikovsky's hypotheses."[40] As Livio Stecchini concluded in a 1963 essay, "The crux of the matter is not the validity of Velikovsky's particular historical interpretations, but whether an entire body of scientific evidence can be rejected on dogmatic premises."[41]

To my knowledge, Velikovsky has figured little, if at all, in historiographies of experimental thought and culture beyond the history of science; he is generally relegated to the dustbin of crackpot thinkers whose theories are considered either ridiculous, at best, or, at worst, pernicious.[42] But if we approach Velikovsky as an experimental historiographer of scientific catastrophe, and thus take his interdisciplinary synthesis as a test case in both documenting and *producing* scientific collision, we get a far different picture of his work. Velikovsky, I maintain, is a conceptual persona who functions as the marker of an epistemic shift—a "revolution"—in the sociology of science. He is a name for, though not the cause of, this shift. Much in the sense that the Marquis de Sade was contemporaneous with the "end of the classical episteme," according to Michel Foucault (see chapter 6), Velikovsky is contemporaneous with a shift in scientific thinking that increasingly attended to the norms, communities, and paradigms of scientific discourse that Michael Polanyi has referred to as the "fiduciary" basis of scientific truth[43]—rather than universalist notions about the experimental verification and progressive accumulation of knowledge that many scientists traditionally upheld. What was Copernican about this revolution was the extent to which it decentered the constitutive procedures of science from the work of individual scientists to the social practices, institutional relations, and criteria of plausibility that composed the broader universe of scientific belief. By this logic, the "pseudoscience wars" that centered around Velikovsky and his contemporaries intensified into the science wars of subsequent decades, which debated the sociological or "extrascientific" determination of scientific theories. The question was not only that of whether legitimate science could be demarcated from pseudoscience but of how, and whether, scientific communities could be demarcated from sociological concerns beyond, beneath, or "outside" the purview of empirical scientific research.

Though his own Copernican ambitions stridently adhered to traditional ideals of verification, Velikovsky's theories nonetheless served as a key test case in corroborating the sociological turn in postwar science studies. His reception from scientists and nonscientists alike dramatized the extent to which extrascientific factors contributed to the outright rejection of his work by members of the scientific community, as much as to the advocacy of his cause by a number of pragmatists, social scientists, and, eventually, student groups and other intellectuals interested in alternatives to establishment science. Velikovsky did not wish to be a marker of a paradigm shift from evidence-based scientific truth claims to sociological discourses about demarcation and "scientific communities." He wanted his theories to be *tested*, not subjected to the fiduciary vicissitudes of scientific culture.

It is curious, then, that Velikovsky's own methodological inheritance would seem to anticipate this fiduciary displacement so insistently. On account of this very paradox, Velikovsky stands as a thinker fundamental to the sociology of science rather than merely a conceptual persona for its debates about scientific insides and outsides. I propose, in other words, the possibility that Velikovsky's theories, with whatever unintentional irony—and indeed, almost certainly unconsciously—*think* this epistemic "revolution" as it unfolded through the rejection and advocacy of his work. For whereas sociologists of science devoted increasing attention to the forms of tacit knowledge and shared intellectual assumptions that organized scientific communities, Velikovsky looked to Freud's experiments in metapsychology as his own reservoir of tacit knowledge—a set of shared psychoanalytic assumptions that addressed, in turn, the problem of how unconscious ideas could bear out traditions and bind cultures together. Not only did Freud's late-career recourse to dodgy biblical hermeneutics prepare the ground for Velikovsky's own research, in other words, but it also posited an allegory of historical amnesia that confronted any such notions about the seamless transfer of expertise or traditions with the disruptive effects of erasure and even violence, whose traces they bore in disguised form. The Freudian insight of Velikovsky's work—and the insight borne out in turn by its hostile postwar reception—was that scientific communities, like the "chosen people" of the Mosaic Bible, perpetuated their shared beliefs through repression and uncanny return rather than through faithful traditions and institutions. This meant not only that communities of knowledge were held together by forces other than conscious reason (or good faith) but that the truth of their tacit assumptions was scandalous and even traumatic.

Velikovsky's scientific project begins, as we will see, with a fundamentally Freudian rereading of the Mosaic Bible. For like scientific "tradition," the biblical narrative of Moses's life privileges an uninterrupted line of transmission whereby a representative patriarch, the bearer of God's laws, passes them along to the faithful. But the truth, for Velikovsky as for Freud, is surprising. According to Freud, the governing function of the Mosaic "law" came neither from God nor from Moses, but instead from a repressed trauma: that Moses the lawgiver was a foreigner murdered by his followers. This was the Copernican stroke of truth in Freud's final work, *Moses and Monotheism*, a book that fundamentally underwrites Velikovsky's career in both animating his research into interplanetary collision and (perhaps unintentionally) describing his own decentered place in the sociology of science. The "Freudian impression" Velikovsky's work bears in its own recourse to biblical hermeneutics allegorizes the sociological revolution in scientific history he sought to create by means of this fundamental displacement. Yet it also suggests that the truth of his theories lay in the extent to which their author would himself be subject to the Copernican "humiliation" his revolution entailed, no longer master in his own house. Velikovsky's postwar reception is anticipated, that is, by the figure of Moses in Freud's final work.

MOSES, MEMORY, AND MASS EXTINCTION

As Velikovsky himself noted frequently, the methodological core of his Copernican catastrophism lay in its latent (though persistent) Freudianism rather than in its manifest interplanetary hypotheses. Born in czarist Russia in 1895, Velikovsky received a degree in medicine from Moscow University before emigrating to Berlin in 1921, where he founded a small press for international Jewish scholarship in the sciences and humanities. Moving to Palestine in 1924, he managed his family's real estate investments and explored what he called "the physical existence of the world of thought," a correlation that his postwar works would literalize in their recourse to myth and religion as the cultural as well as mnemonic trace of planetary trauma.[44] He later traveled to Zurich and Vienna to study psychoanalysis, and completed his training under Freud's former student Wilhelm Stekel, publishing articles in psychoanalytic journals throughout the 1930s. Velikovsky's experiments with science played out on a methodological terrain grounded in metapsychology insofar as Freudianism sought to devise an interdisciplinary synthesis of its own in contemplating collective rather than merely individual psychic mechanisms. Velikovsky considered himself part of the third generation of psychoanalysts, corresponding with Freud's earliest colleagues under the continuing organizational oversight of the then nearly octogenarian Freud.

Velikovsky's work from this period would be foundational for his more explosive later career; his published essays were firmly rooted in metapsychology and applied psychoanalysis, treating literary works, parapsychological phenomena such as telekinesis, and, in particular, collective sociological phenomena. This work culminated in 1937 with the study "Race Hatred," which he presented at the Eleventh International Congress of Psychology in Paris in 1936 and proposed unsuccessfully to publishers in 1940. The premises of the study, which was never published, tacitly undergirded Velikovsky's postwar work insofar as they sought to establish the supra-individual effects of repression: Could a widespread social tendency such as racism be understood as a psychic phenomenon without resorting to universalizing notions of a "collective unconscious" or shared set of cultural myths, as it did for Carl Jung? In arguing for a link between individual and collective psychic mechanisms, Velikovsky's hypothesis in "Race Hatred" adopted a classically Freudian nosology rooted in the repressed knowledge of trauma.

Consistent with the theories of his mentor Stekel, Velikovsky ascribes a neurotic structure to racism and anti-Semitism as social phenomena. His 1937 presentation diagnoses the genocidal imperative as a form of repressed homosexuality, a traumatic kernel of unconscious desire. As he explains, "Freud and Abraham have pointed out that the underlying cause of excessive jealousy is a repressed homosexual tendency. However, hatred, anger, and, in general, every sadistic impulse is the expression of a repressed, unconscious homosexuality, or, in my own terminology, an unsuccessful attempt to overcome the impulse to seek out the homogeneous."[45] Beyond the logical sleight of hand in extrapolating homosexuality to a generalized form of endogamy—a tautological reduction of racism to the expression of a desire for sameness—Velikovsky's proposition is notable for its recourse to repression as a mode of amplification, a medium for translating sociological phenomena into psychoanalytic terms. Racism is tenacious in its social hold because it bears the full psychic intensity of repressed desire; same-sex desire becomes toxic on account of its repression, insofar as it finds expression in disguised form. Given this neurotic structure, "race hatred" cannot simply be countered by a conscious appeal to pacifism, he thus concludes; it has to be treated psychoanalytically on a "mass level." He notes in his diagnosis that "we may ask, why should the sources of collective hatred differ from those of the individual?"—thereby dispelling, at least rhetorically, one of the principal and most divisive concerns in the psychoanalytic enterprise. Velikovsky's search for the cause for such supra-individuation would begin with the study of anti-Semitism and racism in the 1930s and, after the Holocaust, would gravitate toward the genocidal effects of interplanetary collision.

What was especially telling about Velikovsky's approach to such mass psychic phenomena was its evidentiary recourse to texts rather than patients. In a rather stunning dialectical turn, Velikovsky's first step in pursuing this extrapolated theory of repression was to study the psychic imprint of anti-Semitism upon Freud's own dreams, as documented in the foundational text of psychoanalysis, *The Interpretation of Dreams*. In "The Dreams Freud Dreamed," published in the *Psychoanalytic Review* in 1941, Velikovsky proposed that "an important, possibly the most important determination of almost all dreams mentioned by Freud in his inner struggle for unhampered advancement."[46] Yet the road to success was "a difficult one for Freud" on account of his "belonging to an alien race."[47] His professional life was "replete with slights and disappointments." Would success require a Faustian pact with the Christian church, or was it possible to remain a Jew in the face of rabid anti-Semitism? As Velikovsky asked in the conclusion to the essay, "is not the glorious past of a people the phylogenetic wealth of every son of this people?"[48] Such was the problematic whose psychic force occupied Freud's own unconscious in the invention of psychoanalysis; Freud's dreams, and the science of psychoanalysis in turn, bore the impression of both Judaism and anti-Semitism—the effects, rather than the causes, of the more symptomatic "mass" repressions Velikovsky diagnosed in "Race Hatred." Notable here is that Velikovsky sought less to "prove" mass repression by amassing sociological data than to collect data from *The Interpretation of Dreams*—the traces of Freud's own unconscious—that registered the impression of racism within the very science of psychoanalysis itself. His evidence was ultimately philological, an analysis of the effects of repressed trauma upon and within the text. "To reinterpret the dreams of the founder of modern dream interpretation was certainly a daring enterprise," he later wrote, "but I used a method that carried a certain degree of objectivity. Besides, having found the same idea in all sixteen dreams, I believe, following Freud's premise, that those ideas in the dream-thoughts which are most important are probably also those which rear most frequently."[49] The work that anticipated Velikovsky's postwar theories of interplanetary collision and collective amnesia was thus grounded in documenting the persistence of an unconscious thought, the trace forms of both a "phylogenetic" inheritance and its persecution.

Velikovsky's ideas about the structure and significance of collective repression derived, in other words, from an "archival" investigation of psychoanalysis itself, on account of which his Copernican claims about planetary history would extend from his methodological as well as cultural inheritance—which is to say, from Freud, as well as from Velikovsky's own Judaism. But Freud, too, was interested in such inheritances. Indeed, the question of collective repression, collective amnesia, and trace forms of historical memory that animated Velikovsky's theories would likewise figure centrally in Freud's own allegedly crackpot work of metapsychology, *Moses and Monotheism,* portions of which were published in 1937 in *Imago* (the same year as Velikovsky's paper "Race Hatred") and in book form in 1939, after Freud's death.

The indelible impression of Freudian thinking marked the very design and exigency of Velikovsky's overall intellectual project. But nowhere was this impression deeper than in his recourse to Freud's book on Moses. As he noted on numerous occasions, and addressed explicitly in his 1960 book *Oedipus and Akhnaton,* Velikovsky's major work was kindled by Freud's *Moses and Monotheism,* which he read in 1939 and subsequently became, as he put it, "prisoner of an idea." Freud's final book was a scandal in its own right. Written under the twin shadows of fascism and cancer—only one of which he managed to escape—Freud's book proposed that Moses, the leader and lawgiver of the chosen people, was not a Jew at all, but an Egyptian. And not only was he not a Jew, but he was also persecuted by the Jews: Moses was, Freud claimed, murdered by the Israelites, and his religion abandoned, only to be reclaimed years later as the father of monotheism. In the very face of death—and in the very face of Nazi genocide—Freud's final book recast the Torah as a repressive distortion of historical events. More alarmingly still, it recast Judaism as a religion foreign to itself insofar as the source of its law (Egypt) and the patriarchal figure for the Jews' chosen relationship to God (Moses) were both alien to Judaism's traditional knowledge of itself.

In laying out this elaborate counterhistory, Freud argued that the "humiliation" of Judaism this seemed to entail was in fact a powerful truth whose force derived from and testified to the psychic processes of repression and return. Far from a perverse capitulation to anti Semitism or a lapse into persecution mania, *Moses and Monotheism* offered the historically pressing thesis that Judaism was not the invention of one man—or the gift of God to a sole human representative—but instead the accumulated result of historical and even impersonal forces that played out over the course of centuries. The historian Yosef Yerushalmi refers to this displacement of Moses, and the denial of the Jewish origin of monotheism, as the "fourth humiliation" of Freud's litany of scientific revolutions in line with the "series of painful humiliations which the narcissism of mankind has had to endure in order to exchange illusion for reality."[50] A Copernican revolution of biblical proportions, Freud's final work recast religion according to the ideas about scientific truth he ascribed to this series—namely, that such scientific revolutions involved the public encounter with the "humiliating" realization that the

immediate forms and institutions of human knowledge were not only inadequate in themselves but also repressed the truth of historical and impersonal forces that lay beyond their reach.

Velikovsky's body of work at once reproduces the dodgy history and
dodgier metapsychology of Freud's final book and also radicalizes, or rather
completes, Freud's claims about the work of historical repression and the
powerful truth of its cataclysmic effects. This is not to say that Velikovsky
necessarily deduced his "Copernican" ambitions from the structure of scientific revolutions themselves; such a tautology would contradict the very premise of any such ambition, to the extent that scientific revolutions, as Kuhn
wrote in 1962, do not derive "from the logical structure of [existing] scientific knowledge."[51] According to Kuhn, as well as Freud, they instead come
from new claims to attention that throw exiting institutions and paradigms
into confusion. I thus propose that the new paradigm-shifting knowledge that
Velikovsky levied against contemporary science was the "impersonal" turn
prompted by Freud. Consistent with his own reconstructions of cataclysmic
global transformation, in other words, Velikovsky's revolutionary ambition
was prompted by a cataclysmic alien force beyond itself: Freud's *Moses*.
Velikovsky's project was animated by a dogged fealty to the truth event of
this other cataclysm. More than any giant meteor, it was the alien intervention of Moses, Freud's alien bearer of the law, that constituted Velikovsky's
outlandish interplanetary theories and the resilient object cause of his
experimentalism.

Worlds in Collision began, in fact, as a book about *Moses and Monotheism*.
As Velikovsky later recounted it, he came to the United States to do research
on a manuscript entitled "Freud and His Heroes," which, he wrote, was
"inspired by Freud's last book, *Moses and Monotheism*. I disagreed with Freud
and saw in the octogenarian a still-unresolved conflict with respect to
his Jewish origin and his own father."[52] The overarching claim of Velikovsky's
unpublished book—from which he excerpted his 1941 essay on Freud's
dreams—was that Freud's "heroes," Akhenaten, Moses, and Oedipus, offered
further evidentiary grounds for studying the unresolved conflicts of Judaism
and patriarchal inheritance in Freud's work. Having purchased *Moses and
Monotheism* in a Tel Aviv bookstore in 1939, Velikovsky explained, "the reading of this book brought me to the surmise that pharaoh Akhnaton, who
Freud thought to be the originator of monotheism and a teacher of Moses,
was in fact the prototype of Oedipus of the Greek legend. In a few weeks I
had a rather convincing list of supporting evidence, but the meager Tel-Aviv
library did not suffice for the kind of research I needed to do."[53] This insight
eventually led to Velikovsky's fourth book, *Oedipus and Akhnaton*, published

two decades later in 1960, which proposes that the Sophoclean hero and the heretical Egyptian pharaoh were, in fact, one and the same person.

About Moses, however, Velikovsky did not immediately have any especially novel insights, given that Freud's own book on Moses was so definitively full of surprises. Even so, he wrote, "I hoped an idea would come to me in time."[54] Only after eight months of further research on the history of ancient Egypt and Greece at the New York Public Library did an idea arrive: in discussing the biblical location of the Dead Sea with a houseguest, the question of whether a major geological upheaval had occurred struck him as significant. As Velikovsky recalls in his memoir,

> "Actually," I said to our guest, "according to the Book of Genesis, the site of the dead sea was a plain in the days of the patriarch Abraham—the valley of Siddim. But when the Israelites under Moses and Joshua reached the area in their flight from Egypt, they found a lake there. Did not some catastrophe take place beside the upheaval in which Sodom and Gomorrah were overturned? That upheaval is described without mention of a sea being formed."
>
> As soon as I said this, an idea came to me: was there not something here that might be of interest for my unwritten chapters on Moses, one of Freud's heroes?[55]

Velikovsky's project of psychoanalyzing Freud—a far different "return to Freud" than that of Jacques Lacan roughly a decade later—proposed that the unconscious processes of condensation, displacement, and secondary revision proposed by psychoanalysis were at work in the historical record rather than in Freud's mind alone. As Velikovsky explains in the introduction to *Ages in Chaos* (1952), "Ancient history is distorted. . . . Because of the disruption of synchronism, many figures on the historical score are 'ghosts' or 'halves' and 'doubles.' Events are often duplicates; many battles are shadows; many speeches are echoes; many treatises are copies; even some empires are phantoms."[56] Velikovsky's model for such suspicious hermeneutics was, in fact, the applied psychoanalysis of *Moses and Monotheism,* which likewise undertook a psychoanalytic interpretation of biblical history, attributing unconscious processes of distortion to the biblical record of Moses. In *The Pseudoscience Wars,* Gordin proposes that Velikovsky was "plenty mad"—that is, angry, not insane—in response to Freud's argument that Moses was an Egyptian, not a Jew. Such a claim "on the one hand proclaimed the power of psychoanalysis and, on the other, denigrated the origins and destiny of the Jewish people," Gordin suggests.[57] Depicting Velikovsky's work as an "all out assault on *Moses and Monotheism,*" Gordin documents how Velikovsky sought to attack Freud himself, especially his "degradation of Moses," and presents his career as a decades-long struggle with this idea.[58]

But such degradations were only baffling, Velikovsky wrote, if one did not understand Freud's "inner motives."[59] Freud's final work was significant for Velikovsky precisely for the methodological investment in this "degradation," a radical displacement of Moses from the center to the periphery of biblical history and Jewish law. As Yerushalmi notes, Freud's book on Moses clings resolutely to the Copernican "fourth humiliation" in its displacement of biblical tradition in favor of an alien account of "symbolic" truths that draw from Jewish myth and, perhaps most outlandishly of all, from Lamarckian theories about the inheritance of acquired characteristics. Freud asks, "Can a single person create a new religion so easily?"[60] The answer is, flatly, no: the foundling Moses was not himself one of the people whose religion he is credited with establishing. Moreover, Freud explains, the religion he brought to the Jewish people in Egypt was, in turn, an Egyptian one: not the elaborate pantheon of the Eighteenth Dynasty but the rebel monotheism of Amenhotep IV, who renamed himself Akhenaten as a testament to his faith in the sun god Aton.[61] And this religion, along with its bearer, was violently rejected. Much as Akhenaten's name was struck from monuments and his heretical city Tell el-Amarna abandoned, so too was Moses repudiated and erased. Behind Freud's "humiliating" counternarrative, however, lies an insistence about the persistence of historical memory: no less than Akhenaten, the murdered Moses lingered on, he argues, as an anxious myth, a tradition. "The religion of Moses did not disappear without leaving a trace," Freud writes. "A kind of memory of it had survived, a tradition perhaps obscured and distorted."[62] Centuries later the myth of Moses as lawgiver was restored with the full force of unconscious repression: the myth of a phylogenetic origin, an archaic heritage, levied upon the restored "father" of Judaism by the guilty inheritors of his murder.

Freud's final book is not a screed against the ancient guilt of the Jews. It is instead an extension of the psychoanalytic "Copernican revolution" to the Bible itself, a jarring displacement of the sovereign (and predominantly male) figures to whom we still tend to assign historical agency in favor of a more oblique system of historical causes and effects. Asking "how it is possible that one single man can develop such extraordinary effectiveness, that he can create out of indifferent individuals and families one people, can stamp this people with its definitive character and determine its fate for millennia to come," Freud answers that any such presumption would mean a regression toward hero worship. He instead replaces hero worship with a "sociological" explanation—a startling and largely conjectural approximation of

Polanyi's later ideas about the fiduciary basis of scientific communities, here applied to the religions community of the Israelites. "The inclination of modern times," Freud writes, "tends rather to trace back the events of human history to more hidden, general, and impersonal factors—the forcible influence of economic circumstances, changes in food supply, progress in the use of materials and tools, migration caused by increase in population and change of climate. In these factors individuals play no other part than of exponents or representatives of mass tendencies which must come to expression and which found that expression as it were by chance in such persons."[63] Moses becomes the imago or conceptual persona for such overdetermining conditions, particularly in the "establishing of closer connections among different nations and the existence of a great empire."[64] The status of "great man" remains significant, however, since it is far easier psychically to identify with a singular religious figure than the complex tangle of possible determinations. The "truth" of Freud's humiliation of Judaism is less the claim that Moses, the Egyptian, had been murdered by the Jews, than the assertion that Judaism—and the constitution of "the Jews" as a chosen people—is a dynamic, even dialectical, collective formation carried out in Moses's name.

Velikovsky's "idea" was to extend this dynamism to biblical events themselves. In *Worlds in Collision,* he proposes a homologous displacement of divine acts whereby the Torah serves as a disguised, "amnesiac" historical record of celestial activity, the "hidden, general, and impersonal factors" that form its truth. Velikovsky thus extrapolated Freud's Copernican logic from Moses to God himself. Extending the "fourth humiliation" of *Moses and Monotheism* to the physical rather than metaphysical causes for ancient thaumaturgy, Velikovsky thus completed this upheaval through a logical correlation to science as the measure of such impersonal factors. But this would mean that the scientific tradition was no less distorted than the biblical tradition. For if God, no longer master of his own house, was instead a prosopopoeia for hidden, general, and impersonal factors, then the cataclysmic nature of such factors—fire in the sky, radical climate change, inversions of land and sea, a shift of the earth's axis—was also at odds with what Velikovsky called "uniformitarian" presumptions about the earth's history. The traditional assumption that the slow, gradual processes of geological and biological evolution have remained constant over millions of years would no longer hold true. Not only was God subject to Velikovsky's Freudian upheaval, but so too was the reigning ideology of science insofar as it privileged the sovereign vantage point of the present, gauging the unknowable past according to measures drawn from its own restricted experience.[65]

Such shifts in the fundamental conception of planetary as well as biblical history demanded a new understanding of historicity in turn—that is, the very criteria for evaluating and interpreting historical evidence. Scientific and religious traditions were held in place with great conviction; so too could forgotten or repressed historical truths erupt with great psychic force. Freud's final book, whose completion was interrupted by Freud's own exodus from Vienna to London in 1938, was a book about the possibility of collective memory surviving its genocidal erasure. For Freud, *Moses and Monotheism* was an exploration less of the specific "impersonal factors" for which Moses came to serve as a proper name than of the psychic intensity of the tradition through which he came to do so. Yerushalmi notes that "what readers of *Moses and Monotheism* have generally failed to recognize—perhaps because they have been too preoccupied with its more sensational aspects of Moses the Egyptian and his murder by the Jews—is that the true axis of the book . . . is the problem of tradition, not merely its origins, but above all its dynamics."[66] The special power of tradition is that it functions in a way analogous to neurosis, whereby, Freud noted, "something past, vanished, and overcome in the life of a people, which I venture to trace as equivalent to repressed material in the mental life of the individual" returns in disguised form.[67] As Freud put it, "it is especially worthy of note that every memory returning from the forgotten past does so with great force, produces an incomparably strong influence on the mass of mankind, and puts forward an irresistible claim to be believed, against which all logical objections remain powerless."[68] The eventual enshrinement of the dominant tradition of Moses and the Mosaic God of Aton by the Jewish people represented one such return; the religion of Moses "did not disappear without leaving any trace; a kind of memory of it had survived, a tradition perhaps obscured and distorted."[69]

On the one hand, this tradition conceals the "humiliating fact" of Moses's murder, and the abandonment of the Aton religion he gave them, beneath its narrative of a great past representing the Jews as a chosen people.[70] Yet how could tradition bear such effects over the course of millennia? As Freud maintained, the distortions and displacements of tradition grow stronger rather than weaker over time, finding their way "into the later codifications of the official accounts, and at last prov[ing] themselves strong enough decisively to influence the thought and activity of the people."[71] On the other hand, such traditions nonetheless "contain a piece of forgotten truth" from which their distortions emanate.[72] Tradition, in other words, is at once a powerful ideological force for sustaining the "egoistic" myths Freud seeks to overthrow, and, at the same time, the very bearer of a forgotten historical truth that resists such myths with no less force. As the case of Moses dramatizes, the "psychic force" with which a cultural tradition forgets and (mis)remembers a kernel of historical truth extends beyond the individual mind; for the content of the unconscious is already collective, Freud writes, "a general possession of mankind."[73] Freud ultimately resorts to the long out-of-date Lamarckian notion of the genetic inheritance of acquired char- acteristics to account for how repressed historical events—as well as their traumatic repression—can leave their impression on "a people." As both Jacques Derrida and Yosef Yerushalmi have noted, Freud's work on Moses is thus invested in the problem of survival—of what kinds of truth, what forms of historical memory, might survive their obliteration.

Velikovsky extends Freud's Copernican humiliation beyond the phylogenetic inheritance of Judaism to the full planetary scale of human history. His work "completes" Freud's by proposing that the traumatic ker- nel of historical truth was far more widespread than the Oedipal drama of killing off the father of monotheism. For Velikovsky, fully recognizing the dire historical conditions under which Freud wrote and published his final work, the trauma of historical memory was not patricide but holocaust: Shoah, genocide, mass extinction. And like Freud, he looked not to con- temporary dangers—the planetary threat of nuclear war, for instance—but to ancient ones. The trauma referred instead to the global cataclysm of the days of Exodus Velikovsky outlined in *Worlds in Collision*. This was a disas- ter whose traces—and whose genocidal scale—were borne throughout world myth and the incomplete record of global history. "Freud was nearly correct in his diagnoses when he wrote that mankind lives in a state of delusion," he writes in *Mankind in Amnesia*, "but he was unable to define the etiology: in this case, the nature of the traumatic experience."[74] Even though its claims might be fundamentally, even wildly, erroneous, Velikovsky's project was to advocate relentlessly for the force of his etiology with the same intensity as Freud. And thus, in turn, he sought to extend this Copernican humiliation to the field of science as well.

Inspired by Freud's posthumous book on Moses, *Worlds in Collision* was a homologous investigation into the survival of repressed traumatic events through tradition and myth. In this sense, it was a book less about "causes" than about memory and forgetting, which challenged the security of a humanistic worldview by presenting evidence of a "historical truth" of planetary catastrophe that it actively repressed. The prevailing scientific worldview, like world religion, was part of the tradition through which this historical truth was preserved and concealed. Velikovsky would, unlike Freud, levy the critique of repressed and repressive "homogenization" upon his critics, who defended scientific orthodoxy and its "uniformitarian" assumptions against Velikovsky's ideas of sudden, cataclysmic changes during human history. Velikovsky deployed scientific evidence in much the same way that he approached biblical and religious material, upholding its authority but rendering its significance plastic. Freud admitted to the outlandishness of his propositions, though he died before he could ever defend them publicly. Velikovsky, prisoner of an idea, professed no such modesty. Not only were his critics susceptible to repressing historical truth, but their myths about scientific progress and prowess were also the very medium for the preservation of these very truths.

In this regard, Velikovsky's Copernicanism demanded confronting establishment science with its own force of repression. Science, in other words, was not the master of its own house—so much so that the house was in a state of utter collapse, sundered by the very resistance to the kinds of phylogenetic, collective human memory Velikovsky advocated. As he wrote in his memoirs,

> The house of knowledge, stable and everlasting only two decades ago, is now all torn by fissures, with walls bulging or caving in, foundations removed from under the structure, roof collapsing. Ancient history, anthropology, social sciences, philosophy, and psychology, all of them experienced shocks and collapses, though the caretakers of these domains too often pretend that the old values are inviolable. In front of these structures the guardians pretend that all is perfect inside; where a disagreement exists, there is an apparent agreed partition of the territory among the competing proponents. In psychology, for example, adherents of "schools" swear by their chosen maters, having made no progress in a generation, unconscious of the inescapable need—or unwilling—to face at least the issue of racial memories.[75]

The "uniformitarianism" against which Velikovsky argued—that is, the assumption that the slow, gradual processes of geological and historical change have remained constant over millions of years—was the agent of its own destruction. Such uniformity spoke, that is, to a form of repression that lay not only behind "race hatred" (as he argued in the late 1930s) but also behind a faith in scientific progress that could bring about its own apocalyptic form of mass destruction in the age of nuclear weaponry. As Gordin has noted, creationism and other crackpot formations often employ a similarly tautological line of reasoning. Velikovsky was, however, no creationist, and vehemently distinguished himself from them.[76] He argued, by contrast, that sudden, cataclysmic changes have erupted within human history from the intervention of causal forces alien to human understanding, or even earthly continuity, through the interference of heavenly bodies. His Freudian project aimed to reconstruct the obliviated historical memory of such events, thereby challenging the repressive effects of "homogenization" and uniformitarianism on both the empirical and methodological fronts, while also soliciting its psychic force. The truth of human history depended on this messianic challenge, the analytical confrontation of repression with the historical memory of its disavowal.

INSIDE-OUT SCIENCE

Who—or what—determines scientific truth? In the quarter century of debates over Velikovsky's claims, supporters of his work increasingly targeted the "scientific establishment" as a quasireligious orthodoxy whose refusal to subject his theories to rigorous scientific testing demonstrated its dogmatism and self-deluding closed-mindedness. Famously, a 1963 issue of *American Behavioral Scientist* took aim at the politics of science in light of the Velikovsky Affair. In his foreword to the expanded version of the issue, published in book form in 1966, the journal's editor, Alfred de Grazia, summarized the backlash against *Worlds in Collision* and its sequels in terms that dramatized the political consequences of this repressive structure:

> What must be called the scientific establishment rose in arms, not only against the new Velikovsky theories but against the man himself. Efforts were made to block dissemination of Dr. Velikovsky's ideas, and even to punish supporters of his investigations. Universities, scientific societies, publishing houses, the popular press were approached and threatened; social pressures and professional sanctions were invoked to control public opinion. There can be little doubt that in a totalitarian society, not only would Dr. Velikovsky's reputation have been at stake, but also his right to pursue his inquiry and perhaps his personal safety.
>
> As it was, the "establishment" succeeded in building a wall of unfavorable sentiment around him: to thousands of scholars the name of Velikovsky bears the taint of fantasy, science-fiction and publicity.[77]

In likening the scientific establishment to a totalitarian society—from which it differed in degree rather than in kind, De Grazia implies—the editor of *American Behavioral Scientist* proposed to investigate the social and institutional forces at work in Velikovsky's rejection. De Grazia's recourse to the passive voice in his account ("efforts were made," "sanctions were invoked") levies an almost conspiratorial agency upon the construction of this "wall of unfavorable sentiment," as well as cribbing from scientific prose to present seemingly objective results. De Grazia is less interested in singling out individual polemics and persecutors (which was often the case in Velikovsky's own discourse, particularly toward Shapley) than in describing the fields of institutional relations that closed ranks against the heretical author of *Worlds in Collision*.

Though the *American Behavioral Scientist* issue was decidedly pro-Velikovsky and its contributors unapologetically defended Velikovsky's theories at great length, the journal's methodological insistence lay in addressing, as De Grazia put it, "one of the agitating problems of the twentieth century. . . . Who determines scientific truth? Who are its high priests, and what is their warrant? How do they establish their canons? What effects do they have on the freedom of inquiry, and on public interest?"[78] In framing his account of the Velikovsky Affair in such terms, De Grazia invoked contemporary sociological approaches to scientific knowledge that likewise addressed the institutional norms and structures that shaped how "scientific truths" were determined as well as policed. Just as Velikovsky extended Freud's "humiliation" of Moses to a set of impersonal global catastrophes concealed within the religious traditions that obscured them, so too did Velikovsky's defenders seek to demonstrate how scientific tradition likewise repressed its own complex of motives—authority, opinion, prestige, institutional self-interest—under the guise of empiricism and rational inquiry.[79] The scientists who dismissed Velikovsky's theses outright formed part of a "reception system," as De Grazia put it, that "consists of the criteria whereby scientists, their beliefs, and their practices are adjudged by scientists as a community to be worthy, true, and effective."[80] De Grazia's terms recall those of major midcentury sociologists and philosophers of science, such as Robert Merton and Michael Polanyi, who likewise account for the "fiduciary element" of scientific communities. "Whether any particular discovery is recognized and developed further, or discouraged and perhaps even smothered at birth," Polanyi wrote in a 1949 essay, "will depend on the kind of belief or disbelief which it evokes among scientific opinion."[81] De Grazia and other Velikovskians mobilized such insights to implicate scientific opinion for its cryptoreligious function as an institutionalized mechanism of exclusion and inclusion whose "dogmatic premises" were at odds with the Enlightenment ideals it allegedly upheld.[82] Such premises, moreover, clung tenaciously to a "smug . . . framework of celestial harmony and imperceptible evolution" that was, as Ralph Juergens put it, "but an illusion."[83]

Like Freud's destabilization of orthodox religious beliefs in *Moses and Monotheism,* Velikovsky's work incited the ire of the scientific orthodoxy in confronting the "church of Science" with its own bureaucratic tendencies.

For many scientific thinkers, however, De Grazia's confrontation was less a scandal than a confirmation of a revolutionary shift in the structure of scientific beliefs that had already taken place. For Merton, Polanyi, and especially Thomas Kuhn, whose *Structure of Scientific Revolutions* was published the year before the *American Behavioral Scientist* special issue on the Velikovsky Affair, the "fiduciary element" of scientific beliefs, norms, and traditions was evidence of the proper functioning of scientific communities rather than their lapse into delusion or cronyism. For Merton, writing in 1945, the sociological turn in science studies was already a Copernican revolution insofar as it recognized the "discovery" that "truth was socially (historically) conditioned."[84] As Merton noted, "Men of knowledge do not orient themselves exclusively toward their data nor toward the total society, but to special segments of that society with their special demands, criteria of validity, of significant knowledge, of pertinent problems, and so on. It is through anticipation of these demands and expectations of particular audiences, which can be effectively located in the social structure, that men of knowledge organize their own work, define their data, seize upon problems."[85] Such parameters defined the conditions under which scientists, like the members of other communities of knowledge, conducted their research and circulated their results. This did not mean that all truth was socially constructed—far from it; Merton explicitly defended the "special demands" of scientific communities against the hermeneutics of suspicion he attributed to Freud, Marx, and earlier sociologists such as Karl Mannheim and Max Weber in relegating science to merely an expression of underlying social causes. Rather, for Merton social and institutional norms and structures were the very condition for scientific truth insofar as they contributed to the "scientific ethos" according to which scientific communities shared and accumulated knowledge rather than falling victim to "separatism" and "mutual distrust."[86] Polanyi was even more specific in his assertion that such beliefs were the product of "tacit knowledge," the accumulated learning and collective expertise by which the scientific community maintained its integrity as a self-governing system.[87] He concluded that "scientific research—in short—is an art; it is the art of making certain kinds of discoveries. The scientific profession as a whole has the function of cultivating that art by transmitting and developing the tradition of its practice."[88] For Polanyi, as for Merton, science already recognized that its beliefs were cultivated from scraps of experience rather than from some divine imposition of natural law. The "house of knowledge" was held together by such traditions; it would otherwise fall apart entirely.

In his 1965 lecture "The Growth of Science in Society," Polanyi addressed the Velikovsky Affair directly, citing the rejection of Velikovsky's work as an "indispensible" exercise of scientific discipline rather than a delusional or abusive betrayal of principles. In response to the 1963 issue of *American Behavioral Scientist*, Polanyi admitted that "it is understandable that Professor de Grazia was disappointed by the failure of scientists to live up to their professions of giving a ready hearing to any new idea and submitting humbly to the test of any evidence contradicting their current views."[89] De Grazia was right to complain that scientists did not live up to their explicit principles of open-mindedness and commitment to empirical testing; yet he had overlooked the tacit assumptions by which science operated in reality, which necessarily entailed levying advance judgments of plausibility or implausibility to preserve the integrity of scientific institutions. As Polanyi explained, "Journals are bombarded with contributions offering fundamental discoveries in physics, chemistry, biology, or medicine, most of which are nonsensical. Science cannot survive unless it can keep out such contributors and safeguard the basic soundness of its publications. This may lead to the neglect or even suppression of valuable contributions; but I think this risk is unavoidable."[90] Velikovsky's "attractiveness to the public" and brisk sales were no reason to "imperil science" with unbelievable claims, even if some of them might eventually prove to have been true. The house of knowledge necessarily retained its walls, regardless of where its master might reside.

Velikovsky was rejected because his ideas did not immediately conform to scientific notions of plausibility, a judgment that could not itself be proven or demonstrated but which instead reflected the tacit assumptions of scientific belief. Polanyi unequivocally defended these beliefs as the inherited criteria of scientific self-governance that constitute the scientific community: "It is governed by beliefs, by values and practices transmitted to succeeding generations. Each new independent member adheres to this tradition, while assuming at the same time the responsibility shared by all members for re-interpreting the tradition and possibly revolutionizing its teachings."[91] Velikovsky's theories did not themselves amount to a revolution, but were instead a "lay rebellion" against which the scientific community was justified in defending itself. While such a defense may have proven on occasion to be erroneous, it was no less perilous to "pretend that science is open minded." The rules governing scientific life depended on "a large area of hidden and yet accessible truth, far exceeding the capacity of one man to fathom. There must be work for thousands."[92] In confessing that relying on "vague and un-demonstrable conceptions of reality, may sound positively scandalous," Polanyi nonetheless upheld such "tacit knowledge" as the shared tradition upon which science depended for its survival.[93]

Without necessarily intending to do so, Polanyi turned the tables on Velikovsky's Freudian "humiliation" by acknowledging the role of tradition—and the inheritance of acquired epistemological characteristics—as a governing archival function in scientific practice. This was part of science, neither repressed nor disavowed; he instead attributed the pre-Copernican "amnesia" of such causes to Velikovsky's defenders. The revolutionary gesture of confronting scientific belief with its own traditions had already taken place well before Velikovsky's arrival on the scene. In Polanyi's eyes, science already functioned according to the tacit knowledge that bound together its community through journals, institutions, and other impersonal factors. It was Velikovsky, not the scientific community, that fell prey to the delusion of a grand patriarch, a mythical Moses who bore the cosmic law of his people; for Polanyi, the scientific community had already recognized that Moses was a myth.

By 1976, the science fiction author Isaac Asimov—who had definitively labeled Velikovsky as a "crackpot" a few years earlier in his popular *Analog* magazine[94]—could safely conclude that Velikovsky's heretical theories and positions were ultimately "good for science" insofar as they exercised and called attention to such tacit assumptions. In his foreword to the published proceedings of a 1974 meeting of the American Association for the Advancement of Science (AAAS) on Velikovsky, Asimov accepted the political charges levied against the scientific establishment by De Grazia and his fellow Velikovskians in likening the author of *Worlds in Collision* to a heretic excommunicated by an established orthodoxy.

Asimov, in short, admitted it: science *was* an orthodoxy. He was careful to specify that it was a particularly benign sort of orthodoxy, however, and that Velikovsky was a particularly pernicious species of heretic. Whereas religious, political, and socioeconomic orthodoxies could burn heretics at the stake, send them to concentration camps, or prevent them from earning a living, "even the most powerful scientific orthodoxy is not very powerful."[95] Science was, Asimov claimed, "completely helpless if the heretic is not himself a professional scientist—if he does not depend on grants or appointments, and if he places his views before the world through some medium other than the learned journals."[96] Velikovsky had proven, after all, that he could support his career independently through book sales and lectures. Asimov thus shifted the "demarcation problem" of discerning science from pseudoscience on the basis of test-based falsifiability to Velikovsky's unorthodox relation to professional scientific values and beliefs. Because he did not understand "the painstaking structure built up by science," Velikovsky was an "exoheretic," an outsider twice over. Unlike "endoheretics" such as Galileo and Darwin, who were well versed in the scientific traditions of their respective times, Velikovsky was not bound to the tacit assumptions of the scientific community and could thus "appeal over the heads of the scientists to the general public" whenever he became frustrated with his exclusion by the orthodoxy.[97]

Asimov thus naturalized Merton's and Polanyi's justification of scientific communities as an operative rule of thumb for policing the boundaries of the profession. He explained in turn that Velikovsky sought to cash in on his outsider status: "the fact that Velikovsky could then portray himself as a persecuted martyr has cast a Galilean glow upon all his endeavors, and has canceled out any attempt on the part of astronomers to demonstrate, clearly and dispassionately, the errors in the Velikovskian view. All attempts in this direction can be (and are) dismissed as persecution."[98] The opposite, according to Asimov, was in fact the case: charged with the "glow of hedonism," Velikovsky's followers could attack orthodoxy in complete safety and with the pretense of courage. But the orthodoxy "does not, and indeed cannot, strike back," insofar as its recourse to self-governance applied only to the institutional forms and practices of the scientific community itself. Scientific insiders were part of a fragile ecosystem that could only protect itself against "exoheretics"—outsiders—with the methods used to police the members of its own community.

For this very reason, Velikovsky's outsiderism could be accommodated as a benefit rather than a threat, shoring up (rather than humiliating) the self-assurance, or at least the autonomy, of the scientific community. The power of the Velikovskian heresy to "punctuate scientific complacency" was ultimately a good thing, Asimov concluded, insofar as it caused scientists "to bestir themselves for the purpose of re-examining the basis of their beliefs, even if only to gather firm and logical reasons for the rejection of the heresy—and that is good, too."[99] In granting Velikovsky the status of an exoheretic, Asimov strove to recast the scientific orthodoxy as an intentional community reminiscent of J. M. Robinson's Gnostics (see chapter 2), a fragile collective more consistent with the antiauthoritarian ideological prerogatives of the American counterculture than the academic patriarchs who closed ranks against it.

In *The Pseudoscience Wars*, Gordin aptly notes that whereas the AAAS symposium may have been an attempt to shape—rather than staunch—the "countercultural flow" on which Velikovsky's continued appeal was borne, it did not fully succeed in ameliorating the popular distrust of science against which Asimov and the other participants found themselves battling. It instead fueled the popularity of Velikovskian journals such as *Pensée,* which published Velikovsky's retort to the AAAS scientists. The pseudoscience wars did not end with the AAAS symposium or its eventual publication in 1976, nor even with Velikovsky's death in 1979. Indeed, as Gordin argues, in spite of the gradual waning of the Velikovsky Affair from public view in subsequent decades, the pseudoscience wars persist in an era of climate change denial and continued screeds against "junk science" and historical attention to fringe science alike.

My aim here has been less to resolve the pseudoscience wars, or to adjudicate the debates between scientists and Velikovsky and his followers, than to trace the extent to which Velikovsky's catastrophism and the increasingly sociologically inflected thinking of his opponents revolve around the same basic ideas about the impersonal and largely unconscious constitution of traditions of knowledge and historical "truth" alike. Themselves bearing the impression of Freud's final published work, Velikovsky's theories of interplanetary collision propose that our traditional knowledge of the universe—and of human history—was fundamentally alien to itself. Our beliefs in religion, world myth, and science bear the impressions of cataclysmic events whose very extremity rendered them unavailable or even inadmissible to historical self-assurance. Velikovsky's outer-space assertions are neither "inside" nor "outside" the purview of science. Instead, like the other case studies in this book, their efforts to formalize a knowledge that exceeds its historical conditions of possibility are contemporaneous with and provocative of the work of critics, scientists, and other thinkers who interrogated such boundaries.[100] In confronting scientists with the sociological basis of their own truth claims, the Velikovsky Affair had the effect, for some, of shoring up the pragmatic function of such tacit knowledge within the normal functioning of science. Normal science, by this logic, was already Copernican in structure insofar as its worldview necessarily extended to the intricate sphere of hitherto extrascientific factors—institutions, journals, learned societies, economic and political pressures—that both influenced and ultimately constituted the world of science itself. The norms of scientific practice—whether Polanyi's tacit knowledge or Kuhn's paradigms—were already the bearers of inherited alien characteristics.

For others, the project of demarcating scientific insides and outsides remained problematic far beyond the immediate provocation of Velikovsky's work. Surely the kinds of filtration and protection described by Polanyi and others extend to the very heart of scientific work, insofar as it presumes to eliminate extraneous factors from the sphere of experimentation. But any such eliminations necessarily involve reckoning with the demands and limits of the extraneous, the neutral. Critical of the political normalization of science according to criteria considered external to it, sociologists and philosophers such as Donna Haraway, Sandra Harding, and Evelyn Fox Keller have taken issue with the implicit notion that certain kinds of cultural practices were "tacit" rather than formative of scientific objectivity itself. What emerged instead was a portrait of science understood as "situated and embodied knowledges," as Haraway puts it, that posit social dynamics from gender to economics to the role of speculation and belief as determinants in the very work of scientific observation, within the very sphere of experimentation and conceptions of the natural world.[101] "Whereas scientists often express themselves as if the order in which they have faith were already there waiting for them," Isabelle Stengers writes, "what they 'discover' is inseparable from their shadow, from their own presence in the landscape they describe."[102]

For this reason, Gordin notes, "Pseudoscience is not some invasive pathogen that has contaminated contemporary science but that can be fully expunged from the organism with more scientific literacy or better peer review." It is instead "the shadow of science . . . cast by science itself through the very fact that demarcation happens."[103] And it is thus inseparable from the body whose presence in the landscape both causes and seeks to describe it. To what extent, though, might it also be said that science is the shadow of pseudoscience, perpetually striving to distinguish itself from the theories, practices, and beliefs it might all too readily come to resemble? In spite of whatever technological means by which "science" might seek to shore up its identity, the house of knowledge and its shadow are mutually subject to the way they revolve around the sun.

We might do well to consider impressions rather than shadows. In his late reflection on Freud's *Moses and Monotheism,* Jacques Derrida—himself a bête noir of many defenders of scientific integrity—opposes the attempt to conceptualize such criteria and mechanisms of self-governance with the discomfiting open-endedness of an *impression.* Replacing Polanyi's "tacit knowledge" and Kuhn's paradigm with the Foucauldian term "archive"—as the "law of what can be thought and said"—Derrida embraces the haunted, inchoate and religiously laden history of such tacit knowledges, confronting their power to form and structure communities of knowledge with their stammering ineffability. In his own meditation on Freud's *Moses and Monotheism,* Derrida subjects the certainties of such laws to their necessarily speculative worldly existence. In *Archive Fever,* Derrida notes that

> concerning the archive, Freud never managed to form anything that
> deserves to be called a concept. Neither have we, by the way. We have

no concept, only an impression, a series of impressions associated with a word. To the rigor of the *concept,* I am opposing here the vagueness or the open imprecision, the relative indetermination of such a *notion.* "Archive" is only a *notion,* an impression associated with a word and for which, together with Freud, we do not have a concept. We have only an impression, an insistent impression through the unstable feeling of a shifting figure, of a schema, of an in-finite or indefinite process.[104]

The construction of a "house of knowledge" of scientific orthodoxy, to which Derrida refers as an archive, is neither a bulwark against crackpots nor, for that matter, a fully self-governing system unto itself. It is instead a problem, a "notion" that insistently bears impressions but which in itself is never fully where it is supposed to be. This, I maintain, is the historical truth of Immanuel Velikovsky's place in the sociology of science: not as a messianic bearer of revolutionary truth claims, nor as an astronomical interloper, but as the figure whose theories name the infinite or indefinite processes through which tacit, situated, partial knowledges impress themselves, through which they bear and leave impressions. Velikovsky was not himself the author of this truth, any more than Moses or Freud were. He was instead, by his own admission, a "prisoner of an idea," subject to the very fiduciary element that comprised the technology of inheritance, of repressed archival memory, that his interpretive system both exercised and sought to dissolve.

CODA

Thought from Outer Space

"What's next for planet Earth?"
"The next act? The next act is the finale."
—Sun Ra and Henry Dumas, *The Ark and the Ankh* (1966)

D.C. al fine.

The town in which I live recently debated the question of whether to stop fluoridating the public water supply. Local newspaper coverage made sure to report on "both sides" of the problem, citing the decision of the borough manager (an appointed official, not an elected one) to stop fluoridating the water because of its expense and supposed danger: fluoridation involves adding hydrofluoric acid to the water supply, which can be poisonous at high concentrations. Dentists, doctors, and other experts testified to the medical benefits of fluoridated water, especially in a region in which a significant percentage of the population lives below the poverty line (and thus has restricted access to dental and medical care). As is increasingly the case in such public decisions, a number of remarks on the newspaper's online "comments" section cited internet studies about the dangers of fluoridation. Others noted that fluoridation smacked of Nazi-era pseudoscience, or of a communist plot—a seemingly unironic reprise of midcentury conspiracy theories that nonetheless resembled the logic of other "debates" about state policy, such as the state (non)responses to climate change or white supremacy. The problem presented by this local decision was twofold: What was the "right" science about the pros and cons of fluoride treatment in the public water supply, and how could such positions be distinguished? Surely it is not paranoid to be concerned about health and safety regulations. Second, therefore, was the broader question of whether such matters should be determined democratically,

345

subject to the vagaries of public opinion, or whether the decision belonged instead to experts (and if so, which experts?). In the end, the demarcation crisis turns out to have been resolved in advance: the borough manager and the appointed water authority had already made the decision to discontinue fluoridation; the public debate was merely procedural. There had been no Gordian knot to untie. The "experts" in this case turned out, in other words, to be neither medical professionals nor elected representatives, but the appointed body of local leaders (mostly lawyers and business owners) tasked with administering public utilities. In this very local instance, a "debate" that beckoned to scientific authority and conspiracy theory alike ultimately came down to an imposition of power based, residents were told, on the high cost of updating the water treatment facility.

Such anecdotes are both common and, in the grand scheme of things, fairly minor. But major instances come immediately to mind. As I write this, the citizens of Flint, Michigan, the majority of whom are African American, have been without potable drinking water since 2014, when officials switched the city's water source to the Flint River, which is contaminated by automotive industry runoff; the city's aging civic infrastructure also leaches lead, rendering water safety more than a matter of sourcing alone. And this is but one example.[1] From the mass exploitation of indigenous lands and peoples to the refusal to acknowledge or punish state-sanctioned violence against people of color, the administrative override of individual and collective rights may be endemic to the history of governance. I do not wish to naturalize this. For in spite of its long history, such overrides seem only to have accelerated in a global marketplace in which the discourse of rights—whether the right to clean air and water, the right to health, the right to a planetary future, the right to government representation, the right to life and death, the right to thought—are endlessly trumped in favor of "austerity measures" and corporate interests.

I introduce this local anecdote in the final pages of *Outsider Theory* because of the characteristic way in which such administrative decisions appear to hinge upon the failure of scientists, teachers, and intellectuals to convince "the public" that "both sides" of the debate aren't equally valid or, for that matter, equally subject to doubt and suspicion. The notion that public opinion is intrinsically susceptible to beliefs in pseudoscientific ideas—or susceptible to considering scientific theories as debatable "beliefs"—has often been remarked as a fatal lapse into relativism on behalf of a fractured American (and, increasingly, global) public sphere. Yet to the extent that the water fluoridation debate raises red flags—and it should—the problem has more to do with the categorical override of public procedures and institutions of deliberation, governance, communication, and learning than with the resurgence of conspiracy theories about fluoridation as a Nazi or communist plot. The danger is less that the public, the popular media, pundits, policy wonks, and politicians have all succumbed to postmodernism and now debate the extent to which expertise is political or to which "facts" are socially constructed. Rather, the danger is that facts and expertise can be *excised altogether* from the mechanisms of political decision-making. Much political work has been done over the past several decades—from budget cuts and culture wars to "dirty wars" and disappearances—to purge the political process of its messy entanglements with the infrastructures of democratic process, the institutions and networks that give voice to intellectuals, scientists, artists, and concerned citizens. This is especially the case when such voices are those of women, indigenous peoples, and people of color.

How do we—and by "we" here I refer to culture workers, intellectuals, teachers, scientists, critics, artists, journalists, producers of knowledge—respond to such acts of political marginalization? The answer is certainly not to know *less*. "We are being disappeared anyway," wrote Alice Walker in a 2002 lecture. "We might as well make noise. How many of us gathered here have already lost lovers, children, friends, to illness that are a direct result of the way human beings, and the plants and animals they consume, are being forced to live?"[2] Throughout this book I have stressed expanding our set of information about intellectual history and the life of ideas. The media, networks, institutions, and environments within and through which ideas come in contact with each other is continuous with—though not reducible to—the workings of administration and decision-making, the loss and gain of political power. *Outsider Theory* proposes that we attend to the ways such environments not only shape ideas but also arbitrate between them, as well as classifying or enforcing divisions between groups of thinkers. In this regard my work is aligned with other contemporary sociologies of knowledge that acknowledge the radical historicity of the ideas we employ, study, and instrumentalize, as well as the forms and conditions of their deployment: how they come to be vested with ideological specificity, and they come to be known. Radical history means recognizing, as Gabriel Rockhill puts it, "that everything is historical, including our most privileged practices, cherished concepts, and venerated values."[3] Such practices, concepts, and values are part of history, and they participate in history as well. It is not enough to argue about whether or not facts exist or how they are constructed; the point is to account for the means by which facts and nonfacts alike circulate and take on meaning as elements in a historical process.

Acknowledging this both demands and specifies ways to intervene in this process in turn. In *Black Feminist Thought*, Patricia Hill Collins identifies four "domains of power" as critical sites of tactical participation: the structural domain of power that encompasses large-scale social institutions (such as the legal system and the popular media) that reproduce relations of power and reinforce social hierarchies according to segregation by race, class, gender, sexual orientation, language, and immigration status; the disciplinary domain of power that encompasses organizations (such as schools, industries, hospitals, and banks) that manage power relations through bureaucratic hierarchies and the regulation of expertise; the hegemonic domain of power, which comprises the forms and means of shaping ideology, culture, and consciousness; and the interpersonal domain of power that encompasses the routinized, day-to-day practices of how people treat one another and themselves.[4] These are the domains in which intellectuals, scientists, and other culture workers can and must continually reassert themselves as participants within the concrete operations of power, on behalf of new creative solidarities and ethical redistributions of knowledge and power. It is for this very reason that asking new questions about who and what we consider to be "intellectual," "scientific," and "cultural" remains especially urgent. The sociology of knowledge is not limited to description; it both demands and seeks to enable immanent participation in the radical historicity of thought by illuminating its fields of operation.

The literary scholar Mark Seltzer has recently argued that there is no such thing as an outside; we (and who are "we"?) live in a world that "does not *have* a boundary; it *is* a boundary." The operations of this world consist "in renewing, recording, filing, retrieving, reenacting" the question of what might exist outside its own system; the question of what lies beyond is, in fact, the very occasion for the self-examining operations that comprise this "official world."[5] There is no outside, only the sad illusion of our momentary epiphany, our inventive streak, the self-deception of our alienation or individuality or visionary ties to gods, goddesses, or higher beings. These are all effects of the system.

Of course there is an outside. Or rather, of course there are outsides. Even in designating the cultural and experiential field of such questions, the notion of an outside points to the reality of a poetic longing that warrants attention in its own right. Other such notions abound: the search for spiritual or political transcendence; the ruptural effects of art, of thought, of love; the encounter with the limits of one's knowledge; the discovery or recovery of suppressed or forgotten wisdom; the possibility of alternative dimensions, extraterrestrial life, faraway galaxies. Such phenomena are never

free from the self-administering operations Seltzer impugns as the biopolitical function of "the official world," and in this respect I agree with Seltzer's
injunction. Indeed, throughout this book I have argued that such operations comprise the very medium through which speculative or "discontinuous" knowledges move in and out of consideration. Acknowledging
such forms of mediation does not mean, however, that we must now turn up
our noses at the questions they raise, or squander the perception-altering resources they might hold, as if ridding ourselves of such delusions might
constitute a meaningful gesture in itself. Such cynicism represents but one
of the more cartoonish forms of the "hermeneutics of suspicion" as the belief
(and it *is* a belief) in the self-evidence of an act of unveiling or debunking.
By contrast, the administrative forms I have studied throughout this book
are constitutive of the synthetic—albeit necessarily also partial, locatable,
and critical—approach to the study of ideas whereby religion, worldview,
relations, institutional settings, ambitions, and scholarly apparatuses are all
part of the "hybrid" intellectual phenomena under examination. The point
of such an approach is not to gain a totalizing understanding or, through
some kind of epistemological sublimation, to gain the upper hand on the
administrative demiurges of our fallen world. Rather, the point of approaching ideas as synthetic, multidimensional assemblages is to enumerate the
continuities (as well as the discontinuities) between ideas and their environments, their provisional "outsides," in order to render them more knowable
in their radical historicity.

The aim of *Outsider Theory* is to take stock of an intellectual history
subject to its own terms—subject, that is, to the debates about certainty,
relativism, and transformation one finds throughout the past century and a
half, as well as the capacity for error, discontinuity, and revelation that seems
to accompany all intellectual endeavors. In this regard I share many of the
imperatives of a sociologist such as Bruno Latour, whose work argues for a
methodological symmetry that brings to bear all the tools one possesses on
the study of hybrid phenomena such as a scientific discovery or theory, rather
than enforcing a priori separations "between 'sanctioned' and 'outdated' sciences" or artificial divisions between "objective" and "subjective" factors. As
its first principle, such symmetry "uses the same terms to explain truths and
errors," while simultaneously accounting for the human and nonhuman factors—networks, relations—involved in its formation.[6] Latour's argument is
simultaneously that the multiple forms and dimensions of a theory's *Umwelt*
or provisional "outside" should be studied, and that outsider theories are as
legible as any other theory. And yet what emerges from such *methodological*
symmetry is often a discomfiting encounter with fundamental *asymmetries,*

ideas or processes alien to our political beliefs or to one's own epistemological self-assurance: gaps or breaks in knowledge; boredom, fatigue; ideological
discomfiture; anger; seduction. What this means, quite simply, is that
concepts do not always come from where one might suppose they come from;
facts and beliefs do not all fall naturally into line. Such asymmetries, as I
have suggested, can afford new reserves of longing and imagination as well
as presenting further pitfalls for intellectual labor.

For this reason, *Outsider Theory* does not call for an apocalyptic upheaval
in the way scholars understand knowledge. There is far too much apocalypse
already. The task of this book has instead been to beckon toward an expanded
set of meanings and possibilities for thought itself. Efforts to marginalize or
disenfranchise the production of knowledge can have the effect of reducing
the value of intellectual work to political effectiveness or economic gain alone.
Yet as David L. Martin argues, "knowledge production is a deeply political
act" on account of its aversion to such reductions. Martin calls to mind "all
those streams of thought shut down as quaint, deluded, or categorically dangerous blind alleyways of inquiry by the relentless monotheism of modern
science historiography; all those states of being—ecstatic, fractious, excessive,
divine—curtailed, shunned, and ultimately disciplined for being out of step
with a dominant mode of knowledge production whose contemporary form
can only countenance Being shackled to a notion of productivity."[7] To fall
deliberately out of step with this dominant mode is, on the one hand, to enable a more nuanced picture of the inner—and outer—workings of contemporary thought to come into relief, warts and all. It is also, on the other
hand, to exercise on behalf of thought a right to creativity or even opacity—testifying not only to a manifold archive of forms and concepts but
also to an open set of possibilities for their deployment, obscure and propitious. In the words of the novelist Wilson Harris, it is a right too often ignored in the vicissitudes of the present: "Our grasp of time tends—everyone
knows—to incorporate tragic proportions or determined futures and to overlook unspectacular resources of futurity and imagination that may alter perception *through* and away from fixed habit, greed and monoliths of terror."[8]
The task of *Outsider Theory* has been to reclaim some of these resources, however unspectacular they might appear—or however spectacularly obscure
they might remain.

What does it mean, what does it take, to regain one's rights, when such
"rights" entail a reinvention the way one thinks and knows, the way one occupies the cosmos? How, in other words, might we come to think inventively

on a planetary scale—or on an interplanetary scale? This, I propose, is what the composer, jazz pianist, bandleader, mystic, and philosopher Sun Ra (1914–93) asks of his listeners and fellow musicians. In a 1980 poem, for instance, Sun Ra addresses readers with a proposition that they—that *we*—have lost our rights to the "resources of futurity and imagination" on a cosmic scale.

> If I told you, "I am from outer space"
> You wouldn't believe a word I said.
> Would you? . . . Why should you?
> You've lost your way. . . .
> You should have nothing to say.
> You've lost your rights
> To walk on Jupiter and Mars.
> And even other worlds unknown among the stars
> Among the stars.
> You've lost your rights to the pleasant
> To the pleasant things of being.
> You've lost your rights,
> Your cosmo-interplanetary-intergalactic
> External-rights of Celestial being.[9]

I invoke Sun Ra here as thinker for whom the interplanetary—the "cosmo-interplanetary-intergalactic"—proposes the literally outlandish potentiality of outer space as the site of a struggle for rights that might otherwise be lost, erased, or crushed. To Patricia Hill Collins's four domains of power Sun Ra adds a fifth: a speculative domain, the domain of outer space as both a resource for futurity and imagination and, more profoundly still, a realm of political intervention and struggle as well. This is not the place to delve fully into Sun Ra's extensive career and even more extensive archive.[10] My aim in invoking Sun Ra's "thought from outer space" here is instead to dwell briefly on this fifth, speculative domain as the realm of experimental thinking to which outsider theory beckons, and which Sun Ra's cosmic mythos brings to a powerful, synthetic attunement.

Born Herman Poole Blount and known to his friends as Sonny, Sun Ra—whose centenary took place in 2014, bringing renewed popular and scholarly attention to his music and thought—is as famous as a *figure* in the countercultural imaginary of the Black Arts Movement as he is for his long career as a musician and bandleader. With his Afro-futurist recourse to the iconography of ancient Egypt, Sun Ra's massive production of broadsides, poems, hand-labeled records, and public performances espoused a philosophy that "used strangeness to teach us open feeling as intelligence," as Amiri Baraka has put it.[11] My work has everything to do with the vicissitudes of such strangeness; what interests me here is the notion of its deployment as a didactic strategy, a mode of critical unreason that is *instrumental* in the most expansive of senses. "The people will have to change," Sun Ra tells us in another poem:

> The people will have to change their tune
> And that tuning should be in tune with the Inless outer universe
> The endless immeasurable not
> And this is the dual meaning of the phonetic not: note![12]

For Sun Ra, interplanetarity is an *instrumental* phenomenon—or perhaps it would be more accurate to say that it is an instrumental phenomenology, by which I mean a science of consciousness attuned to new possibilities for existence. This instrumentality is both literal in the sense that it plays out in the language and performance of music, and synthesizing in the sense that it takes composite forms and lends itself to collective forms of discipline. It is a rigorous practice we might consider less as linguistic play or a lapse into magical thinking than a thinking of magical thinking, a theory of outsider theory.

Throughout his music, writing, performances, and stage persona, Sun Ra outlines a synthetic discourse that seeks to challenge, rather than simply transcend, the alienating totality of institutional racism and the anthropocentric death grip of late capitalism. Sun Ra's call for "interplanetary" inventiveness likewise demarcates a comprehensive scale of incorporation, an extratotality he envisions as an epistemological and experiential vehicle for both "External-rights" and "Celestial being." Drawing upon ancient Egyptian iconography, biblical incantation, jazz hermeneutics, and space-age myth, this "vehicle" was fueled by a vast archive of readings in black historiography and occult knowledges and was mediated, channeled, through poiesis—a poiesis that took the form of verse and music, ritual and archive, and even the synthesizing form of invented instruments such as the Space Organ that Baraka remembers from the 1960s, with its "Pythagorean connection of Sound to Color."[13] Most poetic of all, perhaps, was the ritualized collective rigor of the Arkestra, Sun Ra's jazz ensemble, whose very name invokes such a liberatory vehicle. I want to insist, however, that this project was by no means restricted to transcendence or escapism, as if deliverance took the form of a metaphorical or metaphysical flight alone. Rather, it comprised a set of practices to be rehearsed, repeated, and continually reorchestrated. The iconography and rhetoric of Sun Ra's interstellar mythos recalls and extends the long tradition of African American *flight* as a tradition of eluding the "geography of containment" of political foreclosure and social death since the Middle Passage. As Michelle Commander has written, such flights, whether physical, mechanical, artistic, or imaginative, assert both a desire for and a right to corporeal and spiritual liberty on behalf of diasporic African Americans.[14] Naming a tradition rather than a proposition, Sun Ra's thought from outer space comprises the material and cognitive practices if synthesizing a virtual infinity of knowledge systems and hermetic traditions. It outlines an instrumental cosmology that both appealed to the inhuman scale of planetary racial politics and demanded the exercise of speculative thinking.

For all the political and intellectual exigency we might wish to ascribe to such "experimental" ways of thinking, I consider it no less imperative to attend to the everyday activities of its creation and circulation. And in the case of Sun Ra and his Arkestra, this everyday had much to do with attunement—that is, the musical and, in many respects, the intellectual discipline of the jazz ensemble derived from a nearly obsessional commitment to rehearsal. It was a philosophical, religious, and political commitment as much as an aesthetic or managerial expediency. It thus extended to a sociological imperative. As Sun Ra put it, "today people are completely out of tune, but the people . . . could sound magnificent if they had the correct composer or arranger, who would know how to judiciously use them and make them play together and obtain a certain sound."[15] And as his biographer John Szwed elaborates in turn, Sun Ra's "concern with precision and discipline took shape against what he saw as an American addiction to freedom and liberty. Freedom had proven itself a plague, a curse, especially for black people, a false idol which they had chased after but which has remained unattainable and ultimately unnatural."[16] In this respect, Sun Ra's thinking resembles a broad array of modern esoteric philosophies that likewise yoked cosmic ambitions to individual and collective practices, from Helena Blavatsky's theosophy, to George Gurdjieff's "fourth way," to the Enochian magic of Aleister Crowley's circle. In the 1950s, Sun Ra and his manager Alton Abraham formed an esoteric study group of their own, the neo-Gnostic Thmei Research group, whose motto was "Seek ye wisdom, knowledge and understanding." But Sun Ra was anything but a self-help guru or professional mystic; his work—as a composer and bandleader as well as Afro-futurist synthesizer and philosopher—was didactic as well as disciplinary.[17]

"You've lost your rights / To walk on Jupiter and Mars." Naming the condition of segregation and colonial domination of the midcentury Jim Crow United States as a global rather than national situation, Sun Ra logically

FIGURE 32. Alton Abraham, notebook marked "Equations." Collection of Sun Ra, Special Collections Research Center, University of Chicago Library, box 3, folder 11.

extends cruelty and exploitation to a totalizing human condition. "It's bad everywhere you go," he explains in a recorded speech. "Leaders have to be given some consideration. It's very difficult to even think about government, man. They've all got their own ideas about what should be. It makes it very difficult for somebody in human form to try to lead people. . . . And unfortunately people mistreat each other. They don't give leaders an example of how they should be treated. They shoot each other. They cut each other. They hate each other. They curse at each other. That's a bad example for people to set for leaders, who see that and might get a very bad impression about people, and not want to lead them, or do anything for them because they're so bad."[18] Already inverting the hierarchy of "leaders" over the people whose example they follow, Sun Ra's portrait of governance stresses the causal function of such models and impressions. Yet rather than defining better models of human comportment—according, say, to a restricted economy of moral or socioeconomic values—Sun Ra's teachings counterpropose an explicitly otherworldly set of historical and epistemological coordinates. He posits a new kind of future alternative to the exploitative futurity implicit in the fallen state of planetary affairs, forging a continuum between ancient Egypt and outer space. This "Alter Destiny" (to cite a track from Sun Ra's 1966 album *Monorails and Satellites*) demanded an alternative set of attunements, a celestial harmonics engineered according to an inhuman, cosmic scale.[19] Another way to approach the problem of governmentality, in other words, was to leave this planet behind and enter the space age. This is how people—meaning Black people, people of color, and only then by extension all those "in human form"—might come to regain the rights lost to cruelty and groundedness: to regain the right to "cosmo-interplanetary-intergalactic / External-rights of Celestial being." Such a speculative recourse to space resonated with the blistering irony that the Cold War "space race" coincided with a civil rights movement punctuated by the murders of Medgar Evers, Martin Luther King Jr., Emmett Till, Malcolm X, the four girls killed in the Birmingham church bombings (Addie Mae Collins, Carol Denise McNair, Carole Robertson, and Cynthia Wesley), and so many others, including Sun Ra's friend Henry Dumas, the writer and fellow Black Arts Movement collaborator who was gunned down by white police in the New York City subway in May 1968 in a case of "mistaken identity." Sun Ra's appeal to space wasn't a fantasy; it was a polemic whose didactic premise was that Sun Ra was *from* outer space and bore its truth.

In a famous scene from the 1974 film *Space Is the Place*, Sun Ra materializes, shoes first, before a group of "black youth of planet Earth" and offers to bring them back with him to outer space. White people, he notes, "are walking there today," having already landed on the moon several years previously. "They take frequent trips to the moon; I notice none of you have been invited."[20] Sun Ra's literally outlandish self-presentation as an intergalactic traveler belies the notion that even the farthest reaches of the cosmos have long been colonized as white, whether in concept or in historical actuality. Any political or imaginative intervention into contemporary so-cial relations thus already demanded interplanetary thinking, by this logic: QED.

At stake in Sun Ra's work, I thus maintain, is the notion that the vast, supramundane possibilities of outer space constitute a right to be exercised in the face of foreclosure, colonization, and exclusion. As Donna Haraway writes in her landmark 1988 essay "Situated Knowledges," the scientific celebration of space exploration has tended to brandish "an ideology of di-rect, devouring, generative, and unrestricted vision, whose technological mediations are simultaneously celebrated and presented as utterly transpar-ent."[21] Sun Ra's vision of intergalactic attunement asserts the right to opacity, to mystery, and to openness in the face of such a colonizing gaze. Less gnostic than agonistic, Sun Ra's thought from outer space seeks to *perform,* to synthesize, the "Alter Destiny" to which his dialectical "poetics of recombination" posits as otherworldly.[22]

In one of the most illuminating summaries of Sun Ra's recourse to outer space, which I will take the liberty here of citing at length, Anthony Reed describes this project in terms that evoke the literalness of Sun Ra's approach to the symbolic languages of his interplanetary mythos:

> We might best understand space as a figure through which Ra
> attempted to form a community rooted in common feeling and
> common dissatisfaction, a common desire to break with the narrowly
> proscribed regime of the possible, in short a figure through which to
> imagine freedom beyond the bounds of extant ideology. In this way, it
> is no metaphor but a catachresis, a figure that invents sense by using
> figures in a more or less arbitrary name to invoke what is otherwise
> unthinkable, or unthought. To use another term key to Sun Ra, it is
> a myth—a caesura of thought aimed at attempting to imagine an
> unimpeded future, which still retains the risks of authoritarianism
> and reactionary formations, but also the promise of something greater
> than itself that cannot yet be named. The difficulty is that, as with any
> catachresis, space must also be taken literally as the introduction of a
> gap or void that punctures ideology's pretense to eternity, and an
> opening for the new.[23]

I would offer here, as a modest adjustment to Reed's articulation, that Sun Ra's recourse to outer space does not itself constitute the exception that Reed names—the break in the regime of the possible—but rather its medium. Outer space, and the epistemological and cosmological sphere it demarcates, is already occupied territory. White people already take frequent trips to the moon. This is not only literally the case, but metaphysically as well: from colliding planets and Gnostic conceptions of an "alien god" to more literal ideas about the cosmic and intergalactic origins of enlightenment that emerged in New Age discourses, to the parapsychoanalytic theories of Carl Jung and Wilhelm Reich, and to the pseudoarchaeology of Erich von Däniken and the space rays of Scientology. The "race for space" is, for Sun Ra, a battle to disrupt the colonization of outsider theory—like the colonization of space—as a white supremacist instrument.[24] Sun Ra thus moves the sphere of contestation, of a demand for rights, into the outer reaches of the imaginary, the fifth domain of power.

The historical space age was rife with alien knowledges that testified to otherworldly sources of intelligence—from conspiracy theories to UFO sightings to sci-fi religious cults to the "occult explosion" of the age of Aquarius[25]—whose possibilities formed a fascinating lure for experimental thinkers in the 1950s, 1960s, and 1970s. Sun Ra's work marks a shift in the "cosmic" thinking of this period, mobilizing the otherworldly concerns of religion, science, and esoterica toward the politicized terms of his interplanetary mythos, which took exception with the long history of colonial exploitation and slavery upon which much contemporary "thought from outer space" continued to draw. It is fascinating to note the ways in which Sun Ra's cosmology becomes a measure of other contemporary efforts to think beyond planetary and humanist terms, particularly in the sciences. Many such interventions, however, are deeply grounded in the very humanisms and capitalist fantasies that "thought from outer space" might claim to transcend. Forms of space-age Gnosticism abounded in the United States and Europe throughout the post–World War II period. In Hollywood alone, for instance, rocket scientist Jack Parsons was an adept in Aleister Crowley's esoteric religious-magical movement, known as Thelema, who invented his own neo-Gnostic spiritual system before accidentally blowing himself up in a botched experiment in 1952.[26] Parsons was a friend of L. Ron Hubbard, the pulp writer and fabulist who incorporated Scientology as a religion in 1953 (after its "scientific" practice was investigated for medical fraud in 1951); this occult world was memorialized by Kenneth Anger in films such as *The Inauguration of the Pleasure Dome* (filmed in 1954), which featured an appearance by Parsons's widow Marjorie Cameron, and *Lucifer Rising* (1972), which was inspired by Crowley's poem "Hymn to Lucifer," as well as Anger's *Hollywood Babylon* books. Parsons lived and held his occult practices in Pasadena, California, which was also the headquarters of the Theosophical Society, founded by Helena Blavatsky and her colleagues in the 1870s and moved to California after World War II by Arthur L. Conger, a

U.S. Army colonel and president of the society since the 1930s. Sun Ra's own sites of activity—Birmingham, Alabama, through the 1940s; Chicago in the 1950s and early 1960s; New York City in the mid- to late 1960s; Philadelphia in the 1970s, amid extensive and protracted tours and residencies—likewise featured major concentrations of theosophical and esoteric groups. Such networks of relations demonstrated the continuities between nineteenth-century and postwar religious inventions that fused Egyptian symbology and Kabbalistic calculation with modern scientific claims and sci-fi imaginaries in the name of accessing otherworldly spiritual knowledge and power. Like Sun Ra's cosmology, such modern "religions" were grand, recombinatory syntheses of heterogeneous ancient symbols and practices that professed to align divine wisdom with advances in subatomic physics and "the dawn of new and important discoveries in the field of psychology," as Helena Blavatsky writes in *Isis Unveiled*.[27]

A survey of contemporary space-age ideas about extraterrestrial or supramundane sources of thought yields a virtual encyclopedia of further explorations in outsider theory, from Immanuel Velikovsky's "interdisciplinary synthesis" of biblical exegesis, world myth, and astrophysics (as discussed in chapter 8), to L. Ron Hubbard's invention of Scientology, as well as to the many other invented worlds and syntheses that comprise the vast terrain of so-called outsider art. There may be few genealogical consistencies between such systems, although there are uncanny resemblances: Hubbard likely read Velikovsky's first book in serial form before quickly penning *Dianetics,* his own book of interplanetary illumination. Sun Ra's disciplinary medium of musical "attunement" is in some ways an analogue to the technospiritual instruments used in Scientology. One of the innovations of Hubbard's religion was its recourse to "personal discipline" in the form of auditing converts to Scientology, thanks to the E-Meter—the "electropsychometer"—designed as "an electronic instrument that measures mental state and change of state in individuals."[28] The function of this "religious artifact" is to separate the immortal, transcendent, and otherwordly part of man—called the thetan, an immortal spiritual being—from the bodily, and to distinguish the good energy produced by its collection of "mental image pictures" from the bad ones we pick up through traumatic experiences. The E-Meter is basically a lie detector, but it also owes much to the "orgone accumulators" invented by the renegade psychoanalyst Wilhelm Reich, whose ideas Hubbard also seems to have ripped off.[29] Yet such technologized forms of Gnostic experience—or what Erik Davis has dubbed *TechGnosis*[30]—promise the sort of individual "freedom" that Sun Ra considered a dangerous lure. And as critics of the Scientology movement have long professed, the only real "attunement" the religion upholds is the sound of money changing hands. Sun Ra's cosmic machinations operate within the same domain, we might say, as Scientology, yet function according to a wholly different set of instrumental practices.

A later example proves even more illuminating: the Swiss writer Erich von Däniken rose to massive celebrity in the 1970s on account of his own outer-space theories, claiming that the great monuments of the ancient past were far too technologically advanced to have been created by "primitive so-cieties" and therefore must have been the products of great geniuses from outer space. The visits of these extraterrestrial geniuses—who look uncan-nily like the spacemen of 1960s NASA voyages—are memorialized as gods in the religion and iconography of ancient civilizations, from Neolithic cave dwellers to ancient Egyptians and pre-Columbian Mesoamerican civiliza-tions. Von Däniken justifies the hypothesis that the technologies and knowl-edge systems of ancient civilizations *were not their own* by comparing the technological discrepancies between contemporary "advanced" (Anglo-European) and "primitive" (indigenous) cultures. As he explains,

> Some parts of our earth are still inhabited by primitive peoples to whom a machine gun is a weapon of the devil. In that case a jet aircraft may well be an angelic vehicle to them. And a voice coming from a radio set might seem to be the voice of a god. These last primitive peoples, too, naïvely hand down from generation to genera-tion in their sages their impressions of technical achievements that we take for granted. They still scratch their divine figures and their wonderful ships coming from heaven on cliffs and cave walls. In this way these savage peoples have actually preserved for us what we are seeking today.[31]

The smug, racist premise of technological superiority explicit in Von Dän-iken's work demonstrates the extent to which the necessarily grounded meth-ods of such "thought from outer space" had already been fully colonized by white supremacy; Sun Ra's approach to outsider theory involved decoloniz-ing not only the mind but also its recourse to myth.

In a manner that harkens to the Copernican ambitions of Ve-likovsky—or, perhaps, Sigmund Freud—Sun Ra emerges as an experimen-tal thinker about the frontiers of human knowledge to the extent that his interplanetary wrest back the far reaches of speculative thought from its ide-ological foreclosure in Hubbard's technocratic self-measurement or Von Däniken's racist fantasy of "advanced" aliens. Sun Ra's interplanetary recla-mation of rights hinges instead on what he calls the "immeasurable equation" of his rigorous dialectical method, which functions at once in his poetic logic, the collective discipline of his Arkestra, and his compositional methods as a jazz artist. The kinds of "vibrations" and attunements to which Sun Ra's interplanetary instruments are dedicated are, after all, musical—designating "soul" as a cultural practice and centuries-long history rather than as a measurable and thus trafficable commodity.

We see a telling example of the agonistic, politically dialecticizing disciplinary practice of wresting esoteric methods from the hands of white supremacy in the broadsheets and leaflets Sun Ra composed during his years in Chicago through his involvement in the Thmei Research group with Alton Abraham. In texts that were rediscovered several months after Abraham's death in 1999, when the contents of his house were rescued from imminent disposal, we witness the development of Sun Ra's "immeasurable equation" as the fruit of an exhaustive, permutational hermeneutics.[32] It is a hermeneutics, we might say, of infinite suspicion. In a broadsheet entitled "The Great Whore," Sun Ra literally calculates the genealogy of the "whore of Babylon" as a religious game of the dozens, which describes the deracinating effects of diaspora as a cosmic game of insulting one's mother:

> Babylon, THE GREAT WHORE, THE MOTHER OF WHORES AND ABOMI-
> NATIONS OF THE EARTH. ... ... Children would call this statement
> "PLAYING THE DOZENS" or "THE TWELVES". ... THE DOUBLE
> DOZEN ... THE TWO TWELVES. .... in the twelve multiplication table.
> 12 is the FIRST. ... 144 is LAST .... THE FIRST is EQUAL to the
> LAST ... ... THE BEGINNING IS THE END. 12 is 144 ...... TO SAY
> THE TWELVES IS THE SAME THING AS SAYING THE ONE HUNDRED &
> FORTY FOURS. 12's equals 144's. .... 144's is 144,000 (ONE HUNDRED
> FORTY FOUR THOUSANDS)
>
> ONE equals a thousand ......
> TEN equals TEN THOUSANDS
> ONE HUNDRED equals ONE HUNDRED THOUSANDS
> ONE HUNDRED AND FORTY FOUR equals ONE HUNDRED AND FORTY
> FOUR THOUSANDS. 144 is 144,000 .... 144 is
> TWELVES. ... TWELVES is DOZENS.
>
> DOZENS IS A NAME GIVEN TO STATEMENTS WHICH CALLS A
> PERSONS MOTHER A WHORE.
> [...] EVERYONE IN THE 144,000 HAS BEEN PUT IN THE DOZENS.
> [...] ALL THOSE IN THAT NUMBER ARE NOW IN SHAME AND DIS-
> GRACE ... THEY ARE CONSIDERED AS LESS THAN NOTHING. THEY ARE
> ALL NATIONS, THEY ARE THOSE THAT HAVE THE BLOOD OF ALL

NATIONS IN THEIR VEINS. THEY ARE THOSE WHO DO NOT KNOW
THEIR ORIGIN, WHO HAVE LOST ALL TRACE OF THEIR TRUE IDENTITY
AND CALL THEMSELVES NEGROES. NEGROES ARE ALL NATIONS.
REVELATION 18.3 . . .[33]

Sun Ra draws the number 144,000 from the book of Revelation, in which 12,000 members of each of the twelve tribes of Israel represent the number to be redeemed in the final judgment. His permutational exegesis thus recasts the wretched of the earth—the diasporic "Negroes" immersed in a cosmic game of insults—as those to be redeemed. Though degraded as the "whores" of Babylon, in other words, the people of the black diaspora reveal their chosen status according to the logic of a multiplication table. This was not a singular premise: Sun Ra's notebooks reveal the extent to which he rehearsed such calculations at length, demonstrating his commitment to deriving—mathematically as well as musically—the means for interrupting what would otherwise amount to a vicious circle, a grim, bottomless condition of perpetual insult.

What is "alien" in this method—the alterity in Sun Ra's version of Afro-futurist "Alter Destiny," as well as the obsessional rigor of his "poetics of recombination," as Brent Edwards describes it—is its promise rather than its premise: we know, or we think we know, that thought does not really come from outer space. But Sun Ra's project of rejecting the planet Earth as a dead place, of abandoning rather than dialecticizing or otherwise engaging the terms of globalization, was proleptically to grant a flight that exercises a *right* rather than a presumption. As Amiri Baraka wrote of Sun Ra, "the possible is obvious, what is desired is the *impossible*."[34] Sun Ra's theory of outsider theory did not propose an impossible revolutionary horizon to be either mustered or mourned. Rather, it enacted a synthesis that introduced the impossible as a science of accidentals, of tonal shifts and scalar permutations: "the impossible," he writes in a 1965 poem, "is a thought / and every thought is real / An idea, a flash of potent fire / a seed that can bring to be / the reality of itself."[35] For Sun Ra, outsider theory is a discipline—but a discipline whose potential yield is the multiplication of such ideas. The poet Nathaniel Mackey defines this manner of discipline as a "discrepant engagement," an expression "coined in reference to practices that, in the interest of opening presumably closed orders of identity and signification, accent fissure, fracture, incongruity, the rickety, imperfect fit between word and world. Such practices highlight—indeed inhabit—discrepancy, engage rather than seek to ignore it."[36] Like the proponents of scientific process and conceptual encounter examined throughout this book, Mackey advocates an intellectual practice that

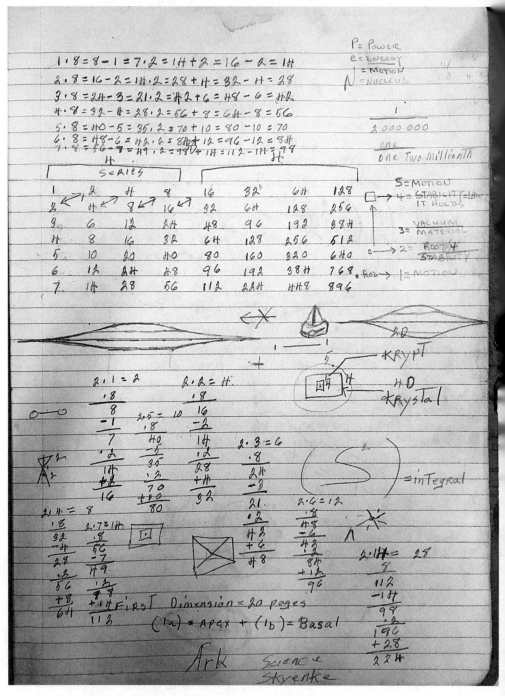

FIGURE 33. Alton Abraham, page from "Equations." Collection of Sun Ra, Special Collections Research Center, University of Chicago Library, box 3, folder 11.

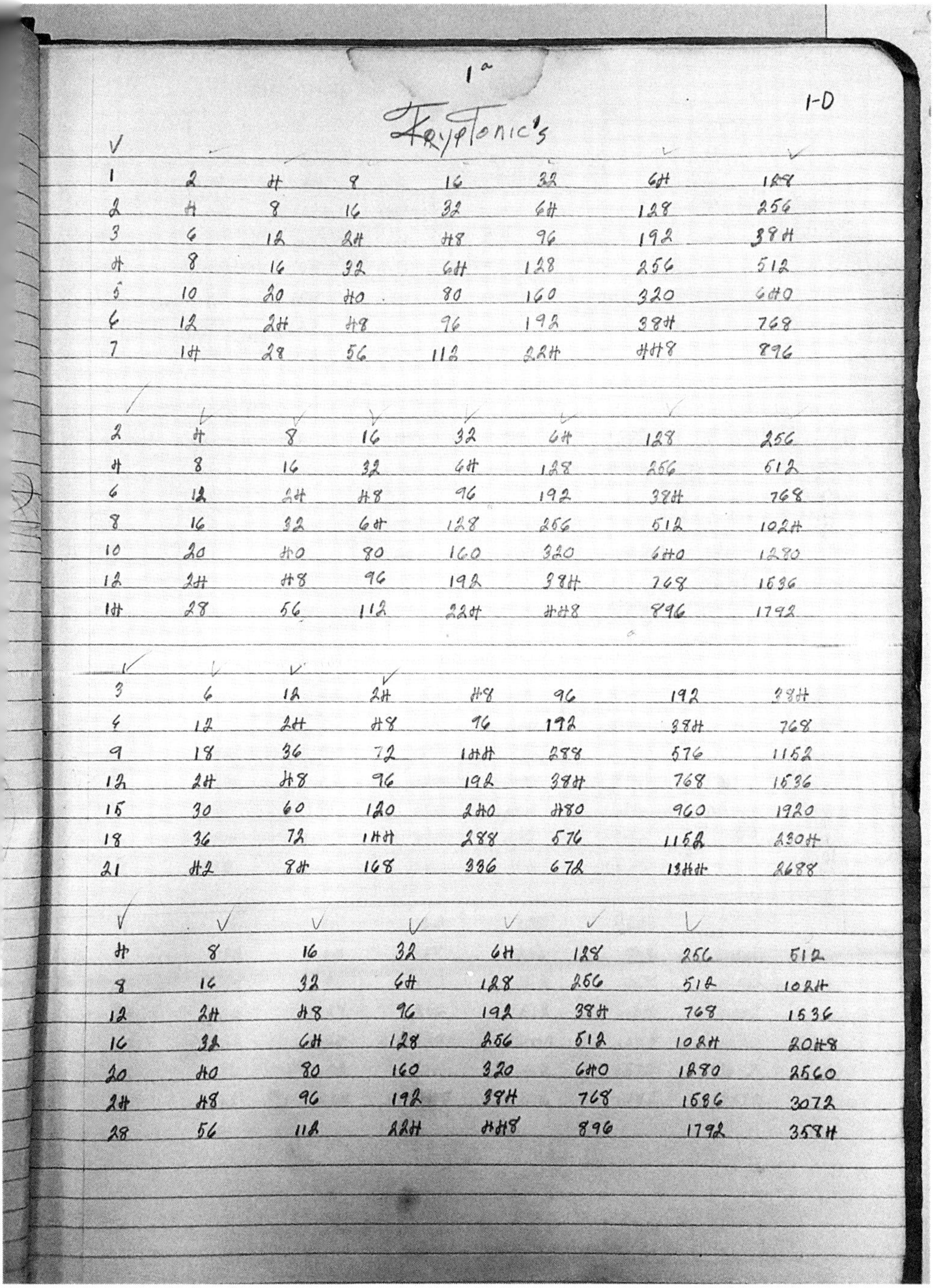

TrypTonic's

V		##					V	V
1	2	4	8	16	32	64	128
2	4	8	16	32	64	128	256
3	6	12	24	48	96	192	384
4	8	16	32	64	128	256	512
5	10	20	40	80	160	320	640
6	12	24	48	96	192	384	768
7	14	28	56	112	224	448	896

2	4	8	16	32	64	128	256
4	8	16	32	64	128	256	512
6	12	24	48	96	192	384	768
8	16	32	64	128	256	512	1024
10	20	40	80	160	320	640	1280
12	24	48	96	192	384	768	1536
14	28	56	112	224	448	896	1792

3	6	12	24	48	96	192	384
6	12	24	48	96	192	384	768
9	18	36	72	144	288	576	1152
12	24	48	96	192	384	768	1536
15	30	60	120	240	480	960	1920
18	36	72	144	288	576	1152	2304
21	42	84	168	336	672	1344	2688

4	8	16	32	64	128	256	512
8	16	32	64	128	256	512	1024
12	24	48	96	192	384	768	1536
16	32	64	128	256	512	1024	2048
20	40	80	160	320	640	1280	2560
24	48	96	192	384	768	1536	3072
28	56	112	224	448	896	1792	3584

FIGURE 34. Alton Abraham, page from "Equations." Collection of Sun Ra, Special Collections Research Center, University of Chicago Library, box 3, folder 11.

"contends with resolution" and "worries resolute identity and demarcation, resolute boundary lines, resolute definition, obeying a vibrational rather than a corpuscular sense of being." Such discrepant engagement thus describes a practical commitment to remaining open to "resonance, dissonance, noise" in order to be "at odds with hypostasis, the reification of fixed identities that has been the bane of socially marginalized groups."[37] As I have suggested throughout this book, this does not mean proposing a lapse into relativism or a sociological attention to the constitution of "facts"; it instead describes a commitment to intervening in the domains of power within which such reifications and hypostases perpetually take place. As Sun Ra teaches us, there may be not only more ideas out there, more ways to participate in the known domains of power, than anthropocentric life admits; there are also other domains we have yet fully to discover, and new communities of thought that have yet to fully take shape. If this is to be the final act for human life on earth, then the time for reclaiming our rights to the "Alter Destiny" within all five domains of power is fully upon us. Sun Ra leaves us, therefore, with a prophecy:

> Advancements will be made
> But it is to be of other dimensions
> These advancements are beyond the measured.
> They are advancement
> It is outside as advancement always it.
> The eternity/cycle/age code is circle
> Return again according to the record
> Repetition of the mirror existence
> Yes, outside of the shadow world
> Advancement shall be made
> With giant strides
> And lightning comprehension
> Potential realization.[38]

NOTES

Unless otherwise noted, all translations are my own.

PREFACE

1. Robert Furneaux, *Ancient Mysteries* (New York: McGraw-Hill, 1977), dust jacket.

2. Martin Gardner, *In the Name of Science* (New York: Putnam's, 1952), 6.

3. Gardner, *In the Name of Science*, 7.

4. The term *post-truth*, the *Oxford English Dictionary*'s word of the year for 2016, was coined by playwright Steve Tesich in "A Government of Lies," *Nation*, January 6, 1992, 12–13. For a field-shifting reappraisal of the way scholars approach oft-disparaged genre fiction, see Janice Radway, *Reading the Romance* (Chapel Hill: University of North Carolina Press, 1984).

5. Robin Wall Kimmerer, *Braiding Sweetgrass: Indigenous Wisdom, Scientific Knowledge, and the Teachings of Plants* (Minneapolis: Milkweed, 2013), 160.

6. Patricia Hill Collins, *Black Feminist Thought: Knowledge, Consciousness, and the Politics of Empowerment* (2000, repr., New York: Routledge, 2009), 14.

7. Harry Frankfurt, *On Bullshit* (Princeton, N.J.: Princeton University Press, 2005), 61.

8. For a discussion of contemporary esoterica in France and the history of this "unification," see Pierre Lagrance and Claudie Voisenat, *L'ésotérisme contemporain et ses lecteurs: Entre savoirs, croyances et fictions* (Paris: Éditions de la Bibliothèque publique d'information, 2005). This is hardly to suggest that the field is ideologically uniform; on the contrary, as in avant-garde art and literature, there have long been right-wing as well as left-wing practitioners of esoterism. Raymond Abellio, for instance, was the nom de plume of Georges Soulès, was a Leftist in the 1930s but an active collaborationist during the Vichy régime who reinvented himself as a left-leaning writer and scholar of astrology and occultism after his pardon in 1952.

9. On this period, see Louis Pauwels and Jacques Bergier, *Le Matin des Magiciens* (Paris: Gallimard, 1960), published in England as *The Dawn of Magic* (London:

Gibbs and Phillips, 1963) and in the United States as *The Morning of the Magicians* (New York: Avon, 1968). See also Theodore Roszak, *The Making of a Counter Culture: Reflections on the Technocratic Society and Its Youthful Opposition* (1969; repr., Berkeley: University of California Press, 1995), esp. 42–83, 155–77, and 239–68. For more recent accounts, see, for instance, Amy Hollywood, *Sensible Ecstasy: Mysticism, Sexual Difference, and the Demands of History* (Chicago: University of Chicago Press, 2002); Sarah M. Pike, *New Age and Neopagan Religions in America* (New York: Columbia University Press, 2006); Jeffrey J. Kripal, *Authors of the Impossible: The Paranormal and the Sacred* (Chicago: University of Chicago Press, 2010); and David Kaiser and W. Patrick McCray, eds., *Groovy Science: Knowledge, Innovation and American Counterculture* (Chicago: University of Chicago Press, 2016).

10. See Roszak, *The Making of a Counter Culture*, 46.

11. On "junk thought," see Susan Jacoby, *The Age of American Unreason* (New York: Pantheon, 2008), esp. 210–41. "Intellectual quackery extends," Jacoby writes, "throughout the landscape of academia; tenured professors in the humanities and social sciences, on the right and the left, are constantly purveying theories that are the philosophical, literary, and artistic equivalent of junk science. That many of the researchers consider themselves intellectuals is sad but unremarkable in the annals of quackery within academia: junk thought with an intellectual patina fosters anti-intellectualism as effectively as junk science with a scientific patina fosters public misunderstanding and suspicion of real science" (230). See also the discussion in the introduction about the "science wars" of the 1990s.

12. For a compelling account of contemporary and postwar debates about the dangers—as well as the inevitability—of popular pseudoscience, see Michael Gordin, *The Pseudoscience Wars: Immanuel Velikovsky and the Birth of the Modern Fringe* (Chicago: University of Chicago Press, 2012). On the Nuwaubian movement, see Susan J. Palmer, *The Nuwaubian Movement: Black Spirituality and State Control* (Farnham, U.K.: Ashgate, 2010).

13. For a discussion of the industrialization of the "hypomnesic" technologies that sustain and reproduce intellectual transmission, see Bernard Steigler, *States of Shock: Stupidity and Knowledge in the 21st Century*, trans. Daniel Ross (Cambridge: Polity, 2015), esp. 1–12, 149–220.

14. Gardner, *In the Name of Science*, 3.

15. See Gordin, *The Pseudoscience Wars*, esp. 204–10. See also Naomi Oreskes and Erik M. Conway, *Merchants of Doubt: How a Handful of Scientists Obscured the Truth on Issues from Tobacco Smoke to Global Warming* (New York: Bloomsbury, 2010).

16. Collins, *Black Feminist Thought*, 17.

17. Frankfurt, *On Bullshit*, 52–53.

18. For a classic investigation of such questions, see Michael Polanyi, *The Tacit Dimension* (1966; repr., Chicago: University of Chicago Press, 2009). See also Diana Crane, *Invisible Colleges: Diffusion of Knowledge in Scientific Communities* (Chicago: University of Chicago Press, 1972).

19. See Donna Haraway, "Situated Knowledges: The Science Question in Feminism and the Privilege of Partial Perspective," *Feminist Studies* 14, no. 3 (1988): 575–99.

20. Arthur Koestler, *The Roots of Coincidence* (New York: Random House, 1972), 11.

21. See Karl Popper, *The Logic of Scientific Discovery,* 2nd ed. (London: Routledge, 2002), esp. 3–26.

22. Though it would certainly have been possible to track down the previous owner of the books, or her family, I did not do so, as I considered it an unnecessary invasion of privacy. My questions are thus purely speculative.

23. On modern collecting practices as "provisional institutions"—the artifactual form of Diana Crane's notion of "invisible colleges"—see Jeremy Braddock, *Collecting as a Modernist Practice* (Baltimore: Johns Hopkins University Press, 2012). See also Diana Crane, *Invisible Colleges: Diffusion of Knowledge in Scientific Communities* (Chicago: University of Chicago Press, 1972).

24. See Educating Humanity, http://www.educatinghumanity.com; and The Conspiracy Zone, http://theconspiracyzone.podcastpeople.com.

25. See, for instance, Daniel Cohen, *Myths of the Space Age* (New York: Dodd, Mead, 1965); John Sladek, *The New Apocrypha: A Guide to Strange Science and Occult Beliefs* (New York: Stein and Day, 1973); Ronald H. Fritze, *Invented Knowledge: False History, Fake Science and Pseudo-Religions* (London: Reaktion, 2010); and David Aaronovitch, *Voodoo Histories: The Role of Conspiracy Theory in Shaping Modern History* (New York: Penguin, 2010), among many others.

INTRODUCTION

1. In *Fantastic Architecture,* Stephen Williams discusses the use of the term *crank* by debunkers such as Martin Gardner and L. Sprague de Camp, citing the *Oxford English Dictionary*'s definition as "a person with a mental twist, an eccentric; especially a monomaniac." As Williams summarizes, "However one chooses to refer to the purveyors of pseudoscience, they do have a similar personal profile. They often work in almost total isolation from professional colleagues, and they exhibit a tendency to paranoia." Williams, *Fantastic Architecture: The Wild Side of North American Prehistory* (Philadelphia: University of Pennsylvania Press, 1991), 16.

2. Patricia Hill Collins, *Black Feminist Thought: Knowledge, Consciousness, and the Politics of Empowerment* (2000; repr., New York: Routledge, 2009), ix.

3. See Georges Bataille, "The Use-Value of D.A.F. de Sade (An Open Letter to My Current Comrades)," in *Visions of Excess: Selected Writings, 1927–1939,* ed. Allan Stoekl (Minneapolis: University of Minnesota Press, 1985), 91–102. For a further discussion, see Arkady Plotnitsky, *Complementarity: Anti-Epistemology after Bohr and Derrida* (Durham, N.C.: Duke University Press, 1994), esp. 17–36.

4. As Jean Dubuffet proposes in *Asphyxiating Culture* (1968), with "a philosophy that would consider fragmentary fields one after the next," thought "once decided upon incoherence, or at least upon a less prolonged coherence," could "find itself endowed with an astonishing burst of energy." This "energy" is, elsewhere in the essay, "animated with a spirit of contestation and subversion" and directed toward "antagonistic aspirations." Dubuffet, *Asphyxiating Culture and Other Writings,* trans. Carol Volk (New York: Four Walls Eight Windows, 1988), 42, 49. For a critique of such avant-garde imperative as a product of the reflexivity of the "field" of art, rather than a break with it, see Pierre Bourdieu, *The Rules of Art: Genesis and Structure of the Literary Field,* trans. Susan Emanuel (Stanford, Calif.: Stanford University Press, 1996), 242–49.

5. Margaret Wertheim addresses the prospect of "outsider theory" in her book *Physics on the Fringe: Smoke Rings, Circlons, and Alternative Theories of Everything* (New York: Walker, 2011). Wertheim likens her study of physics theories by self-taught "outsiders" to the twentieth-century interest in outsider art, citing the largely aesthetic and even spiritual satisfaction of pure scientific inquiry. "This book," she writes, "is an attempt to make sense of theoretical physics outsiders within the context of a society that is enriched, enchanted, and awed by science, but also one that in some respects is intimidated by this force. What does it mean that a man in a trailer park feels the need to reinvent physics from the ground up? What does it mean for the man himself, and for society at large?" (11). Though I admire the concerted attention Wertheim devotes to such theories, my own work seeks to surpass aesthetic contemplation alone, as well as to avoid the implicit condescension of classifying "outsiders" in sociological terms.

6. Roxana Azimi, *La Folie de l'art brut* (Paris: Séguier, 2014), 21.

7. Roger Cardinal, conversation with the author, September 2012.

8. Colin Wilson, *The Outsider* (1956; repr., New York: Putnam's, 1976). Anticipating his own decades-long career as a writer of popular occult books, Wilson posits the outsider as a figure akin to saints and mystics, albeit with a more pessimistic worldview, noting that "the Outsider is always the man who is not susceptible to the general enthusiasm; it may be that he is too short-sighted to see the establishment of Utopia before the end of the century. At all events, he is bound to be a child of his century if he draws his nourishment from its earth; he cannot be a nihilistic pessimist (like Camus and Sartre) in a century when the philosophers are behaving like cowboys at a rodeo" (47). See also Howard S. Becker's sociological approach to such figures in *Outsiders: Studies in the Sociology of Deviance* (New York: Free Press, 1963).

9. Patricia Hill Collins's notion of the "outsider within" to describe the social location of many Black women—but which can also foster "new angles of vision on oppression" through the legacy of struggle and the maintenance of "collectively shared, Black women's oppositional knowledge"—offers a more grounded and politically resilient framework for such generalizable existential resistance to "thrownness." Collins, *Black Feminist Thought,* 14. See also Patricia Hill Collins,

"Learning from the Outsider Within: The Sociological Significance of Black Feminist Thought," *Social Problems* 33, no. 6 (1986): 14–32.

10. Roger Cardinal, *Outsider Art* (New York: Praeger, 1972), 8.

11. Cardinal, *Outsider Art,* 179.

12. Cardinal, *Outsider Art,* 179.

13. As Dubuffet writes, "raw art, primitiveness, liberty must not be conceived of as locales, nor especially as fixed locales, but as directions, aspirations, tendencies. . . . I agree that we are all—and by this I also mean those who received little education, the illiterate—all impregnated with culture, our thought is conditioned and deformed by culture, is to culture what the blade of the knife is to steel. But the blade can adopt a subversive attitude; it can aspire to replace its quality as steel with that of pure will to cut." Dubuffet, *Asphyxiating Culture,* 69–70.

14. Cardinal and Dubuffet are thus not far off in their thinking from Pierre Bourdieu, who describes how avant-garde and "naive" ruptures in the field of art are a very product of its cumulative history. "It is the very logic of the field," he writes, "which tends to select and consecrate all legitimate ruptures with the history objectified in the structure of the field, that is, those ruptures which are the product of a disposition formed by the history of the field and informed by that history, and hence inscribed in the continuity of the field." Bourdieu, *The Rules of Art,* 243. For further (and more sympathetic) discussions of the autopoiesis of such ruptures and the formation of epistemological "insides" and "outsides," see Thomas Kuhn, *The Structure of Scientific Revolutions* (Chicago: University of Chicago Press, 1962); Michel Foucault, *The Archaeology of Knowledge,* trans. A. M. Sheridan Smith (1969; repr., New York: Vintage, 1972); Robert K. Merton, "Insiders and Outsiders: A Chapter in the Sociology of Knowledge" (1972), in *The Sociology of Science: Theoretical and Empirical Investigations* (Chicago: University of Chicago Press, 1973), 99–138; and Cary Wolfe, *Critical Environments: Postmodern Theory and the Pragmatics of the "Outside"* (Minneapolis: University of Minnesota Press, 1998).

15. Gilles Deleuze, *Foucault,* trans. Séan Hand (1986; repr., London: Continuum, 2006), 70. See also Wolfe, *Critical Environments,* 101–17.

16. Cardinal, *Outsider Art,* 46.

17. Cardinal's formulation also differs markedly from Howard Becker's effort to formalize discrete "art worlds" as coherent sociological categories bound together by specific organizing conventions, social formations, and forms of tacit knowledge. "Wherever an art world exists," he writes, "it defines the boundaries of acceptable art, recognizing those who produce the work it can assimilate as artists entitled to full membership, and denying membership and its benefits to those whose work it cannot assimilate." Becker, *Art Worlds* (Berkeley: University of California Press, 1982), 226.

18. Jeffrey Nealon, *Post-Postmodernism, or, The Cultural Logic of Just-in-Time Capitalism* (Stanford, Calif.: Stanford University Press, 2012), 24.

19. This is not to overlook Bachelard's ultimate dismissal of such cultural material beyond its "function" for scientific progress or Prinzhorn's proprietary relation to the materials he collected.

20. Julia Kristeva, *Powers of Horror: An Essay on Abjection,* trans. Leon Roudiez (New York: Columbia University Press, 1982), 1.

21. Édouard Glissant, *The Poetics of Relation,* trans. Betsy Wing (Ann Arbor: University of Michigan Press, 1997), 20.

22. Glissant, *The Poetics of Relation,* 189, 21.

23. For a key study of cultural value through the lens of "rubbish," see Michael Thompson, *Rubbish Theory: The Creation and Destruction of Value* (1979; repr., London: Pluto Press, 2017). I invoke a "rummage heap" rather than a "rubbish heap" or dustbin in order to suggest that the category Thompson designates as rubbish is more expansive, and more malleable, than mere waste. See Jonathan P. Eburne, "Bargain-Basement Thought," in *Against Value in the Arts and Education,* ed. Sam Ladkin, Robert McKay, and Emile Bojesen (London: Rowman & Littlefield, 2016), 97–112.

24. Gilles Deleuze, *Cinema 2: The Time-Image,* trans. Hugh Tomlinson and Robert Galeta (Minneapolis: University of Minnesota Press, 1989), 131–62.

25. Alice Walker, "The Dummy in the Window: Joel Chandler Harris and the Invention of Uncle Remus" (1981), in *Living by the Word: Essays* (New York: Harcourt, Brace, 1988), 32.

26. As Thomas Kuhn writes, a theory "will transcend the known, becoming first and foremost a powerful tool for predicting and explaining the unknown. It will affect the future of science as well as the past." Kuhn, *The Copernican Revolution: Planetary Astronomy in the Development of Western Thought* (New York: Vintage, 1957), 40.

27. On "paper tools" and the everyday labor of theory, see David Kaiser, *Drawing Theories Apart: The Dispersion of Feynman Diagrams in Postwar Physics* (Chicago: University of Chicago Press, 2005), esp. 356–88.

28. Jonathan Culler, *The Literary in Theory* (Stanford, Calif.: Stanford University Press, 2007), 4. For a systematic treatment of the problems of heterodoxy and orthodoxy in the field of critical theory, see Wolfe, *Critical Environments.*

29. Collins, *Black Feminist Thought,* 269.

30. On "zombie concepts" see, for instance, Ulrich Beck and Elisabeth Beck-Gernsheim, *Individualization: Institutionalized Individualism and Its Social and Political Consequences* (London: Sage, 2001), and esp. Jonathan Rutherford, "Zombie Categories: An Interview with Ulrich Beck," 202–13. On zombie concepts and the culture of print, see Jonathan P. Eburne, "Zombie Arts and Letters," in *The Year's Work at the Zombie Research Center,* ed. Ed Comentale and Aaron Jaffe (Bloomington: Indiana University Press, 2014), 389–415.

31. As Jean-Michel Rabaté puts it, writing redemptively about the persistence of critical theory in the humanities, "if Theory is reduced to the ghost of itself, then this is a very obtrusive ghost that keeps walking and shaking its chains in our old academic castles." Rabaté, *The Future of Theory* (London: Blackwell, 2002), 10.

32. Gilles Deleuze and Félix Guattari, *What Is Philosophy?,* trans. Hugh Tomlinson and Graham Burchell (1991; repr., New York: Columbia University

Press, 1994), 22. For a discussion of Deleuze and systems theory, see Wolfe, *Critical Environments*, esp. 87–128. For a masterful investigation into the formation of concepts, see Isabelle Stengers, *Thinking with Whitehead: A Free and Wild Creation of Concepts*, trans. Michael Chase (Cambridge, Mass.: Harvard University Press, 2011). On self-generating concepts, see Gilbert Simondon, *L'individuation psychique et collective* (Paris: Aubier, 1989).

33. Sigmund Freud, "Psychoanalytic Notes upon an Autobiographical Account of a Case of Paranoia," in *Three Case Histories* (New York: Macmillan, 1963), 154.

34. Barbara Herrnstein Smith, *Belief and Resistance: Dynamics of Contemporary Intellectual Controversy* (Cambridge, Mass.: Harvard University Press, 1997), xvi.

35. See, for instance, Richard Wolin, *The Seduction of Unreason: The Intellectual Romance with Fascism from Nietzsche to Postmodernism* (Princeton, N.J.: Princeton University Press, 2004); Roger Scruton, *Fools, Frauds and Firebrands: Thinkers of the New Left* (London: Bloomsbury, 2015); and Daphne Patai and Wilfrido Corral, eds., *Theory's Empire: An Anthology of Dissent* (New York: Columbia University Press, 2005).

36. Ilya Prigogine and Isabelle Stengers, *Order Out of Chaos: Man's New Dialogue with Nature* (1979; repr., New York: Bantam, 1984), 80.

37. Michel Foucault, "Two Lectures," in *Power/Knowledge: Selected Interviews and Other Writings, 1972–1977*, ed. Colin Gordon (New York: Pantheon, 1980), 78–108, esp. 83 and 107.

38. Prigogine and Stengers, *Order Out of Chaos*, 213.

39. Prigogine and Stengers, *Order Out of Chaos*, 20.

40. Paul Feyerabend, *Against Method*, rev. ed. (London: Verso, 1988), 111; emphasis in original.

41. Feyerabend, *Against Method*, 11.

42. For recent studies that likewise sidestep the Popperian "demarcation problem" in favor of a cultural history of scientific institutions, see David Kaiser, *How the Hippies Saved Physics: Science, Counterculture, and the Quantum Revival* (New York: Norton, 2012); Michael D. Gordin, *The Pseudoscience Wars: Immanuel Velikovsky and the Birth of the Modern Fringe* (Chicago: University of Chicago Press, 2012); and Judith Roof, *The Poetics of DNA* (Minneapolis: University of Minnesota Press, 2007).

43. Gaston Bachelard, *La Formation de l'esprit scientifique* (1938; repr., Paris: Librairie Philosopique J. Vrin, 2004), 21.

44. The special issue, minus Sokal's essay, was republished as an edited volume that same year; see Andrew Ross, ed., *Science Wars* (Durham, N.C.: Duke University Press, 1996); see also Paul Gross and Norman Levitt, *Higher Superstition: The Academic Left and Its Quarrels with Science* (Baltimore: Johns Hopkins University Press, 1994).

45. *Intellectual Imposture* is the title for the U.K. edition of Sokal's book, coauthored with Jean Bricmont; in the United States it was published as *Fashionable*

Nonsense: Postmodern Intellectuals' Abuse of Science (New York: Picador, 1998). For an important account of the Sokal affair and a systematic reconsideration of the "bugbear" of relativism, see Barbara Herrnstein Smith, *Scandalous Knowledge: Science, Truth and the Human* (Durham, N.C.: Duke University Press, 2005), esp. 1–17 and 108–29.

46. See Alan Sokal and Jean Bricmont, "Cognitive Relativism in the Philosophy of Science," first published in *Intellectual Impostures* (1998) and reprinted in updated form in Alan Sokal, *Beyond the Hoax: Science, Philosophy and Culture* (Oxford: Oxford University Press, 2008), 171–227.

47. See, for instance, Michael Mann, "I'm a Scientist Who Has Gotten Death Threats. I Fear What May Happen under Trump," *Washington Post,* December 16, 2016, https://www.washingtonpost.com/opinions/this-is-what-the-coming-attack -on-climate-science-could-look-like/2016/12/16/e015cc24-bd8c-11e6-94ac -3d324840106c_story.html?utm_term=.c90f34094b8e.

48. Sokal, *Beyond the Hoax,* xi.

49. On the new "creative economy," see Sarah Brouillette, *Literature and the Creative Economy* (Stanford, Calif.: Stanford University Press, 2014), esp. 1–33.

50. Smith, *Scandalous Knowledge,* 115.

51. See Massimo Pigliucci, *Nonsense on Stilts: How to Tell Science from Bunk* (Chicago: University of Chicago Press, 2010).

52. Walker, "The Dummy in the Window," 32.

53. Bruno Latour, in "Why Has Critique Run Out of Steam? From Matters of Fact to Matters of Concern," *Critical Inquiry* 30 (2004): 225–48, asks (rhetorically) whether his earlier efforts to "show 'the lack of scientific certainty' inherent in the construction of facts" was a foolish mistake, given that it suddenly seemed as though the public is all too willing to discount anything resembling a fact. "While we spent years trying to detect the real prejudices hidden behind the appearance of objective statements," he writes, "I am now the one who naïvely believes in some facts because I am educated, while the other guys are too unsophisticated to be gullible" (227–28). His point is not that scholars should give up on studying the "construction of facts" but—like "every good military officer" (231)—that it is essential to reevaluate the tactics and equipment at their disposal. For Latour, this means recognizing that "constructions" are in fact multiple and complex interrelations with other "constructions" in reality, not that facts are made up. Latour's overall argument is to furnish critique with an expanded data set. "What would critique do," he writes, "if it could be associated with *more,* not with *less,* with *multiplication,* not *subtraction*" (248; emphasis in original). Whereas I admire and share this project of taking an expanded field of data into account when we study how ideas—as well as cultural and scientific "facts"—exist in the world, Latour's polemic against "critique" overlooks how methods, approaches, beliefs, concepts, and *doxa* are likewise multiple and complex constructions in their own right. My issue is therefore not with Latour's tongue-in-cheek militarism (though I do take issue with his presumptions about gullibility), since this militarism

stands in for a necessary militancy in the context of continued culture wars and science wars with literally earth-shattering consequences; my primary issue with his work has instead to do with his reductive picture of thought. That is, Latour's appeal to complexity (which he formalizes elsewhere as actor-network theory) occurs at the expense of a reified practice of "critique" he describes as a cartoonish process of "demystifying" only the objects a critic does not believe in, while remaining "unrepentantly posivitist" for the objects she does believe in and rising to a "perfectly good realist" for what she *really* cherishes (241). According to Latour, the presumption that one can apply utterly different methods of study to different kinds of objects is characteristic of the blindness of the "critical" project of dividing and separating the world rather than studying it in its full complexity. (This critique of critique has given rise in turn to all sorts of "postcritical" movements in humanities scholarship, which it will not be my task to survey here.) Suffice to say that this criticism of "critique" represents a long-standing position in Latour's work that argues in favor of "dealing with things" as assemblages of actants within complex networks rather than according to an epistemological asymmetry that distinguishes between the kinds of scrutiny afforded to different kinds of objects.

In his 1991 study *We Have Never Been Modern,* trans. Catherine Porter (Cambridge, Mass.: Harvard University Press, 1993), Latour argues against the modern separation (or "purification") of intellectual disciplines—and, more broadly, the separation of "nature" and "society," both of which amount to fundamental modes of "critique." He proposes instead a more holistic, interconnected scientific-sociological worldview that views "real" objects and phenomena as fundamentally entangled, imbricated, and immersed in networks of other objects, subjects, and phenomena. Since real-life phenomena such as climate change or moral law tend to be "hybrids" based on close connections between the social and the natural order, their study should likewise trace, even amplify, such points of contact. Latour's ensuing notion of epistemological "symmetry" thus proposes as its first principle to do away with "epistemological breaks, with *a priori* separations between 'sanctioned' and 'outdated' sciences, or artificial divisions between sociologists who study knowledge, those who study belief systems, and those who study the sciences" (94; emphasis in original). Latour's call for a more holistic sociology of knowledge—a self-described "Copernican counterrevolution" (78)—that traces and amplifies the interlocking threads, networks, and human and nonhuman actors/actants of epistemic hybrids has proven influential. Latour has been criticized not only by the likes of Alan Sokal (in whose hoax article Latour is one of the targets), but also by fellow sociologists and anthropologists, for his relative blindness to the history of ideas. A telling issue, for instance, is that he derives his holistic approach to "hybrids" from a generalized set of indigenous "premoderns" to whom he gestures but never grants intellectual autonomy or legitimacy, even in subsequent writings. See, for instance, Zoe Todd, "An Indigenous Feminist's Take on the Ontological Turn: 'Ontology' Is Just Another Word for Colonialism (Urbane Adventurer: Amiskwacî)," Urbane

Adventurer, October 24, 2014, https://umaincertaantropologia.org/2014/10/26/an-indigenous-feminists-take-on-the-ontological-turn-ontology-is-just-another-word-for-colonialism-urbane-adventurer-amiskwaci/.

My own work, while informed by Latour's in many respects, recognizes that the breaks and separations Latour seeks to purge are themselves worthy objects of study and critical attention. Such divisions (whether between nature and society or between and among different objects of study, etc.) are not always the tired automatisms of old-fashioned disciplinary habit, though "discipline" is of course a notable regulatory force in establishing canons, limits, hierarchies, and other forms of distinction. The kinds of divisions Latour rails against are often imposed or guarded by political and economic forces and institutions and, in some cases—especially in their more metaphysical or spiritual guises—can also create sites of refuge and meaning as much as they can be blinding and problematic. My work thus strives to recognize such second-order mediations in their particularity rather than seeking to assimilate them within a singularizing "realism" or, as Latour puts it, a "Copernican counterrevolution."

54. Theodore Ziolkowski, *Lure of the Arcane: The Literature of Cult and Conspiracy* (Baltimore: Johns Hopkins University Press, 2013).

55. Gross and Levitt, *Higher Superstition*, 252.

56. Ishmael Reed, *Mumbo Jumbo* (New York: Scribner, 1972), 104.

57. See, for instance, René Alleau, *Hitler et les sociétés secrètes: Enquête sur les sources occultes du nazisme* (Paris: Grasset, 1969); and Nicholas Goodrick-Clarke, *The Occult Roots of Nazism: Secret Aryan Cults and Their Influence on Nazi Ideology* (New York: New York University Press, 1992).

58. Reed, *Mumbo Jumbo*, 33.

59. C. L. R. James, *The Black Jacobins: Toussaint L'Ouverture and the San Domingo Revolution* (1963; repr., New York: Vintage, 1989), 396.

60. As Andrew Ross stresses in his introduction to *Science Wars,* there is nothing that links creationism with feminism, or Afrocentric history with Holocaust denial, other than the rhetorical excesses of pundits or the persecution mania of allegedly proscience debunkers of postmodern pseudoscience (11).

61. See Wolin, *The Seduction of Unreason.*

1. THE ALIEN KNOWLEDGE OF NAG HAMMADI

1. Jean Doresse, *The Secret Books of the Egyptian Gnostics* (1958; repr., New York: MJF, 1986), 120.

2. Jacques Lacarrière, *The Gnostics,* trans. Nina Rootes (New York: Dutton, 1977), 10, 43.

3. See Hans Jonas, *The Gnostic Religion,* 2nd ed. (Boston: Beacon, 1963), esp. 49–51. This is, of course, a general overview of a heterogeneous set of religious schools and tendencies that have been known as Gnosticism since at least the seventeenth century; the commonality among so-called Gnostic sects, schools,

and practices owes as much to their common suppression (as Christian heresy) as to a categorical unity among them. As I will discuss later in the chapter, the very category of Gnosticism is a composite one that easily falls apart under scrutiny. See Michael A. Williams, *Rethinking "Gnosticism": An Argument for Dismantling a Dubious Category* (Princeton, N.J.: Princeton University Press, 1996).

4. Philip Jenkins, *Hidden Gospels: How the Search for Jesus Lost Its Way* (New York: Oxford University Press, 2001), 22, 23.

5. On the discovery of Darger's oeuvre and its posthumous entrance into the art world, see Klaus Bresendech, ed., *Henry Darger* (Munich: Prestel, 2009) 13–14; and Michael Bonesteel, ed., *Henry Darger: Art and Selected Writings* (New York: Rizzoli, 2000), 13–14.

6. See Michael Moon, *Darger's Resources* (Durham, N.C.: Duke University Press, 2012). On the significance of rubbish as an economic category that enables the transformation in value of physical objects (and ideas) from "transient" (objects with decreasing value over time) to "durable" (objects with stable or increasing value over time), see Michael Thompson, *Rubbish Theory: The Creation and Destruction of Value* (1979; repr., London: Pluto Press, 2017).

7. Vivian Yee, "Outsider's Art Is Saluted at Columbia, Then Lost Anew," *New York Times*, June 7, 2015, https://www.nytimes.com/2015/06/08/nyregion /outsiders-art-is-saluted-at-columbia-then-lost-anew.html?mcubz=0.

8. See Alice Walker, "Looking for Zora" (1975), and "Zora Neale Hurston: A Cautionary Tale and a Partisan View" (1979), in *In Search of Our Mothers' Gardens: Womanist Prose* (New York: Harcourt, Brace and Jovanovich, 1983), 93–116 and 83–92, respectively.

9. Walker quotes this line, citing Elaine Pagels's *The Gnostic Gospels* (New York: Random House, 1979) as the epigraph for the second section of *In Search of Our Mothers' Gardens*, 118. On Walker and Gnosticism, see, for instance, Hedda Ben-Bassat, "Alice Walker's Poetics: Ethic Narratives and Their Gnostic Double," in *Prophets without Vision: Subjectivity and the Sacred in Contemporary American Writing* (Lewisburg, Pa.: Bucknell University Press, 2000), 141–68.

10. Karen Barad, *Meeting the Universe Halfway: Quantum Physics and the Entanglement of Matter and Meaning* (Durham, N.C.: Duke University Press, 2007), 148. In what follows I take Barad's posthumanist notions of "intra-activity" and "agential realism" literally, if somewhat perversely and contentiously, in extending the notion that nonhumans "partak[e] in the world's active engagement in practices of knowing" (149) to the sphere of religious history, whereby the participation of nonhuman factors in the work of knowing extends not only to the metaphysical—as in the case of the inhuman, supramundane, "alien god" attributed to Gnosticism—but also to the scholarly and historical.

11. See, for instance, Amy Hollywood, *Sensible Ecstasy: Mysticism, Sexual Difference, and the Demands of History* (Chicago: University of Chicago Press, 2001), 7.

12. The Gospel of Thomas, trans. Thomas O. Lambdin, in *The Nag Hammadi Library*, ed. James M. Robinson (San Francisco: Harper and Row, 1978), 123.

The discovery of the Gospel of Thomas in Codex II corresponded with fragments from previously discovered Greek texts in the Papyrus Oxyrhynchus (named after the site of its discovery in Oxyrhynchus, Egypt) and thus was one of several sets of cross-references used to date the Nag Hammadi Library, as well as to confirm the authenticity of the Gospel of Thomas. See also chapter 3, note 12.

13. There is no shortage of critical and popular literature on such questions. See Pagels, *The Gnostic Gospels*, xv; Karen L. King, *The Gospel of Mary of Magdala: Jesus and the First Woman Apostle* (Santa Rosa, Calif.: Polebridge, 2003); and Esther de Boer, *The Mary Magdalene Cover-Up: The Sources behind the Myth* (London: Bloomsbury, 2007). For a well-researched if fundamentally skeptical survey of such discourses, see Jenkins, *Hidden Gospels*.

14. See Karen L. King, *What Is Gnosticism?* (Cambridge, Mass.: Harvard University Press, 2003), 58–63; and William Rowe, "Adolf von Harnack and the Concept of Hellenization," in *Hellenization Revisited: Shaping a Christian Response within the Greco-Roman World*, ed. Wendy Hellerman (Lanham, Md.: University Press of America, 1994), 69–98, esp. 76–77.

15. Henri-Charles Puech, "Où en est le problème de gnosticisme?" (1934), in *En quête de la Gnose*, vol. 1, *La Gnose et le temps et autres essais* (Paris: Gallimard, 1978), 147.

16. See G. R. S. Mead, trans., *Pistis Sophia* (London: Watkins, 1896), http://gnosis.org/library/psoph.htm. Offering an extensive outline of the gnostic cosmology, the *Pistis Sophia* became available to readers of Latin and Greek in 1851, in French in 1895, and in German in 1905. For English readers the text was translated by Mead, the prominent English religious historian and theosophist; he began publishing installments in magazine form in 1890, and the full edition appeared in 1896.

17. H. P. Blavatsky, *The Secret Doctrine: The Synthesis of Science, Religion, and Philosophy*, vol. 1, *Cosmogenesis* (1888; repr., Pasadena, Calif.: Theosophical University Press, 2014), xl.

18. For discussions of the heresiological discourse, see King, *What Is Gnosticism?*, 20–54; and Kurt Rudolph, *Gnosis: The Nature and History of Gnosticism*, ed. R. McL. Wilson, trans. P. W. Coxon, K. H. Kuhn, and R. McL. Wilson (New York: Harper and Row, 1987), 9–30.

19. Irenaeus, *Against Heresies*, in *The Ante-Nicene Fathers*, vol. 1, *The Apostolic Fathers with Justin Martyr and Irenaeus*, ed. Alexander Roberts (New York: Cosino, 2007), 316.

20. Irenaeus, *Against Heresies*, 315.

21. For an overview of the history of Gnosticism as a modern concept, see Henry Chadwick, "The Domestication of Gnosis," Gilles Quispel, "Gnosis and Psychology," Carsten Colpe, "The Challenge of Gnostic Thought for Philosophy, Alchemy and Literature," and Harold Bloom, "Lying against Time: Gnosis, Poetry, Criticism," in *The Rediscovery of Gnosticism: Proceedings of the International Conference on Gnosticism at Yale*, ed. Bentley Layton (Leiden: Brill, 1980), 3–16,

17–31, 32–56, and 57–72, respectively. See also Bentley Layton, "Prolegomena to the Study of Ancient Gnosticism," in *The Social World of the First Christians*, ed. L. Michael White and O. Larry Yarbrough (Minneapolis: Fortress Press, 1995), 334–50.

22. Blavatsky, *The Secret Doctrine*, 1:xxiii.

23. See Eric Voegelin, *Science, Politics and Gnosticism*, trans. William J. Fitzpatrick (Washington, D.C.: Regnery, 1977), 23, 30. See also Eric Voegelin, *The New Science of Politics* (Chicago: University of Chicago Press, 1952), esp. 107–61.

24. Rudolph, *Gnosis*, 55.

25. The most gripping, and most canonical, versions of this story are those of Elaine Pagels, who published an account in the *New York Review of Books* in 1979 as part of a series of articles that would become her landmark study *The Gnostic Gospels;* and of James M. Robinson, who researched the story extensively and has offered several detailed versions throughout his career. See also John Dart, *The Laughing Savior: The Discovery and Significance of the Nag Hammadi Gnostic Library* (New York: Harper and Row, 1976), repr. as *The Jesus of Heresy and History: The Discovery and Meaning of the Nag Hammadi Library* (New York: HarperCollins, 1988). For a study of the formation of this origin story, see Thomas Crawford, "Curating Gnosis: Discovery, Power and the Creation of (a) Discipline" (PhD diss., Claremont Graduate University, 2011), esp. 93–116.

26. See James M. Robinson, "Introduction," in *The Nag Hammadi Library in English,* ed. James M. Robinson (San Francisco: Harper and Row, 1978), 21–22.

27. Robinson, "Preface," 21. See also Elaine Pagels, "The Discovery of the Gnostic Gospels," *New York Review of Books,* October 25, 1979, repr. in Pagels, *The Gnostic Gospels,* xiii–xiv.

28. Robinson, "Preface," 23. By contrast, W. C. van Unnik, *Newly Discovered Gnostic Writings: A Preliminary Survey of the Nag Hammadi Find* (1958; repr., Naperville, Ill.: Allenson, 1960), 10, is more measured in its tale of destruction: "It seems that a few pages have been burned, but the greater part was fortunately spared; and although split up into various pieces, it has not thereby suffered irreparable damage."

29. James M. Robinson, "Nag Hammadi: The First Fifty Years," in *The Nag Hammadi Library after Fifty Years,* ed. John D. Turner and Anne McGuire (Leiden: Brill, 1997), 6.

30. Robinson, "Preface," 23. For an analysis and critique of Robinson's presumptions about the "supreme Otherness" of Middle Eastern culture, see Crawford, "Curating Gnosis," esp. 101–2.

31. The most exhaustive study of this drama of recovery is doubtlessly James M. Robinson, "The Jung Codex: Rise and Fall of a Monopoly," *Religious Studies Review* 3, no. 1 (1977): 17–30.

32. One tractate, the Gospel of Thomas, was published in photographic facsimile in 1956, and in English translation with a transcription of the Coptic original in 1959. See A. Guillaumont, Henri-Charles Puech, Gilles Quispel,

Walter Till, and Yassah 'Abd al Masih, trans., *The Gospel According to Thomas* (Leiden: Brill, 1959).

33. Van Unnik, *Newly Discovered Gnostic Writings*, 9–10.

34. According to Bentley Layton, the modern usage of the term *Gnosticism* to describe a discrete set of religious beliefs came from the seventeenth-century Protestant scholar Henry More, who adopted it from Irenaeus's usage in *Against Heresies*. See Layton, "Prolegomena," 334–50.

35. See Jenkins, *Hidden Gospels*, esp. 27–53, 124–47.

36. Adolf von Harnack, *Lehrbuch der Dogmengeschichte*, vol. 1 (1886), trans. Neil Buchanan as *History of Dogma*, vol. 1 (London: Williams and Norgate, 1894), 240. On Harnack and Hans Lietzmann, see Puech, "Où en est le problème de Gnosticisme," esp. 143–45.

37. Harnack, *History of Dogma*, 240–42.

38. G. R. S. Mead, *Fragments of a Faith Forgotten* (1900; repr., New York: University Books, 1960), 22.

39. Mead, *Fragments of a Faith Forgotten*, 20.

40. Mead, *Fragments of a Faith Forgotten*, 22.

41. Jean Dubuffet, *Asphyxiante Culture* (1968; repr., Paris: Editions du Minuit, 1986), 77–80.

42. Kenneth Rexroth, "A Primer of Gnosticism," in Mead, *Fragments of a Faith Forgotten*, xiv–xv.

43. Rexroth, "Primer," xiii.

44. Frances Swiney, *The Esoteric Teaching of the Gnostics* (London: Yellon, Williams & Co., 1909), vii.

45. Swiney, *The Esoteric Teaching of the Gnostics*, 6.

46. Swiney, *The Esoteric Teaching of the Gnostics*, 78; emphasis in original.

47. Swiney, *The Esoteric Teaching of the Gnostics*, 78.

48. Mead, *Fragments of a Faith Forgotten*, 18–19.

49. Mead, *Fragments of a Faith Forgotten*, 21.

50. See Jeffrey J. Kripal, *The Serpent's Gift: Gnostic Reflections on the Study of Religion* (Chicago: University of Chicago Press, 2006), esp. 2–24.

51. Marvin Meyer, *The Gnostic Discoveries: The Impact of the Nag Hammadi Library* (New York: Harper and Row, 2005), 44.

52. Stephen Emmel, "Religious Tradition, Textual Transmission, and the Nag Hammadi Codices," in *The Nag Hammadi Library after Fifty Years*, ed. John D. Turner and Anne McGuire (Leiden: Brill, 1997), notes that the Nag Hammadi codices may not have been bound until the time of their burial, and thus the books are "not necessarily a 'library' in any historically meaningful sense" (36).

53. See Michael A. Williams, *Rethinking "Gnosticism": An Argument for Dismantling a Dubious Category* (Princeton, N.J.: Princeton University Press, 1996); King, *What Is Gnosticism?*; and Puech, "Où en est le problème de gnosticisme?"

54. On the Berlin Codex, see King, *What Is Gnosticism?*, 80–83; Rudolph, *Gnosis*, 26–30; and King, *The Gospel of Mary of Magdala*, 7–12.

55. See Brian P. Copenhaver, ed., *Hermetica: The Greek Corpus Hermeticum and the Latin Asclepius* (Cambridge: Cambridge University Press, 1992).

56. Puech, "Où en est le problème de gnosticisme?," 145.

57. For the initial publication, see Ugo Bianchi, ed., *Le Origini dello Gnosticismo: Colloquio di Messina, 13–18 Avrilo 1966* (Leiden: Brill, 1967). For further discussion, see King, *What Is Gnosticism?*, 167–72; and Rudolph, *Gnosis*, 56–59.

58. Jonas, *The Gnostic Religion*, 49. See also Hans Jonas, *Gnosis und späntiker Geist*, vol. 1, *Die Muthologische Gnosis* (1934; repr., Göttingen: Vandenhoek und Ruprecht, 1964).

59. Nathaniel Mackey, "The Far Side of Mastery: An Interview with Nathaniel Mackey," *ASAP/Journal* 1, no. 2 (2016): 191.

60. The Gnosis Archive, http://www.gnosis.org.

61. The significance of Jungianism, and Jung himself, to the twentieth-century reception of Gnosticism before and after Nag Hammadi is well documented. See, for instance, Gilles Quispel, "Gnosis and Culture," "Herman Hesse and Gnosis," and "Jung and Pauli," in *Gnostica, Judaica, Catholica: Collected Essays of Gilles Quispel*, ed. Johannes van Oort (Leiden: Brill, 2008), 141–153, 243–261, and 567–572, respectively. See also Gilles Quispel, "Gnosis and Psychology," in *The Rediscovery of Gnosticism: Proceedings of the International Conference on Gnosticism at Yale*, ed. Bentley Layton (Leiden: Brill, 1980), 17–31; and Stephan A. Hoeller, *The Gnostic Jung* (Wheaton, Ill.: Quest, 1982). On Velikovsky and the post–World War II discourse on pseudoscience and mysticism, see Michael Gordin, *The Pseudoscience Wars: Immanuel Velikovsky and the Birth of the Modern Fringe* (Chicago: University of Chicago Press, 2012).

62. Jonas, *The Gnostic Religion*, xiv.

2. GNOSTIC MATERIALISM

1. The second stanza of Melville's poem likewise laments the dominion of a fallen world: "Indolence is heaven's ally here, / And energy the child of hell: / The Good Man pouring from his pitcher clear / But brims the poisoned well." Herman Melville, "Fragments of a Lost Gnostic Poem of the Twelfth Century" (1891), in *The Writings of Herman Melville*, vol. 11, *Published Poems*, ed. Robert C. Ryan, Harrison Hayford, Alma MacDougall Reising, and G. Thomas Tanselle (Evanston, Ill.: Northwestern University Press, 2009), 284.

2. Published in 1891, Melville's poem took part in the broad revival of interest in spiritualism and ancient religions in the United States and Europe. Philip Jenkins proposes that Melville's poem refers to the Cathars or Albigensians, groups of Christian dissidents who lived in the southwest of France who were massacred during the Albigensian Crusade (1209–29), a military campaign organized by Pope Innocent III to eradicate Catharism. This history forms the backdrop of Gérard de Sède's popular histories of the Languedoc region, which will be discussed in chapter 3. See Jenkins, "Alternative Scriptures: Melville's 'Lost Gnostic

Poem,'" in *Anxious Bench* (blog), June 19, 2017, http://www.patheos.com/blogs/anxiousbench/2017/06/fragments-lost-gnostic-poem/.

3. Hans Jonas, "Life, Death, and the Body in the Theory of Being," in *The Phenomenon of Life: Toward a Philosophical Biology* (New York: Harper and Row, 1966), 14.

4. Frances Swiney, *The Esoteric Teaching of the Gnostics* (London: Yellon, Williams, 1909), 55.

5. By "truth procedure," I refer to the philosopher Alain Badiou's term for an unfolding generic process in which evidence, concepts, and subjects are mutually implicated and ultimately suspended. "Truth" designates not the immediate judgment a particular set of claims and conditions as either verifiable or false, but instead the formal extension of this mutual implication in the name of an as-yet-unknowable "event," a ruptural break with the endless oscillation of the already known. A truth procedure does not so much resolve into a logical conclusion, in other words, as constitute the form of such a break: an "epistemological rupture," in Gaston Bachelard's terms, that yields new commitments rather than new paradigms or orthodoxies. It thus names an ethical rather than logical pursuit, to be judged not in terms of factual truth and falsehood but in terms of fidelity and, in the case of its foreclosure, evil. Badiou, *Ethics: An Essay on the Understanding of Evil,* trans. Peter Hallward (London; Verso, 2001). Put otherwise, a truth procedure resembles the restlessness of the "unhappy consciousness" we find in Hegel, which strives endlessly toward a higher synthesis; yet it does so without the Hegelian panlogistic master spirit or consciousness that governs such processes from beyond. A truth procedure names the restlessness immanent to the formal extension of a process itself; the event it precipitates is an event within the history of knowledge, which opens up at the point where the endless regime of circulation folds in upon itself. Badiou, *Infinite Thought: Truth and the Return to Philosophy,* trans. Justin Clemens and Oliver Feltham (New York: Continuum, 2003), 49.

6. Roger Cardinal, *Outsider Art* (New York: Praeger, 1972), 179.

7. On the notion of matter as "ontologically agnostic," see Barbara Herrnstein Smith, *Scandalous Knowledge: Science, Knowledge, and the Human* (Durham, N.C.: Duke University Press, 2006), 6.

8. Georges Bataille, "Le bas matérialisme et la gnose," *Documents* 2, no. 1 (1930), trans. Allan Stoekl as "Base Materialism and Gnosticism," in *Visions of Excess: Selected Writings, 1927–1939,* ed. Allan Stoekl (Minneapolis: University of Minnesota Press, 1985), 51. Quotations herein are from Stoekl's translation.

9. Alfred North Whitehead, *The Concept of Nature* (1920; repr., Cambridge: Cambridge University Press, 1961), 29.

10. The Gospel of Thomas, trans. Stephen J. Patterson and James M. Robinson, the Nag Hammadi Library, http://www.gnosis.org/naghamm/gth_pat_rob.htm.

11. A compilation of more than a hundred such aphorisms, the Gospel of Thomas professes to contain "the secret sayings that the living Jesus spoke and Didymos Judas Thomas recorded." Representing the Plato to Jesus's Socrates,

Thomas's written record of these "secret" sayings both articulates and demonstrates their betrayal as secrets: in the process of "coming to know" what is in front of us, all that is hidden will become manifest.

12. See Michael W. Grondin, "An Interlinear Coptic-English Translation of the Gospel of Thomas," n.d., http://www.gospel-thomas.net/x_transl.htm.

13. The Gospel of Thomas epitomizes such mediation; indeed, questions about the text's authenticity and authorship have governed its scholarly reception. Considered to be older than the all New Testament Gospels canonized at Nicaea, with the exception of St. Paul's letters, the Gospel of Thomas is characterized by its negative movement of manifesting and knowing. Promising nonapocalyptic access to the kingdom of God, the "knowing" it advocates as the process of revelation operates on the sphere of vernacular experience: as an event that takes place within our encounter with what is right in front of us, in the phenomena we encounter every day. Greek fragments and other traces of the Gospel of Thomas were recorded in previously discovered Greek fragments from the Papyrus Oxyrhynchus (named after the site of its discovery in Oxyrhynchus, Egypt) and thus composed one of several sets of cross-references used to date the tractates of the Nag Hammadi discovery in general, as well as to argue for the authenticity of the Gospel of Thomas itself. See Henri-Charles Puech, *En quête de la gnose*, vol. 2, *Sur l'évangile selon Thomas* (Paris: Gallimard, 1978). See also Simon Gothercole, ed., *The Gospel of Thomas: An Introduction and Commentary* (Leiden: Brill, 2014).

14. Stefanos Geroulanos, *An Atheism That Is Not Humanist Emerges in French Thought* (Stanford, Calif.: Stanford University Press, 2010), 51; emphasis in original.

15. See Jean Wahl, *Vers le concret: Études d'histoire de la philosophie contemporaine (William James, Whitehead, Gabriel Marcel)* (1932; repr., Paris: Vrin, 2004); 29–33, 200. For a discussion of Wahl's "empiricist mysticism" in the context of French Hegelianism, see Bruce Baugh, *French Hegel: From Surrealism to Postmodernism* (London: Routledge, 2003), esp. 37.

16. See Wahl, *Vers le concret*.

17. See, for instance, Eugène de Faye, *Gnostiques et gnosticismes* (Paris: Leroux, 1913), and especially its attention to dating extant Gnostic documents. On other physical evidence, such as carved gemstones, cf. Charles W. King, *The Gnostics and Their Remains, Ancient and Medieval* (London: Neff, 1887).

18. For an overview, see Geroulanos, *An Atheism That Is Not Humanist*, esp. 51–58. For a career overview of Henri-Charles Puech, see *Mélanges d'histoire de réligions, offerts à Henri-Charles Puech* (Paris: PUF, 1974).

19. On Bataille's work at the Cabinet de médailles, where he held a position from 1924 to 1930, see Laurent Henrichs, "Georges Bataille au Cabinet de médailles de la Bibliothèque nationale," *Bulletin d'informations de l'ABF* 178 (1998): 32–36.

20. Georges Bataille, *Oeuvres Complètes*, vol. 1, *Premiers écrits 1922–1940* (Paris: Gallimard, 1979), 99. For discussions of Bataille's early work as a medievalist, see Jean-Pierre Le Bouler, "Georges Bataille, le Moyen Âge et la chevalerie:

De la thèse d'École des chartes (1922) au Procès de Gilles de Rais (1959)," *Bibliothèque de l'École de Chartes* 164 (2006): 539–60; see also Denis Hollier, *Against Architecture: The Writings of Georges Bataille,* trans. Betsy Wing (Cambridge, Mass.: MIT Press, 1989), esp. 14–45.

21. For a compelling examination of Bataille as a medievalist, and of the relationship between Bataille's dialectic of knowledge and ignorance of contemporary Thomism, see Bruce Holsinger, *The Premodern Condition: Medievalism and the Making of Theory* (Chicago: University of Chicago Press, 2005), 26–56; see also Amy Hollywood, *Sensible Ecstasy: Mysticism, Sexual Difference, and the Demands of History* (Chicago: University of Chicago Press, 2002), 25–112.

22. Holsinger, *The Premodern Condition,* 38.

23. See, for instance, Hollier, *Against Architecture,* 123. See also Stuart Kendall, *Georges Bataille* (London: Reaktion, 2007), 66–75; and Michel Surya, *Georges Bataille: An Intellectual Biography,* trans. Krzyzstof Fijalkowski and Michael Richardson (London: Verso, 2002), 116–25.

24. Bataille, *Oeuvres Complètes,* 1:120–21.

25. Bataille, "Le cheval académique," *Documents* 1, no. 1 (1929): 29; my translation. For a full English translation, see Georges Bataille, "The Academic Horse," in *Undercover Surrealism: Georges Bataille and DOCUMENTS,* ed. Dawn Ades and Simon Baker (Cambridge, Mass.: MIT Press, 2006), 236–39.

26. Bataille, "Le cheval académique," 30.

27. Bataille, "Base Materialism and Gnosticism," 47.

28. Bataille, "Base Materialism and Gnosticism," 48.

29. Bataille, "Base Materialism and Gnosticism," 47.

30. Bataille, "Base Materialism and Gnosticism," 48.

31. Bataille, "Base Materialism and Gnosticism," 46.

32. See Peter Tracey Connor, *Georges Bataille and the Mysticism of Sin* (Baltimore: Johns Hopkins University Press, 2003).

33. Bataille, "Base Materialism and Gnosticism," 46.

34. See Georges Bataille and Raymond Queneau, "La critique des fondements de la dialectique hégélienne," in *Critique Sociale* (1932), trans. Allan Stoekl as "The Critique of the Foundations of the Hegelian Dialectic," in Stoekl, *Visions of Excess,* 105–15; see also Bataille's 1936 contribution to *Recherches philosophiques,* "Le Labyrinthe," trans. Allan Stoekl as "The Labyrinth," in Stoekl, *Visions of Excess,* 171–77. For a discussion of Bataille's Hegelianism, see Rudolph Gasché, *Georges Bataille: Phenomenology and Phantasmatology,* trans. Roland Végsö (Stanford, Calif.: Stanford University Press, 2012), esp. 238–76; see also Baugh, *French Hegel,* 71–92.

35. André Breton, *Seconde Manifeste de surréalisme* (1929), in *Oeuvres complètes,* vol. 1, ed. Marguerite Bonnet (Paris: Gallimard, 1988), 781. See also André Breton, *Manifestoes of Surrealism,* trans. Richard Seaver and Helen Lane (Ann Arbor: University of Michigan Press, 1968), 123, where the term is translated as "an attack of conscience." See also Baugh, *French Hegel,* 51–68.

36. Bataille, "Base Materialism and Gnosticism," 46.

37. Bataille, "Base Materialism and Gnosticism," 49.

38. Bataille, "Base Materialism and Gnosticism," 51.

39. Henri-Charles Puech, "Les 'Prisons' de Jean-Baptiste Piranèse," *Documents* 2, no. 4 (1930): 204.

40. Outlining the long history of magical religious syncretisms in late antiquity, Puech's second article for *Documents* traces the iconography of Gnosticism's "magical monotheism" as an accumulation of figures from Hellenistic, Egyptian, and Assyro-Babylonian magical cults. The result, he explains, is a "pantheistic god." Approached historically, in other words, Gnosticism discloses its discontinuous formation as a religion. Yet Puech's interest also surpasses mere historical understanding; much like this "pantheistic god" itself, his approach would strive to supersede the heterogeneity of Gnosticism's origins and instead take up the concrete problems that animated it as a living cultural system. Henri-Charles Puech, "Le Dieu Bésa et la magie hellénistique," *Documents* 2, no. 7 (1930): 422.

41. Bataille, "Base Materialism and Gnosticism," 45.

42. Puech, "Prisons," 199.

43. Henri-Charles Puech, "Phénoménologie de la Gnose: Collège de France, 1952–1957," in *En quête de la gnose,* vol. 1 (Paris: NRF, 1978), 199.

44. Henri-Charles Puech, "Où en est le problème du gnosticisme?" (1934), in *En quête de la gnose,* 1:143–213.

45. Puech, "Phénoménologie de la Gnose," 189.

46. Henri-Charles Puech, "Préface," in *En quête de la gnose,* 1:xiii.

47. Puech, "Préface," xv. The attention to "practical and concrete sentiments" that managed and oriented the movement of Gnostic thought also characterized Puech's relationship to the material texts of the Gnostic Gospels themselves after the Nag Hammadi discovery. For Puech, Gnosticism's being-in-the-world set the terms of our own approach it its fundamental questions. Whereas James Robinson would later critique Puech for his role in "monopolizing" the Nag Hammadi Library—that is, in policing scholarly access to the Jung Codex—Puech's later scholarship was dedicated to the intensive study of the individual "expressions" of Gnosticism itself. The second volume of Puech's collected works is devoted entirely to the translation and exegesis of a single Nag Hammadi tractate, the Gospel of Thomas, a key text in Codex II.

48. Karen L. King, *What Is Gnosticism?* (Cambridge, Mass.: Belknap Press of Harvard University Press, 2003), 117. See also Puech, "Phénoménologie de la Gnose," 185–214.

49. Puech, "Phénoménologie de la Gnose," 191.

50. Hans Jonas, "Gnosticism, Existentialism, and Nihilism," in *The Phenomenon of Life,* 229.

51. Hans Jonas, *The Gnostic Religion: The Message of the Alien God and the Beginnings of Christianity,* 2nd ed. (Boston: Beacon, 1963), 271.

52. See Samuel Fleischacker, *Heidegger's Jewish Followers: Essays on Hannah Arendt, Leo Strauss, Hans Jonas, and Emmanuel Levinas* (Pittsburgh: Duquesne University Press, 2008), esp. chap. 6.

53. Jonas rehearses this distinction between phenomenology and ontologically minded "contemporary philosophy" in "Heidegger and Theology," *Review of Metaphysics* 18, no. 2 (1964), repr. in *The Phenomenon of Life*, 239.

54. Jonas, *The Gnostic Religion*, 64.

55. Jonas, *The Gnostic Religion*, 65.

56. Jonas, *The Gnostic Religion*, 261.

57. Jonas, *The Gnostic Religion*, 59.

58. Jonas, *The Gnostic Religion*, 60.

59. Whereas Jonas's writing has been deeply influential to the field of Gnosticism studies in general, traditional scholars of early Christianity did not immediately embrace it. Gilles Quispel, for instance, concludes his 1965 review of the third edition of *Gnosis und spätantiker Geist* with the snide remark, "This book has remained very German. [Henri-Charles] Puech in Paris, [Robert] Grant in Chicago, [Erik] Peterson in Rome, [Gershom] Scholem in Jerusalem are rarely mentioned. In a preface the author complains about a lack of response from scholars. But in order to get a response one must be willing to discuss." Gilles Quispel, review of *Gnosis und spätantiker Geist*, 3rd ed., *Church History* 34, no. 2 (1965): 216.

60. Hans Jonas, "Heidegger and Theology," in *The Phenomenon of Life*, 258; emphasis in original.

61. Hans Jonas, *Memoirs*, ed. Christian Weise, trans. Krishna Winston (Waltham, Mass.: Brandeis University Press, 2008), 142.

62. Jonas, *Memoirs*, 142.

63. Jonas asks in *The Gnostic Religion*, "What do the new finds add to our knowledge and understanding of Christian Gnosticism? It is, of course, simply not the case that our evidence hitherto was scanty. The patristic testimony was rich and stands vindicated with every test by newly recovered originals (i.e., texts preserved on their own and not through doxography)" (292). The Nag Hammadi Library, and the other finds that came to light along with it, such as the Berlin Codex, confirmed rather than added to the archive of what was already known about Gnosticism—or at least Christian Gnosticism; for as Jonas insinuates, the Coptic manuscripts preserved only part of the broader phenomenon of Gnosticism, such as the work of the Manicheans or the Iranian Mandeans, who feature prominently in Jonas's own historical survey. Moreover, even as he doubly qualifies the newness of the Nag Hammadi discovery, Jonas also challenges the self-evidence of its status as a library. In terms later taken up by some of the most prominent religions scholars in the field—such as Karen King and Michael Williams—Jonas reminds readers that the Nag Hammadi codices are not "originals" but copies of translations of copies. "This aspect is easily forgotten in the elation over the mere physical age of the writing which happens to come into our hands," he writes, and thus "the reminder is not out of place that nothing in the new sources, being translations one and all (from

Greek into Coptic) equals in directness of testimony the direct quotations in the Greek Fathers (such as, e.g., Ptolemy's *Letters to Flora*), which render the Greek originals themselves—even if a longer line of copyists then intervene between them and our oldest manuscript" (292). Jonas overlooks, however, the libelous heresiological context for such "direct quotations." Yet even so, his inclinations are clear: the authenticity of the Gnostic religion lies not in its textual existence but in its existential bearing, the struggle with historicity that constitutes its burning counterhistorical and supramundane striving. For a systematic argument in favor of Jonas's observation that knowledge of Gnosticism was robust well before the Nag Hammadi discovery, see Phillip Jenkins, *Hidden Gospels: How the Search for Jesus Lost Its Way* (New York: Oxford University Press, 2001).

64. Jonas, *Memoirs,* 187.

65. Jonas, "Heidegger and Theology," 239; emphasis in original.

66. Jonas, "Heidegger and Theology," 247.

67. Jonas, "Heidegger and Theology," 248.

68. Jonas, "Heidegger and Theology," 239.

69. Jonas, "Heidegger and Theology," 261.

70. Jonas, "Heidegger and Theology," 261.

71. The contents of the Berlin Codex 8502 are incorporated in *The Gnostic Bible,* ed. Willis Barnstone and Marvin W. Meyer (Boston: New Seeds, 2006). For a discussion, see, for instance, King, *What Is Gnosticism?,* 80–83.

72. James M. Robinson, "Introduction," in *The Nag Hammadi Library in English,* ed. James M. Robinson (San Francisco: Harper and Row, 1978), 1. The sociologist Theodore Roszak invokes early Christianity in his landmark *The Making of a Counter Culture: Reflections on the Technocratic Society and Its Youthful Opposition* (1968; repr., Berkeley: University of California Press, 1995), describing the contemporary practice of dropping out as analogous to "the quest of third-century Christians (a similarly scruffy, uncouth, and often half-mad lot) for escape from the corruptions of Hellenistic society: it is more a flight *from* than *toward*" (34, emphasis in original). Robinson's revision renders Gnosticism as a flight from Christianity itself as no less "corrupted" an establishment.

73. See James M. Robinson, "Nag Hammadi: The First Fifty Years," in *The Nag Hammadi Library after Fifty Years: Proceedings of the 1995 Society of Biblical Literature Commemoration,* ed. John D. Turner and Anne McGuire (Leiden: Brill, 1997), 3–34.

74. James M. Robinson, "The Rise and Fall of a Monopoly," *Religious Studies Review* 3, no. 1 (1977): 26.

75. Robinson's "liberation" of the Jung Codex from "totalitarian monopolization" was not immune to Voegelin's insinuation of demagoguery; as Thomas Crawford, "Curating Gnosis: Discovery, Power and the Creation of (a) Discipline" (PhD diss., Claremont Graduate University, 2011), puts it, Robinson's account of the liberation not only "inscribes himself as the hero, recoverer, disseminator and organizer of the efforts to understand Nag Hammadi" (109) but also

enables "a symbolic transfer of the mantle of scholarship from German to American soil" (93); see also, generally, 104–10.

76. See Dinitia Smith, "Another Top 100 List: Now It's Nonfiction," *New York Times,* April 30, 1999, http://www.nytimes.com/1999/04/30/books/another -top-100-list-now-it-s-nonfiction.html.

77. Elaine Pagels, *The Gnostic Gospels* (1979; repr., New York: Vintage, 1989), 82.

78. See Pagels, *The Gnostic Gospels,* 46–69.

79. There is no shortage of recent literature, critical as well as mystical, on Mary Magdalene. Part of the Berlin Codex (Papyrus Berolinensis 8502), which was discovered in 1896 but remained untranslated until 1955, the Gospel of Mary has been attributed to the viewpoint of Mary of Magdala. See, for instance, Karen L. King's translation *The Gospel of Mary of Magdala: Jesus and the First Woman Apostle* (Santa Rosa, Calif.: Polebridge, 2003). On the history of representing Mary Magdalene as the complementary "whore" to Mary's "Virgin Mother," see Marina Warner, *Alone of All Her Sex: The Myth and the Cult of the Virgin Mary* (1983; repr., Oxford: Oxford University Press, 2013); see also Esther A. de Boer, *The Mary Magdalene Cover-Up: The Sources behind the Myth* (London: Bloomsbury, 2007).

80. Pagels, *The Gnostic Gospels,* 49.

81. Pagels, *The Gnostic Gospels,* 118.

82. Elaine Pagels, *The Gnostic Paul: Gnostic Exegesis of the Pauline Letters* (Philadelphia: Fortress, 1975), 6.

83. Pagels, *The Gnostic Paul,* 5.

84. Pagels, *The Gnostic Gospels,* 106.

85. Pagels, *The Gnostic Paul,* 53.

3. SO DARK, THE CON OF MAN

1. Dan Brown, *The Da Vinci Code* (2003; repr., New York: Anchor, 2009), 8; emphasis in original.

2. See Brown, *The Da Vinci Code,* 211. See also Michael Baigent, Richard Leigh, and Henry Lincoln, *Holy Blood, Holy Grail* (1982; repr., New York: Bantam Dell, 2004), 306.

3. Brown, *The Da Vinci Code,* 213.

4. See Ted Anton, *Eros, Magic, and the Murder of Professor Culianu* (Evanston, Ill.: Northwestern University Press, 1996).

5. Seznec, Wind, and Yates were art historians who taught at the Warburg Institute in London; Eliade and Culianu were scholars of comparative religion at the University of Chicago; Pagels is Harrington Spear Paine Foundation Professor of Religion at Princeton University. See esp. Frances Yates, *The Rosicrucian Enlightenment* (1972; repr., London: Routledge, 2001); and Jean Seznec, *The Survival of the Pagan Gods: The Mythological Tradition and Its Place in Renaissance Humanism and Art,* trans. Barbara F. Sessions (1940; repr., New York: Harper, 1953).

6. Paul Ricoeur, *Freud and Philosophy: An Essay on Interpretation,* trans. Denis Savage (New Haven, Conn.: Yale University Press, 1970), 31.

7. As we will see in this chapter, this intertwining of history and narrative persists in the novel's reception, wherein fans and debunkers alike appeal to scholars of early Christianity such as Karen King, Elaine Pagels, James Robinson, and others. Rachel Wagner surveys this reception in "The 'Scholar's Code': Biblical Interpretation, Postmodernism, and the *Da Vinci Code,*" in *The Da Vinci Code in the Academy,* ed. Bradley Powers (Newcastle, U.K.: Cambridge Scholars, 2007), 31–47.

8. Mircea Eliade, *Occultism, Witchcraft, and Cultural Fashions: Essays in Comparative Religions* (Chicago: University of Chicago Press, 1976), 64; emphasis in original.

9. See "Brown Wins Da Vinci Code Case," *Guardian,* April 7, 2006, http://www.theguardian.com/media/2006/apr/07/pressandpublishing.danbrown.

10. A partial list of films that seek directly to elaborate on or debunk the claims of Brown's novel include the films *Da Vinci Code Decoded* (dir. Richard Metzger, 2004); *Da Vinci's Darkest Secret* (dir. Philip Gardiner, 2015); *The Da Vinci Deception* (dir. Charles E. Sellier, 2005); *Unlocking Da Vinci's Code* (dir. David McKenzie, 2004); *The Real Da Vinci Code* (dir. Kashaf Chaudhry, 2006); *Is It Real? Da Vinci's Code* (dir. Amy Doyle, 2006), and a History Channel documentary series, The Da Vinci Code: The Total Story, comprising *Beyond the Da Vinci Code; The Templar Code; Da Vinci Code Bloodlines; Opus Dei Secrets Revealed; Mary Magdalene: The Hidden Apostle;* and *The Holy Grail.*

The many books dedicated to exposing Brown's claims include Darrell L. Bock, *Breaking* The Da Vinci Code: *Answers to the Questions Everyone's Asking* (Nashville: Oliver-Nelson, 2004); Dan Burstein, *Secrets of the Code: The Unauthorized Guide to the Mysteries behind* The Da Vinci Code (New York: CDS, 2004); James L. Garlow and Peter Jones, *Cracking Da Vinci's Code: You've Read the Fiction, Now Read the Facts* (Colorado Springs, Colo.: Cook, 2004); Steve Kellmeyer, *Fact and Fiction in* The Da Vinci Code (Peoria, Ill.: Bridegroom, 2004); Martin Lunn, Da Vinci Code *Decoded: The Truth behind the New York Times #1 Bestseller* (New York: Disinformation, 2004); Shawn McDonnell, *Preaching Another Jesus: Decoding Dan Brown's* Da Vinci Code *Hoax* (Morrisville, N.C.: Lulu, 2004); Laurence Gardner, *The Magdalene Legacy: The Jesus and Mary Bloodline Conspiracy: Revelations beyond* The Da Vinci Code (London: Harper Element, 2005); TFP Committee on American Issues, *Rejecting* The Da Vinci Code: *How a Blasphemous Novel Brutally Attacks Our Lord and the Catholic Church* (Spring Grove, Pa.: American Society for the Defense of Tradition, Family and Property, 2005); Kenneth Boa and John Alan Turner, *The Gospel According to* The Da Vinci Code: *The Truth behind the Writings of Dan Brown* (Nashville: Broadman and Holman, 2006); Dillon Burroughs and Michael J. Easley, *The Da Vinci Code* Controversy: *10 Facts You Should Know* (Chicago: Moody, 2006); Rene Chandelle, *Beyond* The Da Vinci Code: *The Book That Solves the Mystery* (Edison, N.J.: Chartwell Books, 2006); James L. Garlow, *The Da Vinci Codebreaker: An Easy-to-Use Fact Checker for Truth Seekers* (Bloomington,

Minn.: Bethany House, 2006); D. James Kennedy and Jerry Newcombe, *The Da Vinci Myth versus the Gospel Truth* (Wheaton, Ill.: Crossway, 2006); Ted Sri and Mark Shea, *The Da Vinci Deception: 100 Questions about the Facts and Fiction of* The Da Vinci Code (West Chester, Pa.: Ascension, 2006); Bowers, *The Da Vinci Code in the Academy;* Sandra Miesel, *The Da Vinci Hoax: Exposing the Errors in* The Da Vinci Code (San Francisco: Ignatius, 2009); and David Aaronovitch, *Voodoo Histories: The Role of the Conspiracy Theory in Shaping Modern History* (London: Harper Element, 2011).

11. See Gérard de Sède, *Le Sang des Cathares: L'Occitanie rebelle du Moyen Âge* (1966; repr., Paris: Plon, 1976), 13.

12. Popular debunkers have derided the novel's scandalous intermixture of biblical fact and historical fiction as both "Gnostic" and "postmodern," to the point of virtually conflating these terms in turn, as Rachel Wagner has noted. See Wagner, "The 'Scholar's Code,'" esp. 38–44.

13. Gershom Scholem, *Major Trends in Jewish Mysticism* (New York: Schocken, 1995), 8.

14. Scholem, *Major Trends in Jewish Mysticism,* 7.

15. Scholem, *Major Trends in Jewish Mysticism,* 8.

16. Brown, *The Da Vinci Code,* 312–13. Brown is ventriloquizing studies of "spiritual" or "goddess" feminism here, such as the work of Carol Christ, Riane Eisler, and Marija Gimbutas that form part of the discussion in chapter 4. Much of this discourse can trace its roots to the reception at the turn of the twentieth century of the *Pistis Sophia,* which figures wisdom *(Sophia)* as female. For a paradigmatic critique of the "eternal feminine" as a patriarchal myth, see Simone de Beauvoir, *The Second Sex,* trans. H. M. Parshley (New York: Vintage, 1989), 179–80.

17. See Elaine Pagels, *The Gnostic Gospels* (1979; repr., New York: Vintage, 1989), 46–89.

18. For a basic introduction to Plantard's work, see Arnaud de l'Estoile, *Pierre Plantard: Qui suis-je?* (Paris: Éditions Pardès, 2014).

19. Jean-Michel Rabaté, *Given: 1° Art 2° Crime: Modernity, Murder and Mass Culture* (Eastbourne, U.K.: Sussex Academic, 2007), 21, 32.

20. Ricoeur, *Freud and Philosophy,* 32.

21. Ricoeur, *Freud and Philosophy,* 343.

22. Rabaté, *Given,* 32.

23. Ricoeur, *Freud and Philosophy,* 4.

24. See Umberto Eco, *Interpretation and Overinterpretation* (Cambridge: Cambridge University Press, 1992). For a recent discussion of the hermeneutics of suspicion summarizing recent neopragmatist (rather than mystical) calls to abandon or at least problematize its critical gesture of "demystification," see Rita Felski, *The Limits of Critique* (Chicago: University of Chicago Press, 2015).

25. Felski, *The Limits of Critique,* 186.

26. Eco, *Interpretation and Overinterpretation,* 23.

27. Eco, *Interpretation and Overinterpretation,* 32.

28. Eco, *Interpretation and Overinterpretation,* 38.

29. Eco, *Interpretation and Overinterpretation,* 39. Eco is paraphrasing—but also adapting—the work of Paul Ricoeur, who writes that the hermeneutics of suspicion "is not an explication of the object, but a tearing off of masks, an interpretation that reduces disguises." See Ricoeur, *Freud and Philosophy,* 30. As I have suggested, moreover, Eco likewise follows Ricoeur in stressing that this mode of interpretation bears a complementary hermeneutics of invention—or, as Ricoeur puts it, a hermeneutics of the sacred. To put it reductively: the ethics of interpretation hinge in both cases on the relation between these oppositional modes.

30. For a sense of Eco's ideas about the political consequences of certain kinds of hermetic semiosis, see his 1995 essay "Ur-Fascism," *New York Review of Books,* June 22, 1995, http://www.nybooks.com/articles/1995/06/22/ur-fascism/.

31. Umberto Eco, *The Limits of Interpretation* (Bloomington: Indiana University Press, 1990), 4.

32. Lila Azam Zanganeh, "Umberto Eco, The Art of Fiction No. 197," *Paris Review* 185 (2008), http://www.theparisreview.org/interviews/5856/the-art-of-fiction-no-197-umberto-eco. For an extensive recent discussion of Brown and Eco that plays on Eco's conflation in its very title, see Douglas Merrell, *Umberto Eco, The Da Vinci Code, and the Intellectual in the Age of Popular Culture* (London: Palgrave Macmillan, 2017).

33. For a more systematic examination of *Foucault's Pendulum* and Eco's hermeneutics, see Carole M. Cusack, "Esotericism, Irony and Paranoia in Umberto Eco's Foucault's Pendulum" (2008), https://openjournals.library.sydney.edu.au/index.php/SSR/article/viewFile/272/251.

34. Brown, *The Da Vinci Code,* 1.

35. Brown, *The Da Vinci Code,* 56–60, 128.

36. Brown, *The Da Vinci Code,* 161–62.

37. Brown, *The Da Vinci Code,* 179.

38. Compare the way Leonardo da Vinci's *Madonna of the Rocks* appears in Dan Brown's novel to some of the more archetypal "primary" interpretations of the painting which, though inspired by Langdon's symbology, nevertheless disarticulate their interpretations from the fictional medium of the novel. The website UFO Digest (http://www.ufodigest.com) directs our attention, for instance, to the phallic and yonic shapes of the rock formations; we thus find one of the archetypal, "symbolic" motifs that saturate Langdon's teaching about the chalice and the blade, the iconography of female and male principles that form, as we will see in chapter 4, the basis for a much different kind of mythohistorical investigation in Riane Eisler's 1989 book of feminist ecological synthesis, *The Chalice and the Blade: Our History, Our Future* (San Francisco: Harper and Row, 1987).

Analogously, Rabaté, *Given,* 23, rightly likens Langdon's morphological interpretation of the painting to Sigmund Freud's wild interpretation of Leonardo's painting *Madonna and Child with St. Anne.* Yet such wild interpretations become plausible in the novel because they are secondary effects of the "real" disclosure, the key hidden behind the painting itself: after the *Madonna of the Rocks* is designated through its anagram ("So dark, the con of man") and discloses its hiding place (Sophie, after finding the key, uses the painting as a shield), the figural economy of the painting itself continues to signify in excess of its utility. Langdon's interpretation works only insofar as the painting also functions as a hiding place for keys and codes that extend beyond the frame into the (fictional) world of Langdon and Neveu. But by keeping this interpretive excess in play, Langdon, and *The Da Vinci Code* more broadly, sketches out a whole secret history in turn: even in one of his most explicitly devout Christian paintings, commissioned by the Milanese Brotherhood of the Immaculate Conception for a chapel in the Church of San Francesco Grande, Leonardo had embedded pagan (and counterhegemonically "feminist") imagery. It was not only Saunière who hid clues in the paintings, in other words, but also the artist.

39. Brown, *The Da Vinci Code*, 1.

40. See, for instance, Daniel Schorn, "The Priory of Sion: Is the "Secret Organization" Fact or Fiction?," CBS News, April 27, 2006, http://www.cbsnews.com/news/the-priory-of-sion/. See also Gérard de Sède, *Rennes-le-Château: le dossier, les impostures, les phantasmes, les hypothèses* (Paris: Laffont, 1988).

41. See, for instance, Christopher McIntosh, *Eliphas Lévi and the French Occult Revival* (Albany: State University of New York Press, 1972).

42. See Baigent, Leigh, and Lincoln, *Holy Blood, Holy Grail*, 306.

43. Baigent, Leigh, and Lincoln, *Holy Blood, Holy Grail*, 18.

44. Baigent, Leigh, and Lincoln, *Holy Blood, Holy Grail*, 20.

45. Baigent, Leigh, and Lincoln, *Holy Blood, Holy Grail*, 310, 312.

46. Jules Michelet, *Satanism and Witchcraft: The Classic Study of Medieval Superstition,* trans. A. R. Allinson (New York: Citadel, 1992), 24.

47. Baigent, Leigh, and Lincoln, *Holy Blood, Holy Grail*, 312–13.

48. See Jenkins, *Hidden Gospels*, 49, and, generally, 48–53. See also Theodore Ziolkowski, *Fictional Transfigurations of Jesus* (Eugene, Ore.: Wipf and Stock, 1972).

49. Gérard de Sède, *The Accursed Treasure of Rennes-le-Château,* trans. Henry Lincoln (Paris: Les Editions de l'Oeil du Sphinx, 2013).

50. Henry Lincoln, "Postface," in Gérard de Sède, *L'Or de Rennes: Signé Rose + Croix, l'énigme de Rennes-le-Château* (1967; updated ed., Paris: L'Oeil du sphinx, 2007), 191.

51. Henry Lincoln, "Preface," in Baigent, Leigh, and Lincoln, *Holy Blood, Holy Grail*, 23.

52. Baigent, Leigh, and Lincoln, *Holy Blood, Holy Grail*, 205.

53. This figure comes from Sède's late account in his unpublished memoir, but is consistent with the figure cited in *L'Or de Rennes* (2007 ed.); Sède writes that he studied the accounting books firsthand. Sède, "La Chimère expérimentale" (unpublished memoir; author's copy), 345; see also Sède, *L'Or de Rennes* (2007 ed.), 54.

54. For a history of French occultist circles, see McIntosh, *Eliphas Lévi.*

55. See Sède, *L'Or de Rennes, ou, la vie insolite de Bérenger Saunière* (Paris: Julliard, 1967), esp. 69.

56. Theodore Ziolkowski, *Lure of the Arcane: The Literature of Cult and Conspiracy* (Baltimore: Johns Hopkins University Press, 2013).

57. Sède, *L'Or de Rennes* (1967 ed.), 13.

58. Sède, *L'Or de Rennes* (1967 ed.), 16.

59. Sède, *Le Sang des Cathares,* 204.

60. Sède, *Le Sang des Cathares,* 11–12.

61. Sède, *L'Or de Rennes* (1967 ed.), 69.

62. Sède, *Le Sang des Cathares,* 142.

63. Sède, *Le Sang des Cathares,* 161.

64. Sède, *L'Or de Rennes* (1967 ed.), 68.

65. Sède, "Avertissement," in *L'Or de Rennes* (1967 ed.), 10.

66. To this end, Sède recounts a compelling anecdote about how Saunière died with his secret intact, having only divulged it to his housekeeper-partner, who likewise died before revealing it. But such final secrets, guarded by death, are ultimately redemptive for Sède, sustaining the enigma rather than withholding a secret that may, in the end, prove hollow.

67. Bruno Latour depicts the cultural overuse of a critical mode dominated by the hermeneutics of suspicion—which, having once gone wild, has now exhausted its relevance—by mock lamenting that nowadays local villagers "are too unsophisticated to be gullible," whereas professors are the naïve one who believe in "facts." "Remember the good old days," he writes, "when university professors could look down on unsophisticated folks because those hillbillies naïvely believed in church, motherhood, and apple pie? Things have changed a lot, at least in my village." Latour's overall argument is that "we" need to expand our critical range by paying attention to the myriad complexities and entanglements of "things" rather than merely categorizing, upholding, or unmasking "facts." It is remarkable to read how much local neighbors, villagers, and "hillbillies" become the targets for his own critique of exhausted methods in turn. Bruno Latour, "Why Has Critique Run Out of Steam? From Matters of Fact to Matters of Concern," *Critical Inquiry* 30 (2004): 228.

68. Sède, "La Chimère expérimentale," 153. See also Anne Vernay and Richard Walter, "Présentation," in *La Main à plume . . . : Anthologie du surréalisme sous l'Occupation,* ed. Anne Vernay and Richard Walter (Paris: Éditions Syllepse, 2008), 20–21.

69. Sède, "La Chimère expérimentale," 153.

70. Gérard Durozoi, "Les Audaces de la Main à plume," in Vernay and Walter, *La Main à Plume,* 6.

71. Léo Malet to Noël Arnaud, 1943, quoted in Durozoi, "Les Audaces," 6.

72. Boris Rybak, "Introduction au surréalisme scientifique ou naissance de l'intraphysique," in Vernay and Walter, *La Main à Plume,* 160.

73. Rybak, "Introduction au surréalisme scientifique ou naissance de l'intraphysique," in Vernay and Walter, *La Main à Plume,* 160–61.

74. Gérard de Sède, "Aperçu d'une encyclopédie surréaliste de l'objet," in Vernay and Walter, *La Main à plume*, 217.

75. Gérard de Sède, "Objectivité théorique et Objectivité lyrique," in Vernay and Walter, *La Main à plume*, 177.

76. Gérard de Sède, *Les Templiers sont parmi nous, ou, l'Enigme de Gisors* (Paris: Julliard, 1962), 118.

77. Gérard de Sède, "Philosophie Marxiste et Philosophie Stalinienne," *Jeune Révolution* 2 (1946), repr. in "La Chimère expérimentale," 204–14.

78. Sède, "Philosophie Marxiste et Philosophie Stalinienne," 205.

79. Sède, "Philosophie Marxiste et Philosophie Stalinienne," 208.

80. Sède, "Philosophie Marxiste et Philosophie Stalinienne," 212–13.

81. In his memoir, Sède notes that in positing his own version of ideological critique in 1946, he had not yet read the work of the Hungarian Marxist thinker György Lukács, whose *History and Class Consciousness* was translated into French only in 1962. Even so, in articulating some of the positions later taken up formally by Marxist thinkers in the 1950s and 1960s, the essay bears continuities with the work of Louis Althusser, whose critique of the excesses of Stalinist orthodoxy in the Lyssenko Affair Sède quotes in his memoir. See Louis Althusser's preface to Dominique Lecourt, *Lyssenko: Histoire réelle d'une "science prolétarienne"* (Paris: François Maspero, 1976), quoted in Sède, "La Chimère expérimentale," 215–16.

82. Sède, "La Chimère expérimentale," 311.

83. In the opening page of the memoir, Sède gives a definition: "Biologists use the term 'experimental chimera' to describe the teratological products created in laboratories, which contain cells from diverse origins." Sède, "La Chimère expérimentale," 1.

84. Sède, *L'Or de Rennes* (1967 ed.), 160.

85. Christian Dotrement, "Lettres d'amour," in Vernay and Walter, *La Main à plume*, 199.

86. Ziolkowski, *Lure of the Arcane*, 5.

87. Ziolkowski, *Lure of the Arcane*, 9.

88. See Felski, *The Limits of Critique*, esp. 14–51.

89. Mary Daly, *Gyn/Ecology: The Metaethics of Radical Feminism* (Boston: Beacon, 1978), 47.

90. Mary Daly, *Gyn/Ecology*, 48.

4. THE CHALICE, THE BLADE, AND THE BIFURCATION POINT

1. These figures are given in Cynthia Eller, *Living in the Lap of the Goddess: The Feminist Spirituality Movement in America* (New York: Crossroad, 1993), 154.

2. Riane Eisler, *The Chalice and the Blade: Our History, Our Future* (San Francisco: Harper and Row, 1987), 105.

3. Eisler, *The Chalice and the Blade*, xvii.

4. Dan Brown, *The Da Vinci Code* (2003; repr., New York: Anchor, 2009), 8; emphasis in original.

5. As Slavoj Žižek has noted, moreover, the power dynamic between Langdon and Neveu never becomes horizontal even in the crudest of senses: any possibility of a sexual relationship between them, for instance, is instead displaced onto Neveu's distant ancestors, Jesus and Mary Magdalene, whose marriage yielded the secret bloodline at the heart of the novel's conspiracy plot. Žižek, *In Defense of Lost Causes* (London: Verso, 2008), 67.

6. A significant precursor to Eisler's work is Lynn Margulis and James Lovelock's "gaia hypothesis," which proposed to study the earth as an integrated, organic whole. On the "gaia hypothesis" and systems theory, see Derek Lee, "Parascience and Revolution: The Paranormal Mind in Twentieth-Century Literature and Science" (PhD diss., Pennsylvania State University, 2018).

7. Eisler, *The Chalice and the Blade*, 9.

8. As Eisler (*The Chalice and the Blade*, 105) explains, "To describe the real alternative to a system based on the ranking of half of humanity over the other, I propose the new term *gylany. Gy* derives from the Greek root word *gyne,* or 'woman.' *An* derives from *andros,* or 'man.' The letter *l* between the two has a double meaning. In English, it stands for the *linking* of both halves of humanity, rather than, as in androcracy, their ranking. In Greek, it derives from the verb *lyein* or *lyo,* which in turn has a double meaning: to solve or resolve (as in ana*l*ysis) and to dissolve or set free (as in cata*l*ysis). In this sense, the letter *l* stands for the resolution of our problems from the freeing of both halves of humanity from the stultifying and distorting rigidity of roles imposed by the domination hierarchies inherent in androcratic systems."

9. Eisler, *The Chalice and the Blade*, xvii.

10. Eisler, *The Chalice and the Blade*, xix, viii.

11. Fritjof Capra, *The Turning Point: Science, Society, and the Rising Culture* (New York: Bantam, 1982), 25.

12. Alice Walker, *We Are The Ones We Have Been Waiting For: Inner Light in a Time of Darkness* (New York: New Press, 2006), 77.

13. Eisler, *The Chalice and the Blade*, 184.

14. See Eisler, *The Chalice and the Blade*, 105.

15. For a more explicitly "holistic" precursor to Eisler's study, see the Jungian project of self-assertion in Edward C. Whitmont, *Return of the Goddess* (New York: Crossroad, 1982).

16. David Loye and Riane Eisler, "Chaos and Transformation: Implications of Nonequilibrium Theory for Social Science and Society," *Behavioral Science* 32, no. 1 (1987): 53.

17. For a study that extends the rhetorical positions of the 1990s culture and science wars to the field of archaeology, see *Archaeological Fantasies: How Pseudoarchaeology Misrepresents the Past and Misleads the Public,* ed. Garrett G. Fagan

(London: Routledge, 2006). As Colin Renfrew writes in the book's foreword, what angers him most about popular pseudoarchaeology "is that the real potential and importance of archaeology as they key to an understanding of the human past has been entirely lost. Why should archaeology be treated in this frivolous and self-serving way, which in other scientific fields would result in a torrent of criticism? Human origins, including the origins of civilization, are a serious matter. For it is only from their serious study that we can hope to achieve a proper understanding of what we are" (xvi). See also Stephen Williams, *Fantastic Archaeology: The Wild Side of North American Prehistory* (Philadelphia: University of Pennsylvania Press, 1991).

18. Eisler is not, it is worth noting, a "new materialist": her version of systems thinking does not grant agency to the earth, or to material things, but is instead interested in the evolution of forms and patterns of social organization as both object and method; hence her language of "models" and "paradigms."

19. Merlin Stone, *When God Was a Woman* (New York: Harcourt Brace Jovanovich, 1978), 1.

20. Eisler, *The Chalice and the Blade*, 29.

21. A. L. Basham, *The Wonder That Was India: A Survey of the Culture of the Indian Sub-continent before the Coming of the Muslims* (London: Sidgwick and Jackson, 1954), 44.

22. Sarah B. Pomeroy, *Goddesses, Whores, Wives, and Slaves: Women in Classical Antiquity* (New York: Schocken, 1975), xii.

23. Pomeroy, *Goddesses, Whores, Wives, and Slaves*, xii.

24. Pomeroy, *Goddesses, Whores, Wives, and Slaves*, 15.

25. Pomeroy, *Goddesses, Whores, Wives, and Slaves*, 15.

26. Margaret Ehrenberg, *Women in Prehistory* (London: British Museum Publications, 1989), 11.

27. Eisler, *The Chalice and the Blade*, 104.

28. Johann Jakob Bachofen, *Mother Right: An Investigation of the Religious and Juridical Character of Matriarchy in the Ancient World* (1861), in *Myth, Religion, and Mother Right: Selected Writings of J. J. Bachofen*, trans. Ralph Manheim (Princeton, N.J.: Princeton University Press, 1967), 61.

29. Bachofen, *Mother Right*, 92.

30. Bachofen, *Mother Right*, 80.

31. Bachofen, *Mother Right*, 74.

32. Bachofen, *Mother Right*, 74–75.

33. Eisler, *The Chalice and the Blade*, 61.

34. Eisler, *The Chalice and the Blade*, 188.

35. Mary Daly, *Gyn/Ecology: The Metaethics of Radical Feminism* (Boston: Beacon, 1978), 386.

36. Eisler, *The Chalice and the Blade*, 164.

37. See Ernesto Laclau and Chantal Mouffe, *Hegemony and Socialist Strategy: Towards a Radical Democratic Politics* (London: Verso, 1985).

38. Eisler, *The Chalice and the Blade*, 53.

39. Eisler, *The Chalice and the Blade*, 47.

40. Capra, *The Turning Point*, 285.

41. Eisler, *The Chalice and the Blade*, 135.

42. Eisler, *The Chalice and the Blade*, 47.

43. Eisler, *The Chalice and the Blade*, 186.

44. Elizabeth Fox-Genovese, "Androcrats Go Home!," *New York Times Book Review*, October 4, 1987, 32. Other critics, in true dialectical form, have sought instead to accuse Eisler of a bad faith in her claims to "partnership," seeing her book as an attack in its own right; a study on feminist misandry lambastes Eisler's book on the claim that it really does attack men, arguing that popular works such as *The Chalice and the Blade* and even *The Da Vinci Code* indicate "a worldview that is not merely profoundly gynocentric but also profoundly misandric." As part of a broader study of the alleged shortcomings of Goddess myths and "ideological feminism," the authors of this critique brandish the old saw of feminist man hating, whereby feminist "ideology" is concomitant with a hatred and diminution of men. See Katherine K. Young and Paul Nathanson, *Sanctifying Misandry: Goddess Ideology and the Fall of Man* (Montreal: McGill–Queen's University Press, 2010), 14.

45. Eisler, *The Chalice and the Blade*, 42. Eisler cites Niles Eldredge and Stephen Jay Gould, "Punctuated Equilibria: An Alternative to Phyletic Gradualism," in *Models of Paleobiology*, ed. T. J. Schropf (San Francisco: Freeman, Cooper, 1972), 82–115. See also Loye and Eisler, "Chaos and Transformation."

46. Cynthia Eller, *The Myth of Matriarchal Prehistory: Why an Invented Past Won't Give Women a Future* (Boston: Beacon, 2000), 7.

47. Eller, *The Myth of Matriarchal Prehistory*, 7.

48. Eisler, *The Chalice and the Blade*, 42.

49. Eller, *The Myth of Matriarchal Prehistory*, 61.

50. For a discussion of this tendency see, for instance, Kathleen Iannello, "Women's Leadership and Third-Wave Feminism," in *Gender and Women's Leadership: A Reference Handbook*, ed. Karen O'Connor (Thousand Oaks, Calif.: Sage, 2010), 70–77.

51. Lynn Segal, *Is the Future Female? Troubled Thoughts on Contemporary Feminism* (London: Virago, 1987), ix.

52. Segal, *Is the Future Female?*, ix–x.

53. Suzanne Heine, *Matriarchs, Goddesses, and Images of God: A Critique of Feminist Theology*, trans. John Bowden (Minneapolis: Augsburg, 1989), 102.

54. Donna Haraway, *Simians, Cyborgs, and Women: The Reinvention of Nature* (New York: Routledge, 1990), 191. The chapter from which this statement is drawn, "Situated Knowledges: The Science Question in Feminism and the Privilege of Partial Perspective," was published in the journal *Feminist Studies* in 1988.

55. Žižek, *In Defense of Lost Causes*, 429.

56. Žižek, *In Defense of Lost Causes*, 428.

57. See Žižek, *In Defense of Lost Causes,* 350.

58. Eisler, *The Chalice and the Blade,* 30.

59. See E. O. James, *The Cult of the Mother-Goddess: An Archeological and Documentary Study* (London: Thames and Hudson, 1959), 229.

60. James, *The Cult of the Mother-Goddess,* 229.

61. Eisler, *The Chalice and the Blade,* 54.

62. Eisler, *The Chalice and the Blade,* 54.

63. Eisler, *The Chalice and the Blade,* 169.

64. See Gere, *Knossos and the Prophets of Modernism,* 216.

65. Gere, *Knossos and the Prophets of Modernism,* 209.

66. On "known unknowns" and "unknown knowns," see Žižek, *In Defense of Lost Causes,* 292.

67. Eisler, *The Chalice and the Blade,* 157.

68. Eisler, *The Chalice and the Blade,* 156–57.

69. Eisler, *The Chalice and the Blade,* 63.

70. J. V. Luce, *The End of Atlantis* (1969; repr., New York: Bantam, 1978), 15.

71. See, for instance, Pierre Vidal-Naquet, *The Atlantis Story: A Short History of Plato's Myth,* trans. Janet Lloyd (Exeter, U.K.: University of Exeter Press, 2007), 23.

72. L. Sprague de Camp, *Lost Continents: The Atlantis Theme* (1954; repr., New York: Ballantine, 1975), 287.

73. Eisler, *The Chalice and the Blade,* 137.

74. Eisler, *The Chalice and the Blade,* xix.

75. Mary Daly, *Beyond God the Father: Toward a Philosophy of Women's Liberation* (Boston: Beacon, 1973), 5.

76. Eller, *The Myth of Matriarchal Prehistory,* 7.

77. Eller, *The Myth of Matriarchal Prehistory,* 3.

78. Eller, *The Myth of Matriarchal Prehistory,* 3, 4.

79. Eller, *The Myth of Matriarchal Prehistory,* 6–7.

80. Heine, *Matriarchs, Goddesses, and Images of God,* 3.

81. Eller, *The Myth of Matriarchal Prehistory,* 8.

82. Daly, *Beyond God the Father,* 11.

83. Daly, *Beyond God the Father,* 11.

84. Daly, *Beyond God the Father,* 12.

85. Daly, *Beyond God the Father,* 5.

86. See Luce Irigaray, *This Sex Which Is Not One,* trans. Catherine Porter and Carolyn Burke (Ithaca, N.Y.: Cornell University Press, 1985).

87. See Michael Gordin, *The Pseudoscience Wars: Immanuel Velikovsky and the Birth of the Modern Fringe* (Chicago: University of Chicago Press, 2012), which is discussed further in chapter 8 of the present volume.

88. Peter Steinfels, "Idyllic Theory of Goddess Creates Storm," *New York Times,* February 13, 1990, http://www.nytimes.com/1990/02/13/science/idyllic-theory-of-goddesses-creates-storm.html?pagewanted=all.

89. Gere, *Knossos and the Prophets of Modernism*, 216.

90. Segal, *Is the Future Female?*, 19–20.

91. Heine, *Matriarchs, Goddesses, and Images of God*, 152.

92. Audre Lorde, "An Open Letter to Mary Daly" (May 6, 1979), in *Sister/Outsider: Essays and Speeches by Audre Lorde* (Berkeley, Calif.: Crossing, 1984), 68.

93. Frances Devlin-Glass and Lyn McCredden, "Inside and Outside the Traditions: The Changing Shapes of Feminist Spiritualities," in *Feminist Poetics of the Sacred: Creative Suspicions*, ed. Frances Devlin-Glass and Lyn McCredden (Oxford: Oxford University Press, 2001), 3.

94. Stacy Alaimo, *Undomesticated Ground: Recasting Nature as Feminist Space* (Ithaca, N.Y.: Cornell University Press, 2000), 8.

95. Devlin-Glass and McCredden, "Inside and Outside the Traditions," 11.

96. Irene Diamond, *Fertile Ground: Women, Earth, and the Limits of Control* (Boston: Beacon, 1994), 20–21.

97. Mary Mellor, *Feminism and Ecology* (New York: New York University Press, 1997), 8.

5. GARVEYISM AND ITS INVOLUTIONS

1. Jacques Berlinerblau, *Heresy in the University: The Black Athena Controversy and the Responsibilities of American Intellectuals* (New Brunswick, N.J.: Rutgers University Press, 1999), 8.

2. Martin Bernal, *Black Athena: The Afroasiatic Roots of Classical Civilization*, vol. 1, *The Fabrication of Ancient Greece, 1785–1985* (New Brunswick, N.J.: Rutgers University Press, 1987).

3. On Bernal's acknowledged debt to black scholarship—and for a genealogy of such scholars, see Maghan Keita, "Believing in Ethiopians," in *African Athena: New Agendas*, ed. Daniel Orrells, Gurminder K. Bhamba, and Tessa Roynon (Oxford: Oxford University Press, 2011), 19–39. See also Keita, *Race and the Writing of History: Riddling the Sphinx* (Oxford: Oxford University Press, 2000).

4. Cathy Gere, *Knossos and the Prophets of Modernism* (Chicago: University of Chicago Press, 2009), 216.

5. Gere, *Knossos and the Prophets of Modernism*, 217.

6. Berlinerblau (*Heresy in the University*, 3–4) notes the inaugural volume's "bewildering hybrid of serious scholarship" that "trespasses across all disciplinary boundaries" and "digresses eruditely" in its survey of "great expanses of scholarly literature." Lefkowitz, on the other hand, attributes this synthesis to inexpertise and an ideological entrenchment in staking claims to the cultural legacy of Ancient Greece. As she writes, "democracy and the other accomplishments of Greek civilization, however real or imaginary, remain so precious to us that virtually every modern civilization has wanted to claim them for itself." Mary Lefkowitz, "Introduction: Ancient History, Modern Myths," in *Black Athena Revisited*, ed.

Mary Lefkowitz and Guy MacLean Rogers (Chapel Hill: University of North Carolina Press, 1996), 6.

7. On Bernal's readership beyond the United States, see the essays in Orrells, Bhamba, and Roynon, *African Athena.*

8. Recasting a political intervention in identitarian, even hereditary, terms, Gere (*Knossos and the Prophets of Modernism,* 218) attributes the *Black Athena* phenomenon in part to Bernal's intellectual lineage, insofar as he "inherit[ed] both the far-left political leanings and the academic abilities of his father." For Gere, in other words, Bernal's study was both motivated by and tolerated on account of his direct bloodline to white, leftist academia.

9. Lefkowitz, *Black Athena Revisited,* x.

10. Lefkowitz, *Black Athena Revisited,* x.

11. Keita, "Believing in Ethiopians," 19.

12. Lefkowitz, "Introduction," 21.

13. Mary Lefkowitz, "Archaeology and the Politics of Origins: The Search for Pyramids in Greece," in *Archaeological Fantasies: How Pseudoarchaeology Misrepresents the Past and Misleads the Public,* ed. Garrett G. Fagan (London: Routledge, 2006), 180. See also Tony Martin, *The Jewish Onslaught: Despatches from the Wellesley Battlefront* (Dover, Mass.: Majority Press, 1993); Mary Lefkowitz, *Not Out of Africa: How "Afrocentrism" Became an Excuse to Teach Myth as History* (New York: Basic Books, 1996); and Mary Lefkowitz, *History Lesson: A Race Odyssey* (New Haven, Conn.: Yale University Press, 1998).

14. Keita, "Believing in Ethiopians," 19.

15. Adam Ewing, *The Age of Garvey: How a Jamaican Activist Created a Mass Movement and Changed Global Black Politics* (Princeton, N.J.: Princeton University Press, 2014), 6.

16. Marcus Garvey, "Address by Marcus Garvey," *Daily Chronicle,* March 26, 1915, in *The Marcus Garvey and United Negro Improvement Association Papers,* vol. 1, *1826–August 1919,* ed. Robert A. Hill (Berkeley: University of California Press, 1983), lix.

17. As Mary G. Rolinson (*Grassroots Garveyism: The Universal Negro Improvement Association in the Rural South, 1920–1927* [Chapel Hill: University of North Carolina Press, 2007], 24) notes, "Many of Marcus Garvey's inspiring words and ideas sounded familiar to his followers because they were not necessarily new. Many of the most important themes of Garvey's speeches, both spoken and transcribed weekly in the *Negro World,* echoed the voices of generations of black clergymen, journalists, and other influential black leaders of the American South."

18. See, for instance, Claudrena N. Harold, *The Rise and Fall of the Garvey Movement in the Urban South, 1918–1942* (New York: Routledge, 2007); and Ewing, *The Age of Garvey.*

19. J. Edgar Hoover to Special Agent Ridgely, October 11, 1919, in *The Marcus Garvey and United Negro Improvement Association Papers,* vol. 2, *August 1919–August 1920,* ed. Robert A. Hill (Berkeley: University of California Press, 1983), 72. On

the federal "investigation" of Garvey, see Theodore Kornweibel, *Seeing Red: Federal Campaigns against Black Militancy, 1919–1925* (Bloomington: Indiana University Press, 1998), esp. 100–131. See also Ewing, *The Age of Garvey,* esp. 107–26.

20. See, for instance, Kwame Nkrumah, *Ghana: The Autobiography of Kwame Nkrumah* (1957; repr., Bedford, U.K.: Panaf, 2002), 45.

21. On Garvey's paranoia, see Robert Bagnall, "The Madness of Marcus Garvey," *Messenger* 5 (1923): 638, 648. On his fascism, see, for instance, Paul Gilroy, *Against Race: Imagining Political Culture Beyond the Color Line* (Cambridge, Mass.: Harvard University Press, 2000), 291; and C. L. R. James, "Marcus Garvey" (1940), in *C. L. R. James on the "Negro Question,"* ed. Scott McLemee (Jackson: University Press of Mississippi, 1996), 114–16.

22. See, for instance, Robert Gooding-Williams's otherwise remarkable *In the Shadow of Du Bois: Afro-Modern Political Thought in America* (Cambridge, Mass.: Harvard University Press, 2011), which makes Du Bois's shadow so long as to occlude Garvey altogether.

23. See Bagnall, "The Madness of Marcus Garvey."

24. Clifford Geertz, *Agricultural Involution: The Processes of Ecological Change in Indonesia* (1963; repr., Berkeley: University of California Press, 1970), 82.

25. Geertz, *Agricultural Involution,* 142.

26. Rolinson, *Grassroots Garveyism,* 8.

27. Marcus Garvey, editorial, *Negro World,* December 3, 1919, in Hill, *The Marcus Garvey and United Negro Improvement Association Papers,* 2:159.

28. Ishmael Reed, *Mumbo Jumbo* (New York: Scribner, 1972), 31. The "crocodile" reference seems to allude to Garvey's 1922 account of (white) deception in "The Future as I See It," in *The Philosophy and Opinions of Marcus Garvey, or, Africa for the Africans,* ed. Amy Jacques Garvey (Dover, Mass.: Majority Press, 1986), 74.

29. As Garvey wrote in a December 1919 editorial, "Five years ago the Negro Universal was sleeping upon his bale of cotton in the South of America; he was steeped in mud in the banana fields of the West Indies and Central America, seeing no possible way of extricating himself from the environments; he smarted under the lash of the new taskmaster in Africa; but alas! Today he is the new man who has proclaimed to the world that the despised and rejected shall rise, not only from his serfdom and slavery, but to rule and to teach man how to live." Garvey, editorial, *Negro World,* December 3, 1919.

30. Marcus Garvey, *The Destiny of the Negro,* in Hill, *The Marcus Garvey and United Negro Improvement Association Papers,* 1:64–65.

31. Marcus Garvey, "A Talk with Afro-West Indians," in *The Marcus Garvey and United Negro Improvement Association Papers,* vol. 11, *The Caribbean Diaspora, 1910–1920,* ed. Robert A. Hill (Durham, N.C.: Duke University Press, 2011), 66.

32. Marcus Garvey, "Articles," in *Marcus Garvey: Life and Lessons: A Centennial Companion to the Marcus Garvey and Universal Negro Improvement Association Papers,* ed. Robert A. Hill and Barbara Bair (Berkeley: University of California Press, 1987), 63. As with the majority of his formulations, Garvey deployed this

argument on numerous occasions. See, for instance, Garvey's 1923 autobiographical statement "The Negro's Greatest Enemy," in Hill, *The Marcus Garvey and United Negro Improvement Association Papers,* 1:3–12.

33. Marcus Garvey, editorial, *Negro World,* December 3, 1919, in Hill, *The Marcus Garvey and United Negro Improvement Association Papers,* 2:159.

34. See, for instance, Paula Giddings, *When and Where I Enter: The Impact of Black Women on Race and Sex in America* (New York: Morrow, 1984), esp. 171–81. See also Amy Louise Wood, *Lynching and Spectacle: Witnessing Racial Violence in America, 1890–1940* (Chapel Hill: University of North Carolina Press, 2009); and David F. Krugler, *1919, The Year of Racial Violence: How African Americans Fought Back* (Cambridge: Cambridge University Press, 2014).

35. See Robbie Shilliam, "Ethiopia Shall Stretch Forth Her Hands unto God: Garveyism, Rastafari, and Antiquity," in Orrells, Bhamba, and Roynon, *African Athena,* 106–21.

36. Reed, *Mumbo Jumbo,* 30–31.

37. On Reed's historiography, see Donald L. Hoffman, "A Darker Shade of Grail: Questing at the Crossroads in Ishmael Reed's *Mumbo Jumbo.*" *Callaloo* 17, no. 4 (1994): 1245–56; and Carol Siri Johnson, "The Limbs of Osiris: Reed's *Mumbo Jumbo* and Hollywood's *The Mummy.*" *MELUS* 17, no. 4 (1991): 105–15.

38. Reed, *Mumbo Jumbo,* 20.

39. See Marcus Garvey, "The Resurrection of the Negro" (1922), in Garvey, *The Philosophy and Opinions of Marcus Garvey,* 67.

40. See Michelle Anne Stephens, *Black Empire: The Masculine Global Imaginary of Caribbean Intellectuals in the United States, 1914–1962* (Durham, N.C.: Duke University Press, 2005), 75–101.

41. Marcus Garvey, "African Fundamentalism," in Garvey, *The Philosophy and Opinions of Marcus Garvey,* 415.

42. Garvey, "The Future as I See It," 77.

43. On Garvey's recourse to black historiography of the late nineteenth and early twentieth centuries, see Wilson Jeremiah Moses, *Afrotopia: The Roots of African American Popular History* (Cambridge: Cambridge University Press, 1998). See also John Henrik Clarke, ed., *Marcus Garvey and the Vision of Africa* (New York: Random House, 1974); Matthew Pratt Guterl, "The New Race Consciousness: Race, Nation, and Empire in American Culture, 1910–1925," *Journal of World History* 10, no. 2 (1999): 307–52; Keita, *Race and the Writing of History;* Winston James, *Holding Aloft the Banner of Ethiopia: Caribbean Radicalism in Early Twentieth-Century America* (London: Verso, 1998), esp. 122–94; Kevin Meehan, *People Get Ready: African American and Caribbean Cultural Exchange* (Jackson: University Press of Mississippi, 2009), 22–51; Tony Martin, *Race First: The Ideological and Organizational Struggles of Marcus Garvey's United Negro Improvement Association* (Dover, Mass.: Majority Press, 1976), 81–88, 110–13; and August Meier, *Negro Thought in America 1880–1915* (Ann Arbor: University of Michigan Press, 1963), 256–79.

44. E. Franklin Frazier, "Garvey: A Mass Leader," *Nation,* August 18, 1926, 147–48, in *The Black Man and the American Dream: Negro Aspirations in America 1900–1930,* ed. June Sochen (Chicago: Quadrangle, 1971), 335, 333.

45. Frazier, "Garvey," 335.

46. W. E. B. Du Bois, "The Black Star Line," *The Crisis* 24, no. 5 (1922): 210.

47. See Wilson Moses, *Creative Conflict in African American Thought: Frederick Douglass, Alexander Crummell, Booker T. Washington, W. E. B. Du Bois, and Marcus Garvey* (Cambridge: Cambridge University Press, 2004), 261–62; and Judith Stein, *The World of Marcus Garvey: Race and Class in Modern Society* (Baton Rouge: Louisiana State University Press, 1991), 48–52.

48. See W. E. B. Du Bois, "The Pan-African Conference: A Report," *The Crisis* 17, no. 6 (1919): 271–74.

49. For a recent mediation on the aesthetics of data presentation in *The Crisis,* see Josh Jones, "W. E. B. Du Bois Creates Revolutionary, Artistic Data Visualizations Showing the Economic Plight of African-Americans (1900)," Open Culture, September 21, 2016, http://www.openculture.com/2016/09/w-e-b-du -bois-creates-revolutionary-artistic-data-visualizations-showing-the-economic -plight-of-african-americans-1900.html.

50. W. E. B. Du Bois, *The Negro* (New York: Holt, 1915), 35.

51. Du Bois, *The Negro,* 9.

52. Lothrop Stoddard, *The Rising Tide of Color against White Supremacy* (New York: Scribner's, 1920).

53. Marcus Garvey, "African Fundamentalism" (1925), in Hill and Bair, *Marcus Garvey: Life and Lessons,* 4.

54. In Jamaica, Garvey drew from figures such as the militant journalist J. Robert Love (1835–1914), who was involved with the Jamaica Cooperative Association (1897) and the People's Convention (1989), and colaunched the Pan-African Association in Jamaica in 1901, as well as Alexander Bedward (1859–1930), a Jamaican Baptist preacher who advocated peasant struggle from the 1890s through the 1920s. See Rupert Lewis, *Marcus Garvey: Anti-Colonial Champion* (Trenton, N.J.: Africa World Press, 1988), esp. 25–39.

55. For further discussion, see Ewing, *The Age of Garvey,* esp. 15–44.

56. "Native Correspondents and Agents Wanted in Every Quarter of the Globe," editorial, *African Times and Orient Review* 1, no. 1 (1912): 2.

57. Marcus Garvey, "Article by Marcus Garvey in the *African Times and Orient Review,*" in Hill, *The Marcus Garvey and United Negro Improvement Association Papers,* 1:31.

58. For a discussion of the 400,000,000 see Hill, *The Marcus Garvey and Universal Negro Improvement Association Papers,* 1:lxxvi.

59. See Hubert Harrison, "Marcus Garvey at the Bar of United States Justice," in *A Hubert Harrison Reader,* ed. Jeffrey B. Perry (Middletown, Conn.: Wesleyan University Press, 2001), 196–97; as Harrison explained in 1923, the UNIA "was not a novel contribution by Garvey. It had been the program of the

Liberty League of which Garvey was a member in 1917 in New York" (196). See also Jeffrey B. Perry, *Hubert Harrison: The Voice of Harlem Radicalism, 1883–1918* (New York: Columbia University Press, 2008), 1–21, 328–40.

60. Hubert Harrison, *When Africa Awakes* (1920; repr., Baltimore: Black Classics, 1997), 40. On the role of Irish independence in early Pan-Africanist discourse, see Guterl, "The New Race Consciousness."

61. Harrison, "Marcus Garvey at the Bar of United States Justice," 196–97.

62. Harrison, *When Africa Awakes*, 91.

63. Harrison, *When Africa Awakes*, 78.

64. Harrison, *When Africa Awakes*, 97.

65. Harrison, *When Africa Awakes*, 98.

66. Harrison, *When Africa Awakes*, 98.

67. Harrison, *When Africa Awakes*, 119.

68. Stoddard (*The Rising Tide of Color*, 4–5) notes that "the late war has taught many lessons as to the unstable and transitory character of even the most imposing political phenomena, while a better reading of history might bring home the truth that the basic factor in human affairs is not politics, but race." See also Harrison, *When Africa Awakes*, esp. 113–15, 140–44.

69. Harrison, *When Africa Awakes*, 144.

70. See, for instance, Aimé Césaire, *Discourse on Colonialism*, trans. Joan Pinkham (New York: Monthly Review Press, 2000).

71. Harrison, *When Africa Awakes*, 113.

72. Harrison, *When Africa Awakes*, 78–79.

73. Harrison, *When Africa Awakes*, 33, 96.

74. Harrison, *When Africa Awakes*, 38.

75. See Du Bois, "The Black Star Line," 210. Harrison, in his 1923 editorial against Garvey, would contest even this claim, noting that the idea for a steamship line had likewise come from a member of the Liberty League. See Harrison, "Marcus Garvey at the Bar of United States Justice," 197.

76. Stephens, *Black Empire,* 103. See also Michelle Commander, *Afro-Atlantic Flight: Speculative Returns and the Black Fantastic* (Durham, N.C.: Duke University Press, 2017).

77. "Certificate of Incorporation of the ACL," in Hill, *The Marcus Garvey and United Negro Improvement Association Papers,* 1:248–52.

78. On the BSL marketing campaign and its critics, see Colin Grant, *Negro with a Hat: The Rise and Fall of Marcus Garvey and His Dream of Mother Africa* (Oxford: Oxford University Press, 2008), 184–217; Moses, *Creative Conflict,* 256–86; and Stein, *The World of Marcus Garvey,* 61–88.

79. See Mustafa Abdelwahid, "Introduction," in Dusé Mohamed Ali, *The Autobiography of a Pioneer Pan-African and Afro-Asian Activist,* ed. Mustafa Abdelwahid (Trenton, N.J.: Red Sea, 2011), 17.

80. Dusé Mohamed Ali, *In the Land of the Pharaohs: A Short History of Egypt from the Fall of Ismail to the Assassination of Boutros Pasha* (London: Paul, 1911), 17.

81. Marcus Garvey, "Editorial Letter by Marcus Garvey," July 18, 1919, in Hill, *The Marcus Garvey and United Negro Improvement Association Papers*, 1:461.

82. Garvey, "Speech by Marcus Garvey," Philadelphia, October 21, 1919, in Hill, *The Marcus Garvey and United Negro Improvement Association Papers*, 2:96.

83. On the history of finance capital in the epistemic and politicoeconomic legacy of the Atlantic slave trade, including the very possibility of a European "public sphere," see Ian Baucom, *Specters of the Atlantic: Finance Capital, Slavery, and the Philosophy of History* (Durham, N.C.: Duke University Press, 2005).

84. On Chief Sam, see Kendra Field and Ebony Coletu, "The Chief Sam Movement, A Century Later: Public Histories, Private Stories, and the African Diaspora," *Transition* 114 (2014): 108–30. See also William E. Bittle and Gilbert L. Geis, *The Longest Way Home: Chief Alfred C. Sam's Back-to-Africa Movement* (Detroit: Wayne State University Press, 1964).

85. "$25,000 Messenger Drive," editorial advertisement, *Messenger,* May–June 1919, 18–19, repr. in *The Messenger* (Westport, Conn.: Negro Universities Press, 1969).

86. Baucom, *Specters of the Atlantic,* 66.

87. See Du Bois, "The Black Star Line"; and W. E. B. Du Bois, "The U.N.I.A.," *The Crisis* 25, no. 3 (1923): 120–22. On the finances of the Black Star Line, see Stein, *The World of Marcus Garvey,* esp. 61–107.

88. Stein, *The World of Marcus Garvey,* 74.

89. Stein, *The World of Marcus Garvey,* 94.

90. See John Henrik Clarke, *Marcus Garvey and the Vision of Africa* (New York: Random House, 1974), 198; and Stein, *The World of Marcus Garvey,* 102–4.

91. See, for instance, Ewing, *The Age of Garvey,* 76–125.

92. Theodore Kornweibel, *Seeing Red: Federal Campaigns against Black Militancy, 1919–1925* (Bloomington: Indiana University Press, 1998), 129.

93. Most notable among Garvey's "diplomatic" acts was his summit meeting in June 1922 with Edward Young Clarke, the imperial kleagle of the Ku Klux Klan, which prompted the leftist editors of the *Messenger*—A. Phillip Randolph and Chandler Owen—to launch a "Garvey Must Go!" campaign. On Garvey's meeting with Clarke and the subsequent intensification of anti-Garvey activism as well as Garvey's own racial ideology, see esp. *The Marcus Garvey and United Negro Improvement Association Papers*, vol. 4, *September 1921–September 1922,* ed. Robert A. Hill (Berkeley: University of California Press, 1985), 679–749, as well as numerous articles in the *Messenger* in 1922 and 1923; see also Stein, *The World of Marcus Garvey,* 153–85; Clarke, *Marcus Garvey and the Vision of Africa,* 193–255; Moses, *Creative Conflict,* 275–77; and Frazier, "Garvey."

94. Stephens, *Black Empire,* 100.

95. See Martin, *Race First,* 41–66. See also Hill, *The Marcus Garvey and United Negro Improvement Association Papers,* 11:lxxiii–lxxvi.

96. Martin, *Race First,* 51.

97. Marcus Garvey, "Epigrams," in Garvey, *Philosophy and Opinions,* 5.

98. Garvey, "Epigrams," 6.

99. See Claudius Fergus, "From Prophecy to Policy: Marcus Garvey and the Evolution of Pan-African Citizenship," *The Global South* 4, no. 2 (2010): 29–48, esp. 30–37.

100. Bagnall, "The Madness of Marcus Garvey," 648.

101. Garvey, "Epigrams," 10.

102. See Ewing, *The Age of Garvey*, 127–242; Frank Andre Guidry, *Forging Diaspora: Afro-Cubans and African Americans in a World of Empire and Jim Crow* (Chapel Hill: University of North Carolina Press, 2010); Harold, *The Rise and Fall of the Garvey Movement;* and Rolinson, *Grassroots Garveyism,* esp. 192–96.

6. THE SADE INDUSTRY

1. Theodor Adorno and Max Horkheimer, *Dialectic of Enlightenment: Philosophical Fragments,* trans. Edmund Jephcott (1947; repr., Stanford, Calif.: Stanford University Press, 2002), xvi.

2. Adorno and Horkheimer, *Dialectic of Enlightenment,* xvi.

3. Adorno and Horkheimer, *Dialectic of Enlightenment,* 100.

4. Adorno and Horkheimer, *Dialectic of Enlightenment,* 16–17.

5. Adorno and Horkheimer, *Dialectic of Enlightenment,* 65–66.

6. Adorno and Horkheimer, *Dialectic of Enlightenment,* 18.

7. Adorno and Horkheimer, *Dialectic of Enlightenment,* 74.

8. Adorno and Horkheimer, *Dialectic of Enlightenment,* 90.

9. Adorno and Horkheimer, *Dialectic of Enlightenment,* 82, 79.

10. Adorno and Horkheimer, *Dialectic of Enlightenment,* 82.

11. Adorno and Horkheimer, *Dialectic of Enlightenment,* 79.

12. Adorno and Horkheimer, *Dialectic of Enlightenment,* 92.

13. See Éric Marty, *Pourquoi le XXe siècle a-t-il prise Sade au sérieux* (Paris: Seuil, 2011).

14. See, for instance, Marie-Françoise Quignard and Raymond-Josué Seckel, eds., *L'Enfer de la Bibliothèque: Éros au secret* (Paris: BNF, 2007), which accompanied a major exhibition of the library's pornographic holdings.

15. See Annie Le Brun, *Sade: Attaquer le Soleil* (Paris: Gallimard, 2014).

16. Jean Paulhan, "The Marquis de Sade and His Accomplice" (1946), in *Justine, Philosophy in the Bedroom, and Other Writings,* ed. and trans. Richard Seaver and Austryn Wainhouse (New York: Grove, 1965), 6.

17. See Richard von Krafft-Ebing, *Psychopathia Sexualis,* trans. Charles Gilbert Chaddock (Philadelphia: F. A. Davis, 1894), 57.

18. Maurice Blanchot, *Lautréamont and Sade,* trans. Stuart Kendall and Michelle Kendall (Stanford, Calif.: Stanford University Press, 2004), 19.

19. Paulhan, "The Marquis de Sade and His Accomplice," 11.

20. Jean-Michel Rabaté, *Jacques Lacan: Psychoanalysis and the Subject of Literature* (London: Palgrave, 2001), 111.

21. Alphonso Lingis ("Translator's Introduction," in Pierre Klossowski, *Sade, My Neighbor,* trans. Alphonso Lingis [Evanston, Ill.: Northwestern University Press, 1991], x) notes that "thinkers began to turn to [Sade's] work [after World War II] in a desperate effort to understand the nightmares the European Enlightenment seemed to have engendered." See also Marty, *Pourquoi le XXe siècle a-t-il prise Sade au sérieux.*

22. Heine also published *Les Infortunes de la vertu,* an early version of *Justine,* with Éditions Fourcade in 1930, a publisher noted for printing works by a number of avant-garde poets and critics.

23. Later literary scholars have, of course, sought precisely to read Sade as an eighteenth-century writer. See, for instance, Norbert Sclippa, ed., *Lire Sade: Actes du premier colloque international sur Sade aux US; Charleston, Caroline du Sud, 12–15 mars 2003* (Paris: L'Harmattan, 2004); Natania Meeker, *Voluptuous Philosophy: Literary Materialism in the French Enlightenment* (New York: Fordham University Press, 2006), esp. 189–221; and Kate Parker and Norbert Sclippa, eds., *Sade's Sensibilities (Aperçus: Histories Texts Cultures)* (Lewisburg, Pa.: Bucknell University Press, 2014).

24. Marty, *Pourquoi le XXe siècle a-t-il prise Sade au sérieux,* 84; my translation.

25. It is worth pointing out in this context that Blanchot's relationship with complicity was, to say the least, complicated: his shift from right-wing journalism in the 1930s to left-wing criticism and literature after World War II (after "abandoning" right-wing politics during the Vichy regime in 1941) points to a discontinuity within his own politics, his own position toward the collapse between reason and atrocity. As Steven Ungar writes in his nuanced assessment of Blanchot's interwar and wartime writings, the desire for "critical distance" is a cultural product that belies the deep entanglements between literature and politics in interwar France. It was a desire for a revolutionary break that, according to Ungar, fueled Blanchot's right-wing journalism and then, in turn, a desire for "critical distance" that fueled his left-wing turn. Sade, we might say, marks such shifts in Blanchot's own politics. See Steven Ungar, *Scandal and Aftereffect: Blanchot and France since 1930* (Minneapolis: University of Minnesota Press, 1995), esp. 110–23.

26. Blanchot, *Lautréamont and Sade,* 7.

27. Ungar, *Scandal and Aftereffect,* 123.

28. Blanchot, *Lautréamont and Sade,* 4.

29. Blanchot, *Lautréamont and Sade,* 2, 165. See also Martin Heidegger, *Elucidations of Hölderlin's Poetry,* trans. Keith Hoeller (New York: Humanity Books, 2000), 22. On Blanchot's recourse to Heidegger, see Ungar, *Scandal and Aftereffect,* 34–59, 121–25.

30. Blanchot, *Lautréamont and Sade,* 5.

31. Simone de Beauvoir, *Must We Burn Sade?,* trans. Kim Allen Gleed, Marilyn Gladys Rose, and Virginia Preston, in *Political Writings,* ed. Margaret A. Simons and Marybeth Timmerman (Urbana: University of Illinois Press, 2012), 95.

32. See Carolyn J. Dean, *The Self and Its Pleasures: Bataille, Lacan, and the History of the Decentered Subject* (Ithaca, N.Y.: Cornell University Press, 1992).

33. Jacques Lacan, "Kant with Sade," in *Écrits: The First Complete Edition in English*, trans. Bruce Fink (New York: Norton, 2006), 645–70.

34. Gilles Deleuze, "Coldness and Cruelty," in Gilles Deleuze and Leopold von Sacher-Masoch, *Masochism:* Coldness and Cruelty *by Gilles Deleuze and* Venus in Furs *by Leopold von Sacher-Masoch*, trans. Jean McNeil and Aude Willm (Cambridge, Mass.: MIT Press, 1991), 45.

35. Deleuze, "Coldness and Cruelty," 78.

36. Deleuze, "Coldness and Cruelty," 77, 63.

37. Michel Foucault, *The Order of Things: An Archaeology of the Human Sciences* (1966; repr., New York: Vintage, 1994), 209.

38. Foucault, *The Order of Things*, 210, 209.

39. Maurice Blanchot, *The Infinite Conversation*, trans. Susan Hanson (Minneapolis: University of Minnesota Press, 1993), 218.

40. Blanchot, *The Infinite Conversation*, 222.

41. On the history of Sade's reception by sexologists, see Will McNamara, "The Marquis, the Monster, and the Scientist: Sade, Sexology, and Criticism," in *Sade's Sensibilities*, ed. Kate Parker and Norbert Sclippa (Lewisburg, Pa.: Bucknell University Press, 2014), 169–94.

42. Maurice Heine, "Introduction aux *Infortunes de la vertu*," in Heine, *Le Marquis de Sade*, ed. Gilbert Lély (Paris: Gallimard, 1950), 61.

43. On Heine's early poetry, see Neil Cox, "La Mort posthume: Maurice Heine and the Poetics of Decay," *Art History* 23, no. 3 (2000): 417–49.

44. See John Phillips, "Old Wine in New Bottles? Literary Pornography in Twentieth-Century France," in *International Exposure: Perspectives on Modern European Pornography, 1800–2000*, ed. Lisa Z. Sigel (New Brunswick, N.J.: Rutgers University Press, 2005), 128.

45. Maurice Heine, *Statuts de la Société du Roman Philosophique*, pamphlet (Paris: n.p., n.d.).

46. See Maurice Garçon and Jean-Jacques Pauvert, eds., *L'affaire Sade. Compte-rendu exact du procès intenté par le Ministère Public* (Paris: Pauvert, 1957). The volume contains testimonies on Pauvert's behalf by a list of notable French authors, including Georges Bataille, André Breton, Jean Cocteau, and Jean Paulhan. See also Emmanuel Pierrat, *Jean-Jacques Pauvert: L'éditeur en liberté* (Paris: Calmann-Lévy, 2016).

47. Heine was certainly far from uninterested in the perversions of Sade's work, as he not only wrote essays about other "scandalous" eighteenth-century writers such as Nicolas-Edme Rétif de la Bretonne, but also penned his own incest novel, *Luce*. See Heine, *Luce ou Les Mémoires d'un veuf* (Paris: Éditions de la différence, 2013). Written in the spirit of Georges Bataille's obscene works of the same period, the novel remained unpublished during Heine's lifetime.

48. Maurice Heine to the Ministre de travail and the Ministre de l'Education nationale, October 16, 1939, Maurice Heine Papers, Bibliothèque nationale de France, NAF 24397.

49. Guillaume Apollinaire, Louis Perceau, and Pascal Pia, *L'Enfer de la Bibliothèque nationale* (Paris: Mercure de France, 1913).

50. Heine, "Préface," in Marquis de Sade, *Historiettes, contes et fabliaux* (1926; repr., Paris: Kra, 1927), 38.

51. Apollinaire, Perceau, and Pia, *L'Enfer de la Bibliothèque nationale,* 7.

52. Apollinaire, Perceau, and Pia, *L'Enfer de la Bibliothèque nationale,* 8.

53. Heine, *Statuts de la Société du Roman Philosophique.*

54. Klossowski, *Sade, My Neighbor,* 28.

55. On Heine's involvement in the Féderation de la Seine, see Henri Dubief, "Contribution à l'histoire de l'ultra-gauche: Maurice Heine," in *Mélanges d'histoire sociale offerts à Jean Maitron* (Paris: Éditions ouvrières, 1976), 87–94. On the "schism of Tours" and the history of the French Communist Party, see Robert Wohl, *French Communism in the Making, 1914–1924* (Stanford, Calif.: Stanford University Press, 1966), esp. 313–54. For the documents pertaining to Heine's party involvement, see Maurice Heine Papers, Bibliothèque nationale de France, NAF 24396.

56. See Dubief, "Contribution à l'histoire de l'ultra-gauche," 88.

57. Maurice Heine, "Introduction aux *120 Journées de Sodom,*" in *Le Marquis de Sade,* 71.

58. Heine, "Introduction aux *120 Journées de Sodom,*" 71.

59. Maurice Heine, "Une thèse de doctorat sur le marquis de Sade" (1932), in *Le Marquis de Sade,* 109–10.

60. Heine, "Introduction aux *Infortunes de la vertu,*" in *Le Marquis de Sade,* 69.

61. Maurice Heine to Louis Perceau, July 31, 1927, Maurice Heine Papers, Bibliothèque nationale de France, NAF 24397.

62. Louis Perceau to Maurice Heine, August 19, 1927, Maurice Heine Papers, Bibliothèque nationale de France, NAF 24397.

63. Maurice Heine, "Projet de Statuts pour l'Association des écrivains bibliographes, traducteurs et commentateurs," manuscript included in letter to Louis Perceau, August 21, 1927, Maurice Heine Papers, Bibliothèque nationale de France, NAF 24397.

64. On the history of bibliophile societies in France, see Raymond Hesse, *Histoire des sociétés de bibliophiles en France de 1820 à 1930,* 2 vols. (Paris: Giraud Badin, 1929–31). For a valuable study of bibliophile societies in France before World War I, see Willa Silverman, *The New Bibliopolis: French Book Collectors and the Culture of Print, 1880–1914* (Toronto: University of Toronto Press, 2008).

65. See Marie Carbonel, "Profession: critique?," *Le Mouvement sociale* 214, no. 1 (2006): 93–111. Heine lists his involvement in the Association Syndicale de la critique littéraire in his letter to the French minister of labor. See Heine to Ministre de travail and the Ministre de l'Education nationale, October 16, 1939.

66. Maurice Heine, "Promenade à travers le Roman noir," *Minotaure* 5 (1934): 1.

67. Maurice Heine, "La Vieillesse de Rétif de la Bretonne," *Hippocrate,* September 1934, 609–10.

68. See Meeker, *Voluptuous Philosophy,* esp. 189–221.

69. Maurice Heine, *Receuil de confessions et observations psycho-sexuelles* (1936; repr., Paris: La Musardine, 2000), 15.

70. Heine, *Receuil,* 16.

71. Heine, *Receuil,* 17.

72. Heine, "Introduction aux *Infortunes de la vertu,*" 68.

73. Heine, "Introduction aux *Infortunes de la vertu,*" 64.

74. Heine, "Introduction aux *Infortunes de la vertu,*" 68.

75. Gilles Deleuze and Félix Guattari, *What Is Philosophy?,* trans. Hugh Tomlinson and Graham Burchell (New York: Columbia University Press, 1994), 64.

76. Blanchot, *The Infinite Conversation,* 218.

77. Maurice Heine, "Le marquis de Sade, persécuté du XVIIIe siècle, ignoré du XIXe siècle, dominera-t-il le XXe?," unpublished manuscript of lecture at the Club du Faubourg, February 10, 1932, Maurice Heine Papers, Bibliothèque nationale de France, NAF 24392.

78. Marty, *Pourquoi le XXe siècle a-t-il prise Sade au sérieux,* 84.

79. Heine, "Introduction aux *120 Jours de Sodom,*" 74.

80. Blanchot, *The Infinite Conversation,* 219.

7. CARTOGRAPHORRHEA

1. For a notable rejoinder to this claim, see Jonathan Glover, *Alien Landscapes? Interpreting Disordered Minds* (Cambridge, Mass.: Harvard University Press, 2014).

2. See, most notably, Maurice Thévoz, *Écrits bruts* (Paris: Presses universitaires de France, 1979), 8, which speculates that "it is internment or social excommunication, and not madness, that constitute the specific condition of the writerly creations" that Thévoz collects in his anthology of "outsider writing." In a valuable critique of "outsider writing," Allen S. Weiss writes diagnoses a literary-historical and art-historical discomfort with interdisciplinarity (with regard to depth psychology in particular) in accounting for the discursive and cultural conditions of such writing. See Allen S. Weiss, *Shattered Forms: Art Brut, Phantasms, Modernism* (Albany: State University of New York Press, 1992), esp. 61–88.

3. As Rachel Adams, Benjamin Reiss, and David Serlin write in *Keywords for Disability Studies* (New York: New York University Press, 2015, 4), "One of the key assumptions of disability studies is that there is no neutral or objective position from which to regard the human body and its differences, just as the 'normal' body is a fantasy belied by the wondrous spectrum of human difference."

4. Georges Canguilhem, *The Normal and the Pathological,* trans. Carolyn R. Fawcett (New York: Zone, 1991), 144.

5. Eve Kosofsky Sedgwick, "Paranoid Reading and Reparative Reading, or, You're So Paranoid, You Probably Think This Essay Is about You" (1997), in *Touching Feeling: Affect, Pedagogy, Performativity* (Durham, N.C.: Duke University Press, 2003), 125.

6. Sigmund Freud, "Psychoanalytic Notes upon an Autobiographical Account of a Case of Paranoia," in *Three Case Histories* (New York: Macmillan, 1963), 154.

7. Eve Kosofsky Sedgwick, *Touching Feeling: Affect, Pedagogy, Performativity* (Durham, N.C.: Duke University Press, 2003), reads this statement in the context of Freud's reduction of "every instance of paranoia to the repression of specifically same-sex desire, whether in women or in men." This has meant in turn that "the traditional, homophobic psychoanalytic use that has generally been made of Freud's association has been to pathologize homosexuals as paranoid or to consider paranoia as a distinctively homosexual disease" (126). Sedgwick aims to interrupt the normalization of paranoia as the dominant critical mode for *antihomophobic* scholarship on account of the way it tends toward totalizing self-reproduction (127). "In a world where no one need be delusional to find evidence of systemic oppression," she writes, "to theorize out of anything but a paranoid critical stance has come to seem naïve, pious, or complaisant. I myself have no wish to return to the use of 'paranoid' as a pathologizing diagnosis, but it seems to me a great loss when paranoid inquiry comes to seem entirely coextensive with critical theoretical inquiry rather than being viewed as one kind of cognitive/affective theoretical practice among other, alternative kinds" (125–26). My own discussion traces methodological reflections in Freud and other psychoanalytic thinkers that resist their own tendency to posit reductive, singularizing explanations; my approach to psychoanalysis, in this sense, might be considered a form of reparative reading insofar as it aims, like Sedgwick, "to understand paranoia in such a way to situate it as one kind of epistemological practice among other, alternative ones" (128).

8. Hans Prinzhorn, *Artistry of the Mentally Ill: A Contribution to the Psychology and Psychopathology of Configuration,* trans. Eric von Brockdorff (Berlin: Springer, 1972), 243.

9. Dr. Guido Weber, quoted in Freud, "Psychoanalytic Notes," 90.

10. Freud, "Psychoanalytic Notes," 151.

11. Freud, "Psychoanalytic Notes," 147.

12. Jacques Lacan, *The Seminar of Jacques Lacan,* vol. 3, *The Psychoses 1955–1956,* ed. Jacques-Alain Miller, trans. Russel Grigg (New York: Norton, 1993), 28.

13. Jacques Lacan, "The Mirror Stage as Formative of the *I* Function," in *Écrits: The First Complete Edition in English,* trans. Bruce Fink (New York: Norton, 2006), 77.

14. Jacques Lacan, "Aggressiveness in Psychoanalysis," in *Écrits,* 91.

15. On Lacan's recourse to cybernetics, see Lydia Liu's "The Cybernetic Unconscious: Rethinking Lacan, Poe, and French Theory," *Critical Inquiry* 36, no. 2 (2010): 288–320. See also Lydia Liu, *The Freudian Robot: Digital Media and the Future of the Unconscious* (Chicago: University of Chicago Press, 2010), esp. chapters 3–5. For a luminous reading of Lacan's complex mathematics, see Arkady Plotnitsky, *The*

Knowable and the Unknowable: Modern Science, Nonclassical Thought, and the "Two Cultures" (Ann Arbor: University of Michigan Press, 2002), 109–56.

16. See Jacques Lacan, *The Seminar of Jacques Lacan*, vol. 2, *The Ego in Freud's Theory and in the Technique of Psychoanalysis, 1954–1955,* ed. Jacques-Alain Miller, trans. Sylvana Tomaselli (New York: Norton, 1991), esp. 175–205.

17. Lacan, *The Seminar of Jacques Lacan*, 2:224.

18. For a humanistic study of nonconscious cognition, see N. Kathryn Hayles, *Unthought: The Power of the Cognitive Nonconscious* (Chicago: University of Chicago Press, 2017).

19. Lacan, *The Seminar of Jacques Lacan*, 2:122.

20. Lacan, *The Seminar of Jacques Lacan*, 3:135.

21. Lacan, *The Seminar of Jacques Lacan*, 3:143.

22. Lacan, *The Seminar of Jacques Lacan*, 3:132.

23. See Jacques Lacan, "The Freudian Thing," in *Écrits*, 334–63.

24. John Haslam, *Illustrations of Madness* (1810), ed. Roy Porter (London: Routledge, 1988), 80.

25. Roy Porter, "Introduction," in Haslam, *Illustrations of Madness*, xxxviii; emphasis in original.

26. Jacob Moreno, "Emotions Mapped by New Geography" (1933), quoted in Manuel Lima, *Visual Complexity: Mapping Patterns of Information* (New York: Princeton Architectural Press, 2011), 76.

27. Mike Jay, *The Air Loom Gang* (New York: Four Walls Eight Windows, 2004), 284–85.

28. For a brief treatment of the resemblance between Matthews's air loom and Tausk's influencing machines, see Christopher Turner, "The Influencing Machine," *Cabinet* 14 (2004), http://www.cabinetmagazine.org/issues/14/turner.php.

29. Victor Tausk, "The Influencing Machine" (1919), in *Incorporations*, ed. Jonathan Crary and Sanford Kwinter (New York: Zone, 1992), 544.

30. Lacan, *The Seminar of Jacques Lacan*, 3:320.

31. Lacan, *The Seminar of Jacques Lacan*, 3:250.

32. Lacan, *The Seminar of Jacques Lacan*, 3:130.

33. Jacques Lacan, "Seminar on 'The Purloined Letter,'" in *Écrits*, 40.

34. Lacan, *The Seminar of Jacques Lacan*, 3:25.

35. See Emily Apter, "On Oneworldedness: Or Paranoia as a World System," *American Literary History* 18, no. 2 (2006): 365–89.

36. Lacan, *The Seminar of Jacques Lacan*, 3:220.

37. Sedgwick, *Touching Feeling*, 136.

38. Lacan, "The Freudian Thing," 339.

39. Jacques Lacan, "The Situation of Psychoanalysis and the Training of Psychoanalysis in 1956," in *Écrits*, 388.

40. Douglas Hofstadter, "The Paranoid Style in American Politics," in *The Paranoid Style in American Politics, and Other Essays* (Cambridge, Mass.: Harvard University Press, 1965), 39.

41. In Hofstadter's account, this includes "minority" movements and revolutionary insurrections—or, it would seem, any notion of politics as class warfare—and thus not merely the totalitarian extremes of fascism and Stalinism alone. In a sense, Hofstadter's own work might be said to betray signs of his own notion of a paranoid style in the sense that his vision of political history designates a conspiracy of conspiracy theories, with his hope for "normal" democracy always under attack from interest groups as well as the Far Right and the Far Left.

42. Sedgwick, *Touching Feeling*, 131; emphasis in original.

43. As Apter, "On Oneworldedness," 371, notes, "Paranoia captures the systematicity of world systems—its folie raisonnante or rationalism of systematized delusion. Very much a symptom of what it critiques, paranoia theory might be said to refer to a delusional model of subjective recognition that apprehends itself in global schemata."

44. Lacan, "The Mirror Stage," 77.

45. Lacan, "The Freudian Thing," 341.

46. For a discussion of the institutional floor plan included in Schreber's *Memoirs of My Nervous Illness*, see Jonathan P. Eburne, *Surrealism and the Art of Crime* (Ithaca, N.Y.: Cornell University Press, 2008), 215–43.

47. Johann Knopf, *Bitte No. 2345 die geheimnisvolle Affären der Mordanschlägen* (Petition No. 2345 the mysterious affairs of the murderous attacks), transcription in *Beyond Reason: Art and Psychosis: Works from the Prinzhorn Collection*, ed. Bettina Brand-Claussen, Inge Jádi, and Caroline Douglas (London: Hayward, 1996), 118–19.

48. Hal Foster, *Prosthetic Gods* (Cambridge, Mass.: MIT Press, 2004), 205; emphasis in original.

49. Jacques Lacan, "Le Problème du style et la conception psychiatrique des formes paranoïaques de l'expérience," *Minotaure* 1 (1933): 69.

50. Gilles Deleuze and Félix Guattari, *Anti-Oedipus: Capitalism of Jacques Lacan and Schizophrenia*, trans. Robert Hurley, Mark Seem, and Helen R. Lane (Minneapolis: University of Minnesota Press, 1983), 5.

51. Insofar as they derive much of their critical insight from the resistance of outsider art to the conceptual rigidity of classical psychoanalysis, their work recasts the visual and speculative work of the insane as a mode of production in its own right, and thus as evidence of their own contentions. On Deleuze and Guattari's recourse to psychotic art, see Daniel O'Hara, "Deleuze and the Art of Psychosis," in *Deleuzian Events: Writing/History*, ed. Hanjo Berressem (Münster, Germany: LIT, 2009), 270–85.

52. Gilles Deleuze and Félix Guattari, "Appendice: Bilan-programme pour machine désirantes," in *L'Anti-Oedipe* (Paris: Éditions du Minuit, 1974), 463.

53. Deleuze and Guattari, *Anti-Oedipus*, 24.

54. Deleuze and Guattari, *Anti-Oedipus*, 366.

55. See Jean-Michel Rabaté, "Loving Freud Madly: Surrealism between Hysterical and Paranoid Modernism," *Journal of Modern Literature* 25, nos. 3–4 (2002): 58–74; also Eburne, *Surrealism and the Art of Crime*, 173–214.

56. Gilles Deleuze and Félix Guattari, *A Thousand Plateaus: Capitalism and Schizophrenia*, trans. Brian Massumi (Minneapolis: University of Minnesota Press, 1987), 13.

57. Deleuze and Guattari, *A Thousand Plateaus*, 17.

58. Deleuze and Guattari, *Anti-Oedipus*, 1.

59. Jacques Lacan, *My Teaching*, trans. David Macey (London: Verso, 2008), 113.

60. Lacan, *My Teaching*, 113.

61. Lacan, *My Teaching*, 112.

8. COMMUNITIES OF SUSPICION

1. Jacques Lacan, "The Freudian Thing," in *Écrits*, trans. Bruce Fink (New York: Norton, 2006), 334.

2. Sigmund Freud, *Introductory Lectures on Psycho-Analysis*, ed. and trans. James Strachey (1917; repr., New York: Norton, 1988), 353.

3. Freud, *Introductory Lectures on Psycho-Analysis*, 353.

4. Jacques Lacan, "The Subversion of the Subject and the Dialectic of Desire," in *Écrits*, 674–76.

5. See Jacques Lacan, "The Situation of Psychoanalysis and the Training of Psychoanalysis in 1956," in *Écrits*, 384–411.

6. See, for instance, Michael Shermer, *The Borderlands of Science: Where Sense Meets Nonsense* (Oxford: Oxford University Press, 2001), 199–214. See also Todd Dufresne, *Against Freud: Critics Talk Back* (Stanford, Calif.: Stanford University Press, 2007).

7. Karl Popper, "Science as Falsification," in *Conjectures and Refutations: The Growth of Scientific Knowledge* (1932; repr., London: Routledge, 2002), 45; emphasis in original.

8. Popper, *Conjectures and Refutations*, 49n3.

9. Paul Feyerabend, *Against Method*, rev. ed. (London: Verso, 1988), 133.

10. See Paul Ricoeur, *Freud and Philosophy: An Essay on Interpretation*, trans. Denis Savage (New Haven, Conn.: Yale University Press, 1970), esp. 32–35.

11. Avital Ronell, *The Test Drive* (Urbana: University of Illinois Press, 2005), 67.

12. Feyerabend, *Against Method*, 133.

13. Sigmund Freud, *Moses and Monotheism*, trans. Katherine Jones (New York: Vintage, 1967), 136.

14. Thomas Kuhn, *The Copernican Revolution: Planetary Astronomy in the Development of Western Thought* (New York: Vintage, 1957), 3.

15. Kuhn, *The Copernican Revolution*, 135. See also Thomas Kuhn, *The Structure of Scientific Revolutions*, 3rd ed. (Chicago: University of Chicago Press, 1996).

16. Evelyn Fox Keller, *Secrets of Life, Secrets of Death: Essays on Language, Gender, and Science* (London: Routledge, 1992), 6.

17. See, for instance, Keller's discussion of scientific "birth" in *Secrets of Life, Secrets of Death*, 39–55.

18. For a full account, see Michael Gordin, *The Pseudoscience Wars: Immanuel Velikovsky and the Birth of the Modern Fringe* (Chicago: University of Chicago Press, 2012), esp. 19–48.

19. Robert K. Merton, "The Perspectives of Insiders and Outsiders" (1971), in *The Sociology of Science: Theoretical and Empirical Investigations,* ed. Norman W. Storer (Chicago: University of Chicago Press, 1973), 101.

20. Immanuel Velikovsky, "Sins of the Sons," Immanuel Velikovsky Papers, Princeton University Special Collections, box 53, folder 8, p. 181. This passage was later published posthumously, in modified form, in Immanuel Velikovsky, *Mankind in Amnesia* (New York: Doubleday, 1982), 37.

21. On such aspirations to messianism, see Jacques Derrida, *Archive Fever: A Freudian Impression,* trans. Eric Prenowitz (Chicago: University of Chicago Press, 1996), 36–37. See also Derrida, *Spectres of Marx: The State of the Debt, the Work of Mourning and the New International,* trans. Peggy Kamuf (London: Routledge, 1994), esp. 73–74, 210–13.

22. See, for instance, Immanuel Velikovsky, *Worlds in Collision* (1950; repr., New York: Delta, 1965), 40–44.

23. See Gordin, *The Pseudoscience Wars,* esp. 135–62.

24. Ignatius Donnelly, *Ragnarok: The Age of Fire and Gravel* (New York: Appleton, 1882). Citing geological evidence, Donnelly argues that major transformations in the earth's surface were not caused by glaciers but by a comet. As Michael Gordin notes, however, Velikovsky himself "was pretty cagey about the Donnelly connection. He does have a footnote in *Worlds in Collision* about it, but that was added when one of the reviewers for MacMillan pointed out the similarities. While he does . . . provide a lot of scholarly references, he was pretty scanty about possible predecessors." Michael Gordin, personal correspondence with the author, June 4, 2017.

25. Editors of *Pensée,* eds., *Velikovsky Reconsidered* (New York: Doubleday, 1976), v.

26. Velikovsky, *Worlds in Collision,* xv.

27. Velikovsky, *Worlds in Collision,* 298.

28. Velikovsky, *Worlds in Collision,* 298.

29. Velikovsky, *Worlds in Collision,* 86.

30. John Lear, "The Heavens Burst," *Collier's,* February 25, 1950, 24, 42–45; John Lear, "World on Fire," *Collier's,* March 25, 1950, 24, 82–85.

31. Norman Vincent Peale, "The Greatness of the Bible," inset in Lear, "The Heavens Burst," 43.

32. Velikovsky, *Worlds in Collision,* 3.

33. Ralph E. Juergens, "Minds in Chaos," in *The Velikovsky Affair: Scientism vs. Science,* ed. Alfred de Grazia, Ralph E. Juergens, and Livio C. Stecchini (Hyde Park, N.Y.: University Books, 1966), 10.

34. Immanuel Velikovsky, "Cosmos without Gravitation: A Revision of the Theory of Gravitation, Preliminary Report," Immanuel Velikovsky Papers, Princeton University Special Collections, box 1, folder 9.

35. For an exhaustive refutation, see Henry H. Bauer, *Beyond Velikovsky: The History of a Public Controversy* (Urbana: University of Illinois Press, 1984), 98–121.

36. Robert K. Merton, "Paradigm for the Sociology of Knowledge" (1945), in *The Sociology of Science: Theoretical and Empirical Investigations,* ed. Norman W. Storer (Chicago: University of Chicago Press, 1973), 11.

37. See David Stove, "The Scientific Mafia," in Editors of *Pensée,* eds., *Velikovsky Reconsidered,* 5–12.

38. There have been no fewer than eleven Velikovsky-oriented journals published since the early 1970s, including *Aeon, Chiron, Chronology and Catastrophism Review, Isis, Kronos,* and *Pensée.* For a listing and description of the journals, see the Velikovsky Encyclopedia, http://www.velikovsky.info/Category:Journals. See also Gordin, *The Pseudoscience Wars,* esp. 179–88.

39. For detailed accounts, see De Grazia, Juergens, and Stecchini, *The Velikovsky Affair;* Horace Kallen, "Shapley, Velikovsky, and the Scientific Spirit," in Editors of *Pensée, Velikovsky Reconsidered,* 21–30; Bauer, *Beyond Velikovsky,* 3–84. The greatest detail is in Gordin, *The Pseudoscience Wars,* esp. 19–78.

40. Livio C. Stecchini, "The Inconstant Heavens," in De Grazia, Juergens, and Stecchini, *The Velikovsky Affair,* 122.

41. Stecchini, "The Inconstant Heavens," 123.

42. See, for instance, John Sladek, *The New Apocrypha: A Guide to Strange Science and Occult Beliefs* (New York: Stein and Day, 1973); and Ronald H. Fritze, *Invented Knowledge: False History, Fake Science and Pseudo-Religions* (London: Reaktion, 2011). A notable exception to this tendency is Vine Deloria Jr., who maintains that Velikovsky "offered a scenario in which a truly planetary history could be constructed." See *Red Earth, White Lies: Native Americans and the Myth of Scientific Fact* (New York: Scribner, 1995), 31–32.

43. Michael Polanyi, "Scientific Convictions" (1949), in *The Logic of Liberty* (Chicago: University of Chicago Press, 1951), 19. Polanyi developed the notion of "fiduciary communities" further in *Personal Knowledge: Towards a Post-Critical Philosophy* (1958; repr., London: Routledge, 2012), esp. 315–42.

44. See, for instance, Immanuel Velikovsky, "Verwandschaft zwischen Sender und Empfänger als erleichterndes Moment in der experimentellen Telepathie," "Über die Zuverlässigkeit des visuellen Merkvermögens," and "The Electrocephalographic Curves of the Discharges of Potential Difference at the Onset of an Epileptic Fit (Petit Mal)," Immanuel Velikovsky Papers, Princeton University Special Collections, box 52, folders 2–8, "Psychological Papers."

45. Immanuel Velikovsky, "Race Hatred," Immanuel Velikovsky Papers, Princeton University Special Collections, box 54, file 20.

46. Immanuel Velikovsky, "The Dreams Freud Dreamed," *Psychoanalytic Review* 28 (1941): 490.

47. Velikovsky, "The Dreams Freud Dreamed," 489.

48. Velikovsky, "The Dreams Freud Dreamed," 511.

49. Immanuel Velikovsky, *Stargazers and Gravediggers: Memoirs to* Worlds in Collision (New York: Morrow, 1983), 28.

50. Yosef Hayim Yerushalmi, *Freud's Moses: Judaism Terminable and Interminable* (New Haven, Conn.: Yale University Press, 1991), 6.

51. Kuhn, *The Structure of Scientific Revolutions*, 95.

52. Velikovsky, *Stargazers and Gravediggers*, 26.

53. Immanuel Velikovsky, "How I Arrived at My Concepts," Immanuel Velikovsky Papers, Princeton University Special Collections, box 40, folder 4, "Thoughts on Various Subjects."

54. Velikovsky, *Stargazers and Gravediggers*, 26.

55. Velikovsky, *Stargazers and Gravediggers*, 30.

56. Immanuel Velikovsky, *Ages in Chaos,* vol. 1, *From the Exodus to King Akhnaton* (New York: Doubleday, 1952), xxii.

57. Gordin, *The Pseudoscience Wars*, 57.

58. See Gordin, *The Pseudoscience Wars*, 60–61, 67; see also Velikovsky, *Oedipus and Akhnaton* (1960; repr., New York: Pocket Books, 1980), 244.

59. Velikovsky, *Oedipus and Akhnaton*, 244.

60. Freud, *Moses and Monotheism*, 18.

61. See, for instance, Freud, *Moses and Monotheism*, 27.

62. Freud, *Moses and Monotheism*, 87.

63. Freud, *Moses and Monotheism*, 136–37.

64. Freud, *Moses and Monotheism*, 137.

65. Immanuel Velikovsky (*Earth in Upheaval* [1955; repr., New York: Pocket Books, 1977], 23–24) notes that "the theory of uniformity, or of gradual changes in the past measured by the extent of changes observed in the present, has, as [Charles] Lyell admitted, no positive evidence in the incomplete record of the earth's crust; consequently the theory, building on *argumentum ex silentio,* or argument by default, required further analogies."

66. Yerushalmi, *Freud's Moses*, 29.

67. Freud, *Moses and Monotheism*, 170.

68. Freud, *Moses and Monotheism*, 107.

69. Freud, *Moses and Monotheism*, 87.

70. Freud, *Moses and Monotheism*, 87.

71. Freud, *Moses and Monotheism*, 87.

72. Freud, *Moses and Monotheism*, 107–8.

73. Freud, *Moses and Monotheism*, 170.

74. Velikovsky, *Mankind in Amnesia*, 33.

75. Velikovsky, *Mankind in Amnesia*, 184.

76. See Gordin, *The Pseudoscience Wars*, 135–62.

77. Alfred de Grazia, Ralph E. Juergens, and Livio C. Stecchini, "Foreword," in De Grazia, Juergens, and Stecchini, *The Velikovsky Affair*, 1.

78. De Grazia, Juergens, and Stecchini, "Foreword," 2.

79. See Alfred de Grazia, "The Scientific Reception System," in De Grazia, Juergens, and Stecchini, *The Velikovsky Affair*, 172.

80. De Grazia, "The Scientific Reception System," 171.

81. Michael Polanyi, "Scientific Convictions," 11.

82. Stecchini, "The Inconstant Heavens," 123.

83. Juergens, "Minds in Chaos," 10.

84. Merton, "Paradigm for the Sociology of Knowledge," 11.

85. Merton, "Paradigm for the Sociology of Knowledge," 34.

86. Merton, "The Perspectives of Insiders and Outsiders," 101.

87. Defending science against the need for governmental or bureaucratic intervention in an age of increasing state control, Polanyi cites the Soviet support of Lysenkoism as its "official" state science as the epitome of such intervention, but the example of ideological interrogation in the era of the Red Scare was no less pressing. See Gordin, *The Pseudoscience Wars*, 79–105.

88. Polanyi, "Self-Government of Science" (1942), in *The Logic of Liberty* (Chicago: University of Chicago Press, 1951), 57.

89. Polanyi, "The Growth of Science in Society," *Minerva* 5, no. 4 (1967): 536.

90. Polanyi, "The Growth of Science in Society," 539.

91. Polanyi, "The Growth of Science in Society," 544–45.

92. Polanyi, "The Growth of Science in Society," 541.

93. Polanyi, "The Growth of Science in Society," 541.

94. Isaac Asimov, "CP," *Analog,* October 1974, 38–50.

95. Isaac Asimov, "Foreword," in *Scientists Confront Velikovsky,* ed. Donald Goldsmith (New York: Norton, 1976), 7.

96. Asimov, "Foreword," 7.

97. Asimov, "Foreword," 14.

98. Asimov, "Foreword," 14.

99. Asimov, "Foreword," 14.

100. As the sociologist Robert McAulay argued in a 1978 essay published shortly before Velikovsky's death, the shortsightedness of accounts of tacit knowledge such as Polanyi's stem from the insistence "that judgments of plausibility, in [Velikovsky's] case and others, rest solely on a basis *internal* to science." The tacit "laws of what can be thought and said" that constitute the self-governing function of scientific communities can also extend beyond their reach: "Advocacy of or opposition to certain theories may, as a consequence, link both scientists and nonscientists alike to a larger community of interest," which beckons to a larger "social and cultural infrastructure" observed by the delimitation of judgments of plausibility to a situation "internal to science." Science, by this logic, could never fully be the master of its own house. Rather, its house of knowledge, the very seat of its self-governance and vehicle of its inheritance, was at once perpetually bound up in and perpetually seeking to distinguish itself from the broader infrastructure that formed its living environment. See Robert McAulay, "Velikovsky and the Infrastructure of Science," *Theory and Society* 6, no. 3 (1978): 322; emphasis in original.

101. Donna Haraway, "Situated Knowledges: The Science Question in Feminism and the Privilege of Partial Perspective," *Feminist Studies* 14, no. 3 (1988): 575–99.

102. Isabelle Stengers, *Thinking with Whitehead,* trans. Michael Chase (Cambridge, Mass.: Harvard University Press, 2011), 117.

103. Gordin, *The Pseudoscience Wars,* 209.

104. Derrida, *Archive Fever,* 29.

CODA

1. As this book was going to press, residents and neighbors in the rural township adjacent to my own began organizing in resistance to a bid by the Nestlé Corporation to purchase water rights from the township and to build a water bottling plant that would enable the company to sell public water at a profit. The bid was sanctioned by the local water authority without public input.

2. Alice Walker, *We Are The Ones We Have Been Waiting For: Inner Light in a Time of Darkness* (New York: New Press, 2006), 116.

3. Gabriel Rockhill, *Radical History and the Politics of Art* (New York: Columbia University Press, 2014), 3.

4. Patricia Hill Collins, *Black Feminist Thought: Knowledge, Consciousness, and the Politics of Empowerment,* 2nd ed. (London: Routledge, 2009), 291–309.

5. Mark Seltzer, *The Official World* (Durham, N.C.: Duke University Press, 2016), 9; emphasis added.

6. Bruno Latour, *We Have Never Been Modern,* trans. Catherine Porter (Cambridge, Mass.: Harvard University Press, 1993), 94–103. See also Bruno Latour, *Reassembling the Social: An Introduction to Actor-Network-Theory* (Oxford: Oxford University Press, 2005), 76.

7. David L. Martin, "Afterword: To Prophesy *Post Hoc,*" in *This Year's Work in the Oddball Archive,* ed. Jonathan P. Eburne and Judith Roof (Bloomington: Indiana University Press, 2016), 391–92.

8. Wilson Harris, *The Womb of Space: The Cross-Cultural Imagination* (Westport, Conn.: Greenwood, 1983), xvi.

9. Sun Ra, "If I Told You" (1980), in *The Immeasurable Equation: The Collected Poetry and Prose,* ed. James L. Wolf and Hartmut Geerken (Wartaweil, Germany: Waitawhile, 2005), 200.

10. For some of the field-defining scholarship on Sun Ra's music and thought, see Brent Hayes Edwards, "The Race for Space: Sun Ra's Poetry," *Hambone* 14 (1998), repr. in Wolf and Geerken, *The Immeasurable Equation,* 29–55; and Brent Hayes Edwards, *Epistrophies: Jazz and the Literary Imagination* (Cambridge, Mass.: Harvard University Press, 2017), 120–53. See also biographer John Szwed's heroic *Space Is the Place: The Lives and Times of Sun Ra* (New York: Da Capo, 1998); and Graham Lock, *Bluetopia: Visions of the Future and Revisions of the Past in Sun Ra, Duke Ellington, and Anthony Braxton* (Durham, N.C.: Duke University Press, 1999).

11. Amiri Baraka, "Sun Ra," *African American Review* 29, no. 2 (1995): 253.

12. Sun Ra, "Challenge" (1972), in Wolf and Geerken, *The Immeasurable Equation,* 94.

13. Baraka, "Sun Ra," 254. On Sun Ra's "instrumental mythos," Szwed, *Space Is the Place,* 95–96, notes that "a few of [the instruments] were homemade, more were foreign, picked up on travels about the country, and some were not that unusual. . . . There was the flying saucer, lightning drum, space gong, space harp, space-dimension mellophone, space drum, space bells, space flute, space master piano, intergalactic space organ, solar bells, solar drum, sunhorn, sunharp, Egyptian sun bells, ancient-Egyptian infinity drum, boom-bam, mistro clarinet, morro, alto sax, spiral percussion gong, cosmic tone organ, dragon drum, cosmic side drum, and tiger organ."

14. Michelle D. Commander, *Afro-Atlantic Flight: Speculative Returns and the Black Fantastic* (Durham, N.C.: Duke University Press, 2017), 7–8.

15. Sun Ra, "Sun Ra 1," *Jazz* 265 (1970): 31, quoted in Szwed, *Space Is the Place,* 308–9.

16. Szwed, *Space Is the Place,* 308–9.

17. On Sun Ra's erudition, see Edwards, *Epistrophies,* 133–45; Szwed, *Space Is the Place,* 131–41; and Marques Redd, "Astro-Black Mythology: The Poetry of Sun Ra," in *Esoterism in African American Religious Experience,* ed. Stephen C. Finley, Margarita Simon Guillory, and Hugh R. Page Jr. (Leiden: Brill, 2015), 227–45.

18. Sun Ra, "The Shape of the World Today," spoken word recording, https://www.youtube.com/watch?v=AmpgKIJl9NY.

19. Sun Ra, "The Alter Destiny," *Monorails and Satellites* (Saturn Records, 1966). For a discussion of "Alter Destiny," see Anthony Reed, "After the End of the World: Sun Ra and the Grammar of Utopia," *Black Camera* 5, no. 1 (2013): 127–30.

20. *Space Is the Place* (1974), dir. John Coney, written by Sun Ra and Joshua Smith (Harte Recordings, 2015).

21. Donna Haraway, "Situated Knowledges: The Science Question in Feminism and the Privilege of Partial Perspective," *Feminist Studies* 14, no. 3 (1988): 582.

22. Edwards, *Epistrophies,* 145.

23. Reed, "After the End of the World," 121–22.

24. See Michelle D. Commander, "The Space for Race: Black Exile and the Rise of Afro Speculation," *ASAP/Journal* 1, no. 3 (2016): 409–37.

25. See Ned Freedland, *The Occult Explosion: From Magic to ESP—The People Who Made the New Occultism* (New York: Putnam's, 1972).

26. On Jack Parsons, see John Carter, *Sex and Rockets: The Occult World of Jack Parsons* (Port Townsend, Wash.: Feral House, 1999).

27. H. P. Blavatsky, *Isis Unveiled: A Master-Key to the Mysteries of Ancient and Modern Science and Theology,* vol. 1 (1877; repr., Pasadena, Calif.: Theosophical University Press, 1976), 335.

28. "What Is the E-Meter and How Does It Work?," Scientology, http://www.scientology.org/faq/scientology-and-dianetics-auditing/what-is-the-eme ter-and-how-does-it-work.html.

29. On Wilhelm Reich and his theory of orgone energy, see James E. Strick, *Wilhelm Reich, Biologist* (Cambridge, Mass.: Harvard University Press, 2015); and Christopher Turner, *Adventures in the Orgasmatron: The Invention of Sex* (New York: Farrar, Straus and Giroux, 2011).

30. See Erik Davis, *TechGnosis: Myth, Magic, and Mysticism in the Age of Information*, 2nd ed. (Berkeley: North Atlantic, 2015), esp. 133–70.

31. Erich von Däniken, *Chariots of the Gods?* (1968; repr., New York: Berkeley, 1980), 31.

32. See John Corbett, "Rescuing the Treasures of a Dead Jazz Legend," Literary Hub, June 13, 2017, http://lithub.com/rescuing-the-treasures-of-a-dead-jazz-legend/.

33. Sun Ra, "The Great Whore," typed broadside with manuscript additions (c. 1950s), Alton Abraham Collection, University of Chicago Special Collections, repr. in *The Wisdom of Sun Ra: Sun Ra's Polemical Broadsheets and Streetcorner Leaflets,* ed. John Corbett (Chicago: WhiteWalls, 2006), 92–93.

34. Baraka, "Sun Ra," 255; emphasis in original.

35. Sun Ra, "The Potential" (1965), in Wolf and Geerken, *The Immeasurable Equation,* 309.

36. Nathaniel Mackey, *Discrepant Engagement: Dissonance, Cross-Culturality, and Experimental Writing* (Cambridge: Cambridge University Press, 1993), 19.

37. Mackey, *Discrepant Engagement,* 20.

38. Sun Ra, "Prophecy" (1965), in Wolf and Geerken, *The Immeasurable Equation,* 317.

INDEX

Note: Page numbers in *italics* indicate figures.

Abellio, Raymond (Georges Soulès), xviii, 365n8
Abraham, Alton, 353, *354,* 360, *362–63*
academia, xix, 13–14, 18–20, 21–22, 59, 114–15, 117, 120, 124–25, 127, 134–37, 156, 163, 167, 171, 186–87, 195, 201, 203–4, 287, 310, 340, 366n11
Accursed Treasure, The. See *L'Or de Rennes* (Sède)
Adler, Alfred, 307
Adorno, Theodor, 237–39, 240, 241, 242, 244, 245, 248, 250, 260, 262, 263
African Communities League (ACL), 226, 227, 230
African Times and Orient Review (magazine), 219, 220, 221, 226, *228*
Afrocentric history, 24, 32, 166, 186, 201–4, 219, 235, 236, 374n60
Ages in Chaos (Velikovsky), 310, 329
air loom (Matthews), 278–79, *280,* 281–83, 285, 291, 292
Alaimo, Stacy, 197
Albigensian Crusade, 118, 136, 143, 379n2
Ali, Mohamed Dusé. *See* Mohamed Ali, Dusé
'Ali, Muhammed, 48–50, 61

alien, the, xi, 1, 4–5, 9, 17, 20, 23, 25, 27, 32, 39–40, 43, 47, 61, 64, 65, 68, 70, 74, 75, 76, 80, 81, 85, 90, 92, 93, 94, 97, 98, 99, 100, 101, 102, 105, 108, 109, 166, 167, 172, 174, 175–76, 177, 183, 205, 208, 269–70, 276, 297, 317, 321, 326, 327, 328, 330, 335, 341, 350, 357, 359, 361
alienation, 4–5, 6, 11, 23, 75, 76, 92, 101, 108, 110, 120, 125, 279, 281, 287, 289, 348, 352
Aline and Valcour, or, the philosophical novel (Sade), 31, 253
Alleau, René, xviii, 374n57
amnesia, historical, 5, 201–11, 220, 312, 314, 323, 326, 327, 331, 333, 339
androcracy, 159, 161, 177, 195, 196, 246, 393n8, 395n44
Anger, Kenneth, 357
Anti-Oedipus (Deleuze and Guattari), 291, 298, 299, *300, 301,* 302, 303
anti-Semitism, 134, 325–26, 327
Apollinaire, Guillaume, 240, 243, 252, 254–55, 260
Apter, Emily, 289, 411n43
archives and archivization, xiii, xvi, 2, 9, 27, 42, 44, 47, 52, 53, 54–58, 59, 61, 62, *63,* 64, 78, 79, 84, 90, 96, 104,

archives and archivization (cont.)
107, 109, 116, 119, 122, 146, 147, 150, 176, 243, 252, 254, 259, 261, 302, 326, 339, 342–43, 350, 351, 352

archons, 39, 44, 80, *81*, 82, 85, 86, 93, 96, 97, 98, 99

Arkestra. *See* Sun Ra

Arnaud, Noël, 149

art brut, 3–6, 7, 55, 408n2

Asimov, Isaac, 339–40, 341

Association des écrivains bibliographes, traducteurs et commentateurs (The Association of bibliographic writers, translators, and commentators), 259, 407n63

Atlantis, xix, 19, 135, 165, 187–90, 198

avant-garde, xviii, 3, 8, 20, 27, 32, 76, 78, 151, 193, 252, 297, 321, 365n8, 368n4, 369n14

Azimi, Roxana, 4

Babelon, Jean, 78, 79, 80

Bachelard, Gaston, 8, 10, 19, 24, 29, 83, 84, 150, 152, 369n19, 380n5

Bachofen, Johann Jakob, 165, 172–75, 177, 180, 182, 183, 186, 189, 193

Badiou, Alain, 380n5

Bagnall, Robert, 233, 399n21

Baigent, Michael, 118, 134–35, 136, 138, 141

Baraka, Amiri, 352, 361

Barthes, Roland, 31, 240

Basham, Arthur, 168, 169

Basilides, 55, 56, 82

Bataille, Georges, 3, 8, 10, 28, 31, 64, 70, 71, 74, 75, 76–90, 91, 92, 93, 94, 100, 102, 105, 106, 109, 173, 240, 252, 406n47; and base materialism, 71, 74, 76, 78–83, 85, 86, 88; and coins, 76, *77*, 78–82, 84, 85; and *Documents*, 74, 76, *77*, 78, 79, 80, *81*, 86; and heterology, 8–9, 10, 80

Bateson, Gregory, 162

Beard, Mary, 159

Beauvoir, Simone de, 4, 31, 156, 237, 240, 244, 247, 251, 252, 263, 264, 388n16

Becker, Howard, 4, 368n8, 369n17

belief, xiv, xv, xvi, xviii, xx, 8, 16, 17, 18, 19, 21, 24, 42, 43, 46, 53, 54, 55, 58, 62, 69, 70, 73, 75, 83, 84, 93, 96, 97, 98, 99, 100, 101, 106, 108, 110, 113, 116, 117, 119, 123, 128, 130, 134, 136, 154, 163, 167, 173, 176, 177, 181, 182, 188, 189, 191, 192, 193, 194, 222, 224, 250, 259, 263, 313, 317, 320, 321, 322, 323, 334, 336–37, 338, 339, 340, 341, 342, 346, 349, 350

Berlin Codex, 59, 100, 107, 384n63, 385n7, 386n79

Berlinerblau, Jacques, 201, 397n6

Bernal, Martin, 25, 202–4, 205; and *Black Athena*, 202–4, 398n8

biblical history, xiii, 32, 113, 312–13, 314, 315, 316, 324, 327, 329–31, 332

bibliography, 25, 116, 240, 251, 252, 254–55, 259–60

bibliophilia, xvi, 15, 24, 30, 31, 244, 253, 254, 256, 260, 407n64

Bibliothèque des curieux, 255, 260

Bibliothèque nationale de France, 77, 78, 81, 122, 133, 138, 240, 241, 242, 243, 251, 252, 254–55, 269, 381n19

bifurcation point (Prigogine and Stengers), 29, 72, 178, 184, 185, 190, 205

Black Arts Movement, xviii, 32, 351, 355

Black Athena (Bernal), 202–4, 398n8

Black nationalism, 30, 203, 204, 205, 206, 221, 222, 225, 232, 233, 235, 237

Black Star Line (BSL), 30, 204, 205, 213, 221, 225, 226, 227, *228, 229*, 230, 231, 232, 233 blade. *See* dominator model

Blake, William, 27, 53, 55

Blanchot, Maurice, 10, 31, 240, 241, 242, 244, 245–48, 250–51, 255, 263, 264, 405n25

Blavatsky, Helena Petrovna, xix, 27, 44, 45, 55, 56, 353, 357, 358

Blood of the Cathars, The. See *Sang des Cathares, Le*

Blount, Herman Poole. *See* Sun Ra

Blyden, Edgar Wylmot, 25, 215

Boehme, Jakob, 70

books: bibliophile societies, xvi, 24, 30, 31, 253–56, 260, 407n64; material construction, xxiii, *38*, 42, 43, 47, 50–52, 58, 59, *63*, 64, 95–96, 102, 103, 226, 254, 259–60, 375n12; publishing, xxiii, 20, 24, 31, 50, 51, 52, 59, 62, 95–96, 101, 103, 149, 226, 227, 231, 241, 244, 251, 252–61, 262, 310–11, 312, 335; secondhand, xiii, *xv*, xxiii, xxiv, 137

Bourdieu, Pierre, 6, 23, 368n4, 369n14

Bousset, Wilhelm, 56

Breton, André, 84, 252, 406n46

Brown, Dan, 28, 29, 113–33, 134, 136, 137, 138, 141, 142, 147, 153, 154, 155, 159, 160, 165, 166; and *The Da Vinci Code*, 28–29, 65, 113–26, 128, 129–30, 132–33, 134, 135, 136, 137, 139, 144, 153, 154, 155, 159–61, 165, 172, 387n10, 389n38, 395n44; lawsuit against, 116, 118, 137

Bruce, John E., 212, 230

bullshit, xiv, xvii–xviii, xix, xx, xxii, 21, 24. *See also* junk thought; rubbish

Buñuel, Luis, 252

Bush, George H. W., 166, 185

Butler, Judith, 167, 183, 240

Camp, L. Sprague de, 188–89, 367n1

Campbell, Joseph, 27, 174

Camus, Albert, 4, 368n8

Canetti, Elias, 289–90

Canguilhem, Georges, 270

Capra, Fritjof, 162, 164, 165, 178, 183, 190, 191

Cardinal, Roger, 4–7, 9, 13, 18, 23

Carter, Angela, 240

Carter, Howard, 38

cartography. *See* maps

Catharism, 118, 142, 143, 144, 153, 379n2

Céline, Louis-Ferdinand, 9

Césaire, Aimé, 223

chalice. *See* partnership model

Chalice and the Blade, The (Eisler), 29, 159–98, 202, 389n38; critical reception of, 29, 164, 166, 171, 178, 179–84, 189, 193–95, 201, 202

Cherisey, Philippe de, 133, 134

Chief Sam. *See* Sam, "Chief" Alfred Charles

"Chimère expérimentale, La" (The chimera of experiment) (Sède), 153–54, 392n81

Christ, Carol, 164, 388n16

Christianity, 27, 29, 37, 39, 42–45, 46, 47, 52, 54–55, 56, 60, 62, 67, 68, 69, 70, 74, 75, 76, 77, 81, 82, 84, 85, 86, 88, 90, 97, 98, 100–101, 103, 104–10, 113–14, 116, 119, 120, 121, 122, 123, 129–30, 137, 144, 146, 161, 238, 326, 379n2, 384n63

Claremont Colleges Library, *38, 49, 53, 62, 63*, 103–4

Clement of Alexandria, 44

codex. *See* books: material construction

coins, 76, *77, 78*–82, 84, 85

Collins, Patricia Hill, xvi, xx, 2, 13, 348, 351, 368n9

Commander, Michelle, 353

communism, 151–52, 177, 184–85, 189, 253, 257–58, 289, 345, 347, 416n87 conceptual persona, 204, 242, 244, 247, 249, 251, 263, 264, 265, 269, 307, 322, 323, 331

Conger, Arthur L., 357–58

conspiracy, xxiii, 23, 26, 113–14, 116, 117, 118, 119, 121, 122, 123, 124, 125, 128, 132, 133, 132, 141, 155, 206, 271, 273, 279, 285, 288–89, 290, 291, 336, 345, 346, 347, 357, 411n11

Copernican revolution. *See* revolution, Copernican

Copernicus, Nicolaus, 305, 306, 307, 308, 310, 311. *See also* revolution, Copernican

Corbin, Henry, 83, 84

Corbu, Noël, 139, *140*

Corpus Hermeticum, 59

"Cosmos without Gravitation" (Velikovsky), 12, 317–18, *319*

counterculture, 75, 90, 100–104, 121, 142, 164, 191, 202, 254, 269, 297, 312, 321, 340, 351, 365n9, 385n72

crank, 1, 213, 367n1

Crete, 185–88, 189, 202

Crimes of Love (Sade), 251, 254

Crisis, The (magazine), 214, 215, *216, 217, 218,* 230, 401n49

Crowley, Aleister, 27, 353, 357

Culianu, Ioan, 115, 386n5

Culler, Jonathan, 13

cultural evolution, 17, 18, 23, 54, 56–57, 159, 162, 163, 164, 166, 171, 172, 175, 178, 179, 180, 187, 190, 198, 205

cultural transformation theory, 166, 167, 171, 172, 176, 177, 178, 179, 180, 182, 183, 184, 185, 187, 190, 191, 192, 196, 197, 201

culture wars, xxii, 15, 19, 124, 125, 149, 163, 164, 166, 167, 178, 181, 182, 186, 195, 201–2, 215, 235, 236, 237, 347

Cussler, Clive, 122

cybernetics, 14, 275, 276, 290, 301, 302, 303, 409n15

Daly, Mary, 156–57, 164, 176, 192, 194, 195, 196, 197; and methodicide, 194–96, 197

Däniken, Erich von, 32, 135, 311, 357, 359

Darger, Henry, 4, 40–41, 375nn5–6

Darwin, Charles, 22, 166, 179, 306, 340

Da Vinci Code, The (Brown), 28–29, 65, 113–26, 128, 129–30, 132–33, 134, 135, 136, 137, 139, 144, 153, 154, 155, 159–61, 165, 172, 387n10, 389n38, 395n44

Davis, Erik, 358

Dead Sea Scrolls, xiii, 38, 46, 52

deep ecology movement, 183, 192

Deleuze, Gilles, 6, 10, 11, 14, 31, 248–49, 251, 263, 278, 288, 291, 298–99, *300, 301,* 302–3, 370n32; *Anti-Oedipus,* 291, 298, 299, *300, 301,* 302, 303

Derrida, Jacques, 333, 342–43

Devlin-Glass, Frances, 197

diagrams, 272, 274, 278, 279, *280,* 281, 282, 283, 285, 291, 292, 299–300, 370n27

dialecticism, 11, 28, 31, 68, 69, 70, 72, 74, 75, 76, 78, 82, 83–85, 88, 89, 92, 110, 117, 120, 123, 129, 150, 151–53, 179, 180, 220, 237–40, 242–43, 248–51, 260, 263, 274, 285, *286,* 288, 290, 291, 292, 326, 331, 356, 360–61, 382n21, 382n34

Dialectic of Enlightenment (Adorno and Horkheimer), 237–39, 242, 244, 248, 250, 260, 262, 263

Dialogue between a Priest and a Dying Man (Sade), 243, 253, 256

Diamond, Irene, 197–98

Diop, Cheikh Anta, 202, 203

disability, xx, 1, 3, 4, 5, 24, 269–70, 408n3

Documents (journal), 74, 76, *77,* 78, 79, 80, *81,* 86

dominator model, 159, 160, 162, 163, 168, 171, 175, 177, 178, 179, 180, 181, 183, 184, 186, 192, 193, 194, 210, 223, 248, 393n8

Donnelly, Ignatius, xix, 188, 313, 413n24

Doresse, Jean, *38, 49,* 51, *53, 63,* 103

Doresse, Marian, 49, 63

Dossiers Secrets (Plantard and Cherisey), 122, 133–34, 138, 141, 146

Dotrement, Christian, 154

"Dreams Freud Dreamed, The" (Velikovsky), 326–27

Du Bois, W. E. B., 211, 213, 214–15, 225, 228, 232, 401n49

Dubuffet, Jean, 3, 4, 5–6, 7, 9, 13, 55, 368n4, 369nn13 14

Dumas, Henry, 345, 355

Durozoi, Gérard, 149

Earth in Upheaval (Velikovsky), 310, 415n65

Eco, Umberto, 116, 125–29, 132, 133, 136, 141, 142, 143, 144, 145, 147, 150, 154, 155, 156; and *Foucault's Pendulum,* 116, 125, 127, 128, 132, 289n33

ecofeminism, 29, 159, 162, 163, 164, 166, 167, 179, 183, 184, 192, 196–98, 202

École pratique des hautes études, 51, 74, 86

Edwards, Brent Hayes, 361, 417n10, 418n17

Ehrenberg, Margaret, 170, 171

Eisler, Riane, 29, 159–68, 170–73, 175–98, 201, 202, 210, 242, 388n16, 389n38, 393n6, 393n8, 395n44; *The Chalice and the Blade,* 29, 159–98,

202, 389n38; and dominator society, 159, 160, 162, 163, 168, 171, 175, 177, 178, 179, 180, 181, 183, 184, 186, 192, 193, 194, 210, 393n8; and gylany, 161, 162, 190, 393n8; and human survival, 159, 160, 178, 179, 187, 190, 191, 198; and partnership society, 160–61, 162, 163, 165, 170, 171, 175, 178, 179, 180, 184, 185, 186, 190, 191, 192, 193, 395n44

Eldredge, Niles, 180

Eliade, Mircea, 115, 117, 386n5

Eller, Cynthia, 180–81, 192, 193–94, 195

empiricist mysticism (Wahl), 68, 73, 74, 84, 89, 381n15

Enfer. *See* Bibliothèque nationale de France

Engels, Friedrich, 175, 182

Enlightenment (rationalist intellectual movement), 126, 187, 190, 237–39, 241, 242, 243, 244, 245, 246, 247, 248, 249, 250, 258, 260, 263, 271, 336, 386n5, 405n21

enlightenment (state of consciousness), 16, 32, 39, 54, 55, 58, 89, 106, 113, 118, 126, 194, 357, 358

Epiphanius, 93

epiphany, 37, 39, 41, 42, 46, 47, 48, 50, 52, 53, 61, 62, 65, 104, 109, 128, 348

epistemology, ix, xvi, xvii, xviii, xxii, xxiv, 7, 8, 14, 15, 16–20, 22, 23, 24, 25, 26, 27, 31, 32, 33, 40, 53, 62, 68, 74, 79, 81, 82–85, 104, 117, 126, 127, 130, 135, 139, 149, 156, 166, 167, 168, 184, 189, 195, 197, 201, 215, 221, 223, 235, 242, 244, 249–50, 252, 255, 262, 263, 264, 265, 269, 273, 278, 287, 289, 298, 301, 303, 307, 309–12, 322–23, 339, 349, 350, 352, 355, 356, 369n16, 372n53, 380n5, 409n7

errance. *See* errantry

errantry, ix, 1, 9, 11, 172, 198
Espezal, Pierre de, 78
Estes, Clarissa, 164
Evans, Arthur, 185, 186, 202
evil, 45, 80, 81, 82, 83, 309, 380n5
Ewing, Adam, 204, 398nn18–19,
    401n55, 403n91, 404n102

fascism, 46, 96, 97, 145, 159, 206, 234,
    239, 243, 289, 299, 327, 371n35,
    389n30, 399n21, 411n41. *See also*
    Nazism
Faye, Eugène de, 56, 381n17
Felski, Rita, 125, 156, 388n24
Feyerabend, Paul, 18–19, 20, 21, 22,
    24, 73, 305, 308
Fleuret, Fernand, 255
Foster, Hal, 297–98
Foucault, Michel, 10, 17, 22, 24, 31,
    166, 183, 240, 249–50, 263, 322,
    369n14
Foucault's Pendulum (Eco), 116, 125,
    127, 128, 132, 289n33
Fox-Genovese, Elizabeth, 179–80,
    181, 188
Fragments of a Faith Forgotten (Mead),
    53, 54–55, 57–58
Frankfurt, Harry, xvii, xviii, xx–xxi, 23
Frazier, E. Franklin, 213
Freud, Sigmund, xix, 14–15, 31, 122,
    123, 124, 127, 141, 144, 145, 165,
    172, 174, 175, 177, 190, 271–78, 281,
    288, 290, 291, 297, 299, 303, 305–8,
    310, 312, 320, 323–35, 336, 337, 339,
    341, 342–43, 359, 389n38, 409n7,
    409n15; *Moses and Monotheism*,
    327–30, 331, 332, 333, 337, 342; and
    the Schreber case, 14, 271–73, 276
Furneaux, Rupert, 17–18

Galileo (Galileo Galilei), 305, 311, 340
Gardner, Martin, xiv–xv, xviii, xiv,
    367n1

Garvey, Amy Jacques, 212, 232
Garvey, Marcus, 10, 15, 25, 30, 166,
    202–36, 239, 242; and African
    Communities League (ACL), 226,
    227, 230; and Black Star Line (BSL),
    30, 204, 205, 213, 221, 225, 226,
    227, *228, 229,* 230, 231, 232, 233,
    234; critics of, 30, 206, 208, 212–13,
    221, 227, 230, 233, 234, 399n21;
    federal investigation of, 205–6, 209,
    226, 231, 398n19; and *Negro World*
    newspaper, 204, 205, 212, 221, 222,
    225, 226, 398n17; speeches and
    writings, 207, 208, 209, 210–11, 212,
    219, 220, 226, 227, 232–33, 399n29;
    and Universal Negro Improvement
    Association (UNIA), 30, 202, 204,
    205, 207, 208, 209, 210, 211, 212,
    213, 214, 220, 221, 222, 225, 226,
    228, 230, 231, 232, 233, 234, 401n59
Geertz, Clifford, 206, 230
Gere, Cathy, 186–87, 195, 202, 203,
    398n8
Geroulanos, Stefanos, 73, 381n18
Geworfenheit (thrownness), 5, 92, 94,
    97, 368n9
Gill, Madge, 4
Gilroy, Paul, 206, 399n21
Gimbutas, Marija, 161, 164, 183, 191,
    195, 202, 388n16
Glass, Philip, 321
Glissant, Édouard, 9, 10, 350
gnosis, 27, 39, 42, 43, 44, 46, 47, 48,
    50, 58, 60, 61, 62, 64, 68, 71, 72,
    88, 89, 90, 93, 97, 106, 107, 358
Gnostic Gospels, The (Pagels), 37, 38,
    42, 43, 45, 47, 48, 52, 53, 64, 100,
    102–7, 110, 113, 119, 121, 175,
    375n9, 377n25, 383n47
Gnosticism, 10, 15, 25, 27–28, 32,
    37–65, 67–110, 113, 116, 118, 119,
    120, 121, 126, 127, 173, 175, 176,
    194, 195, 242, 258, 340, 353,

357–58, 374n3, 376n21, 378n34, 383n40, 383n47, 384n63; definitions of, 38, 39–40, 42–44, 46, 48, 54–55, 59–62; as fantasy of power, 46, 47, 54, 55–56, 69, 99, 101, 102, 126, 129, 258, 385n75; as heresy, 27, 28, 37, 39, 43, 44–47, 52, 53, 56, 60, 62, 64, 65, 67–68, 70, 74, 76, 82, 83, 86, 100, 104, 105, 106, 107, 108, 110, 175; and nineteenth-century religious history, 27, 43–44, 53–54, 56, 69, 70, 73, 86, 100, 121

Gnostic Religion, The (Jonas), 37, 61, 90, 92, 96, 98, 100, 374n3

goddess religion, 28, 29, 106, 115, 119, 129, 130, 160, 161, 163, 164–65, 166–68, 169, 170, 172, 174, 176, 180, 181–82, 183, 185, 186, 187, 191, 193, 195, 197, 348, 388n16, 395n44

Goethe, Johann Wolfgang von, 27, 53, 55, 121, 173

Gordin, Michael, xx, 311, 312, 318, 321, 329, 334, 340, 341, 342, 366n12, 371n42, 379n61, 398n87, 413n18, 413n24

Gospel of Matthew, 45, 72

Gospel of Thomas, 41, 42, *63*, 72, 105, 375n12, 377n32, 380n11, 381n13, 383n47

Gould, Stephen Jay, 162, 180

grail. *See* Holy Grail

Graves, Robert, 27, 174

Grazia, Alfred de, 335–36, 337, 338, 339

Grondin, Michael, 72

Gross, Paul, 20, 24, 371n44

Guattari, Félix, 10, 14, 31, 263, 278, 288, 291, 298–303, 370n32, 411n51; *Anti-Oedipus*, 291, 298, 299, *300, 301*, 302, 303

Guénon, René, xviii

Gurdjieff, George Ivanovich, 27, 353

gylany, 161, 162, 190, 393n8

Haraway, Donna, 20, 183, 342, 356, 395n54

Harding, Sandra, 183, 342

Harnack, Adolf von, 43, 53–54, 56, 60, 81, 86

Harris, Joel Chandler, 11

Harris, Wilson, 350

Harrison, Hubert, 212, 215, 221–25, 232, 235, 401n5, 402n74

Harrison, Jane Ellen, 165

Haslam, John, 279, *280*, 281, 288, 289

Hayford, J. E. Casley, 219

Hegel, Georg Wilhelm Friedrich, 25, 28, 31, 46, 53, 55, 70, 72, 73, 74–75, 76, 78, 83–84, 85, 89, 90, 94, 152, 166, 179, 180, 209, 215, 248, 249–50, 251, 380n5, 381n15, 382n34

hegemony, 110, 121, 129, 142, 144, 169, 177, 179, 190, 192, 193, 194, 208, 348

Heidegger, Martin, xix, 4, 16, 61, 70, 72, 73, 75, 83, 90, 91–94, 96, 97–99, 101, 108, 246

Heine, Maurice, 244, 246, 249, 251–65, 288, 406n47, 407n55; and l'Association des écrivains bibliographes, traducteurs et commentateurs, 259, 407n63; and the Société du roman philosophique, 244, 246, 248, 249, 253–54, 256–58, 259, 260, and syndicalism, 257–58, 259–60, 262, 264, 265

Heine, Suzanne, 182, 193, 195, 196, 407n65

Hellenism, 43, 53–54, 60, 77, 80, 81, 82, 172, 174, 202, 383n40, 385n72

Henderson, Hazel, 164

heresiology, x, 27, 28, 37, 39, 43, 44–47, 52, 53, 56, 60, 62, 64, 65, 67–68, 70, 74, 76, 82, 83, 86, 100, 104, 105, 106, 107, 108, 110, 114, 116, 124, 175, 340, 374n3, 376n18, 384n63, 397n1 hermeneutics, biblical, 54, 59, 104, 107–9, 210, 311, 316, 318, 323, 324, 352, 360

hermeneutics of suspicion, 19, 45, 119–20, 123–29, 135, 136, 138, 139, 142, 144–47, 149, 150, 153, 155–56, 160, 168, 290, 308, 317, 329, 337, 349, 360, 388n24, 389n29, 391n67

hermetic semiosis (Eco), 125–27, 128, 129, 133, 136, 141, 150, 389n50

Herodotus, 172, 174

Hesiod, 172

heterodoxy, xvi, 2–3, 23, 44, 47, 53, 55, 57, 67, 77, 81, 100, 109, 113, 155, 188, 191, 370n28

heterology, 8–9, 10, 80

Historiettes, contes et fabliaux (Sade), 243–44, 253, 254

Hofstadter, Richard, 269, 289, 411n41

Holocaust, xiv, 46, 94, 95, 237, 245, 325, 327, 333, 364n60

Holy Blood, Holy Grail (Lincoln, Baigent, and Leigh), 29, 118, 133, 134–38, 139, 141, 142, 153

Holy Grail, 25, 28, 29, 114, 116, 118, 119, 121–22, 133, 134, 144, 146, 155, 160, 236

home rule, 205, 214, 219, 222

Hoover, J. Edgar, 205, 398n19

Horkheimer, Max, 237–41, 242, 244, 245, 248, 250, 260, 262, 263

Hubbard, L. Ron, xix, 32, 311, 357, 358, 359

humiliation, 308, 320, 324, 327, 330, 331, 332, 333, 336, 339, 340

Hurston, Zora Neale, 41, 375n8

Husserl, Edmund, 72, 152

I Ching, 162, 165, 166, 191

Illustrations of Madness (Haslam), 279, *280*, 281–82, 288, 289

influencing machine, 281–83, *284*, 285–86, 289, 292, 293, 298, 410n28

Infortunes de la vertu, Les (Sade). See *Misfortunes of Virtue, The*

involution, 23, 30, 206–8, 212, 230, 235, 239

insanity. *See* madness

Irenaeus of Lyon, 44–45, 72, 378n34

Irigaray, Luce, 31, 194

Jacoby, Susan, 14, 16, 29, 366n11

James, C. L. R., 30, 206, 399n21

James, E. O., 175, 180

James, William, 72, 73, 74, 83

Jarry, Alfred, 134

Jay, Mike, 282–83

Jenkins, Philip, 28, 40, 42, 46, 47, 52, 379n2, 384n63

Jesus, 41, 42, 43, 72, 104, 105, 107, 113, 114, 121, 122, 123, 129, 132, 134, 137, 380n11, 393n5

Jonas, Hans, 25, 28, 37, 39, 43, 52, 61, 64, 68, 70, 71, 73, 75, 90–100, 101, 102, 108, 109, 374n3, 384n59, 384n63; *Gnosis und spätantiker Geist,* 90, 92, 95, 96, 384n59; and *The Gnostic Religion,* 37, 61, 90, 92, 96, 98, 100, 374n3; and pseudomorphosis, 97

Judaism, 39, 84, 91, 94–96, 106, 107, 120, 324, 326–33

Juergens, Ralph, 317, 321, 336, 414n39

Juliette (Sade), 238–39, 241, 248, 252, 253

Jung, Carl, 27, 32, 51, 58, 60, 65, 102, 164, 166, 175, 325, 357, 379n61, 393n15

Jung Codex, 51, 58, 102–3, 377n31, 379n61, 383n47, 385n75

junk thought, xvi, xviii, xxi, 341, 366n11. *See also* bullshit; rubbish

Justine (Sade), 238–39, 261, 405n22

Kaiser, David, 12, 365n9, 370n27, 371n42

Kant, Immanuel, 6, 73, 247, 249, 262

Keita, Maghan, 203, 204, 307n3, 400n43

Keller, Evelyn Fox, 309, 342, 412n17

Kimmerer, Robin Wall, xvi–xvii

King, Karen L., 90, 376n13, 384n63, 387n7

Kleber, Franz Josef, 292, *293*, 297, 298

Klossowski, Pierre, 31, 240, 241, 249, 252, 256–57, 258, 263, 405n21

Knopf, Johann, 293, *294, 295, 296*, 297, 298, 411n47

Koestler, Arthur, xxi

Kojève, Alexandre, 83

Kornweibel, Theodore, 231, 298n19

Koyré, Alexandre, 83, 84

Krafft-Ebing, Richard von, 258, 261, 262

Kristeva, Julia, 8–9, 240

Kuhn, Thomas, 308–9, 328, 337, 341, 342, 369n14, 370n26

Lacan, Jacques, 15, 31, 154, 183, 240, 247, 248, 262, 263, 269, 273–78, 283, 285, *286*, 287–88, 290–92, 297, 298, 299, 300, 301, 302–4, 305–7, 329; and "return to Freud," 277, 278, 288, 306, 329

Laclau, Ernesto, 177

Latour, Bruno, 20, 125, 147, 349, 372n53, 391n67

League of Nations, 205, 212, 214

Le Brun, Annie, 31, 240

Lefkowitz, Mary, 202, 203–4, 219, 235, 236, 397n6

Leigh, Richard, 118, 122, 134, 135, 136, 138, 141

Lély, Gilbert, 244, 254

Lettick, Birney, 314, *315, 316*

Levitt, Norman, 20, 24, 371n44

Lewy, Hans, 95

Lichtheim, George, 95

Lietzmann, Hans, 54, 378n36

Lincoln, Henry, 118, 134–36, 137–38, 141, 142, 155

Lorde, Audre, 196

L'Or de Rennes (Sède), 118, 136–39, 142, 144, 146–47, 152–53, 154

Loye, David, 165, 395n45

Luce, J. V., 188–89

Lysenko, Trofim, xix, 24, 416n87

Mackey, Nathaniel, 10, 62, 361

madness, 1, 3, 4, 15, 24, 206, 233, 234, 250, 265, 270–71, 272, 279–81, 287–88, 291, 297, 299, 329, 399n21, 408n2, 411n51. *See also* paranoia; psychosis; schizophrenia

Main à plume (wartime resistance group), 148–50, 391n68

Malet, Léo, 149

Manicheanism, 86, 179, 182, 384n63

Mankind in Amnesia (Velikovsky), 333–34, 413n20

Mannheim, Karl, 337

maps, 5, 15, 31, 122, 154, 215, *216, 217, 218*, 272, 278, 281–83, 290–98, 300–303

Marcel, Gabriel, 74, 83, 381n15

Marcion, 56, 82, 88, 101

Martin, David L., 350

Martin, Tony, 204, 232, 390n13, 400n43

Marty, Éric, 240, 242, 243, 244, 245, 264, 405n21

martyrdom, 42, 105, 109, 238, 276, 311, 340

Marx, Karl, 28, 46, 123, 145, 152, 307, 308, 337, 392n81

Marxism, 70, 76, 95, 148–52, 153, 167, 180, 181–82, 183–84, 222

"Marxist Philosophy and Stalinist Philosophy" (Sède), 150–52

Mary Magdalene, 43, 105, 114, 132, 134, 155, 376n13, 386n79, 393n5

Masoch, Leopold. *See* Sacher-Masoch, Leopold von

masochism, 248–49

materialism, base (Bataille), 71, 74, 76, 78–83, 85, 86, 88

materialism, dialectical, 28, 76, 85, 151–52

matter, 28, 39, 44, 64–65, 67–72, 74, 78, 81, 82, 84, 85, 88, 93, 375n10, 380n7

Matthews, James Tilly, 278–79, *280, 281–83*, 285, 288, 291, 292, 298, 410n28

McCredden, Lyn, 197

Mead, G. R. S., 27, 45, 54–58, 60, 102, 376n16; *Fragments of a Faith Forgotten*, 53, 54–55, 57–58

Meeker, Natania, 261, 405n23

Mellor, Mary, 198

Melville, Herman, 67–70, 76, 81, 82, 379nn1–2

mental illness. *See* madness; paranoia; psychosis; schizophrenia

Merton, Robert, 22, 310, 320, 336, 337, 340, 369n14

Messenger (magazine), 227, 399n21, 403n93

method and methodology, xxi, 3, 6, 7, 9, 10, 12, 15, 16, 18–19, 20, 21, 25, 26–27, 29, 58, 64, 65, 71, 73, 75, 77, 79, 80, 83, 84, 85, 88, 89–90, 96, 107, 109, 115, 119, 125, 126, 134, 141, 144, 148–52, 153, 154, 155, 162–63, 164–67, 168–72, 176, 177, 181, 182, 184, 187, 189, 191–98, 204, 214, 215, 243, 247, 262, 264, 271, 273, 276, 278, 290, 299, 303, 305, 306, 308, 311, 320, 323, 324, 326, 330, 335, 336, 349, 359, 360, 361, 372n53, 391n67, 394n18, 409n7

methodicide (Daly), 194–96, 197

Meyer, Marvin, 59, 385n71

Michelet, Jules, 135–36, 165, 173

Michell, John, 135

Middle Passage, 26, 30, 207, 225, 353

Mina, Togo, 51

Minoan civilization, 185–89, 193, 194, 202, 203

Misfortunes of Virtue, The (Sade), 252, 253, 259, 262, 405n22

Mitchell, Juliet, 299

Mohamed Ali, Dusé, 212, 219, 226, 235

Mohr, Jakob, 283, *284, 285*, 298

Montagu, Ashley, 179

Mor, Barbara, 164

Moreno, Jacob, 281, *282*

Moses, 98, 312, 313, 323–24, 327–31, 332, 333, 336, 337, 339, 342–43

Moses, Wilson, 400n43, 401n47, 402n78, 403n93

Moses and Monotheism (Freud), 327–30, 331, 332, 333, 337, 342

Mother Right. See Bachofen, Jakob

Mouffe, Chantal, 177–78

Mumbo Jumbo (Reed), 25–27, 208–10, 211, 219, 224, 236, 399n28

Mussolini, Benito, 206

mysticism, xiv, xviii, 2, 8, 16, 27, 29, 33, 41, 42, 43, 45, 46, 54–56, 58, 65, 68, 73–74, 75, 82–83, 84, 89, 102, 110, 113, 115–23, 125, 127, 128, 133, 135, 147, 150, 151, 153, 156, 164, 165, 185, 196, 273, 283, 351, 353, 365n9, 368n8, 379n61, 381n15

myth, xv, xviii, xxii, 9, 17, 23, 26, 28–29, 30, 40, 41, 42, 46, 47, 48, 52–53, 61, 64, 82, 89, 92, 98, 99, 115, 117–19, 120, 121, 123, 125, 133–47, 148, 149–51, 154, 155, 156–57, 164, 165, 169, 172, 173–76, 177, 180–82, 183, 185–90, 191, 192, 193, 196, 197, 201, 204–6, 236, 237–39, 245, 258, 291, 307, 312, 313, 314, 316–18, 324–25, 330, 332–34, 339, 341, 351, 352, 356, 357, 358, 359, 418n13 mythomorphic facts (Sède), 119, 133–47, 148, 149, 155, 157

Nag Hammadi, Egypt, 27, 37, 40, 42, 48–49, *49*, 51, 377n25
Nag Hammadi Library, xiii, 27, 28, 37–52, *38, 53*, 54–62, *63*, 64–65, 67, 68, 70, 71, 72, 73, 75, 76, 78, 94, 95, 96, 100–105, 107, 108, 113, 114, 175, 377n25, 381n13
National Association for the Advancement of Colored People (NAACP), 207, 214–15, *218*
nationalism, Black. *See* Black nationalism
Nazism, xiv, 23, 75, 91, 93, 94–96, 97, 98, 148, 149, 182, 201, 237, 245, 327, 345, 347, 374n57
Nealon, Jeffrey, 7, 8
Negro World (newspaper), 204, 205, 212, 221, 222, 225, 226, 398n17
Neolithic prehistory, 160, 161, 163, 167–71, 174, 175, 176, 178, 180–81, 193, 359
Neoplatonism, 54, 59, 82, 107
Neumann, Erich, 175
New Age movement, xviii, 2, 23, 26, 29, 32, 90, 101, 102, 122, 162–64, 166, 167, 183–84, 187, 190–92, 197, 357, 365n9
Newton, Isaac, 12, 16, 162
Nietzsche, Friedrich, 3, 10, 113, 123, 186, 239, 308, 371n35
Nkrumah, Kwame, 206, 399n20
Nordau, Max, 25, 209

Oedipus, 249, 291, 298–99, 303, 328, 329, 333
Oedipus and Akhnaton (Velikovsky), 321, 327, 328–29
120 Days of Sodom (Sade), 244, 248, 253, 258, 262, 264

orthodoxy, 22, 29, 32, 38, 39, 43–44, 46, 53, 54, 68–69, 70, 72, 74, 75, 77, 80–82, 85, 86, 98, 101, 104–6, 109, 121–22, 123, 125, 134–35, 139, 151, 155, 175, 177, 311, 321, 334, 335, 337, 339–41, 343, 370n28
outsider art, 1, 2–11, 18, 40–41, 42, 55, 155, 272, 288, 291, 297, 358, 368nn4–5, 369nn13–14, 369n17, 375n5, 375n7, 408n2, 411n51

Pagels, Elaine, 28, 46–47, 59, 64, 70, 75–76, 101, 104–10, 115, 121, 375n9, 377n25; *The Gnostic Gospels*, 37, 38, 42, 43, 45, 47, 48, 52, 53, 64, 100, 102–7, 110, 113, 119, 121, 175, 375n9, 377n25, 383n47; *The Gnostic Paul*, 104, 106–8
Pan-Africanism, 203, 207, 212, 214–15, *217*, 221, 233, 234, 402n60
paranoia: as clinical diagnosis, 2, 14–15, 31, 206, 236, 270, 273–78, 283, 286–88, 345; political, 206, 234, 269, 279–82, 288–90, 291, 411n41; as system, 14–15, 270–71, 272–75, 278, 285, 286–88, 299, *300, 301*, 411n43
paranoiac discourse, xviii, 14–15, 270–73, 278, 286–88, 294, 297
paranoid interpretation, 31, 116, 133, 141, 206, 270–74, 286–90, 317, 409n7
Parker, George Wells, 202, 215
Parsons, Jack, 357–58
partnership model, 160–61, 162, 163, 165, 170, 171, 175, 178, 179, 180, 184, 185, 186, 190, 191, 192, 193, 395n44
Paul, St., 28, 103, 104, 106–9, 381n13
Paulhan, Jean, 31, 241–42, 244, 252, 406n46
Pauvert, Jean-Jacques, 254
Peale, Norman Vincent, 315

Perceau, Louis, 243, 254–55, 259, 407n63

Pere Ubu (rock band), 321

Pia, Pascal, 243, 254–55

Pigliucci, Massimo, 22

Piranesi, Giovanni Battista, 86, *87*, 88

Pistis Sophia, 44, 45, 54, 105, 376n16, 388n16

Plantard, Pierre, 122, 133–34, 138, 146, 147, 153

Plato, 187–88, 189, 204, 380n11

pneuma, 39, 47, 55, 56, 60, 61, 67, 68, 72, 82, 91, 99, 100, 106–10, 279, 282

Poe, Edgar Allan, 154, 275, *286, 409n15*

Polanyi, Michael, 321, 332, 336–39, 340, 341, 342, 366n18, 416n87, 416n100

Polotsky, Hans-Jakob, 95

Pomeroy, Sarah, 169–71

Ponzi, Charles, 230

Popper, Karl, xxi, xxii, 12, 15, 22, 272, 307–8, 371n42

Porter, Roy, 281, 291

postmodernism, 6, 10, 16, 19–22, 24, 141, 179–90, 197, 202, 347, 388n12

prehistory, 28, 160–61, 163, 166, 167–79, 180, 181, 183, 184, 185, 186, 189, 193

Prigogine, Ilya, 17–18, 162, 178, 190

Prinzhorn, Hans, 8, 272, 369n19

Prinzhorn Collection, 283, *284*, 292, *293, 294, 295, 296*

prosopopoeia, 147, 243, 246, 306, 331

Protocols of the Elders of Zion, 134

pseudoarcheology, 32, 164, 176, 185, 188–89, 236, 357, 367n1, 393n17

pseudomorphosis (Jonas), 97

pseudoscience, xiv, xvii, xviii, xix–xx, xxi, xxiii, 1, 2, 15, 32, 33, 46, 116, 164, 180, 194–95, 196, 201, 272, 307–9, 311–12, 318, 320, 322, 329, 339, 340, 341–42, 345, 346, 366n12. *See also* Gordin, Michael

psychoanalysis, 8, 12, 14–15, 25, 27, 31, 32, 46, 51, 85, 123–24, 144–46, 154, 155, 172, 206, 270–78, 283–304, 305–8, 312, 313, 314, 319, 320, 323, 324–27, 328, 329–30, 358, 409n7, 411n51

psychosis, 10, 31, 271–78, 281–86, 287, 288, 289–91, 292, 293, 297, 298, 299–303, 411n51

Puech, Henri-Charles, 28, 44, 51, 59, 61, 64, 70, 71, 74, 75, 77, 78, 84, 86–91, 92, 93, 100, 101, 102–3, 106, 109, 377n32, 381n13, 383n40, 383n47, 384n59

Pythagoras, 16, 352

Quispel, Gilles, 51, 103, 376n21, 377n32, 379n61, 384n59

Rabaté, Jean-Michel, 122–23, 124, 242, 370n31, 389n38

"Race Hatred" (Velikovsky), 325, 326, 327, 334

racism, xv, 11, 25, 32, 204, 205, 223, 230, 325–26, 352, 359

Raiders of the Lost Ark (film), 65, 115

Ramirez, Martín, 4

Reagan, Ronald, 166

Recherches philosophiques (journal), 74, 77–78, 83, 84, 86, 90, 94, 382n34

Reed, Anthony, 356

Reed, Ishmael, 25–27, 28, 155, 208–11, 219, 224, 230, 236; *Mumbo Jumbo*, 25–27, 208–10, 211, 219, 224, 236, 399n28

Reich, Wilhelm, xviii, 32, 357, 358, 419n29

religious symbology, 114, 117, 123, 124, 137, 142, 156–57, 160

Rennes-le-Château, 118, 136, *137*, 138–39, *140*, 141, 142, 144, 145–47, 153–54

Rétif de la Bretonne, Nicolas-Edmé, 261, 262, 406n47

"Return to Freud" (Lacan), 277, 278, 288, 306, 329

revolution: Copernican, 290, 305, 306–7, 308–12, 320, 322–24, 327–28, 330, 337, 372n53; epistemological, 40, 52, 71, 194, 195, 243, 246, 249–52, 263, 288, 290, 305, 306–7, 308–12, 318, 320, 322–23, 324, 327–28, 330, 337, 338–39, 343, 370n26; French, 239, 240, 242, 243, 244, 245, 246, 249–51, 262–63; political, 21, 40, 84, 92, 101, 148, 151, 171, 177, 178, 180, 193, 194, 195, 196, 206, 209, 210, 212, 221, 239, 240, 249–50, 361, 405n25, 411n41; scientific, 306–7, 308–12, 318, 322–24, 327–28, 337, 370n26

Rexroth, Kenneth, 55–57, 106

Ricoeur, Paul 115, 123, 124, 126, 308, 389n29

Rimbaud, Arthur, 148

Robinson, James M., 49–50, 52, 64, 70, 75, 101–4, 109, 340, 377n25, 383n47, 385n72, 385n75, 387n7

Rogers, J. A., 25, 202, 212

Rolinson, Mary G., 207, 398n17

Ronell, Avital, 10, 308

Rosicrucianism, 55, 128, 134, 139, 146, 155, 386n5

Rowling, J. K., xix

rubbish, xix, 370n23, 375n6. *See also* bullshit; junk thought

Rudolph, Kurt, 48, 376n18, 378n54, 379n57

Rumsfeld, Donald, 185

Rybak, Boris, 149

Sacher-Masoch, Leopold von, 248–49, 406n34

Sade, Donatien Alfonse François, Marquis de, xix, 1, 3, 10, 15, 24, 30, 31, 237–65, 269, 270, 288, 322; *Aline and Valcour, or, the philosophical novel*, 31, 253; *Dialogue between a Priest and a Dying Man*, 243, 253, 256; *Historiettes, contes et fabliaux*, 243–44, 253, 254; *Juliette*, 238–39, 241, 248, 252, 253; *Justine*, 238–39, 261, 405n22; *La Nouvelle Justine*, 245; *The Misfortunes of Virtue*, 252, 253, 259, 262, 405n22; *120 Days of Sodom*, 244, 248, 253, 258, 262, 264

sadism, 248, 251, 253, 265, 325

Sam, "Chief" Alfred Charles, 227, 235, 403n84

Sang des Cathares, Le (Sède), 143–44, 153

Sartre, Jean-Paul, 4, 91, 152, 264, 368n8

Saunière, Bérenger, 136, 138, 139, *140*, 141, 143, 144, 145–46, 147, 151, 154, 399n66

schizoanalysis, 11, 298–303

schizophrenia, 2, 11, 272, 274, 278, 283, 288, 298–99, *300, 301*, 303

Scholem, Gershom, 95, 115, 120, 122, 384n59

Schreber, Daniel Paul, 14, 271–73, 276, 278, 279, 283, 411n46

Schuyler, George, 230

science wars, 15, 19, 20, 22, 25, 322, 366n11, 371n44, 372n53, 374n60, 393n17

Scientology, 32, 357–59

Scott, Judith, 4

Sède, Gérard de, 29, 118–19, 122, 133–57, 242, 379n2; "La Chimère expérimentale," 148, 152, 153–54, 392n81; *Le Sang des Cathares*, 143–44, 153; *Les Templiers sont parmi nous*, 150, 153, 155; *L'Or de Rennes*, 118, 136–39, 142, 144, 146–47, 152–53, 154; and the Main à plume group, 148–50, 391n68;

Sède, Gérard de (cont.)
  "Marxist Philosophy and Stalinist
    Philosophy," 150–52; and mytho-
    morphic facts, 119, 133–47, 148,
    149, 155, 157; "Theoretical Objec-
    tivity and Lyric Objectivity,"
    150–54
Sedgwick, Eve Kosofsky, 125, 271,
    287, 289–90, 297, 302, 409n7
Segal, Lynn, 182, 195, 197
Seltzer, Mark, 348–49
Serres, Michel, 10, 11, 20
Sertima, Ivan Van, 202
Seznec, Jean, 115, 386n5
Shapley, Harlow, 310, 321, 336,
    414n39
Sjöö, Monica, 164
Smith, Barbara Herrnstein, 16–17, 20,
    22, 371n45, 380n7
Snow, C. P., 22
Snowden, Frank, 25, 202
Société du roman philosophique
    (Society for the Philosophical
    Novel), 244, 246, 248, 249, 253–54,
    256–58, 259, 260
sociogram (Moreno), 281, *282*
sociology of science, x, 18, 309–12,
    318–20, 322–24, 336–37, 341–43,
    347, 349, 364, 369n14, 372n53,
    416n100
Sokal, Alan, 16, 19–22, 371nn44–45,
    372n53
speculation: financial, 203, 205,
    212–13, 221, 225–31; as theory, xvii,
    xxi, xxii, 1, 10, 12, 14, 16, 21, 28,
    32, 73, 74, 76, 90, 93, 110, 118, 119,
    120, 132, 135, 137, 141, 151–54,
    164, 165, 167, 169–79, 180, 182,
    183, 184, 185, 188, 190–95, 196,
    201, 202–3, 205–8, 209, 212–13,
    232, 233–36, 258, 271, 274, 275,
    285, 287, 303, 311, 342, 349, 351,
    353, 355, 359

Spengler, Oswald, 209, 215
Stalinism, 46, 147, 148, 149, 150–51,
    185, 289, 411n41
Starhawk, 164
Stecchini, Livio, 322, 414n39
Steinberg, Sam, 41
Stekel, Wilhelm, 324, 325
Stengers, Isabelle, 10, 17, 19, 20, 21,
    22, 24, 162, 178, 190, 191, 201, 342,
    370n32
Stephens, Michelle Ann, 225, 232
Stoddard, Lothrop, 210, 215, 223–24,
    402n68
Stone, Merlin, 164, 167, 191
Sun Ra (Herman Poole Blount), 25,
    32, 345, 350–65; and equations,
    354, 359, 360, 362, 363; poetry of,
    351, 352, 356, 360, 361, 364
surrealism, 29, 83, 84, 118, 138, 142,
    148–51, 153, 154, 240, 244, 252–53,
    382n35
suspicion. *See* hermeneutics of
    suspicion
Swiney, Frances, 37, 56–57, 68
syndicalism, 24, 257–60, 262, 264–65,
    407n65
systems theory, 6–7, 14, 18, 161, 162,
    164–65, 167, 171, 178, 181, 187,
    190, 191, 196, 197, 370n32, 393n6
Szwed, John, 353, 417n10, 418n13

Tausk, Victor, 282–83, 285, 297,
    410n28
Templar Knights, 55, 121, 128, 136,
    143, 150, 153, 155
Templiers sont parmi nous, Les (Sède),
    150, 153, 155
"Theoretical Objectivity and Lyric
    Objectivity" (Sède), 150–54
theory: as conceptual apparatus,
    12–13, 14–15, 204, 205, 208, 213,
    234–35, 270–74, 278, 289–90, 291,
    302; as mode of intellectual inquiry,

2, 3, 6, 11–13, 14–15, 69, 71–72, 90, 119, 124, 135, 151–52, 161–62, 164–67, 169, 173, 176, 177, 178–80, 187, 204, 251, 270–74, 286–87, 290, 291, 302, 307, 317, 349, 352, 361, 368n5, 370n26, 370n31, 372n53

thinking machines. *See* cybernetics

Thmei Research Group, 353, 360

Tito, Josip, 148

Toffler, Alvin, 164, 191

Traylor, Bill, 4

trivialization, xvi, xvii, 22, 41, 122, 124, 133, 176, 177, 189, 192–94, 198, 202

Trotsky, Leon, 177

Trotskyism, 118, 142, 147–48, 150, 152

Uexküll, Jakob von, 6–7, 14

UFOs, xiv, xvii, xxiii, 23, 357, 389n38

Umwelt, 6–7, 12, 100, 349

universal history, 25–29, 207, 211, 212, 215, 234

Universal Negro Improvement Association (UNIA), 30, 202, 204, 205, 207, 208, 209, 210, 211, 212, 213, 214, 220, 221, 222, 225, 226, 228, 230, 231, 232, 233, 234, 401n59

Unnik, Willem Cornelis van, 50–51, 377n28

utopia, 18, 20, 84, 151, 160, 167, 176, 178, 179, 182, 184, 189, 192, 197, 202, 204, 368n8

Valentinus, 45, 55, 56, 82, 88, 101, 105, 106, 107, 108

Vandenhoeck und Ruprecht (publishers), 95–96

Velikovsky, Immanuel, 12, 25, 31–32, 65, 305, 309–43, 358, 359; *Ages in Chaos,* 310, 329; "Cosmos without Gravitation," 12, 317–18, *319; Earth in Upheaval,* 310, 415n65; *Mankind in Amnesia,* 333–34, 413n20; *Oedipus*

and Akhnaton, 321, 327, 328–29; "Race Hatred," 325, 326, 327, 334; *Worlds in Collision,* 32, 309, 310–11, 314–15, *315, 316,* 318, 320, 321, 328, 331, 333, 335, 336, 339

Velikovsky Affair, 32, 312, 320–21, 335–41

Vidal-Naquet, Pierre, 188

Vinci, Leonardo da, 129, 130, *131,* 132, 141, 156, 389n38

Voegelin, Eric, 46, 47, 54, 55–56, 69, 99, 101, 102, 126, 129, 258, 385n75

Vollard, Ambroise, 254, 260

Wahl, Jean, 28, 64, 70, 73, 74, 75, 83–84, 86, 381n15

Walker, Alice, 11, 23, 41–42, 163, 164, 347, 375n9

Whitehead, Alfred North, 72, 74, 83, 90, 201

white supremacism, xvi, 25, 26, 30, 204, 206, 207, 209, 214, 223–24, 345, 357, 359–60

Wilson, Colin, 4, 368n8

Wind, Edgar, 115, 386n5

witchcraft, xviii, xx, 55, 165, 173, 175, 210

Wittig, Monique, 157

Wölfli, Adolf, 4

Wolin, Richard, 33, 99, 371n35

Wollstonecraft, Mary, 53

Worlds in Collision (Velikovsky), 32, 309, 310–11, 314–15, *315, 316,* 318, 320, 321, 328, 331, 333, 335, 336, 339

Yates, Frances, 115, 386n5

Yerushalmi, Yosef, 327, 330, 332, 333

York, Malachi Z., xix

Ziolkowski, Theodore, 23, 141, 155–56

Žižek, Slavoj, 167, 183–85, 190–93, 393n5

zombie categories, 13, 26, 370n30

Jonathan P. Eburne is associate professor of comparative literature, English, and French and Francophone studies at the Pennsylvania State University. He is editor of *ASAP/Journal* and the author of *Surrealism and the Art of Crime,* as well as coeditor of four additional books.